Cranes of the World

LAWRENCE WALKINSHAW

Cranes of the World

Library of Congress Catalog Card Number: 79-159423

ISBN: 087691-047-9

Published by Winchester Press
460 Park Avenue, New York 10022

PRINTED IN THE UNITED STATES OF AMERICA

To all of the people throughout the world who helped make this study possible, I dedicate this book.

CONTENTS

PREFACE

I have been fascinated by cranes all of my adult life. This book was written with the hope that it will transmit to the reader some of the abiding interest and sense of wonder these great birds stir in me. These pages represent an attempt to catch the imagination of the general reader as well as provide information needed by ornithologists. I do not believe the two readerships are mutually exclusive—there is a human story to be told that accompanies the scientific observations and descriptions, and to this must be added to the long, colorful history of cranes as well as photographs of their striking beauty and their often wild and remote habitats. It is all of this, as well as the strictly scientific information contained here, that I wish to share with all who read this book.

My first crane observations were made in September, 1921, watching a group of three Sandhill Cranes coast over a cornfield. It was not until nine years later, however, on a visit to the "Big Marsh," or "Junction Swamp" in Convis Township, Calhoun County, Michigan that I had a sight of cranes which completely changed my life.

Roaming over a ridge from which groves of old beech had recently been lumbered, I heard a loud call vibrating from the marsh ahead, reverberating between the bordering woods. What made this wild, haunting call? Wading forward through the muck and water at the ridge's base, pushing aside dense sedges and grass that hot afternoon, I saw ahead of me three tremendous birds, almost four feet tall, drawn up to their full height as if at attention, watching intently. Immediately they took to the air, flying with extended necks and feet, moving with slow deliberate downward wingstrokes, contrasting with a rather quick up stroke, to a far corner of the marsh. Only their loud, sonorous, trumpeting call came drifting back. This was the home of the Greater Sandhill Crane. The next spring I found my first nest on May 5, and thereafter, except for 1932, have found from one to 15 nests in Michigan annually.

During March, 1938, I made my first trip to Florida and spent a week on the Kissimmee Prairie, locating three nests of the Florida Sandhill. From Kenansville to Okeechobee, we had to open gates as we made our way through a largely roadless expanse of sand, mud, water, and saw-palmettos, sleeping in old buildings or ranchers' work shanties. In 1940 I found three nests of the Mississippi Sandhill Crane on a visit to Jackson County, Mississippi and became acquainted with that bird. During 1941 we went to the far West, studying the cranes in Idaho, Utah, Oregon and Wyoming. In 1942 Bernard W. Baker and I spent three weeks in the extreme wilderness of central Alberta. Since then I have visited Cuba and the Isles of Pines twice, visited Alaska, Banks Island and other regions of Canada's Northwest Territories, Saskatchewan, Texas (several times), New Mexico, Nebraska (twice), Wisconsin (thrice), and Ontario, as well as making many trips to Florida and northern Indiana observing all the subspecies of the Sandhill Crane and the Whooping Crane on both its summering and wintering grounds.

During 1961-1962 my wife and I visited Africa, beginning at Cairo and stopping in every country to the south until we reached Natal, South Africa. In South Africa we found or observed 25 nests of the three native crane species: Stanley, Crowned, and Wattled. On a visit to Sweden, Poland and Denmark during 1963, we observed some 21 nests of the Common Crane. Then in 1965, on a trip across Africa from west to east entering at Dakar, I observed eight nests of the West African Crowned Crane in northern Nigeria, and a few days later saw two nests of the Sudan Crowned Crane in central Ethiopia. Shortly thereafter, in India, I observed Sarus Cranes and eight of their nests, and later in Japan, I saw the Japanese Cranes.

In September 1968, I retired from my dental practice and my wife and I flew immediately to Queensland, Australia where in this drought-stricken land we noted three nests of the Brolga and one of a newly-arrived exotic invader, the Burmese Sarus Crane. Brolgas were also present at Darwin. Then in central India I saw the first Siberian White Cranes at Keoladeo Ghana Bird Sanctuary. In southern Kyushu I studied the White-naped and Hooded Cranes for a month. Six weeks were then spent near Kushiro, Hokkaido, in northern Japan watching groups of Japanese Cranes. By this time, I had seen, at first hand, all of the world's cranes except the Black-necked Crane, a rare central-China and Tibetan species.

I had seen nests of all the American species and subspecies, and of all those in Africa but the East African Crowned and Demoiselle Cranes. I had seen nests of both Sarus Cranes, of the Australian and Japanese Cranes. The White-naped Crane was observed nesting in a large enclosure in the Detroit Zoological Park. My studies had taken me to libraries, museums and zoos throughout the world, and I have also been fortunate enough to go over records of observations received from many institutions and many individuals.

ACKNOWLEDGMENTS

Many people have helped greatly in the work on The Cranes of the World, far too many to list here, I wish to thank them all but especially some who helped me in getting acquainted with regions, securing transportation, housing, and food. First many thanks to my own family, chiefly to my wife Clara who went with me to most of the regions visited and helped in making observations, taking photographs, in regular living routine. I wish to thank our children, James Walkinshaw and his wife Janet; our daughter, Wendy and her husband Dr. Lowell M. Schake, even to our grandchildren, especially Ron Walkinshaw who helped with canoe trips. And many thanks to Dr. Salim Ali, Dr. George Archibald, Dr. John W. Aldrich, Fred Bard, Mr. and Mrs. William Barnes, Dr. and Mrs. Andrew J. Berger, Gavin Blackman, Mr. and Mrs. Arne Blomgren, Mr. and Mrs. Rudyard Boulton, Bruce Cook, Rod Drewein, William A. Dyer, Dr. Andrej Dyrtsch, Dr. Ray Erickson, Dr. John George, Billie Gill, Andreé Griffin, Tsuneo Hayashida, Dr. and Mrs. George Heinsohn, Uno Hedstrom, Ronald Hoffman, Mr. and Mrs. Tom House, T. Iwamatsu, Dr. Henry Kyllingstadt, Dr. Hugh Lavery, E. Gordon Male, Dr. and Mrs. H. Masatomi, S. Matano, Dr. and Mrs. R. M. Naik, Graham Newton, Dr. Nick Novakowski, Dr. Miles D. Pirnie, Dr. and Mrs. Vlad Rydzewski, Dr. and Mrs. P. O. Swanberg, Dr. and Mrs. G. Samuelsson, Dr. and Mrs. S. Satsuki, Dr. and Mrs. Victor W. Smith, Godfrey Symons, R. Takahashi, Dr. and Mrs. Emil K. Urban, Col. and Mrs. Jack Vincent, Nils Wellberg, Lovett Williams, Jr., Keiki Yoshazaki, Akio Yoshida, and to the following people who gave me photographs to use, Dr. Salim Ali, William Barnes, Gavin Blackman, Bruce Cook, Toshiaki Harada, Dagmar Hruskova, T. Iwamatsu, Fred Lahrman, Dr. Hugh Lavery, Dr. and Mrs. Wolfgang Makatsch, Alan Schroeder, P. O. Swanberg, Eizi Takabayshi, M. Phillip Kahl and Lovett Williams, Jr.

I also wish to thank The American Museum of Natural History, The British Museum (Natural History), Chicago Natural History Museum, Florida State Museum, Museum of Comparative Zoology, Michigan State University Museum, and the University of Michigan Museum of Zoology and the Canadian Wildlife Service, the United States Fish and Wildlife Service, the Michigan Audubon Society, Hokkaido Crane Preservation Board, Bombay Natural History Society, and the Keoladeo Ghana Bird Sanctuary.

Without the help of these people and organizations I would not have been able to have done this work.

INTRODUCTION

The cranes, as a group, are very old. Fossils have been found dating from the Eocene period, some 40 to 60 million years ago. Even the Sandhill Crane in its present form and size lived during the Pliocene period in Nebraska, a period extending as far as nine million years back.

Fifteen of the approximately 8,600 world bird species are cranes. They inhabit all of the continents except South America and Antarctica as well as several major islands, such as Japan, New Guinea, western Cuba and the adjacent Isle of Pines. North American cranes are found from the Arctic south to central Mexico and southern Florida, depending upon the season. In Asia, and in northern and central Europe (Palaearctic Region) eight species are known to breed but only two in North America (Nearctic). Three of these species breed northward from the Arctic Circle (the Holarctic Region). Four species breed in central and southern Africa (Ethiopian Region) while one breeds in the India-Burma area (Oriental Region) and two (one until just recently) in Australia (the Australasian Region).

Two species winter in northern Africa, travelling south at times as far as Lake Chad, and being found regularly along the White and Blue Nile in Sudan and Ethiopia (southern Palaearctic Region, Ethiopian Region), in Asia into India, Burma and surrounding countries to Viet Nam (southern Palaearctic and Oriental Regions). The breeding cranes of Africa, India, Burma and Australia are resident, not migrating into other countries.

Cranes have disappeared or been extirpated in many regions. Often this has been caused by encroachment upon their habitat, by drainage, or by hunting. Yet a number of species, in recent years, have increased in numbers because of better protection, the creation of sanctuaries, and continued newspaper, radio and television educational programs. In fact, the preservation of the rare Whooping and Japanese Cranes, both of which were near extinction, and the tremendous increase in the numbers of the Sandhill Cranes, show how enlightened conservation activity can work wonders against the often destructive efforts of other men.

Cranes have long been kept in captivity. Egyptian tomb drawings indicate that young birds were reared by man thousands of years ago. During the past 150 years records have been kept of these species in many zoological parks. During this time all species of cranes but three (Black-necked, Siberian and Hooded) have been known to breed successfully. Possibly the Chinese have bred these three without our knowledge. In addition many birds have mated with cranes of other species so interesting hybrids have been produced. One of the first descriptions of cranes breeding in captivity was written by Emilius Hopkinson in 1926 (H.F.&G. Witherby. London, *Records of Birds Bred In Captivity*). He listed ten species. Since then the Wattled and Whooping Cranes have been bred in United States, along with Sandhill, White-naped, Sarus, Stanley, and both Crowned Cranes. The Demoiselle breeds regularly in Czechoslovakia, the Manchurian has been bred in both Europe and Japan and probably in China. Because of the large number of cranes in collections, exotic cranes may escape on different continents. George Lowery saw two wild Stanley Cranes in southern Louisiana; W. A. Dyer (who made a photograph) and Gordon Male and later H. V. Hines have

seen paired Gray-Crowned Cranes in central Florida. Sarus Cranes have been reported breeding in Massachusetts while similar escapes have been seen in Europe and probably an Australian Crane in southern Siberia. The Canadian Wildlife Service and the U.S. Fish and Wildlife Service have combined their efforts to raise Whooping Cranes from eggs taken from the wild with good success, and have reared Sandhill Cranes from the same source. They are now working on releasing some of these in regions where they may produce young which can go free, for it is very doubtful that any hand-reared crane will do very well in the wild unless started first by its parents, for they become imprinted strongly by the people with whom they associate. It has been found that by taking one egg from a set of two, the wild birds rear as many young as normal since only one chick generally survives, and the extra eggs thus obtained have produced a comfortable flock of captive Whooping Cranes. I was one of the first to fear this procedure because of the wildness of wild cranes. But they apparently have not deserted their nests when visited by a helicopter, as they often do when a blind is built near their nest or when too many human visits are made on one or more days. Thus we are continuing to learn a great deal about our cranes at the time of this writing. This knowledge will soon be forthcoming.

Stanley Crane chicks, Giants Castle, Natal, South Africa, Jan. 2, 1962. Approximately at 7,000 ft. in the Drakensberg Mountains. Nest built of pebbles. Note weakness of babies. They are unable to stand, so they sit on their haunches.

Australian Brolga at fresh water pond, Yarrowmere Station, Queensland, Australia, Jan. 4, 1969. Note Black Swan, Stilt and ducks.

To avoid ambiguity, scientific names will be used frequently to refer to cranes by genus and species. Listed below are the 15 living cranes of the world and their scientific names:

1. The Common, or European Crane *(Grus grus)*
2. The Black-Necked Crane *(Grus nigricollis)*
3. The Hooded Crane *(Grus monachus)*
4. The Sandhill Crane *(Grus canadensis)*
5. The Japanese, or Manchurian, Crane *(Grus japonensis)*
6. The Whooping Crane *(Grus americana)*
7. The White-Naped Crane *(Grus vipio)*
8. The Sarus Crane *(Grus antigone)*
9. The Australian Crane, or Brolga *(Grus rubicundus)*
10. The Siberian White Crane *(Grus leucogeranus)*
11. The Wattled Crane *(Bugeranus carunculatus)*
12. The Demoiselle Crane *(Anthropoides virgo)*
13. The Blue, or Paradise, Crane *(Anthropoides paradisea)*
14. Dark-Crowned Crane *(Balearica pavonina)*
15. Gray-Crowned Crane *(Balearica regulorum)*

More detailed information, including subspecies and distribution, is given near the end of this Introduction, where nomenclature applied to extinct species known only from fossil evidence is also given.

Except for the Japanese Crane, which is resident in southeastern Hokkaido, Japan, all cranes breeding in northern latitudes migrate southward to warmer regions in autumn. In March, April or early May, they migrate northward again, In far northern latitudes above the Arctic Circle, most cranes nest in June. In Scandinavia, because of the warming trend of the Gulf Stream, *Grus grus* nests most often in May and early June. Across Asia, North America and the remainder of Europe, at latitudes between 45° N. and 61° N., cranes nest during May: in southern Georgia and Florida, south of 30-31° N., from January until April. In many regions of central India, Australia and central Africa, cranes nest during the rainy season. Because of the cold at high altitudes, *G.canadensis tabida* in Colorado, and *G.nigricollis* in Tibet and inner China nest in June and early July. Yet some *A.paradisea* nest in the Drakensberg Mountains at heights up to 7,000 feet in Natal, South Africa at practically the same time as others nest at lower elevations. The Wattled Crane in most regions most often nests at the season opposite that of the Crowned and Stanley Cranes. In Natal, South Africa, *B.carunculatus* has been found regularly setting when heavy ice surrounded the nests while a few of that species nest during the same period as *Balearica regulorum* and *Anthropoides paradisea.*

All *Grus* except *G.rubicundus* nest north of the Equator. During recent years some *G.antigone sharpii* moved into northern Australia. All *Balearica* are found south of 12-13° N. latitude, as is *Bugeranus* generally. *Anthropoides virgo* breeds entirely north of the Equator; *A.paradisea* entirely south of it.

Fossil discoveries show that *G.antigone* was formerly found in Europe; a close relative of *Balearica* in France and Florida; and *G.americana* from Northwest Territories, Canada, south to California, New Jersey, and Florida.

During spring, cranes have been observed migrating northward along a high pressure weather system, with flight most often beginning during mid-morning. One observed group ate ravenously for two or three hours early mornings. Between 9:30 and 11:00 a.m. families, groups and singles suddenly began flight, ascending by great spirals in broken formation, up and up. Some leveled off at about 1,000 feet, joined into formation, and headed northward; more groups spent 10 minutes or more spiraling higher and higher, some until they were only visible through binoculars. Then, forming a V pointed in the direction of flight, less often a straight line and at times a diagonal line, they began swiftly drifting northward. To me, there are few sights more thrilling than a flock of these great birds taking wing.

In Japan, *G.vipio* and *G.monachus* have been observed departing every spring for many years. Going to watch the cranes leave is for many Japanese a springtime ritual. I watched a group of 90 *G.vipio* in late February, 1969, leave Kyushu for Korea. The birds circled until they were twice as high as the surrounding mountains, and when almost invisible, began crossing the open sea. I watched a heavy flight of *G.canadensis canadensis* which had originated south of Lubbock, Texas in early March, 1968, as it gained elevation, apparently searching for better thermals until its members seemed satisfied and shaped quickly into formation again, between 1,000 and 2,000 feet above the earth, and disappeared to the north. During March, 1967, I noted *G.canadensis*, probably *tabida*, at 1,000 feet flying slightly northwestward until out of sight over St. Cloud, Florida, while at another time, late March, 1932, in Ionia County, Michigan, a group of cranes was flying so high, I could follow it only by its members' continuous bugling. H. V. Hines (Letter, November 18, 1970), as he flew his plane over Sebring Air Terminal at 11:00 a.m. March 1, 1966, observed a flock of 53 Sandhill Cranes. He climbed to 1,700 feet, determined that the birds were flying northwesterly, and continued in that direction for 20 miles, when he turned back, satisfied they were migrating. The cranes paid little attention to the plane when he neared their formation.

Cranes fly a mile or more high, and at such heights their formations would pass unnoticed except for their continuous bugling. European Cranes have been observed by airplane pilots while migrating over the North Sea at 4,300 meters. Observers in the Himalayas at 20,000 feet noted cranes flying south a mile or more above them.

Wattled Crane.

Top: Sarus Cranes; White-naped Cranes.

Bottom: Sandhill Cranes.

Sandhill Cranes.

Stanley Cranes.

Top: West African Crowned Cranes; Whooping Cranes.
Bottom: Nest of Crowned Crane; European Crane chick.

Cranes cross the Mediterranean regularly spring and fall, apparently flying several hundred miles or more on each leg of their journey.

In autumn, migration often continues in shorter hops. Food may have much to do with this. Coming from the Arctic, Sandhill Cranes begin arriving in Saskatchewan in mid-August, when wheat is ripening. Here, as other cranes often do in northern climates, they do considerable grain damage, eating and trampling it as they forage. But cranes also do much good. One morning I watched Jo, the captive Whooping Crane at Aransas Refuge, Texas, eat over 800 grasshoppers in less than two hours. Hand-reared Sandhill Crane my family raised in Michigan devoured 300 to 400 grasshoppers and crickets a day, beginning when it was two months of age, throughout August and September. European Cranes have been noted devouring cockchafers every spring and summer while many cranes eat harmful seeds. At various times cranes have been noted eating a wide variety of foods: frogs, snakes, small birds, birds' eggs, small mammals, crayfish, snails, shrimp, small fish, roots, tubers, earthworms, melons, sweet potatoes, beetles, and more. And of course they need liquid refreshment, often returning to water once or twice daily to drink.

In winter, spring and autumn their first morning flight from the night roost spot, which is most often in the shallows of some body of water, takes them only a short distance to flat higher land, where they loaf and preen, before continuing their flight to feeding areas. There they eat from one to three hours, return to drink if necessary, loaf and preen during mid-day heat, then in mid- or late afternoon fly again to the feeding region. Here they remain until around sundown when again they fly to the night roosting spot. At times some stop on the flat region near the water, then fly in to roost at dark or nearly so. Some cranes, such as *G.americana* and *G.leucogeranus* often feed in water not far from their night roosting place. Although many cranes, such as *G.monachus, G.vipio* and *G.canadensis* roost in rather compact flocks in winter and spring, family groups often feed regularly some distance from the main flock, as do the two white species mentioned above. A trespasser into the family group is immediately attacked by the male of the family. Even the more gregarious species do not allow others of their kind to approach closer than six or eight feet while feeding or roosting.

Cranes are strongly territorial. In winter this territory may be no more than a few meters on each side of the individual bird or family. In spring and summer it may be several hundred acres of marsh or highland. Although both birds defend the territory, the male does by far the most. Attack is often forewarned through display and is so quickly anticipated that the attacked bird moves away simultaneously. At times the attack begins by ruffling the feathers and preening (false preening) the back, wings, above or below. From this the bird suddenly assumes an attack stance, with the neck arched and the bill pointing downward. Almost immediately he attacks the other, rushing at him with extreme vigor. Often this rush is adequate, the other bird retreating to a safe distance, which in winter can be a few meters away, but in summer or spring means abandoning the attacker's territory. At times a short battle follows. In this, the sharp toenails are the deadliest weapons but the bill and wings are often used as well. The flapping wings can throw the opponent off balance, and the bill can stab the opponent on the skull, from which observed deaths have been recorded.

Cranes have a unique dance. The Crowned Cranes often begin it by bobbing their heads up and down. Sometimes this ends the display. Many cranes pick up objects with their bill, hold them momentarily, and drop them, or else throw them into the air, at times catching them and repeating the performance. Sometimes they throw an object several times, then follow with spectacular bounces. These bounces carry the birds high into the air, at times eight or ten feet. Some birds jump slightly backward; some jump sidewise and whirl; some even jump slightly forward. Throughout the head is held high, the legs, slightly bent, hang motionless below; the wings are slightly spread, waving or motionless. Often bows follow or are mixed with more bounces. Again the bird or birds whirl around and around.

Grus canadensis in immense winter or spring flocks call continuously when dancing. They dance after daylight, later in the morning after eating, and again during the afternoon and evening. Cranes will dance at any age, in any season, and often when disturbed, showing it is used also as distraction display. For some time prior to the breeding season the pairs often dance more than at other seasons. A baby six day old *Grus canadensis* my family reared, and a ten-month old Crowned Crane, when released in early morning from their pens, both danced all over the yard.

Cranes apparently become mated in the nonbreeding flocks formed each spring when parents leave their last season's youngsters. These lone birds, or twins, join with other similar birds and roam the country. Sometimes they may roost in the same spot nightly in the same marsh all summer, feeding on neighboring fields by day. Again they will move from marsh to marsh, depending on circumstances. Existing evidence indicates that most cranes do not breed until four or five years of age. An occasional one, however will breed at three years. Once they take up a marsh, if not disturbed by outside interference, a pair and their successors may remain there for years. Cranes are very long lived. In zoos they have been known to reach advanced ages. One Siberian Crane brought to the Washington, D.C. zoo at an unknown age lived there 61 years, while Common Cranes have lived known ages of 43, 42 and over 40 years. Many Sandhill Cranes have been known to live 24 or more years, as have Manchurian, White-Naped, Crowned and Stanley cranes, while one Australian Crane lived at least 47 years. Once a crane pair is established they remain together as long as both remain alive. This has been observed in captivity, and it is presumed to be true in the wild. Consequently, some pairs may nest for many many years in their favorite territories. Novokowski with the Whooping Crane and the author with the Greater Sandhill Crane have shown that territories are occupied by the same birds for as long as 10 or perhaps 20 or more years.

Most cranes lay two eggs and nest every year. During extremes in weather, drought and high water they may not nest. Sometimes only one egg is laid. The Wattled Crane is found with one egg about as often as two. The Crowned Cranes often lay three; something other species only very rarely do. Occasional Crowned Cranes in South Africa have been found with four. Incubation requires between 28 and 36 days and although the eggs are usually laid two days apart, the chicks hatch on successive days. These now remain with their parents for about nine or ten months. They learn to fly at different ages according to the length of day and other factors. In temperate climates it is around 70 to 100 days. In the Arctic much less; in the tropics a longer period is needed.

Adults try to teach their chicks to eat by offering food to them, dropping it at times, then reoffering it until the chicks learn to pick it up themselves. But adults have been noted feeding young when they were all of nine months and older. But generally, chicks quickly become capable of getting their own food as the family group roams. Most cranes prefer to nest in shallow marshes but when the chicks hatch parents often lead them onto dry surrounding prairies or pastures to feed, returning to the marsh at night to roost in the shallow water. For about three months the young cranes sleep sitting down, but thereafter they stand in shallow water. In both positions they tuck the head into the feathers between the wing and body. After beginning to stand, most often do so on one leg.

When flying, the feet trail out behind the tail and the head is held fairly straight out front. During severe cold I have observed both *Grus japonensis* and *G.canadensis* fly with their feet drawn into the breast feathers. Fred Bard has observed this with *G.canadensis* and P. O. Swanberg with *Grus grus grus*. When this is done the tail is spread slightly more than normal.

Cranes are born with beautiful brown or gray down and can run around within a few hours. Within six weeks they acquire new gray feathers, usually brown-tipped. Although some of these are retained, most are lost by the time the bird is five months old. The primaries, secondaries and rectrices* are not lost at this time. From observations of hand-reared birds, these are lost every two, or in some instances, three years. Often all the flight feathers are lost at once leaving the birds flightless. Since this happens at the breeding season, the birds are often grounded with their offspring. Only a few weeks, however, are required to acquire the new feathers and flight is resumed.

Cranes like to bathe and often will soak for many

*Tail feathers

minutes then spend several hours preening and rearranging their feathers. Even when not bathing they often spend hours each day preening. They also dig in the earth with their long bills looking for insects, roots and tubers. Sometimes they seem to do this just to dig. At times they follow this by preening, rubbing the soil over their feathers. Many of the grayish cranes thus acquire a brownish or reddish stain over their entire body, giving them a much better protective coloration. I do not believe the white cranes do this for they are nearly always perfectly white.

Thus the gray and brown cranes are better camouflaged while nesting than are the white and blue ones. Those with white or partly white heads are conspicuous on their nests and in their marshes. Conspicuous coloration must have reduced the numbers of the three white species for they appear to be the rarest of all.

Another salient characteristic of Cranes is the tremendous voice which they utter often continuously when flying, on occasion when on the feeding grounds, and at times even when changing places at the nest, for both birds incubate. Most can be heard from one-half to three miles by a person with good hearing. At break of day from their roost they utter a loud call, a rendition of either *Kurroooo, Karroooo, Garoooo* or a goose-like honk. The crowned cranes sound more goose-like while the Siberian White Crane has a beautiful *toyoya* call. The Crowned Cranes and the Siberian White Crane differ from the others in that they do not have the

Australian Brolga dry-season flock at Pallarenda Town Common, Townsville, Queensland, Australia, Oct. 12, 1968.

A pair of White-naped Cranes giving unison call. Male with raised secondaries, primaries held stiffly at sides. This is similar to G.antigone, G.rubicundus, G.grus, G.americana and Anthropoides paradisea. Arasaki, Kagoshima Prefecture, Japan, Jan. 1968. (Photo by Eizi Takabayashi.)

trachea convoluted inside the breast bone. These convolutions definitely give the voice much more resonance.

The future of the cranes of the world is both bright and gray. First, in those areas where strenuous conservation efforts have been mounted, some species have been brought back from the edge of extinction and other species have begun positively to burgeon. However, large birds with only fair-to-middling natural protective devices will always remain in relative danger. Cranes fit perfectly into this category, and beyond that they are noisy (see above) and they make for rather good eating. So it will always be a struggle for these birds to maintain their position on the earth. If man adopts a protective stance toward cranes—as he has in Japan and parts of the U.S.—they will prosper. If man allows himself to become a predator of these birds—as he has in the U.S. and other countries in the past and as he still is in many areas—the world population of cranes could be virtually destroyed in not too many years. Hopefully, the knowledge that comes from the scientific community joined to the enthusiasm and readiness to fight that has come and is coming from groups of interested citizens like the Audubon Society, will result in an environment in which the cranes and other birds of the world can thrive.

CLASSIFICATION

The Order (one of the 28 Order classification of birds), *Gruiformes*, to which the cranes belong consists of 12 Families: *Mesoenatidae* (Mesite Family), *Turnicidae* (Hemipode-quail Family), *Pedionomidae* (Collared-hemipode Family), *Gruidae* (Cranes), *Aramidae* (Limpkins), *Psophiidae* (Trumpeters), *Rallidae* (Rails), *Heliornithidae* (Finfoots), *Rhynochetidae* (Kagu Family), *Eurypygidae* (Sunbitterns), *Cariamidae* (Cariama Family), and Bustards (*Otididae*). The *Gruidae* are separated into two subfamilies, the *Gruinae* and *Balearicinae*. The *Gruinae* are again divided into three Genera, *Grus*, *Anthropoides*, and *Bugeranus*. Some ornithologists add a fourth, *Tetrapteryx*. The *Balearicinae* are all found in one Genus, *Balearica*.

Following are the living world Cranes (Summer and winter distribution given):

SUBFAMILY Gruinae

GENUS GRUS

1) *Grus grus*. Common or European Crane.
   A. *Grus grus grus*. Europe to western Siberia. Winters in northern Africa, Spain, southeastern Portugal; more rarely in some other Mediterranean countries, south to central Sudan and Ethiopia.
   B. *Grus grus lilfordi*. Central, and to some extent eastern, Siberia. Winters chiefly in China, and northern India.
2) *Grus nigricollis*. Black-necked Crane. Western China, Tibet. Winters in Tibet at lower elevations and in northern Viet Nam.
3) *Grus monachus*. Hooded Crane. Central Siberia. Winters in East China, southern Japan, and occasionally in Assam.
4) *Grus canadensis*. Sandhill Crane.
   A. *Grus canadensis canadensis*. Northeastern Siberia, northern Canada, (including northern Ontario), Alaska, and Arctic Islands. Winters in southern California, Baja California, eastern New Mexico, Texas to central Mexico. Rarely in Japan.
   B. *Grus canadensis rowani*. Central portions of Canadian prairie provinces. Winters in Texas.
   C. *Grus canadensis tabida*. British Columbia, northwestern United States, north central states. Winters in southern California, central New Mexico and central Florida.
   D. *Grus canadensis pratensis*. Resident in southern Georgia and peninsular Florida. At present the bird resident in southeastern Mississippi is included here, although it is definitely different.
   E. *Grus canadensis nesiotes*. Resident in western Cuba and Isle of Pines.
5) *Grus japonensis*. Japanese or Manchurian Crane. Resident in southeastern Hokkaido, Japan and migratory in continental Asia. Summers in Manchuria and southeastern Siberia. Winters in South Korea and eastern China.
6) *Grus americana*. Whooping Crane. Wood-Buffalo

Park, North West Territories, Canada. Winters principally at Aransas National Wildlife Refuge, on Texas Gulf Coast.

7) *Grus vipio.* White-naped Crane. South-central Siberia, northwestern Mongolia, Manchuria. Winters in eastern China, South Korea, and Kiushiu.

8) *Grus antigone.* Sarus Crane.
A. *Grus antigone antigone.* Resident. North and central India, southern Nepal.
B. *Grus antigone sharpii.* Resident. Burma, SE Asia, formerly Philippines. Recently found in northern Queensland, Australia.

9) *Grus rubicundus.* Australian Crane or Brolga. Resident (migratory during droughts), Southern New Guinea, northwest, north, northeast and south Australia.

10) *Grus leucogeranus.* Siberian White Crane. North central Siberia. Winters in central India, eastern China and at times in southern Kiushiu.

GENUS BUGERANUS

1) *Bugeranus carunculatus.* Wattled Crane. Resident. Southern Ethiopia south to eastern South Africa except not found in Kenya, Uganda and Tanzania.

GENUS ANTHROPOIDES

1) *Anthropoides virgo.* Demoiselle Crane. Northern Algeria, perhaps in Tunisia. SE Europe across central Siberia to Mongolia. Winters in Sudan, some in Nigeria, Ethiopia, India, Burma, China. Rare at Lake Chad.

2) *Anthropoides paradisea.* Blue or Paradise Crane. Resident. South Africa, chiefly in east. Some altitudinal migration.

SUBFAMILY *Balearicinae*

GENUS BALEARICA

1) *Balearica pavonina.* Dark-Crowned Crane.
A. *Balearica pavonina pavonina.* Resident. West Africa, Senegal to Lake Chad, northern Nigeria, Cameroon.
B. *Balearica pavonina ceciliae.* Resident, Southern Sudan, southwestern Ethiopia. Occasional in both northern Uganda and Kenya.

2) *Balearica regulorum.* Gray-Crowned Crane.
A. *Balearica regulorum regulorum.* Resident. Southern Congo to South Africa.
B. *Balearica regulorum gibbericeps.* Resident. Kenya, Uganda, Tanzania, eastern Congo.

FOSSILS

Brodkorb (1967) has summarized the fossil cranes of the world:

Family Gruidae *Vigors*

Gruidae Vigors, 1825, *Trans. Linn. Soc.* London, Vol. 14, p. 488 (family; type *Grus* Pallas).

Subfamily Geranoidinae *(Wetmore)*

Geranoididae Wetmore, 1933 (May 15), *Condor,* vol. 35, no. 3, p. 115 (type *Geranoides* Wetmore).

GENUS GERANOIDES WETMORE

1. *Geranoides jepseni* Wetmore
Geranoides jepseni Wetmore, 1933 (May 15), *Condor,* vol. 35, no. 3, p. 115, fig. 22 (type from South Elk Creek; distal end of left tarsometatarsus, Princeton Univ. no. 13257). LOWER EOCENE (Willwood formation). WYOMING: Bighorn County: South Elk Creek.

Subfamily Balearicinae *(W. L. Sclater)*

Balearicidae W. L. Sclater, 1924, *Systema avium ethiopicarum,* vol. 1, p. 110 (family; type *Balearica* Brisson)—*Balearicinae* Peters, 1934, Checklist Birds World, vol. 2, p. 154 (subfamily).

GENUS PARAGRUS LAMBRECHT

Paragrus Lambrecht, 1933, *Handbuch Palaeorn.,* p. 520 (type by monotypy *Gallinuloides prentici* Loomis).

2. *Paragrus prentici* (Loomis)
Gallinuloides prentici Loomis, *Amer. Jour. Sci.,* ser. 4, vol. 22, p. 481, fig. 1-3 (type from head of Elk Creek; distal end of right tibiotarsus, femur, proximal end of fibula, phalanges, ungues,

West African Crowned Crane at Vom, Northern Nigeria, Aug. 15, 1965.

Amherst College Museum). LOWER EOCENE (Willwood formation). WYOMING: Bighorn County: head of Elk Creek, 10 miles W of Otto.

GENUS ALETORNIS MARSH

Aletornis Marsh, 1872, Amer. Jour. Sci., ser. 3, vol. 4, p. 256 (type Aletornis nobilis Marsh, designated by Hay, 1902, Bull. U.S. Geol. Surv., 179, p. 527).

3. Aletornis nobilis Marsh

Aletornis nobilis Marsh, 1872 (Oct.), Amer. Jour. Sci., ser. 3, vol. 4, no. 22, p. 256 (type from Grizzly Buttes, distal end of left tarsometatarsus, Yale Peabody Mus. no. 63). MIDDLE EOCENE (Blacks Fork member of Bridger formation). WYOMING: Uinta County: Grizzly Buttes on Smiths Fork, 1 mile SW of Mountainview.

4. Aletornis marshi (Shufeldt)

Grus marshi Shufeldt, 1915 (Feb.), Trans. Connecticut Acad. Arts Sci., vol. 19, p. 41, pl. 15, figs. 144-147 (type from Henrys Fork, distal end of right tibiotarsus. Yale Peabody Mus. no. 888). MIDDLE EOCENE (Twin Buttes member of Bridger formation). WYOMING: Uinta County: Henrys Fork.

5. Aletornis pernix Marsh

Aletornis pernix Marsh, 1872 (Oct.), Amer. Jour. Sci., ser. 3, vol. 4, no. 22, p. 256 (type from Henrys Fork, distal end of left tibiotarsus, Yale Peabody Mus. no. 64). MIDDLE EOCENE: (Twin Buttes member of Bridger formation). WYOMING: Uinta County: Henrys Fork.

GENUS ORNITOCNEMUS ZIGNO

Ornitocnemus Zigno, 1876, Mem. 1st. veneto Sci., vol. 20, p. 445 (type by monotypy Ornitocnemus robustus Zigno)...

6. Ornitocnemus robustus Zigno

Ornitocnemus robustus Zigno, 1876, Mem. Ist. veneto Sci., vol. 20, p. 445 (type from Monte Zuello, distal end of tibiotarsus). MIDDLE EOCENE (Lutetian). ITALY: Monte Zuello.

7. Ornitocnemus geiseltalensis (Lambrecht)

Palaeogrus geiseltalensis Lambrecht, 1935, Nova Acta Leopoldina, n.s. vol. 3, no. 14, p. 361, pl. 1. fig. 1 (type from Cecilie Mine, fragmentary right tibiotarsus and tarsometatarsus, Geiseltal-

museum). MIDDLE EOCENE (Braunkohle des Geiseltales). GERMANY: Saxony: Grube Cecilie near Halle/Saale.

8. Ornitocnemus hordwellienis Lydekker

Grus hordweillienis Lydekker, 1891, Cat. Foss. Birds Brit. Mus., p. 165, fig. 36 (type from Hordwell, distal portion of right tibiotarsus, Brit. Mus. no. 30333). UPPER EOCENE (Hordwell beds) ENGLAND: Hampshire: Hordwell.

9. Ornitocnemus excelsus (Milne-Edwards)

Grus excelsa Milne-Edwards, 1871, Ois foss. France, vol. 2, p. 24, pl. 75, 76, figs. 1-2 (type from Chavroches and Langy, coracoid, humerus, radius, ulna, carpometacarpus, tibiotarsus, tarso metatarsus, Paris Mus.). LOWER MIOCENE (Aquitanian). FRANCE: Dept. Allier: Chavroches and Langy (Milne-Edwards, 1871): Saint-Gerand-le-Puy (Lambrecht, 1933, Handb. Palaeorn., p. 519, fig. 155A).

Genus Eobalearica Gureev

Eobalearica Gureev, 1949, Doklady Akad. Nauk SSSR, vol. 64, no. 2, p. 249 (type by monotypy Eobalearica tugarinovi Gureev).

10. Eobalearica tugarinovi Gureev

Eobalearica tugarinovi Gureev, 1949, Doklady Akad. Nauk SSSR, vol. 64, no. 2, p. 249 (Ferghana). UPPER (?) EOCENE (Ferghana beds). UZBEK SSR: Ferghana sink.

GENUS GERANOPSIS LYDEKKER

Geranopsis Lydekker, 1891, Cat. Foss. Birds British Mus., p. 166 (type by original designation Geranopsis hastingsiae Lydekker).

11. Geranopsis hastingsiae Lydekker

Geranopsis hastingsiae Lydekker, 1891, Cat. Foss. Birds British Mus., p. 166, fig. 37 (type from Hordwell, left coracoid, Brit. Mus. no. 30331). UPPER EOCENE (Hordwell beds). ENGLAND: Hampshire: Hordwell.

12. Geranopsis elatus Milne-Edwards

Geranopsis elatus Milne-Edwards, 1892, C.R.2. Congress internat. Orn. Budapest, p. 72 (type from phosphate de Chaux, tibiotarsus). According to Lambrecht (1933) a synonym for G.hastingsiae Lydekker. UPPER EOCENE or LOWER

OLIGOCENE (phosphorites du Quercy). FRANCE: plateau of Quercy.

GENUS PROBALEARICA LAMBRECHT

Probalearica Lambrecht, 1933, *Handbuch Palaeorn.*, p. 519 (type by monotypy *Grus problematica* Milne-Edwards).

13. *Probalearica problematica* (Milne-Edwards)

Grus problematica Milne-Edwards, 1871, *Ois. foss. France*, vol. 2, p. 30, pl. 76, fig. 3-7. (type from St.-Gerand-le-Puy, rostrum; referred sternum from Gannat, coll. Marquis de Lazier). LOWER MIOCENE (Aquitanian). FRANCE: Dept. Allier: Gannat and Saint-Gerand-le-Puy (Milne-Edwards, 1871).

14. *Probalearica crataegensis* Brodkorb

Probalearica crataegensis Brodkorb, 1963 (Sept. 20), *Quart. Jour. Florida Acad. Sci.*, vol. 26, no. 2, p. 163, pl. 1, figs. h-1 (type from Tallahassee, distal end of right tibiotarsus, Brodkorb no. 8503). LOWER MIOCENE (Hawthorne formation). FLORIDA: Leon County: Tallahassee, north of "Runaway Track," Switchyard B, Seaboard Airline R.R., in SE ¼ of NW ¼ section 3, Township 1 South, Range 1 West.

GENUS PLIOGRUS LAMBRECHT

Pliogrus Lambrecht, 1933, *Handbuch Palaeorn.*, p. 522 (type *Pliogrus germanicus* Lambrecht, designated by Brodkorb, 1952, *Condor*, vol. 54, p. 175).

16. *Pliogrus germanicus* Lambrecht

Pliogrus germanicus Lambrecht, 1933, *Handbuch Palaeorn.*, p. 522, fig. 156 (type from Eppelshiem, distal end left tibiotarsus, Mus. Preussischen Geologischen Landesanstalt zu Berlin). LOWER PLIOCENE (Dinotheriensande). GERMANY: Mainz basin: Eppelsheim.

17. *Pliogrus pentelici* (Gaudry)

Grus pentelici Gaudry, 1862 (read March 3), *C.R. Acad. Sci. Paris,* vol. 54, no. 8, p. 504 (type from Pikermi, 2 cervicals, proximal end of coracoid, humerus, ulna, index, pelvis, sacrum, distal end of femur, proximal half of tibiotarsus, both ends of tarsometatarsus, Paris Mus.). LOWER PLIOCENE (Pontian). GREECE: Attica: Pikermi (Gaudry, 1862). LOWER PLIOCENE:

(marnes de la Croix-Rousse). FRANCE: Croix-Rousse, on right bank of Saone near Lyon (Depéret, 1887)? LOWER PLIOCENE *(Hipparion fauna, lower Pannonian).* HUNGARY: County Fejer: Esterházy, cave near Csákvár (Kretzoi, 1957, *Aquila,* vol. 63-64, pp. 244, 248, figs. 50-51).

Subfamily Eogruinae *(Wetmore)*

Eogruidae Wetmore, 1934 (Apr. 7), *Amer. Mus. Novitates,* no. 711, p. 3 (type *Eogrus* Wetmore).

GENUS EOGRUS *WETMORE*

Eogrus Wetmore, 1934 (Apr. 7) *Amer. Mus. Novitates,* no. 711, p. 3 (type by monotypy *Eogrus aeola* Wetmore).

18. *Eogrus aeola* Wetmore

Eogrus aeola Wetmore, 1934 (Apr. 7), *Amer. Mus. Novitates,* no. 711, p. 3, figs. 2-5 (type from Chimney Butte; right tarsometatarsus, Amer. Mus. no. 2936). UPPER EOCENE (Irdin Manha [Ulan Shireh] formation). INNER MONGOLIA: Shara Murum region, Suiyuan Prov.: Chimney Butte, 5 miles N of Arshanto Obo; Camp Margetts, 25 miles SW of Iren Dabasu (Wetmore, 1934). LOWER OLIGOCENE (Ardyn Obo beds). OUTER MONGOLIA: near Ardyn Obo (Wetmore, 1934)?

19. *Eogrus wetmorei* Brodkorb

Eogrus sp. Wetmore, 1934, (Apr. 7), *Amer. Mus. Novitates,* no. 711, p. 12 (40 miles SE of Iren Dabasu).

Eogrus wetmorei Brodkorb, 1967 (June 12), Bull. Florida State Mus., vol. 2, no. 3, p. 150-151 (type distal portion of tibiotarsus, Amer. Mus. no. 2949). UPPER MIOCENE (Tung Gur formation). INNER MONGOLIA: Prov. Chahar: 40 miles SE of Iren Dabasu.

Subfamily Gruinae *(Vigors)*

Gruidae Vigors, 1825, *Trans. Linn. Soc. London,* vol. 14, p. 488 (family; type *Grus* Pallas)— *Gruinae* Bonaparte, 1831, *Saggio di una distribuzione metodica degli animali vertebrati,* p. 24.

GENUS GRUS *PALLAS*

Grus Pallas, 1766, *Misc. Zool.* p. 66 (type by tautonomy *Ardea grus* Linnaeus).

20. *Grus conferta* A. H. Miller and Sibley

Grus conferta A. H. Miller and Sibley, 1942 (May 15), *Condor,* vol. 44, no. 3, p. 126, fig. 50 (type from Black Hawk ranch, distal end of left tarsometatarsus, Univ. California Mus. Paleo. no. 34715). UPPER LOWER PLIOCENE (Siesta formation). CALIFORNIA: Contra Costa County: Black Hawk Ranch, Univ. Calif. locality no. v-3310.

21. *Grus nannodes* Wetmore and Martin

Grus nannodes Wetmore and Martin, 1930 (Jan. 20), *Condor,* vol. 32, no. 1, p. 62, figs. 23-25 (type from Sherman County, distal portion of left carpometacarpus, Univ. Kansas Mus. no. 3757). MIDDLE PLIOCENE (Edson beds, Ogallala formation). KANSAS: Sherman County, section 25, T. 10 S., R. 38 W.

22. *Grus bohatshevi* (Serebrovsky)

Sarcogeranus bohatshevi Serebrovsky, 1940, *Doklady Acad. Sci. URSS,* vol. 27, no. 7, p. 767 (type from Binagady; type skull, Azerbaijan Acad. Sci. no. 2) — *Leucogeranus bohatschevi* Serebrovsky, 1941, *Doklady Akad. Nauk URSS,* vol. 33, no. 718, p. 473, fig. 767...LOWER PLEISTOCENE (Kirov beds). AZERBAIJAN: Binagady.

23. *Grus melitensis* Lydekker

Grus melitensis Lydekker, 1890, *Proc. Zool. Soc. London,* p. 408, pl. 36, figs. 2-2a, 4, 5a-b (type from Zebbug Cave, proximal half of left coracoid, fragmentary left innominate, Brit. Mus. nos. 49365, 49322m). MIDDLE PLEISTOCENE (cave deposit). MALTA: Zebbug Cave.

GENUS BAEOPTERYX *WETMORE*

Baeopteryx Wetmore, 1960 (July 7), *Smithsonian Misc. Coll.,* vol. 140, no. 2, p. 6 (type by original designation *Baeopteryx latipes* Wetmore).

24. *Baeopteryx latipes* Wetmore

Baeopteryx latipes Wetmore, 1960 (July 7), *Smithsonian Misc. Coll.,* vol. 140, no. 2, p. 6, pl. 2, figs. 1-3, pl. 3. figs. 1-3 (type from Wilkinson quarry, right tarsometatarsus, U.S. Nat. Mus. no. 22505). LOWER PLEISTOCENE. BERMUDA: H. Bernard Wilkinson Quarry, south and west of Coney Island, Hamilton Parish (Wetmore, 1960); Government quarry (Brodkorb coll.).

25. *Baeopteryx cubensis* K. & H. Fischer

Baeopteryx cubensis K. & H. Fischer, 1968, *der Falke,* 15, 270-271, a flightless crane from the Pleistocene of Cuba, 18 craniums, humerus, other wing bones, femur and other leg bones, Institut für Paläontologie, and Museum of the Humboldt University, Berlin. PLEISTOCENE, Quaternary Period. Rio Cuyaguateje at El Abismo, the Pio-Domingo cave, Pinar del Rio, Cuba.

In addition to the discovered extinct forms, Brodkorb listed neospecies of Gruidae from Pleistocene and prehistoric sites:

1. *Bugeranus carunculatus* (Gmelin) from (Southern) Rhodesia.
2. *Anthropoides virgo* (Linnaeus) from France and Azerbaijan.
3. *Grus grus* (Linnaeus) from Ireland, England, Denmark, Germany, Italy, Azerbaijan, and Java.
4. *Grus canadensis* (Linnaeus) from St. Lawrence Island, Alaska, Washington, California, Arizona, Wyoming, North Dakota, South Dakota, Nebraska, Iowa, Illinois, Ohio, New Jersey, Georgia, Florida, and San Juan de Aragon, Mexico.
5. *Grus americana* (Linnaeus) from California, Idaho, North Dakota, Illinois, Michigan, Kentucky, Virginia, and Florida.
6. *Grus antigone* (Linnaeus) from France and Germany.
7. *Grus leucogeranus* Pallas, from Azerbaijan.

Chapter One

THE EUROPEAN CRANE

(Grus grus)

Ardea Grus, Linnaeus, *Syst. Nat.* 10th ed. 1, 1758, p. 141.
Type locality: Sweden.
Vernacular names. The Crane, The European Crane, The Common
Crane (English); der Kranich, Kranich, (German); Trana (Swedish);
Kraanvogel (Dutch): Tranen (Danish); Trane (Norwegian); la Grue
Cendree (French); Grulla (Spanish); Ja Kurjen (Finnish); серый
журавль (Russian); Kurotsuru クロヅル (Japanese).

The European Crane has long been well known to man the artist, as well as
man the hunter. It is recognizably portrayed in Egyptian tombs from every
period of that country's ancient history. In one case, even a small chick is
depicted. The Demoiselle Crane also appears, but not as often. The Common
Crane was drawn by prehistoric men in Spanish caves. It was described during
Biblical times, and was known well by early Greeks and Romans. It is truly
a bird that has captured the hearts of men. It is still a very popular bird, much
loved in many regions, especially in Norway, Sweden, parts of Poland and
Germany. All over Europe ornithologists continue to amass knowledge of its
winter and summer distribution, its flights, its nesting activities, and other
behavior.

Because of damage to wheat crops, it is less liked in the Russian wheat belt
and parts of Germany. Because it raids survival food crops in Sudan and
Ethiopia during winter, it is even less liked there. Large flocks of European
and Demoiselle Cranes invade crop areas across India and Pakistan, where

European Crane on nest, near Backhammar, Sweden, May 16, 1963

the Sarus Crane is much more favored because it tends .to remain in or near jheels (irrigation impoundments) and ponds, though at times, it too, invades grain fields. Apparently the Siberian White Crane does man no economic damage, since it seldom if ever leaves its winter marshes. Here it both roosts and feeds, by night and by day.

I saw my first European Cranes when Dr. Vlad Rydzewski took me from Wroclaw northward to the Barycz Valley, Poland during early May 1963. Here for about a week's time Dr. Andrej Dyrtsch, Adam Mrugasiewicz and I visited one small marsh after another. We traveled by car, motorcycle, and bicycle, as well as on foot. After visiting two old nests, found earlier by Adam, we searched for new nests, two of which we found; but none now contained eggs. Each day we saw lone or paired cranes, but found no nests with eggs.

Polish marshes in this region are grown to sedges (*Carex* sp.),* reeds (*Phragmites communis*), marsh

marigold (*Caltha palustris*) — then in blossom — and are bordered by deciduous trees and bushes, including many alders (*Alnus* sp.), very much resembling crane marshes of southern Michigan. Weather conditions, including amount of precipitation, the humidity, air temperature are also very similar to southern Michigan, which of course is one of the areas in the U.S. with the best natural conditions for the Sandhill Crane.

Vocalizations by the European Crane were quite similar to the American Sandhill Cranes, but as I learned, their regular 'unison call' differed greatly. This was the most marvelous sound. I have never heard another crane call to approach it.

*Here, as throughout the book, when a number of species of the same genus are mentioned collectively, the abbreviation for species will replace an enumeration of possible specific terms. A glossary of ordinary and scientific names of plants and animals mentioned is at the end of the book.

From Poland we went to Denmark, where we found that only a few cranes had been seen since a fire in 1957 had rampaged through their prime roosting area. At the next stop, in Sweden, our host, P. O. Swanberg took me to crane marsh after crane marsh.

We stayed two weeks. The first day, May 15, 1963, we went to a small marsh near Vreten, to the farm of Arvid Gökstorp. We arrived by daylight, watched a gray form walk out of the *Phragmites,* and disappear in the light ground fog amongst the *Carex* vegetation. Later we saw a large bird fly across to a patch of reeds but again lost it, so we separated. Soon a crane flew across the marsh, faded amongst the cattails and Phragmites. We joined again, drove to the opposite side, waded into the rather deep marsh and soon found the nest, my first European Crane's nest with eggs. The marsh, contained reeds (*Phragmites communis*), cattails (*Typha latifolia*), marsh marigold (*Caltha palustris*), and other plants familiar to me, identical to those I had left behind in southern Michigan crane marshes. Also present were plants related to those I knew from my home: *Spiraea ulmaria, Iris pseudacorus, Filipendula ulmaria, Uronica anigallus, Carex* sp., *Equisetum* sp., with bordering bushes, alders (*Alnus glutinosa*), spruce (*Picea excelsa*), and some white birch (*Betula alba*).

Only one pair of cranes resided in this marsh. They were some distance from any other crane marsh. These conditions were similar to those of a pair of Sandhill Cranes I had studied at length in Bellevue Township, Eaton County, Michigan. Neither pair of birds called during my observations, and a local man reported that he had never heard these cranes call. Apparently cranes call much more when associated with others of their kind, perhaps a defensive mechanism.

We were in a different marsh during the afternoon, this time grown mostly to *Carex,* with scattered *Equisetum sylvaticum* and white birch; the narrow marsh bordered by extensive ridges grown park-like to pines (*Pinus silvestris*). Tord von Essen met us here and showed us a nest with two eggs. Inside these eggs chicks were peeping. The adults screamed their disapproval some 100 meters away, until after we had left the region.

The next day we went northward to Bäckhammar and Kristinehamn. Here Nils Wellberg had already found several crane nests which he showed us that day and on successive days. There was one nest (1 egg) in Skogamossen, another (2 eggs) at Uppsjön, two nests in Stormossen (each 2 eggs) and nests with 2 eggs in two other small bogs. Each Mosse was surrounded by forests of mostly pine, some spruce, at times white birch, alders, etc., and grown to fine Carex, grasses, *Equisetum,* in places short *Phragmites communis, Sphagnum, Comarum palustre, Andromeda polifolia, Vaccinium oxycoccus, Menyanthes trifoliata, Carex acuta,* and many other plants. The water was just slightly acid, registering a pH 6.0-6.6.

On May 17, Swanberg and I left for Gårdsjö where Gustav Andersson had already found another crane nest. Following him through a beautiful pine woodland we came to a small marsh about 10 acres, or 4 hectares in area, waded through shallow water where almost pure sedge, *Carex acuta* grew with smattering of *Myrica gale, Eriophorum polystachion, Menyanthes trifoliata,* and some *Caltha palustris;* pine forest reached to within 20 meters of the nest — the same forest that completely surrounded the region. Although most of the forest was pine, there were scattered white birch and spruce. The nest was a very neat pile of *Carex.*

On May 18, Swanberg took me to some southern marshes. At Jönköping Knut and Tord von Essen took us to a nest were *Carex* sp., *Andromeda polifolia, Vaccinium oxycoccus, V. vitis-idaea, Empetrum nigrum, Menyanthes trifoliata, Equisetum limosum,* and many gnarled old pines were the conspicuous plants. Here two downy chicks greeted us as the parent flew a short distance into the surrounding pine woodland. There, it joined its mate, and the two bugled their disapproval until we departed. That afternoon farther south near Varnamo, Filip Josefsson showed us the location of another nest, this time across a wide ditch in an extensive marsh grown with grass and sedge. Later we went to Kavsjön south of Kävsjö. For many years this had been an extremely successful refuge. We camped in the pine woods. (Quite typical of the usual camping expedition: it rained most of the night.) The following rather rainy morning we visited two nests in this large marsh. At one, I caught a downy two-day old chick and heard another, while at the second nest, one egg had hatched, the second was hatching. Later from the tower Swanberg and I watched birds at two additional nests far out along the edge of a marshy lake border. That afternoon we left Kävsjön, "the Big Quagmire," and the next day said farewell to the Swanbergs at Kristinehamn, where we spent several days with Nils Wellberg and Gösta Samuelsson working on crane nests found earlier by Wellberg. He took me repeatedly to blinds, where he acted as go-away person, by his departure lulling the cranes into returning. At times I reciprocated and left him in the blind. At another nest my wife and I spent the entire time from daylight until dark, a very long day in Sweden in late May, watching a pair of cranes at a nest.

The rest of our trip to Sweden consisted of lonely hours tramping through bogs and fields, interspersed with marvelous hospitality from people like the Blomgrens, Hedstroms, and Lindmarks. We went through many *myrs* that are typical of Arctic Sweden. Grown up with fine *Carex*, and some grass *(Molinia coerulea),* isolated by pine and spruce forests that in many places held pockets of small birch, they were desolate places except for the occasional appearance of the glorious cranes that lived, widely separated, in the area.

A typical day was June 5th. As I worked around a small lake, in the distance I heard the unison call given by a pair of cranes. I moved to a secluded spot from which I could watch. A lone crane came over the trees, landed near a group of small ponds, and disappeared. I moved closer, until it spotted me and

Nesting territory of Grus grus *in Barycz Valley, central Poland, May, 1963*

went into distraction display, dropping its wings and walking about in a crouched position. After an hour spent in fruitless searching for a nest, I retreated again into the spruce woodland. The bird had by now disappeared, so all I could do was wait.

At 5:10 p.m. I heard the unison call again—this time farther northwest. I was not sure of the exact direction and continued to wait. Hours wore on, the sun set at 11:00 p.m. and periodically I tried for some sleep. Each time, though, the cold woke me soon, and I was awake for the sunrise at 12:17 a.m. Patience rewarded me at 2:30 a.m., when I heard the unison call again and began working through the spruce woods. Soon I came into a much larger open myr, also entirely surrounded by spruce forest. As I entered it, a crane flew into view through the low ground fog and made its way around a point of woods where it joined its mate and both called several times. I made my way there, but found no nest, so returned to where the first bird had been. Here, in an area treacherous with sedge-covered areas of deep mud and water, I began working along the two-foot wide solid ridges, also grown to sedges and grasses. I knew I had selected the right one when just before 4:00 a.m. I found the nest with its two eggs. Even though the light was still rather weak photographs were taken, notes made of eggs, nest, and locality plants. And as I left the birds uttered their bugles of disapproval.

In several regions, at Hatten, Spatnovare, Lakaträsk, even in Muddus National Park, well above the Arctic Circle, we saw cranes but found no nests. In some regions we spent hours of search without success, in sharp contrast with those in which we found nests almost immediately.

BEHAVIOR IN SPRING.

The finest description of the European Crane's springtime activities that I have ever read was written by Sieber in 1932. Parts of it are reprinted herewith, since it has been out of print for some time and is difficult to find.

My knowledge of the Common Crane is based on many observations made over a period of 25 years. All accounts deal with birds which made their home here in the heath of Mark Province, Brandenburg, Prussia (near Berlin) and whose behavior is naturally adapted to local conditions. In other territory and surroundings the biological behavior...may be different. I should like to emphasize mainly the great confidence of the crane in man in my district. The reasons for that confidence are that there is a permanent closed season and that a tame crane named "Peter" lived in our household since the summer of 1920. Since our bird enjoys full freedom to move around, it is known by every crane living in the area surrounding our forester's farm which is situated in solitude amidst the woods. They all appear right after their arrival in the month of March on the field behind the house searching for food. Until three years ago my crane possessed also full flying power which enabled him to visit fen and bog, and he used to stay away from the farm for more than three weeks during the pairing and hatching season. Three years ago one of his wings was broken by a migrant. But that does not keep him from taking excursions by foot for many hours. The behavior of my bird toward man has influenced all the wild cranes so much that they can be approached in fields to within a distance of 30 to 50 steps. The wild mate of Peter came even to the gate of the farmyard when he was fed and for short moments she appeared even in the middle of the yard. With his call the tame bird attracts the wild ones, and they are easier to observe when he stands among them in the fields because the wild cranes are influenced to a certain degree by his behavior.

The cranes arrive here during the first part of March even if it is a (cold) spring, as it was in 1929. I have marked the following dates of arrival: March 10, 1918; March 6, 1928; March 12, 1929; March 4, 1930; March 8, 1931; March 19, 1932. In 1928 I witnessed their return. At noon, March 6th I was with Baron von Berlepsch at the edge of an elevated fen of about 40 hectares. Suddenly we heard the well-known "Kruh," and we saw 8 silvery cranes in the brightness of the sun close above our heads, gliding one after the other down to the fen. The experience of witnessing the arrival of the proud birds left a deep impression on me despite the fact that I am used to hearing and seeing the cranes daily during the warm season. At other times their presence became known to me only after I heard their loud trumpeting.

I am led to the assumption that the older birds which have already been mated arrive in pairs. I see paired birds standing around in bog and fen from the first day of their arrival, whereas unpaired birds, probably the younger ones, stay together in small flocks, at least in the beginning. I could not determine the age at which the cranes become mature enough to breed. My tame bird was 5 years old when he went out to look for a mate; but he had often joined the unpaired birds in the spring preceeding years. Any research on that question is difficult because both parent birds are of exactly the same appearance and, in my opinion, it is also impossible to distinguish between their voices. Any difference in size, although often quite substantial, is individual only, My Peter has had at least 3 different mates since the year 1925, of which the first one (1925, 1926) was very small and graceful, with quite light plumage and an abnormally high pitched voice. This female followed the tame crane in a very obvious way. I am almost certain that these two birds had young. In 1926 the loudly calling female stood about twenty steps before the yard door as early as…the 26th of February. The male flew right out to her, and for weeks they prowled all over the vicinity of the house together; toward the end of March he returned alone in the evenings, and if he was locked up the female came for him with loud calls early in the morning. In April, my bird stayed away entirely but I did not find the nest although I had reliable signs of his presence in the large bog. I presume that it was after the appearance of the young that he began staying, for shorter and shorter intervals, at the farm. He did not take part in the rearing of the young birds. It was only in the first week of August that the female appeared during the day with the fledged young birds on my field. As soon as they came down, the tame bird joined them and he came to the farm only to get his food.

At the arrival of the cranes in the beginning of March almost the whole countryside is still covered with ice and snow. Thus we had, in 1928, after they had come on March 6, a cold period from March 8th until March 22nd, with strong east wind and snow lying a hand's breadth high. Since the temperature fell, especially at night, to −7°C., bog and fen were covered with ice and the ground was frozen solidly.

In spring the cranes seek their food on nearby fields. First they feed among the young sprouts of rye and later in oat fields. It is always said that they feed on insects, grain, etc., but mainly on the sprouting green of fields and bogs. I represent the opposite opinion. During the entire spring, until the time when oats are about a hand's breadth high, at which time the young are about to hatch, the cranes stand daily among the green grain of my fields and at the farm. There are always a few around and I have counted sometimes up to 23 of them. When I took over the job an old coachman ran out as the birds settled down and chased them with a cracking whip, as my predecessor had, because of the supposed damage, instructed him to do. But I let the

Grus grus grus *at nest preening in a moment of inattentiveness at nest, near Bäckhammar, central Sweden, May 23, 1963.*

birds do as they please and could never observe any damage. Careful search sometimes found a single plant had been pulled up, but I never found that the cranes had torn off the young green or eaten it. I am sure under the sprouted plants there were hair worms or larvae of cockchafers. Moreover, one finds little funnels the size of a thimble in soft ground between the birds' large footprints, as proof of their rooting for insect larvae. I believe cranes here feed on insects by preference. Cranes sometimes pick up kernels of grain which are lying around. But since seeds are drilled everywhere nowadays, eating grain hardly needs to be considered.

My tame bird picks up a kernel sometimes when we feed the hens. For the rest of it is surprising how moderate he is in his eating habits. His hunger must be very strong in order to make him change from his dignified pace to a more rapid one. Often I leave him alone because I have no time to wait until he eats his slice of bread in very small pieces while he looks around warily between bites. I have never observed him rushing to the food and swallowing greedily as is the custom of the poultry. When dusk falls he cannot see very small pieces anymore. Every crane has an abundance of time; 'do not hurry' seems to be their motto for all actions.

I would like to comment some more about the 1928 spring. During the severe winter weather after March 8th there was nothing to be seen or heard of the cranes for awhile. Only on March 17th I found that the birds had stayed quietly the entire time in a deep-lying narrow marsh about a kilometer long, which was protected by two ridges. The sun rose above the southern ridge, thawing the northern edge of the gully about a hand's breadth wide. There I found track after track in the snow and an immense number of characteristic funnels in the black soil of the bog. Under the bare ice along the entire edge of the marsh were thousands of fen frogs which had gone into the water to spawn during the first warm days of March. Among them swam some water bugs, water scorpions and larvae of the dragonfly, all attracted by the sun shining over the ridge of the hill. It appeared that the cranes had managed to live there...contrary to their usual habits they had been absolutely silent.

It seems that the digging in the soil has been little observed yet, but it is a favorite way with the crane while searching the food. The part of the heath where I live has been infested for some ten years with quantities of larvae of the cockchafer. This provides a wide field of action for the cranes. In two years which precede the flight of the cockchafer my crane is always busy uprooting tufts of grass on a meadow which is used as pasture, sliding the appearing larvae into his throat with a graceful swing.

As soon as July comes, the wide green meadows are swarming with grasshoppers, crickets and locusts, and the cranes are occupied exclusively in a search for insects. Naturally they take at the same time every mouse, young bird, lizard and blindworm but no frogs.

My tame crane lies in wait for mice which he observes hiding. His usual slowness changes to the quickest dexterity when a soaring insect, a flying young bird or a bird with a broken wing is to be captured. I have never seen a stagbeetle escape which came within reach of his beak. Larger pieces, as camp mice, little birds, etc., he dunks into water after he has worked on them with his beak so that they can slide down easier. When the blueberries ripen one sees the cranes among the bramble eating the berries. But insects are always their favorite food.

In some sense cranes are omnivorous, but with some individual differences. My bird liked to eat rats for years. After he had pulled out the tongue, he excavated them, beginning with the mouth down to the smallest pieces until only hide and tail were left. But lately he will not even touch one.

I knew a tame crane which—through misunderstanding of his feeding needs—had been fed nothing but small fish. He had thrived nevertheless very well. But wild birds would probably obtain fish rarely and then only by accident.

Cranes require quantities of water to satisfy them. They drink frequently and copiously if water is available. On the other hand I have often seen old birds with their young in dry parts of the woods kilometers away from water. My tame crane likes a frequent bath even in the middle of winter. I have not observed such a habit among wild birds, but that does not mean they do not bathe. In bog and fen they are for the most part removed from our observations.

The birds make their presence known mainly through their voices which during the mating season are often heard even during the nights. Schuster has already appropriately described the calls, which vary very much on different occasions. There are always variations of 'Kr' and 'Kruh' in which the vowel 'u' is sometimes clear and accented, sometimes wholly absent. The 'Kr' without a vowel which becomes at last just a purring, expresses covetousness.

...it is my opinion that the old birds which have already been mated, return paired. That does not prevent the males from having hard fights with their rivals. In my specific area there are about eight pairs and perhaps six or seven unmated birds which I presume are all young. These are probably the attackers which start the fights. But a few days after arrival the whole question has been settled and I can see all eight pairs standing peacefully together on a comparatively small part of my field. Between the partners of a pair there are from time to time little love skirmishes during which the females always run for a short distance from the aggressive males.

The young single birds stay together but separated from the old ones. The preliminary approach before a pair is formed seems to take quite a time. The first endeavors to attract a female consist, it appears, in the continuous marching behind the courted female. I should like to call this stalking (*Hinterhersteigen*) after her. Heinroth has described very well this grave stalking march with thighs pressed outwards, erect ornamental feathers, and highly lifted legs.

The stalking goes on for hours and days so that it becomes tedious to the observer. Very frequently there are several birds which strut along one after the other at some distance apart. It is remarkable that every bird turns his head and beak ostentatiously in the opposite direction as if he would pretend to be completely indifferent. If the first bird stops, all the others do the same, and they act as if they had to preen themselves thoroughly to the exclusion of everything else. Heinroth very appropriately calls this acting 'mock preening' (*Scheinputzen*). My tame bird does this behavior when he intends to make an attack. In such cases he 'struts on parade' moving in smaller and smaller circles about his victim. As soon as he is close enough he starts 'mock preening,' and then suddenly lunges forward.

Toward the end of March and the beginning of April the pairs are always found in the vicinity of their chosen nesting sites whenever they are not feeding together in the fields....

It is true that about three to five pairs often breed on the bog which is about forty hectares in size. I believe this is possible because the bog is divided by spits of land and by vast reed thickets into several solid and separated plains of marshy fen which bear no vegetation other than peatmoss, cotton grass, mossberries, sundew and tube mushrooms. The adjoining lake to the north and the almost treeless meadows to the south which resemble typical prairies, provide free passages in various directions for flying in and out, so that the birds do not have to cross the breeding territory of their neighbors. Apparently this is an essential condition. On the smaller bog to the south and on the kilometer-long narrow marshes, I have never found more than one nesting pair, so that one must assume that the birds like a rather extensive breeding territory.

I should like to insert here some of my observations on the 'dancing' of the crane. The dance is executed by a single bird as well as in pairs and groups, sometimes even outside of the mating season. A bird dancing alone, opens his wings, traces the figure eight with fast steps, turns around and runs back, retracing the eight, stops, bows low several times, jumps about a meter high to the right and to the left while his long legs dangle down in the opposite direction; then he picks up a piece of bark or reed grass or any other object in reach, throws it high up, catches it, then, with a last jerk, stands erect very quietly, shakes his plumage, and the whole performance is over. It is easy to make tame birds dance if some person starts out with dancing movements. If there is enough space the bird may also run in a large circle or in an ellipse.

Bengt Berg denies the dance but he is not justified. He has watched cranes in the bogs of Lapland. In the reeds, bog, and swamp it is difficult for a crane to dance. Had he watched the birds more intensely or had he had a chance to become familiar with them somewhere else, as in bare open places of the peat bogs or in the fields of the Mark Brandenburg, he would never have made his statement.

(Author's note—While working over Common Crane marshes of Sweden and Poland, I never for the six weeks I was there observed a single dance by any cranes. This was during the nesting season, when birds were setting on eggs, the period when they try to be the least conspicuous. I am sure they had danced considerably prior to their arrival and prior to their nesting activities. For Sandhill Cranes dance considerably immediately after arrival, often at the leat provocation, and in these cases as Sieber has stated, by lone birds, by pairs, or by groups. At times during migration, when immense concentrations occur, and also during winter, an entire congregation will participate in such dances, like a bunch of bouncing balls.)

If following Schuster one is to distinguish between early and late hatching birds, we have to consider the cranes here mostly in the first group...I have found most nests ready and containing eggs in the first half of April. At this time there is no vegetation in the marsh so that the nest stands at first open and unprotected, but later on it often cannot be seen any more with higher plants surrounding it. Nests are occasionally placed in clumps of marsh marigold (*Caltha palustris*) which float on the water and are anchored loosely. In such cases the nest remains open and unprotected all the time because the marigold sinks deeper as the nest is built higher.

The young hatch around May 6th. The pair which Schuster observed had its young in 1929 on May 8th. Both young birds must have hatched almost the same time because a picture taken by forest assistant Beninde on May 6th shows the nest with both eggs in it. In 1930 the nest of the same pair stood in a narrow bog close to the bank. The hatching period was unquestionably much prolonged that year by cold and rainy weather and by some work done in the vicinity of the nest. In the last third of the hatching period the old birds stayed away frequently for as long as half a day. Nevertheless, on May 9th I saw a young bird, already dry, sitting beside the other egg. The latter had already been pecked open, and both of the young, the one inside the egg, too, peeped loudly. At my careful approach the free one tried to come towards me. It fell awkwardly over the edge of the nest between the leaves into the mud where it made unsuccessful efforts to come to me through the entanglement of leaves and stems of marigold while it kept up its loud peeping. I

Grus grus grus *turning eggs, working with nest material. Central Sweden, May 16, 1963.*

was desperate and did not know how to help. At last I waded closely to the little runaway, grasped him and put him back into the nest; when I, quickly went away. The next morning I looked into the nest from behind a trunk over the ridge...but could see only the egg. When I scanned the region with the glass I saw both old birds at a distance of about 50 meters from the nest in search of food among the foliage under old beech trees on the opposite hill. They had the young bird between them stumbling along in its thick little legs. I retired without having been detected, but, unfortunately I found a few days later that because of the many disturbances the old birds had not incubated the second egg any more. The opening in the egg had not been enlarged and the young bird inside was dead.

Otherwise both young ones come out regularly. It seems that enemies bother the crane very litt.e The usual predators are probably afraid of the sharp strokes of the crane's wings and kicking of their legs. The beak does not make a dangerous weapon. It is true that my tame bird returns in spring with his head hacked all over from his fights but these are only surface wounds which look worse than they really are. This bird has now been staying on the farm for 12 years, of which he has spent many a night in the forest without being harmed by a fox. Hens spending a night outdoors are almost always victims of a predator.

The old birds in my district take their young right after hatching to nearby parts of the woods which resemble a park with only a few very old oaks and birches, where it is quite dry and there is a meadow-like growth of very high grass. The little ones must first swim through the water-belt around the nest; the adult swims well whenever it does not want to take off. I do not know if the old birds stay overnight in the woods with their young. In these light woods which provide a far-reaching view for the birds, I often find families with small young that can move only slowly in the tall grass, shortly before nightfall, far away from fen and bog. But the big gray figures match so completely with the countryside after dusk that they vanish from the view of the most conscientious observer. Furthermore they are silent and retiring during the entire time the young are dependent, and even during the day one is often aware of the presence of the young only through movements of grass. Therefore I cannot offer a guess on how the night is spent by families as long as the chicks are small.

The leading of the young ones is done from the start in such a way that each old bird leads one of the young ones. They stay in sight and in communicating distance of each other, but they are often 100 meters apart. If one surprises these pairs the adult birds fly off at a rapid pace in different directions, then when they believe the young ones are safe, they take off without a sound. If one comes suddenly quite close, the old ones, like so many animals, pretend to be injured and try to distract the onlooker from the young by drooping their wings and by pitiful stumbling. In great danger and in case of very close approach to the young the old birds will come very near the observer and try to attract attention to themselves by strange movements, as lying flat on the ground with their wings spread out, trampling the ground on one spot, pretending to eat very eagerly and moving the head from one side to the other while holding it closely to the ground. Most of the time they succeed. The little ones know very well how to hide and disappear like a flash. They are seen one moment and vanish in the next, ducking... in the grass, resting flat against the ground.

However, I have also found families with newly hatched chicks, where the two parents cared for both young together. I have also found that chicks which hatch at the same time both remain in the nest... (for a short time). Also one sees the individual leading only the one young when first hatched; later on, all four birds stay peacefully together.

I have never seen the young birds fly before the first week of August. According to the growth of their plumage they should be able to fly long before that but apparently they do not dare to take off, but would rather rely on their fast running. In early August one sees families flying either singly or united onto the fields after the grain has been harvested. When the corn is standing, fields are avoided because the birds desire a free view to assure their safety. From that time on until their departure all birds spend the night in the bog and fen. Each arriving family is received by the others with loud trumpeting. Also every day at dawn they raise their powerful voices. The flourish of trumpetings fits wonderfully into the mood of the country, and one may stand reverently time and again to listen to the loud trumpetlike serenade which arises from all parts of the great bog. The huge figures can be seen often during daytime standing in open regions of peat bogs, where they rest and preen.

During the molting season the cranes prefer extreme privacy. I never found a bird in this condition.... They must stay in thickets of reeds and rushes. Since it is the same time during which they have the young with

them, there is complete silence in the district and not a single bird can be heard... My tame bird, a male, sheds his large feathers every other year either during early or late June....

The time of departure of the cranes varies with the year. I see departing flocks from the first of October until late November. These flocks consist of various numbers, from ten and twenty up to several hundred. Many days flight after flight passes over, often four or five groups are in sight at the same time. It seems as though the individual flocks stay in sight of each other. Some also travel at night...These flocks travel from east to west across my field close to the large bog. Most flocks break up when they discover the fen. With loud calls every bird flies in gigantic circles in the sky.... A few minutes later the flight gathers again with one bird leading and they proceed in their previous order.

It happens very seldom that a big group rests or spends the night on the bog. As a rule they stop over in fields in order to rest and search for food. As conspicuous as the departure is, so the arrival is quiet; suddenly one day in the early part of March birds are again on the fields.

Description. Breeding Adults.

Sexes alike. A large long-necked, long-legged gray bird with a black neck and a white streak extending from the face down the posterior side of the neck. In flight, like all other cranes, flies with both neck and feet extended.

Forehead and lores, which are black, and crown, which is red, sparsely covered with fine black hairlike feathers, sparsest on the crown. This bald spot recorded on two specimens (CNHM), one taken April, the other in November, extended 78 and 72 mm anteriorly-posteriorly, from the base of the upper mandible back. One specimen was from Sardinia, Caglian, Italy; the other from Wadi Natroun, Western Desert, Egypt. In three specimens of *G.g.lilfordi* (all five above birds males) (CNHM), all from China, this measurement was 65, 64, and 60 mm, while in three females (CNHM) (all from China or India) this measurement was 63, 76, and 70 mm long. The posterior half of this area, approximately, was covered with red skin. Behind this, the nape is covered with slaty-gray feathers for about 65-70 mm. The chin, throat, and anterior portion of the neck, black or very dark gray, extending from the base of the lower mandible, 217, 310, 217, and 264 mm on four of the above male specimens. From behind the eyes, extending above the crown, below onto the auriculars, including the ear coverts, white, extending around behind the gray nape, then down the neck to upper back. Remainder of plumage, slaty-gray, darker on the back, and rump, lighter on the wings and breast. The back often tinged with brown. Alula, primaries, and terminal portions of primary coverts, tips of secondaries, tip of tail, edges of upper tail coverts, some scapulars at times, black. Bases of rectrices, slaty-gray. Innermost greater coverts much elongated, rami separated, and drooping. This plumage, without primaries and secondaries, acquired by a complete molt every year, late July to early October. A few inner secondaries, some greater coverts and some outer wing-coverts are lost between December and February.

Bill straighter than in *G.canadensis*, thicker, as well as shorter, pointed, with upper mandible ridge broad and flat at the basal two-thirds. Gonys with very gradual slope. Nostrils in deep nasal groove. Tibia and tarsus slender, the bare portion of the former nearly half bare. Four toes, the hind toe slightly elevated. Each toe with a downcurved, sharp claw. There is a small web between the middle and outer toes. Leg black. Toes black above, greenish, brownish or flesh colored below. Bill of fresh specimen, (A.O.Hume, BMNH, Hissar, Punjab, India) was pale plumbeous with greenish tinge. E.C.S. Baker adds, at base of both mandibles, yellowish above. Eye, according to Hume, yellow; to Baker, orange-red; red-brown or crimson. One bird I observed in Sweden had a yellow eye; its mate had reddish-orange eyes.

Chicks, when two to three months old, acquire a rather gray plumage, but nearly every feather has a tawny or rufous tip while the entire head and neck feathers are tawny or rusty colored.

From August until early October this plumage is nearly all lost. The primaries, secondaries and rectrices are not lost. E. C. S. Baker (1928) wrote, "the edges of the grey feathers isabelline* or rufescent isabelline; the sides of the head and neck and hind neck pale rusty rufous; feathers cover the bare skin on the nape whilst the crown also is more

or less covered with the same; the drooping inner secondaries are wanting."

The Eastern Gray Crane, *G.g.lilfordi* is paler in color, Blaauw (1897) could see insufficient evidence to differentiate it from the common crane, but the two forms have been retained because of the paler coloration of the adult bird. All other plumages seem exactly alike.

Downy Chick

Downy chick. The chick is covered completely with thick, soft down. Dorsally it is deep chestnut, darkest down the back of the neck, along the mid-dorsal line, over the back of the wings, the back, and the width of the rump, then extending down the sides to below the wing level. Narrow, similarly colored strips, about one or two mm wide, extend semicircularly from either side of the base of the bill, five to eight mm below and posterior to the eye, then up over the crown where they join. The head is lighter chestnut, some portions having been described as "Ocheraceous-tawny to Cinnamon" in color, while the ventral side, from the base of the bill to the region below the tail, is lighter, in some places tinged with gray, others almost white. On the anterior side of each wing attachment is a region of white. At the bend and tip of each wing is a small claw. The eye is dark brown. The bill and legs, flesh colored at first, soon darken, become grayish with a tinge of blue. The tibial-tarsal joint remains flesh colored at least two or three days. There is a yellowish tinge at the base of the upper mandible.

Downy European Cranes on nest at Dumme Mosse, near JonKoping, southern Sweden, May 18, 1963. Nest found by Knut von Essen.

---

*A pale yellowish brown.

COPULATION

I have seen four species of cranes copulate and several photographs of a fifth, the last, *Grus grus grus*. From photographs the Common Crane resembles both the Greater Sandhill Crane in Michigan (*Grus canadensis tabida*) and the West African Crowned Crane (*Balearica pavonina pavonina*), in Nigeria. About two weeks before eggs are laid, possibly sooner, the breeding urge reaches a peak.

Normally the pairs have fed for some time together, side by side, day after day, and roosted together at night. About the time nest building is in progress in Michigan—the first warm days of March—the female crane during early morning suddenly stops in front of the male, her back toward him. As she stops she raises her head and bill, pointing them forward and upward. Sometimes she spreads her wings slightly. Littlefield (1970) observed that the male sometimes went into this stance first. The female

Common Cranes on feeding grounds, near Lake Hornborgasjön, Sweden, April 16, 1971. (Photo by Dr. P. O. Swanberg.)

holds this position for several seconds, not moving her head from side to side but holding it perfectly still. The male, who has hitherto been slow and deliberate, quickly comes to life, advancing to the female, who at times crouches slightly with wings half-spread. When he mounts he stands either on the rump, lower wings or lower back and with slowly beating wings copulates with her. I never have heard any calls given by *G.c.tabida* but they do utter a low rapid purring according to George Archibald. The Common Crane performs copulation in exactly the same position as does *G.c.tabida,* and *B.p.pavonina.* With *Grus japonensis* the female at times lies flat against the ground with wings spread while the male mounts. Prior to this the male gives a distinctive call, different from any other I have ever heard —a penetrating *"Kurr-kurr-kurr-kurr-kurr."* The Japanese Cranes performed copulation on the winter feeding grounds when snow was often a foot or more deep. But within a few days they turned up missing from the region, their young birds being deserted for the first time. With the Sandhill Crane in Michigan, the young birds had disappeared for some time, the adults had been back usually about two weeks and were just beginning to build nests, with every pair on its own breeding territory.

Franden (1958) reported that the male crane in approaching the female gave a loud "Krå, krå, krå." In Sweden copulation apparently often takes place on the feeding grounds near Hornborgasjon, in Västergotland, probably some distance from the nesting grounds.

NESTING BIOTOPES

Makatsch (1959) said central European crane marshes are grown to sedges, grasses and *Phragmites,* bordered by oak, beech, birch and pine woodlands. In the Barycz Valley, western Poland, sedge grown crane marshes were usually isolated by woodlands, mostly oak, birch, pine and alder. The cranes nested in the open regions but at times in wet swamps among trees.

In northern Jutland, Denmark, cranes nested betwen 1948 and 1956, when a fire swept the Kragskovhede region. The birds returned for a few days in 1957 but disappeared shortly thereafter. They had not returned by 1963 when we visited the region. (C. Koch, verbal). This region was grown heavily to heath plants: *Carex, Eriophorum,* and grasses; the openings surrounded by groups of forest, largely birch and alder. Although ditched, the land was poorly drained and flat. Probably the bogs at Lille Vildmose region (Lat. 56°50′N.), where cranes were also reported nesting in Denmark, were similar.

The biotopes of Sweden, Norway, Finland and northern Russia vary from south to north but little at the same latitudes. Few cranes nest north of 68°N.Lat. Most all bogs, myrs, and mosse, up to this latitude are surrounded or nearly surrounded by forest, chiefly spruce (*Picea excelsa*), pine (*Pinus sylvestris*), birch (*Betula alba, B.nana*), and some alders (*Alnus* sp.). All regions were flat with surrounding woodlands only slightly higher in south and central Sweden but extending in northern Sweden from the bog borders even onto the mountain valleys and up the low mountains.

Southern marshes of Sweden, like those of Poland, and Germany, are similar to Sandhill Crane marshes of southern Michigan, Wisconsin, and Oregon. Northern bogs are more like those of northern Michigan, Ontario, Minnesota and Alberta.

The marsh near Vreten, Sweden was only partly surrounded by forest, mostly birch and alder with a few isolated spruces. Much of this marsh was surrounded by cultivated fields. The marsh plants, many exactly similar to North American ones, were reeds (*Phragmites communis*), cattail (*Typha latifolia*), sedges (*Carex* sp.), marsh marigold (*Caltha palustris*), *Filipendula ulmaria, Iris pseudacorus,* and others.

Slightly south of here, at Tidaholm, a nesting marsh was a stream valley grown mostly to sedges, with a bordering forest chiefly of pine, with some birch. At Jönköping in Dumme Mosse, the bordering pines were old and gnarled. Even the raised marshy center had scattered pines, all encircled by an open marshy moat containing sphagnum moss, *Carex, Equisetum limosum, Equisetum* sp., *Andromeda polifolia, Vaccinium oxycoccus, V. vitis idaea, Empetrum nigrum,* and in places, more scattered plants such as *Menyanthes trifoliata.*

At Kavsjön, forest of pine with some birch and alder surrounded the region. Along one side a road had been built, and between this and the marsh an observation tower stood, but few people entered the marsh. It was grown heavily to *Equisetum limosum, Equisetum* sp., sedges, marsh marigold, groups of willow (*Salix repens, Salix* sp.), and in places to reeds and a few cattails.

In the Kristinehamn-Bäckhammer region, all mossen were surrounded by pines, associated with some spruce, white birch and unidentified bushes. The bogs were dense with *Carex*, including *C. acuta*, and grasses; in places with shorter reeds, in others with sweet gale (*Myrica gale*), cotton grass (*Eriophorum polystachion, Eriophorum* sp.), *Comarum palustre*, and marsh marigold.

In the Arctic regions from Harads to Gällivare, myrs were covered with sphagnum moss, along with varying numbers and associations of other plants, including *Menyanthes trifoliata, Vaccinium ulginosum, V. vitis idaea, V. oxycoccus, Andromeda polifolia, Ledum palustre, Rubus chamaemorus, R. arcticus, Betula pubescens, B.nana, B.alba, Scirpus caespitosus, Molinia coerulea*. Most often forests of pine and spruce in pure stands surrounded the myrs, producing exceedingly good isolation. These soft, treacherous myrs were divided by solid, slightly raised, interconnected ridges, one to four feet wide, grown much more densely to grass, sedges, and low birches, and so connected that a person could walk from one to another. But one misstep off the firm ridges would sink the walker into a deep quagmire. The grassy ridges in some regions also supported scattered scraggly pines, standing eight to twenty feet apart. These ridged bogs often were very extensive, with many isolated regions among them formed by the maze of clumped spruces growing through them. Many years, ice remains over the clearings through much of the crane nesting season, while few people penetrate them and predators are scarce. Bogs of Norway and Finland and probably Russia over the same latitudes are very similar. Wolley (1859) described a region at Latitude 68°N. opposite the Finnish village of Yli Muonioniska in a great marsh called 'Iso Uoma,' a soft bog in which, except where the bog-bean grows, one generally sinks up to the knees, or even to the middle. It is intersected by long strips of firmer bog-earth, slightly raised above the surrounding level, bearing creeping shrubs, principally of sallow and dwarf birch, mixed in places with *Ledum palustre, Vaccinium ulginosum, Andromeda polifolia, Rubus chamaemorus*, grasses and *carices*, mosses and also a few bushes or treelets of the common birch, and these quite numerous in some parts of the marsh.

THE NEST

The European Crane's nest often depends on the surrounding vegetation. It is always placed in or very near water, which is usually only a few centimeters deep. It is placed in a bog, mosse, myr, heath, or marsh. It can be in an open spot several hundred meters from the nearest bushes or trees; or directly adjacent to a tree or bush. Sometimes it is well hidden by tall or even short ground vegetation, at other times it is quite conspicuous.

Nests are smaller in Arctic Lapland. Wolley (1959) describes several Arctic nests (Lapland, Lat.68°N.) which he found in 1853 and 1854. One was made "of very small twigs mixed with long, sedgy, grass; altogether several inches in depth, and perhaps two feet across." A second was "about two feet across, was fairly flat, and chiefly of light-coloured grass or hay, loosely matted together, scarcely more than two inches in depth, and raised only two or three inches from the general level of the swamp." Another nest "was on a little elevation not more than one stride across, and only raised a few inches above the water.... The nest, as usual, was of the kind of sedgy grass which grew in the same marsh as the nest. Some of the pieces had been pulled up by the roots. It was twenty-seven inches across (68.6 cm), and three or four inches (7.5-10 cm) in thickness, perfectly flat, dripping wet in the lowest layers."

Berg (1930) described a nest, "scarcely to be called a nest. It was placed on the one and only grass hummock between two or three outermost willow bushes. On the hummock was a flat bed of withered grass." This was also in Swedish Lapland. He described a more southern nest in Sweden as placed in a white birch wooded island "on a mound of sward, which was as flat and broad as an altar."

Nest of Grus grus grus *near Tidaholm, Sweden, May 15, 1963. Tord von Essen found the nest.*

Hoffman (1936) described and showed photographs of a nest near Brandenberg, Germany, built entirely of *Phragmites communis.* Makatsch (1959) showed and described several nests, many built of *Phragmites,* others of sedges, grasses and other plants in the Oberlausitz, East German region.

Adam Mrugasiewicz showed me two crane nests in the Barycz River Valley, Poland. Both were built in open marshes adjacent to a bush or tree at the very edge of the woods. One was a large mass, one meter across, 15 cm tall and nearly flat, of round rushes (*Scirpus* sp.) built in 10-15 cm of standing water, surrounded by similar vegetation used in

nest construction. The second nest was 65 cm across, 8 cm above the water, located in 38 cm of standing water and only 10 meters from nearby alders.

One nest at Kavsjon, southern Sweden, was built beside a one-meter tall willow. Materials used were *Carex, Equisetum* sp., *E.limosum.* It was placed in 12 cm of standing water, measured 11.5 cm above the water and 92 x 92 cm across, and was hollowed out about three cm. Another nest in the same marsh was even smaller; 60 x 42 cm across, 15 cm above the surrounding water, placed on top of a natural mound exactly the size of the nest and surrounded by 45 cm of water. The vegetation around both of these nests was only 15 to 18 cm high while at a nest nearby at Draftånge it was up to one meter in height.

A nest at Jönköping in Dumme Mosse was placed in 15 cm of water. It was a huge pile of *Carex, Equisetum* and other surrounding plants pulled up from the immediate neighborhood. Some of the sedges had been pulled out by the roots. Twenty-seven cm tall, it measured 127 x 127 cm across, and was nearly flat on top.

Another large nest at Vreten was placed in 32 cm of standing water but surrounded by water one-half meter deep. It was built of *Carex,* some cattail, and some reed, slightly hollowed out on top for the eggs. It measured 100 x 98 cm across, and 19 cm above water level.

A nest near Tidaholm was only two meters from a small stream, its top 23 cm above the water which around it was only 10 cm deep. It measured 117 x 106 cm across, and was built mostly of surrounding *Carex.* Another nest near Gårdsjö, located in a four-hectare mossen was closer than usual to surrounding trees—only 20 m away. It was a large pile of mainly *Carex acuta,* a small clearing around the nest showing where all the nearby plants had been pulled out and piled into the mass. Water 20 cm deep surrounded the nest, which rose 8.5 cm above water, and measured 119 x 104 cm across. It was almost flat, being but slightly hollowed on top.

Seven nests near Bäckhammar (found by Nils Wellberg) were piles of surrounding vegetation, principally *Carex, Myrica gale, Phragmites communis, Equisetum* sp., *Eriophorum* sp., etc. Four measured across 75 x 77 cm, 94 x 107 cm, 70 x 78 cm, and 118 x 119 cm. Five averaged 10.01 (4...15) cm above water level and water around them averaged 26.2 (8...60) cm deep. One nest was built chiefly of *Phragmites* (pieces generally 5-12 cm long) and placed in a water-soaked, woods-surrounded, mosse some 6 hectares in size; another was placed in a similar sized mosse amid short *Equisetum* and *Carex* (about 12 cm tall), 150 meters from surrounding trees; two nests were placed in the same long, narrow, mosse (about 10 kilometers long by ½ to 1 kilometer wide). One was built mostly of *Carex* sp., with a very little sweet gale and was situated about 150 meters from the surrounding woods. The second,

about 2 or 3 kilometers away, was built mostly of *Carex.* Another nest found by Wellberg was built of short pieces of *Phragmites* and *Carex.* None was built in tall vegetation.

Four nests in Norrbotten were built in varying sized myrs, the nesting territory surrounding each ranging in area from 50 to about 400 hectares. Each nest was built on a mound of solid ground or on a ridge. All were placed in short (less than 30 cm) *Carex* or similar vegetation, and all except one were built adjacent to a pine or a low dwarf birch. Isolation of both nest and nesting territory was insured by dense, surrounding spruce or pine forest. Nests were built of grass *(Molinia coerulea), Carex,* and *Equisetum,* often with wads of sphagnum moss mixed in—some plants incorporated into nests had been pulled roots and all from the nearby soft marsh. No nest was more than 100 meters from some part of the surrounding forest. Water beside the ridges averaged from 14 to 61 cm deep. The nests were 4 to 28 cm thick and, measured across, the four were 65 x 65 cm, 61 x 62 cm, 63 x 96 cm and 62 x 65 cm respectively, much smaller than nests farther south. Southern nests were crane-made islands.

The average mean measurements of 20 nests (16 in Sweden, 2 each in Finland and Poland) taken at the widest and narrowest aspects were: 81.7 extremes: 61-127 x 92.0 extremes: 62-127 cm across at the base and 12.58 extremes: 2-28 cm high. The average water depth at 18 Swedish nests was 29.36 extremes: 8-60 cm. Nests in the Arctic always seem associated with deeper water, even though placed on dry ridges.

Dementiev and Gladkov wrote (1951) of Russian nests: "The nests usually are established a great distance from each other, at 5 to 6 km, and only in rare instances does it come about that several pairs nest closer one to the other than by two or three km. In the northern part nesting cranes are side by side with nests of geese and ducks with which the cranes get along peacefully. For the nest site they choose a dry place amidst the marsh—rushes, with reeds or bushes (may be) nearby, but around the nest it is always an open clearing, which lies on the ground. ...Sometimes it is a simple small scooped spot in the soil covered with a thin layer of dry stems of grass, reeds or clubgrass, but more often a heap of care-

Nest of Grus grus grus *at Rödingsträsk, Norrbotten, Sweden, May 31, 1963.*

lessly piled twigs lined with straw-like layers of dry grass and reeds, or a compact trampled down heap of humified reeds, almost perfectly flat. The diameter is about 80 cm. Height 20-30 cm (Khar'kovskaya Oblast, Somov, 1897). During several summers cranes nest in the same marsh, with some pairs occupying the same nest — even, with one pair, when the eggs had been taken and the nest ruined the previous year."

EGG LAYING

Behm (1908) wrote that a pair of *Grus grus* came to Skansen Zoological Gardens, Stockholm, Sweden during mid-September 1893. There the pair nested each year, 1895 through 1908. This region is quite similar in climate to nesting regions at the same latitude in Sweden. Table 1 gives the records of this crane pair. Eggs were laid on an average of 2.4 (3.3) days apart, but extremes ranged between one and 14 days, usually not more than four. Birds in the wild may nest earlier.

Dementiev and Gladkov wrote (1951): "Little is available concerning the hatching dates. As a rule one can compute that egg sets occur (are laid or set on) from early April to mid-May. In northern European Russia laying begins in late April or early May; in the Ukraine, during the second half of April to early May. Eggs were found in Moscow Oblast in Voskresensk Region, (Lat.56°N, Long. 39°E) on 2nd May...; in Minsk Province (Lat.52°N, Long.27°E) April 29, 1905 (2 well incubated eggs),

May 14, 1905, and June 5, 1903 (in each set was one pipped egg...); in Novgorodsk Oblast in middle May. If bothered the birds duplicate reproduction but greatly delayed....The space between laying of the eggs is about 2 days.

"Incubation begins, apparently, with the laying of the first egg. The first young hatched 2 days before the second in Moscow Oblast. During the period of incubation, cranes manage a very secretive mode of life. The female does most of the incubation, but the male is always around the nest alertly on watch, giving advance notice by bugling loudly if danger comes, and he relieves her for short periods when she feeds...Incubation requires about a month (29-30 days)."

Incubation period

Behm (1908 — see Table 1) recorded incubation periods at Skansen, Sweden, at ten different nests by a captive pair. These eggs required 27 to 35 (averaging 30.3) days to hatch. Makatsch (1959) wrote that Niethammer gave the incubation period "28-31, usually...29-30 days," while Makatsch, from his own observations at Oberlausitz gave an average of 30 days. The British Handbook gave 28-30 days.

Clutch size

The Common Crane lays two eggs — rarely one, even more rarely three. Niethammer (1942) reported 200 clutches. Five consisted of one, and 195 of two, eggs. Fränden (1958) reported that the usual number in Sweden was two, while Makatsch (1959) stated the usual number in Germany was two. In a letter (22 July 1964), Makatsch reported to me that he had found 36 eggs sets, of which all contained two eggs except one with one egg and one with three.

In the British Museum (Natural History) 17 clutches from Germany, including Prussia and Pomerania, averaged 1.88 eggs (1x3 13x2 3x1). From southern Russia there were ten sets (8x2 2x1); from Norway, Sweden and Finland, four sets, all two eggs; from Spain, one complete set of two eggs. During May and June 1963, I saw 13 completed sets

in Sweden (12x2 1x1) and obtained records of ten other clutches (10x2). From available records I find records of 292 sets (574 eggs) of which 278 consisted of 2 eggs, 2 of 3, and 12 of 1 egg; averaging 1.97 eggs per set.

Egg Size, Shape, and Color

Following are measurements of many museum eggs, measured by me in Sweden and as recorded there and elsewhere by others:

		length diameter
U.S.S.R. (So. European)	16 eggs	97.29x62.47mm (BMNH)
Finland	5 eggs	97.6 x60.86mm (BMNH)
Sweden	26 eggs	94.4 x60.03mm (LHW)
Sweden	106 eggs	93.3 x59.7 mm (Rosenius)
Germany	100 eggs	96.4 x59.3 mm (Hartert)
Germany, Prussia, Pomerania	29 eggs	96.47x61.54mm (BMNH)
Spain	16 eggs	99.38x61.13mm (BMNH)
Norway	1 egg	93.7 x64.4 mm (BMNH)
Turkey	1 egg	92.3 x61.8 mm (BMNH)
Total	300 eggs, mean dimensions	95.34x60.05mm

Nest and eggs of European Crane, Gårdsjö, Sweden, May 17, 1963. Found by Gustav Andersson.

Common Crane eggs taken in the past in Spain (BMNH), and those from southern Russia, averaged larger than those from regions in between. The largest were from Spain, they measured (length by width): 109.4x63.9, 107x61, and 105.9x60.9 mm; while three from south European Russia measured 94.1x64.8, 95.1x65.4, and 93.9x64.9mm. The smallest egg, from Prussia, measured 84.7x58.3mm. Two I measured in Sweden were, respectively, 84.9x59.7 and 92.2x56.1mm. Extremes of the 22 eggs I measured in Sweden were: Length, 84.9 to 104.8mm; width, 56.1 to 63.1mm.

Makatsch (op.cit.) gave the average weight of 40 eggs as 183 (extremes: 144-211) grams. Dementiev and Gladkov (1951) reported the weights of two eggs as 167.4 and 200.0 grams in Russia. During May and June 1963, I weighed 22 eggs, mostly near hatching time. They averaged 157.3 (from 133.4 to 206.6) grams. One egg, at Kavsjön, the day before hatching, May 18, 1963, weighed 141.3 grams. (It measured 90.4x60.2mm) The two largest Swedish eggs were at Rödingsträsk, Norrbotten, May 31, 1963, which weighed 203.6 and 206.6 grams. (They measured, respectively, 104.4x62.6 and 104.8x 63.1mm.) Eggs were ovate, long ovate, less often pointed ovate, and at times, subelliptical in shape.

Makatsh (1959) wrote: "There are three different distinguishable color types of crane eggs:

"1. Ground color: Olive-brown with a tinge of greenish or reddish; frequently too, a reddish-brown. The spots extend over the entire egg with the majority at the larger end and fewer at the smaller end. Spots are rather coarse, irregular in size, brown or reddish-brown, while at the blunt end they frequently are black-brown, with an underflecking of gray-brown. There are small warts at the larger end. The pores along the length around many eggs frequently are scarcely recognizable with a pocket lens.

"In this group belong the eggs of all cranes except those of *Grus antigone, Grus rubicunda* and *Balearica.*

"2. Ground color is whitish, perhaps with a tinge of gray or Isabella-color*; spots weak loam-brown with underfleckings of violet-gray. In this group be-

*A yellowish-brown off-white.

Eggs of Grus grus grus *Bäckhammar, Sweden, May 17, 1963. One of the nests found by Nils Wellberg.*

long the eggs of *Grus antigone* and *Grus rubicunda.*

"3. The eggs...are bluish-white normally without any spots. Above the bluish-white calcareous shell, there extends still another much less pronounced white plainlike region...In this group are found eggs of *Balearica.*"

In Sweden I observed 23 eggs in 13 different nests. Nine of these had a greenish cast to the dark olive-brown color. These were from five different sets. Twelve eggs from six other sets had a much whiter or grayer tinge to the ground color. Most of these light colored eggs were from Norrbotten. All eggs were heavily spotted but some much more heavily than others. Some were flecked with dark olive-brown, gray-brown, gray, lavender, black-brown, and even black. Some had rather fine dots, with many more near the larger end, while some had extremely large splotches at the larger end. Some had splotches nearly one cm across. On all, the spots radiated from the larger to the smaller end. The darker eggs resembled very much those of the Lesser Sandhill Crane and Stanley Crane.

Eggs of cranes are almost invariably placed in the center of the nest, where there is a slight depression. Relationship of one egg to the position of the other and the distance they were apart is given in Table 2.

The nesting season lasts for about one month. Its dates in a particular place can be generalized from the dates of egg findings.

Incubation Behavior

Both male and female incubate the eggs. On the rainy morning of May 19, 1963, P. O. Swanberg and I watched several pairs of cranes at their nests from the tower at Kävsjön. Two pairs had young but at two other nests the birds changed places at 5:28 a.m. and 6:02 a.m. One crane flew from behind some bordering trees and across the marsh, to alight beside the nest. The birds changed places silently. The second bird flew back in a reversal of the route the first had used. At the second nest, one bird, standing about 32 meters from the nest, abruptly walked over to it. The incubating crane rose, and together they sounded their unison call. The second bird then walked away a short distance and began to feed as the first bird settled onto the nest.

Near Bäckhammar, at Uppsjön, my wife and I watched a pair continuously for 18 hours on May 21, 1963. The birds changed places only three times, at 6:24 and 8:01 a.m., and at 1:17 p.m.

Crane observations at Uppsjön Värmland, Sweden, 21 May 1963, 0300-2100 hrs.

0300. -1°C., frosty and clear. One crane standing 100 meters NW of nest; other setting on nest. A snipe is winnowing; a redwing and cuckoo are singing; water rails, and wood pigeons call.

0314. Female (smaller bird) roosting in shallow water near nest. She suddenly flies about 1 kilometer from the marsh to a field east of the road to feed.

0315. Two cranes, a long distance away, call in unison.

0320. Sun rising. Black grouse at height of display on other side of mosse

0335. Black grouse temporarily lessening activities.

0345. Male crane raises head and looks around.

0356. Male raises head again, looks all around.

0401. Male, as he sits on eggs, begins preening.

0445. Male stand up about one minute, working with eggs, then sits down. Black grouse nearly inactive.

0455. Male stands up again for 10 seconds. Black grouse silent; Snipe winnowing; Curlew continue to call.

0602. Male stands up, turns eggs. After 2½ minutes sits down.

0624. Female flies into marsh, lands 50 meters south of nest. She drinks then walks to nest as male rises and walks away about 6 meters silently, then flies east over trees to same field where female has just fed. Female down onto eggs in 15 seconds.

0642. Female stands up, walks away from nest a few meters, returns.

0720. Curlew lands near nest. No crane action. Cool and windy now.

0732. Male flies into marsh, lands 100 meters south of nest.

0745. Male drinks, then preens. Feeding as he goes, he works toward nest.

0750. Male flies east of nest, zigzagging back and forth in pursuit of the curlew, which stays ahead of him in their race across the marsh.

0801. Male returns to nest on foot. Female rises, works with eggs. Silently male walks onto nest as female leaves. She walks 110 meters north of nest, then stops and preens. Later she feeds in the shallow water. She stretches first one wing, then the other, and at 0856 flies back to feed in the same field. Male watches her go.

0901. Male stands, works 2 minutes with eggs, settles down.

0959. Male rises, preens, then works with eggs 1½ minutes; settles down.

1043. Male stands, preens, works 2 minutes 25 seconds with eggs.

1211. Male preens and works with eggs 2 minutes.

1301. Female lands 300 meters east of nest, then flies to within 100 meters and walks slowly to it.

1317. Silently they change places; the female walking in; the male walking away. As he leaves, he stops, picks up some sedges, and tosses them sidewise over his shoulder back toward nest. They land in water near but not on it.

1325. Male stops pulling sedges, flies 300 meters south of nest.

1415. Male flies some distance along the marsh border. Clouds forming in west as male begins feeding near our observation tower.

1445. Male flies to field to feed.

1510. A mallard lands near the tower in a pool, but flies when it sees us. Swallows, white-rumped martins flying over all of the marsh. Snipe winnowing; curlew calling.

1615. The female rises and quickly leaves the nest, going about 100 meters, as if frightened. She returns, but again quickly goes away about the same distance. We soon see a young boy walking along the bog's edge. As soon as he becomes visible (on two occasions), the female leaves the nest; once 7 minutes, the second time, 5 minutes.

1650. Black grouse clucking at edge of woods.

1720. Clouds becoming heavier; a light rain begins falling.

1815. Female rises for 40 seconds, works with eggs. She reaches out along the edge of nest, pulling in more materials.

1922. Cuckoo begins calling steadily. A starling flock flies over bog. Cloudy and windy, rain has ceased.

2035. Male flies into marsh, lands 500 meters from nest to spot where female spent the previous night. Here he preens.Black grouse dancing again.

2100. Male preens. He does not go to nest. Female setting. Sun has set. Night clear.

At a myr 12 kilometers southwest of Gällivare, Norrbotten, Sweden, I stayed nearly 24 hours in the vicinity of a crane nest, on June 5, 1963. I watched one bird of a crane pair fly over a spruce woodland into a lake situated in a marshy clearing at 1:52 p.m. At 5:10 p.m. he returned to the nest and with his mate, gave the unison call. The sun set at 11:00 p.m., and rose again at about 12:17 a.m. It was a clear cold night. At 2:30 a.m. the pair called in unison again when the sun was still very low and the temperature a few degrees above freezing. From what I could observe, these birds probably changed places four or five times during a 24-hour period. They were largely inactive during the midnight dusky period. One bird roosted about 500 meters from the nest, behind a spruce-grown point, so that he was unable to even see the nest. The other bird remained like a gray ball during the period of dusk and low sun, neither moving much nor looking around.

Nils Wellberg found a Common Crane nest in Stor Mosse April 27, 1963. It contained two eggs. On May 16, he showed this nest to P. O. Swanberg and me. They put me in a blind Nils had built at 12:30 p.m. After they left, the only sounds were the continued monotonous call of a cuckoo, calls of whimbrel and curlew, and the songs of a willow warbler and a reed bunting. At 1:25 p.m. I noted a lone crane standing 100 meters away, turning his head from side to side as he seemed to inspect everything everywhere. He then walked swiftly away but soon a unison call split the air. When the pair gave this call the male called Krooaa-krooaa-krooaa-krooaa-krooaa, the female simulataneously Krrr-krrrr-krrr-krrrr-krrr-krrr-krr. The male seemed to be the aggressor, and the call of the female was slightly behind his.

From my notebook for May 16, 1963:
1328. Only 10 meters from the blind a crane walks swiftly by, going directly to nest. It turns the eggs, alternately stamping its feet up and down several times, then sits down. It is the female. At 1345 she begins preening. The only noise now is wind blowing through the pines above me.
1420. The female rises suddenly, walks swiftly away into the mosse and eight minutes later the male, carefully measuring each step, comes to the nest. He is much larger and darker, with eyes a reddish-yellow; hers are a deep yellow. He turns the eggs and sits down. Later he watches two jets as they fly overhead.

He is very alert, watching out all the time, but pays no attention to the click of my camera shutter. Finally he lowers his head until it is no higher than his body.
1601. I look through a small hole in the back of the blind. There, only a short distance away, stands the female, alternately watching and preening. She begins walking around the blind, crossing through the pine point which extends into the mosse where it leaves the main woods.
1658. The female comes from the woods side, walking swiftly to the nest. Silently she sits down on the eggs as the male begins feeding away from the blind in the mosse. The sun is getting quite low and the temperature is ideal.
22 May 1963. Cool and slightly rainy. In blind 1300-1730 hrs. Both birds at the nest, run away at our arrival with wings drooping and outspread, showing pronounced distraction display. Shortly afterwards I hear one give a *purrr* call from behind the blind and not too long afterwards the female comes to the nest and begins incubating and brooding, for there is now a newly hatched chick in the nest and one egg.

Stormosse, near Bäckhammar, Sweden, May 23, 1963. European Crane standing at attention over eggs.

1501. The female feeds the chick some small particle that I cannot recognize.

1700. She rises and feeds the chick a piece of egg-shell, talking softly to him: *Purr, purr, purr.*

1705. She repeats the procedure, sits down and pecks at the edge of the nest.

23 May. Clear and cool. The birds are wilder. The baby crane is gone.

0925. Twice the cranes give the unison call about 300 meters away.

1025. The two cranes now stand about 100 meters from the nest. I cannot see the chick. A jay (*Garrulus glandarius*) just flew from the bordering woodland, landed on the edge of the nest. Both cranes flew right to the nest, moving with surprising speed. The intruder did not even have time to hop once. He didn't stay. The behavior change in these slow birds is almost unbelieveable.

1107. The male has come to the nest and begun incubating. He is there even as I leave. The female somewhere off in the mosse must have the other young. Now the second egg is almost hatched. The young should be out in a very few minutes. The eggs had hatched on 22 May about 0700 hrs, and on 23 May at 1730 hrs, respectively.

The Young

Table 1 gives hatching dates for the eggs of a captive pair of cranes at Skansen. The average dates during a ten-year period were June 4-6. (Extremes: May 30-June 1 to June 13-15.) The eggs in these nests hatched two days apart on 3 occasions; on successive days, 4 times; and on the same day, once. In the wild, in southern Sweden, some eggs observed during 1963 hatched as follows:

Småland, Kavsjön; About May 16-17, 1963.

Småland, Kavsjön; May 18-19, 1963.

Småland, Jönköping, Dumme Mosse; May 17-18, 1963.

Västergötland, Tidaholm: About May 17-18, 1963.

Västergötland, Gårdsjö: May 21-22, 1958 (Gustav Andersson).

Västergötland, Gårdsjö: May 16, 1961 (Gustav Andersson).

Värmland, Bäckhammar, Stormosse; May 22-23, 1963. Swanberg (letter) gave May 16-23 as normal hatching in central Sweden.

Dementiev and Gladkov (1951) wrote:
Incubation begins, apparently, with the laying of the first egg (in a nest discovered in Moscow Oblast, the first egg hatched two days before the second. Yevt-

yokhov, 1928). During the period of incubation, cranes have a very secretive mode of life. The female does most of the incubation but the male is around the nest alertly on watch, giving advance notice in case of danger, by loud crying. During short periods he relieves her while she feeds. If frightened from the nest the female flies directly away, or back and forth. Sometimes she runs a few steps and later flies up...Incubation requires about a month (29-30 days.)

The young hatch in central parts of the European USSR early in, or during, mid-May, up to late June (in a Moscow Oblast nest, first young hatched 22 May and the second 24 May...In Minsk Oblast, 14 May 1905, and 5 June 1903, eggs were hatching (Shintnikov, 1913). In Voronezh District (Lat. 52°N, Long. 39°E) 3 or or 4 day old chicks were encountered, one on 26 May, the second on 22 June (Ognev, 1924). The male and female are both strongly attached to the chicks...At hatching time young weigh about 120 grams. By three days the weight has increased only about 10 grams; later...by 12 days a young weighed 560 grams; at 16 days, 800 grams; at 26 days, 1350 grams; at 32 days, 1880 grams; at 70 days, 3500 grams; at 170 days, 4800* grams; here it reached its peak, equal in weight to adults. The first feathers appeared on the wing at 15-17 days; at 30 days the entire chick was still covered with down, feathers showing only on the wing; at 40-43 days, young are fully covered with feathers with down here and there.

As soon as the young becomes stronger, parents take them from the nest into the rushes, into weeds near a river, or into shrubbery. When the young are able to fly, parents and young fly out to feed in nearby grain fields or into meadows, but to rest (at noon and night) they fly back into the reeds. During early July, in the central European USSR, young begin to fly. In late July, families begin a nomadic mode of life. In early August families gather into flocks in preparation for migration.

The average weight of three young less than one day old was 105.3 grams; the average wing measurement of four such young, from the bend to the end of the longest down, 35.6 mm; tarsus, 46.7 mm; exposed culmen, 21.75 mm.

When first hatched a chick is helpless, but becomes able to crawl off the nest and hide after only a few hours. They are able to swim almost immediately. By one day of age they are capable of actively running about and swimming. At first they walk, half-crouched, wings held out and away from the body. By their second day they are able to stand erect, hold the wings much closer to the body and run and swim dexterously. Their call is exactly like

---

*wts. apparently from Heinroth, 1928.

that of other downy cranes I have heard, a shrill *peeep* with a trill to it. When comforted, this call has much more of a trill and is dragged out over a longer period of time. The adult often responds with a low, guttural, *purrr.*

VOICE

Descriptions of the chick vocalizations are given above, along with the attentive *Purrr* call of the adult. The alarm call is a rendition of the *Krrr* or *Groooa* but much shriller.

In large flocks of Common Cranes the noise at times is tremendous. Each bird or pair seems to try to outdo the others. Often it is hard to differentiate individual calls, although at times individual calls can be separated easily. Most calls consist of some formation of the syllables, *Kraah, Kruk, Kurrr, Groooh,* or *Krrrr.* Sometimes only a single call is given; again they may repeat it many times, usually five to eight times. Sometimes lone birds call a very shrill *Kraaa-tuk-tuk-tuk-tuk-tuk* or *Kruk-kruk-kruk-kruk* or *Krooh-krooh-krooh-krooh* or one bird gives one call and its mate another in unison. This "unison call" may be given in winter, during migration or on the breeding grounds, and is at times given when the birds change incubation duties. It is a beautiful call and can be heard two or three kilometers with ease. One bird often gives the following, strongly accented on the first two syllables, *Kraaa-gro, kraa-kraa-kraa* while the female, if it is she answering, often gives a similar, less penetrating call, or one of the above renditions. A call given by individual birds while feeding is a *Kruk,* periodically repeated while other birds give similar calls nearby. Many calls are similar to those of the Sandhill Crane, but the "unision call" is much different, more like that of the Sarus Crane. This call, the "Doppelschlag" of German writers, is outstanding.

When giving the unison call the birds stand a few feet apart, throw their heads back with bill pointing upward, often slightly rearward, each bird giving vent to his own call simultaneously. As they give it they throw their chests forward, display their inner secondaries high over their rumps, and even ruffle the other secondaries outward from the body side-wise as the male lowers his primaries along both sides like those of a strutting turkey gobbler, so they nearly touch the ground. This could be called the "strutting unison call." I have seen this performed by *Grus grus, Grus vipio, Grus leucogeranus* (not so pronounced a performance), *Grus antigone,* and *Grus rubicundus.* The Sandhill Cranes rarely, if ever, display as much. They hold their secondaries tight against their side, the primaries showing little or not at all. I have seen the unison call given by all members of the genus *Grus* (except *G.nigricollis,* which I have never seen) and by *Anthropoides paradisea. Bugeranus carunculatus,* a very silent bird most of the time, occasionally gives a unison call, but I never have seen it given by *Balearica.* Often cranes give the call when changing incubation duties; again they may give it over and over on the feeding grounds prior to nesting; or in a flock, during fall, winter, or spring. The untrained listener might well think only one bird was calling, not two. Often when one pair initiates it, others follow suit.

Duet or unison calling by Common Crane pair, near Lake Hornborgasjön, central Sweden, April 20, 1971. (Photo by P. O. Swanberg.)

THE MOLT

The Common Crane, like other cranes, molts regularly once a year. Some years, however, the complete molt takes place during two periods. Apparently this is very similar or identical to the molt of *G.canadensis.* Cranes are hatched out in America, Europe and Asia at about the same time and at about the same latitudes. When born they are covered with beautiful rich chestnut or tawny down. This down in the Common Crane is browner throughout than that of the Sandhill Crane, which has a gray undertone. The Japanese, White-Naped, Whooping and Wattled Cranes seem to have a brown plumage like the Common Crane. The Australian Brolga, the Paradise, Demoiselle, and sometimes the Sarus are even grayer than the Sandhill Cranes, and there seems to be little or no tawniness in these birds except on the head.

Infant cranes grow rapidly the first two months. Their down becomes lighter colored, approaching a tawny color even in Sandhill and Paradise Cranes. The Brolga remains, except for the head, almost completely gray. Crowned Cranes are chestnut and tawny without gray.

At two weeks of age primaries begin to show, the rectrices shortly thereafter. At the tip of each there remains a long beautiful downy plume, giving the young bird a lacy appearance. At one month, *Grus grus* primaries are 15 to 22 mm long, with down 50 or more mm long adhering to the ends. At two months many gray feathers are showing over the entire body, many of these with tawny tips. The primaries, outer secondaries and the rectrices are black. The head is completely feathered. By three months of age this plumage is complete, the primaries and rectrices lose their plumes entirely, and the brown feather tips lend the bird a brownish appearance.

At three months of age the post-juvenal molt begins, and lasts for two months. All of the body down is lost, and all the feathers except the primaries, outer secondaries, and rectrices. These feathers are retained at least two years, possibly longer on occasion.

Heinroth (1928) commented that cranes in Germany become quite well concealed during the period when flight feathers are lost, and they seldom vocalize then. Once he found a multitude of freshly lost feathers on May 21, in Kremmener Moor near Berlin. (On June 4, 1963, at a myr 30 kilometers northeast of Harads, Norrbotten, Sweden, I found a crane which flew weakly from the ground where a group of trees grew in the marsh. On the ground where it had stood there were 10 feathers, three of which were secondaries, two upper wing coverts, and three under wing coverts.) Heinroth stated that two captive cranes, a brother and sister, molted their flight feathers in mid-May of 1923. One, "Trana," molted these again June 7 to 8, 1925, while the second, "Pancraz" molted them May 5-6, 1926. Of course they molted the other body feathers regularly each August-October.

Big flocks of Common Cranes collect each August on inaccessible islands and in marshy districts. After the molt 2,000-4,000 collect in fields of ripened wheat causing notable devastation.

Cranes, at least *Grus* and *Anthropoides,* apparently become flightless when they lose their primaries, outer secondaries and rectrices almost simultaneously. Since this happens only every second or third year, there are always flying cranes during the period that others have lost their flight feathers. Blaauw, from his own experience and from observations by Lord Lilford, described this molt (of primaries and some secondaries) in *Grus grus, G.-japonensis, G.vipio, G.americana, G.leucogeranus, G.antigone antigone* and *Anthropoides paradisea.* He told how numbers of Paradise Cranes were captured regularly in South Africa by simply rounding them up into an enclosure over which they were unable to fly. This molt is also found in *Grus canadensis,* probably in all subspecies. Littlefield tells (1970) of finding 32 Sandhill Cranes at Malheur National Wildlife Refuge, Oregon, on May 28, 1966. Twenty-nine of them flew away, some with great difficulty. Two birds flew only a short distance. One individual observed had lost all its primaries. By June 11, all members of this flock were capable of flight. One at a nest on June 5, 1966, was also flightless while its mate flew rapidly away.

The feathers are apparently all dropped in very few days—perhaps only one or two, and the new ones emerge so quickly that the birds are flightless for only a very short period of days or weeks. One Whooping Crane which remained on Aransas Wildlife Refuge, Texas during one summer became flightless. This bird was captured after a chase but quickly died. It had lost the power of flight by molting its primaries and many of its secondaries.

From existing evidence, it appears that cranes molt once a year, the primaries, outer secondaries and rectrices being lost at least one month or more prior to the remainder of the feathers and then only every second or third year. The flight feathers may not be lost until the birds reach breeding age or nearly so.

DIET AND FEEDING BEHAVIOR

Dementiev and Gladkov (1951) wrote that Common Cranes subsist on: "...a vegetable and fruit diet...in the north in spring...cranberries, shoots of grain, young grass shoots, aquatic plants and their roots, bread grains such as wheat, peas and oats. Small amounts of food...are different insects, such as beetles and locusts, and frogs, snakes, mice, mollusks, worms, birds' eggs, sometimes even small birds (once among digested materials, remains of *Acrocephalus paludicola*...). In family groups in June, when young are sufficiently grown, and later in small flocks, cranes fly, trumpeting loudly, to feed in the nearest grain fields each evening and morning. If there is no grain near at hand they fly to a meadow, a steppe, even a salt marsh steppe or sandy region, where they catch locusts and other insects. When resting they return to the marshy reeds. They drink water in large quantities and if there is no water available at the feeding region, they fly some time during a 24 hour period to a place where it is."

To this I might add that in wintertime in Spain, cranes show a liking for acorns.

In the Handbook of British Birds it is reported that Common Cranes eat vegetable matter, roots of grasses, pieces of aquatic plants, as well as insects, Coleoptera (*Aphodius, Geotrupes* and *Agriotes*) and *Diptera* (54 *Tipula* larvae in one stomach), mollusca (*Arion*, water snails, etc.). On the Continent they eat grain of all kinds, oats, barley, wheat, rye, peas,

beans, buckwheat, acorns, olives (272 olive stones in one stomach in Tunisia), berries of *Oxycoccus, Empetrum*, rice, leaves of grass, clover, rape, mallow, nettle, chickweed, *Arum*, and sedge seeds. Animal food recorded included insects: *Orthoptera* (Locusts, grasshoppers, crickets, *Gryllotalpa*) *Odonata, Lepidoptera* (caterpillars), Coleoptera (beetles), Geotrupes, earthworms, amphibia (frogs), reptiles (lizards, slowworms), young birds an aquatic warbler (*Acrocephalus paludicola*) was once recorded, and small mammalia such as field-voles and shrews.

Makatsch (1959) reported under the heading of usefulness and harm done by the Common Crane that Naumann stated the species destroyed many insects and their larvae, as well as grasshoppers, beetles, and snails. Considerable harm was done to

Common Crane taking its turn at incubation, Bäckhammar, Sweden, May 16, 1963.

39

grainfields in Germany by the large concentrations of cranes in the fall. In the Castile region collected cranes have yielded several beetles, bones, and from 200 to 500 kernels of partially germinated grain. In northern Germany on the Baltic Island of Rügen, much damage has been done to grain crops, but often this damage was wrongly associated with cranes when geese were responsible.

Sieber (1932) and Christoleit (1939) both stated much damage attributed to cranes was found to be minor when the fields were studied—the crops matured at the normal rate with the normal output. But cranes in gross concentrations can do much damage to corn, wheat, oats, and at times barley, when these are ripening and left on the field near where the birds concentrate. This also happens in winter in Sudan. I talked with the Curator of Birds at Khartoum Natural History Museum who reported that large concentrations often occurred on the White and Blue Nile Rivers above that city and at times in the fall they did considerable crop damage. In most regions this might be abated by earlier removal of grains.

RANGE AND BREEDING DISTRIBUTION

Grus grus grus is known to be currently breeding in Russia west of the Volga, between Lat. 50° and 68°N, western Kazakhstan S.S.R., Finland, Norway, Sweden, northwestern Poland, and eastern Germany. A few pairs are reported in western Germany, many more pairs in western Germany. Today none nest in Austria, Yugoslavia, Albania, Czechoslovakia and Italy. But the species is still found in fair numbers in the Russian Caucasus, as well as in Asia Minor, including several regions in Turkey. The form breeding in the European part of the Molotov Oblast may be *Grus grus lilfordii*.

Formerly found in Ireland, and up until about 1600 in the English fen country (Blaauw, 1897; Cott, 1953), the Common Crane was reported in southern Spain until about 1954 (Bernis, 1960); northern Denmark at least from 1938 until around 1962 (Jensen, 1952; Koch, verbal). It breeds in a

few scattered western German regions (H. Makowski; Makatsch, 1959), commonly in Eastern Germany (Makatsch, 1959, and letter). The last breeding in Hungary was 1892 (Keve and Udvardy, 1951).

This form winters from south central Spain, southeastern Portugal, northern Morocco, across the Mediterranean shore of Africa sparingly to Egypt, more densely in the White Nile valley south of Khartoum, Sudan, some on the Blue Nile, then in central Ethiopia in the lake country, and sparingly in eastern Turkey, eastern Iraq and western Iran.

Breeding and summer distribution

NORWAY.

The majority of *Grus grus* in Norway are found in the Gudbrandsdal and Østerdal valleys, at Dovrejell, Atna Lake and possibly at Nordlie (H. Holgersen, letter, March 19, 1963). Definite records are:

Finmark. Schanning (1916) and (Holgersen, *op.cit.*) observed cranes in Övre Pasvik in June 1902; on Skogeröy Island in the Varangerfjord, June 11, 1905, and on the Sammattimyra at the Pasvik River, May 23, 1915. Collett (1920) gave locations as: Alta, Kistrand, North Cape, and Övre Pasvik, in June and July.

Troms. Collett (1920) listed Skjervöy, 1821; Målselvdalen, July 1890.

Nordland. Found at Saltdalen, 1865 (Collett, 1920); also found between Nordland and Tröndelag, possibly at Namdal (Collett).

Nord Trondelag. Found nesting in Upper Ogndal east of Steinkjer, and at Nordlie (Krogh, 1950). Also at Verdal (64°N) observed July 29, 1920 and a nest with 1 egg and 1 chick the week of July 7-14, 1924. From 1935 annually observed in summer at Ogndal where 1 young was observed in 1941 and another nest with 2 newly laid eggs, June 14, 1943. At Sparbu, on August 6, 1940, 4 birds were observed and on August 22 and 29, 1941, 2 more in the same place (Överland, 1947).

Opland. At Dovrefjell, Fokstumyra (62°N), Lövenskiold (1947-51) and H. Holgersen (letter, December 30, 1953) observed 2 adults in July 1943. One year a newly hatched chick was found on June 2, while during another year the first egg was laid June 1. Holgersen wrote there are 1 to 3 pairs at Fokstumyra and some birds are found in the Gudbrandsdal valley. Mountfort (1957) observed three nesting here May 8, 1951.

Hedmark. Lövenskiold listed this bird from the Gudbrandsdal and Österdal valleys (60-62°N). Hagen and Barth (1951) reported it breeding annually in the

Atnasjö region, just east of, partly within, Rondane Mountains, southeast of Dovre. Three well known localities are Atnasjömyrene, Skjellamyrene, and southeast of Finnsjö. A nest with 1 egg (hatched June 5) was found near Musvollkollen in 1947. In June, 1948 a juvenile crane was observed between Finnsjö and Storetjöhn. In 1949 a pair with a fully-fledged chick was seen at Atnasjömyr in late summer. One pair observed July 8, 1951 on the Skellåmyr must have had young.

County Telemark. Nested during 1917 at Tinn (Lövenskiold).

County Buskerud. Two pairs nested at Normannslågen on Hardangervidda in 1887 and 1888. A single bird was seen in 1934. Listed from Hallindal valley (Lövenskiold).

County Rogeland. A crane was observed August 15, 1952 in Hjelmeland, Ryfylke (Holgersen, *op.cit.*)

County Akershus. Near Oslo. Formerly it bred here but not for many years (Lövenskiold).

Haftorn (1971) gave no breeding records from Troms or Nordland, but said it bred at Sandstad on Hitra in Nord Trøndelag, between Lillehammer and Rena, an area of 58,500 hectares and west of Nuten at Rjotomyrene, Romsdale fylke, at Trollheimen (1951-1953) and Surnadal (1966).

SWEDEN.

Norrbotten. Muonion, Isovuoma and Kartovuoma (68°N); Wolley (1859) found 4 nests (each 2 eggs).

Pajala (67°25′N) P. O. Swanberg (letter October 28, 1951) found a nest (2 eggs) June 9, 1951.

Boden (65°45′N). Sven Wahlberg (verbal) observed cranes regularly here in summer, early 1960's.

Harads (66°10′N). Arne Blomgren (verbal) found nests, May 20, 1945; May 3, 1950; May 15, 1963. Blomgren and I found a nest, May 26, 1963 at Spikeberg (Spikselan near Harads). (All 2 eggs.)

Rödingsträsk (66°N). I found a nest (2 eggs) May 31, 1953.

Lillå (66°20′N). I found a nest (2 eggs) May 27, 1963.

Hatten (near Harads). Blomgren and I observed cranes here several times during May and June 1963.

Lakatrask (66°20′N). Gunnar Blomgren and I found June 4, 1963, a lone crane which could barely fly and on investigation of the spot it came from found several flight feathers, including mostly secondaries and upper and lower wing coverts.

Muddus National Park. (67°N). The species is fairly common here (Blomgren and Wahlberg, verbal). Arne Blomgren, Sven Wahlberg and I observed 4 cranes on June 2, 1963.

Laisdalen (66°20′N). P. O. Swanberg (letter, December 31, 1962) found a nest (2 eggs) June 3, 1962.

Lule Lappmark. Gallivare, 12 kilometers west (67°-25′N). I found a nest (2 eggs) June 5, 1963 and observed several cranes.

Värmland. Krinstinehamn and in southeastern Värmland and in Narke, Nils Wellberg (1965) found 16 nests (one had 1 egg; the others 2) during the 1963 summer. He showed nests to P. O. Swanberg and me as follows: Upsjon, April 28, 1963; Skog Mosse, May 11, 1963; Stor Mosse, May 11, 1963 and May 16, 1963; Korsbacken, April 26, 1963; Skogstorp, May 17, 1963. Wellberg (verbal) also had found a number of nests prior to 1963, and many since then, in these same regions.

Skaraborg. Gårdsjö (58°+ N). Nests were found by Gustav Answeaaon, May 4, 1958; April 10, and June 7, 1959; April 14, 1960; April 20, 1961; and May 13, 1963. The latter nest shown to P. O. Swanberg and me.

Skövde. North of Vreten, farm of A. Gökstorp. Gökstorp (verbal) observed cranes here for many years. P. O. Swanberg and I found a nest (2 eggs), May 15, 1963.

Tidaholm. Tord von Essen found a nest (2 eggs) during May, 1963. showing it to Swanberg and me, May 15, 1963.

Småland. Jönköping, Dumme Mosse Knut and Tord von Essen found a nest (2 eggs), May 14, 1963, and showed it to Swanberg and me May 18.

Kafsjon. Southeast of Kävsjö. Four nests were found, May 18, 1963. One had an egg and newly hatched chick, a second 2 newly hatched chicks; birds were incubating eggs on the third and fourth nests (Knut and Tord von Essen, Filip Jacobsson, P. O. Swanberg and L. H. Walkinshaw).

Forsheda. Southwest, at Draftånge. Filip Jacobsson found a nest (0 eggs), May 4, 1963 showing it to Swanberg, the von Essens and me, May 18.

Lima. (60°55′N, 13°22′E). A young bird, unable yet to fly, was ringed July 13, 1958. It was recovered March 27, 1960, at Soest, Westphalia, Federated German Republic (51.34°N, 8.06°E). (Osterlof, 1964.)

General. (Sveriges Fåglar, 1962.) Breeds sparsely in Småland, Bohuslän, Västergötland, Östergötland, Värmland, Närke, Västmanland, Sörmland, Uppland, Gästrikland, fairly common from Dalarna and Hälsingland to Lapland. Has also bred in Skåne, Blekinge, Dalsland and Gotland.

Rosenius (1937) wrote: Earliest egg dates for 64°N Lat. are April 24 and 28. Commonly eggs are fresh in mid-May, with latest June 22, (possibly second laying); for 68°N Lat.: earliest, May 20, (eggs incubated 2 or 3 days), May 23, (incubated about 2 weeks).

FINLAND.

Wolley (1859), Wolley and Newton(1905-1907), and Oates (1902), recorded nests from the Lappi district as follows: Sodankyla (67°N, 27°E), a nest (1 egg), May 20, 1856. Several others, some possibly in northern Sweden: Isovuoma, June 15, 1853 (2 hatched eggs);

May 20, 1854 (2 eggs). Kartovuoma, June 29, 1853 (eggs hatched), and May 23, 1854 (2 eggs). Lahovuoma, near Muonioniska, June 5, 1857 (2 eggs). Laulivuoma, June 8, 1858 (2 eggs). Alamanavuoma (2 eggs), May 18, 1859. Lahi Järvi, June 10, 1862 (1 egg) and still another (2 eggs) at Kittila (67°45′N, 25°E) in June, 1862.

Lappi District. Kittila. Kreuger (1930) reported two nests: one had 2 eggs during 1918 and the other in 1917 with 1 egg.

Oulu District. Linfors (1930) recorded egg dates: Korsnas (63°N, 21°E), May 11, 1921 (2 eggs); May 18, 1927. Suomussalmi (65°N, 29°E): June 13, 1927 (2 eggs).

Pudasjärvi (65.5°N, 27°E). Wasenius (1929) recorded a set (2 eggs).

Pielisjarvi. Cranes were reported in this region July 20, 1933 and June 22, 1935. (Ornis Fennica, 1936, 84.)

Lars von Haartman (letter, April 19, 1963) stated prominent breeding localities today are: Kristinestad (62°N), Risnäsmossen (45 kilometers from Kristinestad); Hanhikeidas (35 kilometers from Kristinestad) several pairs; and Sanemossen (60 kilometers from Kristinestad) where there are up to 50 non-nesting and several nesting pairs of cranes.

In Finland this bird breeds countrywide except for the far north. Merrikallio (1955) estimated a nesting population in Finland of 8,500 pairs.

FEDERAL REPUBLIC OF GERMANY (WEST GERMANY).

Henry Makowski (letter, 1970) listed the present breeding regions for *Grus grus* in Western Germany. There are 4 breeding zones, with 15 nesting places and 16 breeding pairs besides two to three pairs which cross between East and West Germany, which may nest one year in the former, the next year in the latter:

Zone 1. *Lower Saxony. Gifhorn.* (52°30′N, 10°50′E). Five nesting places; 6 breeding pairs.
Zone 2. *Lower Saxony. Ulzen.* (52°45′N, 10°50′E). One nesting place; 1 pair irregularly breeding.
Zone 3. *Lower Saxony. Luchow-Dannenberg.* (53°N, 11°20′E). Six nesting places; 6 breeding pairs.
Zone 4. *Schleswig-Holstein. Herzogtum Lauenburg.* (53°30′N, 10°50′E). Three nesting places; 3 breeding pairs.

GERMAN DEMOCRATIC REPUBLIC (EAST GERMANY).

Wolfgang Makatsch (letter, 1970) and G. Meyer

*Meyer, G., 1968. Erfassung der Kranichbrutplätze in den drei nordlichen Bezirken der Deutschen Demokratischen Republik 1962-1968. *Naturschutzarbeit in Mecklenburg,* 11, pp. 32-34.

(1968)* estimated the breeding cranes in Eastern Germany as:

City and Environs	Number of Pairs	
Besirk Rostock	about 7	(1967)*
Schwerin	about 110	(1967)*
Neubrandenburg	about 112	(1967)*
Potsdam	about 50	(1969)
Frankfurt/Oder	about 10	(1969)
Cottbus	about 25	(1969)
Magdeburg	about 10	(1969)
Dresden	about 2	(1969)
Leipzig	about 1	(1968)
Halle	—	
Erfurt	—	
Gera	—	
Suhl	—	
Karl-Marx-Stadt (formerly Chemnitz)	—	
Total	327 pairs	

Formerly the Crane nested in what is now East Germany in the Sprottauer district and the Oberlausitz in Schlesian (67 breeding pairs reported in 1905; 49 breeding pairs reported in 1923; and 15 pairs recorded, but probably more present, in 1948. Makatsch, 1959).

Hoffman (1936) reported regular nesting in Brandenburg. Niethammer (1942) reported there were once many cranes in north Germany, from East Prussia (now Poland) along the "North Sea" — probably the Baltic Sea (Makatsch, *loc.cit.*) Now these birds are found south of there, from the River Oder to Lausitz across to the middle Elbe. Formerly they bred at Koschentin and Waischnik in Oberschlesian, in Vehner by Oldenburg, and were reported in 1878 in the Rheinland. In the Oberbayern they once nested at Erdinger Moss, the Dechauer Moss,

European Crane settling down onto nest in Phragmites. *Oberlausitz, East Germany. (Photo by Isle Makatsch.)*

Murnever Moss, the Moss by Schledorf and the big Filz near Rosenheim, but these places have long been abandoned (Makatsch). In 1926 they were found breeding in Schleswig-Holstein and in Oberschlesian and one pair during the breeding time in Teichwalde, county Guttentag (Niethammer).

DENMARK.

Kragskovhede (about halfway between Frederikshavn and the Skaw), North Jutland (57°30′N). found here from 1938 up until 1962. He also presented a photograph as evidence, of a half-grown young bird found June 25, 1952. C. Koch (letter, February 26, 1964) gave the same information and reported cranes stayed there until 1962, when a fire burned out the entire surroundings, after which the birds were not seen again. I visited this region in May, 1963, but saw no cranes. Koch sent me a photograph of a nest with 2 eggs taken June 18, 1953.

Cranes still nest at Lille Vildmoss (56°50′ N. — Swanberg, letter, 1972). Salomonsen and Rudebeck (1963) reported cranes formerly bred in many parts of Denmark.

Migration, Spring.

Salomonsen and Rudebeck (1963) reported that many cranes pass over the eastern part of Denmark in spring but few ever land. Most birds pass over in just a few days, even all in a single day at times. They fly from the Baltic island of Rugen, Germany to southern or middle Sweden.

Migration, Fall.

Only a few cranes pass over Denmark in the fall, then between late August and October. Occasionally they land.

A young crane ringed in Denmark was captured in southern France (Salomonsen and Rudebeck, 1963).

POLAND.

Pomerania. Dr. Holland and others (BMNH) took several sets of eggs from this region (possibly some or all in East Germany or in northwestern Poland). The eggs were taken May 10, 1857 (1 egg); May 14, (2 eggs), 23, (2 eggs), 25 (3 eggs), and 28 (2 eggs) 1873; April 1875, (2 eggs); April 1877 (2 eggs); April 24, 1878 (2 eggs); April 20, 1879, (2 eggs); April 30, 1881, (1 egg); and April 24, 1888, (2 eggs).

Makatsch (1959) wrote that more Common cranes breed in East Prussia than any other place in middle Europe. At the beginning of the present century there were at least 300 pairs, perhaps more, nesting in this region, and during 1935 probably the same. They are seldom found in West Prussia. Makatsch adds that Baer wrote of 100 breeding pairs in approximately 27 definite nesting places. The Pomeranian region has been one of the most outstanding breeding regions since prehistory, and is still used extensively.

Farther south, in the Barycz River Valley, cranes also nest. Mrugasiewicz and Witkowski (1962) found several nests here in recent years, and during early May 1963 I spent several days with Adam Mrugasiewicz and Andrej Dyrez in this region. We saw 2 cranes near Zmigrod in the valley on three of the five days we were there, but never more than a pair at one time. We observed two nests from which either young had hatched, or the eggs had been taken by predators. Both of these nests had been found by Mrugasiewicz during late April and both had had 2 eggs.

The average egg date for Poland was April 28 (11 records).

U.S.S.R.

Northward to 68°N Latitude; Kola Peninsula northward to the basin of the Imandra and Pazi rivers (Gebel', 1902); Solovetskiye Peninsula (Polyakov, 1929); and Arkhangel'sk Oblast northward to the tundra. Distribution extends into the southwest part of the Timanskoy tundra up to the Pesha River (Semenov, 1939), middle and lower Pechora River northward to Ust'Usa (66°N), Ust'-Tsil'mi and, it is possible, to the Polar Circle (Dmokhovskiy, 1933). Further to the east, cranes apparently *lilfordi*, dwell on the Ob. The birds nesting in the European part of the Molotov Oblast may belong to *lilfordi*. Southward *G. grus grus* reaches to Volyn', Podoli, Kiev, Poltava Oblast and to the central part of Dnepropetrovsk (in Pavlodar and in the reserve in Koncha-Zaspa, in the lower reaches of the Dnieper (Sharleman, 1930); but it does not reach Zaporozh'ya (Val'kh, 1897). Apparently isolated colonies are found in Sivashe and Prisivash'e (Vorontsov, 1937). It does not now nest in the Crimea, there is an old egg set (BMNH) taken in Crimea. In Astrakhan it does not reach kilometer 150 (Bostanzhoglo, 1911). In Zavolzh'e it still is the related form. The boundary between the subspecies is not exactly cleared up, and it is possible they may go even more westerly. Northward it goes to the middle of Povolzh'yo, quite possibly even to the Suri Basin. There were isolated colonies in the Balkans (Serbia, Bosnia, Albania, Macedonia), in Dobrudzja, in the lower reaches of the Dunaya and in Vengrii, in northern Italy (Venice), and southward. In Spain it was found in Andalusia and in northern Africa, in Tunisia. (Quoted from Dementiev and Gladkov, 1951.)

SPAIN.

Breeding: Andalusia, Laguna de la Janda. Col. L. H. Irby (Oates, 1902) deposited eggs in the British Museum (Natural History) taken from here in May, 1871 and April, 1877 (each 2 eggs), as well as another set without data (1 egg), and from Casa Viejas, May 2, 1871, 1 egg, besides 3 other eggs taken in May, 1871.

Saunders (1871) reported the species abundant on the marshy plains of Doñana from autumn to spring, with considerable numbers remaining to breed. He took one set of eggs (BMNH)(Oates, 1902).

Bernis (1960) reported cranes bred at La Janda up until 1954, while they discontinued doing so at the Marismas at the end of the last century. In the past there were several locations in central Spain where cranes nested (see map).

TURKEY.

There is an egg set (1 egg) in the British Museum (Natural History) taken June 9, 1841 at Erzumum (40°N, 41°E).

Cecil Kersting (letters, 1959, 1960) observed Common Cranes at Gòlbasi Lake, 20 kilometers south of Ankara (39°N, 33°E) April 26, 1959; May 19, 1959 (2); May 23, June 13-14, July 25, August 1, 1959; none thereafter in that year. He saw from two to seven cranes each trip during the next year on May 14, (4); May 15, (7); June 5, (2); June 7, (12); June 8, (3); July 2, (10); July 3, (15); July 9, (3); July 23, (8) July 30, (11); August 6, (3−1 quite brownish);

September 3-4, (2); and September 17, (51 — this group much wilder). See Warncke (1970).

ITALY.

Giglioli (1881) described the annual breeding of a few pairs of Cranes on an extensive marsh along the Adriatic Sea north of Venice. It is not known if it is still used.

CZECHOSLOVAKIA AND SE EUROPE

From 1920 to 1925 Cranes bred in two places in Czechoslovakia. They may still breed there in small numbers. Makatsch wrote (1959) that there were isolated breeding places yet in Yugoslavia. But in Bulgaria, Albania, and Greece, the bird is missing. It bred at Dobrudzja, near Sofia; near Batak on the north slope of Rhodope Mountains; and at Hochmoor near Vlasina in East Serbia. Niethammer had reported it at Livno in Northwest Bosnia (Yugoslavia) and at the Malik Sea south of Ohrid in Albania. Keve and Udvardy (1951) wrote that the last breeding record for Hungary was in 1892. Now they do not breed in southern Europe (Makatsch).

WINTERING

The Common Crane winters chiefly in Africa, Spanish Morocco, Morocco, Algiers, Tunisia, isolated places along the Mediterranean, central Sudan, and Ethiopia; less so in Spain and Portugal; possibly in Italy, Iraq, Iran and Palestine.

SPAIN.

Bernis (1960) reports many wintering regions in south western Spain and southeastern Portugal, with unknown numbers of birds crossing to northern Morocco. He lists about 150 positive wintering regions in Spain: 43 on river banks, 42 along small lakes and ponds, 15 on top of slight hills, 10 in marismas and many others on open plains. He estimates 4,500 cranes winter in Spain and 5,000 in the Iberian Peninsula. In addition, a small number wintered around two small lakes in the north of the Province of Malaga, and at swamps and small lakes along the lower Ciguela River.

In addition to the regular Spanish wintering grounds, cranes are found slightly farther north until quite late in the year in pseudo-wintering spots where populations may fluctuate, then disappear. The usual wintering regions, all very much alike, consist of plains of slight hilly country in which great stretches of ilex-woods alternate with corn and legume fields, or with extensive pastures.

Saunders (1871) reported breeding cranes were common in the marshes of Doñana, with larger numbers in winter. Irby (1895) saw 4,000 flying over the mountains 32 kilometers NNW of Tarifa, March 11, 1874, wind westerly. Chapman and Buck (1893) noted a similar flight March 20, 1891 over Coto Doñana, wind westerly. Riddell (1945) said a few pairs still bred in Laguna de la Janda. In a nearby cave were neolithic drawings of cranes and their nests. He also reported cranes arriving in late September and during October, departing northward at the end of March.

SPAIN-MOROCCO.

Bernis (1960) estimated from questionnaires sent to many people that 10,000 cranes crossed a region 50 kilometers wide between Spain and Morocco, beginning some 5 to 15 kilometers west of Tarifa. Sometimes birds crossed in both directions during the winter. K. D. Smith (1965) observed Cranes in Morocco at Oued Massa, November 15, 1962; 2 flocks (13 birds) arriving from the direction of Tarifa at Cape Malabata, east of Tangier January 13, 1963. Birds wintered near Lac Zima and Sedd el Mejnoun, (32°N, 7.5-9°W) where they fed on the plains, roosting at night in the lakes; in 1963, 11 were noted February 24, and 23 on December 30, at Lac Zima; in 1964, 33 at the Sedd el Majnoun, January 1, 13 on January 2, and 38 on February 27, at Lac Zima. Twenty were seen flying south January 14, 1964, near Larache.

Lathbury (1970) reported the flights across the straits west of Gibraltar were local and irregular, yet Brudenell-Bruce saw birds crossing Zaharas de los Atunes regularly in November, December, sometimes in January, occasionally in February, and once each in March and April. Flight was not clear cut—birds sometimes flying northward in November. Flocks consisted of 10 to 20—once 60, birds. He assumed the drainage of Laguna de la Janda may have had considerable effect on recent concentrations.

PORTUGAL.

Tait (1924) reported Cranes wintered in the valley of the Tagus and the Alemtejo. Bernis (1960) thought about 500 wintered in southeastern Portugal.

FRANCE.

A few Cranes formerly wintered in the Les Landes region but due to recent development, this may also have been abandoned.

ITALY.

Cranes formerly, wintered here. Walter (1965) reported a lone bird in mid December 1961 in Cugliari Province, Sardinia.

ALGIERS, TUNISIA.

Payn (1948) reported wintering in Algeria near Constantine, while Snow (1952) attributed cranes in northern Tunisia as belonging to this species. Guichard (1956) saw two on February 5, near Tripoli and 17 near Tauorga, Libya, February 11. In both cases they were near the sea flying west.

ETHIOPIA.

There is a specimen (BMNH) taken January 27, 1900, by J. J. Harrison at Buffa Lake, central Ethiopia; another male and female were taken February 14, 1905, by P. C. Zaphiro at Lake Helen, Harar; and a bird was taken December 31, 1913, by W. P. Lowe at Senga on the Blue Nile (in Sudan) while another female was taken somewhere in Ethiopia (specimen Haille Selassie I University Museum). K. D. Smith (1960) said a few winter in Eritrea. Cheeseman and Sclater (1935) wrote that flocks visit the high plateau and stay through the winter.

SUDAN.

The chief concentration of this Palaearctic species in winter occurs along the White and Blue Niles south and southeast of Khartoum. It does not reach as far south as Malakal for we saw none there nor even 80 miles north of there at Khor Adar in February 1962.

These birds congregate in immense flocks on mud flats, river bars, plains, and durra, as well as wheat and cotton locations. Most remain somewhat north of the range of *A. virgo*. Berg (1930) presented photographs of great concentrations along the Nile River south of Khartoum and reported they were chiefly between 13°N Lat. near El Dueim, Abu Seid, southward to where trees grew along the Nile banks.

Berg (1930) reported that great numbers of Demoiselle and Gray Cranes spend the winter along the White Nile, and probably to some extent on the Blue Nile south of Khartoum. The shallow, muddy lagoons and bars along the Nile river offered water and night roosting regions, while unharvested grain could be secured from nearby fields. Berg wrote:

"The great hour of day approaches. The tumult of the cranes swells until it becomes positively deafening.... The lot beyond is a troop of demoiselle cranes...with a hoarser call in higher pitch than that of our own cranes, though not nearly so harsh as the strident blast of the crowned cranes... Ranged up behind them stands the huge host of European cranes. In my imagination I had pictured hundreds. There are certainly over two thousand... The greater part are assembled on the mudbank near the shore. It's only a short way from solid ground. Smaller troops stand on watch in the shallow water that laps the mudbank, one as an advance guard, and the other posted at the army's head. And where the water is sufficiently shallow thousands and tens of thousands of all conceivable kinds of wading-birds stand among them or run about between their long legs and right underneath their crowded bodies... the moment has arrived for the great dispersal... The number of voices is multiplied; the uproar swells in volume, minute by minute...The crowned cranes standing in file farthest away on the mudbank begin moving about impatiently here and there and join in the concert with a shrill double-toned burst of horn music. It seems all the others had been waiting for this. As if at a signal the whole army pauses to listen intently. The multitudes become possessed with restlessness. Urging and questionings are to be heard in their voices. The files arrange themselves in a manner unknown to me. And with a mighty roar resembling thunder or a

cataract, swelling in tremendous crescendo, phalanx after phalanx rises and wings its way against the morning breeze.

"Since that time I have often come across them clamoring on stormy nights on the Nile when the river was tossed about like a sea; on the desert edge near Gjebel Auli; in leisurely flight on still evenings when they were returning from the fertile fields in Durrah-land near El Dueim; during hot midday hours when they had paused to rest and were quenching their thirst in the company of marabou storks; near About Zeid....''

Mathiasson (1963) watching from Tutti Island, Khartoum, Sudan, from February 12 to April 12, 1961, counted 630 *Grus grus* and 141 *A. virgo* flying northward, the former chiefly west of the river; the latter east of it.

Ticehurst, Buxton and Cheeseman (1922) reported *G. grus* not uncommon in winter on passage through Mesotamia. While Meinertzhagen (1949) says it was not seen in Arabia but on the plains near Port Sudan. Safriel (1968) gave one record (over a 9-year period) for the fourth week in January, for Israel.

PALESTINE.

Tristram (1868) reported many cranes wintered in Palestine, roosting at night atop several acres of hillocks. During late evenings and early mornings, and often during the night, they were very vociferous. If a jackal or hyena howled, the entire congregation trumpeted loudly.

IRAQ.

Meinertzhagen (1924) and Chapman and McGeoch (1956) found this bird common in the Habbaniya-Ramadi region on the Euphrates, during January, 1954. Allouse (1953) claimed it a winter visitor.

MIGRATION

In late February, more so in March and April, diminishing to stragglers in May, crane migration starts from the winter regions. From Morocco, Spain, and Portugal, migration proceeds northward flying over Spain, then northeast, crossing both

France and Germany to the breeding grounds—a distance of roughly 1600 to 2400 miles. Most cranes begin migration in the morning, after they have eaten. (I noted this with both *G. c. canadensis* in Texas and *G. vipio* in Kyushu, Japan, while others have noted the same.) They prefer to fly when the sky is clear and a light tail wind accompanies them from a high pressure system. They normally fly from 48 to 58 km per hour (Meinertzhagen, 1955). Normally they fly the remainder of the day on which they start and all through the first night, probably for a period of 14 to 21 hours without stopping. (Sandhill Cranes leaving Tahoka Lake or Big Springs, Texas, fly to the Platte River, Nebraska; *G. vipio* leaving Kyushu flies until it reaches at least northern South Korea; apparently *G. c. tabida* flies from Gainesville, Florida to southern Michigan.) Migration records of Common Cranes in Europe almost invariably are of birds in the air. Probably many Cranes are never seen nor heard for at times they migrate at extreme heights (Hurzeler observed Cranes at 4,300 meters—13,779 ft., over the English Channel, September 16, 1950, wind WNW, at 35-40 kilometers per hour), even up to 15,000 ft. (Meinertzhagen, 1955). Donald (1924) noted cranes (apparently *G. leucogeranus)* crossing the Himalayas above 20,000 feet, and Dementiev and Gladkov (1951) reported *Grus grus* crossed the Glavily Range in the Caucasus Mountains (4,000 meters).

Payn (1938) observed cranes migrating March 16, 1937 at Tangier, Morocco (several other records are listed under winter movements), while the species was observed by both Lilford and Irby (Moreau, 1953) flying over the Mediterranean at Adra, about 150 miles east of Gibraltar, once on   March 16.

C. A. White observed five parties flying northeast, high over Teboursouk, 70 miles southwest of La-Marsa, Tunisia, in spring, while Kiepenheuer and Linsenmair (1965) noted migration March 14 and April 13, along the Tunisian coast.

Lilford (1875, 1887) reported large flights northeast of the Straits of Bonifacio (between Sardinia and Corsica) during fine weather on April 30, and other large flocks flying north into the Straits of Messin a (past Taormina), southeastern Sicily on March 16. Brandolini (1950) reported flight over Italy, April 16, 1948. Finis (1952) in 1944 observed

flights at Brindisi (Lat. 40.5°N; Long. 18°E) on March 4, (20); 12, (20); 22, (60); and 24, (1) flying north-northeast or east. Foschi (1954) observed migration April 16, 1949 near Collezione. Alexander (Libbert, 1938) also noted a flight passing Taormina, possibly in the spring. W. B. Alexander also observed a stream travelling north across the Mediterranean some distance off shore from Palestine on March 19, while Dorst recorded a northwestward flight over the western Black Sea (Moreau, 1953). Stresemann (1956) gave records of 100 birds going north, March 27, 1943; of 200 to 250 going west over Iraklion; of a migration on March 10; and of flights (50 to 70 birds) going west; on March 11, of five flights, 200 to 250 Cranes; and on March 21, 10 a.m., 60 birds flying toward the west. Sielmann (1945) noted 3 cranes on April 1, all over Crete. Moreau (1953) reported cranes regularly flew the 300 miles across the eastern Mediterranean going right over Cyprus. Marchant (1941) saw flocks (28, 15, 2, and 50) between March 2, and April 5, 1939, crossing Hurghada on the Gulf of Suez.

Cecil Kersting noted cranes in Anatolia, while Wadley (1951) reported 17 feeding on the ground April 21, 1946. Collman and Croxall (1967) noted about 400 on the Evros Delta, 160 miles from the Bosphorus, March 19 (1964-1965), and like Geyr von Schweppenburg (1934) believed the birds passed by the Dardanelles. Muave (1938) reported cranes March 2 and April 12 near the Bosphorus. Chapman and McGeoch (1956) saw two flocks (about 50 each) flying north over Habbaniya, Iraq, March 27, 1954, while Marchant (1963) reported one of the spectacles of Iraqi ornithology was the migration of *Grus grus* up the Tigris, past Mosul and Ain Zalah in late March. He reported seeing a flock of 100 pass Baghdad on March 30, going northwest, but had not seen any of the birds in autumn.

Pasburg (1959) recorded seven cranes March 12, south of Kazvin and four March 21, west of Robat Karim, Iran. Feeny, Arnold and Baily (1968) said thousands fly north across the Caspian region in spring, but that autumn records are scarce.

Lambert (1961) reported flocks of cranes flying by day March 27-29, 1960 at Burgas Lake (south of Sofia), Bulgaria. Mountfort and Ferguson-Lees (1961) saw an immature crane flying with pelicans

Nesting site of Common Crane at Laisdalen, Lapland, Sweden, 66° 20′ N. lat., June 3, 1962. (Photo by P. O. Swanberg.)

over Lake Burgas June 4, and wrote that Petrov and Zlatanov reported thousands on spring migration through the Dobrudzja where a few still nested on the Rumanian side of the Danube.

Schenk (1938), said that over Hungary spring migration is rapid, culminating in the second half of March.

U.S.S.R.

Dementiev and Gladkov (1951) reported cranes wintering in Transcaucasia fly south in spring into the mountains. Otherwise migration proceeds northward and begins from the south and southwest in two waves. At Lenkoran the first birds appeared March 16 to 19, with a heavy flight March 24 to 26, along the middle course of the Arak River; from February 24, to April 6, in Armenia near Yerevan and Nakhichevan March 26; near Tbilisi March 12 to 15, with heavy flight observed March 15 to 20, (Radde); at Kavkaz flight was observed as late as May; in southern and southwestern Ukraine from the second half of March until mid-April; at Podoli March 30-31, but from March 24, (1906) until April 6, (1899, 1909).

At the Koncha-Zaspa Preserve, flights averaged April 9, with the earliest recorded on March 25, 1925, and the latest, April 18, 1928; at Pavlodar, between mid-March and mid-April. At Rostov-on-

Don one early spring (1906) March 5. Later, due to a cold snap, flight discontinued until March 16, with a massive flight occurring between March 20 and 31; in Khar'kovskuyu *oblast*, March 16-17, a heavy flight April 1-2, with flights completed in second half of April; in the Moscow *oblast* (21 years' observation) average was April 10, (March 31, 1924 to April 20, 1920); the average flight at Ivanovskuyu *oblast* April 10, with heavy flight, April 18-19; in Norgorodskuyo *oblast*, April 11; in Pskovskuyo, April 13-14; in the southern part of Kirovskoy *oblast*, the second half of April; in the environs of Cherdivi, May 6, 1827; on the Ob, April 25, 1873; below Ust'Tsilma a flight was observed May 21 to 25.

Dementiev and Gladkov wrote that in the fall—inlate July or early August—families join into small flocks and begin a nomadic type of life, roaming far from nesting regions, even down out of the mountains into lower country. As northern birds arrive, local ones join them and these flocks roam, slowly migrating southward. Sometimes they remain until frosts come. They feed on grain fields, roosting at night on river bars and in marshes. On favorable days they fly high in the sky, so far at times that they can only be heard. On cloudy days they fly at low altitudes. Flocks become much larger than spring flocks, from a few tens up to hundreds. They remain separated a short distance when flying. These flocks begin to come from the north in the second half of August and continue through September, even into October—at times late in the month (October 23, Kirovskaya *oblast)*. In the central zone they fly the first days of August, even as early as July (Moscow *oblast*, flock of 44, July 14). On August 22, 1894 there was an immense flight (Semenov). Intensive flight extends through September, and is generally completed by late September or early October, although scattered single flocks are often observed even later.

They continue that in Ethiopia cranes make their appearance in autumn as early as September (September 7), and in Nubia in late August and throughout September, with some flying over all winter. They begin flying back as early as February in Nubia, while in Ethiopia late birds have been seen flying in mid-May.

Cranes fly at miscellaneous times of day and night. If they encounter extreme cold in spring they discontinue northward flight and turn back south for a few days. Usually they fly in a V-formation, like the well established crane-wedge. Flocks reach highest numbers in fall. During heavy flight, flock after flock flies over in a short interval of time. If a flock is very large, clusters sometimes break off, forming several groups which fly a short distance apart. Generally a flock consists of 10 to 50 individuals, infrequently up to 400 or more. In such cases they fly in long wavy lines or at obtuse angles, often in several lines. They proceed at a great height, particularly in spring, rarely stopping where there are no people. Before descending they circle several times, even rising upwards, then make their descent. Sometimes they descend when crossing some large marsh and whirl about in the air, but continue without stopping. They fly straight over mountains. In the Caucasus Mountains they have been observed flying over the Glavily Range at an elevation of 4,000 meters at Kazbek and El'brus (Radde). They must fly at this elevation normally at times, for Hürzeler, 1950, wrote of observing 80 cranes flying in V-formation at an elevation of 4,300 meters over the North Sea between Dover and Boulogne when he was flying that region.

Some cranes winter in Mesopotamia, in Zagroshe and Iran. Radde (1885) found a group wintering in Zakavkaz'ye, on the Mugansk Steppe. Spangenberg observed them during January and February in pairs in northern Beli near the Iranian border of U.S.S.R. Tavetskov (1901) found them at 300 meters on the lower reaches of Khrami River, and it is possible that they winter in Crimea in small numbers (Dementiev, 1951).

Mester (1961) reporting for the middle Westphalia, Germany migration:

1) During the spring, over a period of 13 years, 1948-1960, there were more birds passing over in March than in autumn.

2) Exact numbers at night could not be told, but he estimated 10 per cent flew by night. More than half of them travelled between 4 p.m. and 6 p.m. in spring; in the fall the greatest flight density occurred during the forenoon.

3) They flew in the crane-wedge going about 20

kilometers per hour because of high winds, although they tried to find more ideal conditions by flying higher at times.

4) In October, one time, a flight turned around and flew back along its course. The line of travel of the birds observed by Mester turns along the Ruhr Valley (apparently the birds follow valleys when possible).

5) The middle of Westphalia is slightly north of the 'ideal center' of the flat course of the flight. In the German district it is farther north in spring than in the fall. Possibly this because the hills to the south are cooler in spring.

Schien (1950) said spring migration in Germany observed from 1927 to 1950 occurred between March 9, (1937) and March 31, but birds usually passed through between March 18 and 25. Numbers varied between seven and 100, and flight directions were east, northeast, and east-northeast.

During spring migration cranes may pass over Denmark in a short period of time, sometimes all in just one day (Salomonsen and Rudebeck, 1963). By the last of April and early May they have scattered all over the land to breed. Most birds pass over the eastern portion of Denmark.

Mascher, et al. (1962) noted that some of the bird flocks they recorded by radar were cranes at an estimated elevation of 650 to 1,650 feet as they passed over southern Sweden. Ehrenroth (1965) reported total cranes over Skagen's Lighthouse, Lake Vanern, during 34 days in 1962 was 12; during 93 days in 1963, 118.

One of the greatest spring concentrations of *Grus grus* for many years has been the one at Hornborgasjön, Sweden (Lat. 58°20′N). Cranes seldom stop in autumn, but in spring they arrive during the first two or three weeks of April, reaching concentrations of several thousands, depending on the severity of the weather, between the 16th and the 24th of April. P. O. Swanberg, (letter, October 28, 1951 and published records, 1970) sent me the following record of dates and number of birds observed:

1939. April 8, 1; April 25, 614; May 1, 70 in one flock; another flock not counted.

1940. April 18, 235; April 28, 500, after very severe winter and late spring.

1941. April 18, leaving by hundreds; April 23, 1,000.

1943. April 10, 2; April 12, 73; April 14, several hundred.

1948. April 10, 300-400; April 16, about 3,000; April 18, 1,000; April 27, 15.

1950. April 9, at least 500, probably 700-800.

1966-1969 are listed on the accompanying chart, which shows numbers, and peaks of density. Swanberg estimated about 5,500 cranes used the region in 1967, and 5,700 in 1968. The birds roost at night in the shallow waters of Hornborgasjön and feed on nearby fields during the daytime.

Farther north, at Gärdsjö (Lat. 59°N), cranes arrived on a nesting marsh April 14, 1958; April 1, 1959; April 4, 1960; April 4, 1961; April 11, 1962; and April 7, 1963 (Notes by Gustav Andersson). At Harads, Norrbotten, (Lat. 66°N) Arne Blomgren (unpublished) reported first cranes as follows: April 22, 1943; April 28, 1945; April 22, 1947; April 30, 1948; April 22, 1949; April 19, 1950; April 23, 1951; April 24, 1952; April 24, 1953; May 2, 1954; April 28, 1955; April 25, 1956; April 21, 1957; April 27, 1958; April 28, 1959; April 18, 1960; April 30, 1961; April 12, 1962; April 13, 1963.

The mean arrival date was April 23, (extremes: April 12-May 2). In autumn Andersson observed flights on September 24, 1955 and October 17, 1956.

Holmström, et. al. (1947) reported migration during the last half of August, through September and often prolonged into October. Some years cranes returned in late March, but more often in early April. In Uppland (north of Stockholm) they return in mid-April; to Muonio (north of the Arctic Circle) between May 3 and 9, once as early as April 27.

The first attempt to investigate the European migration was made in Sweden, by Professor Sundevall (1871) who in 1844 published a paper "Om Tranans flyttning." His 1871 paper was based on wider information, drawn from all over Europe.

Although a few small groups or single flocks are seen in southern Sweden in the fall, the largest concentration occurs at Öland (Late 56+°N; Long. 16°E) where 1,000 to 2,000 stop (P. O. Swanberg, letter, October 28, 1951). During the fall of 1961, Ehrenroth, et. al., (1965) noted cranes twice in Värmland: September 3, (258) and November 19, (1); while Edberg (1965) recorded migration through Kalmar Sound between Öland and the mainland,

Common Cranes dancing, April 20, 1971, Lake Hornborgasjon. (Photos by P. O. Swanberg.)

giving flight directions and numbers of birds as north, 53; south, 152; east, 11; west, 70.

At Ottenby Bird Station (south end of Öland) numbers of cranes flying over the sea in autumn were: 1947, 1,900; 1948, 1,260; 1949, 3,419; 1950, 2,206; 1951, 1,753. During 1951, flight dates and number of birds (in parentheses) were as follows: September 7, (9); 8, (275); 9, (299); 10, (422); 11 (11); 13, (21); 19, (117); 20, (372); 21, (62); 22, (25); October 2, (42); 3, (98).

FINLAND.

Bremer (1927) gave spring arrival of cranes at Finby, southwest Finland as follows: April 12, 1901; April 17, 1902; April 24, 1903; April 16, 1904; April 24, 1905; April 13, 1906; April 25, 1909; April 4, 1911; April 18, 1912; April 21, 1913; April 14, 1914; March 30, 1916; April 17, 1917; April 12, 1918; April 15, 1922; April 14, 1923; April 16, 1924; April 16, 1926.

The median arrival was April 15 during the 18 years that observations were made.

Renvall (1926) gave records at Helsinki (Lat. 60°N; Long. 25°E): April 10, 1925, (3 p.m., 20 birds flying NE at 100 meters); April 14, 1925 (noon, 25 flying NE at 100 meters); April 23, 1925 (20-21 flying NE); April 24, 1925 (7:30 a.m., 10-12 flying N; and at 3:20 p.m., 4 flying at 150 meters NE); April 28, 1925 (1 flying N at 150 meters). On September 25, 1923 he observed 40 birds flying south at 4 p.m.

Kärki (1915) showed that the cranes arrived later than the swans. At Savonlinna (Lat. 62°N; Long. 29.5°E) arrival dates from 1899 until 1924 were: April 1-7, 3 flocks; April 8-14, 3 flocks; April 15-21, 17 flocks; April 22-30, 20 flocks; early May, 11 flocks. Latest flock: May 13, 1917.

Böök (1929) gave spring arrival dates at Padas-joelle as April 17 and 18, 1926 (cranes flying N); April 28, 1926 (17 going N); April 25, 1927 (2:30 p.m., 48 flying NE at 100 meters) (7 p.m., 28 flying NE at 100 meters) (8:30 p.m., 19 flying NE); April 26, 1927 (noon, 52 flying NE; 2 p.m., 60 flying NE at 300 meters); May 3, 1928 (10:30 a.m., 50 going N at 300 meters); May 4, 1928 (8:33 a.m., 52 going N at 150 meters). Böök (1931) in the same region observed cranes April 17, 1930, and (1932), on April 22, 24, 27, and 29, and May 2, 1931, while (1933) he

gave April 26, 27, and 28, 1932, and (1934) April 14 and 30 and May 1, 2, and 4, 1933.

At Jyväskylan (Lat. 62°+ N, Long. 25°+ E), Tah-vonen (1932) observed cranes May 2, 1924; April 24, and May 1, 1925; April 25, and May 3, and 15, 1927; as well as June 15, 1925; while Hortling (1927) observed one on April 12, 1927 at Ayrapaanjarvi.

Vappula (1930) gave these records for Tikkuri-lassa near Koelaitoksella: April 30, 1929 (noon, 30 flying N; 12:30 p.m., 75, circling for some time then going N). Others were observed May, 2 1929 (3 p.m. 60 going N); May 7, 1929 (lone bird flying N at 10 a.m.); and September 26, 1929 (2 p.m., 30 flying E).

Federley (1929) wrote at Esbo near Mankån that he had observed cranes flying on April 20, (5); April 23, (5); April 27, (13); April 29, (flocks of 15, 38 and 60); and in fall, September 3, (7); September 13, (4); September 16, (12); and September 22, (42).

In *Ornis Fennica* (13:50, 1936) crane migrations given for 1934 at Padasjoella were April 14, 15, 18, 19, 21, 22, and 25; and for fall, August 26, 28, and 29, and September 3, 9, 10, 13, and 14. For spring 1935, April 25, 26, and 27, and June 2, and for fall, August 29, and September 2, 8, 9, 10, and 12.

Putkonen (1936) during 1935 observed cranes April 3 to June 12, at Ayrapaanjarvella.

Cranes begin to leave Finland (Böök, 1926) in late August. A summary of the 1925 flight is given: Forty-one flocks totalling 1,303 individuals were observed on the following dates:

August 28, (1 flock); September 8, (4); September 9, (1); September 10, (5); September 11, (1); September 12, (6); September 13, (7); September 15, (2); September 16, (1); September 17, (6); September 18, (1); September 19, (3); September 20, (1); September 28, (1); October 5 (1).

The largest flock was 75, the smallest two, cranes. There were 25 flocks with 20-75 individuals; seven flocks, with 10-19; nine flocks, two to nine, with the average flock size 31.7 individuals. Six flocks were observed before 11 a.m., 29 flocks between 11 a.m. and 5 p.m., and six flocks after 5 p.m. Nine flocks were flying at an elevation of over 200 meters; 32 flocks between 100 and 200 meters; none below 100 meters. Five flocks were flying SW; one flock N; and 35 flocks directly S.

South of here some migrations proceed directly across the U.S.S.R.; other birds cross along the islands at the north edge of the Baltic Sea to Sweden.

NORWAY.

Lövenskiold (1947-1951) wrote: "Arrival in S Norway about mid-April, sometimes as early as March. About mid-April flocks of 15-20 birds are no rare sight in the Oslo region, flying northwards. Abmigration in August/September."

Records published in the Lillehammer and Hamar newspapers, 1949-1952 showed typical migrations: In 1950, April 12, (5); April 22, (6); April 23, (31); April 28, (25); April 29, (7); each group in a single flock, while in 1952: April 28, (18-20); May 22, (30 in two flocks).

Hagen and Barth (1951) recorded 15 cranes flying over Atnabru, April 28, 1951.

At Hamar a fall-migrating flock of nine was observed September 11, 1949 (H. Holgersen, letter, December 31, 1953).

GERMANY.

Geyr von Schweppenburg (1934, 1955), Libbert (1936, 1938, 1948, 1957, 1961), and others have shown that autumn migration of the crane crosses Germany from East Germany, Poland, Sweden and other countries to the E and N, then crosses France toward Spain. Bernis (1960) showed this continued on a wide front, except to the northwest, across Spain to a wintering ground in southwest Spain, southeast Portugal and northwest Morocco. Libbert (1936) and (1961) describes the German migration in detail. It crosses Germany from northeast to southwest between September and November. Observations in 1958 showed the cranes crossing chiefly between October 11 and 24. Tremendous numbers were observed on October 17, 18, and 19.

THE NETHERLANDS.

Cranes migrate over Holland regularly, their numbers varying from year to year. During autumn of 1963 large numbers were reported around the country and in Belgium (Burton, 1970). A few are recorded regularly, as in these reports by Ten Kate (1964): Zuthaven, Zutphen, January 1, about 30

Common Crane at nest, Oberlausitz, East Germany. (Photo by Ilse Makatsch.)

individuals. Hilversum, NW, March 10, 12 individuals. Kampen, April 28-29, (1) Ramspol, August 23, (6); September 20, Schouwen, Inlagen, and October 13-14; at Amersfoort, (25).

SCOTLAND.

A crane was shot May 14, 1906, at Stornoway, Isle of Lewis, Outer Hebrides (*Ann. Scott. Nat. Hist.*, 1907, 84); another was observed April 21-May 20, 1953 on the west coast of Benbecula (Campbell, 1956). The latter observer also reported the bird May 22-24, 1953, in North Unit, west of Knockinterran. Another lone bird was noted at Birsay, Orkney, May 17-27, 1955 (Balfour, 1956).

ENGLAND.

Turner (*Avium Praecipaurum quarum apud Plinium et Aristotelem mentis est, brevis et succinta historia.*, Coloniae, 1544) mentioned the breeding of the crane in England as not unusual. Blaauw, 1897), quoting Professor Alfred Newton, believed the breeding place was in the fen districts of the Cambridge locality. H. B. Cott (1953), wrote that this bird bred in East Anglia up until about 1600, but as early as 1534 it was found necessary to protect the eggs by law.

More recently, cranes have been observed in migration: A pair at Lilford Hall, Northamptonshire, May 27, 1937 (Moody, 1937); at Normanton Park, Oakham, Rutland, April 27, 1940 (Bolam, 1940); at Blythburg, Suffolk and later at Brampton, September 8, 1949 (C. B. G. Benson, 1950); one at Westwood Marshes, Suffolk, September 14-24, 1949 (Tucker, 1950); another in both Norfolk and Suffolk, in 1951 (*Brit. Birds,* 1953, 46: 149); one was found dead April 5, 1954 at Auburn, Yorkshire (G. J. Brown, 1955); one was seen at Westleton Heath, near Minsmere, Suffolk, May 25 and 26, 1955 (Wolfendale, 1956). A large invasion occurred in autumn 1963 when about 500 cranes visited England, arriving between Beachy Head and the Isle of Wight and dispersing over Sussex, Hampshire, Somerset, Dorset, Devon, Cornwall, Essex, Cambridgshire, and Kent (Burton, 1970).

IRELAND.

Lydekker (1891) stated crane remains were found in kitchen middens at Ballycotton, County Cork.

NORTH AMERICA.

Alaska. Kessel and Kelly (1958) recorded the first bird (probably *G. g. lilfordi*) photographed by Earl L. Schene, at Fairbanks, April 24, 1958.

Alberta. Wishart and Sharp (1959) recorded a single bird December 11, 1957 at Cavendish (Lat. 50.75°N; Long. 110.5°W) from where it departed December 20. Another was seen March 20, 1958 at Stirling Lake, Lethbridge (Lat. 49.75°N; Long. 113°W) while on September 19, 1958 one was photographed with two Sandhill Cranes at Athabasca (Lat 55°N; Long. 113.5°W).

New Mexico. A lone bird was seen in a flock of 600 Sandhill Cranes on the Bitter Lakes Wildlife Refuge, Roswell (Lat. 33.5°N; Long 104.5°W), March 10, 1961 (Monson, 1961).

FRANCE.

Thomson (1953) described how cranes had been seen migrating along the Bay of Biscay at St. Jean de Luz where the coast bends westward. Cranes, with many other birds, followed SSW on a broad front overland.

Poncy, (1941) reported a crane flight over France through the Valley of the Saone, when birds began arriving October 15 and 16, in flocks of 50 to 200, with an enormous band October 17, and many more birds on October 18. Some migrants were in evidence until December 10.

Mayaud (1964) reported a heavy 1963 crane flight, when birds crossed Holland and England over the valley of l'Oise in early October, continuing to the end of November. Wille (1964), Etchécopar and Hüe (1964) and Cuisin, all have described some phase of migration across France.

ITALY AND THE MEDITERRANEAN.

Brandolini (1955) reported Cranes in December 1952 at Parti di Bagnacavallo, while Finis (1952) in southern Italy, reported cranes October 28, 1943 (flying high SW); and November 18, 1943 (30 going SW). Foschi (1954) reported four passing Magliano (Forli) October 25, 1953; as well as a migration October 25, 1946 at San Zaccaria di Ravenna il. Moltoni (1957) reported flights over the island of Pantelleria, October 14, 1953 and November 1930. Wille (1964) reported cranes in Italy in autumn, 1963.

At Capri Bird Observatory, *Grus grus* was seen November 2, 1961 (28) and a flock heard during the night. Lundberg (1963), and Engström (1963) noted a flock (5) flying SE, October 15 in the afternoon and three on October 30, 1960.

Munn (1932) described how an adult and an immature Common Crane landed at Albufera of Alcudia, Balearic Isles, October 17, 1930. Both were shot four days later. They were quite unknown to the inhabitants. Stresemann (1956) reported cranes over Crete, autumn of 1941 and 1943.

C. A. White (Moreau, 1953) recorded 18 cranes passing south over Bizerte, Tunisia, October 12, while Payn (1948) reported first flocks passing over Cape Bon September 3, 1943, and thereafter small flocks were seen almost daily flying south. Many of these flocks, he said, came down into marshes and newly-sown cornfields as they moved to central Algeria.

Feeny, et al., (1968) recorded ten cranes in V-formation, the last day they were in the field (as they wrote, perhaps migration was just beginning) September 19, at Meyan Keleh, at the south end of the Caspian Sea. Sage reported a large flight September 8-9, 1958, at Khanaqin, Iraq, while Ticehurst, et al., (1926) reported great numbers in the Mosul district of Iraq, at the end of November and early December, flying southwest. Smith (1960) noted first cranes bordering the estuary of Oued Messa, Eritrea, November 15, 1962. Passburg noted first three then six birds flying west of Ahmadabad, Iran, October 9.

Buxton (1916) noted large flocks crossing the Dardanelles into Turkey in October, 1915, and neither Geyr von Schweppenburg (1934), nor Steinfatt, Nisbet and Smout (1957) saw any birds crossing the Bosphorus, but believed many flew across at the Dardanelles.

Some cranes stop off west of Alexandria, but most move on into Sudan. Gray and Demoiselle Cranes arrived at Khartoum September 3, 1934; three small parties were seen October 5, 1939 at Gezivetel Fil. G. K. F. Madami saw a small flock October 1, 1941 at Gezira Research Farm. During November, 1943 they did considerable damage; on October 10, 1961, Ahmed El Sayed and Dr. G. Treichel, 30 kilometers east of Khartoum, observed some 20,000 cranes, mostly A. virgo, but some G. grus (Sud. Nat. Hist. Mus.).

Cheeseman and Sclater (1935), wrote at Machigo, 5 miles southwest of Lake Tana, Ethiopia, (el. 6,500 ft.) that a large migration arrived the night of October 9-10, 1926. Flocks were heard every 30 seconds after dark, all flying SSE toward the small Abbai Valley. Again at Dangala, October 10, 1928, cranes passed overhead all night. Two days later flocks were seen passing SSE during the daytime. (Records from eastern regions could be of either A. virgo or G. grus.)

Summarizing autumn migration as done by Libbert (1936):

A large flight goes from Sweden and near by

Common Crane at nest with chick, Oberlausitz, East Germany. (Photo by Ilse Makatsch.)

across Germany, France, and central Spain to southwest Spain, southeast Portugal and northwest Morocco. Another flight passes southward through eastern Poland (Sierakowski et al. (1967).

Birds rarely cross the Balearic Islands, but do cross about 150 miles east of Gibraltar into Morocco.

A flight does occur across Capri, Corsica, and Sardinia, going to Algiers and Tunisia.

Another flight crosses the Adriatic to Italy at Brindisi, then across Sicily to Tunisia.

A strong flight crosses eastern Hungary and across the southern Danube, with no records farther south in the Balkans, and none crossing at the Bosphorus.

Birds cross Anatolia, and cross the eastern Mediterranean in several places, having been noted over the Cyclades, Crete, and Cyprus, at times far distant from land.

Flight passes over the Yaila Mountains in the Crimea (Pusanov, 1933).

Flight goes over the Caucasus Mountains, over Iraq and to some extent into Eritrea.

An extensive flight goes around the south end of the Caspian Sea.

In spring, flights are apparently reversed, but seem to avoid the Caspian region. Farther east, extensive flights cross Afghanistan from the Punjab; some cross Nepal and the Himalayas, and others fly farther east into western China. More rarely, some birds fly along the east coast.

THE EASTERN GRAY CRANE. *Grus grus lilfordi.*

Grus lilfordi. Sharpe, *Cat. Birds British Museum,* 23, 1894, p. 250 (in key), p. 252.
No type nor type locality designated but specimens listed from Ob River, Siberia; India; Nepal, and Swatow, China; (Peters, 1934). Eastern Siberia (Dementiev and Gladkov, 1951). General color pearly-gray, the inner secondaries lighter.
Grus grus lilfordi. Koslova, *Birds of southwest Transbaikalia, Northern Mongolia, and Central Gobi.* 1932, Part 3, Ibis, 13th ser., 2, 4. 567-596. Dementiev and Gladkov, *Birds of the Soviet Union,* 2, 1951.
Dolgushin, *Birds of Kazakhstan,* Vol. 1, Acad. Science Kazakhskoi SSR, Alma-Ata, 1960.
Megalornis grus lilfordi. Baker, *The Game Birds of the Indian Empire.* Part 5. Journ. Bombay Nat. Hist. Soc., 1928, 32: 402-407.
Vernacular names. The Eastern Gray Crane, Lil-

ford's Crane, (English); Grauer Kranich (German); Kuranch, Kurch (Hindi); Kunj (Sind); Kullam (Deccan); Kulangi (Tel.);

Range and Breeding Distribution. Eastern Siberia from Kazakhstan and the Yenisey basin eastwards possibly to the Kolyma. Winters in northern India, east to Assam, northern Viet Nam, China and Taiwan.

Dementiev and Gladkov (U.S.S.R.: 1951) reported: The northern boundary extends to the Ob at Obdorsk (Salekhard, Lat 66°358N; Long. 66°35′N; (Shostak, 1926), to the rivers Taz (Lat. 67°30′N; Long. 79°E), and Yelaguy (Skalov and Sludski, 1941). On the Yenisey, it is possible to the Turukhansk (Lat. 65°25′N; Long. 88°E), somewhat to the south of the Lower Tunguska (Lat. 63°40′N; Long. 90°10′E), the Vilyuy, Lena up to the mouth, and her tributary the Aldan Verhoyansk (Lat. 67°35′N; Long. 133°E), and the Indigirka, up to the mouth of its tributary Moma (Lat. 66°N) (Mikhel, 1935). How far it goes to the east of the Indigirka is not elucidated (on the Kolyma some cranes nest and some of these may be the Gray Crane rather than the Candian Crane, but in collections there are no specimens from there). In the Anadyr (Lat. 64°40′N; Long. 177°30′E) they do not nest. Concerning the nesting of the Gray Cranes in Kamchatka (Long. 160°E), the Koryatskoy Peninsula (Lat. 62°N+; Long. 170°E), and the Okhotsk seacoast, there is no information. In Primorya and Priamur it does not nest.

The western boundary is not exactly cleared up. Southward it goes to the Volzhsko-Ural'sk Steppes (Lat. 51°15′N; Long. 51°20′E). In the south it reaches to 47°5′N Lat., reaching Samarskiye Lake, El'ton (Lat. 47°N; Long. 50°E), Novouzensk Steppe (Volchanetskiy, 1937). On the Ural—up to its middle reaches; the Khobda, Ilek (Lat. 51°35′N; Long. 53°25′E), Emba (Lat. 47°30′N; Long. 56°40′E) rivers but how far it goes along the Emba to the south is not known (Sushkin). Farther to the south its boundary reaches to the northeastern coast of the Aral Sea, the delta of the Syr-Darya (Lat. 46°N; Long. 61°E), Kamishly-bash, Lake Teli-Kul', Sary-Su (Lat. 46°N; Long. 67°E), Chu, Ozera Issyk-Kul', Alma Ata (Lat. 43°N; Long. 77°E), Ili, Zaysan (Lat. 48°N; Long 84°E), Emilsk, the valley foothills of the Tarbagatai Range (Lat. 46°30′N; Long. 82°30′E) (Khakhlov), Altay (Lat. 53°30′N; Long. 91°45′E), Cyani, Tannu-Tuva (Lat. 51°N; Long. 92°E) (Sushkin, 1938), Khanga, Pribaikal, Dauria, Lake Tarey-Nor, Rivers Onon and Argun (Lat. 53°20′N; Long. 121°30′E).

Farther to the east there is no positive information about the nesting of this crane. Some flight of cranes has been observed near Mariinsk (Lat. 51°40′N; Long. 140.15°E) (Shrenk, 1860), and in the valley of the Ussuri (Lat. 42°N; 132°E) (Maak). Isolated colonies are found in Transcaucasia and Asia Minor, in Dzhava-kheity, in Armenia at Lake Sevan (Lat. 40°20′N; Long. 45°E), at the source of the Kura (Lat. 40°N;

Long. 47°E), at Lake Chaldir, in the valley of the upper reaches of the Araks, in the northern part of Iran—at Kotursko-Urmiysk region, and in northeast Turkey at Lake Adzhin-Tuz-Gol (Lat. 38°N; Long. 33°E).

Koslova (1933) wrote of this species in southwest Transbaikalia, northern Mongolia, and central Gobi: "Passes through in both spring and fall. Nearest breeding localities are valleys of the Onon and Argun rivers. The migration through southwest Transbaikalia and the Tola River valley (Lat. 46°N; Long. 105°E) is very marked, but at Lake Orok-Nor it is considerably less. The first flocks are usually seen about the middle of April. Large companies of cranes arrive from the north in August and stay in Mongolia for some time, keeping to the largest river valleys, where they rest and feed before continuing their journey."

In *Birds of the Eurasian Taiga and Tundra* (p. 346), cranes were reported April 10, 1926 flying at 1,057 meters elevation by the Gobian Altai.

Dolgushin (1960) wrote:

It is known that the two subspecies are found in Kazakhstan, most often the light subspecies, *G. g. lilfordi* Sharpe, and only in the west very close to the border of Kazakhstan may one meet specimens of the nominal form—*G. g. grus* L.

...Between the Volga and the Ural rivers it nests to the south to Kamysh-Samarsk Ozera (Lat. 49°N; Long. 52°E), and Kalmykov. Southward, in the desert, adjoining the Caspian Sea, apparently it does not nest, but reaches the Volga delta. Further east it nests—to the south on the middle Emba, nesting everywhere near the Kustanay Steppes to the northern boundary of the *oblast*, then to the south to the lower regions of the Irgiz, Turgay, and ChelkarTengiz(Lat. 48-50°N; Long. 60-64°E). Further nesting is done along the edges of marshes and lakes in northern Kazakhstan, in the Kokchetav region (Lat. 53°30'N; Long. 70°E.), at Kurgal'dzhino (Lat. 50°N), at Shubar-Teniz, and beside lakes near Karaganda (Chushkal' Dar'ya Steppe and others). Common on Pavlodar Steppes (Lat. 51°N; Long. 75°E), and everywhere in the valley of the Irtysh (Long. 69°30'E). It nests next to lakes in Chingiz-Tau and Kalbinsk Altai, as well as Zaysan and at Chernom Irtysh, many places on the Altay (Lat. 53°30'N; Long. 91°45'E), over the majority of Marka-Kulya and the lower reaches of the Burkhtarm,Katon-Karagaya. It nests in the Chiliktim (Tarbagatay). It is common in the Alakulskoy Valley. Uncommon as a nester in the lower reaches of the Chu, it nests in the Biylyookul'skoy hollow on the lower Sary-Su. Also on islands and the coastline of the eastern portion of the Aral Sea, at the delta of the Syr Darya and on the Kamishlibash Lake. Along the Syr Darya—the entire length, from Kazalinsk to Chiili—it is found at the beginning of the summer migration. A nest was found by N. A. Zarudni at Lake Chushkakul near Turkestan. Few are found in the high mountains. It nests in the Altai, up to 2,500 meters. In the greater part of Tien Shan it does not nest. But on Kegeni, it is found normally at 1,800 meters. In Kazakhstan it is found everywhere but is not common.

Dolgushin added that it was common along the east shore of the Caspian Sea and in Ust'Urt, and in Kazakhstan during migration almost everywhere along the valleys but not in high mountains.

Close to China, on Keles and Golodno steppes, arrival occurs at times in late February but more frequently early in March. At Karatau, at Dzhuvalinskoy, and at Chayane, flight was observed from early in March to early May. Birds customarily flew in flocks of 30-40 individuals, at times in smaller groups of from three to ten individuals, or on occasion with up to 60 in a flock. At Lzhulek first groups were observed April 7. On the lower Chu only a few flocks were observed in April at Barsa-Kel'mes (Aral'skoe Sea). In the Ili valley and on the Ili delta cranes were seen in early March but the flight was weak and dropped down greatly by May. Below Alma-Atoy, flight appeared later, sometimes in late March, more often in early April. Throughout the *oblast* flights were similar to these arrival dates.

Dementiev and Gladkov wrote (1951):

This species has been observed farther to the north. For example, on the island of Wrangel, at Novosibirsk Islands, on the delta of the Indigirka, on the northern Ural, below 68°30'N Latitude and in 1908 (Molchanov, 1911) and twice in 1942, at the southern island of Novaya Zemlya (Uspenski).

In Armenia, when some birds are nesting, others are migrating, in mid-April. The flight in the west goes even earlier. In the lower Ural first birds appear in late March, near Chalov and on the Emba in early April and even into May. A heavy flight occurs near Chalov during the second half of April (Sushkin1908). Beginning flight in the region of Bugurslansk, Kuybishevsk *oblast* starts in middle or late April (Karamzin, 1909), and in central Povolzh'ye (Volga region) begins around March 28, to mid-April (Volchanetskiy and Yal'tsev, 1934). In central Asia, migration is very early. In Turkmenistan, flight begins early in March, with heavy flight late in the month and in early April (Dementiev, 1950). At Tadzhikistan, April 1 to mid-April (April 11, Ivanov); on the lower Syr Darya April 7, 1928 (Spangenberg and Feygin).

At Semirech'e, very early; on the river Kaskelen, March 20, near Alma-Ata, March 30, with a heavy flight on April 8; near Dzharkent, April 4-8; on the river Leschanoy April 1-4; at Semirech'e by May 10, heavy flight is completed, and flying is done only by individual pairs or alone (Koreev and Zarudniy). In Iliysk region, March 28, (Shestoperov, 1929). At Irgiz, from April 12 to May 8, (Sushkin, 1908); at Naurzume, early in the second half of April (Mikheev, 1938). At Lake Chani, April 28, (Danilovich, 1935). In the Omsk region, early part of second half of April to early May. At Altay, in the second half of April (April 20, Teletskoe Lake; April 25, Bele, Folitarek and Dementiev, 1936); April, 9 and 17, northern Novenskoe (Lavrov, 1911). At Yelague April 15, 1932 (Skalon and Sludski, 1941); at Vitim May 8; at Yakutsk from May 1. Latest dates of arrival: May 6, 1918 and 1925; May 7, 1921 (Skalon). At Olekmu, April 29 (3 year average); at Ust'-Mae, 2 year average, April 7; at Abage, April 9, (4 year average); at Tatta, May 2, (4 year average); at Ust'-Aldansk, May 9, (4 year average); at Viluysk, May 4, (4 year average); at Verkhoyansk, May 9, (2 years) (Skalon, Vorob'eva, 1931; Tugarinov, 1928). On the Indigirka, at the mouth of the Moma, May 10, 1929 (Mikhel, 1935).

A great difference in arrival dates is found between west and east Siberia and also in eastern and western parts of central Asia and in Kazakhstan, apparently explained by winter distribution of the Gray Crane and the distance of the flight path.

Fall flight. At Yakutsk return flight begins in late August to early September, often passing swiftly over in just a few days...At Verhoyansk (Lat. 67.5°N; Long. 134°E) (Skalon) first flocks flew on September 6, 1935; at Olekminsk (Lat. 60°N; Long 120°E) September 6, 1937, and the flight was completely ended September 15. At Abaga, the first flock flew August 25, 1928. Flight continued until September 1; at Churancha, first flight was September 2, 1929; at Tatta September 13, 1929 and August 28, 1930; at Megezhen, September 4, 1930 and at Vitim (Lat. 58°N; Long. 112.5°E), September 5. At Aldan (Lat. 58°N, Long. 125°E), August 28, (Vorob'eva, 1928); at Yakutsk (Lat. 62°N, Long. 130°E), late August until mid-September. On the upper reaches of the river Taz (Long. 80°E) birds were flying in late September (September 29, 1929, Skalon and Sludski, 1941). At Minusinsk (Lat. 53°N, Long. 92°E) region and in Altai, flight went in late August through September and even up to the second half of October (October 12 and 13, 1935, Altaysk Preserve, Folitarek and Dementiev, 1935; October 16 flight of many flocks from Novensk Zmeinogorsk District, Averin and Lavrov, 1911). At Kuznetsk, August 25 (Zalesski, 1930). At Altay...birds did not skirt the mountains, flying low above them at 2,200 meters. In the Zaysan valley (Lat. 47°N)...late August to October 3. Direction of flight to south (Sushkin, 1938). On the Kirghiz Steppes (Lat. 42°N) local birds depart in August, but flight is observed into September; in Naurzum... September 20, heavy flight September 23 up to first of October (Mikheev, 1938). At Semirech'e and Ilisk

regions...mid-September to mid-October. At Syr-Darya near Dzhulek birds appeared August 7, 1938 (Spangenberg and Feygin, 1936). At Kisyl-Kum, second half of September. In Turkmenistan, late August (August 5 on Tedzhen River—Lat. 37°N, Long. 61°E, Zarudniy, 1896), a heavy flight in second half of September (Dementiev, 1950). At Tadzhikistan they flew from mid-August to September (August 17-September 1, Ivanov, 1940); Fedchenko in 1870 observed a large flight in September flying southwest...

On the delta of the Volga and at the Caspian seacoast, cranes appear...in late September...continuing intensively into the latter part of the first half of October ...flying southwest. Apparently birds out of Bashkir fly along the Caucasian Caspian seacoast over the main Caucasus Mountains. At Kavkaz crane flight was observed...in mid-September up through late October and early November. On Lake Sevan (Lat. 40°N, Long. 45°E)...flight occured in the second half of September. Return flight is largely dependent on approaching frost in the south country; where conditions are suitable for feeding and existence, the birds delay for a long time.

Ecology. Reproduction. Not distinct from the Western Gray Crane in nest construction, number and hatching of eggs...The time of reproduction: In Armenia...at Lake Gilli June 26, two well developed eggs were found (Dal'); on the Lower Syr-Darya, sets were started in late April; at Lake Teli-Kul on May 21, 1927, a set of two eggs was found (Spangenberg and Feygin, 1936); on the Upper Ili, in the first half of April, a set of two eggs was found, and on April 13, two nests. In one there were 3 eggs; the other had 1 (Shestoperov, 1929). At Barabinsk Steppe a set was found in the first half of May and concluded in mid-June; in the region of Kainsk a nest with one egg was found on May 24. On May 26 and 29, nests with eggs were found—one nest with 2 eggs—at Lake Sartlan on June 10 (Johansen, 1907); At Altai-in Katon-Karagae an incubated set of 2 eggs was found May 7, 1931 (Spangenberg). The eggs measured: (2 eggs) 103.5 x 63.0 mm (Armenia, Lake Gilli, Dal'); (6 eggs) 88.8-96.0 x 57-61 mm, averaging 93.05 x 59.5 mm (Barabinsk Steppe, Johansen, 1907, 1930); (3 eggs) 98.5-102.8 x 60.5-62 mm., averaging 100.8 x 61.1 mm (Ili, Shestoperov, 1929); (2 eggs) 83.2 x 53.8 and 81.0 x 54.2 mm (Lake Teli-Kul; Spangenberg and Feygin, 1938); (2 eggs) 88.1 x 61.4 and 88 x 60 mm (environs of Katon-Karagaya-Lat. 49°N, 85°E, Spangenberg). Weight: (6 eggs) 150-200 grams, average 182.4 grams (Barabinsk Steppe, Johansen, 1907, 1930); (2 eggs) 151 and 155 grams (Lake Teli-Kul, Spangenberg). The eggs are somewhat smaller than those of the Western Gray Crane. The average weight of 8 eggs was 175.0 grams (151-200 grams). The average measurements of 13 eggs was 94.8 (81.0-103.5) x 60.59 (53.8-63.0) mm.

Baker (1928) reported two sets of two eggs taken north of the town of Yeniseysk.

Dementiev and Gladkov (loc. cit.) wrote:

In Armenia at Lake Gilli first young hatched in very late June and in early July (weight of newly hatched young, 100 grams, Dal'); in late July in western Siberia the first flying young appeared. At Altai (Chuysk Steppe) first flying young were seen July 31 but non-flying young were still seen two or three weeks later (Sushkin, 1938). In the first half of August first families begin to collect in flocks.

Molt. General scheme like that of the western crane. Adults have (in Altai) a molt observed the second half of July through mid-August, quills and tail having already been changed.

Nutrition. The same as the Western Gray Crane with only slight variations in relation to available vegetable food. For instance, cedar nuts (they were found crushed in the eosaphagus and stomach of a crane at Altai Preserve; Folitarek and Dementiev, 1938).

CHINA

Winter. In the British Museum there are specimens from northern Yunnan, February 7, 1899, and from Konang-Tcheou-Wan, January 28, 1933.

Caldwell and Caldwell (1931) reported this bird wintered in China in the Yangtse basin and southward, in Yunnan, south Shansi, Shensi and Anhuei. In Kwangtung it is common in flocks from October to February.

La Touche (1931-1934) wrote:

> N. E. Chihli (wintering and migrant). Yangtse Valley, Fohkien, Kwangtung, Yunnan (winter).
> In March, early in April, and again in October, the Eastern Common Crane passes in immense numbers up and down the north east China coast. On October 15, 1915, I saw and heard flocks passing over Chinwangtao continuously from 4:30 p.m. til past 8 p.m.
> Small parties winter on the Chihli plain, particularly near Chinwangtao, and I believe, on the plains throughout China to South Yunnan. Styan writes that it seems to be uncommon on the Lower Yangtse; Père David reports small parties found in winter in the Northern Provinces; a few have been shot at Foochow (I had one dated March 18, 1909), and I met with small flocks in winter on the plains behind Swatow and on the coast of NE Kwangtung. On the Mengtsz plateau great numbers winter every year; they feed on the remains of the crops and on the sweet potatoes. Farther south they are common in Indo-China and winter abundantly in Northern India. The summer quarters are in Turkestan, Eastern Siberia, Dauria, and Manchuria...

JAPAN.

One specimen was taken in Japan (Austin and Kuroda, 1953) at Ibaraki Prefecture, November 10, 1928. In addition, there are many sight records from Kyushu, one at Akune in 1928 and another 1929, and two single birds were seen at Arasaki, Kagoshima, in 1936, 1937, 1938 and 1939. During the winter of 1968-1969 five birds spent the winter there. One, apparently a male, was mated with a Hooded Crane and they had their hybrid youngster with them daily in their foraging for food out in the region where *Grus monachus* fed on the cultivated fields. During recent years they apparently have been increasing slowly in numbers in the Arasaki region. Much of the time they remained apart but as often they accompanied *G. monachus*. I did not see them associate with *G. vipio* at all.

KOREA.

The "Hand-List of Japanese Birds" (1958) records the species from Kogendo, Keikido, and Chuseido.

INDIA.

Specimens (BMNH) exist from Guzarat (Bombay), December 18, 1892; Sirsa District (Punjab), November 13, 1869; Jhellum, near Jelapur, November 21, 1871; and Hissar (Punjab), December 13, 1867.

Baker (1928) wrote: "In India, the Common Crane is only known to us as a winter migrant, arriving generally about the second or third week in October; Hume records their arrival on one occasion as early as October 3, whilst Doig says that in Sind, many birds arrive as early as the end of August, though this must be exceptional They begin to leave again by the middle of March, the bulk of the birds moving about the end of that month and a few staying on until the end of April. These late birds Hume thought were young birds.... In the east of India the few cranes that are to be seen arrive in November and I do not think that I have ever seen them after the second week in March. In North-west India they are often found in very great numbers, said sometimes to be in many hundreds."

Col. Ticknell, quoted by Blyth, (1881) wrote:

> The crane is, in India as in Europe, a bird of passage, appearing about November in the plains of Hindostan, and departing in February. It is common throughout the Bengal presidency during that period, but does

not extend far to the eastward. I never observed it in Arracan, nor in any part of Burma or Tenasserim. It spreads over the open parts of Tirhoot but avoides the more wooded country of eastern Poorneea, Bhaulia, and Dhaka; and is altogether unknown to the vast forests of the Teraie, the Morung, the Soonderbuns, and Chittagong. It keeps far away also from hills—even the low and scantily-clad ones of Chota Nagpore, where, in many years of wandering, I have never seen this bird.

Throughout the Punjab and the North-west Provinces, and Central India, from Oudh inclusive, as far south as Moongher, it is found in great flocks. How far it extends to the west and south-westward, I know not. Jerdon speaks of it as occurring in the Dukhun in parties of six or eight to twenty. These are probably stragglers from the main army. It keeps entirely to open, dry country, in the vicinity of the Ganges and other large rivers which have extensive sand flats bordering their streams. During the day they are generally observed high in the air, seldom coming to the ground unless in the most solitary places, when they rest on isolated sand islets in the river, or on the highest parts of wide barren tracts, clear of any covert which might conceal the approach of an invader; and at all times they are most wary and difficult of approach.

...I once, indeed, met with a striking exception to this wary habit of the crane in keeping, during the day, out of gunshot in the air. In January, 1845, as I was one day riding along the Trunk-road (as the old Government road from Calcutta to Delhi is called), in the district of Manbhoom, near the village or chowkee of Niamutpoor, I came in sight and within point-blank ball shot of a host of these birds collected in a rice stubble field. There was a prodiguous concourse of them, amounting probably to a thousand. They were making a deafening clamour, and seemed in great agitation, while every now and then a party of them would take wing and fly off, generally to the eastward, towards the Damoodur river, but many went in other directions. The country in the vicinity was open and wild, with bushes scattered about, and here and there a cultivated patch; the hour early in the morning. By sunrise they had all disappeared. I was told by the villagers that as night fell the birds would return and reassemble in the same spot, and that they had been in the habit of doing so for many years...The people of the vicinity are...no shikaries, and the report of a gun was probably a sound almost unknown in that part of the district.

In India, after filling their crops with the gleanings from the rice and vetch stubbles, the cranes retire at or soon after sun rise to sand flats or islets in large rivers, or to open downs inland, where no covert affords means of approach to an enemy. And there they may be seen through a telescope, preening themselves, lazily stretching forth their legs or wings, or sitting dozing on their heels. One or two, however, keep on the alert, their heads raised on high; and these, to judge by their size and flowing plumes, are old males.

I did once, and only once, catch these birds napping. They had selected in the Kalichowk, a stream or branch which joins the Mahanuddee to the Granges (Malda district), an islet of sand and clay for their diurnal repose, which, from its banks being scarped, allowed a boat to creep along under the shore unseen from the *terre pleine* of the island. Selecting a spot for landing which was not above a hundred yards from the nearest of the birds, I made them drop my little dinghee down to it, then, jumping ashore, scrambled up the bank, and at once ran as hard as I could pelt towards the birds. Firing both barrels into the flock as they rose some fifty yards off, I was fortunate enough to wing one, which fell into the river. It swam well, and reached the shore opposite, where some fisherman were assembled, who attempted to seize it as it landed; but the bird made such a vigorous use of its beak that it held its assailants at bay till I reached the spot. It was a young male, its tertial plumes not fully developed, and its stomach was found crammed with oorid (a kind of vetch).

Hume, quoted by Baker (1928) stated:

Cranes feeding as they do so much in cultivation, very soon get used to the cultivators moving about in their small carts or with their bullocks and frequently do not trouble to keep out of gun-shot of these familiar objects. Accordingly, advantage is taken by this both by Indian and European sportsmen who approach under cover of bullock cart or bullock and thus get shots at birds which would otherwise be impossible to approach. At other times birds may be driven towards the sportsmen but to do this with any success a few beaters only must be employed...

Cranes are very omnivorous in their diet but probably on the whole prefer a vegetarian meal to any other. Different shoots of all kinds of crops, especially rice, are greedingly eaten and in some cases, when the flocks are numerous and large, they cause considerable damage to crops. They are said to be especially fond of water melons and destroy even more of these than they eat. In addition to all kinds of aquatic plants, grain and shoots, they will eat any small reptile and all kinds of large insects and it has been alleged that on occasion they even catch fish. They feed principally in the very early mornings and late evenings whilst, where they are much disturbed, they feed a great deal during the night more especially when there is a moon. During the hot hours of the day they resort to the banks of rivers and tanks where they have a wide view all round them and there pass the time away dozing and often standing on one leg in shallow water with their head and neck tucked away into the feathers of the back. Directly they fly towards their feeding grounds and become very noisy, constantly uttering a loud trumpet-like call but during the day they seem to keep more or less silent.

Like all their family this bird indulges in dancing during the breeding season and at odd moments even during the winter months, when the attitudes, bowings and scraping indulged in during these performances are often very ludicrous.

A flight of these birds when moving for any distance is always carried out in regular formation, either a long line or a wide "V," the leader at the apex apparently changing place every few minutes with one of the other birds in the rear. When flying short distances from one feeding ground to another, this formation is not always observed and the birds move in indiscriminate flock.

CHINA.

There are specimens in the Chicago Natural History Museum from Szechwan, Ngang Kou Pa, December 1, 1931; from Chu Tsu Chan, October 22, 1931; from Kansu, Titao, March 4, and 7, 1925; from Chekiang, Chu-chow (Lat. 28.5°N; Long. 120'E), November 18, 1926; from Fukien (Lat. 26°N; Long 118'E), December 5, 1930. In the British Museum (Natural History) there are specimens from Konang Tcheou-Wan, China, January 28, 1933; near Yunnan City, Yunnan, February 7, 1899; Swatow (no other data); Chingwangtao, March 12, 1913. In the Museum of Comparative Zoology there are three specimens from NE Chihli; two from Hsieh Chia Ying, January 4, 1915; and one from Shanhaikwan, December 15, 1915. Caldwell and Caldwell (1931) wrote: Range—Eastern Siberia, wintering in Yangtse Basin to south and west China and northwest India. Recorded from Mongolia, western Manchuria, and the Amur region; Chihli, April and October; Fukien, March; west Szechwan, April; Yunnan, south Shansi, Shensi, and Anhuei, in winters; Kwangtung, common in flocks October to February; Hainan, November." Stresemann, et al. (1938), observed this bird and G. nigricollis, in western Kansu in March and April. Swinhoe (1861, 1870) noted small parties at Swatow, in Naochow and Hainan where they were abundant and fed chiefly on sweet potatoes.

MANCHURIA.

A specimen (CNHM) was taken April 18, 1938 at Kirin, Harbin, on the Sungari River.

VIET NAM.

Delacour, Jabouille and Lowe (1928), Delacour (1929), Delacour and Jabouille (1931), and Wildash (1968), reported this bird common during the months of February and March in Annam, the northern portion of what is now South Viet Nam.

BURMA.

There is a specimen (BMNH) taken at Myitkyina in February 1933. Stanford and Ticehurst (1939) and Stanford and Mayr (1941), both reported large numbers on cultivated plains east of Irrawaddy from Waingnaw to Talawgyi. Fall migrants arrived one year November 10; another, November 1, at Kamaing. They feed in long lines on paddy stubble, in early March.

NEPAL.

Two specimens (BMNH) were taken at Hodgson.

INDIA, PAKISTAN.

Rattray (1899) reported countless numbers of the Common Crane and A. virgo going up the Kurram Valley in April 1898, flying high. Seldom did they rest, but once a severe storm farther up the valley drove them back. Ali (1945) reported it a winter visitor and passage migrant. Earliest record, September 13, in Kutch. In the British Museum (Natural History) there are specimens from Etawah (Lat. 26.5°N; Long 77.5°E), Sirsa (Lat. 29.5°N; Long. 75°E), Hissar (same region), Kathiawar (Lat. 22.5°N; Long 71°E), Guzaret (Lat 23°N; Long. 71°E), Jheelum, near Jelapur, Punjab, all between October and January while one in Chicago Natural History Museum was taken at Lurishban, Dured.

Whitehead (1911) reported this bird at Sehore, Central India. Currie (1916) noted it at times during cold weather near Lahore, Punjab (Pakistan), and during migrations in March. Whistler (1916, 1918) noted birds also in Punjab, in the Gujranwala and Ambala Districts. Whistler and Kinnear (1936) reported Sharpe neither designated a type or type locality for G. g. lilfordi, but reported only two birds were then located in the British Museum collection and both were from Punjab. Consequently one must have been the type, and they selected the one from River Jhelum, near Jelalpur. Frome (1947) reported this bird as occasional near Delhi in winter but a score of V's (of 30-50 birds each) flew along the River Jumna at sunset in mid-October (1931-1947), while *A. virgo* was observed in the same region from November to April 15.

Waite (1948) reported *Grus grus* and *A. virgo* frequently crossed the mountains in Punjab in August and September. Records are: 1938, August 15; 1939, August 22; 1940, August 27; 1941, August 26; 1943, August 21; 1944, August 28; 1945, August 28; 1946, September 2 and only twice in spring; February 29 and April 5. Dharmakumarsinhju (1955).

Measurements

Grus grus grus

Adult male. Eight specimens (CNHM, NR) (Sweden, 3; Russia, 1; Italy, 2; Poland, 1; Egypt, 1). Wing, 547.6 (507-597) mm.; exposed culmen, 109.0 (104-116) mm.; from base of nostril, 77.3 (71-84) mm.; tarsus, 228.8 (202-252) mm.; tail, 189.3 (168-210) mm.; bare tibia, 111.1 (88-121) mm.; middle toe with claw, 110.0 (98-123) mm.

Adult female. Three specimens (BMNH) (Ethiopia, 3). Wing, 536 (529-546) mm.; exposed culmen, 107.3 (104-113) mm.; tarsus, 224.3 (205-238) mm.; tail, 186.3 (178-197) mm.; bare tibia, 93.3 (70-111) mm.; middle toe with claw, 104.3 (103-105) mm.

One male (NR) taken September 24, 1934 at Ottenby, Öland, Sweden weighed 5,095 grams; one female taken December 31, 1913 (BMNH) at Senga, Blue Nile, weighed 13 lbs (5,895.8 grams), had a wing expanse of 84 in. (213.4 cm), and total length, 45.5 in. (115.6 cm).

Grus grus lilfordi

Adult male. Twelve specimens (CNHM, 5; BMNH, 6; MCZ, 1) (China, 7; India, 4; Manchuria, 1). Wing, 547.9 (512-608) mm.; exposed culmen, 103.4 (95-112) mm.; from base of nostril, 77.2 (69-81) mm.; tarsus, 229.7 (206-249) mm.; tail, 197.7 (185-215) mm.; bare tibia, 103.5 (91-125) mm.; middle toe with claw, 97.2 (84-106) mm.

Adult female. Seven specimens (CNHM, 3; MCZ, 4) (China, 4; India, 2; Manchuria, 1). Wing, 533.7 (521-550) mm.; exposed culmen, 98.7 (96-104) mm.; from base of nostril, 73 (72-74) mm.; tarsus, 219.7 (201-242) mm.; bare tibia, 99.0 (84-117) mm.; middle toe with claw, 98.8 (88-112) mm.

Chapter Two

THE BLACK-NECKED CRANE

(Grus nigricollis)

Grus nigricollis, Przevalski, *Mongol i Strana Tangutow*, St. Petersburg, 1876. Vol. 2, p. 135.
Type locality: Koko Nor (Ching Hai), Tsinghai Province, China, Lat. 37°N.
Vernacular names: The Black-necked Crane, The Tibetan Crane (English); Schwarzhalskranich (German); la Grue de Prjevalsky (French); Zwarthals Kraanvogel (Dutch); Trung-trung (Tibetan); Katung (Ladaki); журавль черножечнеч (Russian); Okuro zuru ナグロ'ブル (Japanese).

The Black-necked Crane is found in some of the least traveled portions of the world, and because of this is little known. Its actual summer range is the higher mountain valleys of the Himalayas and neighboring ranges. It has wandered over into Kashmir, extends eastward into western China, and is probably found in most of Tibet. Farthest north records come from Koko Nor (Tsing Hai). It has been found between longitudes 78° and 101°East and between latitudes 28° and 37°North.

In winter it moves down to lower elevations in Tibet such as Lhasa (elevation 12,200 feet) while birds from western China move southward — some even southeastward — as far as Hanoi and Hadong, North Viet Nam. Generally it winters north of the winter range of *Grus grus lilfordi.*

During the spring migration it has been seen in Sikang Province, China, at Seshu, March 14; on the Upper Yalung Steppe, March 20. It reaches the **Sikang breeding grounds by April 20,** while in Kansu Province, China, at Heitsuitse, it was found April 28, 1929, and April 11, 1930. In Tsing Hai

Province, China it was recorded as early as March 30. In Tibet it moves up the mountains to the higher plateaus, 13,000 feet and more at the end of March and early in April.

In the fall the birds return to the lower valleys in mid-October (Ludlow, letter, February 20, 1951). In Sikang and Yunnan, China, they migrate in late September and early October (Schäfer, 1938).

The Tibet migration is altitudinal; in Tsing Hai it migrates a considerable distance southeastward, some birds reaching almost to sea level in Viet Nam during winter as compared to the high elevation where they are found in summer. Probably this crane nests at higher elevations than any other.

The birds in winter form into large flocks sometimes. Schäfer wrote (1938) that in Yunnan, China, these cranes wintered by the thousands but their winter range was generally immediately north of the wintering grounds of *Grus grus lilfordi*. During migration they followed the river courses. Here the birds were very wild.

Ludlow reported flocks of 200 to 400 in the neighborhood of Lhasa in winter and at Tsatang on the Tsangpo, he observed flocks of 200 on March 21. The cranes fed during the day on open fields, retiring at night to a sandy spot on the river a few hundred meters from his camp. The native Tibetans never molested them and they were exceedingly tame. In contrast, at Gyangtse, soldiers often shot at them and here they became very wild.

Farther west in Tibet, Salim Ali (1946) observed near Lake Manasarowar, that the birds did considerable leaping, prancing and bowing around each other during the breeding season. Schäfer (1938) and Ludlow (1928) often observed dancing cranes also. The male, somewhat taller than his mate, showed considerable interest in her and after nesting began, Schäfer noted, was much more watchful than the female. Often he walked up higher on a nearby mountainside, sometimes 200 meters or more, watching approaching men. Once under good cover, a male at 40 meters flapped his wings, bent his head so that it nearly touched the ground, then ran around in a circle with his toes pointed inward. This definitely was a demonstration similar to that of other cranes prior to attack. From what photographs are available, the male carries his inner

secondaries raised slightly over his back as does the male of *Grus grus*. No one has recorded the stance of either male or female while giving the normal Unison Call or other calls.

The Nesting Biotope.

The Black-necked Crane nests in the mountain valleys of Tibet and southwestern China, in marshes, marshy lake borders, even in open lakes dotted with small muddy islands, at an elevation of from 3,800 to 4,500 meters or more. When nesting begins, very little vegetation has begun to grow because of the extreme early-season cold. In fact, many nesting situations never grow to much more than a little short grass. In many regions little muddy islands in the cold open lakes offer the safest nesting sites for the birds, since here mammal predators cannot reach them but they are close enough to shore so that they can lead their downy chicks to dry land after they hatch. In other regions, lower in elevation, marshy lake borders and open marshes offer nesting habitat similar to that used by the majority of world cranes.

THE NEST

Two types of nest have been described. (1) A grassy or muddy island in some lake in one of the higher valleys where normally little or short vegetation grows during summer. Very little if any nesting material is used. Sometimes the birds pile up mud and then deposit the eggs on this black mass. At other times short neighboring dead grass is used, while at others a minimum of material is carried from a short distance away and placed in the hollow on top of the little islet. Dresser (1906:347), Ludlow (1928:220), Schäfer (1938:109), and Ali (1946:305) all described this type of nest. Although the usual island had a hollowed out spot on top, Schäfer described some that were exceedingly flat, where the eggs were visible for a long distance.

(2) The second type of nest, more typical of crane nests, is a huge pile of vegetation pulled from the immediate vicinity and piled in shallow marsh or lake border. Meinertzhagen (1927) wrote that two nests he saw were huge pads of material, some 91

Black-necked Crane near nest at Lake Manasawar, western Tibet, July 1945. (Photo by Salim Ali.)

Nest and eggs of G. nigricollis, *the Black-necked Crane on Wild Yak Steppe, 4,600-4,700 m, July 1935. (Photo by E. Schäfer.)*

cm in diameter and 25 cm above water level. Ludlow wrote (letter, February 20, 1951) that after he published his Tibet records he found many nests built of a mass of rushes and dried dead grasses, from 61 to 69 cm across and located in marshy situations.

The Eggs

One or two eggs are laid. Most sets in collections consist of one egg but actually there are probably two laid more often. Baker (1928; 1929) wrote:

"The bird breeds on the same ground as the Bar-headed Goose and sometimes its own nest is surrounded by the large down-covered nests of these birds.... The eggs are two in number and closely resemble those of the Common Crane except in being much bigger. Most of those I have seen are rather dingy olive-brown or purplish-brown with secondary, or underlying, markings of purple-grey or reddish-grey.... Twelve eggs average 101.2x64.1 mm; maxima *105.3x63.4* and 103.2x*69.1* mm, minima *96.4*x64.1 and 99.3x*59.6* mm."

Ludlow wrote (1928) "The ground colour is dark olive, boldly blotched with dark brown. Three eggs average 106.2x62.6 mm." He also wrote (letter, 1951) that sometimes two eggs are laid but as often only one.

In western China, Schäfer (1938) wrote: "End of May, also in that season when heavy frosts still come at night, the first eggs are laid. Even in mid-June, these cranes, when snow falls at these elevations, have well brooded eggs, some with fully developed embryos. The chief breeding season falls during June, July and August."

Schäfer (1938) also said there are large scattered rust spots on the eggs, as in *Bubo*. They have a light brown background, spots of reddish brown and purple-gray, and are smeared with black earth. Two measured 99.0x63.0 and 106.0x62.5 mm. Shells weighed 23.0 and 21.0 grams. Some eggs had brownish-olive-green, one had brown-olive-gray, for the background. The largest part of the shell showed a crystal-like structure, had a thickness of 0.6 mm and a membrane thickness of 0.06 mm. The pores were comma shaped, a characteristic of crane eggs. In a transverse section of the egg the Mamillen

layer was blue green and the Mamillen heads, magnified 20 times, showed very well.

Salim Ali (1946) found one egg at Ding Tso, Tibet, which was greenish-gray or olive-gray in color with rough splotches of faint reddish-brown all over, more densely at the broad end. It measured 107x66 mm.

Makatsch (1959) gave the average measurements of 23 eggs as 102.6x62.8 mm, and the Schönwetter weight at 22.0 grams.

Ludlow (letter, February 20, 1951) wrote that young birds remained with parents during the first winter, all feeding in one group.

Range and Breeding Distribution

Range

Inner Asia, from Kashmir east to Tsing Hai Province, China, south to upper Yalung River, China, westward to Ding Tso, Tibet, in summer. The lower Tibetan valleys, Yunnan Province, China and Tonkin Province, Viet Nam; possibly northern Burma and upper Assam.

Breeding Distribution.

KASHMIR.

Tsokar Chumo Lake, Rupshu (Lat. 33.25°N; Long. 78°E—El. 4,541 meters=14,900 ft.), three seen, one shot, June 2, 1919 (Ludlow, 1920). Occurs in Ladakh, observed early June at Tso Kar in Rupshu, during June 1925 at Puga (Lat. 33°N; Long. 78.5°E —El. 4,359 meters=14,300 ft), June 10, 1925 at Shushal (Lat. 33.75°N; Long. 78.75°E—El. 4,425 meters=14,500 ft.), at Chakar Talao, May 26, 1925 (Meinertzhagen, 1927).

Osmaston (1927) reported it from Tsokar Lake, Rupshu, during early June, several pairs near Shushal east of the Indus in early July, and the third week in June at Tso Moriri.

Walter Koelz (letter, March 19, 1947) wrote that he observed the species at Shushal, Puga, Hanle and Tso Kar and found a nest with two eggs in July at Tso Kar.

CHINA.

Inner Tibet: Tsing Hai Province. Observed at Koko Nor (Lat. 38°N; Long. 100°E – El 3,200 meters =10,500 ft.) a beautiful salt lake surrounded by mountains with extensive marshy areas about its shoreline – according to Przevalski, the northernmost region where this species is found. He also found the bird at Schuga River (Lat. 36°N; Long. 96°E), at Baga-syrtyn Nor, west to the Syrtynechan Desert (Lat. 39°N; Long. 94°E), along the Hwang Ho (Yellow River) (Lat. 36°N; Long. 100°E) (Deditius, 1886).

Stresemann, Meise, and Schönwetter (1938) report breeding at Koko Nor, June 18, 1930 and reported the species from northwest Kansu, found by Walter Beick from 1926 to 1933, giving arrival dates at April 28, 1929 and April 11, 1930.

Sikang Province. Schäfer (1938) reported this crane as nesting on Wild Yak Steppe, at Dsogchen Gomba; Dre-tschu Gomba; Jalung Steppe (Lat. 31-35°N; Long. 96-99°E – El. 4,400 to 4,700 meters).

FARTHER TIBET.

Gyangtse and Lhasa (Lat. 29.30°N; Long. 89.5-91°E – Els. 4,041 and 3,721 meters). Abundant (Walton, 1906). Eggs taken June 12, 1905 from this Tibet region were identified by Captain Steen (Dresser, 1906).

Hram Tso. A nest (C/2) June 2, 1908. Birds observed in 1906 and 1909 by Bailey (1909) at Gyangtse and Chumbi.

Yatung to Gyangtse. Two pairs observed and breeding reported at Dochen Lake (Battye, 1935).

Yamdrok Tso and Gyangtse. Observed in 1933 and in 1934 at Tsona (Ludlow, 1937). Gyangtse, Lhagyari and on the Tsangpo, March 21, at Chera, 200 observed (Ludlow, 1944).

Harm Tso and Kala Tso. Observed (MacLaren, 1947) May, 1946.

Lhasa. Downy young found and birds observed in lower valley of the Tsangpo (Ludlow, 1928).

Tingri (El. 15,000 ft.). A pair observed July 7, 1924. Longstaff and Norton photographed a pair June 15, 1922 on Tinki Plain (Hingston, 1927).

Lake Manasarowar and Mt. Kailas. Observed in June, 1945 at Ding Tso, Lejandak Tso, and Gyan-

ima Tso. A nest found at Ding Tso, June 25, 1945 (1 egg). All about Lat. 31°N; Long. 81°E – El. 4,575 meters (Ali, 1946).

Ten definite egg records are: May 15, 1926 (C/2), May 15, 1926 (1 egg) Hram Tso, Tibet (BMNH); June 1, 1923 (C/2), Bham Tso, Tibet (BMNH); June 2, 1908, (1 egg), Hram Tso (El. 14,000 ft.) (BMNH) (Bailey, 1909); June 3, 1909 (C/2), Rham, Tibet (El. 14,300 ft.) (BMNH); June 12, 1905 (C/2) Lhasa region (Dresser, 1906); June 15, 1910 (1 egg), Gyangtse, Tibet (BMNH); June 18, 1930 (nest), Koko Nor, Tsing Hai Province, China (Stresemann, Meise, and Schönwetter, 1938); June 25, 1945 (1 egg), Ding Tso, Tibet (Ali, 1946); early July (2 eggs), Tso Kar, Kashmir (Walter Koelz).

The average egg date for the ten sets would be about June 8, without the Kashmir set, around June 3, for southern Tibet.

Winter Distribution.

The Black-necked Crane winters in the lower valleys of southern Tibet, south to Yunnan Province, China and Tonkin Province, Viet Nam, probably into northern Assam and possibly northern Burma.

In Tibet it is found in Kyi Chu Valley; Gyangtse; Yamdrok Tso; Tsona (Lat. 28°N; Long. 91°E – El. 4,361 meters); at Tsetang (Lat. 29°N; Long. 92°E – El. 3,614 meters); Temo Gompa (Lat. 29.5°N; Long. 94.5°E); Yigrong Tso (Lat. 30°N; Long 95°E – El. 2,226 meters); Dongtse; Nyang Chu Valley (1923-1926), (Ludlow, 1927).

YUNNAN.

An adult male was taken February 1, 1899, by A. W. S. Wingate (Ogilvie-Grant, 1900).

Two live examples were observed at Yunnanfu (La Touche, 1924). It was also reported from Yunnan by Stevens (1930).

At Yungning, two female specimens were taken, one in December, 1929, the other in January, 1930, by Dr. Joseph F. Rock (Riley, 1931).

Schäfer (1938) found it in winter at Yungning, Likiang, and Tali, in Yunnan Province, and listed it as possible from northern Burma. He wrote that it wintered here by the thousands, but generally

Hooded Cranes in flight, Kagoshima Prefecture, Japan. (Photographer unknown)

stayed immediately north of the wintering grounds of *Grus grus lilfordi.*

KOREA.

Kuroda (1917) and Mori (1917) recorded a specimen of this crane taken at Kapung, Kyonggi Do, February 21, 1917 and purchased for the Seoul School Collection. Kuroda (1917b) listed it again. Later, Delacour and Hachisuka (1928) examined it and declared it a hybrid between *G. japonensis* and *G. vipio.* Austin (1948) considered it a melanistic *G. japonensis.*

VIET NAM.

Delacour (1924) observed *G. nigricollis* near Hanoi. Later Delacour and Jabouille (1931) reported finding it at Hanoi and Hadong, Tonkin, and two live specimens were caught.

ASSAM.

Betts (1956) wrote that a flock of 30 or 40 of these cranes had wintered annually within human memory in the Apa Tani Valley, arriving in mid-December and leaving in March. They fed in the paddy fields and were extremely wary.

MIGRATION

CHINA.

At Keshu, Sikang Province, March 14. On the Upper Yalung Steppe March 20 and present on all breeding territories in northern Sikang by April 20. (Schäfer, 1928.) Also observed in Kansu Province, China, March 30.

TIBET.

Migration occurs at the end of March to early April altitudinally from the lower valleys, 3,600 meters in elevation and over, up to the valleys 3,900 meters in elevation up to 4,750 meters in elevation.

In mid-October they fly back to the lower valleys (Ludlow, letter February 20, 1951). In Sinkiang and Yunnan Provinces, China, migration occurs in late September and early October.

The Tibetan migration is altitudinal; in Tsing Hai migration takes the birds a considerable distance southeastward. Many birds reach Hanoi and Hadong, Viet Nam, in winter. Ludlow reported flocks of 200 to 400 in the neighborhood of Lhasa in winter and at Tsatang on the Tsangpo he observed flocks of 200 on March 21, all feeding during daytime on open fields, retiring at night to sandy river bars.

DESCRIPTION.

ADULT. Sexes alike, the male slightly larger. Crown and lores, naked, red and covered with varying numbers of black hairlike feathers. Remainder of head and upper part of neck, extending down the neck 140 to 270 mm, black. A white or very light gray spot, about 39 mm anteriorly-posteriorly and 22 mm vertically, extending from the posterior and lower edges of the eye, sometimes having a narrow line over the eye, feathered. General color, a very pale ashy gray, whiter when feathers are older, just before the molt. The shafts of the back feathers have dark brown lines, often with yellowish margins. Underparts, almost pure white, less yellowish than the upper parts. Tail, black. Upper tail coverts, grayish. Under tail coverts, white. Primaries and innermost prolonged secondaries, black. Inner webs of outer secondaries, black or mottled black and many of the greater coverts over the secondaries more or less black on inner webs. Inner secondaries, falcated, elongated, slightly decomposed, and erectile. Scapulars, sometimes with black mottling on terminal quarter. Small wing coverts, inside and outside, pale gray. Bill greenish-horn or grayish-horn color, yellowish towards tip. Legs and feet, black. Iris yellow.

Measurements

MALES.

Eight specimens (BMNH, CNHM, MCZ, UMMZ): Exposed culmen, 120.5 (110-129) mm; wing 623 (569-677) mm; tail, 245.3 (200-284) mm; tarsus, 247.4 (226-262) mm; bare tibia, 89.8 (82-102) mm; middle toe with claw, 111 (104-117) mm; expanse (1), 203.4 cm; length (1), 110.9 cm.

FEMALES.

Seven specimens (BMNH, CNHM, USNM): Exposed culmen, 116.4 (111-124) mm; wing, 606.5 (585-628) mm; tail, 226 (214-239) mm; tarsus, 231.7 (214-252) mm; bare tibia (2), 86 (75-97) mm; middle toe with claw, 100.2 (84-106) mm.

Chapter Three

THE HOODED CRANE

(*Grus monachus*)

Grus monacha, Temminck, *Planches Coloriées.* Livr. 94, 1835, pl. 555.
Type locality: Hokkaido and Korea. Type in Leiden Museum, Leiden.
Vernacular names: The Hooded Crane (English); Nabezuru ナベヅル
(Japanese); монах журавль (Russian); Mönchskranich (German); la Grue moine (French); de minniks Kraanvogel (Dutch).

DESCRIPTION.

ADULT.

A very dark crane with white head and neck. Forepart of crown bare, extending about 60 to 67 mm posteriorly from the base of the upper mandible. The bare part red (brighter during the breeding season) and covered with black hair-like bristles. Upper eyelid bare and horn-colored. Remainder of head and neck pure white, tinged at times with a little gray during the non-breeding season. From the posterior edge of the bare red forehead, the white extends posteriorly down the neck from 125 to 232 mm.; on the anterior neck from the base of the lower mandible 140 mm. In one individual the white extended 224 mm on the posterior side. Usually the white in back extends down 5 to 8 cm farther than in front. Often the white changes abruptly to the black-gray of the back and breast. General color, above and below, slaty gray with some brownish and grayish tinge above and a slightly different gray tipping each feather. Primaries, secondaries, tail and tail coverts, black. Inner secondaries lengthened, falcated, decomposed, and drooping. Bill yellowish horn-color, shiny at the tip. Legs and feet almost black. Soles of feet olive-green. Iris hazel-yellow to orange-brown but usually showing yellowish.

Hooded Crane, feeding on edge of rice field, Arasaki, Kagoshima Prefecture, Kyushu, Japan, Feb. 12, 1969.

CHICK.

Unknown.

SUBADULT.

With some brownish and much grayish wash, much more pronounced in the head and neck. No bare spot on top of head until about one year of age. This future bald area covered with black and white feathers the first year. Iris, brown.

Measurements.

Adult male.

Seven specimens (AMNH, 2; BMNH, 3; CNHM, 1, USNM, 1): Exposed culmen, 103.7 (99-107); from base of nostril (2), 77; wing (chord), 506.0 (479-525); tail, 178.6 (171-186); tarsus, 209.3 (194-222); bare tibia, 86.5 (80-97); middle toe with claw, 95.8 (90-98) mm.

Adult female.

Nine specimens (YIOZ, 2; AMNH, 2; BMNH, 1; CNHM, 2; MCZ, 2): Exposed culmen, 95.4 (89-101); from base of nostril, 70.5 (2); wing, 487.9 (453-560); tail, 163 (159-167); tarsus, 208.8 (199-223); bare tibia, 80.0 (72-86); middle toe with claw, 93.3 (79-101) mm. Weight (1, UMMZ, 2,460 g).

Distribution.

The Hooded Crane occurs during summer in central Siberia, from Tomsk eastward to Lake Baikal. Its exact nesting regions remain unknown. It winters in southern Honshu, Japan at Yashiro and at Arasaki, near Izumi City, Kyushu, Japan also in southern Korea, southeastern China, occasionally in northern India and possibly in upper Burma.

SUMMER.

Dementiev and Gladkov (1951) summarized the Siberian summer range (also summarized by Johansen, 1907 and 1930, and Zalesskogo, 1921):

(1) Anikina, in the Spasskom region, 14 kilometers south of Tomsk, June 14, 1893.

(2) Near Novosibirsk, at North Kochenevo (Lat. 56°N; Long. 85°E), one was obtained.

(3) Near Tomsk, one was shot in mid-May 1915.

(4) Near Tomsk, at the city of Popovoy, a pair was observed in late April and early May, 1917.

(5) Near Tomsk, at the city of Petrovoy, one was obtained May 18, 1917.

(6) At Papadeykino, a village near Tomsk, one was taken May 16, 1918.

(7) At Tomsk, three were observed May 5, 1920.

(8) At Yenesei one was observed with a flock of *Grus grus*, June 19, 1920.

(9) At the river Ket adjacent to the Ob, one was taken in 1921.

(10) Nested in (Krokhaleva) at Lake Chan'u. However the organized Tomsk University Expedition of 1909 failed to find any birds there. Nor have there been any found since.

Dementiev and Gladkov (1951) add that: "In east Siberia in TransBaikal and especially in Dauria the Black Crane is encountered during nesting time in greater numbers than in western Siberia. On the south shore of Tarey-Nor it was met by Stegman (1928) in pairs, to all appearances nesting birds, and simultaneously large flocks by unmated birds. It was found in large numbers by Dolgushin (1941) in summer on the steppes of Lake Dauria. A female was taken June 30, 1925, at Tarey-Nor (Zoological Institute Academy of Science, CCCP). A young male was taken June 18, 1939 at Popova on Lake Zun-Aralantuy Borsinskij region, Chitinskoy Oblast. It nested according to Molleson (1896) on the upper reaches of the Chikoy and Iro rivers but later investigations show during recent time this is not the case. It was observed on the middle course of the Amur, a few pairs in Bureynski Mountains and on the river Selbachi (at the beginning of the state boundary, Radde, 1863). It was taken in northern Manchuria in the first part of July 1933 near Khaylar.

WINTER.

"It passes regularly through Mongolia and N.W. China. Styan writes that it is the commonest crane in the Yangtse and that it is found all along the river in winter. I never met with it, and Wilder only records one example in the Peking Academy Museum." (LaTouche, 1933).

"This crane is said to haunt open plains and marshes but to be nowhere very numerous, whilst even when migrating it collects in small parties only. According to David and Oustalet it migrates in pairs or in flocks of a half dozen to a dozen. The flock I saw in Cachar numbered seven, and those I saw on the Subansire were in two flocks of seven and eight respectively. In each of these instances the birds were on the move and though I shot one in Cachar I could get nowhere near those on the Subansire, though I spent a whole day trying to get at one flock which kept moving downstream and settling every half mile or so. The other flock rose when first disturbed and went right away at once, flying very high in a line and loudly trumpeting at the start. The flock I saw at Cachar seemed very tired as if they had flown far. They pitched very headlong on the banks of the stream I was boating down and stood still as if exhausted. Even after I had shot and secured one, the remaining six kept pitching among the short reeds on the river side, though they would not allow me to get within a hundred yards. Their call seemed to me much like that of the Common Crane and their flight also very similar." (Baker, 1928).

Formerly the Hooded Crane wintered over much of Japan. During recent times it has become scarce. Apparently there are only two Japanese regions where the birds now winter: At Yashiro in Yamaguchi Prefecture, southern Honshu, and at Arasaki, near Izumi City, in Kagoshima Prefecture, Kyushu.

In the "Hand-List of Japanese Birds," published by the Ornithological Society of Japan, it is stated: "Found in: Hokkaido (Sapporo, Hand-1. 1942), Honshu (Tokyo, Hand-1. 1922), Ishikawa (1926-Tori, No. 67), Yokohoma (Seebohm 1890,) Yashiro-mura in Yamaguchi (W.V.), Kyushiu (Nagasaki, three specs.—Ibis, 1884), Arasaki (W.V.), 'Japan' Leyden and Brit. Mus."

A hybrid Crane at Arasaki, March 3, 1969. Father (left) G. g. lilfordi; *Mother,* G. monachus.

"Distribution abroad: Sakhalin, Korea (Genzan, Keikido, Fusan, Moppo), Quel- part I."

"Formerly common winter visitor. Now a few hundred birds regularly winter at Yashiro-mura in Yamaguchi and Arasaki in Kagoshima."

For many years crane arrival and departure records have been kept at both Yashiro (Honshu) and Arasaki (Kyushu). At Izumi City, the Mayor, Tooru Shibuya, the Crane Warden, S. Matano, who kept the records, gave me their records for the Arasaki region from 1938 to date, with more complete data for the winter of 1964-65, which are presented

in full in Tables 2, 3, and 4 for the three species which spent that winter there.

The people from Yashiro, Yamaguchi Prefecture, sent the author the following information:

Cranes in olden times were loved by all Japanese people and considered an omen of good fortune and longevity. They can still be found at Kushiro in Hokkaido (*G. japonensis*), at Izumi near Kagoshima in Kyushu and at Yashiro, Yamaguchi Prefecture. Although there are fewer cranes at Yashiro than at Izumi, they are very tame and stalk freely in the vicinity of farmers' houses. Everyone in Yashiro loves a crane as he does his own child, as if they were their own friends.

Yashiro is located on a high table-land, 320 meters above the sea and 8 kilometers north from the Railroad Station 'Takamizu,' on the local line 'Gantoku-Sen' of the Tokaido Main Line. It consists of 400 houses with 400 hectares of rice and vegetable fields.

We think that cranes used to fly over all parts of Japan in olden times and because of that we find 46 odes in the 'Man-yo-shu,' an old Japanese anthology composed about cranes...It seems that cranes flew down to the rice fields at that time. From other odes we can tell that cranes used to fly along the seashores, lakesides, and moorlands where there were many pools of water. Since some of these odes were written 1,500 years ago it seems that they must have been flying over at that time.

In the time of feudal lords, cranes were caught at random. Consequently the village people set up some regulations to protect them. Afterwards the governor of Yamaguchi Prefecture announced the prohibition of crane hunting, and the Yashiro District was designated as a natural preserve by the Ministry of Home Affairs in 1920. Because the farmers were not rich, they set up a group in 1919 to pay for food and for a correction fund. After this was done cranes increased year by year.

Dementiev and Gladkov (1951)) wrote of *Grus monachus:* Nesting and migratory bird. Found in winter in China. It is there during mid-November remaining until April. From Japan the cranes fly across southeast Korea to the maritime provinces of Siberia. In south Ussuri-land the Black Crane appears in small numbers in flocks of 3-11 individuals at the close of the second half of April and the flight extends to mid-May. Thus in the upper part of the Sungachi in 1869 first birds were flying on April 23, passing through rapidly. Further flight proceeds northwest to Lake Khanka and up the middle course of the Amur. Birds wintering in China apparently fly up the coast of China (In Chzhili bird flocks were observed in April and October). Then the crane flight, in large numbers, is observed far from the seacoast in Kalgan and the entire extent from Kalgan to Lake Dalay-Nor. First birds were observed there

Hooded Cranes beginning flight, Arasaki, March 3, 1969.

Hooded Crane pair feeding in rice field, Arasaki, Feb. 12, 1969.

March 27, 1871, with a heavy flight the same year in the first half of April (Przhevalsky). Flying cranes were observed in May on the south shore of Lake Baikal, along the Onon and Argun. In west Siberia it was observed from the first day of May, even once at the end of April, in 1917 near Tomsk (Johansen, 1930).

In the fall they leave western Siberia from the second half of August up until the first of September... At Karachi (Lake Kolosovo, Mali, Yarkul, Termakul) two Black Cranes were observed September 2-4, 1927, and four on September 8; in the neighborhood of Tomsk, September 7, 1919 (3 cranes, Zalesski, 1921); August 20, and later in early September 1920 on the Ob near the village of Ziryanskoe... on the left tributary of the Chulim in Minusinck district it was taken October 15, 1912 (Tugarinov). Encountered in flight in spring and in autumn on the middle course of the Chulim (reported, Anikina—Johansen, 1923), rare in flight at Kurchume, it was encountered in flight in the upper reaches of the Nazhney Tunguski (one specimen taken, Thachenko, 1937). It was taken in flight in September on the northeast shore of Baikal in the environs of Kudaldov (Shulpin, 1936). It was observed in flight on the south shore of Baikal, on the Onon, and the Argun, from late August up to the middle of September and in August on the north shores of Tarey-Nor.

Tacanowski (1893) wrote: "Radde found it in the Gobi Desert and in the mountains of Dauria on the Amur. Dybowski has considerably extended the range of this crane by supplying specimens from several regions of Dauria and from Kuttuk in northern Baikal. Probably Pallas's name *G. vipio* applied to this species in spite of several contradictions in the author's description."

Ivanov (1929) reported there was a specimen in the Zoological Museum from the Tungus and in the collection of Chekanov. And that the Yakutsk hunters persistently answer that they have only two species of cranes, i.e.: *G. grus* and *G. leucogeranus* helped disclaim the nesting of *G. monachus* at the latitude of Yakutsk and that some records from that region were discounted because specimens had been misidentified.

This is one of the least known cranes. Much information has been obtained in its winter behavior in Japan, where the people have protected and studied it for years. During World War II its numbers diminished, but since then have gradually increased. The birds do some damage to wheat and rice, but much of the grain they eat is probably waste grain left in fields after harvest. It spends five or six months in Japan before it starts back to Siberia.

Johansen (1961) reported it is found in Siberia on the wooded steppes of the Taiga regions, apparently in small or large marshes. Descriptions of two eggs from Siberia have been recorded, but the measurements indicate them as larger eggs than those laid by larger

75

cranes such as *G. vipio* and *G. leucogeranus*. However, four eggs laid in England in captivity and now in the British Museum (Natural History) averaged 91.25 x 58.97 mm in measurement. The four measured respectively, 86.0 x 57.7, 93.0 x 59.5; 94.7 x 59.7, and 91.3 x 59.0 mm. These eggs in both ground color and markings are colored much like those of *Grus canadensis*. Johnasen (Dementiev and Gladkov, 1951) reported buying an egg from the vicinity of Tomsk.

Nothing is known concerning the nesting, length of incubation, or any stages of the breeding of this species. It is found in central Siberia in summer.

In the full grown adult the trachea is well convoluted in the sternum. The voice is quite similar to that of the Sandhill Crane but shriller. The birds give unison calls at times quite similar to those of the Sandhill, give the low guttural 'Garraw' call when flying, and a low 'Purrr' when caring for their young or as a reassurance call to their mates. The young have a call similar to that of other cranes, even in the first winter after their birth, but do not give it as often as do some other species.

Besides grain, *Grus monachus* in winter eat insects, snails, and grubs, which they remove from soil and old logs.

The approximate number of cranes at Yashiro ranged in winter: 30 in 1870; 50 in 1911; 70 in 1918; 100 in 1921; 160 in 1924; 350 in 1940; 200 in 1966.

The natural surroundings at Yashiro are suitable for cranes in winter. Here the tableland valley is towered over by mountains and here the birds find adequate food and suitable roosting at night. The Yashiro people have found 30 different roosting spots in their studies. The climate is quite similar to that in Siberia in summer. And the locality is safe for the birds.

In the morning the people awaken to the call of the cranes. They are the largest wild birds in the vicinity. Most crane families consist of two parents and one or two young, nearly full-grown on arrival. Each family has its own territory, separated from other families and from the larger groups of non-breeding cranes which always feed and roost together.

Furnished with unhulled rice and snails, the cranes also secure loaches and insects from the fields. Their bill holes are evident in the soil where they dig and around decayed wood where they probe.

Before they migrate, they seem to save energy. When flying they proceed in a straight line or V-formation in groups of 40 or 50. Flying up and up, beginning to sail without falling, they gradually disappear from sight.

On winter evenings they fly in a V-formation back to roosts, usually departing early in March when winds become favorable. In group after group they depart toward Siberia, most often during the morning hours."

In Kagoshima Prefecture, Kyushu, both *Grus vipio* and *Grus monachus* wintered at Akune up until about 1930 when they completely abandoned the region, moving to the Arasaki vicinity. The possible decrease in crucian fish (carp) may have had some effect on the former species departing but the latter species may or may not feed on these fish. But since then both species have returned each fall to Arasaki. First Hooded Crane arrivals were recorded by S. Matano, the Crane Warden, on October 20, 1964; October 21, 1965 (1); October 15, 1967; October 13, 1968. Later arrivals during the 1964 autumn are given in Table 2, departures in spring of 1965 in Table 3, while peaks are given for the Arasaki region since 1938 in Table 4. The peaks of *Grus monachus* have varied only by 25 birds during the past four winters (1965-1968). In the spring the Hooded Crane remains later than the White-naped. Last birds were observed March 18, 1965 (2) 1,087 left between February 25 and March 9, 1969; March 19, 1968; and mid-March 1969.

Hooded Cranes roost at night in a rather compact group in two or more of last year's rice fields, now covered with one to four inches of water. Arasaki is an extensive rice growing region adjacent to the sea. The White-naped Cranes roost in a separate compact group in a neighboring rice field that is also flooded with shallow water. As a rule the species do not associate either while feeding or while roosting.

Shortly after the break of day Hooded Cranes begin flying to their feeding regions, rice and wheat fields two to ten kilometers from the roosting site. Wheat (180 kilograms per day) and small crucian fish (carp) (60 kilograms per day) are placed on a field less than 1 kilometer from the roosts of both species. The White-naped Cranes usually go to this immediately and feed in a rather compact group for several hours. Often they scramble along like a flock of chickens devouring the available food. Because of this they are more popular with the people at Arasaki and Izumi than the Hooded Crane. This species begins flying shortly after daylight and by sunrise has nearly or completely abandoned the night roost. They spread over the immense valley in small groups, often families, separated from others. Often they feed for hours on one field if not disturbed, or else change to another field for another long period of time. Whether the same groups come back each day to the same fields no one knows but certain regions seem favored more than others. They feed on both wheat and rice remaining from the season's harvest, and probably on available insects.

Hooded Crane in flight, Arasaki, March 3, 1969.

When the new crops are planted, they do consider-able damage to both wheat and rice, another reason for their unpopularity. They continue this sort of feeding even into March, when the crops have be-come so high that often only the birds' heads and necks can be seen. They continue to feed during the entire day on these fields. A few fly back to the roost before sundown, but the great influx comes between sundown and dark. As in the morning the birds usually fly over a few hundred feet above ground,

often silent, more often one or more birds in a flock, calling moderately as they fly. Flight is direct from the feeding region to the roosting spot. Often if they are flying higher up they make one or two circles before alighting. Some groups cross over 300 meter hilltops to reach the spot, and so have to make sev-eral circles before alighting.

Chapter Four

THE SANDHILL CRANE

(Grus canadensis)

The Sandhill Crane is one of the oldest living birds. Bones, exactly like those found in present day birds have been found in Pliocene and Pleistocene deposits, some four to nine million years old. The species may also have nested in the Valle de México where subfossil eggs were recently discovered. DeCampo (1944) considered these about 1,000 years old. During colonial times the species wintered and possibly nested in the Atlantic seaboard states. Later it disappeared as a nesting bird from southwestern Ontario, from Ohio, Indiana, Illinois, Iowa, Nebraska, North and South Dakota, eastern Montana, southern Alberta, southern Saskatchewan, and probably much of southern Manitoba; in the south from Louisiana and possibly southern Alabama; and from much of southern Cuba and from many places in Florida.

Six subspecies have been described. They are found from the Isle of Pines, Cuba, to northern Canada, and west to northeastern Siberia. They occur from Florida to California, but there are many regions where none are found. Three forms are non-migratory, the Cuban, the Mississippi and Florida subspecies.

Lesser Sandhill Cranes in flight, Feb. 24, 1968, Muleshoe National Wildlife Refuge, Texas.

Three others migrate. The Greater Sandhill Crane in the eastern part of its range apparently migrates into Florida in winter to further complicate matters.

These migratory forms do not agree with Bergemann's Rule, because the continental birds decrease in size with decreasing mean temperatures of their breeding habitat. The smallest birds nest in the Arctic.

The most characteristic differences between the subspecies are those of size, slight plumage variations, and geographical range. The largest, the Greater Sandhill Crane, *Grus canadensis tabida,* nests in the northern United States, but less often in southern Canada. The next largest, the Florida Sandhill Crane, *G. c. pratensis*, nests only in Florida, and southern Georgia. The Mississippi bird has been found only in Jackson County, Mississippi. The Canadian Sandhill Crane, *G.c.rowani,* nests in central Canada. A similar-sized Sandhill Crane, *G.c.-nesiotes,* nests in Cuba and the Isle of Pines, while the smallest and nominate form, the Lesser Sandhill Crane, *G.c.canadensis,* nests in the Arctic.

Weight is no criterion between the different forms, for birds vary considerably — probably due to diet and season. Stephen (1967) showed that in a large series from Saskatchewan there was an overlap in many Sandhill Crane measurements and in weights. He showed that where one measurement agreed with the breeders from that region, possibly one or two other measurements failed to do so. The differences among the three migratory forms is apparently chiefly that of size. Measurements of 469 sexed birds, both male and female, from all regions of North America, show the following differences:

(1) *Grus canadensis canadensis* is much the smallest bird and it has the shortest bill, seldom over 100 mm in length, the shortest tarsus, seldom over 200 mm, while the bare tibia and the bill from the posterior edge of the nares to the tip are also shorter. Even the wings average 2 to 3 cm shorter than in other migratory forms.

(2) *Grus canadensis rowani* is the next in size. It seldom has a bill exceeding 125 mm in males; 120 mm in females and seldom (once) below 100 mm in either sex. The tarsus is about midway between the nominate form and the next.

(3) *Grus canadensis tabida,* the largest form never has a wing chord measurement below 490 mm

Florida Sandhill Crane (Grus c.pratensis) *on nest, April 7, 1972, Adams Ranch, near Kenansville, Osceola County, Florida.*

when fully grown, a bill below 121 mm (males), in fact only four of 44 measurements were below 125 mm, and 2 females out of 29 below 120 mm.

(4) *Grus canadensis pratensis,* a non-migratory form, is slightly smaller than (3) with a shorter wing, longer tarsus and bare tibia. It also has the feathers of the back of the head and occiput deep mouse gray instead of light mouse gray as in the preceding form. Mississippi birds are darker than some birds found in Florida.

(5) Grus canadensis pulla, the Mississippi Sandhill Crane was described by Aldrich (1972).

(6) *Grus canadensis nesiotes,* the Cuban form, is non-migratory and smaller than the Florida bird. Only twice in 13 measurements did the tarsus exceed 220 mm (both sexes), while in Florida birds none went below 220 mm.

Stephen (1967) wrote:

"The range of measurements given for *G. c. canadensis* males (Walkinshaw, 1965) overlaps the distribution of measurements of Last Mountain Lake specimens by 38.2 per cent in length of bill...15.4 per cent in length of bill from tip to the posterior of nostril...and 10.6 per cent in length of tarsus... The range of measurements given for *G. c. rowani* males (Walkinshaw, 1965) overlaps the distribution of measurements of Last Mountain Lake specimens by 29.5 per cent in length of bill ...*G. c. rowani* males occupy only 33.3 per cent and 46.8 per cent of the distribution of measurements of bill from tip to posterior of nostril...and tarsus...of Last Mountain Lake specimens. The range of measurements given for *G. c. tabida* males...overlaps the distribution of measurements of Last Mountain Lake specimens by 2.0 per cent in length of bill...0.2 per cent in length of bill from tip to posterior of nostril... and 64.4 per cent in length of tarsus... Extremes of measurements of 46 adult male sandhill cranes taken in New Mexico (Boeker, *et al* 1961) overlapped the measurements of Last Mountain Lake specimens by 75.2 per cent in length of bill from tip to posterior of the nostril, and 17.6 per cent in length of tarsus....At least 75 per cent of the Last Mountain Lake sandhill crane specimens could not be assigned to one subspecies (Mayr, *et al,* 1953); the measurements of adult males follow a normal distribution, indicating a single population; there is a lack of diagnostic characters."

From the above information it is evident that *G. c. tabida* does not now reside in Saskatchewan if, in fact, it ever did. But the author has gone over records of hundreds of measurements since Stephen published his material, and I still feel that *G. c. rowani* should be separated from *G. c. canadensis.* Four regular measurements have been used (1, 2, 4, 5 – see below) where available and when these were not available, three measurements (1, 3, 4) which many other authors have used. Since Stephen used a slightly different tarsus

measurement, these measurements cannot be compared. With the many more weight records available than formerly, these do not prove diagnostic.

The five measurements taken were: (1) The wing (the chord from the bend to the longest primary). (2) The exposed culmen from where the black hairlike feathers begin, to the tip. (3) From the posterior edge of the nostril to the tip of the upper mandible. (4) The tarsus, from the tarsometatarsal-tibiotarsal joint division to the last scute at the joint of the tarso-metatarsal-foot region. (5) The bare-tibia-tarsus. These show this size variation very well. From these it is evident that Arctic birds quite small, those from central Canada larger, but birds from the northern United States are the largest of all. I cannot find any difference in size between the birds described by Peters (1925) and those from southern Michigan described as *Megalornis canadensis woodi* by H. H. Bailey (1930). Bailey differentiated his birds by color alone and did not measure any. Red coloration of plumage is not reliable since the birds often decorated themselves considerably with iron-stained water and dirt.

LIST OF MUSEUMS AND COLLECTIONS
FROM WHICH SPECIMENS WERE SEEN

AGP – A. G. Prill Collection; AMNH, American Museum of Natural History; AW, Alex Walker Collection; BMNH, British Museum (Natural History); CM, Carnegie Museum; CNHM, Chicago Natural History Museum; CSAS, Case School of Applied Science; Colo. MNH, Colorado Museum of Natural History; FSM, Florida State Museum; HBC, H. B. Conover Collection; HPI, H. P. Ijams; LCS, L. C. Sanford Collection; LBB, Louis Bishop Collection; LHW, L. H. Walkinshaw Collection; LW, Lawrence Weller Collection; ME, Miller Empey Collection; MCZ, Museum of Comparative Zoology; MMNH, Minnesota Museum of Natural History; MPM, Milwaukee Public Museum; MSU, Michigan State University (courtesy of Dr. M. D. Pirnie and Carl Madsen); MVZ, Museum of Vertebrate Zoology; NMC, National Museum of Canada; UHM, Museo Poey, University of Habana Museum; UISB, University of Idaho, Southern Branch; UMMZ, University of Michigan, Museum of Zoology; USF&WS, United States Fish and Wildlife Service; USNM, United States National Museum; U. of I., University of Iowa Museum.

The author has previously written (1949):

Little natural color variation is distinguishable among adults of the four subspecies of Sandhill Crane (since then I have described *G. c. rowani* – author), except that *tabida* is somewhat lighter than *pratensis*...

The Lesser Sandhill Crane. Edwards (1750) portrayed the "Brown and Ash Colour'd Crane" from Hudson Bay, the bird later described as *Ardea canadensis* by Linnaeus (1758); "sincipite nudo papilloso, corpore cinereo, alis extus testaceis. *Grus fusca canadensis* Edw. av. 133, t. 133. Habitat in America septentrionali."

The following description of bill and bare parts of head was taken from a male collected July 2, 1930, at

Lesser Sandhill Cranes at roosting lake, Muleshoe National Wildlife Refuge, Texas, Feb. 24, 1968.

Southampton Island, Hudson Bay, by Sutton (1932). The specimen had been dead four hours; the color terms are from Ridgway:

"Bare space of crown, loral, and orbital region of varying shades of *red* or *red-orange, orange-rufous, bitter-sweet pink,* and *begonia-rose,* fading anteriorly into the *drab gray* or *grayish olive* base of the upper mandible, through *light purplish gray* and *light grayish blue-violet* toward the tip, with suffusions near the nostrils of *light russet vinaceous;* under mandible *drab gray* at the base, fading into *grayish olive* and *pale glass-green* toward the tip, eye *cadmium-orange* in a narrow ring about the pupil, merging quickly into *bright grenadine red."*

The bare space of the crown, forehead, and lores extends about 10 to 15 mm above and behind the eye, a papillose skin covered sparsely with short, black hairlike bristles. The occiput is pallid to pale mouse gray; hind neck, back, rump, wings, and tail are light to pale mouse gray, washed on the back, scapulars, wings, and tertials with fawn, wood brown, and buffy brown (often entirely washed with a brownish stain produced by ferric oxide—see above). The chin and upper throat are white or pale gull gray, blending into the grayer cheeks. The breast is mouse gray, the abdomen lighter than the breast, the sides and under wing pallid mouse gray. All the feathers of neck, back, scapulars, upper wing coverts, breast, and abdomen are edged for about 8 to 10 mm with pale to pallid mouse gray.

The primaries and greater upper coverts are dark gray to slaty gray or black, the coverts with an ashy bloom, the primary shafts dark gray. The tarsi and toes (Ridgway and Friedmann, 1941) are "dull greenish blackish to very dark olive."

The Greater and Florida Sandhill Cranes . . . The Greater Sandhill Crane *(tabida)* was first described by Peters (1925), who distinguished it from *pratensis* as follows:

"Similar to *Megalornis (Grus) canadensis pratensis* (Meyer) but paler throughout especially on the occiput and back of neck which are pallid mouse gray to pale mouse gray instead of light mouse gray to mouse gray; the underparts particularly the lower breast and abdomen are appreciably grayer..."

The Cuban Sandhill Crane. Outram Bangs and W. R. Zappey described *Grus canadensis nesiotes* in 1905:

Canadian Sandhill Cranes (G.c.rowani) at Fawcett, Alberta, Canada, May 29, 1942.

"Characters—similar to the Sandhill Crane of Florida ...in color, but slightly darker and not so clear a gray on back; smaller with shorter tarsus; beak somewhat stouter and heavier."

Plumages vary little except in the shades of gray between the six subspecies. But there is a definite distinction in size and geographical ranges.

The downy chick of all six subspecies is similar

Sometimes there is a variation in the amount of buff or gray but this seems to be more individual than racial. Following is the description:

Bill, dull flesh color with a darker tip at hatching, becoming darker on the second day, even darker on the third and fourth. The general down color is tawny. The occiput is burnt sienna, changing abruptly at the end of the widow's peak to tawny, with much shorter down on forecrown and forehead. The anterior portion of the forehead and sides of the face are a light buff white or lighter gray in adults with a slightly darker line beneath the eye, enlarging to a spot of chestnut on each loral region.

"From the occiput to the rump and on top of the wings, the down is much darker than that on the rest of the body; a region on the upper back, somewhat diamond-shaped, narrowing to a stripe on the center back, and becoming diamond-shaped again on the lower back and rump, is mikado or sayal brown, whereas the hind neck and sides have a dark gull gray cast. The throat is white, or nearly so, shading to a deep gull gray on the neck, which shows some mixture of tawny toward the sides, changing to dull grayish white on the breast and under wings, and wing. Some young are more buffy, some more gray underneath."

When 53 days old a crane raised by the author's family showed the juvenal plumage well advanced on July 2. The forehead, occiput, hind neck, and back were tawny to ochraceous tawny. The scapulars and wing coverts were deep gull gray, the primaries slate black to black. The base of the upper mandible was vinaceous-cinnamon, the rest of the bill pinkish buff, the legs and feet a darker pinkish buff. Many feathers of the wing and tail had had long tawny plumes projecting beyond the normal ends. As the bird became older it became grayer then molted from August 1 to mid-October into the light to pallid mouse gray plumage quite similar to that of the adult plumage. But the bird did not lose its primaries and rectrices.

THE LESSER SANDHILL CRANE. *Grus canadensis canadensis*
Ardea canadensis Linnaeus, *Syst. Nat.*, 10th ed. 1, 1758, p. 141.
Type locality: North America. Hudson Bay, *ex. Grus fusca canadensis* (Edwards, *Nat. Hist.*, 1750.)
Vernacular names: The Lesser Sandhill Crane, The Little Brown Crane (English)); К а н а д с к и ж у р а в л ь (Russian); Grulla (Mexican); der Canadische Kranich (German): de Canadeesche Kraanvogel (Dutch); la Grue du Canada (French); Tattidgak (Nunamiut dialect at Anaktuvuk); Kutchilkag (meaning color of body red) (Eskimo dialect at Hooper Bay); Go-cheé-sel-kuck (Kuskokwim Eskimos); Lat-slhuk (western Alaska Eskimo); Tuds-le-uk (St. Michael); Tut-tíd-ri-gu (Point Barrow Eskimos) (Eskimo names from Gabrielson and Lincoln, *Birds of Alaska)*; Tadiiak or Tadigak (Banks Island Eskimos (Manning, Höhn and McPherson, *Birds of Banks Island)*; Kanada zuru カナヅル (Japanese).

DISTRIBUTION

Previously the author summarized (1949) many of the summer and specimen winter records as well as migratory specimen records of the Sandhill Cranes. Later, (1960) the available sight and specimen records of the species in migration east of the Mississippi River were summarized. Dementiev and Gladkov (1951) summarized the Siberian records. More recently Boeker, Aldrich and Huey (1961), and Buller and Boeker (1965) gave the migration procedure through the Great Plains and the winter distribution of the Lesser Sandhill Crane in eastern New Mexico and western Texas.

This smallest subspecies of the Sandhill Crane is found farthest north and west in summer, reaching extreme northeastern Siberia; Wrangell Island; much of western Alaska; northern Canada, including Banks and Victoria, and some other islands; south and west to the Bering Sea Islands; some of the Aleutians; south possibly to northern Kamchatka; Cook Inlet, Alaska; and probably to southern Mackenzie; Keewatin; Southampton Island; western Hudson Bay; and possibly even to the Hudson Bay watersheds of western and northern Ontario.

It winters from southern California, eastern New Mexico, western Texas, southeastern Texas, south into Mexico to Jalisco, Guanajuato, San Luis Potosi, Baja California and northwestern Sonora, and possibly even farther south. One wintered at Arasaki, Kagoshima Prefecture, Japan, during the 1963-64 winter and one at Akan, Hokkaido during the 1969-70 winter. In each case with other species of cranes.

Winter

More Lesser Sandhill Cranes winter in Texas than in any other region. The majority winter in western Texas and eastern New Mexico, on the grassy high plains, the "Llano Estacado" of the early settlers. This high plain region comprises 20,000,000 acres, in Texas alone, all at an elevation of 3,000 to 4,500 feet, sloping gently to the southeast. Its surface is spotted with 'playa lakes' often several feet deep, many 40 or more acres in size. Average rainfall is 15 to 21 inches, varying from as little as 12 to as much as 45 inches. Severe droughts sometimes

Mississippi Sandhill Crane settling down onto eggs, north of Ocean Springs, Jackson Co., Miss., April 20, 1940.

plague the region. Possible frost periods last 140 to 186 days annually, with temperatures at times well below zero in midwinter. Gould (1962) wrote that the soils vary from clays in the north to sands on the Southern High Plains, with underlying caliche accumulations at depths of 2 to 5 feet.

These plains have been classified as mixed-prairie, short-grass prairie, and in some regions, tall-grass prairie. Plant communities vary on the hardlands,

mixed lands, sandy lands, draws and caliche breaks with varying successional patterns.

The most abundant native grasses are buffalo-grass (*Buchloe dactyloides*), blue grama (*Bouteloua gracilis*), sideoats grama (*B. curtipendula*), black grama (*B. eriopoda*), little bluestem (*Andropogon scoparius*), western wheatgrass (*Agropyron smithii*), Indiangrass (*Sorghastrum* sp.), switchgrass (*Panicum* sp.) and occasionally, sand dropseed (*Sporo-*

bolus cryptandrus). Any or all of these might have originally been sandhill crane food. This region is usually free of brush, but mesquite and yucca have invaded some regions and cedars some others. In this treeless region, the Lesser Sandhills winter. Concentrations also occur in parts of southern California, Baja California, Sonora, even south to Jalisco. Some winter in southeastern Texas and Tamaulipas.

Tahoka Lake, typical of lakes of the western Texas region, lies a hundred feet below the level of the surrounding tableland, extending over a mile in a southwest-northeast direction. It displays receding muddy shores in winter, and behind these are high ridges. There are no cottages along its shoreline, and no motorboats or skiers race over its surface. The nearest ranch houses are one-half to one mile away and these are few. Its waters are alkaline.

Mississippi Sandhill Crane in flight in typical habitat, Ocean Springs, Miss., April 18, 1940.

Lesser Sandhill Cranes in flight migration time, North Platte River, near Hershey, Nebraska, March 26, 1954.

For many years it has provided isolation in a region where visibility is almost unlimited. In it, like in many similar lakes, the Lesser Sandhill Cranes roost at night. Except for some pasture land close to its southwest border where a few juniper-like cedars and dead grasses occur, the surrounding land is extensively farmed. Cotton, sorghum and wheat are the main crops. The land is plowed in winter but many fields remain as left when harvested the previous fall. Many of these are sorghum. Over

5,000,000 acres of sorghum are planted in Texas alone much of which is raised on this tableland.

Paul's Lake, on the Muleshoe National Wildlife Refuge, Bailey County, Texas, although smaller, is similar to Tahoka Lake and is used by even more Sandhill Cranes. It consists of a shallow alkaline lake with a dark, muddy shoreline. Most adjoining lands are in pasture. East and west of the lake about a mile are lands planted each spring to sorghum, other grains, and cotton.

At Bitter Lakes Wildlife Refuge, Roswell, New Mexico, where a few scattered lakes get much water from the Pecos River, Sandhill Cranes also winter.

Extensive mud flats, river bars or lake shores with large areas of shallow water, where disturbance is at a minimum, produce winter roosting regions as well as migration stopovers for Sandhill Cranes. Grain is raised somewhere in the vicinity of most wintering areas. In former days there was no grain, yet huge concentrations occurred then as now. No one knows what foods were used then, but apparently native grass seeds, grasshoppers, other insects and roots were used. Now, without the grasses, cranes feed on the nearest substitutes, sorghum, corn, wheat and barley. They also feed extensively on grasshoppers when they occur on the grassy regions (Muleshoe personnel, 1967).

There are several essentials for wintering regions:
(1) There must be mud flats, large stretches of shallow water or isolated sand bars in rivers or lakes where the cranes can roost at night and get drinking water by day.
(2) The birds like a region adjacent to the night roost area where they go early mornings from the night roost. Here they loaf for 15-20 minutes.
(3) There must be feeding grounds nearby; as close as one-half mile or as far as 12 to 18 miles away.
(4) There must be little disturbance in the roost region.
(5) Favorable weather is preferred.

Daily behavior may vary some, but in general it differs little in winter or during migration. Cranes fly from their shallow water roosting spot around daylight. If a feeding ground is available one-half mile away or a little more they usually fly directly to it; if it is much more, they often fly to some nearby field, where they preen, at times call, dance, chase their neighbors or watch for impending danger. Then later they fly to their feeding field. At night they roost in a large group, each bird standing on one foot about six feet from its nearest neighbor. When sleeping they tuck their head deftly among the scapular feathers at the bend of the wing. Such a night was recorded on February 23-24, 1968 by the author:

On February 23, 1968 at 1600 hours a gray mass of about 15,000 Sandhill Cranes stood on the hillside south of Paul's Lake, Muleshoe Wildlife Re-

George, a pet female. Florida Sandhill Crane cared for by Gordon and Mary Male, Timberlane, Polk County, Florida, November 1966.

fuge, Texas, as I drove by. Without frightening them I passed behind a knoll one-half mile east and watched the arrival of new birds. The incoming flight was almost entirely from the southeast, a few flocks from the east. Nearly all birds were 300 to 400 feet above ground, a few flocks up to 1,000 feet. The higher ones, as they neared the lake, dropped quickly down; others side-slipped from one side to the other as they lost altitude. Approaching flocks flew in diagonal lines, V-formations, and in irregular masses. When the great mass arrived, flocks were strung from the eastern to the western horizon, nearly all at right angles to the flight direction. Some birds were bugling in each flock and those on the ground were making so much noise individual birds could not be heard. The time, flock sizes, and number of individuals arriving were:

5:45 p.m. One flock, 28 cranes arrived.
5:53 p.m. Two flocks (4, 2) arrived.
5:58 p.m. Three flocks (2, 2, 32) arrived. One flock of 3 flying out.
6:02 p.m. Two flocks (16,56) arrived. Eight flocks (1-28) out. Total out, 106 cranes.
6:10 p.m. 66 flocks (1-370), total, 2,059 individuals in; 5 birds out.
6:20 p.m. 20 flocks (1-144), totaling 425 birds flew to roost.
6:26 p.m. 16 flocks (17-200), totaling 947 individuals in to roost.
6:37 p.m. Not much flight; ducks flying out; sunset.
6:46 p.m. 18 flocks (ll-360), totaling 1,755 cranes in to roost.
6:50 p.m. 31 flocks totaling 2,039 individuals in to roost.
7:00 p.m. Many flocks in to roost, estimated 5,379 birds.
7:07 p.m. 28 flocks in to roost, extimated number, 1,286 individuals in.
7:12 p.m. 6 flocks (7-141), totaling 260 individuals in to roost.
Total cranes to roost, 5:45-7:12 p.m.: 14,292 individuals.

Departure the following morning from the night roost at Muleshoe National Wildlife Refuge, Texas was: (February 24, 1968; sky, clear; the morning frosty; no wind but it began blowing shortly and increased during morning, slackening during early afternoon; temperature over 60°F by early afternoon; sunrise, 7:30 a.m.).

Individual cranes called off and on all night; I had no way of knowing whether the same birds or different birds were calling. At dusk and near daylight the birds made much more noise. Sometimes I could barely hear anything else because of the extreme noise.

6:10 a.m. Small groups began flying from Paul's Lake onto the dry sidehill. This continued for the next hour so that nearly all the cranes were on a nearby hill, the morning roost site.
7:12 a.m. A lone crane flew from the hillside up to about 400 feet elevation, and calling, disappeared to the southeast. Almost immediately 20 other groups totaling 147 cranes flew, about 75% to the southeast; 25% to the east. Flock sizes varied between one and 25.
7:20 a.m. Fifty-four flocks (1-350 individuals) in about

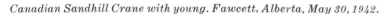

Canadian Sandhill Crane with young. Fawcett, Alberta, May 30, 1942.

the same proportions flew from the hill-time roost. Total: 1,100 during five min.

7:25 a.m. About 90 flocks, totaling 678 cranes, flew at about the same height directly away to the southeast (two to 20 birds in a flock, one or more in the flock calling.).

7:27 a.m. The heaviest flight out, about 2,091 in 185 flocks (1-250).

7:30 a.m. Twenty flocks (1-75) flew out, totaling 429 birds.

7:31 a.m. Sun rising. About 123 flocks (1-150, plus individuals), totaling 2,374 cranes flew out in the next 12 minutes.

7:43 a.m. About 162 flocks (1-200 plus), totaling 2,587 cranes flew out followed by a lull.

8:10 a.m. During the next ten minutes, 133 flocks (1-50), totaling 1,015 cranes flew SE, fewer to the E, and a very few to N.

8:20 a.m. During the next five minutes, 23 flocks (1-18), totaling 536 out.

8:25 a.m. During five minutes, 34 flocks (2-80), total, 506 cranes out.

Sandhill Crane chick, Ft. Smith, Northwest Territories, Canada, June 6, 1964, note short tarsi.

8:30 a.m. During seven minutes, 657 birds (49 flocks) out.

8:37 a.m. During 13 minutes, 22 flocks (1-34), of 206 individuals out.

8:50 a.m. Many flying, 41 flocks (2-75), total of 450 individuals out.

9:10 a.m. Two flocks (37, 38) flew to SE. There were still about 2,000 on the hillside which left shortly. But almost as soon lone individuals or small groups began arriving back at the lake. On return they usually flew to water and began to drink. As the morning progressed, family groups returned. They remained apart from the larger mass. And while the youngsters drank, dug in the mud with their bills, and moved about unconcerned, the parents, either one or both, stood at attention watching everything everywhere about them. But shortly other groups came in and when I left the blind about 3 p.m., there were over a thousand in the lake again, a few on the nearby hillside. They all stopped calling, and watched with extreme alertness but did not fly. After I had reached the car, out of their sight, the entire mass took to the air, triggered off by some disturbance. They climbed into the sky, circling higher and higher until they were barely discernible, but their voices came back to me as I left. Later they circled back to the roost region.

Cranes increased at Bitter Lakes Wildlife Refuge, New Mexico, from 5,772 in December 1942 to 10,559 on March 5, 1943; by March 17, to 11,000. All had left by April 2. During 1944 there were 6,000 on March 12, and the last observed April 11. (Charles Keefer, U.S. Fish and Wildlife Service Notes.) The U.S. Fish and Wildlife Service also recorded 15,975 on November 3, 1961; the next week, 10,845; 6,040 by December 6. Similar counts have been recorded yearly.

At Muleshoe National Wildlife Refuge, Bailey County, Texas, the 1942-1943 winter concentration increased from 8,000 to 15,000 before spring. On December 15, 1960, 42,000 cranes were counted. Here a peak of 55,000 was reached. More recently, since hunting of this bird began in 1961, many of the counts have been published. Boeker, Aldrich and Huey (1961) wrote that there were 149,702 Sandhill Cranes in eastern New Mexico and western Texas regions, December 31, 1960; 142,110 on January 30, 1961 and 92,164 by February 15-17, 1961. Boeker, *et al*, (1961; 1962) and others gave these counts between 92,164 and 216,000 cranes. The highest count made by the U.S. Fish and Wildlife Service and other organizations was made in 1967: 216,000 cranes.

Cuban Sandhill Crane at dry-land nest, near Los Indios, Isle of Pines, May 4, 1951.

Boeker, *et al* (1962) reported wintering regions in November-December 1961 occurred in the following Texas counties: Aransas-Calhoun, Cameron, Castro, Colorado, Comal, Cottal, Frio, Ft. Bend, Goliad, Hardeman & Wilbarger, Harris, Henderson, Jackson, Kleberg, Lavaca, Nueces, Reeves, Refugio, Sutton, Throckmorton, Wharton and Young. I observed the species also in January 1944 in Carson and Randall; in February 1968 in Lubbock counties.

Cranes in other portions of Texas may be either *G. c. canadensis* or *G. c. rowani*. Counties where cranes have been found other than west Texas are: Bailey, Calhoun, Cochran, Dallas, Gaines, Gillespie, Hidalgo, Hockley, Howard, Jackson, Kerr, Lynn, Nueces, Refugio, Reeves, San Patricio, Terry, Travis and Willacy. In New Mexico this bird is found in Chaves, Eddy, Lea and Roosevelt counties; in California in Marin (formerly), Merced, Los Angeles (formerly), Kings, Orange, Imperial, San

Bernardino and San Luis Obispo counties; in Arizona in Pima County; in Mexico, it has been found regularly in Baja California, specimens from Cerro Prieto; in Sonora at Alamos; in Chihuahua (on the plateau, 400 mi south of Juarez—Arnold Small, letter April 22, 1968); in San Luis Potosi at Rio Verde; and in Jalisco at La Barca (see Walkinshaw, 1949).

The known winter range of *G. c. tabida* varies greatly. No records or few are available from Texas nor eastern New Mexico. The species has been found at Los Banos, Merced County, California (Maillard, 1921) from the Carissa Plains, Soda Lake (Eben McMillan, letters, December 14, 1955; January 10, 1956; December 1960 and April 12, 1968) but not as abundantly as *G. c. canadensis*. The largest known concentration in winter is at the Bosque del Apache National Wildlife Refuge, San Antonio, New Mexico. During the 1960s, 7,500 of these birds were found roosting in the marshes feeding on nearby fields, as well as in the marshes. This bird also winters in either or both southern Georgia and central Florida. Here there are no known *G. c. canadensis* nor *G. c. rowani*.

Florida Sandhill Crane (George) in pre-attack pose. Anyone who petted her had to watch out. Polk County, Florida, November 1966.

Nest of Cuban Sandhill Crane, Los Indios, Isle of Pines, Cuba, May 1, 1951.

Eben McMillan (*loc cit*), over a period of 30 years has observed winter crane concentrations at Soda Lake, Carissa Plains, San Luis Obispo County, California. Some years, 500 are present, other years, 5,000, while more recently, up to 10,000 cranes have gathered there.

They roost in Soda Lake, a shallow sink some five miles long and one-half mile wide with many narrow arms, some 25 yards across, extending out from the sides. In summer this is dry or nearly so, but in winter it fills up with runoff rains from nearby hills, so that there are several inches of water in the narrow arms. Nearby farmers raise wheat, the newly planted and old stubble fields offering best feeding conditions to the cranes. But new alfalfa fields are also used for grazing.

The cranes go to roost around sunset, making considerable noise, become quiet during the night, but again do much calling about daylight. They leave then for neighboring fields. One morning in January, 1947 McMillan counted 3,200 cranes in flocks of one to 300 flying out in one hour and 15 minutes. At no time were there less than three flocks in sight at once. The orderly exodus usually required between 40 and 60 minutes.

A portion of this region was subdivided in 1960

and many new houses were built on two and one-half acre lots. Thus far this has not deterred the roosting cranes.

McMillan also wrote that there were other groups of cranes throughout the San Joaquin and Sacramento Valleys in winter, but none concentrated nor remaining in a given locality for any length of time. Some birds come and go into the great California valleys but probably few cranes come south in winter without spending some time on the Carissa Plains.

During 1958 cranes first appeared October 23, during 1959, on September 29; in 1960, on October 10. Most birds have left by March, the first leaving in late February, but some have remained until May 1 and in 1941, three stayed until May 23.

The majority of these birds are very small, indicating that they are *G. c. canadensis* while a few are very large, showing that both expected races do occur there.

At Aransas National Wildlife Refuge, Austwell, Texas, wintering Sandhill Cranes have been found to be largely *G. c. canadensis*, with some *G. c. rowani*. They feed on surrounding fields. Refuge notes include the following résumé:

1938: First arrival, October 20; 300 wintered; last (20), March 17, 1939. One *G. c. canadensis* found dead December 12.

1939: First October 12, (13); winter peak, 600; last (1), April 20, 1940.

1940: November 1 through winter (100-200). Two cripples: (one, *G. c. canadensis;* second, larger); last, April 18, 1941.

1941: First, October 9; October 26, (several hundred); last, late March 1942.

1942: First (8), August 25; October (750); December (500); as well as January and February; last (100), March 23, 1943.

1943: First, October 11, (3); peak, 350; last, March 15, 1944 (6).

1945: January to March (500); last, March 22, (10). In fall, first, October 18, (18); 300 into winter; last, March 29, 1946 (300).

1946-47: Winter peak, 300; last, April 11, 1947 (3).

1947: Cranes roosted on tidal marsh east of refuge headquarters, in the fall. Winter peak, 300; last, April 20, 1948 (35).

1948: First (1), October 12; winter peak, 500; last (11), April 21, 1949; one bird remained into the summer.

1949: First (5), October 4; winter peak, 300.

1950: Winter peak: 200; 3 observed into March.

1951: First (2), September 14; peak, 400, October 24 with 250 through the winter and last (3), March 15, 1952.

1952: First (12), October 14; 856 counted on December 31; estimated peak, 1,000; last (3), March 20, 1953.

1953: First (3), October 10; peak, 350; last (16), March 19, 1954.

1954: First (3), October 10; 2,800.

During February and March, 1968, the author was in Lubbock, Texas. On February 24 a small flock of Lesser Sandhills passed northward over the western part of the city; on March 4, the author counted between 900 and 1,000 cranes in groups numbering from 40 to 200 flying between 400 and 1,000 feet. Often low-flying flocks broke formation, circled up and up gaining altitude, then regained V-formation and proceeded northward. On March 8, the author's daughter counted 3,200 cranes going northward, and a few more flocks periodically in the following days up until March 17. All flew at about the same altitude or reached it by circling; all flew on bright, clear days, when winds were light or southerly during a high pressure period; all flew over between 11:30 and 12:30 a.m., and often in V-formation flocks following immediately behind similar-shaped flocks. All flew directly northward. Seldom did cranes pass over this part of the county except during this period.

Edith R. McLeod (1954) described a concentration of Sandhill Cranes in spring at Meiss Lake, Siskiyou County, California, where about 1,500 Lessers begin arriving late in February or the first week in March, sometimes well into April. She wrote that the cranes had used this region in both spring and fall as far back as local farmers could remember.

The birds from California must migrate across British Columbia. Those from Central Mexico, New Mexico, and Texas cross Colorado, Kansas, Nebraska, Wyoming, Montana, and the Dakotas, to southern Saskatchewan, and into southern Alberta and Manitoba. In these southern Canadian latitudes, the greatest concentration occurs at Last Mountain Lake, Saskatchewan. But here they remain only for a few days (Munro, 1950) then proceed farther northward.

The spring migration has been recorded from

Nest and eggs (eggs lighter colored than canadensis, rowani *or* tabida *eggs). Ocean Springs, Miss., April 18, 1940.*

Lincoln County, Nebraska in the *Nebraska Bird Review*, by the Charles Summer family, William Rapp and the author as follows: March 5, 1937; February 22, 1938; March 8, 1939; March 11, 1940; March 7, 1947; March 16, 1948; February 25, 1949; February 24, 1950; March 11, 1951; February 27, 1952; February 2, (greatest concentration, March 20-25) to May 6, 1953; February 1, to April 19, 1954; February 18, 1955; February 16, 1957; February 20, 1958; February 13, 1959; March 8, 1960;

February 14, to April 20, 1961; January 13, to April 17, 1962; February 6, to April 10, 1963; February 14, to April 22, 1964; February 9, to April 26, 1965.

At Hastings, Adams County, Nebraska, Rapp (1951) gave the earliest record (24 years) as March 1, 1930 and the latest April 11, 1937. Following that early dates have been: March 4, 1951; February 26, 1952; February 26, 1953; February 9, 1954; February 24, 1955, February 17, 1956, February 10, 1957; February 18, 1958; March 18, 1959; March 13,

1960; March 1, 1961; February 7, to April 13, 1962; February 17, 1963; March 1 to April 5, 1964 and February 25, to April 26, 1965.

Following 1953 and 1954 Nebraska visits, the author published (1956):

> We found the cranes roosted in shallow water or on sand bars in the Platte and North Platte Rivers at night. They flew into the rivers just prior to dark. Shortly after daylight in the mornings they flew from the rivers to some neighboring fields. After about 15 to 90 minutes they began flying to grain fields. During the day we often found them in cornfields where they had fed. Also they were in the hayfields, or plain plowed ground, and in fall wheat fields where they usually were preening and loafing but sometimes dancing. Sometimes on warm sunny days, large flocks congregated and much dancing ensued. On fewer occasions, in mid-day we found large groups, in a great gray mass, just "sitting" down. These flocks were immense...
>
> ...The areas where the cranes were found were from Grand Island and Doniphan (W. E. Eigsti) on the east, to Cozad on the west. From Cozad west to North Platte we found seven cranes in 1953; none in 1954. In 1954 we drove this distance at dusk when cranes are usually flying and saw none. The greatest numbers during both years were in the neighborhood of Hershey. We found a small group as far as Kingsley Dam north of Ogallala. We found all the cranes in the river valleys. At North Platte in 1954 we did see a few small groups leave toward the north but had no evidence that they stopped anywhere nearby. We drove for hours during midday in the sandhills looking for cranes but found none.

Buller and Boeker (1964) wrote: 'The North Platte, South Platte and Platte Rivers and adjacent grainfields from Llewellen to Grand Island constitute an important way station for spring migrating cranes. Birds enroute north usually arrive in the Platte River Valley about mid-February, and during the third week of March measurements of this population have ranged from 240,000 (1958) to 120,000 (1963). Departures begin within 1 or 2 weeks of the peak population date."

During 1953, the author and associates counted 60,124 cranes and during 1954, 52,894 along the Platte and North Platte Rivers (Walkinshaw, 1956a). In these concentrations, no one knows how long each bird stays, nor each group, nor how often new birds arrive. The turnover could be fast; the numbers tremendous.

The cranes came to roost after 5 p.m., the vanguard in small groups, an immense flight just prior to sunset, and some not arriving until after dark. Here they roosted in shallow water up to about ten inches (25 cm) deep, each bird just out of reach of its nearest neighbor. One night I slept in a duck blind in the middle of the North Platte River, in the center of one of these concentrations. The cranes bugled off and on all night, and if I snored, they bugled in return and woke me up. As daylight approached their calls drowned out all other noises and shortly they began to fly in small groups, continuing long after sunrise. They went into neighboring fields, often immediately adjacent to the river where they stood, often in groups, each bird separated from its nearest neighbor by several feet. They preened, danced, and often called. Some birds showed dominance over other birds but the attacked neighbor usually jumped only a few feet into the air and landed in a new spot several feet from his attacker and other cranes. As the light intensity increased, the birds began flying, some into neighboring alfalfa fields, where they browsed; others into old corn fields, where they ate loose corn left the previous fall by the mechanical corn-picker.

David A. Munro (1950) wrote of their behavior in Saskatchewan:

"The spring migration of sandhill cranes through Saskatchewan is fairly rapid...birds were seen for only two to seven days at any one point during the spring. The heaviest migration seems to proceed in a northwesterly direction, touching the following points: Last Mountain Lake, Quill Lakes, Lake Lenore, Sandwith, Midnight Lake and Meadow Lake. Smaller numbers...pass through Yorkton, Arborfield and Nipawin. That these are regular flyways is suggested by the fact that migrant sandhill cranes are rarely seen at points such as Foam Lake, Saskatoon and Waskesiu which lie outside the two main routes of passage..."

He gave migration records from April 23 until May 12, 1947, from Last Mountain Lake, Connell Creek, Nipawin, Sandwith, Middle Lake, and Big Quill Lake. That same spring, W. A. Tholen and the author observed a flock of 41 birds, May 27 at Last Mountain Lake, near Hatfield, 6 miles NW, 28N, 23W2.

Fred Bard, Jr. sent me the following records of first observations and concentrations from Regina,

Greater Sandhill Crane nest in cattails. Malheur National Wildlife Refuge, Oregon, May 15, 1941.

Nest of Florida Sandhill Crane on small island, Okefenokee National Wildlife Refuge, Georgia, March 13, 1960.

Saskatchewan (17N, 19-20W2): May 5, 1913; April 12, 1914; April 8, 1920; April 12, 1921; April 29, 1922 (big migration); April 29, 1925 (big flock); April 11, (May 2, – hundreds) 1926; April 24, 1928; April 13, 1930 (6)(April 27, – many flocks); April 12, (hundreds – more flocks April 15, 19, and 30, and May 1) 1932; April 15, 1935; April 13, 1936 (April 17, flocks of 35 over city at noon, flying NW at 3,000 feet); April 8, 1937; April 13, 1938 (4 flocks); April 13, 1939; April 18, 1940; April 6, 1945 (many); all observed by F. G. Bard, Sr., F. G. Bard, Jr., H. H. Mitchell, E. H. M. Knowles.

First sizable flocks were observed by Maurice Street at Nipawin (51N, 14W2), Saskatchewan: April 21, 1933; April 20, 1934; April 22, 1935; April 29, 1936; April 20, 1937; April 25, 1938; April 27, 1939; April 20, 1940; April 23, 1941; April 19, 1942; April 28, 1944; April 21, 1945; April 12, 1946; April 27, 1947; April 21, 1948; April 4, 1949; April 13, 1950; April 12, 1951; April 21, 1952; April 24, 1953; April 16, 1954; April 26, 1955.

Sandhill Cranes arrive in Alaska almost as soon as in central Saskatchewan. In the interior, mostly at College and Fairbanks, often at Creamers

Scanty nest and eggs, Lesser Sandhill Crane, 20 mi. SE of Sachs Harbour, Banks Island, Canada, June 16, 1964. Nest is on top of large sand dune.

Dairy, Dr. Brina Kessel gave the following arrival dates: April 28, (4)(May 5-65) 1952; April 30, (3) (May 12-12) 1953; April 27, (2)(May 18-15) 1954; April 26, (1)(May 11-27) 1955; April 29, (2)(May 12-300 flying over Big Delta) 1956; April 27, 1957; April 28, (May 19-14, and May 26-2, June-100) 1958; April 22, 1959 (10); April 26, (several)(April 26-30) 1960; April 26, (1)(April 30, 120-130 at Mile 1376, Alaska Highway; May 7, 5,500 between Delta and Gerstle River) 1961; April 18, (10)(April 22-30; May 3-100) 1962; April 26, (15)(April 30-80; May 5-8,000 near Tok and 14,000-15,000 on Taylor Highway between Tok and College-Weeden) 1963; April 28, (1)(May 1-97 between Fairbanks and Tok-Weeden)(May 2-2,500 on Taylor Highway-Weeden; 5,000 at Big Delta-Argy) 1964; April 22, (Big Delta)(May 7-many at Tok) 1965; April 29, (9)(May 8, 4,000 at Tok-Weeden) 1966; May 1, (1)(May 5-6, 2 flocks at Tok, 300 and 40-50) 1967.

Early arrival dates in other Alaskan regions have been: Wrangell, February 29, 1920 (8)(A. M. Bailey, 1927). Ft. Kenai, May 4, 1869 (Cooke, 1914). Bethel, May 4, 1946 (H. Kyllingstad). Hooper Bay, May 7, 1924 (Conover, 1926). Mt. Village, April 29, 1943 and 1944 (H. Kyllingstad). St. Michael, May 2, 1875 (Turner, 1886). Nome, May 10, 1907 (spec., C.N.H.M.). Humphrey Point, May 17, 1914 (W. S. Brooks, 1915:388).

In Siberia, at Anadry Bay, Belopolski (1933) observed first cranes May 16, 1931 and at Bering Island a specimen was taken May. 18, 1914 (A.M.N.H.).

An early date for Escape Reef, Yukon Territory, Canada, by R. M. Anderson, was May 13, 1914. At Ft. Providence, Mackenzie, April 28, 1905 one was seen (Preble, 1908); another on the Middle Branch Mackenzie River, May 9, 1933 (Porsild, 1943). On Banks Island, Manning (1956) recorded birds May 17, 1952 at De Salis Bay and May 12, 1953 at Sachs Harbour—where G. Clouvidakis recorded the birds' first appearance May 15, 1964 (Walkinshaw, 1965b).

First cranes often arrive at Fairbanks in pairs. Farther west they often appear in pairs and immediately go onto their territories. The first 1953 pair on Banks Island (Manning, et al, loc cit) were observed on territory. I observed paired birds on

Greater Sandhill Crane nest, with chicks hatching, near Henry, Caribou County, Idaho, May 24, 1941.

territories in early June and one group of three flying over Sachs Harbour to the northeast. There were no larger groups. Yet in the region of Tok and Big Delta, Alaska, sometimes several thousand cranes appear in flocks. And they sometimes reach Bering Straits in flocks. These may build up because of adverse winds or weather conditions, as described by Breckenridge and Cline (1967):

There are a few published reports...of Sandhill Cranes, presumably Grus c. canadensis, moving westward in spring across the Bering Strait. The large numbers we encountered, however, seemed especially noteworthy. Flocks of 12 to 1,200 birds were seen daily in the area (May 14 to June 4). The presence of pairs and small groups suggested that some might nest locally, but most of the flocks were heading out over the sea ice toward Siberia. On the morning of May 23 the temperature of 30°F, the 30 to 40 mph winds, and a fairly heavy fall of snow, combined to produce wintry conditions. We spent the morning on the lee side of a

Greater Sandhill Crane standing on nest, Phyllis Haehnle Memorial Sanctuary, Jackson County, Michigan, April 28, 1963.

100

rocky ridge near the top of Wales Mountain. By noon the snow had stopped, the wind abated somewhat, and the sky began to clear. Small flocks of cranes appeared far below us moving out over the sea ice. More and larger flocks began coming from the east along the mountain sides, some flying directly toward us and veering aside to pass around the cliff where we sat. On passing the last point of land many of the flocks appeared "reluctant" to fly out over the ice-choked strait at low levels. The cranes broke their formations and began circling, gaining altitude to perhaps 1,000 feet, from which elevation the Diomede Islands and the Siberian mainland would be plainly visible. They then re-formed in long lines and proceeded across the strait. Far out over Lopp Lagoon to the north, other lines of cranes, perhaps as much as two miles long, were also moving westward. Often two or three layers of birds circled above us as the early arriving flocks reached higher levels and the later ones followed. The flight continued throughout the afternoon.... We estimated that between 15,000 and 20,000 birds were involved in this flight.

SUMMER HABITAT

The Alaskan tundra, home of many Lesser Sandhill Cranes, extends for boundless miles. For cranes, the most important portion lies from the Seward Peninsula to the Kuskokwim Mountains. Some smaller scattered regions are also used. This treeless tundra, broken periodically by cold deep rivers, drains into the larger Yukon and Kuskokwim rivers. Winter snows and summer rains keep the soil, which is only a few inches above permafrost, soaked continuously. Between the rivers are countless lakes, varying from small ponds to those several miles long. Sometimes small streams run from one lake to another. Everywhere else is tundra. The higher tundra is often rather rugged or quite rolling. Sometimes, parallel ridges extend down to the lower tundra. In between, ravines carry meltwater from the spring thaw. Extensive regions are nearly flat, yet lake covered, while other regions have few lakes. On this high tundra are scattered clumps of alders, short sedges, grasses, much moss, including reindeer moss, Labrador tea, dwarf birch, crowberry, salmonberry, blueberry, mountain cranberry, fernwort, and often in dense patches, cotton sedge.

The low tundra is wetter, has more lakes (especially near the sea), has many small streams, even little channels flooded regularly by brackish tides. This tundra grows more to sedges and grasses. It provides almost limitless vision because the ground cover is so short.

Brandt (1943) described nesting regions at Igiak Bay, Alaska and nearby Hooper Bay as follows

"Vast marshes border the Askinuk Mountains on the south, and are separated from the base of the mountains by both Igiak Bay and its tributary river of the same name. The Magak Flats, as the natives call this region, are a wide expanse of countless ponds and lakes with low, level, grassy tundra between, which in the distance looks very marshy. It is not really as wet, however, as it appears, because the watery areas are well defined, while the surrounding land is high and dry."

Near Fairbanks, cranes nest in muskeg. This muskeg, sedge- and moss-grown, has scattered regions of bushes, and, often, irregular borders of spruce. Here the cranes move out onto the cultivated land during the day to feed except during the nesting season. These muskegs, varying in size, are quite similar to those throughout northern Canada south of the tundra regions.

Dementiev and Gladkov (1951) report cranes in northeastern Siberia nest in tundra, extensive marshes, the shores of lakes, rivers, and seas, and grassy gentle slopes of hills up to 1,000 meters or more above sea level. These regions are very similar to Alaska.

Along the southern regions of Banks Island, Canada, where many cranes occur, the birds use areas where the snow disappears earliest. This region slopes up from the sea, becomes quite rolling then levels off inland. It is completely treeless, almost bushless, but is grown up with very short plants. Even the willows are only a few centimeters tall.

Many regions of southern Banks Island are covered with sand, often blown into dunes and knolls—some, three to ten meters in height usually rounded on top, completely dry, and often grown up with scattered dune grass. Most of the cranes nest on these dunes.

Besides the above habitats, cranes also use extensive marches in parts of Canada and Alaska, where sedges and grasses are the predominant plants. Here the birds nest in shallow water.

PRENESTING BEHAVIOR

Sandhill Cranes arriving on their nesting grounds in the Arctic have a very limited season. They move onto their territories immediately, defending them against other cranes. When they first arrive they make a good deal of noise, and do much flying back and forth, with the paired birds constantly side by side. Since there is no darkness and little dusk in most regions, this goes on continually, but usually in spurts, with periods of rest between. During the rest periods the pair feed on their own territorial tundra.

In a few days they become quieter, and by late May in western Alaska, and early June on Banks Island, they have started to nest. Apparently birds often use the same site, or one very near it, year after year. Most nests certainly do not take very long to build for all the material in them can be dragged together by a pair in a few minutes.

At Johnson River, west of Bethel, Alaska, steep irregular banks, 12 to 15 feet, separate the low from the high tundra. Narrow irregular points, only a few meters wide, sometimes 100 meters or more in length, jut out into the low tundra. Since larger mammals seldom climb up their steep banks or walk out onto them they offer wonderful isolation for cranes to nest. A nest I found was built in a slightly hollowed-out spot, amongst the grass, moss, and crowberry. Only a few pieces of cotton sedge, some grass and moss were used. There were no bushes anywhere. The crane could see for nearly a mile in any direction. The nest measured 33 x 38 cm across.

Along the Kashunuk River, farther west in Alaska, many poorly vegetated sandy knolls dot the tundra. On top of each of these highest mounds there is usually a hollowed-out spot. On three of these, I found nests. Here the cranes placed only a few grass stalks, twigs, etc. from nearby plants, so few that usually the two eggs lay on bare ground. Again the crane could see for long distances. These nests varied between 35.1 and 43.1 cm in diameter.

The second type of nest is a haystack-like pile of grass, sedge and neighboring plants, built in a small marsh or pond. Brandt (1943) reported that 12 of these nests varied in height, 10.1 to 20.3 cm; measured 30.5 to 45.7 cm at the top; 71.1 to 121.9 at the base; and 3.8 to 7.62 cm, depth of bowl. Sauer and Urban (1964) described a similar nest along a small lake shore on St. Lawrence Island. Farther south I found a similar one near Fort Smith, Mackenzie, Northwest Territories. This was a huge pile of sedges (Carex, sp.), rushes (Scirpus validus), and grasses, 62 x 69 cm across, 8 cm tall, located in 30.5 cm of water and surrounded by hip-high dead rushes, grasses and sedges.

In the other type of nest, the setting bird remained motionless quite often, with head extended forward along the ground. I know I passed one nest several times as the bird sat before I finally found it June 8, 1946. At other nests, the birds walked away from their more conspicuous ridge nests so that it required some time to search for the proper mound. Usually the second bird was only a short distance, less than a mile, from the nest, and both birds walked around, sometimes with drooping wings, sometimes calling, but often flying about silently or calling.

At Sand Creek and Fish Lakes, east of Sachs Harbour, Banks Island, I found two different types of nests. The first was built on top of a tundra knoll in a hollowed-out spot. My description of this nest (1965) follows:

"As I walked across the tundra, suddenly a crouched crane with lowered head was running with outspread wings only 40 feet from me. The bird ran between this point and one several hundred feet away and when I left trotted parallel to me for a short distance. Only once did she call a shrill "Karoooo-karoooo-karoooo." There were many Long-tailed Jaegers (Stercorarius longicaudus) all through the surrounding tundra. As I left they began flying back toward the nest. The crane turned and immediately trotted back. Three minutes after I left it, she was standing over, and soon settling down onto the nest.

"The nest was merely a few pieces of creeping willow torn from nearby plants. It was built on top of a mound which, though small, was still the highest tundra mound in the vicinity, and not very far from the shore of a small tundra lake. The nest depression was 37 cm across, slightly depressed for the eggs.

"Between Fish Lake and Sachs River, June 13, 1964. Two eggs."

I found in June 1964 three other nests on Banks Island. They were built on top of sand dunes, each in a separate extensive dune region. Usually, however, they were not too far from surrounding tundra. All crane territories here contained some tundra, and all but one, regions of sand dunes. Amongst the dunes, I tracked cranes to their nests or scanned from the top of some high dune until one was spotted. In one such nest six miles southeast of Sachs Harbour, June 16, 1964 there were two eggs. The parent flushed at 500 feet, flew a short distance, and paced back and forth silently until I left the region. Then she uttered a series of bugles, but her mate was not seen. On June 21-22 I watched this nest from three-quarters of a mile away throughout the night. It was clear but bitter cold. The bird that was on the eggs at 8:00 P.M. was still there the following morning. At 7:32 A.M. the second bird came from the tundra about one mile away, flying directly to the nest dune. The setting bird rose, they gave the 'Unison Call,' the second bird flew back onto the tundra about three-fourths of a mile away, and the incoming bird settled immediately onto the eggs. During the night, the setting bird rose at 8:15 P.M. for one minute and at 10:55 P.M. for two and one-half minutes to work on the nest and eggs. Otherwise she did not stand during the night though the sun was quite high in the sky even at midnight.

The nest measured 43 cm in diameter, was built of pieces of dead dune grass, in the slight sandy depression on top of the highest dune. Besides the two 1964 eggs, it contained remnants of egg shells, indicating that two eggs might have hatched in the same nest in 1963.

THE EGGS

Brandt wrote that amongst the variety of shapes of these eggs, the normal type was elongate ovate to ovate, but a few were ovate pyriform, elliptical ovate, and even cylindrical ovate. Often eggs were long and slender. He wrote that the shells had a faint to marked luster with a hard, strong texture, sometimes with a slightly greasy or porous surface, and often finely pitted. Occasionally eggs had some roughness at the large end, well-defined pimples and warts, of a color similar to the egg shell.

The ground color was of two types, one greenish, the other brownish, the ratio about five to one. The eggs with a greenish ground color were smoky gray to olive or deep olive buff, while the brownish eggs were more avellaneous brown.

The primary markings ranged in size from minute dots to great hazy confluent caps; the surface was well freckled with small spots or with large blotches. These often were elongate, parallel with the long axis, but not spiraled. In some eggs blotches were fused and blurred. The primary spots ranged from rood brown to walnut brown to hazel and chestnut brown. Underlying was often a distinct purplish cast so that some eggs had a beautiful violet bloom. These markings ranged from light purple drab to pallid purple drab. Additional blotchy markings were found on other eggs, hay brown to light seal brown. Measurements of 40 eggs were: Average, 91.9x58.67 mm. Extremes, 100.58x61.7; 78.2x57.6; 88.4x63.2; 95.7x54.3 mm.

I find records of measurements of 91 Alaskan eggs which averaged, 90.82 (77.4-101.0)x57.52 (44.0-63.2) mm. while eight eggs from Banks Island averaged, 86.23 (82.4-90.0)x54.9 (52.1-57.1) mm. The average of the 99 eggs was 90.45x 57.32 mm. See Tables 5 and 6.

Two fresh Alaskan eggs averaged 152.4 grams in weight; three in mid-incubation, 145.0 grams; two near hatching, 119.1 grams; two during mid-incubation from Banks Island averaged 123.1 grams. Weight extremes in Alaska were 118.3 and 155.0 grams.

I previously published a record of an egg set in the United States National Museum (No. 22880) taken at Cape Lisburne, Alaska, latitude 69°, May 1, 1886. I feel there must be some mistake in this data for there is no other egg record after this until May 23. During many springs, cranes have not arrived at that latitude by May 1. The average of 69 other Alaskan egg dates was June 14, varying between May 23 and August 1. There were four May dates, 64 for June, one for July, one for August 1 from Alaska. On Banks Island there were six nest records with eggs, all for June, all of which hatched probably in early or mid-July. These egg dates were June 13, 13, 15, 16, 19 and 21. I previously published a record of a female bird collected along the east branch of the Mackenzie River with an egg in her ovary, June 2, 1910 (R. M. Anderson).

In 77 Alaskan sets, 68 had two eggs, nine had one, averaging 1.883 eggs. I find records of ten sets (8x2; 2x1), averaging 1.800 eggs per set from northern Canada. For the entire Arctic, of 87 sets (76x2; 11x1) the average was 1.873 eggs per set.

INCUBATION AND THE YOUNG

This bird nests where there is 24-hour daylight. Both parents incubate, the female most often at night. Most eggs hatch after June 20.

Two nests June 8 and 9, 1946 at Johnson River, Alaska, must have had had young by late June, while four nests at Chevak, Alaska that month probably hatched later for on June 21 they showed no signs of hatching nor did any of those near Sachs Harbour, Banks Island, June 13-19, 1964. Young cranes in the Arctic must grow much faster than those farther south because all cranes leave Banks Island and Siberia by late August or early September when snows begin to cover the land. Probably some young fail to mature because of the early cold.

Parents are very attentive to their young even into the winter. On February 24, 1968, I watched several pairs with young at Paul's Lake, Muleshoe National Wildlife Refuge, Texas, where they associated with the huge winter concentrations. They flew with the others to the grain fields in the morning, returning between 10 o'clock and early afternoon to drink. On arrival, they landed usually in a remote spot, some distance from the larger group. Here they kept continuous vigilance over the young. During this time the young began drinking, digging in the mud with their bills,

paying no attention to outside activities. Each family was separated a few meters from each other group, but in each group one adult always stood alert. On June 14, 1964, a group of three cranes migrated over Sachs Harbour, Banks Island. As they disappeared into the snowy interior, I was confident they were a family group from the previous summer. Yet, on June 16, 1964, I watched another pair, just east of there, drive from their territory a lone bird which could have been an offspring from the past year. All other birds I observed, either in Aaska or on Banks Island (except a small flock of non-breeders at Creamer's Dairy farm), in June were in pairs or single birds from some nesting territory. None tolerated either neighboring birds nor their last year's young on their territories.

AUTUMN MIGRATION

Dementiev and Gladkov (1951) described the Sandhill Crane departure from northeastern Siberia. About the 20th of August, the cranes in the Anadyr region, young with their parents, began to flock, and by late August started flying back. This lasted up until mid-September. Last birds were observed at the mouth of the Tanyurere River in 1931 on September 15; at Novomariinck, September 9, 1932; and at Anadyr Bay in 1930 the flight was between August 29 and September 13. In one region there was 18 cm of snow the day prior to departure.

I wrote (1949) "Jaques . . . observed about 20 Sandhill Cranes crossing Bering Strait August 27, 1928, a bright day with a cold northwest wind, following a storm during which much new snow fell on the Siberian side. He saw two more flocks, of 12 and 20, on August 30, 1928 (wind south). The intervening days had been stormy, and East Cape was again covered with new snow. All the cranes were flying southeast in the direction of the Diomedes and Cape Prince of Wales, crossing the strait at its narrowest point. Dice observed large flocks along the Kuskokwim River near Bethel, Alaska, August 18, 1912; in late August, over Nulato, Alaska, Helmericks . . . observed large flocks, three gigantic fans of them, comprising perhaps 3,000 cranes, some flying so high they were not visible except with field glasses. Charles Sheldon . . . said cranes were . . . on the Upper Toklat, near Mt. McKinley, Alaska, in the autumn . . . from September 10 to early October . . ."

Rand reported flocks over northern British Columbia in the fall of 1943: flocks were heard going over Summit Pass on September 1; near Muskwa, a flock of 150 on September 16; and seven flocks varying in size from 35 to 91 cranes, on September 17, between 9 and 5. "Some were only a couple of hundred yards up; others were nearly out of sight; all were in a V or a diagonal line formation, and the calls of even the highest came plainly to earth."

Sandhill Cranes were observed leaving Banks Island, at Castel Bay, August 24, 1952; near Back Point, August 18, 1963, while four were seen September 1, 1953, 30 miles south of Russell Point on the east coast (Manning, et al., 1956).

Farther south D. A. Munro (1950) reported Sandhill Cranes migrated through central and southern Saskatchewan, August 1 up to October 19 (1945-1947) while Stephen (1967) wrote that migration occurred between August 9 and October 30 (1961-1963), with peaks of 18,000 from the third week in August until the middle of September. He estimated the average cumulative number of crane-days before grain threshing in the Last Mountain Lake district to be about 350,000.

Sandhill Cranes cause damage in autumn migration to the Saskatchewan spring wheat before it ripens in early September. Since cranes begin arriving by early August and this peak is reached long before September 1, damage is quite severe. The worst damage is in the Last Mountain Lake region. Recent means of combating this have been the use of automatic acetylene exploders and an open season on the birds. The cranes causing this damage are *G.c.canadensis* and *G.c.rowani*. Grain was found in gullets of 93 percent of 190 shot specimens; food consumption of captive wild cranes indicated that one bushel of wheat would supply food for at least 200 cranes for one day (Stephen, *loc cit.*). He also stated that the high-

est number of cranes observed foraging in grain fields was 4,365 per 100 acres, although the most frequent size was 100 or less per quarter section. A mean distance of 5.79 $\pm$ 0.1622 (SE) feet was observed between individual cranes, but the space occupied by individuals was inadequate to describe fully the observed dispersion of cranes. He estimated the minimum foraging requirements for the region to be 412 acres. Cranes as usual foraged on closest fields first. The cost of operating an acetylene exploder was $43.83 annually per quarter section; total for the region, $3,769. If left undisturbed, the cranes would produce damage amounting to $5,843.

In the Horsehead Lake region, North Dakota, Carl Madsen summarized his 1965 study (1967): Fall migrants fed almost exclusively on grain, much more rarely a few insects. Wheat, barley, and possiby corn were selected grains. Even though there was an abundance of wild seed, cranes did not feed on grass and other seeds. They fed on both harvested and unharvested fields. In the unharvested fields they did some damage; in the harvested ones they ate only the scattered waste grain. During years of normal weather conditions they did little damage, but if crops were late considerable damage could be done. Damage was cut to a minimum when desired grains were not raised near the roost regions. These cranes flew from one to five miles each day from the night roost to grain fields. It also helped if harvested fields were left unplowed until all grain fields were harvested, thus giving the birds waste grain on which to feed. The majority of his cranes proved to be *G.c.rowani* and a few *G.c.canadensis*.

FOOD

Much has been discussed on food during autumn in migration. In winter these cranes feed considerably on grain, including milo, kaffir and sorghum in New Mexico and Texas; on fall wheat in California; in all regions on some insects including grasshoppers when they are common. They browse also on alfalfa fields. In spring, in Nebraska, they feed mostly on corn left on the ground from the previous fall's harvest. And as they proceed northward corn and wheat are used considerably along with browsing and a few insects.

When they reach Alaska and Banks Island there are a few insects in evidence but their chief diet seems to be browsed vegetation. They are supposed to eat lemmings when these are common and they will eat, if available, eggs, embryos, and chicks of willow ptarmigan (*Lagopus lagopus*) and blue goose (*Chen caerulescens*), breaking up the eggs and dismembering the chicks prior to swallowing them (Harvey, *et al*, Mss.). They also report the cranes along western Hudson Bay ate corms of sedge (*Carex*) or cottongrass (*Eriophorum*).

Manning, *et al.*, (1956) reported that stomachs of birds examined contained nothing or a small amount of unrecognizable vegetable matter. The one I collected in 1964 contained a small amount of unrecognizable vegetable matter and a few small pebbles. In late summer many berries are gleaned from the bearberry and crowberry plants on the tundra.

DISTRIBUTION

In summer this subspecies has been recorded from Siberia at Anadyr Bay, along the Anadyr River, the Anadyr Mountains, Cape Tschukoss, Providence Bay, Seniavine Strait, Koljuchin Bay, Cape Bolschoi Baronowski, Balagan, Sebddij Strait, East Cape, possibly lower Kamchatka and the mouth of the Kolyma River; Wrangel Island; from Bering Sea Islands: St. Lawrence Islands, St. Matthew Island, St. Paul Island, Nunivak Island, and the near Islands, Aleutians; from Alaska, from Point Barrow, Meade River, Chipp River, Colville River, Humphrey Point, Wainwright, Cape Lisburne, Tigara, Noatak River, Kowak River, Cape Prince of Wales, Lopp Lagoon, Wales, Cape Mountain, Teller, north of Nome, Norton Sound, Black River, Hooper Bay, Igiak Bay, Chevak, Kashunuk River, Nushagak River, Johnson River, St. Michael, Quinhagak, Goodnews Bay, Circle, Ft. Yukon (1953 and 1954, Alaska Nest Record Cards), Kotzebue Sound, lower Colville

River, Humphrey Point, Marten Lake (1962, Alaska Nest Record Card), Umiat, Upper Mouth Birch Creek (Lat. 66°31′ N.; Long. 116°05′—1962, Alaska Nest Record Cards), College (1967, Alaska Nest Record Card), Minto Lakes (Alaska Nest Record Card—thanks to Dr. Brina Kessell).

In northern Canada the subspecies has been found along the entire Arctic shore, nesting in favorable places. Observations and nests have been recorded from Yukon Territory at Shoalwater Bay, Tent Island, North Coast, while in Mackenzie from the Mackenzie River Delta, at Tuktuyaktok, East Branch, Liverpool Bay, Harrowby Bay, Baillie Island, Cape Bathurst, Lower Anderson River, Langton Bay, Franklin Bay, Cape Parry, Wise Point, Croker River, Bernard Harbor, Peel River, Ft. Wrigley, Ft. Simpson, Big Island, Great Slave Lake, Mission Syne, Slave River Delta, Buffalo Lake, Nyarling and Little Buffalo River, Wood Buffalo Park, Thelon River, Prairie Lake, Thelon Game Sanctuary.

In Franklin the species has been recorded at Banks Island: Mercy Bay, Cape Kellett, Sachs Harbour, Kellett River, Bernard and Thomsen Rivers, Sachs River (Manning, *et al*, 1956), Fish Lakes, Sachs River east of Sachs Harbour, Sand Creek (Walkinshaw, 1965), from Victoria Island at Walker Bay and Wollaston Peninsula, from Melville Sound, Parry Bay, Boothia, Felix Harbour, Melville Peninsula, Igloolik, Crozier River, Iglulik Island, Nerdlernaktoq Island, Frozen Strait, Garry Bay, Bylot Island, Baffin Island at Navy Board Inlet, Pond Inlet, Cumberland and Exeter Sounds, Kingwah and Kingnite Fiords, Kangerkslukjuak and Piling.

In Keewatin the birds have been observed from Perry River, Queen Maud Gulf, Beverly Lake, at Hudson Bay: Mistake Bay, Cape Eskimo, Nunalla, Cape Herd, Southampton Island, Cape Low, 4-Rivers, Ranger River, Coral Inlet, South Bay, Coral Inlet, Koodlootak River, 6 miles west of Boas River, Roe's Welcome Shore, Bay of God's Mercy, Monica Point, Ranger Brook, Coats Island, McConnell River.

Sandhill Cranes (subsp.?) have also been found or nested in southern Alaska, at Kupreanof Island, Big John Pass, between Kupreanof and

Kuiu Island, Sergief Island and Kalgin Island (Gabrielson and Lincoln, 1959), in Wood-Buffalo Park, Alberta, on the Slave River, the Alberta Plateau and the Peace River and a breeding female with two eggs of this supspecies was collected at Crescent Lake, Yorkton while many records are available from Churchill, Manitoba and some from Ilford (Walkinshaw, 1949).

In migration birds have been taken as far east as Rhode Island, South Carolina, and Prince Edward Island. In winter the subspecies has been recorded from California: at San Francisco Bay region, Merced County, San Joaquin Valley, Corcoran, Kings County, Los Angeles, Newport, Orange County, Colorado River, and Salton Sea, Imperial County.

These birds were found near Tucson, Pima County, Arizona, and records from New Mexico and Texas are given earlier. In Mexico, specimens have been taken at Cerro Prieto, Baja California; at Rio Verde, San Luis Potosi, and at La Barca, Jalisco. Annabel (1966) tells of hunting these birds at Campo 12, near Huatabambo, Sonora where they also occur throughout the winter.

Robert Wheeler (Wheeler and Lewis, 1970), with a group of six assistants operated some three to six rocket-net traps and banded 542 cranes most of which were *G.c.canadensis* along the Platte River, Overton, Elm Creek, Bertrand, Hershey and other regions, in Nebraska, 1965-1968 inclusive. Already some returns have come in.

Their inventory of cranes in the springs of 1957-1970 along the Platte River region were: March 28-29, 1957, 180,000; April 7-8, 1958, 240,-800; March 21-22, 1959, 147,496; April 4, 1960, 125,870; April 21, 1961, 136,276; March 21, 1963, 101,925; March 30, 1964, 156,028; March 30-31, 1965, 80,315; March 24-25, 1966, 123,087; March 22-23, 1967, 126,043; March 22, 1968, 169,194; April 2, 1969, 154,978; and March 26-27, 1970, 193,600. They wrote Crane distribution is not uniform along the river. Three regions were used. The greatest was along the Platte River from Grand Island westward to Lexington, with an average of 1,520 cranes per lineal mile; second between North Platte and Sutherland, with an average of 1,733 cranes per lineal mile and third on a 5-mile stretch at the west end of L. McConaughy and Lewellen where on the North Platte River slightly more than 2,000 cranes occurred.

THE CANADIAN SANDHILL CRANE
Grus canadensis rowani

Grus canadensis rowani. L. H. Walkinshaw, *Canadian Field-Naturalist*, 1965, *79*, 181-184.

Type locality. Fawcett, Alberta, between the Pembina and Athabasca Rivers.

Type specimen, Chicago Natural History Museum, Chicago, Illinois, June 1, 1943, male.

	Date		Location	
Banded	Recovered	Banded Nebraska	Recovered	
March 28, 1966	September 5, 1966	Overton	4 miles SW Wadena, Saskatchewan, Canada	
March 26, 1968	November 9, 1968	Elm Creek	Madera, Chihuahua, Mexico	
March 25, 1968	November 8, 1968	Elm Creek	15 miles SW Littlefield, Texas	
March 20, 1968	September 16, 1968	Bertrand	Delta Junction, Alaska	
March 22, 1968	November 9, 1968	Elm Creek	8 miles W Littlefield, Texas	
March 21, 1968	June, 1968	Elm Creek	Tuktoyaktuk, North West Territories, Canada	
March 25, 1968	November 16, 1968	Elm Creek	10 miles E Bula, Texas	
March 24, 1968	December 15, 1968	Elm Creek	32 miles NW Big Springs, Texas	

Migrating Sandhill Cranes in southern Saskatchewan in spring are of two races. A smaller form, *G.c.canadensis*, remains into late May at times but passes northward generally in early May to the Arctic. *G.c.rowani*, the Canadian Sandhill Crane, which comes early, remains only a few days before proceeding into the central portion of the Province, into central Alberta or central Manitoba. Some of this form may occur in eastern British Columbia and northern Ontario. Stephen (1967) found only 0.2 to 2 percent of cranes in southern Saskatchewan were *G.c. tabida*. He believed *G.c.canadensis* and *G.c.rowani* were indistinguishable. From specimens he and others took, the bill measurements (males) showed about 56 percent of birds were *G.c.rowani* while about 72 percent fitted into this category from measurements taken from the posterior edge of the nares to the bill tip; a little higher from his tarsal measurements (these he measured differently from the normal technique so that they were longer than usual). Even then 19 percent of them fitted in with *G.c.canadensis*.

I have previously shown (1965) that with the available small group from museum collections, the summer birds of the central Provinces were definitely larger than the summer birds from the Arctic. From specimen records, spring migrants move from eastern Texas (a few from eastern New Mexico and west Texas, rarely from western Louisiana) northward into central Nebraska. Here the birds near Grand Island and Hastings region seem to be larger than those farther west. Then they move across South and North Dakota into Saskatchewan and southern Manitoba, then onto the breeding grounds in April or early May. Fall migration follows a reverse pattern (see Huey, 1960; Boeker, Huey, and Uzzell, 1962; Buller and Boeker, 1965; Madsen, 1967; Buller, 1967).

Prenesting behavior is little different than that of other cranes. The birds move directly onto their territories and in a very short time begin nesting. In the southern portion of their range, these cranes nest in large open marshes often surrounded by open fields or prairies. Farther north they nest in muskeg country or in open marshes surrounded by forest.

A typical prairie marsh at Saltcoats, Saskatchewan, irregular in contour, is covered during nesting time with shallow water but in spring is covered nearly knee high with dead sedges and grasses. The marsh offers good nesting cover; the neighboring fields are feeding regions.

Baker and I (1946) described a typical muskeg bog at Fawcett, Alberta. Here habitats were: running water (rivers); open water (lakes); marsh; muskeg; lowland brush; spruce-tamarack, aspen; jack-pine ridges. The muskeg is generally surrounded by the jack-pine ridges, open water, spruce-tamarack forest or lowland brush or combinations of these. It is covered heavily with moss, through which often protrude small willows (*Salix* sp.), dwarf birch (*Betula* sp.), with crisscrossing or parallel rows of tamarack ridges only a few inches above the treacherous bog regions. In between the scattered tamaracks are a few dwarf birches producing necessary nesting cover. The cranes often nest right on these dry ridges. There is a great similarity between these and the crane regions of northern Sweden. But one nest we found was on a hummocky island in open water at the edge of the muskeg.

THE NEST

The nests in the prairie regions, some in open marshes farther north, are haystack-like piles of dead grasses, sedges, and nearby plants hidden in shallow water amongst the standing, dead rushes, etc. A similar nest in Wood-Buffalo Park I have described under *G.c.canadensis*.

The two nests were found at Fawcett, Alberta, I have previously described (1949) along with others found by William Rowan and Frank L. Farley: "I found an egg at Fawcett, Alberta, that was on no nest at all. It had been laid on a small island covered with thick short grass. William Rowan (letter), in describing the many nests he found in this region, said that if the cranes 'used 50 straws at a time they treated themselves generously; they hardly make a nest, in fact.' Frank L. Farley (letter) reported of the nests he found at Fawcett: 'They are nothing but about twenty bits of snake grass laid crisscross on a narrow ridge that is common on the northern muskegs.' A nest found by Bernard W. Baker during May 1942 in this region consisted of a few sticks of the surrounding dwarf birch about 20 to 45 cm. long and many wads of the moss that grew all about. (This nest measured about 45 cm across and was perfectly dry but near boggy water.) A nest found by Frank L. Farley farther south in Alberta, at Spotted Lake, was more typical of those in the prairie country; it was a large mound of material."

THE EGGS

In color, shape, and markings these eggs differ little from those of the other Sandhill Cranes. I am including the records here from British Columbia as well as those farther east in Canada. Five British Columbia egg records average May 25 (extremes May 9 and June 15). All contained two eggs. Regions where cranes have been found in summer in British Columbia are: Lulu Island, Quinsam Lake, V.I., Oyster River, V.I., Bobtail Lake, Punthesakut Lake (*see* Munro and Cowan, 1947; Walkinshaw, 1949).

The earliest egg record for Alberta is May 3, the latest June 8 (average, May 17). There were 10 sets of 2 eggs; one set of 1 egg. Three sets hatched May 28-29; May 29-30; June 7-8. Actual nesting regions were Athabaska, Spotted Lake, Innisfail, Fawcett.

In Saskatchewan egg records varied between April 11 (1914) at Grayson and July 1 at Yorkton, averaging May 20. Out of 32 complete egg sets, there were three of one and 29 of two eggs. Breeding regions were Lac Ila a la Crosse, Kutawagan Lake, Big Quill Lake, Dafoe, Calder, Grayson, Balgonie, Tyvan, Fillmore, Instow, Saskatchewan plains, Willowbrook, Crescent Lake, Carlton, Rokeby Marsh, Saltcoats, Yorkton, Rousay Lake, McNichol Slough (See Houston, 1949; Walkinshaw, 1960).

The average of six Manitoba nests was May 31, May 19 to June 12). In five complete sets, four were of two eggs, one of one egg. Breeding regions were Lake St. Martin, Carman, Sperling, Boyne Marsh, Eden and Norfolk.

Egg records from western central Canada ranged between April 11 and July 1. There were five sets of one egg; 48 of two eggs. The average measurements of 22 eggs from Alberta, Saskatchewan, and Manitoba was 91.69 (85.3-102.0) X59.27 (54.6-65.0) mm. Three eggs, all near hatching time, averaged 173.0 grams in weight.

THE YOUNG

Young resemble the other chicks at hatching and thereafter. Hatching dates for Alberta are given above; for Saskatchewan, downy chicks have been found at Dafoe, June 24, 1915; at Kutawagan Lake, June 5, 1920; and at Calder, June 20, 1945; at Carman, Manitoba on June 21, 1901. See Table 7.

FOOD

A great deal has been written about the food of this and the former subspecies in Saskatchewan, (Munro, 1950; Stephen, 1967) and in North Dakota (Buller, 1967; Madsen, 1967). With the former bird they do considerable damage on wheat in Saskatchewan, some in Manitoba, and some in Alberta in the fall in late August and early September. Arriving in North Dakota they usually find the wheat harvested but do damage to corn. Farther south they disperse more, and so they do not do as much damage as does *G.c. canadensis* in winter. Also, there are not as many of them as of that subspecies.

This bird winters apparently in southeastern Texas, Aransas Refuge, the Brownsville region, even to southwestern Louisiana (spec. ROMZ). Less often they are found in western Texas and eastern New Mexico. Distribution in Mexico is not known.

THE GREATER SANDHILL CRANE
Grus canadensis tabida
Megalornis canadensis tabida. J. L. Peters, *Auk*, 1925, 42 , 122.
Type locality. Valley of the South Fork of the Humboldt River, Nevada.

Type specimen, May 19, 1859, male. Museum of Comparative Zoology, Harvard University, Cambridge, Massachusetts, U.S.A.

Greater Sandhill Cranes, largest of the entire Sandhill group, are the breeding cranes of northern United States—approximately Latitude 40° (Nevada) to 50° (southern British Columbia, possibly still in Manitoba and northern Minnesota), and from Longitude 84° (Michigan) to 122° W. (central Oregon and northern California; British Columbia). The birds formerly nesting in southern Ontario were this form. Those now in northern Ontario are not known but indications are that they are *G.c.rowani* (specimen NMC, from A. E. Allin, letter).

Although roving cranes are found in summer, such as in Tennessee (Butts, 1936; Edney, 1940), the majority of Greater Sandhill Cranes migrate earlier in spring and later in fall than do more northern birds. Many Greaters are nesting, some even have young, when *G.c.canadensis* leaves southern Canada in spring.

The winter range of the Greater Sandhill Crane has been little known. It was surmised eastern birds wintered in Florida (Walkinshaw, 1960), wintering on Payne's Prairie (six miles south of Gainesville), probably more on the Kissimmee Prairie, Florida, possibly some in the Okefenokee Swamp, southern Georgia. There are winter specimens in both the American Museum of Natural History and the Museum of Comparative Zoology with light gray occiputs, taken in Florida.

During recent years, cranes have been observed regularly flying in March over Gainesville Florida and central Georgia, at times in eastern Tennessee, across Indiana and in fall a reverse flight in October and November. One fall bird, now in the Smoky Mountain National Park, from Knoxville, Tennessee, was *G.c.tabida* (I examined the bird). More proof came in 1968-1969. Lovett E. Williams, Jr. marked and banded about 100 Sandhill Cranes on Payne's Prairie, Florida. Two of these marked birds were seen in March 1968 at Boyce Lake, Washtenaw County, Michigan (by Dr. Miles D. Pirnie and Ronald Hoffman), and I

observed two in the same region, August 11, 1968. Ronald Hoffman observed two more July 6, 1969 at Phyllis Haehnle Memorial Sanctuary, Jackson County, Michigan, and others have been observed in Tennessee and Minnesota. Birds were marked with aluminum bands above the leg-joint and also with green streamers on the wing.

During March-May 1970 four marked cranes, including one pair and two other individuals were found in N.E. Jackson County, N.W. Washtenaw County, Michigan all very localized while in marshes one and a half to five miles away and farther no marked birds were found. These birds, showed their affinities to each other during both summer and winter for all were marked at Gainesville, Florida in winter.

Behavior in winter differs little from that of local Florida birds. During daytime they feed on the prairies; during the night they roost in some shallow pond or marsh. When they fly north, many Florida Cranes already have young, or are on eggs. Field differentiation of races is impossible.

Greater Sandhill Cranes arrive in late September and during October at Bosque del Apache National Wildlife Refuge, Socorro, New Mexico. They roost at night in shallow marshes and ponds, standing in six to eight inches of water, usually a short distance from shore or over the entire pond. They fly between 4 P.M. and dark to roost, usually arriving between 6 and 7:30 P.M. Here they do considerable calling until after dark, when they become quieter. Near daylight, all seem to break into trumpeting again. Shortly they begin flying to their feeding ground, in groups of two to 15 individuals. By ten o'clock they have all departed. They feed on mature wheat, barley, or corn, crops which have been harvested. They browse on alfalfa and eat some insects, such as grasshoppers. They feed from one-half to four miles from the roost region until about noon, when they begin flying back to the roost marsh for drinking water. These groups continue to fly back and forth all afternoon. A few roost in family groups, but the majority roost and feed in a large flock. It is not uncommon to find the entire group feeding in one grain field or roosting in one pond. By mid-February they start northward, the big migration following immediately, while late birds have been seen on March 1 (1963). First autumn birds appear between September 24 and 26, at the latest September 27 (1963). Numbers vary in winter, but concentrations of 5,500 to 7,000 occurred in the winter of 1964. A few Lesser Sandhill Cranes have been captured here, but the majority have been Greaters. (Refuge personnel.)

Sandhill Cranes concentrate in large numbers at Jasper-Pulaski Game Preserve, northern Indiana; late September to early December in the fall; early March to mid-April in spring. Southern Michigan cranes arrive almost simultaneously, depart later than fall Indiana peaks. Indiana specimens have been found to be *G.c.tabida*. The Jasper-Pulaski region is in direct line between central Florida and central Wisconsin. Mumford (1950) and I (1949, 1950b, 1956) have given these spring records. This is only a stopping place.

At Jasper-Pulaski cranes feed in fall on wheat and corn fields, harvested earlier that year. In spring they feed on corn, left from the past fall, on pasture-lands, or insects which are scarce. They roost at night in a shallow lake on the refuge; feeding during daytime on the refuge or neighboring farms, flying back and forth morning and evening. Sometimes they feed five miles from the roost, again one-half mile. No one knows how many individuals visit the refuge, how long individual birds remain, nor the rate of turnover. Peaks occur in late March in spring; late October or early November in fall.

In Indiana, where Greater Sandhill Cranes are observed regularly in migration, Mumford (1950) and Gregory (1967) have given many notes on behavior. Gregory stated that he has seen flocks of cranes flying over his orchard 2½ miles southwest of Mooresville, Morgan County, on many occasions. In spring flight occurs between March 11 and 27, chiefly between 11:15 A.M. and dusk. Average date was March 17. In fall 15 flocks (average size, 42.7 (8-100) were observed or heard flying between October 17 (1966) until December 18 (1966). Fall flights were always seen on clear, relatively calm days, usually within 24 hours of a cold front passage. Spring flights could not be associated with any frontal system, and the cloud factor and wind direction varied. Fall groups flew higher (some out of sight) than spring groups, and flocks were larger. There was more confusion in the fall as birds often circled higher and higher (apparently searching for better thermals). Spring flocks fly directly toward Jasper-Pulaski Game Preserve (about 90 miles NNW). Fall cranes are never seen before 11 A.M. and not after 3 P.M. (except for 1964), apparently leaving Jasper-Pulaski during the morning, after they eat. Spring birds fly between mid-morning and late afternoon.

I observed six Sandhill Cranes, definitely migrating, in Osceola County, Florida, at 10 A.M., March 15, 1967. Flying slightly west of north at about 1200 feet, they crossed the north-south length of Alligator Lake. Approaching the north end they descended some and at 400 feet crossed the highway, then disappeared to the north.

Nearly always in March, sometimes in late February, cranes have been seen migrating over central Georgia. They usually were flying between 150 and 700 feet elevation and to the northwest. Few cranes in Georgia (except in Okefenokee) are observed on the ground.

In eastern Tennessee a few cranes have been observed in the air; a higher percentage on the ground. The same holds true in the fall. In the fall of 1942 a flock of 50 remained three days on a wheat field near Knoxville. The farmer who shot one from the flock did not know the birds. The specimen was placed in the Smoky Mountain National Park Museum. I observed it and confirmed that it was *G.c.tabida*. There are very few records from western Tennessee, a few from Kentucky, western Ohio and western Illinois, but many from Indiana. East and west of this region cranes are extremely rare, except on the Great Plains, through Rocky Mountain valleys, and along the west coast.

Greater Sandhill Cranes arrived at Malheur National Wildlife Refuge, Oregon, over an eleven-year period, between February 7 (1959) and February 28 (1957) (average February 19) (Littlefield, 1967). At Ruby Lakes National Wildlife Refuge, Nevada, Greater Sandhills arrived on territories, March 12, 1964. March 11, 1965, March 14, 1966; March 11, 1967; February 29, 1968) (neary one month later than at Malheur—Donald E. Lewis, Refuge Manager). At Red Rocks Lake National Wildlife Refuge, Montana, first birds were observed April 3, 1964; April 12, 1965; March 28, 1966; April 6, 1967; and April 9, 1968, sometimes when snow was still two feet deep. At Jasper-Pulaski Game Preserve, Indiana, cranes first appear in late February or early March, while heavy concentrations occur in late March and early April. In central Wisconsin cranes arrive later than in Michigan, and even later usually in Minnesota. At Reesor, Ontario, John Enns (letter) reported cranes arrive in mid-May when it is still cold.

Usually cranes fly over Michigan when the weather is good, but once I heard a group flying northward, March 27, 1932 over Woodbury, Ionia County. It was a cloudy, stormy day; the birds were among the lower clouds.

PAIR FORMATION

I wrote (1965):

"Little is known about pair formation in cranes, a few things are evident. Young cranes, coddled for their first year, are under constant supervision of their parents. As the coming breeding season arrives, these young suddenly find themselves turned upon and driven from the home territory by their parents. They then soon form small flocks which feed on open fields and marshes during the day and roost at night in some isolated marsh, remote from other crane territories. In these flocks, apparently, new pairs are formed. When about three years old, these newly paired cranes depart from the nonbreeding flocks.

"*Establishment of territory: Breeding age.* Before they nest, these young mated birds often spend one or more summers on their new territories, usually marshes uninhabited by other cranes. Thus there is no defense problem. Some times, however, they enter a marsh where there is a crane population. Since the breeding pairs are busy for about four months, incubating eggs and caring for young, the newly formed pairs have the advantage. Although driven away many times they persistently return to their favorite niche and in time are accepted. During 1961 a group of nonbreeding sandhill cranes . . . roosted in the center of the Haehnle Sanctuary, Michigan. One pair, accepted finally by surrounding pairs, remained during the late summer. During April and early May 1962 a pair, probably this new one, worked diligently day after day building a nest. They maintained this territory throughout the nesting season but never had any eggs.

"Griswold (1962) wrote that cranes sometimes lay fertile eggs when three years old, but that the average in zoos is probably closer to six. Sieber (1932) reported that a tame male European Crane (*Grus grus grus*) bred in Germany when five years old. Two Michigan sandhill crane eggs (same nest) sent to the Audubon Park Zoo, New Orleans, Louisiana, by the U. S. Fish and Wildlife Service in connection with their whooping crane studies, produced two young, which four years later produced two healthy offspring of their own (These also nested three years later and produced one young.).

"Once a territory has been established, a crane pair will apparently continue using it unless there is too much disturbance. Although few wild cranes have been banded, they apparently return to their same nesting marsh for many years (Sieber, 1932). From the location of nests, the similarity of eggs, the behavior of the adults, the majority of crane pairs at Haehnle Sanctuary seem to be the same each spring.

"Cranes usually remain paired for life. Pratt (1963) wrote that Fred W. Stark had at San Antonio Zoological Gardens, Texas, a pair of sarus cranes that produced 43 young during 21 years, 1943-1963. In 1963 the female died. Two weeks later the male acquired a new mate. Sieber (1932) had a wild crane which nested near his house in Germany for many years and had, during this period, three different mates.

"Migratory cranes return to Michigan in pairs.

Although gregarious in fall and winter, and though they may return in flocks, they immediately disperse onto the breeding territories in pairs. At Haehnle Sanctuary, Michigan, Harold Wing found no cranes the night of March 10, 1961. Early the following morning I found all six pairs on territory. On March 11, 1964, I found two pairs on territory.

"Between arrival and nesting, most cranes are very active and at times very noisy. They defend their territories with considerable vigor. Except for feeding periods they spend most of their time on their territories. On three occasions, all very warm days, I observed pairs copulating at Haehnle Sanctuary—once on March 18 and twice on March 30—always on their own territories."

Twice since then I have observed copulation—on April 4, 1964 (two pairs). The times were 6:30, 7:20, 7:59, 8:59 and 9:14 A.M. In each case the female approached the male and with her head and neck held out and forward at a 45 degree angle, she stood with outspread wings in an erect position. The male approached swiftly and as she crouched, he hopped gently onto her rump. With wings half-spread and slowly beating, he copulated with her. In only a few seconds they stood near each other and preened.

Littlefield and Ryder (1968) observed copulation 25 times and throughout daytime. Usually the female initiated copulation but at times the male did so. They also observed dancing associated with copulation, once preceding and following, once following copulation only. Normally there was no dancing.

TERRITORIES

Most crane territories fall under Type A, defined by Hinde (1956): "A large breeding region within which nesting, courtship, and mating and most food-seeking usually occur." There are some differences. It is apparent that cranes require three separate territorial divisions (1) A nesting division (2) a roosting spot, and (3) a feeding division. Each section depends on the density of breeding cranes, there may be variations during

the breeding season also. When there is one pair to a marsh, there is no problem. But in some of the larger, more favorable marshes, several crane pairs may nest in close proximity. During recent years the Phyllis Haehnle Memorial Sanctuary, Michigan, has been such a marsh. Here five to seven breeding pairs of Sandhill Cranes nest each summer within an area of much less than one square mile (640 acres). But even here territories have apparently been maintained for many years. The boundaries vary little from year to year. The actual marshy portion used has been 260 acres. The average wet marsh territorial size during the five-year study period, 1959 through 1963, was 43.5 (8-67) acres.

The average territorial size of 76 Lower Peninsula nest regions has been 132 (8-480) acres and for 13 Upper Peninsula pairs, 210 (20-450) acres. Some of these larger marshes have been completely occupied. (In Mississippi and Florida, seven Florida Sandhill Crane territorial sizes averaged about 103 (15-300) acres. Four in Idaho averaged about 161 acres.)

In Phyllis Haehnle Memorial Sanctuary, Michigan, over a period of 11 years, 260 acres of wet marsh were used each year, except for three years, when nonbreeders utilized a few acres in the center of the lake which were little used by breeding cranes anyway. Additional drier marshes were used to some extent so that the total wet and dry marsh used each year varied from around 300 to 340 acres. These drier regions were used more after the young hatched. Five to seven pairs of cranes nested during this period in the 260 acres so that an average of 71 territories (counting the territory of each pair each year) was 39.62 acres (1,603 acres) ranging between 8 and 67 acres and at times up to 90 acres wet and dry land combined. One territory (A-1) has been the same from 1948 until 1969 except for 8 acres taken by a pair during the 1959 season. This pair remained there only the one year then disappeared. Territory C-3 is slightly larger in 1969 than it was in 1959. Territory G-7 was enlarged from about 25 acres in 1948 to 57 acres for many years, then narrowed down again 1966-1969 until the birds were using about 25 acres in 1968-1969.

The territory was still adequate for food and other activities, and had one of the best regions for nesting in the entire lake, a patch of cattails just about the right size. Pair E-5 used 57 acres in 1959 which decreased to about 29 acres in 1967 and 20 in 1968 and 1969. The last two years they had no eggs even though they built a nest in 1968. Pair D-4 moved in next to E-5 in 1961 and gradually usurped some of their territory and then some of G-7's territory, so that they had 60 acres, more land than both of the others in 1968-1969. The territory of Pair B-2 has changed periodically, for different pairs have moved in next to them and usurped varying parts of their territory. The last pair in 1968 were still there in 1969. These strange pairs often used different sections of B-2 territory, sometimes a little from D-4. They differed in behavior and the eggs were different so that it appeared as though they were there at the most only three years. Some years there were no birds here at all.

Littlefield and Ryder (1968) wrote: "The size of territories varied with the density of birds in a particular area. The smallest territory was three acres, while the largest contained 168 acres. Eight territories were mapped on aerial photographs (as I did) . . the average size was 62.0 acres."

Fresh water (pH 5-7.6) is essential on crane territories. In a marsh or bog, water most often surrounds the nest. Preferred depths are between two inches and two or three feet. This offers protection to the nest and a roosting site. Plants, usually dead during the nesting season, consist chiefly of sedges (*Carex* and *Scirpus* several species), grasses (many species), cattails (*Typha latifolia*, less often *T.angustifolia*), rushes (*Scirpus acuta* in Oregon; *S.validus* in some Idaho and Michigan marshes), and reeds (*Phragmites communis*). Central Wisconsin marshes are similar to southern Michigan marshes, but in northern Michigan, although a few are similar, most crane breeding regions are bogs. Plants here consist of Labrador tea (*Ledum groenlandicum*), leatherleaf (*Chamaedaphne calyculata*), swamp laurel (*Kalmia polifolia*), bog rosemary (*Andromeda glaucophylla*), trailing arbutus (*Epigaea repens*) wintergreen (*Gaultheria procumbens*) while

neighboring trees are tamarack (*Larix laricina*), black spruce (*Pinea mariana*) and pines (*Pinus resinosa, P.banksiana,* and *P.Strobus.*)

C. A. Hurd (letter, June 5, 1969) wrote that in Routt County, Colorado, willows (*Salix* sp.) help produce better isolation to nesting Sandhill Cranes. Here the birds nest year after year in the exact spots they have in previous years, in mountain valleys far from most humans.

Littlefield and Ryder (1968) wrote that most Oregon nests are located in pure stands of mixed of dead bulrushes (*Scirpus acuta*), *Sparganium eurycarpum*, or cattail (*Typha latifolia*).

Concerning the roosting spot on the territory, I wrote (1965):

"Usually the roosting spot is part of the nesting territory. It is used for daytime roosting where the birds rest and preen and for nighttime roosting where the non-incubating bird sleeps. It is usually covered with shallow water, 4 to 12 inches deep. Often it is surrounded by deeper water or large expanses of marsh. Many times patches of sedges, grasses, rushes, reeds, and/or cattails grow over and around it, usually dead ones from the previous season. During warm years, new plants also cover it. The exact roosting spot may vary by a few feet or more night by night, or be different for the two birds.

"Sometimes the cranes fly to the roosting spot; sometimes they wade. At Haehnle Sanctuary, Michigan, the Greater Sandhill Cranes went to the roosting spot long before dark. On 16 different nights during late April and early May (1959-1963) the average time was 5:59 P.M. (extremes 3:40 to 7:30 P.M.). In addition the roosting spot was used often during the day. (During the five-year period the average night roost was 461 (59-916) feet from the nest site."

Concerning the Feeding Territory, I also wrote (*loc cit*):

"Cranes feed considerably on their nesting territory and at times near the roosting site. They, however, often feed some distance from the nest. This more remote feeding territory, often a field, may be less than one-half mile or much more from the actual nesting territory. During the prenesting periods both cranes of the pair often fly in early morning to these more distant feeding territories. After incubation begins, each takes its turn, while the other bird is incubating. After the young hatch most feeding is done near the nest, but the birds often lead the young into areas where food is more plentiful.

"At the south end of Haehnle Sanctuary, there is one extremely favorable feeding area often used by three pairs of cranes. Often there are skirmishes in this area and the pairs seem to regard it as subdivided, but they do wander over boundaries and at times two or three birds may be feeding within a short distance of each other. The superabundance of food here is apparently the reason the Mud Lake marsh is used by so many crane pairs. Here frogs (*Hyla crucifer*; *rana pipiens*) are numerous, and several snails (*Helisoma trivolvis*; *H.anceps*; *H.campanulatum*) are exceedingly abundant. Regardless of this communal feeding territory the cranes feed also in neighboring fields, each pair using a separate field. Sometimes to get to these fields they fly completely over the territory of another pair or pairs."

DEFENSE METHODS

"Small birds advertise their presence on their presence on their territories by singing. Cranes do not have a true song, but make their presence known by a penetrating call. When several pairs nest in close proximity . . . such as the Sandhill Crane at Haehnle Sanctuary, many of them give the call each morning during the breeding season. One pair often calls in unison and immediately all or nearly all others respond. In marshes remote from other breeding cranes, the nesting pair may not call for days. Here they are often very quiet."

DISPLAY

Prior to the nesting season, cranes are often very conspicuous, they call regularly, often dance and display in front of each other. Both birds enter into the dance. This is a series, sometimes only a hop or two, again very many, stiff-legged jumps into the air with half outspread wings, often accompanied with much bowing of the head. Usually they leap four to twelve feet into the air, landing somewhere near their mate, over and over again. At times the second bird enters the dance and both bound up and down, bowing and jumping for several seconds or minutes. Although cranes do this in winter in their gregarious flocks, they most often do it more just prior to nesting. Captive cranes sometimes can be stimulated to dance by a person copying the same movements.

DEFENSE

When a strange crane lands on a territory of another, the owner shows sudden concern. Sometimes he moves quickly toward the stranger. With bill pointing groundward, neck arched swan-like, inner secondaries raised over his back, he struts stiff-legged toward the interloper. If the bird is from a far distant territory, or some other marsh, he usually flies immediately. If from a neighboring territory, usually he does not fly. At this time they sometimes face each other in combat using beating wings, stabbing bill, and clawing feet. The battle ordinarily lasts only a few seconds, after which both birds usually retreat into their own territories. Evidence that damage can be inflicted, however, was when a young male was killed by an old established male at W. K. Kellogg Bird Sanctuary (R. D. VanDeusen, verbal).

Actual approach for defense is accomplished by one of two methods. Sometimes the nonincubating crane of a pair flies leisurely up from the marsh just above the vegetation, then increases his speed as he heads in the direction of the interloper. In all my observations, the intruder begins flying away at this point, with the rightful owner in hot pursuit.

At other times the nonincubating crane feeds aimlessly through the marsh, working toward the other bird. When about 100 to 200 feet away, he starts toward the other with great strides. Approaching with spread or beating wings and loud calls, he chases the other bird into the air, eventually from his territory, and often from the marsh. Later he returns to his own territory and utters many reverberating victory calls.

On several occasions tolerance was shown to a third crane on territory, possibly an offspring from the past year. Eventually these birds disappear, but at times during the nesting season, I have seen them roosting at nights only a few feet from their parent.

I have also seen Greater Sandhill Cranes chase Great Blue Herons and Canada Geese from Michigan territories.

NESTING

When paired Michigan cranes arrive in spring they immediately go to their own territories. During the first March or April warm spell they begin building nests. If the weather continues cool, they usually remain static, but I have found eggs as early as April 2 after which ice formed for several days on their nesting ponds, ice sufficient to hold the weight of the birds when they came and went to their nests. Usually when they begin laying, the most severe weather has past. However, many nests are built earlier. Some birds build their nest in two days, others take two weeks and many add materials after eggs are laid. If excessive rains follow, much material is added. First nests take longer than later ones.

I have watched cranes build nests many times. They stand side by side or only a few feet apart, pull up nearby dead vegetation with their bills, swing it sidewise or over their shoulder toward or onto the nest. Sometimes they pick up this same material again and toss it onto the nest. Thus they produce an accumulation of materials. They work only for a short period, usually a half hour or less, then wander away and feed. Sometimes they return the same day to continue building but often they wait until the next day. Most birds work during the early or mid-morning. At times they climb onto the nest, walk around on it, work with the materials, and as it gets larger even sit down for a short time.

All nests in water are huge piles, nearly always surrounded by knee- to shoulder-high dead vegetation. If deep snows have packed it down, it produces poorer cover. Sometimes it is sparse in the region. In this case they pull up nearly all of it, making the nest appear as a small island; others in dense vegetation are almost impossible to see where they have pulled surrounding vegetation. I have found two nests on top of muskrat houses. The rest were built by the birds themselves, except for four placed on little islands. The water depth when 144 were found averaged 25.3 (0-250) cm deep at the edge of nests. Average height to the rim was 13.6 (1.5-31) cm. The average diameter at the widest and narrowest spots were 100.5x122.4 cm. Extremes were 35 and 274 cm. All were flat or only slightly depressed and the top portion narrower than at water level.

In southern Michigan I have observed 174 nests to date, 62 were in sedges (*Carex* sp.); 66 in cattails (mostly *Typha latifolia*, a few *T.angustifolia*); 29 in rushes (*Scirpus validus*); 10 in water willow (*Decodon verticillatus*); 4 in fine dead grasses; 2 in *Juncus* sp.; and one in a mixture of plants. All were built with materials closest by. Often nests were in pure stands, at times a few other plants were scattered lightly amongst the almost pure stands.

In Oregon Littlefield (1966) reported both male and female participated in nest construction, that birds picked materials up with their bills, tossed them over their shoulders and as the materials accumulated, one, usually the female, stood on or beside the nest rearranging it. He observed both sexes setting and shaping the nest before it was completed. Materials were added after laying at times. He observed it required one to fourteen days to build nests.

Littlefield and Ryder (1968) showed that Oregon nest materials were chiefly dead vegetation surrounding the site. Sixty-two nests were built amongst *Sparganium eurycarpum* (61 were built of this material); 28 nests were built of rushes (*Scirpus acuta*) (25 were surrounded chiefly by this plant); 11 were built of grass and forbs (11 were placed in this combination); 11 were built of cattails (*Typha latifolia*) leaves (6 built amongst cattails); while 4 nests were built in a combination of burreed and bulrush; 3 in a bur-reed-grass combination; and 3 others in a wider combination of plants.

THE EGGS

Greater Sandhill Crane eggs are larger than those of the other subspecies, lighter colored usually than Lessers, darker colored than the southern subspecies eggs. The ground color varies from Wood Brown, Dark Olive Buff, Deep Olive Buff to Light Olive Buff. They are lightly to heavily spotted with shades (darker than the ground color) of Lavender, Clove Brown, Bone Brown, Pale Violet Plumbeous, Army Brown, Tawny Olive, Black and occasionally shades of gray. On many the markings are definite, in others they are blurred; on all the spots are concentrated more at the larger end, sometimes in a cap. In some the markings are small, in others large extensive scrawls, or a mixture of both.

The shape is most often oval, at times elliptical oval, more rarely almost elliptical, a few are long and narrow. Preston (1953) reported two eggs in the Carnegie Museum (Florida Sandhill) had a standard avian oval in shape. One measured, 93.6x62.0 mm., had a c_1 value of 0.1135 and a c_2 value of -0.0298, where elongation (length/breadth) was 1.57 (1.56-158) (Preston, 1969). Twenty-two Upper Peninsula of Michigan eggs of *Grus canadensis tabida* averaged in measurements, 94.81 (76.0-104.6) x 61.20 (58-65) mm (elongation, 1.549). Three fresh eggs averaged in weight, 196.6 grams. In southern Michigan, 264 eggs averaged in measurements, 94.96 (86-108) x 60.84 (54.5-65.7) mm, and the average weight of 143 (all nearly fresh) eggs was 196.19 (165.1-219.2) grams. At hatching, six eggs averaged 156.9 (149-168.5) grams. Twenty-seven Oregon and Idaho eggs averaged 97.78 (88.9-105.9) x62.41 (57.5-66.0) mm while two fairly fresh eggs averaged 190.1 grams in weight and six at hatching time, 169.9 (160-175) grams. Five early Iowa eggs averaged 99.0 (98.3-100.6) x61.4 (59.5-64) mm in measurements.

Although there are variations in shapes and measurements and similarities at times I have studied many eggs in eleven up to 20 years now at Phyllis Haehnle Memorial Sanctuary, Jackson County, Michigan. Here, although the birds were not marked, territories have been occupied in many cases the entire time most probably by the same birds from their behavior, the shape, color, similarity of egg markings and the use of almost the same identical territories year after year; nesting roosting and feeding places being identical or nearly so. On a number of occasions the same nests have been used for as many as three times while in others they have been widely scattered over the territory. The similarity of the size of eggs on the different areas can be portrayed by the information in Table 7A, where the eggs of several females are shown barely overlapped in measurement even when one used the elongation formula (length divided by breadth). In addition the ground color of each was slightly different from the others and the markings were even more different. One female A-1 has always laid eggs with very fine spots widely scattered over the entire egg. Harold Wing and I found her first nest in 1948 and the eggs in May 1972 were colored almost identical to the 1948 eggs and all the sets I have examined during the interim were similar. The same held true with the eggs on D-4, C-3 and E-5 territories. A new pair took over in the north end of the lake in 1968. The female laid two eggs and a single one in 1969 in the same identical nest. These eggs were longer than usual and narrower (F-6). The elongation records of these females were as follows:

Egg-set sizes are given in Table 6. In northern Michigan there were 19 sets of 2 eggs; 2 sets of 1 egg. In the Lower Peninsula, there were 6 sets of 1 egg; 155 sets of 2; 1 set of 3 eggs. Average egg-set sizes in northern and southern Michigan were respectively, 1.905 and 1.975. Littlefield and Ryder (1968) gave the mean clutch size at Malheur National Wildlife Refuge, Oregon in 1966 (52 clutches), 1.923 and for 1967 (56 clutches), 1.912. The average of 140 Oregon and Idaho clutches including those of Littlefield and Ryder, was 1.935 eggs per set while 186 Michigan clutches averaged, 1.966.

Nests in several areas in southern Michigan that had one egg and later two have been as follows: May 7, 1939 (probably a second nest); May 1, 1941; April 7, 1946; April 27, 1949; April 8 and

21, 1962; April 4, 1964; April 23, 1965; April 2, 1966; April 8, 1967 and April 8, 1967, average, April 15. Earliest eggs were found on April 2 and one nest with two infertile eggs (still under incubation) was found July 1 (This bird probably had set since April). Of 155 southern Michigan records, 108 were found in April, 45 in May, 1 in June and the 1 in July. The average was April 25.

Littlefield and Ryder (1968) gave total days when cranes were found on eggs in Burns County, Oregon, in 1966, April 11 to July 4, 84 days; in 1967, April 10 to June 13, 64 days.

In southern Michigan incubation was checked on the following nests:

(1) April 27, 1949 (1 egg; 2nd egg laid later did not hatch). No. 1 egg hatched May 28. Incubation period, either 31 or 32 days.

(2) April 8, 1962 (1 egg; 2nd egg laid later did not hatch). No. 1 egg hatched May 6. Incubation period 28 or 29 days.

(3) April 21, 1962 (1 egg; 2nd laid either April 22 or 23). Both eggs hatched May 21 when one young was still wet. Incubation period 28 or 29 days.

(4) April 4, 1964 (1 egg at least) hatched May 4-5. 30 or 31 days.

(5) April 24, 1965 (1 egg; 2nd egg laid either April 25 or 26). One egg hatched early morning; the second in afternoon, May 24, 28 or 30 days.

(6) April 2, 1966 (pair setting on egg or eggs). The birds were still setting May 1.

(7) April 2, 1966 (1 egg; second egg laid either April 3 or 4; 1 egg infertile; second hatched about May 3. Incubation required 29 or 31 days.

(8) April 8, 1967 (1 egg); second egg laid either April 9 or 10. Hatched, the second egg May 10. Incubation required 30 or 31 days.

(9) April 8, 1967 (1 egg); second egg laid either April 9 or 10. Hatched, May 11 (31 or 32 days.

(10) April 6, 1968 (1 egg); second egg laid either April 7 or 8; hatched, May 6 or 7. Incubation required between 28 and 30 days.

At Haehnle Sanctuary, where five to seven pairs have nested from 1959 to 1969, I found 66 of their nests (3 were not found). These birds laid eggs at different times on different territories. For example the female on territory A-1 nearly always laid eggs first and eventually was first to have young. Female G-7, on adjacent territory, was nearly always the latest.

In northern Michigan first eggs were found May 7 and 9, 1943, while hatching eggs were found May 29, 1952; May 24, 1952; June 23, 1952 (second attempt), May 27, 1961 and May 21, 1967.

The average hatching date for southern Michigan was May 13 (May 2-June 10). Sometimes both eggs hatched the same day, more often on successive days; rarely two days apart. Following are actual hatching dates:

May 15, 1932 (2 eggs); May 21, 1933 (1 egg); May 28, 1935 (2 eggs); May 21, 1936 (1egg); May 19-20, 1940 (2 eggs); May 20, 1940 (1 egg); May 17, 1941 (1 egg, E. M. Brigham, Jr.); May 10, 1942 (2 eggs); May 13, 1944 (2 eggs); May 3, 1946 (2 eggs); May 2, 1948 (2 eggs); June 10, 1948 (1 egg); May 28, 1949 (1 egg); May 3, 1952 (2 eggs); May 4, 1952 (two nests each with 2 eggs); May 15, 1954 (2 eggs); May 18, 1954 (2 eggs); May 8, 1958 (2 eggs); May 4, 1959 (2 eggs); May 15, 1959 (2 eggs); May 19-20, 1959 (2 eggs); May 1-3, 1960 (2 eggs); May 11-13, 1960 (2 eggs); May 15-17, 1960 (2 eggs); May 18, 1960 (1 egg); May 19-20, 1960 (2 eggs); May 10, 1961 (two nests, each 2 eggs); May 11, 1961 (2 eggs); May 15-16, 1961 (2 eggs); May 27-28, 1961 (2 eggs); May 6, 1962 (1 egg); May 10-11, 1962 (2 nests, each 2 eggs); May 15-16, 1962 (2 eggs); May 21, 1962 (2 eggs); May 4-5, 1964 (2 eggs); May 7, 1964 (1 egg); May 8, 1964 (2 eggs); May 8-10, 1964 (2 eggs); May 9, 1964 (2 eggs); May 13, 1964 (2 eggs); May 16, 1965 (1 egg); May 24, 1965 (two eggs in two nests); May 24-25, 1965 (2 eggs); May 3, 1966 (1 egg); May 9-10, 1967 (2 eggs); May 10-11, 1967 (2 eggs; May 16-17, 1967 (2 eggs); May 6-7, 1968 (2 eggs); May 13-14, 1968 (2 eggs); May 14-15, 1968 (2 eggs); May 8, 1969 (1 egg); May 9-10, 1969 (2 eggs); May 11-12, 1969 (2 eggs each in two nests—Ronald Hoffman).

On the day of hatching, 10 young averaged 114.2 (98.5-132.3) grams in weight while 10 when one day old averaged, 116.1 (102.2-133.5) grams. Following are weights and measurements of 71 *Grus canadensis* when downy chicks. All were less than two days old, except two from the Isle of Pines which were probably about three or four days old. See Table 7.

ATTENTIVENESS

I wrote (1965):

"The attentive period of cranes at the nest is often regulated to some extent by the bird that is not incubating. The bird at the nest seldom leaves unrelieved. Thus, the length of the period of feeding, especially if the bird feeds some distance from the nest, may influence the attentive period .... The longest feeding period was the first in morning. The extremes for the Sandhill Crane at Haehnle Sanctuary were; for the first daily period, 69 to 645 minutes; for the second, 37 to 430 minutes; the third, 49 to 405 minutes; the fourth, 46 to 148 minutes; and the fifth, 84 to 125 minutes.

"Water is essential to cranes. Often on returning to the nesting marsh, cranes stopped to drink immediately. Thereafter, they seldom hurried and sometimes took much time before going to the nest. Sometimes they fed in the marsh; sometimes they bathed; at times they just stopped to preen.

At Haehnle Sanctuary I watched Sandhill Cranes on 11 different days at 17 different nests ... I timed 76 daytime incubating periods. Where it was possible to ascertain the sex (74 cases), the males were at the nest for 41 periods averaging, 215.3 minutes (range 46-645); the females for 33 periods, averaging 194.6 minutes (37-450).

"Based on the birds leaving the nests in the morning or going onto it at night, however, the females more often remained on the nests at night, being there in 36 (64.3 per cent) of 56 cases ... The males were there in the remaining 20 cases. The length of time between the average time of the last evening change (1603 hours) and the first morning change (0642

hours) was 879 minutes. Actual recorded times at four nests, at night when males were incubating, were 864, 867, 1,027 and 1,033 minutes (average 947); and at one nest with a female incubating, 898 minutes. The five-nest average was 938 minutes. The eggs were always incubated at night, even the night following the laying of the first egg.

By day, based on 20 periods of observation with an average beginning of 0512 hours and an average ending of 1854 hours, the eggs were incubated 97.6 per cent of the time (variation 92.5 to 99.4), and of this incubation, 52.3 per cent was done by the males (33.3-90.6).

On 62 occasions when males approached the nests to incubate, they flew to the nest 13 times (21 per cent) and walked there 49 times (79 per cent). In 48 cases females flew to the nests 17 times (36 per cent) and walked there 31 times (64 per cent).

The birds when leaving sometimes flew immediately from the nest; at times they stood beside their nests and preened for a time before flying. This period of preening lasted up to 47 minutes (average, 12 minutes) for the males and up to 65 minutes (average, 17) for females.

When walking to a nest, cranes usually move very cautiously, stopping every few feet to look around. At times, they approach without hesitation, walking directly to the nest. Sometimes they fly to a spot near the nest, then complete the trip on foot. On occasion I have seen one crane fly to a nest, whereupon the other bird would rise and fly away almost simultaneously, so that it appeared that only one crane was flying. This also sometimes happened when the birds walked."

When first settling onto the eggs the birds often rise and settle down many times before getting properly adjusted. They always straddle the eggs while incubating. They are also very alert watching every moving thing. Often in case something looks suspicious, their head is lowered so that it is barely visible, but they are still able to watch. If someone approaches a nest, the incubating bird often lays its head on the nest in front of itself so that it looks like a brown mass. Many times I have approached 15 to 20 feet of a nest without the bird flying. In such cases birds usually fly a short distance away; at other times they walk away, with or without distraction display.

Sandhill Cranes change incubation places at the nest once to seven times daily. On 29 dawn to dark observation days, the average was 3.6 times (once, 1 time; twice, 2 changes; eight times, 3 changes; seven times, 4 changes; three times, 5 changes; three times, 6 changes; and once, 7 changes.). Although cranes could change places after dark, I doubt that they do. Many times I have found the morning bird roosting in exactly the same spot where it stood at dark the previous night. They may change during dawn or dusk.

Calling at the nest. Cranes seldom call while incubating, but they do at times. Sometimes calls by one pair stimulates many others to call. Sometimes a lone individual calls from a nest as though expecting an answer from its mate. When there are only a few cranes in a region, they are much quieter. Where the population is large, there is much calling. Nearly all calls given during incubation are when the birds change places, at which time they call simultaneously, so that it sounds as though only one bird is calling. The unison call is given by many species of cranes. The male Sandhill Crane cries out, *Kar-roo-kah-roo-Kah-roo-kah-roo*, while the female calls, *put-tock—put-tock—put-tock—put-tock*. Number of syllables vary but the female continues as long as the male calls. His call at this time is shriller than hers. He holds his wings slightly raised (not nearly as much as many cranes) and holds his head up with bill pointing slightly backward. The female stands erect but holds her bill usually in a horizontal position or nearly so. Usually she repeats a call every time he utters it.

Often when approaching the nest the birds give a low snore or *Purrr* call. They give this when calling the young to them also. They often give a single goose-like bugle and when in large concentrations utter many single bugles so that the entire mass may produce much noise.

Before hatching, young birds give a low chicken-like *Peeep* and they continue giving this until the next March, 10 months after hatching.

THE YOUNG

When young Sandhill Cranes hatch they stay in the nest about 24 hours. At first they are very weak, when first hatching they lie beneath their parent half curled up, as they were inside the egg. Gradually they become stronger so that when even six hours old they are capable of crawling away from the nest, waddling and swimming, in case of danger but will return immediately when the parent returns. They require much heat for the first two days, and little food, if any, the first day. The second day they begin to eat small items, handed them by mouth by their parents as they roam around near the nest site. If the first egg hatches a day or two ahead of the second, the first-hatched chick often roams away with one parent while the other (usually the female) retmains to incubate the remaining egg. But more often both young remain at the nest site then leave with both parents. In cases where there is dissension between the two chicks, one may be lost at this time. But if the parents are alert they at times separate the young, each parent taking one then come back together towards evening when they brood them. At first, when standing they remain slightly crouched, head erect or lowered, wings drooping.

Usually young birds are lead onto drier land when they hatch and the families often roam either in a drier marsh or onto dry fields where hay or grain has been cut. They must consume thousands of insects at this time for a young crane, we reared when about two months old ate 193 grasshoppers and katydids, 58 crickets, 10 earthworms, one moth, and 2 other insects as well as some grain and calcium in one and one quarter hours in the evening and usually she ate more in the early morning.

The young Greater Sandhill usually begins to fly when three months of age, some possibly sooner. Thereafter, the family groups, three or four birds are easily found for they roost at night in shallow marshes flying shortly after daylight to a neighboring field to feed.

Littlefield and Ryder (1968) wrote:

"Most chicks were out of the egg within 24 to 36 hours following initiation of pipping, but one chick took 48 hours and was very weak and died shortly afterward."

The young left the nest almost immediately after the second chick was hatched, and for the first several weeks were kept 15 to 50 feet apart by the parents. The female brooded both young during the night. Hyde (1957) reported seeing two chicks leaving a nest together, but only one on the next observation. He suspected that the older chick killed the younger bird. He also found that an assault by an older chick leaves the younger one panicky up to an hour. On one occasion he observed a chick in such a state fleeing across a 12-foot stream, finding a crack in a fence, and running several hundred yards through a meadow before being caught. At Malheur N. W. R. aggressive behavior was observed between two chicks on one occasion.

This aggressive behavior by a chick may not always be the oldest chick because often the second chick to hatch is the largest and strongest. While the parent (most often the female) is brooding them there is no danger of such behavior but the minute she stands it can happen but fortunately it does not happen every time. No one knows what percentage of chicks behave in this manner. No one knows whether this holds true for just the Sandhill Cranes or for all cranes. But one thing is certain, a small percentage of cranes each year do raise two young, a larger percentage one young and almost as many no young.

Following are records of survival of young until August and September from 1952 through 1968 by my work or that of Harold Wing, others, and I, or Cottrilles and I (Walkinshaw and Wing, 1955; Walkinshaw, Cottrille and Cottrille, 1960; Walkinshaw and Hoffman, 1972). See Table 8.

POPULATION

Littlefield and Ryder (1968) discussed the fact that at Malheur National Wildlife Refuge, although only two dead adult Sandhill Cranes were found during two years, the population has not increased.

However, the population has increased tremendously at Malheur since I visited it in 1941. In addition many new marshes in Oregon are now used by the species. Farner (1952) said Sandhill Cranes were rare migrants (probably) over Crater Lake National Park, a flock being seen March 30, 1936; but G. W. Gullion (1947) reported a nest with 2 eggs May 25, 1941 a few miles south of Three Sisters Mountains in western Deschutes County, Oregon, while Roest (1957) observed two birds July 10, 1954 at Swampy Lakes, about 14 miles west-southwest of Bend, Oregon. Thatcher (1947) also found cranes in Douglas County, Oregon in June and July 1945. Many mountain meadows in Oregon, Idaho and Nevada can thus be used. In southern Michigan, the crane population has also exploded. Where there were only 27 to 35 pairs nesting in 1944 (Walkinshaw, 1949) there are probably over 100 pairs now. This increase has not used the same marshes only as much as occupied territories and food have allowed, but have spread into new marshes, in the same counties but even into new counties so that the present breeding region is double that of 1944. Protection by farmers, interest, much more intense than formerly, and the creation of refuges by state, and federal governments and by societies interested in protection of endangered species have accounted for this increase. If the birds have a wintering region where they are safe, a nesting area where they are not endangered by illegal shooting, casualties are so rare and predation so low in most regions, cranes should continue to increase unless present uses of insecticides and pesticides produce a heavy toll. If nests are disturbed eggs are sometimes lost to predators because the birds at times will stay away for an hour or more. Cooling of eggs under normal temperatures does no harm to eggs for many hours. I once had a pair of cranes which remained away from a nest all day long at Haehnle Sanctuary and the eggs hatched within 24 hours of the time those in another nest where the eggs in both nests were laid the same days.

However, if eggs are left exposed, and crows

(*Corvus brachyrhynchos*), other crow species, or ravens (*Corvus corax*) are nearby, they are almost sure to devour contents of eggs. Littlefield and Ryder (1968) found this to be the case in Oregon especially where heavy concentrations of cranes occurred. Here males congregated some days in corners of their territories at one point where six territories met, apparently not returning to take their incubation turns as they battled and guarded territorial boundaries. The females thus had to leave their nests to get food and when they were gone, Ravens devoured the eggs. Only one of these six nests was successful. Evidence of this higher population causing difficulties is also shown in the percentage of success or failure in nesting. During two years 58 of 110 nests were lost to predation. Ravens destroyed 21 nests (19.1 percent), raccoons, 18.2 percent, and coyotes, 3.6 percent. The causative agent in 13 was unknown. This indicates the crane population at Malheur has reached a saturation in numbers.

In Michigan where cranes have probably expanded and populations are smaller this does not occur. I have followed 126 nests until they hatched or were terminated in Michigan, 93 produced young (73.81 percent) of 240 eggs, 185 hatched (77.08 percent) and 179 left the nest (74.58 percent). Of the six young that did not leave, 3 were drowned and 3 died of unknown causes. Concerning the eggs, 28 were infertile (8 nests had all eggs infertile; 6 of 2 eggs; 2 of 1 egg) (14 nests had 1 of 2 eggs infertile). Of the other 27 eggs, 22 were taken by predators; 2 were flooded; 3 were unknown. The most common predator was the raccoon and at most nests where eggs were taken I found a scat or scats of raccoons. The eggs in one nest in northern Michigan was apparently taken by a Raven and the eggs in one southern Michigan nest by a Crow.

In addition to the above nests, during my early studies, 18 eggs and 3 young were deserted because of human interference, not always mine. By more careful behavior at nest sites and remaining away from them as much as possible, I have not had a pair desert since 1943. Two nests since then have been deserted when others worked with them or tried to photograph the birds. If a blind is not tolerated, I have almost immediately taken it down. The deserted nests and eggs are not listed in the above totals.

VOICE

The voices of the subspecies of *Grus canadensis* vary so little that I am unable to tell them apart. At times there is a difference between individuals, but this happens seldom. The usual call given by the downy young is similar to that of other crane chicks—a sharp *peeep* with a burr to it that becomes more of a *peeer* during the second and third month. This is retained until the bird is 10 to 12 months of age, when it acquires the bugle call of the adult, possibly due to the trachea now extending well into the breastbone as it does in the adult. This extension definitely aids the quality, volume, and tone of the call. All Grus except *G.leucogeranus* apparently have the trachea convoluted inside the breastbone, some species more so than others. The tracheas of *Anthropoides* and *Bugeranus*, like that of *G.leucogeranus* enter into the depression of the keel of the sternum, then bend backwards around the *mons interclavicularis* then bend back into the lung region. The trachea of *Balearica* goes directly into the lungs without any convolutions. Consequently adults of *Balearica* have a much different voice.

The call given by all adult cranes when calling their young or when given as a call of reassurance to the mate or young is a low guttural snore or *purrrr*. The Sandhill gives this note. *Graauw* is often given early mornings and late evenings, when flying to and from the night roost, one or more birds from a flock call a sharper single *Garroooa*, repeating it periodically. Early mornings, often a series of these calls is given shortly after daylight from the roost region and at times after the birds have arrived on the feeding area. The alarm call is similar to this but much shriller. The Unison Call as given by the male resembles the above syllable but is repeated over and over; as given by the female it is a series of double notes, *Put-tock—put-tock—put-tock—put-tock—put-tock*. Although this is given when the birds change brooding or incubation duties, it is also given at roost, on fields, in winter, in summer or at any season.

The male *Grus canadensis* does not display his secondaries nearly as much as do such species as *G.Grus*, *G.japonensis*, *G.antigone*, *G.rubicundus* although he does raise them to some extent. He does not strut the primaries. The female, like others, does not raise hers at all.

Sometimes birds give a goose-like call when at roost or in flight; some birds in captivity I have heard give a low clucking when nearby. All cranes have a large repertoire of calls. Many are seldom heard.

FOOD

Sandhill Cranes prefer fresh water and are seldom found where water is saline or brackish. They seem to prefer water about pH 4.5 to 7.6, and do not use water that is too alkaline. They drink as do chickens, dipping their bills into the water, shoveling it forward, raising it quickly above the body then swallowing. Often they do this several times when returning from a long period of feeding.

They are omnivorous, eating a large variety of things—grain, roots, browsed vegetation, snails, crayfish, mice, other small mammals and birds, frogs, snakes, toads, and many kinds of insects.

During winter they often feed on grain, browsed vegetation, roots, acorns (in Florida), and a few of the above items. During spring they feed on loose grain remaining from the past season's harvest while it is still cold, but also eat roots of marsh plants. As the ground thaws they begin to dig for earthworms, eat any insects they can find, eat snails, frogs, tadpoles and snakes. As the season advances crickets, grasshoppers, spiders, flies, and other insects are devoured with relish.

I am sure that *Grus canadensis* eats young Redwinged Blackbirds because adults of that species despise them so. Male Redwings are continually pecking them on the head, even riding on their backs as they peck. Redwing nests are at an optimum height for a crane and could easily be emptied by a bird. Betty Cottrille at a blind watched an adult crane devour the eggshells from which a young crane had just hatched.

Cranes do much digging with their bills, which makes a tool strong enough to penetrate several inches below ground. More often they feed from visible food on or above the ground surface. Some insects which they pick up, such as millipedes, they do not care for and immediately shake out of their mouths. Some birds appear to have food likings that others of the species do not share.

During late summer they feed on newly harvested wheat, rye, barley and oat fields, but definitely prefer the wheat. When corn ripens though, they leave the wheat for it. In Texas, and New Mexico they like sorghum, maize and associated crops as well as corn.

DISTRIBUTION

I previously published (1949, 1960) the distribution of this species. During historic times it was found in eastern Canada and United States regularly. Coues (1883) wrote that in 1792 Sandhill Cranes occurred commonly in New Hampshire, and considered as one of most common waterfowl in Vermont in 1794. Brewster (1901) recorded one killed either in 1896 or 1897, the first for the state in over 100 years.

Since 1930 the bird has increased in numbers probably due to protection on both winter and summer grounds, so that it has widened its range considerably, probably to somewhere near where they formerly were. The following records I have found:

ONTARIO.

1772: Mouth of Severn River. Forster (1772) indicated the bird nested.

1862: Kent Co. Two adults with 2 chicks (Mc-Illwraith, 1894).

1869: Rondeau. Specimen collected by J. Oxford (Nat. Mus. Canada).

1872: Toronto. A pair collected by G. Warren (Roy. Ont. Mus. Zool.).

1882: Mitchell's Bay, St. Claire Flats. A pair observed (Allin, 1943), and a specimen of *G.c.canadensis* taken at Beaumaris.

1890: Leeds Co., Mud Creek. A pair shot (J. Thompson). Escott. Flock flying over (Toner *et al*, 1942).

1892: Thunder Bay Dist., Silver Island. One shot from flock of 5 (Allin, 1943).

1893: Mt. Forest, reported in April (Allin, 1943).

1935: Gore Bay. Mounted spec., said to have been taken earlier (Williams, 1942).

1939: Ft. William, 50 mi. SW, September 30, 4 flying over (Allin, 1943).

1941: Port Arthur, 30 mi. NE, September 6, (2) Allin (1943).

1950: Junction of Asheweig and Winisk Rivers (Lat. 54.25°; Long. 87.5°). C. A. Elsey observed cranes as follows: May 9, (2); May 11 (1); May 16 (heard); May 17 (2); May 22 (2). Indians reported Cranes nested. (Baillie, 1951 and letter from Elsey, March 10, 1952).

Nikip L., near the headwaters of the Severn R. (Lat. 52.5°; Long. 91.5°). A. T. Cringan worked here steadily from June 6 until September 9 and heard cranes on June 20 and August 26 and observed two on August 3 (letter, February 14, 1952).

Wawa Lakes, between Kapuskasing and Moosonee. A. S. Hawkins observed 2 cranes June 24 (letter, February 14, 1952, and Baillie, 1951).

1952: Thunder Bay Dist., Lappe, spec. taken Oct. 9, 1952 was *G.c.canadensis* (Baillie, 1953).

1955: North shore of Lake Ontario, Oshawa Marsh, May 8, one (Baillie, 1955).

1957: Point Pelee, Oct. 5, one (Bennett, *et al*, 1958).

1958: Moosonee, 9 mi. east, May 23, two; May 24, one (Gunn, 1958). Ft. William, W. Zaroski saw one on June 13 (Allin, 1959).

1959: Dorion (Lat. 48.8°; Long. 88.5°) One observed April 30 (Allin, 1959).

1960: Simcoe County, Orillia Twp, October 22, (1) obs. (Devitt, 1962:154).

1961: Sandhill Cranes were seen April 22, 1961 (2) at Ft. William; 15 more May 2; two more on May 13 at Pool L., Manitoulin Island (Woodford and Burton, 1961).

Ghost River Lake (Pledger L.), 8 mi. NE

(Lat. 50°45'; Long. 83°40'). An Indian, Simeon Metat shot a Sandhill Crane and saw 40 others as well as a nest and two eggs near his trap line during the spring. Ghost River Post, 10 mi. SW (51°30'; 83° 25'). Raphael Spence saw a Sandhill Crane's nest with eggs during the 1961 spring. During 1962, 25 per cent of the trappers in this area saw 10 birds throughout the entire Cochrane region, but they saw no nests.

Port Arthur, 25 miles east, three were seen October 1, 1961 (Woodford and Lunn, 1962).

1962: Albany River, at mouth of Chippie River (Lat. 51°30' N; Long. 83°25' W). Andrew Gagnon observed cranes both during 1962 and 1963 summers.

Paipoonge Twp., one crane observed April 19, 1962 (Allin, 1962) and the next day two near Grand Marais, Minnesota.

At Reesor (Lat. 49.5°; Long. 83.1°), John Enns (several letters) first saw cranes in 1962.

1963: Enns saw first cranes for the year April 21 (2) and last, September 4.

1964: At Reesor, Enns again saw first cranes April 27 (2) and last June 7 (2).

1965: Enns saw the first crane May 12. He also saw them at Hearst.

1966: Enns again saw cranes at Reesor, April 24 (2) and Carl Madsen and I visited him and saw one and two on May 28 and one on May 29. Again he saw cranes near Hearst (Lat. 49°45' N; Long. 83°35' W).

1965: Missinaibi R., about where Lambert and Mahoney townships meet (Lat. 50°30' N; Long. 82°15' W). Alverik Peltonen and others (Department Lands ond Forest) saw a pair of Sandhill Cranes with two chicks about 18 inches tall, July 18.

Pitukupi L. (Lat. 50°45' N; Long. 84°05'). Gerald M. Hendry saw groups of four and three cranes from August 10 until September 11, 1965. where there had been none in 1964. They were feeding on wild rice (Department Lands and Forest):

Near Atikokan, September 20, 1965 (Allin, 1965) four were seen, one of which was injured (The spec. sent to Nat. Mus. Canada was *G.c.rowani*).

1966: A lone crane was seen in Sibley Provincial Park, May 8, 1966 (Allin, 1966).

Six flocks of Sandhill Cranes (total 51) flew over Ignace (Lat. 49.5° N; Long. 91.7° W) September 26, 1966. Goodwin (1966) also reported 4 at Mattawin R., west of Ft. William, September 11, 1965.

1967: Goodwin (1967) reported another bird at Point Pelee, May 12 and one at Long Point, May 16-18.

Cockburn Island, Lake Huron. Mr. Hamlin (Battle Creek) told me he saw two Sandhill Cranes in the center of this island during the 1967 summer.

Six flocks of 3 to 10 birds, a total of 51, flew over Ignace, and one was collected September 26, 1967 (Denis, 1967:20).

1969: Carl Lumsden (letter) found two nests about 80 miles northwest of Moosonee (each had 2 eggs). (See Lumsden, 1971.)

MAINE, Scarboro, October 25, 1966, through January 1967, May 23 and 25, 1967 (Woodruff and Emery, 1967a; 1967b; 1967c). Another was seen at Brunswick October 9, 1961 (Bagg, and Emery, 1962). Lone cranes were seen at Ashland, Leeds Junction and Harpswell during the 1967 summer and at Kittery Point September 12, 1967 and at Wells, September 24, 1967 (Woodruff, and Emery, 1968:10).

VERMONT. One was seen near Addison, September 6 to 19, 1961 (Carleton, 1962).

MASSACHUSETTS. Three were reported at Yarmouthport, April 18, 1961 (Bagg, and Emery, 1961). A lone bird was seen at Concord-Acton, Middlesex Co., October 23, 1967. One was seen at Cuttyhunk, September 21, 1963 (Bagg and Emery, 1964, 8); another at Williamsburg, October 9, 1963 (Carleton, 1963:16). Another was seen at Chatham, October 19, 1964 and one October 20, 1964 at Falmouth (Bagg and Emery, 1965:8).

CONNECTICUT. One was seen at Stratford, December 20, 1963 (Carleton, 1964:341).

NEW YORK. At Whitehall, a lone crane was seen from mid-February to March 26, 1967 (Carleton, 1967:400) and another May 16, 1965 at Phoenix (Carlton, 1965-456).

NEW JERSEY. Two were seen at Light House Pond, Cape May County, October 1 and 6, 1958 (Choate, 1959; Scott and Potter, 1959; Potter, 1959) and a flock of 31 flying October 14, 1962 at Watchung Ridge behind Bound Brook (Carleton, 1963.

MARYLAND. The first Maryland record was a bird (*G.c.canadensis*) shot near McDaniel, Talbot County, November 19, 1961 (Scott, and Cutler, 1962).

WEST VIRGINIA. A crane (*G.c.tabida*) was shot in September, 1934 at Point Pleasant, Mason Co. (Brooks, 1944). Another was seen at Canaan Valley, Tucker County, October 15, 1967 (Hall, 1968:38).

PENNSYLVANIA: A lone bird was seen April 28, 1963 at Port Clinton Fire Tower (F. R. Scott, and Cutler, 1963:395) while one was seen October 10, 1967 at Greencastle, Franklin County.

NORTH CAROLINA. Two Sandhill Cranes were shot at Lennon's Marsh, Robeson Co., November 19, 1957 and parts given to North Carolina State Museum (Davis, 1958) (Grey, 1963:78).

SOUTH CAROLINA. A specimen (*G.c.canadensis*) taken by A. T. Wayne Oct. 18, 1890 came from Eston Co., at Mt. Pleasant (Sprunt and Chamberlain, 1949). At Pon-Pon, across the Edisto River, from Willtown Bluff, four cranes were seen in 1957; eight in 1964 and 14 on December 30, 1966 (Dick, 1967). I previously listed two other records (1960) from North Santee R., Rice Hope Plantation, December 19, 1941 (spec. *G.c.tabida*) and Hasty Point Plantation, Georgetown Co., November 23, 1928.

GEORGIA. Here again the increase of migrating cranes is evident from the large number of records in recent years. I listed the records (1960) up until that time from Charlton, Bibb, Jones, Jasper, Fulton, Dawson and Habersham counties in spring as well as the Augusta region and from Fulton, Forsyth, Jones, Irwin, Chatham, Ware, Charlton and Camden counties in fall.

Since then the species has been observed in spring as follows: Irwin County, Osierfield (M.

Hopkins 1960:10) observed 113 flying at 1600 hrs. on March 10, 1960 (1962:9), March 8 and 19, 1962 (total 95), (1964:21) flocks of 89 and 150 on March 7, 1964 (1965:71), March 1, 1956 a flock of 48 and a flock of 31 and 26 on March 15, 1965. All were flying NW. At Decatur, DeKalb County, P. B. Smith (1960:10) saw 40 flying March 13, 1960, while Peters (1961:29-30) recorded migrations of 20 at Zebulon, Pike County, and 3 flocks, totaling 75, at Decatur, DeKalb County, March 5, 1961. Chamberlain (1961:319) recorded 30 over Augusta, Richmond County, March 19, 1961. K. Weaver (1962:9) recorded 21 over Milledgeville, Baldwin County, March 10, 1962. Boulware and Edwards (1963:35) saw a flock of 22 over Hall County, October 28, 1962. Hopkins (1964-21) heard cranes at Fitzgerald, Ben Hill County, March 14, 1964. Fink (1965:96) reported 4 cranes on the ground at Atlanta, Fulton County, November 12 and 13, 1965, and Hamilton (1965:71) saw flocks of 23 and 100 at Dawnville, Whitfield County, March 18, 1965. Parnell (1966:28) and Trammer (1965:113) reported a flock of 48 at 10 A.M. flying at 500 feet at Athens, Clarke County, October 26, 1965 and Hall (1965:378; 1966:423) reported a flock of 75-100 over Dalton, Whitfield County, March 2 and more March 7, 1966.

TENNESSEE. A few recent Tennessee records follow. Spring: Chattanooga, in Cumberland, Anderson, Knox and Shelby counties and from Anderson, Bedford, Sevier, Shelby-Tipton, and Union counties in the fall (Walkinshaw, 1960). One was seen November 13, 1959 and one spent the winter at Knoxville, Knox County, while migrating cranes were seen over Chattanooga March 14 and 15, 1960, March 12, 1961 and October 18, 1962 (Hall, 1960:36; 1960:311; 1961:329; 1963:33).

KENTUCKY. Wilson (1923-131) reported Sandhill Cranes migrated rather commonly by Calloway County at that time but thereafter it has been scarce. Records since my 1960 article have been: At Louisville, Jefferson County, one crane was seen September 17 and 18, 1960 while one was seen at Bowling Green, Warren County, April 8 and 9, 1961 and eight at Glasgow, Barren County, March 24, 1961 (Mumford, 1961:45,414).

Petersen (1966:514) reported two cranes at Green County, March 3, 1966.

In Indiana the species has been exceedingly abundant during migration; in Illinois less so but fairly common in the northeastern corner while a few records continue to come from Ohio, especially in the west.

The Greater Sandhill Crane has not nested, so far as is known, in Ohio since 1926, in Indiana since 1929, in Illinois since 1890, in Iowa since 1905, in Nebraska since 1884, in South Dakota since 1910, in North Dakota since around 1917, and probably since the same time in eastern Montana and Wyoming; in Arizona, since 1886, possibly as late as 1910; in Utah the bird may possibly be nesting but the most recent record is a nest found at Fish Springs, Juab County, May 4, 1940 (Bee and Hutchings, 1942).

The species still nests in both northern and southern Michigan, in central and northwestern Wisconsin, northern Minnesota, central Manitoba, central and northern Saskatchewan and Alberta, throughout parts of British Columbia, western Montana, north and western Wyoming, northwestern Colorado, southern and central Idaho, northern Nevada, eastern and central Oregon, northeastern California and a few scattered places in Washington State. These I have summarized before (1949), but more recent records are listed:

MICHIGAN. In Michigan the Greater Sandhill has increased in both the Upper and Lower Peninsulas. These regions are 200 to 250 miles apart. In northern peninsula the species has been found in Marquette, Alger, Luce, Chippewa, Schoolcraft and Mackinac counties.

C. J. Henry photographed a Sandhill Crane at its nest in Schoolcraft County, in May ....; I found a nest with 2 broken eggs, May 28, 1952 and Wm. Dyer and I found a downy chick (T47N, R13W, Section 19) June 23, 1952. At Sleeper Lake, Chippewa County (T48N, R10W, Section 33) I found nests May 21, 1943, May 23, 1952, May 17, 1968. In Mackinac County (T44N, R9W, Section 3) I found a nest, May 24, 1952 and in Chippewa County (T45N, R5W, Sections 10, 15 and 25) I found nests May 22, 1952 (two nests, one with two newly hatched chicks), May 2, 1958, May 27, 1961 (at least one chick), May 19, 1967, May 20, 1967 (two nests, one with one egg—all the rest had two).

In the Lower Peninsula of Michigan cranes have increased considerably. In addition to nesting rather abundantly in Jackson, Calhoun, Washtenaw and Clinton counties, to a lesser extent in Livingston, Ingham, Eaton, and Barry counties, the birds have now been found nesting or with chicks in Gratiot, Shiawassee, Kalamazoo and St. Joseph counties and have been seen in summer in Oakland, Allegan, and Hillsdale. I published (1949, 1965a;1965b) records of many of these nests.

WISCONSIN. The Sandhill Crane has been found in greater numbers in more recent years, after a low during the period probably between 1910 and 1940. Just prior to 1940 some refuges were established, and since then others, so the birds have managed to increase and spread into new regions. It has been found in summer or nesting in the following counties:

Adams, Burnett (Breckenridge), Dane, Dodge, Green Lake, Jackson, Jefferson, Juneau, Marathon, Marquette, Monroe, Oconto, Racine, Shawano, Walworth, Waukesha, Waushara, and Wood.

MINNESOTA. The Sandhill Crane has been found in summer, its nest observed or young in the following counties:

Aitkin, Anoka, Clay, Clearwater, Grant, Jackson, Kittson, Lac Qui Parle, Pennington, Pine, Polk, and Roseau.

COLORADO. A. M. Bailey and R. J. Niedrach (1965) wrote: This species and *G.c.canadensis* both migrate over Colorado, the former in the western portion; the latter in the eastern portion of the state. Nests of the former have been found in the northwestern portion.

Routt County. Cooke (1897:62) reported nesting here. C. A. Hurd (letter, June 5, 1969) reported finding nests in Crane Park; California Park, Jackadowsky Creek; Armstrong Creek; First Creek; Hahn's Peak region; North of California Park, branch of Adams Creek; Green Creek region; Silver City Creek.

Cranes usually return in early April. One flock (30) came into the Yampa Valley during the first week of April, spent several days in Section 8-6-87, courting and talking, then broke up into twos, threes, or fours, crowding the snow line as it thawed. By May 7-12, they reached their nest sites. They use the same site on which to nest each year. Nests are built on tiny islands in beaver dams with low willows for cover (Forest Service spraying of willows may produce some habitat damage). All nests have had two eggs. Young (they hatch about mid-June) are taken to higher land daytimes to feed. After they have grown up and can fly by mid-September killing frosts are common. About this time a vociferous crane will rise, begin circling, higher and higher, while the other birds answer him. Then they all begin rising to join him and all disappear until the next April.

The first state record was in the San Juan Mountains, March 30, 1822 (Bailey, and Niedrach, 1965).

Buller (1967:6) wrote that "Sandhills using Prewitt Reservoir, peaked at about 20,000 birds in 1962 and 1963. In 1962, these birds stopped off for about 1 week, whereas the 1963 migration used this way station for about 4 weeks. The 1964 and 1965 fall migration practically bypassed Prewitt Reservoir, but with 5,000 birds stopping overnight in 1965. Bonny Reservoir and the Arkansas Valley serve as way stations for smaller numbers (500 to 2,000) of migrating sandhills. Kansas way stations also host small numbers of cranes."

Scott (1956:44) reported 200 Sandhill Cranes at Monte Vista Natl. Wildlife Refuge November 25, 1955; (1962:435,496) he reported 500 at Grant Junction, Colo., the second week of April 1962, they tried to repopulate the species at Monte Vista Refuge, March 15 (p. 475). Huey 1964 Scott (p. 376) reported 1,100 Sandhills at Monte Vista Refuge, March 15 (p. 475). Huey (1965:640) reported one bird with 200 others October 3, 1962 and with 483 others on October 4, 1962 at Monte Vista Refuge, was formerly marked at Socorro, New Mexico at Bosque del Apache Refuge. Scott (1967:443) reported cranes moving across Colorado March 11 (90 birds) and 4,000 on March 31, 1967 at Monte Vista while

(p. 591) he reported 2 stayed there all summer. Williams (1968:58) reported one at Loveland on October 19, 1967 while Scott (1968:74) reported 1,500 at Monte Vista, October 22-November 4, 1967.

WYOMING. Sandhill Cranes nest regularly in Yellowstone National Park and on and around the Elk Range, Teton County. Brown (1942:21) wrote few cranes were found in Wyoming between 1920 and 1931 but thereafter numerous observations were made at Jackson Hole, Yellowstone and the regions immediately south of there. Caslick (1955:82) reported numerous pairs in Hayden Valley and other parts of Yellowstone and two nests (both C/2). I (1949:175) previously reported nesting at Yellowstone National Park in the Bechler River district, at Yellowstone Lake and near the Lower Falls. Also cranes were observed on Gibbons Meadows, north of Old Faithful, and nesting was reported at Jackson, Teton County. Scott (Wilson and Norr, 1949:246) observed birds July 4, 1949 at Targhee National Forest.

George F. Wrakestraw (letter, September 8, 1969) reported birds and nests were found on tributaries of Green River in Sublette and Sweetwater Counties, the Bear River in Uinta County and Lincoln County, the Salt River in Lincoln County, the Snake River in Teton County while numerous nests were observed in Canada Goose studies along the Bear River near Cokeville while cranes appeared to be increasing.

In migration, *G.c.canadensis* is found chiefly in the eastern part of the state. Buller (1967) reported large numbers often stopped off here but most fall-migrating sandhills did not stop in 1962 and 1963. From 1,600 to 6,000 birds stopped at Reservoirs in Albany, Platte, and Goshen Counties.

MONTANA. Sandhill Cranes formerly nested or occurred in Flathead, Lake, Glacier, Beaverhead, Gallatin, in Bitterroot Valley and either in Lewis and Clark or Broadwater counties (Walkinshaw, 1949:175).

Davis reported the birds on their breeding grounds, May 28, 1955 and a pair near Logan, Gallatin County, July 9, 1955 (Rogers, 1955:390) while a pair had downy chicks June 12, 1960 at Ennis Lake, Madison County, where they arrived on April 16, 1961 and nested again in 1962, when 5-day-old chicks were seen June 3. Nine birds were still observed here in 1965 and they apparently nested in 1966 and had 2 chicks, June 11, 1967 while another pair with young were seen near Belgrade, Gallatin County (Rogers, 1958-371; Red Rocks Lake, April 8, 1958; October 14, 1958, 1959: 49,444; 1960:466; 1961:427; 1962: 495; 1965:565; 1966:586; 1967:588). Rogers (1963:51) reported the birds at Lolo, Missoula County in 1963 and at Kamloops near Bozeman. Bull (1959:411) reported about 400 in mid-June 1959 at Red Rocks Lakes, Beaverhead County.

Gammell and Gammell (1950:22,248; 1951:24; 1952:24; 1949:213) and Gammell and Huenecke (1955:35; 1956:33) reported the species in migration (probably *G.c.canadensis* mostly) at Lake Bowdoin National Wildlife Refuge, Phillips County, 35,000, September 15 to November 12, 1949, the peak the last few days of September and first of October; none in the 1950 fall; September 20 with the peak, October 9-17, 1953; only a few in 1954; a small flock in 1954; a small flock October 19, 1955; large flocks in 1956 fall, September 16 (first) with the peak of 50,000 October 5 and 6.

A large flight occurred at Medicine Lake Refuge, Sheridan County—20,000 on April 11-18, 1950, 7,000 between September 28 and October 22, 1950; 15,000 were here April 10, 1949 (the peak) while 15,000 were found the last few days of September and first few days of October, 1949 at Fort Peck Refuge, Fort Peck, Montana; a flock of 12,000 built up in the fall of 1951. They were first seen on October 8.

IDAHO. The first Idaho nest reported by Lewis and Clark (Coues, 1893, 1022, 1041, 1295) was located in what is present day Idaho County, May 20, 1806 (with hatching chicks). There is an egg taken May 6, 1860 (U.S.N.M.) at Sinyakwateen Depot (Clark Fork of Columbia River). Merrill reported possible nesting at Ft. Sherman, Kootenai County (Lat. 47°40' N; Long. 116°30' W); while Merriam and Stejneger (1891:91) reported chicks in June 1871 at Ft. Lapwai, Nez Perce County, and eggs in May 1877 near Olds Ferry, Snake River, Washington County. Merriam took a female bird, August 6, 1872 at Henry's Fork,

Snake River (1873:702) and Victor Jones (letter) reported a nest at Stanley, Custer County, in June 1940 and another nest June 21, 1938 at Driggs, Teton County. Sugden reported nesting in Warm River, Fremont County and Carter (1936) from Blaine County. Sugden (*loc cit*) also found a nest (C-2) May 16, 1900 at Bannock County. He (1938:18) reported nests at Soda Springs, Caribou County June 2, 1935 (C/2, C/2) and reported the species was seen here back August 27, 1843. Stanley G. Jewett (letter) took a specimen July 1, 1930 at Gray's Lake, Caribou County, and V. Jones and I (Walkinshaw, 1949:175) found three nests (all C/2 except one egg in one nest hatching) May 24, 1941. Sugden reported also that another nest was found in Caribou County.

Huey (1965:641) reported that several cranes banded in Socorro County, west central New Mexico in January 1969 were sighted in Idaho.

R. C. Drewien (1969) summarized the breeding numbers and distribution of this species in eastern Idaho and Lincoln County, Wyoming as follows: (Tables 11 and 12).

UTAH. Sandhill Cranes summered in Cache Valley, Cache County, August 30, 1843 (Sugden, 1938:18). They were observed by Stansbury (1852:205) on Antelope Island, Davis County, June 15, 1850 and found by Ridgway June 23 to July 2 and July 16 to August 16, 1869 at elevation 6,500 feet on Parley's Peak, Wasatch Mountains. Ridgway also reported the species breeding in the Salt Lake Valley, Salt Lake County. Sugden wrote (1938:19) they bred on the Jordan River, Salt Lake County, at Strawberry Reservoir in Wasatch County where they were observed up until 1937 (D. I. Rasmussen, Sugden, letter). They again nested here (Nest, C/2) June 29, 1969, nest found by Conservation Officer, Don S. Paul but the nest was deserted (1 egg now in Museum, University of Utah).

Cranes were found at Fish Springs, Juab County where a rancher, Claridge (Sugden, 1938:19) observed nests with eggs regularly and Bee and Hutchings (1942:68) found nests, April 30, 1939 and May 4, 1940 (both C/2). Henshaw (1875:467) found the species here in July and August, 1872. Sugden saw the birds here, May 17, 1936. He and I saw one here May 11, 1941.

Bee and Hutchings (1942:68) also reported chicks in 1939 at Lehi, Utah County while Lockerbie (1944:109) reported birds here in 1944.

NEVADA. Elko County, Humboldt Valley, Simpson's Lake: eggs (U.S.N.M.) and specimen. (Baird, 1876:380). South Fork of the Humboldt River, type specimen. (M.C.Z.), May 19, 1859 (Peters, 1925:122); eggs (U.S.N.M., May 27, (1859?)) Ruby Lake, male specimen, May 22, 1928 (Ellis, 1935:86; Linsdale, 1936:50). Independence Valley, observed (W. J. Hoffman, 1881:248). Ruby Valley, observed August 28-September 3 (Ridgway, 1877:361). Ruby Lakes National Wildlife Refuge, 50 pairs and nests during 1930s and early 1940s (Dill, U.S. Fish and Wildlife Service). During 1950 summer, 15 Sandhill Cranes were counted at Ruby Lakes (Wilson and Norr, 1951:31), while 10 pairs were reported in 1962 (Scott, 1962:496) and a number of pairs still nest here (1969).

Cranes arrived at Ruby Lakes, February 25-March 5 (1938-1942) and left November 3. Cranes arrived here March 18, 1949 (Van den Akker, 1949:179). Cottam (1936:122) reported a few fly down Pahranagat Valley each fall, and a flock of 15 were observed 10 miles south of Alamo, in November 1924. At Sheldon Antelope Refuge, Nevada 46 were seen November 30, 1949.

A specimen of *G.c.canadensis* was taken at Ash Meadow, Nye County (Fisher).

CALIFORNIA. The Greater Sandhill Crane has been found breeding in northeastern California in Siskiyou County: Lower Klamath Lake, Meiss Lake, Tule Lake (Walkinshaw, 1949:174) (Naylor, *et al*, 1954:226; McLeod, 1954:227). Modoc County: Goose Lake, Jess Valley, Pit River Valley, Steele Swamp, Surprise Valley, Boles Meadow, Upper Roberts Reservoir, Cowhead Lake, Wood Valley, Ash Valley (Naylor, *et al*, 1954:226). During 1948 to 1953 inclusive, 24 to 107 cranes occupied this region and there were 9 to 39 nesting pairs (Naylor, *et al*). Cranes remained at Merced Refuge during the 1965 summer (Chase and Paxton, 1965:574). Cranes were observed in summer at Tulare Lake, Kings County. (E. A. Goldman, 1908:202), and at Buttonwillow, Kern County (Grinnell, Bryant and Storer, 1918:281).

In winter the species or *G.c.canadensis* have' been found in recent years in Imperial County, South end of Salton Sea, but gradually becoming scarcer; rarely in San Diego County; in Orange County rarely; in the past in Los Angeles County, but recently at El Monte, San Gabriel River Wildlife Sanctuary; rarely in Santa Barbara County; commonly and increasing in San Luis Obispo County; Kern County; Kings County; Monterey County; Fresno County; Inyo County, in Death Valley (1 bird); Tulare County; Merced County; San Joaquin County; Marin County; Solano County; Sacramento County; Sonoma County; Sutter County; Butte County, Tehama County (regular on Christmas bird counts at Red Bluff); and the same at Redding, Shasta County.

Naylor, *et al* (1954:226) reported nestings as follows (variable due to amount of rain). See Tables 9 and 10.

Naylor continues: "The large number of cranes recorded in 1952 (107) may have been due to the generally wet season and a late cold spring retarding the nesting season about two weeks. This may have resulted in more cranes staying in California that normally would have gone farther north. The opposite may have occurred in 1953 when a warm early spring caused early northward migrations of most waterfowl . . . a decrease in population even though water conditions were ideal."

OREGON. Nesting: Harney County: Malheur National Wildlife Refuge, Frenchglen, Malheur Lake, Blitzen Valley east of Steens Mountains; Grant County, near Strawberry Mountain; Lake County: Warner Valley, Adel, Silver Lake, Syncan Marsh, Summer Lake, Seller's Marsh. Dayton Hyde has much information on this region.

In winter cranes have been found at Portland, December 26, 1948 (2); December 29, 1957 (20), (Audubon Field Notes, Christmas bird counts); at Tillamook, Tillamook County December 26, 1949 (6) while Lewis and Clark (Gabielson and Jewett, 1940:229) observed them at the mouth of the Columbia River, the winter of 1805-1806.

At Malheur Refuge, Harney County, Littlefield and Ryder (1968:4) reported migration during the 12 previous years: average, February 19, extremes, February 7 and 28. Here Lesser Sandhills

remain much longer. Scott (1967:527) reported 3,000 at Burns, Harney County May 1, 1967 when Greaters are nesting. Scott (1965:405) reported 5,000 in March, 1965. Farner (1952) reported a flock of 45 over Crater Lake National Park, March 30, 1936.

WASHINGTON. Summer observations or nests have been found at Orcas Island, San Juan County; at Nisqually Plains, near Ft. Steilacoom, at Coulee City, Grant County; Ft. Simcoe, Yakima County (nest and eggs, C/2), and in Walla Walla, Benton and Klickitat counties (Walkinshaw, 1949: 173). Jewett, *et al*, 1953 reported it formerly nested north at Okanogan and Fort Colville, Stevens County, east to Calispell Lake (Stevens County) and Spokane Bridge, south to Prescott, Walla Walla County, and Rockland; and west to Cashmere, Chelan County, Fort Simcoe, Camas, Clark County, and Grand Dall. Formerly it bred both east and west of the Cascades.

THE FLORIDA SANDHILL CRANE
Grus canadensis pratensis

Grus pratensis. F. A. A. Meyer, *Zool. Annal.,* 1794, *1,* 286, 296.

Type locality. Paynes Prairie (Alachua Savanna), Alachua County, Florida (Pierce Brodkorb, *Auk,* 1955, 72, 207).

The Florida Sandhill Crane, the 'Whooping Crane' of many Florida cattlemen, although most common in central Florida, has been found from Homestead northward as far as the Okefenokee Swamp of southern Georgia on the east and Wakulla County on the west. The cranes occurring in southern Alabama may belong to the Mississippi race. Cranes formerly nested in extreme southern Louisiana.

In Florida, cranes are found on the wide-open prairies. At times they may walk into oak groves to eat acorns. They roost at night in shallow ponds and feed during the daytime on the drier grassy regions. Near sundown they fly to roost, dispersing again shortly after daylight. Often they roost in large groups, which at times remain isolated from the northern birds (flocks of sev-

130

eral hundred have been found in July); again, they may roost with birds from the north.

Lovett Williams, Jr. (1972) has shown that large groups of northern birds spend the winters south of Gainesville, on Payne's Prairie and vicinity, where the Florida subspecies also nests. I found a concentration of cranes near Lake Istopoga, Highlands County, Florida, from November 15, 1969 (57), through the winter (247 birds observed on February 9) until March 9 when the flock dwindled to 42; then to 21 on March 20 and 7 on March 25. From behavior these were northern birds. They fed, drank, loafed, in the daytime, and roosted at night in a group. A few separated pairs remained nearby in small neighboring marshes and ponds. These latter birds were there into late April when we visited the region last, but the larger group had vanished.

Williams (1972) captured around 200 Sandhill Cranes by use of drugs, placed bands on their right legs, marked them on one or both wings with green plastic streamers. Ronald Hoffman found several in northeastern Jackson and northwestern Washtenaw counties, Michigan in 1968, 1969 and 1970. I saw my first marked birds in Lyndon Township, Washtenaw County, Michigan, in August 1968. At a 1970 nest found by Hoffman, both parents were marked, one on the right wing only, the other on both wings. Williams reported his marked birds had been seen in Tennessee, Georgia, Kentucky, Indiana, in migration and in Michigan, Wisconsin, Ontario, and Minnesota in summer.

The Florida bird requires an isolated region, where it is generally open so they have a commanding view, where they can easily vanish by walking into surrounding parklike forests or among the saw palmettos, or where they can fly just above the vegetation to some remote position.

These Florida prairies, the chief home of the Florida Sandhill Crane, are great stretches of openness. Here and there they are grown to cabbage palms (*Sabal palmetto*), either lone scattered trees or groups of them (hammocks) often intermixed with immense stretches of saw-palmettos (*Serenoa repens*). Intermixed with these are often a few pines, generally *Pinus palustris*, at times *P.elliotti*, the former often in immense forests, sometimes growing parklike with or without saw-palmetto. In other places woodlots of live oak (*Quercus virginiana*), more rarely water oak (*Q. nigra*), grow. In the lower damper regions redbay (*Persea borbonia*), gum, and in place cypress (*Taxodium distichum*), maple (*Acer rubrum*), and other trees are present. Sometimes trees are in "hammocks," again lone ones are scattered amongst the hammocks with heavily wooded regions intermixed.

On the Kissimmee Prairie the cranes nest in both the small ponds and the large marshes. Their preference seems to be undrained ponds, two to ten acres, grown to varying stages of density with many different plants. The most conspicuous, giving the most cover, are sedges, grasses (*Andropogon* for one), joint grass (*Paspalum*), often large dense beds of saw grass (*Cladium jamaicense*), *Scirpus lacustris*, *Eriocaulon decangulare*, *E.compressum*, *Lachnocaulon anceps*, *Xyris smalliana*, often thick stands of pickerelweed (*Pontedaria lanceolata*), accompanied with more scattered growths of *Juncus* (more than one species), *Gyrotheca tinctoria*, *Iris savannarum*, *Nuphar advena*, *Drosera brevifolia*, in places almost or completely shaded by St. John's Wort (*Hypericum fasiculatum*), in other places with a few scattered *Lyonia lucidia*, *Vaccinium* sp., *Nymphoides aquaticum*, *Utricularia inflata*, in deeper water, water-lilies (*Nypphaea odorata*) as well as the yellow one.

Occasional regions are grown to bushes such as buttonbush (*Cephalanthus occidentalis*), willows (*Salix*, including *S.caroliniana*), waxmyrtle (*Myrica cerifera*), elderberry (*Sambucus simpsonii*) or these intermixed with trees. Trees are often draped with Spanish moss (*Tillandsia usneoides*), with undergrowths of poison ivy (*Rhus toxiodendron*), Virginia creeper (*Psedera* sp.), grapevine (*Vitis aestivalis*, *V.munsoniana*), *Smilax rotundifolia*, *S.laurifolia*, etc.

In the nesting regions described by Richard L. Thompson (1970) found on the Loxahatchee Wildlife Refuge, 145,525 acres of Everglades habitat, a small population of cranes nest in a rather different type of habitat. Here the birds nest in one region chiefly where the wet prairie tree island zone is located. Thompson wrote: "This portion of the Everglades began as the bottom of a Pliocene sea during which a complex earth stratum of marl, shell beds, and limestone was formed . . . The growth and decay of both plant and animal life for some 5,000 years formed one of the largest single bodies of organic soil in the world. The elevation above mean sea level slopes from about 17 feet at the north end of the refuge to 11 feet at the extreme southern boundary. The difference in elevation allows a north-to-south movement of water supplied basically by 142.2 cm of annual rainfall and supplemented by Flood Control District pumping in times of extreme rainfall or drought."

He wrote further: "Vegetation is generally within one of the six physiographic divisions . . . composed of wet prairie communities of relatively low stature plants interspersed with thick stands of sawgrass (*Cladium jamaicensis*) and slough aquatic communities which support white water lilies (*Nymphaea oderata*). This complex is further broken up by thousands of tree islands varying in size from a few trees to several hundred acres."

In the Okefenokee National Wildlife Refuge, southern Georgia, scattered forests and 'Houses' (trees growing in thick groups in marshy regions) isolate the extensive aquatic prairie regions where cranes are found. Here saw grass, white and yellow water lilies, maidencane, never-wet (*Orontium aquaticum*), arum (*Peltandra virginica*), redroot, iris, buttongrass, grasses, sedges and mosses all help produce nest cover while surrounding trees and "houses" are of swamp black gum, loblolly bay (*Gordonia lasianthus*), sweet bay, red bay, cypress, loblolly pine (*P.taeda*), water oak, magnolia, and sweet gum (*Liquidambar styraciflua*), extensive regions of slash pine (*P.caribaea*) and long-leafed pine on the flatlands.

THE NEST SITE

In the Kissimmee Prairie region nearly all nests are built in shallow water, in a small pond, or along the shore of a small lake—less often in a large extensive marshy region. These are always or nearly always surrounded by the prairies now pastured regularly to cattle. In the Okefenokee Swamp and at Loxahatchee, nests are usually placed in much more extensive marshy regions and often in deeper water. These regions are subject to inundation by excessive rainfall more and at times may suffer some from extreme drought.

On the Kissimmee Prairie many nests are placed in clumps of pickerel weed, or they may be surrounded by St. John's wort. In some regions they are roughly isolated by sawgrass and by other vegetation while at Okefenokee such growth as maidencane, arrowhead, sawgrass, produce the isolation. Apparently maidencane and pickerel weed produce cover for nests at Loxahatchee.

In one pond in Polk County, Florida the center was grown to a thick dense mass of pickerel weed surrounded for about five to ten meters by open water, where herds of cattle pastured and watered daily, often loafing for hours in the vicinity. In the midst of these herds, a crane fed, unperturbed. From his nest two eggs hatched March 24-25 (1967), and as we passed by on March 27, both adults with their two downy chicks trudged toward another marshy region, at least one-fourth mile from the nest pond. Florida nests described by Holt (1930:170-178), by D. J. Nicholson and Sprunt (1954:136) were very similar to those I have found. Nicholson (Sprunt, 1954:136) reported cranes sometimes nest in pine flats on dry ground, using a few wisps of grass and a few dead palmetto leaves. Sprunt (1963:6) reported such a nest, April 11, 1956, the first either he or Marvin Chandler had ever seen. Holt found such a nest in 1924.

THE NEST

Twenty-seven of the twenty-nine nests I have observed on the Kissimmee Prairie, central Florida, and in the Okefenokee Swamp, southern Georgia, were in shallow water. Two Georgia nests were built on small islands less than one meter from water. Water depth around nineteen nests averaged 29.4 (10.1-62) cm in Florida and at eight nests in Georgia, 25.54 (0-46) cm; the average for the twenty-seven nests: 28.2 cm. Thompson (1970) gave average water depth around 44 nests in Loxahatchee National Wildlife Refuge as 25.0 (2.5-99.1 cm). The average record for seventy-seven nests of which I have records was 25.1 (0-99.1) cm.

The nests were made of the available materials and measured in diameters (measured at widest and opposite sides) between 36 cm and 216 cm. The average was 89x90.1 for six nests in Georgia, 102.6x121.2 cm at sixteen Florida nests, and for the twenty-two nests 94.4x121.9 cm. The average height of nests above water was 11.7 cm at eighteen Florida nests (extremes, 7.6 to 24 cm) and at eight Georgia nests, 9.75 (0-15) cm., but those in water averaged 13.6 cm.

All nests were nearly circular in shape, somewhat larger at the base, slightly less so at the water level and a little less at the top. All were nearly flat but with a depression in the center in many cases for the eggs. In Georgia, nests were built of maidencane, saw grass, moss, hardhead, arum, and some water lilies. All were some distance from surrounding bushes and trees, well out in the open marsh, as were those in Florida. But Florida nests were often in small ponds only a few dozen meters from the surrounding prairie; in general, they were also well out from shore in a less accessible portion of the pond or marsh. The most available materials were used and the usual nest appeared like a small haystack in the water. Much of the surrounding vegetation was pulled up for several meters in all directions. If the vegetation was dense, nearly all the materials used came from within only a few meters, and were piled onto the site; if vegetation was more sparse, the majority was pulled, sometimes within a radius of five or more meters. Sometimes when the pickerel weed was exceedingly dense, the birds merely tramped down a thick mass of dead stalks without pulling up any. Although maidencane was the most common plant used in Georgia and found by Thompson to be used most regularly in Loxahatchee National Wildlife Refuge, on the Kissimmee Prairie pickerel weed was found used in fifteen of nineteen nests, in most of these almost entirely (since it was the most common plant in the vicinity). But one nest was built almost entirely of *Equisetum*, four almost entirely of grasses (*Andropogon* sp.), and one of pickerelweed, joint grass, and other plants; still another was built of *Juncus* and *Scirpus*.

Hypericum is much tougher but is used at times, pieces of branches having been broken off and piled around the border. Sphagnum moss, often common, is often mixed in with other vegetation. Sometimes in thick pickerelweed and other vegetation, long approaches or runways were formed.

Sometimes abandoned nests or extra nests are found within a few meters or a long distance from the occupied site. Often if a nest under construction is found, it will be abandoned and another built. I have never found more than one nest in a pond on the Kissimmee Prairie, but evidence pointed to two pairs using a marsh near Lake Wales, Polk County, Florida. Here I found a nest in late February 1970 from which the young had hatched. On March 19 I again visited this region, captured a one-month-old youngster and heard another pair call farther back in the marsh. During June another youngster, 26 cm tall, was captured at a shopping center only a short distance from this marsh (there was no other marsh anywhere in the region).

EGGS

I found a nest with one egg (possibly an incomplete set) in the Okefenokee National Wildlife Refuge, Georgia, March 13, 1960, and the same day another set with two eggs. On April 1, 1945 we found two nests with two eggs and one with one egg (on later visits the same) while the next day a nest was found with two newly hatched chicks indicating eggs were laid there around March 1 and 2. On April 5, 1945 I found two more nests; one a new nest without eggs, the other with only one egg (probably an incomplete set). Young would not have hatched in these until the first week in May.

In the Kissimmee Prairie region, there are two December egg records (Indian River County, December 10, 1932; Polk County, December

1967) ; I have records of five nests in January (Okeechobee County, January 10, 1929; Orlando, January 28, 1923; Indian River County, January 28, 1932 (2 eggs), January 19, 1933 (2 eggs); I found a nest with two hatched young on February 24, 1970 which must have had eggs laid in it about January 20-25.) Thompson (1970) wrote that the earliest nest with eggs found during their study (1964-1968) was February 6, but several nests at Loxahatchee National Wildlife Refuge had eggs in January, while one had eggs December 28, the latest was April 27. One nest had young hatched the second week in January, 1958. The majority were found between early February and mid-March. I find the following for the Kissimmee Prairie region and central Florida; December, two records; January, 5 records; February, 27 records; March, 63; April, 17; May, 3; and June a record of newly hatched chicks. For the entire population I find actual egg dates for 127 nests: December, 3; January, 6; February, 27; March, 66; April, 21; May, 3; and June, 1. The average is 12-13 March.

In my study there are records of six nests with 1 egg; fifty-four with 2, and two nests with 3, averaging 1.967 eggs per set. Thompson (1970) wrote they found 118 eggs in 64 nests. The average for the 126 nests was 1.888 eggs per set (20x1; 106x2; 2x3). Six Georgia nests (1x1; 5x2) averaged 1.833 eggs.

In Florida 28 eggs measured in the field averaged 93.86x60.35 mm in length and width. Nine eggs averaged in weight 165.3 (138.9 at hatching to 185.4, fresh) grams. Nine Georgia eggs averaged 93.02x59.08 and 161.6 grams. The average of 107 Florida eggs (CNHM, AMNH, MCZ, Holt, 1930; J. C. Howell and mine) averaged, 92.46 (80.9-104.0)x59.33 (53.7-67.0) mm in measurements. This does not agree with Tables 5 and 6 because of new data added to text.

Florida Sandhill Crane eggs usually are lighter colored than eggs from farther north. The ground color is pale olive buff, olive buff, gray to ecru drab. Some have a greenish cast, but the majority have the buffy or brownish cast. Eggs are often sparingly covered with fine spots, again with elongated splotches. Markings are thickest at the largest end. The underlying portion as described by Bent (1926:245) is drab gray, ecru drab, or vinaceous drab with overlaid markings of Isabella color, saccardos umber, Rood's brown, and brownish drab. Some markings are closer to lavender while others are gray or black. The smooth shells have little grass, are often pitted, again covered with a few pimples. Shapes vary; most are ovate to long ovate, but many are ovate-elliptical and some are long-elliptical. Preston (1953:166-179) described crane eggs as oval. Many eggs are quite blunt at the larger end.

The period of incubation, similar to other Sandhill Cranes, requires 28 to 31 days. One nest Hal Comstock and I found in Indian River County contained one egg on March 7, 1970. A second egg was laid on an undetermined date later, probably March 8 or 9. On April 5 one chick hatched and the other the next morning after around 29 days incubation period.

Both birds incubate, changing every two to three hours. Usually the male incubates in the early morning; the female all night. In Polk County, Florida, during 1967, the male began incubating at 7:26 A.M. on March 11 (they gave the unison call when changing); on March 17 (silent) at 7:07 A.M.; on March 21 at 7:09 A.M. (silent). On March 21 I found another nest when the pair called as they changed at 8:00 A.M.

Birds fed from 400 feet to two or more miles from the nest. One pair fed on a flat, wet region only 400 feet from the nest, probing with their bills into the ground and picking food from the grass. Another pair fed about one mile (1.6 km) from the nest; at a third they fed about ¾ mile away; at a fourth nest the female fed 400 feet away. At a nest in Polk County, Florida, in late February 1970, the birds fed ¼ mile from the nest; at another nest in Polk County they fed (one at a time, as usual) about one mile away; at one nest in Osceola County they fed from ¼ to one mile away, but at another the birds nested over two miles from this region and fed in the same general area. In DeSoto County a pair was feeding about ¼ to ½ mile away; in Okeechobee County two pairs fed from 400 feet to 1,500 feet.

The bird not incubating usually roosts a short distance from the nest, often only a few meters away. On 54 visits to Florida Sandhill Crane nests in Florida and southern Georgia, I saw one crane at the nest 21 times; one on the eggs, the other standing nearby on 14 visits; one bird setting, the other only a short distance away on 12 visits; on only 7 occasions was one bird so far away that it did not join its mate soon after the bird flushed from the nest.

In only the large marsh southwest of Kanansville, March 21-22, 1938 and in the Okefenokee National Wildlife Refuge, Georgia, have I found several cranes roosting in the nesting marsh, other than the nesting pair. They always roost at night in shallow water, on an island surrounded by water on a river bar.

YOUNG

At one Florida nest (Polk County) it required 19 to 20 hours for the two young to hatch after they had pipped the eggs (Gordon Male, William A. Dyer) April 7, 1968, one egg pipped some at 3:15 P.M.; hatched April 8, 11:15 A.M. The second egg pipped a little at 11:15 A.M. April 8, hatched 9:15 A.M. April 9. At the nest found March 7, 1970 in Indian River County, neither egg was pipped on April 1, but on April 5 one young was out, and the second well on his way—he hatched the following morning.

Young resemble those of the Greater Sandhill but some may be a lighter tawny color. Measurements of five chicks less than 24 hours old were: wing, 34.2 (33-35) mm; exposed culmen, 23.3 (21-25) mm; tarsus, 45.6 (43-49) mm; bare tibia, 20.5 (30-21) mm. In weight three birds averaged 100 (96.0-110.0) grams.

Hatching at one nest in the Okefenokee was April 1-2, 1945, but at many it must have been mid-April or up to May 1. In Florida hatching occurred at one nest March 28-29, 1938; at another March 24-25, 1967; at still another, April 8-9, 1968; at another, April 5-6, 1970; and another, March 28, 1970 and by February 20, 1970 at still another. Hatching occurs from mid-January (Thompson, 1970) until mid-June. The average, about April 2 (mid-January-mid-June).

Sutton (1946: 100-101) described the downy chick (May 27, 1945) from Osceola County, Florida. "It was too young to stand firmly, appeared to be wholly unafraid, and cheeped in a high, fine voice. If put in strong sunlight, it promptly sought shade. It took small grasshoppers from the hand but did not swallow them expertly. Given a pan of water, it waded about, sat down and drank deeply, but did not go through the motions of taking a bath. After eating four small grasshoppers, it became drowsy, sank to its belly, and let its head sink farther and farther forward until one side of the face rested on the grass. In this attitude it napped briefly but soundly, with eyes closed.

"Standing, it held its head moderately high and let its wings hang limp. On sitting down it rested on its heels and lifted its head, or sank to its belly and let its head rest between its shoulders. Its plumage was foxy red-brown, brightest on the back, paler on the face, belly and sides, with a white spot in front of each wing. The forehead and crown were fully feathered. The feet were brownish pink. The basal half of the bill was pinkish flesh color, the terminal half horn gray, the egg-tooth grayish white. The eyelids were dull bluish gray, the irides light gray with a faint greenish or bluish cast, the pupils milky gray rather than black."

This nest never held more than one egg and was thought to be late because of extreme drought that year.

FOOD

Since there is little grain farming in the regions of these crane marshes, they do no or little damage to crops.

They feed extensively in Florida on the wide-open prairies, digging with their bills for hours in the hard ground. Some of this probing is for roots but much must also be for insects. I have observed birds in fall, feeding on acorns beneath live oak trees. They also eat earthworms, crickets, grubs, etc.

A. H. Howell (1932:199) reported:

"Examination of seven stomachs of the Sandhill Crane in the Biological Survey indicated a preference on the part of the birds for a vegetable

diet. Animal food in the contents amounted to
only about 2.5 percent comprising carabid beetles,
dragon-fly nymphs, caterpillars, ants, and craw-
fishes. Four birds from Florida had eaten chiefly
tubers of a sedge (*Cyperus* sp.) and fine buds
and rootlets of an unidentified plant, with a few
seeds of saw grass. N. B. Moore . . . records his
examination of six stomachs . . . in which he
found only vegetable matter, chiefly the bulbs and
roots of a Sagittaria, with a few seeds. Bryant
. . . states that the food . . . in spring consists
largely of a root called "pink-root," growing in
wet savannas. Baker . . . reports finding a frog, a
toad, a lizard, and a snake in stomachs examined
at Micco."

Red-root (*Lachnanthes tinctoria*) is a favorite
food item in the Okefenokee Swamp. They often
feed on fresh burns apparently picking up
scorched insects, lizards, etc. In the Okefenokee
they feed on blueberries in season.

DISTRIBUTION

The Florida Sandhill Crane has been found
nesting in the Okefenokee National Wildlife Refuge, in both Charlton and Ware counties, Georgia
(summarized by me in 1949); and throughout
favorable regions in peninsular Florida.

THE MISSISSIPPI SANDHILL CRANE
Grus canadensis pulla

Grus canadensis pulla. John W. Aldrich. A new
subspecies of Sandhill Crane from Mississippi.
1972, Proc. Biol. Soc. Washington, Vol. 85, No.
5, pp. 63-70, August 30, 1972.

Type locality. Jackson County, Mississippi.
Type specimen. Adult female, USNM No. 564841
in the National Museum of Natural History.
Hatched May 15, 1969, from egg taken May 7,
1969, about 7 miles northwest of Fontainebleau,
Jackson County, Mississippi. Reared at Patuxent Wildlife Research Center, Laurel, Maryland,
leg band No. 49; wing tag No. 207. Died there
September 15, 1971.
During the past century cranes apparently
bred in southern Louisiana. These birds could

have been of this race or another; the same with
those found in southern Alabama, which, however, were much closer to the Mississippi range.
Definite records were given of cranes in southern
Louisiana by McIlhenny (1897: 287), Beyer, Allison, and Kopman (1908: 176); Alfred M. Bailey
(1918, 11). Bailey and Wright (1931: 193) and
Arthur (1931: 233) listed cranes with chicks in
Cameron Parish 1917 and 1918. Young were also
recorded in July 1919 by Figgins (1923: 673) at
Black Bayou; birds were recorded by Kopman at
Calcasieu Pass; while Cooke (1914: 11) and Bent
(1927: 253) both recorded nesting formerly in
Terrebonne Parish at Houma. These records by
outstanding ornithologists of their times cannot
be discounted. The Sandhill, like the Whooping
Crane, then vanished from Louisiana as a breed-
ing bird. A few northern cranes may winter there.

In Alabama the situation is similar. Imhof
(1962: 206) gave sight records from Elberta,
Romar Beach (June 18, 1958), Orange Beach
(June 23, 1960), from southern Baldwin County
(August 16, 1960) besides several winter records
but apparently there are as yet no specimens
from that state, although Arthur (1931: 233)
claimed a specimen from Louisiana.

During the spring of 1938, E. A. McIlhenny
(1938) visited friends at Fontainebleau, Mississippi. During his visit, they mentioned that Sandhill Cranes nested in the vicinity. McIlhenny
doubted this but investigated and found a setting
bird on a nest on April 8. That year his friends
found 11 nests throughout the region. Two
chicks were rescued after a seven-inch rain. All
the remaining eggs and young were destroyed.
The two were reared by McIlhenny but later
when they died apparently no atttempt was made
to save the specimens. Thus no specimens, except
a downy chick I saved when it died in April 1940
(UMMZ), were placed in any museum. During
late April 1940 I spent a week in the region and
found three nests (1949 and 1960: 42-43). On
another Mississippi visit March 29, 1960 I located
another nest in the same region.

During the course of studies made on cranes in
the United States and Canada in work on propagation of the endangered Whooping Crane, many
regions were visited and studied. Since a new

highway was crossing this Mississippi region, it was selected as one for study. Jacob M. Valentine, Jr., and Robert E. Noble undertook this work. Since there were no specimens of the bird, several eggs were taken from nests and hatched in the new Endangered Species Propagation Laboratory at Patuxent, Maryland. As suspected, the birds were much darker than birds from the north, darker even than Florida cranes. Considering that all birds were reared under similar conditions, color, not size, differentiated this subspecies from others and it was described by J. W. Aldrich.

Valentine and Noble in their five-year study reported this population consisted of fewer than 48 birds in 1968. Between illegal shooting, the crossing of a new superhighway right through the heart of the crane nesting region, the loss habitat to pine plantations, and the loss of more to housing developments, these birds were being hard pressed. Their survival now stems on whether they extend their range, or whether a portion of their breeding region is set aside and managed as a refuge for them. Thus far all have been found west of the Pascagoula River and east of the Harrison-Jackson county line.

HABITAT

Valentine and Noble (loc. sit.) reported: "There are two localities that the cranes use as nesting habitat. The two are separated by the forested Old Fort Bayou drainage system. One is found about four miles north of Ocean Spring; the other is located just north of Highway 90 between Fontainebleau and Gautier. The Ocean Springs breeding area is about thirteen square miles and the Fortainbleau, fifteen. A few cranes may nest northwest of the Ocean Spring nucleus.

"Two plant communities important to the ecology of the cranes are the savannas and the swamps. The greatest in extent is the savanna, commonly called 'Pine Barrens,' 'Flat-woods,' 'Pitcher-plant Land,' or 'Wet Prairies.' These are grasslands with scattered longleaf pine (*P.palustris*), cypress (*Taxodium distichum*), and slash pine (*P. elliottii*). Some common plants are wiregrass (*Aristida* spp.), toothache grass (*Ctenium*

aromaticum), pitcherplant (*Sarracenia* spp.), sundew (*Drosera* spp.), club moss (*Lycopodium alopecuroides*), pipewort (*Eriocaulon* spp.), yellow-eyed grass (*Xyris* spp.), golden-crest (*Lophiola americana*), red-root (*Lachnanthes caroliniana*), milkwort (*Polygala* spp.), meadow beauty (*Rhexia* spp.), snakemouth orchid (*Pogonia* spp.), and grass pink (*Calopogon pulchellus*).

The wooded depressions, known locally as 'ponds,' are dense to open swamps with cypress, slash and longleaf pines, and shrubs such as wax myrtle (*Myrica cerifera*), several hollies (*Ilex* spp.), swamp cyrilla (*Cyrilla racemiflora*), buckwheat tree (*Cliftonia monophylla*), sweetbay (*Magnolia virginiana*), and others. The swamp herbs are sphagnum (*Sphagnum* spp.), pennywort (*Centella asiatica*), bracken fern (*Pteridium aquilinum*), beakrush (*Rhynchospora* spp.), and others. The larger swamps such as Ben Williams Pond and Perigault Swamp are well known as nesting and feeding grounds for the cranes. Little Bear Pond and Bear Pond and many other breeding regions are now so overgrown with trees and brush that cranes no longer use them."

Even when I was studying the cranes in 1940, Ben Williams Swamp was quite heavily wooded. Many young cypress trees and along the border tall long-leafed pines grew. The open regions were grown to heavy stands of grass, pipewort, scleria, pitcher plant, some *Calopogon* spp., etc. There were no palms and no palmettos. There was no grazing through the region and much of the area for some time has been planted to long leafed, slash and other pines.

Valentine and Noble (loc cit) wrote:

"Within or along the edges of the swamps and in depressions in the savannas are small marsh communities, scarcely distinguishable from the savannas but usually containing marsh plants such as scleria (*Scleria* spp.) and sedge (*Carex* spp.) in addition to grasses. The land use within the breeding range is silviculture, There are a few small farms mainly for raising cattle. Within the feeding range in the pine hills, the soil is slightly better drained and corn is raised, on small farms.

"The home range of the crane [is] the narrow

coastal lowlands known as the Pamlico Plain. This formation, usually less than 20 miles wide, extends from the Florida parishes of Louisiana into Florida. The land form originated from alluviation and marine deposition during a period of high sea levels in the latter part of the Wisconsin Glacial Period. The plain is delineated on its northern edge by a wave and stream scarp 15 to 20 feet higher than the plain. Elevation near Fontainebleau ranges from 10 up to 40 feet with an average about 20 feet. At Ocean Springs crane area it is higher, with an average of 40 feet. Drainage is irregular, water courses anastomosing in the marshes and swamps. Some drain into the Pascagoula system, others into the estuarine bays. In between, Old Fort Bayou passes through so that many small bayous extend out from it.

"Soils generally are association of Rains-Lynchburg-Plummer-Goldsboro. The savannas are largely Rains, highly acid with pH 4.0 to 5.0. The soil is black to dark gray loam, with a subsoil of gray sandy and clay loam, poorly drained with a water table close to the surface . . . Much soil has been unclassified."

Valentine and Noble stated that Eugene Hilgard, State Geologist of Mississippi, passed through this region in May 1855 but did not report cranes (1860). But John King reported to me in 1940 that between 1898 and 1940, the period when he lived there, cranes were always present. In 1940 I estimated there were about 25 birds nesting. Turcotte (1947) estimated 30, then in 1961 less than 50 birds. Harold Wing and I counted 15 in groups flying October 24, 1952 into the Bayou Castelle region to roost. Noble counted 32 in one pasture October 8, 1965, then 42 on another date and 42 during January 1967 near Freeman's farm (Valentine and Noble). Their counts during 1968 were 17 breeding pairs and 10-14 non-breeding birds for a total population of 44 to 48 cranes. There was no winter increase.

NESTING

Whereas most crane nests found in United States and southern Canada are in extensive open marshy regions or bogs, the cranes of Mississippi have always been known to nest in wooded marshes, which eventually became typical swamps. All or almost all nests have been in shallow water among grasses, sedges and associated plants, but in every case trees grew just a few feet from each nest. During 1938 when McIllhenny studied the cranes and during 1940 when I was there, these trees were so small that often the region seemed rather open. The nests were placed in the most open regions of the marshes. The nest I found March 29, 1960 was located where the trees had reached such stature, when the crane left the nest, that it had to dodge amongst them as it flew out of sight. At most or all nests, when not disturbed, cranes walked to and from their nests, and much of the time they were rather silent.

Valentine and Noble (loc cit) reported during their study that most of the active nests were in relatively open savannas, grasslands kept free of trees because they were wet much of the time. Often these were solid stands of nutrush (*Scleria baldwinii*), almost an indicator for potential nesting environment.

They found eleven nests in marshy swales of savannas and three on the edges of swamps. Many inactive nests were found in the same type of savannas, swamp edges, and small water-filled openings within the swamps. Four or five inactive nests were found in semi-permanent ponds or waterholes. Most were found in areas that would be surrounded by water if it rained. Part of the 1965, 1966, and 1967 nesting seasons, many of these regions were dry because of extreme drought.

McIllhenny (1938) found that all nests were flooded by a six to seven inch rain. During a severe rainstorm on April 18, 1940 one nest I was watching was nearly inundated, but the birds built it above the increase of water depth. One day the water reached 30 cm in depth around the nest; the next day it dropped to near normal, 15 cm.

As in many other world regions, the vegetation when nesting begins is rather dead, it becomes fresh from new growth as the month the birds are setting progresses.

Nests are of the most available materials, sedges, grasses, etc. Valentine and Noble found *Scleria, Carex, Panicum* and *Andropogon* were all used, but bits of sphagnum, twigs, red-root, golden-crest, and pitcher plant may be a part. The nests I found were made almost entirely of grasses and sedges, scleria, etc., pulled up from the immediate neighborhood.

Water depth varies with rainfall at nests but the average depth at four nests was 17.5 cm. Measurements of nests varied 61x54 to 140x95 cm across and from 3 to 18 cm above the surrounding water. The average for 10 nests was 99.5x85.45 cm across and 12 cm high. Nearly all had a slight depression in the top for the eggs. Everyone working with this bird has found extra nests near the occupied ones.

EGGS

Similar to other Sandhill Crane eggs in both size, shape, and color, the average measurements of 16 eggs was 95.90 (89-104) x 58.55 (56.2-59.0) mm, the average weight of six eggs (some fresh, two near hatching) was 147.9 (121.1, hatching-162.2, fresh) grams. Of 31 complete sets of eggs, the average was 1.839 eggs per set (6x1; 24x2; 1x3).

The earliest nest with eggs was March 29 (1960) while late ones have been found up until June 10 (Valentine and Noble, Mss; Walkinshaw, 1960). Another nest I observed must have had eggs laid in it around March 18-20, the average of known dates was April 13-14 (March 19-June 10).

The general color of eggs was similar to Florida Sandhill Crane eggs, not as olive-colored as eggs farther north but more drab such as "drab gray," "ecru drab," with darker overlaid markings such as "snuff brown," and "brownish drab." The shape was similar to other cranes, ovate, ovate-elliptical but at times long-elliptical.

Valentine and Noble (loc cit) reported an egg laid between April 13-14 hatched May 14, 1965 (30 days) while of two eggs laid, one by April 18, a second on April 19, 1967, the first egg hatched at Patuxent Research Center May 18. Assuming this egg was laid either April 17 or 18, incubation required 30 or 31 days.

Both parents incubate, for I watched them do this at a nest April 20, 1940. Normally one bird stayed at the nest all the time unless driven away by some human.

Known success of this subspecies has been very bad. During 1938, ten nests were found with 2 eggs; one nest with 3. Although nine or more eggs hatched, a two-hour rain of six to seven inches destroyed all but two, which were rescued, otherwise they too would have died. All in all, only 23 eggs hatched in the wild from 47 eggs, and only 15 young survived to leave the nest. Probably the average success is much better than this, for the species has survived in about the same numbers for the past 30 years.

YOUNG

The average hatching date for 27 eggs at 17 different nests (my observations, plus those by McIllhenny and Valentine and Noble), was May 16 (extremes April 20 and June 19). Four eggs hatched in April; 20 eggs in May and three in June.

Young were peeping inside unpipped eggs the night of April 18, 1940, but the next day both eggs were pipped, one more than the other, and the first chick was out at 6 A.M. on April 20 while the second hatched that afternoon between 1 P.M. and 2 P.M. The downy chick weighed at 105.0 grams at 6 A.M. and 103.0 grams at 2 P.M. The second young weighed 93.4 grams at 2 P.M. (he had never been fed). Wing measurements were 34 mm for the older and 31 mm for the younger. Culmens measured 22 mm each.

When first hatched, chicks can barely stand and if they do they remain half crouched with drooping wings. They still are able to scramble off the nest by 8 hours of age and can swim if necessary. As usual they hold their head erect at times but often lower it and when brooded lie on their belly. The reddish brown down is much deeper color on the rump, back and upper side of the wings. Down is lighter colored on the head, breast and sides and beneath the wing. The flesh colored feet become darker as they get older. The irides are dark gray appearing at times almost black. On the bend and at the tip, characteristic of crane chicks there are small claws apparently aids in clambering through thick rushes.

VOICE

The voices of these birds, to my ears, were very similar to other Sandhill Cranes and all the calls given by others are given at times by them but often they are exceedingly quiet. Sonograms are not available yet for comparison.

FOOD

Probably these cranes do little damage. They do feed on corn fields after it has been cut but probably eat loose waste grain left in the fields. They are vegetable eaters chiefly. Valentine and Noble (loc cit) wrote: "In spring and summer the cranes feed in the same savannas they nested in and along the edges of the swamps and the more mature pine stands. They were often flushed from the ponds in the larger swamps. They feed on roots, greens, seeds, berries, insects, amphibians, crayfish, and small reptiles. We found redroot pulled up by the cranes. Crayfish are quite abundant in the region.

"Ten droppings picked up on May 2, 1966 from one spot were washed, dried and examined. The dried material consisted of leaf tips from grasses and sedges (36 cc.), 89 dewberry (*Rubus,* sp.) seeds (5 cc.), and very fine sand (1 cc.), presumably grit."

SURVIVAL

This region was first lumbered during the period following the civil war during the 1870's. Then during the period 1915 to 1920 the pine was cut off through much of the region. Probably the region was burned severely during this period but when I first saw it in 1940, although there were many savannas and several open marshes, fires apparently were kept under control. Turpentine and free range was characteristic during these days but since then a paper company has taken over leases on most of this land and fires are kept to a minimum while new plantings have taken place across the savannas so that more and more habitat has decreased. Pine plantings were began during the 1950s and continue up until the present. The earliest ones are now getting so tall that cranes have moved to different openings. Several housing developments are under way, encroaching the region from both Ocean Springs and Pascagoula. These bring more and more people into proximity to the cranes and of course some are bound to be detrimental to their survival.

The only way to have this crane survive is to establish a refuge, or possibly two of several thousand acres, having both open marsh and dry savanna, where possibly some corn might be raised for fall and winter food. These of course should be patrolled regularly to eliminate poaching.

THE CUBAN SANDHILL CRANE

Grus nesiotes. Outram Bangs and W. R. Zappey, *Birds of the Isle of Pines.* Amer. Nat., 1905, 39, p. 193.

Type locality. La Vega, Isle of Pines. Male specimen, May 8, 1904, Museum of Comparative Zoology, Harvard College, Cambridge, Mass.

The Cuban Sandhill Crane, resident throughout its limited range, is found in western Cuba and on the Isle of Pines. It is nowhere abundant, and in places completely missing, it is fairly well known to native Cubans. It is smaller than the Florida subspecies.

Because they live in dry isolated regions, most of these cranes may never visit a marsh, getting their drinking water from small streams, springs, and rain-pools. They roost at night and feed by day on dry land. Most of their territories are sparingly grown to shrubs and trees, often somewhat park-like, often rather flat but at times rocky and mountainous.

These birds make less noise than other Sandhill Cranes but at times in the early morning, an entire population may begin bugling, their resonant calls ringing from every direction.

Nothing is known about the early breeding behavior but it is probably much like that of the Florida Sandhill. I found pairs on territories when we were there in March 1945 and in about the same identical regions in April-May 1951. Peter Smellie reported that near his house beside the Cañada Mountains, pairs had nested in the same vicinity for many years. And they also remained throughout the year selecting each spring the same local region in which to nest.

All nests I found were on dry land. With rare exceptions, cranes on the continent nest in shallow water except in the Arctic. The regions here where I found nests and observed families were nearly level, sparingly grown to grasses. The cranes usually flew when flushed only a short distance from the nest; again they faded amongst the trees and bushes on foot, periodically trumpeting their defiance. The incubating bird usually joined its mate, and the two birds walked back and forth just out of sight, on occasion flying over to inspect us as we examined the nest. One nest was built on top of a small mountain, on a flat rock amongst large boulders, and shaded by tropical pines. All nests were built of needles of this pine, in one case these radiated spirally from the center as though the birds had turned around and around while setting. Others reported these mountain nests also. Still others found nests in flat regions, one man finding a nest in Sabana Grande, an immense open prairie, during the rainy season. It was built in a pool of water. Since mammalian predators, including dogs, were absent or scarce, the birds were bothered little except by an occasional human being.

The mountain nest measured 96 by 134 cm across and had a runway 9 cm wide, 56 cm long, extending out between the rocks. The pine needles were about 8 cm deep, and the nest, like the others, was slightly depressed in the center. The nest at Siguanea was more poorly constructed of a few needles, with the eggs resting mostly in sand. But the third nest was again a thick pile of dead needles. The three nests averaged 98 by 67 cm in width and about 4 cm thick and all were nearly circular in shape.

Besides a growth of live grass, most regions had dry dead grasses at the nesting sites. Live vegetation nearby included scattered tropical pines (*Pinus tropicalis*), an occasional *Pinus caribaea*, palmettos (*Acoelorraphe Wrightii*) and scattered bushes including *Hypericum stypheloides*, rompe ropa (*Tabebuia lepidophylla*), *Byrsonima verbascifolia*, *Ouratea elliptica*, *Kalmiella aggregata*, with here and there a few bottle palms (*Colpothrinax Wrightii*).

The ovate shaped eggs are very similar to those of the Florida Crane but smaller and possibly lighter colored with fewer spots. The measurements of seven eggs averaged 87.94x57.13 mm and the weight 133.2 (108.1-158.2) grams. Gundlach (1875) gave the extremes in measurements as 82 to 95 mm in length and 59 to 60 mm in width. The 'pale olive buff' ground color is spotted with 'wood brown,' 'dark olive buff,' and 'lavender' spots, all rather small and widely scattered over the entire surface. Five sets consisted of two eggs each.

No one has recorded the actual laying dates but there are a number of hatching dates: May 20, 1904, a newly hatched chick (Bangs and Zappey, 1905; 194); young birds observed several times in May (Gustav Link in Todd, 1916: 208); a crane taken when downy in mid-May 1943 (Walkinshaw, 1949: 102); two nests with eggs April 30 and May 1, 1951 and small downy chicks, April 23, 26, and 28, 1951 (Walkinshaw, 1953: 4-7). These observations indicate that eggs are laid in late March or early April and that the average hatching date comes at the end of April up to the middle of May. Once, possibly a second attempt, young hatched in mid-July.

Both male and female incubate the eggs and both care for the young, the entire family remaining together until the following breeding season.

Four miles southeast of Los Indios, Isle of Pines, May 4, 1951, I spent the day in the blind. The cranes came back to the nest about 8 A.M., departed and returned again at 10:26 A.M., the female incubating until 1:56 P.M. During this period of three hours and 30 minutes she stood up only twice, at noon hour for 30 seconds, and at 1:39 P.M. for one minute, turning the eggs on each occasion. The male then walked to the nest and changed places at 1:56, remaining there until after 4 P.M., when he left the nest for three minutes to pick up some food from the ground. He, too, turned the eggs at 2:20 P.M. for one minute.

The young, similar to other Sandhill Cranes, appeared darker than downy chicks of the Florida Sandhill. Wing measurements of three individuals when two or three days old were, 36.16 (35-37) mm; tarsus, 47.8 (41-51.5) mm; middle toe (with claw), 36 (35-37) mm; height, 21.8 (20.5-23) cm; and exposed culmen, 27.8 (24.5-33) mm (different chick than in Table 7).

The greatest concentration of cranes probably either in Cuba or the Isle of Pines is in the region southeast of Los Indios. I found eight pairs here, in a region 3x4 miles (3,108 hectares), the closest pairs being about one-half mile apart. In the region about four miles northeast of Los Indios, between and including the Sierra de Madelena to the Sierra de la Cañada, a distance of between six and seven miles there were five pairs, so widely scattered there were no territorial problems. In the region near Ensenada de la Siguanea, northwest of Los Indios, there were three pairs in about two square miles. We found no other concentrations like this.

Many local people estimated there were probably 100 cranes on the Isle of Pines in 1951. We don't know what the population is today. On the main island of Cuba, the population is much lower. Probably the greatest concentration occurs near the Gran Cienega de Zapata. Local people here told me in 1951 that there were more on two islands, Cayo del Masio and Cayo de Diego Perez, just south of the Zapata Peninsula, but they did not know how many.

Unless drastic proctective measures have been taken this bird could be in dire circumstances.

FOOD

Each pair of cranes fed together or with their young during the breeding season after the eggs had hatched. When setting, the non-incubating bird wandered away on foot, feeding usually within one-half mile or slightly more. They seldom flew. The female apparently incubated most often at night feeding after daylight when the male relieved her. After two or three hours she returned to the nest and the male fed for about the same length of time. After that they changed more often until night when the male stopped a few feet from the nest where he spent the night. After the young hatched the entire family fed in the same general region until the following spring when the parents began nesting again.

Gundlach (1875:294) reported that food consisted of insects, insect larvae, snails, reptiles, nesting birds, tender roots and herbs, seeds—especially the seed of *Byrsonima* sp., and of various palms, as well as berries, fruits, etc. He never found traces of fish.

Gustav Link (Todd, 1916:209) reported the birds "feed on worms, insects, lizards, etc., and may often be observed on recently burnt tracts, picking up the lizards which have perished in the fire." Barbour (1923:59) said cranes ate "the scorched reptiles and burnt insects, as well as the succulent roots and beetle larvae found in the denuded soil of fresh burns."

We found both pairs and non-breeding birds at times flew onto fresh burns when they were near their territories.

DISTRIBUTION

Resident and non-migratory in western Cuba and western Isle of Pines. Birds have been observed in Cuba at:

Pinar del Rio: Viñales, Guane, and Mendoza (Gundlach, 1875:293) (Barbour, 1923:58; 1943: 48) (Walkinshaw, 1953) (Dr. Abedardo Moreno, letter, July 18, 1944).

Habana Province: Ariguanabo, Laguna Arigu (one spec.) (Moreno, letter).

Matanzas Province: Alacranes, Union de Reyes (Barbour, *loc cit*). Cienega de Zapata (Gundlach, 1875:293) (Moreno, 1941:4).

Las Villas: Santa Tomas. Spec. M.C.Z., March

11, 1933. Cayo del Masio and Cayo de Diego Perez (obs.) (Walkinshaw, 1953:3).

Santa Clara: Cienfuegos, Soledad Plantation. Obs. (Harold Brown, and Vogel, 1936:85). Aguada de Pasajeros: Male and female specimens (Univ. Habana, Museo Poey, Habana).

Camaguey: Jucaro. Obs. (Barbour, *loc. cit.*), Ciego de Avila: Obs. (Danforth, 1935:425). Camaguey (Puerto Principe), Spec. (U.S.N.M.), captured alive by Helen Hatfield, May 1900, died December 17, 1908, in the U.S. Natl. Zool. Park.

Isle of Pines: Eggs (U.S.N.M.), by Poey and Gaudlet; egg (M.C.Z.), 1858, by J. Gundlach; male spec. (Acad. Natl. Sci., Phila.), January 26, 1931, by J. Bond; downy chick (M.C.Z.), May 20, 1904, by O. Bangs, and W. R. Zappey. Nueva Gerona: Juv. (U.S.N.M.), July 8, 1900, by Palmer and Riley. 'Sabana Grande': Rept. March 1945; winter 1950-51 (Walkinshaw and Baker, 1946:135; Walkinshaw, 1953:4). Santa Barbara: Obs., March 1945 (Walkinshaw and Baker, *loc. cit.*): Read (1913b:125); three spec. (M.C.Z.) March 28, 29, 1917. Santa Barbara, 10 miles west): Yg., May 1943 (Walkinshaw and Baker,

loc. cit.). Pine River (Neuvas River): obs. July 12, 1911 (Read, 1913a: 123). West McKinley: Obs. 1908 (Read, 1911b:113). McKinley to Cañada Mts.; Obs., December 4, 1910 (Read, 1911a: 7). Los Indios: 3 specimens (Carnegie Museum), October 24, 1912 and May 3, 1913 (Todd, 1916: 205-208; and letter); young birds in 1930s, by L. Hedin (Walkinshaw, 1949:185); Observed March 20-22, 1945 (Walkinshaw). Los Indios (4 miles NE): Nest, young just hatched, April 23, 1951; 2 young out of nest April 26, 1951 (Walkinshaw, 1953). Los Indios (4 miles SE); Nest, 2 eggs, May 1, 1951 (Walkinshaw, 1953). Sierra de la Cañada: Eggs, late April 1932 by P. Smellie (Walkinshaw, 1949:185); two pairs, one with 2 chicks, April 28, 1951 (Peter Smellie, W. A. Tholen, L. Walkinshaw). Rio Mahagua region (NW of Los Indios): Observed, April, May 1951; nest with two eggs, April 25, 1951 (Walkinshaw and W. A. Tholen). La Vega: Type spec. (M.C.Z.), May 8, 1904 (Bangs and Zappey, 1905:193). Pasadita: Spec. (M.C.Z.), 1904 (Bangs and Zappey, *loc. cit.*); observed rarely in 1951 by residents (Walkinshaw, 1953:3).

THE JAPANESE CRANE

(Grus japonensis)

Ardea (Grus) Japonensis, P. L. S. Müller, *Natursyst. Suppl.*, 1776, p. 110.
Type locality: Japan.
Vernacular names: The Japanese Crane, Manchurian Crane (English); Tancho ダンチョウ (Japanese); Ussuriland Crane Уссурилана журавль (Russian); Mandschurenkranich (German); la Grue de Montigny (French); de chinese Kraanvogel (Dutch).

The Japanese Crane has long been more than an object of wonderment in its native land. Many verses, Haiku from 500 years ago and Waka from 1,500 years ago, pertained to *Tancho*, the Japanese Crane and other cranes. *Tancho* especially has been a symbol for years of longevity. Where the turtle was supposed to live for 10,000 years, the crane lived for 1,000. Since most cranes pair for life, they have also been a symbol of marital solidity. And since they are so devoted to each other, they are a symbol of love. The cranes are mentioned and displayed at wedding ceremonies in many areas of Japan; they are loved and respected by a large proportion of the people. And so their future is almost assured. The Japanese people are so imbued with the beauty and behavior of the cranes that these birds should be able to maintain their status for many generations. If all the cranes throughout the world had such respect, there would be no problem of extinction; but alas, some of the huge birds in such large concentrations in fall and winter produce much damage to agriculture. And the farmers are not slow to anger. But the Japanese show their love for their cranes when they feed them all through the winter.

Japanese Cranes landing at winter feeding ground, at Mr. Yamazaki's farm, Akan, Hokkaido, Japan, March, 1969.

The Japanese Crane is found in two separate regions. There is a resident population in eastern Hokkaido around Kushiro City and Nemuro. There is a second population in Asia, breeding in the region of Lake Khanka, in southeastern Siberia and northern Manchuria, which migrates in winter to northern South Korea and eastern China. These birds have been called the Manchurian Cranes, the Ussuriland Cranes of the Russians. Rarely, one individual or several birds migrate to southern Kyushu and to Formosa. (It has been proved now that none migrate across for there are no extra unaccounted birds there.)

DESCRIPTION.

Adult. One of the three predominantly white cranes, it is pure white with black secondaries. The innermost secondaries are pointed, somewhat pendent, with some more or less decomposed and erectile. Cheeks, throat and neck are ashy black in males, pearly-gray in females, extending down the neck but farther on the posterior than on the anterior. Beginning just below and back of the eye, a broad white band extends from the ear coverts and occiput down the hind-neck to a sharp point. The bill is olive-green or greenish-horn in color, lighter at the tip. Legs are slaty-black or grayish-black. Iris is dark brown. Forehead and crown are bare, red, brighter at certain seasons, and covered with black hairs down nearly to the eye. Larger than *Grus grus*.

Subadult and Juvenile. Following the downy stage, plumage is partly tawny, white, cinnamon-brown, rusty or grayish. The neck-collar is coffee-brown or grayish. Secondaries are dull black, mixed with brown. Crown and forehead are covered with gray and tawny feathers. As in the adult, primaries are white, but tipped with black. The primary greater coverts for the outer six feathers are tipped with black, and this may persist until the second or third year. Bill and legs are similar to those of the adult but lighter colored.

Downy chick. Tawny-brown or cinnamon-brown down covers the entire body. This down is darker on the body, shoulders and rump, and tawnier on the head and neck. Cheeks are light gray and tawny — mixed. A grayish tinge to the lower parts makes it appear lighter. A spot at the insertion of the wing is almost white. The bill is flesh-colored, with a yellowish tinge at the base. Feet and tibio-tarsal joint are bluish, but with yellowish-flesh color predominant. Legs are bluish the first day, changing to flesh-color the next day or two. Eyes are dark brown.

When the bird is about a month old, it is much tawnier, tinged with gray and almost light gray on the upper neck and face. The top of head is rather tawny.

Measurements

Adult male (average of 8 specimens: AMNH, 2; BMNH, 1; CNHM, 2; MCZ, 1; USNM, 1; YIOZ,1) Exposed culmen, 159.0 (151-167); From base of nostril to tip of upper mandible, 123-132; wing (chord), 618.6 (560-670); tail, 240.5 (2); tarsus, 285.7 (267-301); bare tibia, 134.2 (120-155); middle toe with claw (4), 127.2 (120-135)mm.

Adult female (average of 11 specimens, BMNH,1; CNHM,1; LM,1; MCZ,2; USNM,5; YIOZ). Exposed culmen, 150.9 (135-167); From base of nostril (2), 127.0; wing (chord), 609.0 (557-635); tail, 241 (2); tarsus, 271.9 (255-297); bare tibia, 110.9 (81-135); middle toe with claw, 126.4 (114-137) mm.

Japanese Cranes near night roost, the Akan River (some birds still in water where they roost at night). The pair in foreground with their last year's chick have come out onto the snow before they go to feeding area. Akan, Hokkaido, Japan, March 8, 1969.

Adult Japanese Crane in flight, Akan, March 20, 1969.

One adult female had a wing expanse of 244.5 cm and was 127.5 cm in length. A subadult female had a wing expanse of 229 cm and was 129 cm in total length. Heinroth (1922) gave weights of adult birds between 6 and 7 kg (13-15 lbs.) Dementiev and Gladkov (*loc. cct.*) gave 9-10 5 kg, even 15 kg. wing formula 3 > 2 = 4 > 5 > 1 > 6 > 7 — 11. Inner secondaries about 100 mm beyond primaries.

DISTRIBUTION

Summer. Dementiev and Gladkov (1951) and Vorobiev (1954) reported the Ussuriland Crane nested only in the Maritime Kray, in the vicinity of Lake Khanka and in the Ussuriland lowlands, probably up to Ussuri River, possibly even in some regions to the Amur. Shulpin, however, did not find *Grus japonensis* on the Amur nor in Mariinsk, while Shrenk (Dementiev and Gladkov, 1951) reported it on the lower Amur at the mouth of the Gorin and near Chelmok both in July and September. Shulpin also reported that it was found west of the Amur, possibly as far as the Zeya River.

Vorobiev (1954) reported it nesting on the Prikhankayskooyoo Plains, with a few in the Ussuri River valley, in damp meadows and impassable swamps on the Lower Lefu, and the Lake Khanka Plains, along the lower River Iman and the Rivers Moolingche, Taikhoolinkhe and Abootsinkhe, the left tributary of the Ussuri, and probably at the conclusions of the Rivers Ussuri and Sungari. Przevalsky (1876) also reported it at Lake Khanka, even by the second half of March, when snow completely shrouded the land.

In Manchuria *Grus japonensis* is found on the Sungari River, possibly in the Khalkhin-Gol valley, even in central Manchuria at Ysitsikar, where Piechocki (1958) saw a lone individual and said the birds frequent these central plains.

In Japan (Japanese Hand-List, 1958) it was reported from Hokkaido: Iburi, Chitose, Sapporo; Honshiu: Miyagi; Kiushiu: Nagasaki, Kagoshima; from Sakhalin (Kaibato-*Tori*, no. 45: 472), from Korea: Kogendo, Kokaido, Keikido, Chuseinando, Keishonando, Moppo; from Formosa: near Rato in Taihokushu). These records include both winter and summer.

147

Winter. In Hokkaido the Japanese Cranes move back in autumn from breeding marshes a few miles to corn and wheat fields where they winter especially around Ôhtu (5 birds counted); Akan (67); Hororo along the Yama Kawa (21); Shimosetsuri (24); Shimohororo (38); Tsuru Koen (9); Nemuro (10). Winter counts are made annually in early December by the members of local Crane Clubs formed by teen-age students in the different schools near where the cranes are found. In the first of these counts 1949 to 1954, when none were counted at Nemuro and Ôhtu, numbers ranged between 33 and 52. Then there was a gradual increase until 1960, when the numbers leveled off between 147 and 200. Since the birds lay only one or two eggs annually there is no problem of any population explosion! They may have reached their saturation point now, although new breeding regions were found by aerial survey during 1972 and the winter count reached 222, though 24 birds have been lost in four years (H. Masatomi, G. Archibald).

A few birds winter in Korea (C. M. Fennell, letter, January 13, 1966 reported *G. japonensis* is not abundant but some are found still in the eastern region near Kangnung, Kangwon-do, about 32.2 km north, a region now off-limits to hunters). A group of twelve spent the fall of 1965 here, but four were shot or trapped during the previous winter. Ben King (verbal) saw some in the Demilitarized Zone near Panmunjan.

The December count made by the Hokkaido schoolchildren, in 1968-1969 totaled 171 birds, of which 26 were young. This number was slightly lower than what Masatomi, Hayashida and I found. At the different feeding regions numbers vary, indicating that some birds move from one to the other at times.

During the long cold winter nights the cranes roost in Hokkaido's swift-running rivers, on sandbars or in shallow water. During the daytime they often return to drink the cold water. Early mornings they fly from the water onto a flat, snow-covered re-

A group of Japanese Cranes in cornfield, near Akan, Oct. 16, 1965.

gion shortly after daylight; some go directly to the feeding grounds. Those that go onto the flat may preen there for several hours, more or less, then join the others on the feeding regions. These cranes are the only northern-hemisphere cranes that remain resident in severe winter conditions.

In March of 1969 I had the opportunity of studying the Japanese Cranes on Hokkaido at first hand. We made many observations; some of the more interesting and significant are reprinted here:

March 16, 1969:

5:45 a.m. Cranes still in Akan River roosting. Water open – river very swift. Temperature, for day, high, 2.5°C.; low, −4.5°C. Official sunrise at 5:31 a.m. Clear. There was adequate food on field.

5:56 a.m. First crane heard calling from river a slow
Garrooo – 3 times.

5:58 a.m. A lone crane called a rapid *Garoooa – garoooa – garoooa.*

6:14 a.m. Sun came over ridge. One crane called *Karooo.*

7:00 a.m. Cranes began leaving water, walking in snow up on flat region in the sunshine.

7:15 a.m. 6 cranes flew from river up onto bank; others walked out so nearly all stood now on the bank, a few yet in river. All stood on one leg.

7:23 a.m. First cranes flew to food field, 2 adults + 2 young; 2, 2 adults + 1 young. None fed, all stood on one leg and preened.   9

7:25 a.m. 2 adults, 1 young flew to feed area.   3

7:29 a.m. 3, 8, 3 flew to food region. No cranes called. A few now began to feed on grain.   14

7:32 a.m. 2, 2, 1 flew to food.   5

7:36 a.m. 2, 4, 19, 6, 5 flew from river region (1 km away) to food.   36

7:45 a.m. Mr. Yamazaki took out a large bag of corn; scattered it over snow which

Japanese Cranes in flight against Akan Mountains, March 6, 1969.

was about one foot or more deep now. Most of cranes walked away about 60-65 m, watched. No calling.

7:47 a.m.   3 cranes flew back to river. Most stood on one foot. They always shook the foot they raised beneath their breasts.

8:20 a.m.   Mr. Yamazaki now took out a box of small mud fishes. Threw them into snow much closer to buildings. The cranes now did not run away but came closer and closer so they were only 5-10 m from him and as soon as he was gone all dashed forward for the fish.

8:41 a.m.   3 flew back to river; 3 walked thru hedge. Cranes when it was cold, like this morning, often flew with their feet tucked into the feathers below — not trailing behind as they usually fly.

8:45 a.m.   A male stood in precopulatory pose, body erect, head and neck upward and slightly forward. He called a sharp *Krr-krr-krr-krr-krr-krr*. The female approached him and he hopped gently on her as she crouched some in the snow. He maintained his balance by slowly beating his wings. This required only a few seconds and he stepped off. He danced around the female, making several circles. Then they preened. When they began copulation, many cranes in close proximity hurriedly approached them but all stopped when he dismounted.

9:05 a.m.   One group of 3 which had moved farther away when food was taken out now came working back over the snow on foot. Young birds always came to the food first. I could now count 11 young.

9:15 a.m.   3 birds flew to river.

9:20 a.m.   2 cranes flew to river then 2 and 2.

9:24 a.m.   4 cranes flew down river some distance.

9:30 a.m.   7 cranes flew up river; 3 to river nearby.

9:36 a.m.   5, 4, 2 flew to river.

9:40 a.m.   2, 2, 2, 5, 1 flew to river; the first three groups walked 60 m before flying. Usually the birds walked away 10-20 m before flying.

9:43 a.m.   2 flew to river.

9:52 a.m.   All 13 remaining cranes walking away and all flew to river at 9:55. One pair circled high overhead. 67 cranes were counted during morn-

ing. All feeding was done between 7:29 a.m. and 9:52 a.m.

March 13, 1969:

Time	Observation	Count
1:48 p.m.	I arrived at the Yamazaki house. Tsuneo Hayashida was there but he said there had been no cranes for 2 hours now. Clear, wind, moderate, SE, very little thawing: Temp. −5.2° to −10.4°C.	0
2:06 p.m.	4, 3 cranes flew to food, just clearing trees, silent.	7
2:25 p.m.	3, 3, 4 cranes to food from river.	17
2:35 p.m.	3, 3 cranes to food from river.	23
2:43 p.m.	2 cranes to food from river. Only call given usually a barely audible *Kurrr* and always uttered only by one bird in a flock.	25
2:50 p.m.	2 cranes flew to food; 6 were walking slowly away.	27
2:53 p.m.	6 cranes flew back to river.	21
2:58 p.m.	1, 2 cranes flew back to river.	18
3:10 p.m.	2, 2, 3, 2 cranes flew to food from river. One bird circled twice, calling a shrill *Garrooo — garrooo* as it did.	27
3:15 p.m.	2 flew in from river, some chasing in group.	29
3:18 p.m.	2 flew in from river.	31
3:25 p.m.	1 (yg.), 1 (yg.), 2, 3, 3 flew back to river; 5 flew to food (This is the first independence of young I have noted).	26
3:31 p.m.	3 flew to river. Before flying, one of the group, usually the male gave a low *Kurrr*. A dog came near the group, all began running away with heads erect. One called a sharp alarm call, *Garoooa*. When 50-60 m away they stopped, watched the dog; several danced.	23
3:38 p.m.	Dog tried to catch crow — no luck.	
3:48 p.m.	2, 1 to food from river.	26
4:05 p.m.	3 flew from river to food; 2 flew to river. When the dog moved away the cranes all began converging on him; when he moved toward them, they moved back a few meters.	27
4:10 p.m.	5 flew to food from river (about 75 crows also feeding).	32
4:14 p.m.	3, 3 cranes flew to food from river.	38
4:19 p.m.	3 cranes to food from river.	41
4:27 p.m.	3, 2 cranes flew to river.	36
4:28 p.m.	5, 3 cranes landed over fence from food; 4, 2 flew to river.	38
4:33 p.m.	2, 1, 1, 4, 2, 1, 1 cranes flew to river.	26
4:41 p.m.	3, 1 cranes flew to river.	22

The writer and his wife with Hiromichi Ito, Principal Tsutoma Kamada and members of the Middle School Crane Club, which feeds the Japanese Cranes and helps other children make the annual early December count, October 1965.

4:48 p.m.	2 cranes flew to river, one giving usual low *Krrr.*	20
4:51 p.m.	6, 2 cranes flew to food from river.	28
4:53 p.m.	1, 3, 2, 2 cranes flew back to river (sun behind mountain)	20
5:18 p.m.	Crows all flying away.	
5:23 p.m.	3, 5 cranes flew to food; 1 flew away	27
5:28 p.m.	9 cranes flew to food.	36
5:32 p.m.	2 cranes flew to food; 3, 1 flew away.	34
5:34 p.m.	2 cranes flew to river.	32
5:35 p.m.	Official sunset	
5:37 p.m.	3, 3 cranes flew to food; 1, 3 cranes flew away.	34
5:44 p.m.	3, 3 cranes flew to river.	28
5:46 p.m.	4, 2 cranes flew to river.	22
5:47 p.m.	3 cranes flew to river.	19
5:50 p.m.	2 cranes flew to river.	17
5:51 p.m.	17 cranes flew to river.	0

March 16, 1969, at Shimosetsuri:

4:10 p.m.	Cranes fed on a flat field adjacent to school where the children fed them. There were 11 cranes feeding here.	11
4:12 p.m.	2 cranes flew to food.	13
4:17 p.m.	3 cranes came to food, flying in.	16

4:24 p.m.	2 cranes came to food, flying.	18
4:34 p.m.	2 cranes came to food, flying.	20
4:38 p.m.	3 (including 1 young), 1 crane to food, flying.	23
4:44 p.m.	1 crane came to food, flying in.	24
5:26 p.m.	4 cranes, bullied by a dominant male flew to Setsuri Gawa (River) to roost. (Official sunset, 5:30).	4
5:43 p.m.	3 cranes went back to river to roost (800 m away).	7
5:51 p.m.	11, 2 cranes flew to river.	20
5:54 p.m.	2 cranes flew back to river to roost.	22
5:58 p.m.	2 cranes (the last) flew back but landed on a field adjacent to the Setsuri River. It was so dark we could barely see them but they went shortly into river for night. Freezing again Temp. −3°C. Wind nearly gone.	24

From existing records, this bird is found frequently in central Manchuria in summer, has decreased in the Maritime Kray in U.S.S.R., but has increased considerably in eastern Hokkaido.

A pair and youngster of Japanese Cranes. Akan, March 10, 1969. The pair are giving unison call; male with wings held over his back—not with drooping primaries like G.americana, for example. Female in center. Females hold their wings against their sides.

Austin and Kuroda (1953) wrote:

"This, the noblest and finest of all the Japanese birds, was apparently a not uncommon breeding bird throughout Japan in feudal times. It was wiped out almost everywhere early in the Restoration, but a small group managed to survive in the extensive, almost inaccessible marshes just inland of Kushiro, Hokkaido, where it is still resident and non-migratory. This site was investigated for the first time by H. Saito in 1924 (*Tori*, 1926: 16-19). It is a deep, fresh-water marsh of about 3,000 acres extending from Zesshin village north to the Kutcharo plain. It freezes from December to April, but a few spring holes remain open through the winter. The cranes that live there wander but little, which is their salvation. Occasionally in very severe winters when spring holes freeze over, a few birds stray past Cape Erimo to the Ishikari Plain, where they usually starve to death. Two birds were seen in Kitani in late September 1926; and again on 15-16 September 1937, probably post-nuptial wanderers."

"In 1924 Saito estimated the population as fewer than 20 birds and he found six nests, three of which were in use. On the strength of his report the site was made a National Monument in 1925. Thanks to its inaccessibility the birds are seldom disturbed. The population increased to about 30 in 1934. Saito was able to visit the area again in 1949, and found 35 or 36 cranes still there. (He reports incidently, that they are now quite tame.) The breeding area can be reached easily in winter on skis, but in spring, summer, and fall it is almost inaccessible."

The Japanese people's protectionist attitude in Hokkaido is the greatest aid to the survival of the species. Adult people admire, respect, study, feed and protect the cranes and by example teach children, who help feed and count them. Even small youngsters are imbued with the idea that the birds must be protected and saved. Because of this human attitude, the Japanese Crane now feeds fearlessly close to houses, in fields, in back yards, except during the breeding season.

When the waste grain on harvested fields gives out in early winter, the birds are given supplementary food by certain designated farmers, or by school groups. Here the birds congregate in groups and families, often feeding in close proximity, only a few feet apart. They feed during early morning, again during midday, and a third time late in the afternoon (this is evident in the Tables). Leaving food regions they often return to rivers to get drinking water, but at times they eat snow. At night they go to roost between sundown and dark.

I observed that the birds did considerable dancing on wintering grounds. When the temperatures climbed above freezing on March 15, then to 2.5°C. on March 16, I noted copulation for the first time. (1969, 8:45 A.M.). Yamazaki observed it March 18 at 8:00, 8:20, 8:50 and 9:50 A.M. The next week many birds returned to their nesting marshes, deserting their past seasons young for the first time (this was noted in counts on the feeding region, which were 63 to 67 birds March 8 to 16 with either 6 or 7 young. On March 20 there were only 36 — 11 young — and on March 25 a flock of only 18 of which 9 were young; by April 4 the flock consisted of 17 birds of which 14 were young). During 1968 Hayashida reported copulation was first observed on March 6 to 8, while eggs were laid in one nest March 23.

H. Masatomi (1971, 1972) discussed behavior of this bird in Hokkaido as did Hayashida (1973).

Migrations

This bird migrates in Asia. Dementiev and Gladkov (1951) wrote:

"In the Maritime Province it migrates very early —from the second half of March up to the middle of April. In 1869 first birds were noted on the Sungachi March 16 and migration was strongest between the 6th and mid-April, when a few flew (Przevalsky, 1870). On the Ussuri and Suyfun first birds were flying 13 to 15 March in pairs or small flocks (Dorries)."

In Hokkaido cranes migrate only a few km even before snow has thawed and streams all thawed out and they remain on these nesting grounds until September and October. Dementiev and Gladkov (1951) said, in Siberia:

"The return flight in autumn is very dragged out, from September, even sometimes in August, to November, up to December. On the Amur and at the mouth of the Ussuri, late cranes were observed 14 September 1854....In other years on the Ussuri it has been observed in November with uninterrupted flights going south. The river at this time was already covered with floating ice, a later flock of 4 was observed apart in December...on the shores of the Ussuri (Tazanowski, 1875).

La Touche (1933) reported that Styan found the Manchurian Crane on some of the wildest marshlands on the Yangtse and at Poyang Lake in winter. He also recounted and experience of Pere David who said the crane was such a great rarity in China, that a live pair was offered to him at Peking, for 1,000 teals (at that time £320). During seven years at Chinwangtao in northeast Chihli, La Touche heard of only two being obtained, one of which was shot in November 1916. He said these cranes usually came in October and when traveling usually flew in formation like geese but more slowly and irregularly, and at a very great height. Their penetrating call was usually heard long before the birds became visible. During winter many were snared for export to other parts of China and to Japan.

In eastern Siberia, Dementiev and Gladkov wrote (1951) that the usual biotope is large clearings, not always marshy, overgrown with small bunches of reed grass (*Calamagrostris neglecta*). Some are shallow river borders, almost without thickets. They also wrote:

"Soon each pair begins nesting [where] they live until the fall migration. In distinction from the Daurian Crane (*G. vipio*) the Manchurian Crane is inclined to nest, not in the narrow valleys, but in the clearings on the plains (Przevalsky). In the outlying southern districts at Lake Khanka in the tremendous expanse, pair separates from pair, a considerable distance by many kilometers. Pairs respond to one another though producing a morning and sometimes evening trumpeting performance between themselves...One is able to hear (it) at 3-4 kilometers (Shulpin)."

THE NEST

Dementiev and Gladkov (1951) wrote:

"A nest, with young (found) by Shulpin at the mouth of the Lefu, near Altinovki, was located amidst an extensive marshy lowland... The marshy ground was somewhat covered with hummocks, with short, barely green grass, with moss scattered here and there. Amongst this growth was a clearing about four meters across within which was located the nest. The clearing was the work of the cranes; grass had been pulled up, stamped and trampled into the spot and laid in a disorderly flat spread, somewhat leveled by the birds feet. This was 98 cm in diameter, perfectly flat, in a level place...and built of small pieces of nearby plants."

Saito (Austin and Kuroda, 1953) reported: "The nest, 90 cm. at the base, 60 cm. at the top, is built on the ground on a base of heavy alder twigs with thinner ones on top, into which green reeds are entwined as they grow around it, and lined in the center with stems and leaves of grasses and the same reeds."

Iwamatsu (1963) showed photographs of several nests from Hokkaido. These nests were about the same width at the top as at the base, and measured 111 and 122 cm across as did most nests. But the one we found at Shimochanbetsu was one of the largest crane nests I have ever seen. It was 7 m in circumference, 198 to 212 cm across, about 85 cm above water, which was 20 cm deep. It was in the center of a large clearing made by the birds themselves, 15 to

153

20 m across where the birds had dragged masses of *Phragmites* into a huge pile. The *Phragmites* were approximately 376 cm in height, completely concealing the nest except from the top or near the top of a nearby foothill from which we located the bird setting on the nest. The top of the nest was about 100 cm across; the center depressed about 6 cm for the eggs. The nest was made entirely of *Phragmites* except for some few plants that may have come along when the birds dragged the *Phragmites* into the pile.

Biotope Used for Nesting. Takeo Iwamatsu (1963) described the Kushiro regions in Hokkaido: "...the vast and desolate view of the Kushiro Shitsugen [a kind of swamp where the water plants are piled up for thousands of years without decomposition because of coldness] is located north of Kushiro City, Hokkaido, and covers an area of 20,000 hectares. The River Kushiro and its many tributaries wind their way through the marsh, and combined with countless interspersed ponds make a vast jungle of the *Kitayoshi (Phragmites)* and other plants, inaccessible to any man and animal.

"At the snow-thawing season or after heavy rain, dry land and water becomes indiscriminate, and turn into *zero-meter area*. With the duck-weed upon it, the swamp looks shallow at first glance, but once you step into it, you are sure to sink as deep as the breast."

Iwamatsu reported that along the meandering River Chiruhashiai, bordering marshes appear like floating islands in a lake. It is impossible during the breeding season to get into the region except by *choro*, a small boat. Another similar marsh is found at Lake Furen, Nemuro Province.

I observed these marshes in October 1965 and March-April 1969. Professor H. Masatomi, R. Y. Takahashi, A. Yoshida (Chairman of the Kushiro Branch of the Hokkaido Crane Preservation Board) and T. Hayashida took me to many of the marshes in Hokkaido. Many of the regions were upper reaches of streams, nearly all of which drained eventually into the great Kushiro Marsh.

Many marshes exceed 50 hectares in size; the great Kushiro Marsh extends 30 km in length, 2½ to 20 km in width. No one is sure just how many Japanese Cranes nest in it. Often the size, extent or geographical barriers, such as a natural stream, a low mountain range, a highway, even a small stream at times, form territorial boundaries for the cranes. At Otanoshike, a narrow about 10 km long marsh, only one pair of cranes nest. Many nesting marshes are not subject to heavy flooding; others are built in the midst of deep water, all are put in water except those at the Crane Park (Tsuru Koen).

Territorial sizes range between thirty-five and several hundred hectares. In upper reaches the birds nest well out from shore; in the Kushiro Marsh cranes often nest in about the geographical center of their territories. Most regions are well away from humans.

Along the borders many shrubs often grow, some two to four meters high, while often low mountain ranges or hills border one or two sides. In some cases lake borders are used. Some plants near nest sites are: *Equisetum palustre, Lobelia sessilifolia, Phragmites longivalvis,* and most common, *Phragmites communis.* Some grasses and some sedges (*Carex* sp.) also grow here. In spring only dead plants from the past season produce cover, usually reeds, some 15 to 250 cm in height.

Hayashida (verbal) noted most nests were the same width at the top and at water level. All were slightly depressed in the top center for the eggs. Since *Phragmites* was the most common plant in nest vicinities, it was used most often for nest construction. The dead stalks were torn to pieces, by the birds and piled onto the nest site. Often the nest region was quite denuded of tall vegetation. Some pieces in the nest were 14 to 30 cm long; others only 2 or 3 cm. Water varied between a few centimeters up to a meter or more in depth.

During the warm March 1968, a female laid her first egg March 23. During 1969 one laid April 1 — both at Tsuru Koen. The average of five laying dates was April 3. Egg records all fell between March 23 and May 19. There were twelve April records and six May records besides the one for March.

R. Y. Takahashi (verbal) reported eggs were laid at Tsuru Koen during the early morning, most often about 0630 hours. Incubation started immediately. Since nights are often very cold eggs would be frozen if unattended. Eggs are laid usually two days apart.

Eggs

Eggs are oval, some somewhat elliptical in shape. Some sets are unspotted, milky-white in color, while others are drab-gray, pale vinaceous, even light brown color with spots of darker brown, brownish-drab, dark umber, and dark gray. The shell is smooth, with little or no gloss, with fewer pits and pimples than most crane's eggs.

Usually two eggs are laid, but occasionally there is only one. The average of 22 sets was 1.955 eggs per set (21x2;1x1).

The average measurements of 17 eggs were 101.17 (94.8-108.0)x64.88 (61.2-68.8) mm. Kiyuso (1942) gave the average, as 102.9 (99-108)x64.1 (61.2-70.2) mm and weights between 255 and 273 grams. Ten eggs weighed by Hayashida and me, averaged 231.7 (210-250) grams.

On April 14, 1969, T. Hayashida and I watched a lone Japanese Crane fly from the Otanoshike Marsh to Lake Koitoi at 3:55 P.M.; and the same bird or another fly back the same course at 5:55 P.M. to spend the night in a rather open pool (sunset was at 6:02). On April 16 at 4:45 P.M. a bird flew the same course again, from Koitoi to the pool to spend the night. Since there had been a pair here April 6 when the region was frozen almost solid and covered with some snow, it appeared that a nest might be around the low mountain range. On April 17 I watched the (apparently) male crane fly from the pool at 4:49 A.M. to exactly the same region. The birds did not call but apparently changed places. They changed again at 7:25, 11:39 and 1:44. At no time did they call. During most of the day the non-incubating bird fed in the region of Koitoi River along the stream or in a neighboring field.

A pair at Shimochanbetsu appeared on their nesting grounds on March 23, 1969. The two birds came daily to feed back of Katsumi Nagata's home, but on March 31 and thereafter only one bird at a time came to feed. We found the nest with two eggs about two km from his house April 13. One bird left at 8:30 A.M., the second bird came back at 8:37 for food. At 10:45 we were in a low range of hills and heard them give the Unison Call, and shortly we found their nest.

R. Y. Takahashi (verbal) reported that at Tsuru Koen the cranes changed places usually twice, at about 9:00 A.M. and 4:00 P.M., but sometimes they changed four times. Here the non-incubating bird roosted near the nest at night. Mr. Nagata said the bird at Shimochanbetsu roosted about 1 km from the nest; at Otanoshike the bird roosted about 4.8 km away.

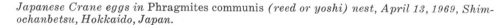

Japanese Crane eggs in Phragmites communis *(reed or yoshi) nest, April 13, 1969, Shimochanbetsu, Hokkaido, Japan.*

Young

Takahashi and Hayashida reported that Japanese Crane eggs are pipped for two to three days prior to hatching and that the young remain in the nest another two to three days. Following this the parents lead them carefully away from the nest site, feeding where possible on drier areas or marsh borders. Some, according to their nesting territories, must continue to live inside large marshes. From this time on the parents care for them without fail. At times parents have even offered food to a bird as old as 10 months, but when he was about ten and a half to eleven months old they suddenly deserted him. The parents flew back to their old nesting grounds in late March. The young began concentrating in a group at the old winter region, eating supplementary food placed by specified persons.

Hatching dates were: April 23-25; May 2-15 (Tsuru Koen-R. Takahashi); May 1-3, 1969 (Takobu-Dr. H. Masatomi); May 7, 1968, May 6-8, 1969 (Tôro Ko, T. Iwamatsu); May 3-5; May 19, 1954 (Miyajima-zaki-T. Iwamatsu); May 3-5, 1969 (Shimochanbetsu-Dr. H. Masatomi); May 20, 1959 (Furen Ko); May 3-June 6 (Kushiro-T. Hayashida); May 17, 1968 (Yamahana-T. Hayashida). The average was May 8.

Young are capable of swimming when only two or three days old (Iwamatsu, 1963; 1967). They also are capable of picking up much food when just a few days old, although parents often pick it up and offer it to them many times daily.

In southeastern Siberia, along the lower Lefu, Przhevalsky found young had hatched in mid-June 1869. By July 20, 1858 Maak found young, large in size, near Cape Tsifyak on the Ussuri, but they were still unable to fly (Dementiev and Gladkov, 1951).

The young Japanese Crane grows much during the first month, becoming a lighter tawny color and acquiring very long tarsi, so much so that the tibio-tarsal joint appears out of proportions to the rest of the bird. But by the second month the remainder of the bird has acquired growth so it now appears normal.

VOICE

The downy chick gives a shrill *peeep*, often with a burr to it, at times more like a *peeer* call. It resembles the call of other downy crane chicks. It retains this call until 11 or 12 months of age when it acquires the adult call.

Similar to *Grus grus*, but even more like *Grus canadensis*, in winter a single *Garroooa*, the adult *Grus japonensis* sounds at times three or more syllables, almost exactly alike. During flight it gives a low, guttural *Kurrr*. The alarm call is shriller than the normal call. As the bird gives it, it usually stands at attention, with body, neck and head erect. All neighboring cranes also become immediately alert. When reassuring its mate, one of a pair often gives a guttural low *purrr*, and both parents often give this when calling the downy chick to them. The "Unison Call" is similar to that of *G. canadensis*. The male, displaying secondaries much more, calls *Garroooa-garroooa-garrooa-garroooa-garroooa*, varying the number of syllables. He holds his head erect, and under favorable conditions struts around the female. Simultaneously, she utters a *Tuk-tuk-tuk-tuk-tuk-tuk*, generally as long as he calls. This call is often given on the winter and spring feeding regions and again on the breeding grounds. It is given at times when the birds change places at the nest. Another call, given by one of a flock as the birds prepare to fly, is a low *Kurrr* barely audible a hundred meters away. When giving the "Unison Call," the male extends his secondaries high above his back, with the primaries normally well concealed beneath, and extends his head upward, backward bill pointing forward. The female, with bill pointed upward, holds her wings, against her sides.

FOOD

During the spring and summer, Japanese Cranes feed extensively on small mudfishes. Professor T. Abe of Tokyo told me that these are probably *Misgurunus anguillicaudatus*, but that some may be other loaches such as *Lefua* sp. and *Cobitis* sp. Parents feed chicks on some of these along with other items, including many insects. They eat frogs, the common Hokkaido one being *Rana temporaria temporaria*. At Tsuru Koen at times they feed the chicks on salamanders, *Salamandrella keyserlingii*, but usually on *Hynobius retardatus*. In fall and winter they again return to buckwheat and corn, loose grain in recently harvested fields. Later they resort to supplementary food. On many mornings schoolchildren and designated farmers rise before dawn, carry the food to the same feeding region used for years, scatter it on the ground or snow, then often linger to gaze at the birds for awhile.

THE DANCE

All cranes dance, the Japanese Crane much more during late winter or early spring. Both pairs and young birds dance, often the latter more than its parents. Young non-breeding cranes usually dance even more. Pairs often dance opposite each other, hopping and jumping together for several minutes. More birds dance after eating than before. Sometimes after the morning food has been consumed, dancing is started by one individual, then taken up by others until the entire flock hops, skips, and jumps all over the region.

I have noted seven or eight different steps in relation to the dance or pair behavior of cranes in general: (1) jumping; (2) bowing; (3) spreading of

Japanese Cranes dancing wildly prior to breeding season. Akan, March 13, 1969.

wings; (4) whirling or twisting; (5) legs dangling; (6) head bobbing; (7) neck weaving; (8) billing. The Japanese Crane apparently does little turning, nor head bobbing, neck weaving nor billing. Jumps and bows are usually in the direction the bird faces; if the bird hops, it goes in one direction, seldom turning.

Often one of a pair dances when the other does not. Sometimes the dancing bird, either the male or female, dances for several minutes around its mate. At times the mate seems indifferent, at others even annoyed. I saw one bird peck its mate severely after it had danced around him for several minutes. One or both birds may dance after copulation. Sometimes one or both birds of a pair dance as a Distraction Display near eggs or chicks when a potential enemy, such as a man, approaches. At times like these they may also throw around vegetation or clods.

Some birds produce much noise when dancing; others are quiet. Some cranes in a group seem to have a synchronized jumping, many doing it in rapid succession or simultaneously; some seem to jump alternately. Sometimes a pair faces each other; again they face in different directions. I classify dancing in different categories:

1. *Play.* Energy release. This is definitely the reason some cranes dance. When we raised a young Sandhill Crane in 1942, the chick danced all over our yard when released from its night pen in the morning of its sixth day. A penned 10-month-old Crowned Crane released in the early morning in Zambia behaved very similar before settling down to eat.

2. *Adult.* Birds approaching maturity dance more. This was evident in Hokkaido when *G. japonensis* youngsters, 10 to 10½ months old, danced all around their parents, or around other birds again and again all day.

3. *Communal.* Birds in large flocks seem to dance more. Flocks occur during the non-breeding seasons, and especially in winter I have observed this when it appears at times as though birds all through the flock are jumping up and down. This occurs especially in flocks of *Grus canadensis*, *G. grus*, *G. antigone*, *G. rubicundus* and *G. japonensis*. This does not appear to have anything to do with territorial behavior.

4. *Opposite dancing.* One or both birds of a pair may dance opposite each other. Some stand (*G. antigone*) and both birds weave their necks back and forth simultaneously. *G. japonensis* dance opposite each other many times, or only one of the birds dances.

5. *Fall dancing.* This may be done by a non-mated bird trying to attract another of the opposite sex, especially in flocks of non-breeding birds. It may have no significance. Again it may be merely play.

6. *Distraction display.* In the vicinity of eggs or young, both cranes or one often dance, again one or both pick up clods or vegetation, hold it in their bills or toss it around. All this serves to divert the attention of a potential enemy.

TERRITORY

Crane territories may be classified according to different conditions or seasons. Some of these territories vary considerably with numbers of the same species present, probable amount of food, even at times to the humor of the birds involved. Territory is evident even with young birds. In this case dominance is strongly evident. A male crane has at least five different territories:

1. *Territory around himself.* At times I have even seen a crane peck at its mate when it approached too closely. This, of course, does not happen very often. The male also maintains this territory against all other birds of his kind.

2. *Territory around his mate.* In general he guards her zealously, often almost with jealousy. He not only guards her but protects her against danger. In this case the territory moves with the birds as in 1.

3. *Territory on the feeding region.* This is not defended as much as some but is a definite area, more so during the breeding season when for example *Grus canadensis* in southern Michigan feed on separate fields bordering their nesting marshes, seldom using the same field.

4. *Territory in a flock or at a roost.* Here again cranes have a very small territory but it is definitely guarded and protected. If it is approached too closely, any bird shows concern and attacks.

5. *Territory around the nest or young.* Often this is

Two first-year Japanese Cranes dancing, late March 1969, Akan. They have been just deserted this week by parents and are forming a flock of similar aged birds.

Attack and Escape by Japanese Cranes, April 13, 1969, Shimohororo, Hokkaido, Japan.

tremendous in size, up to 1,000 acres, more or less. Again it is as small as 8 acres. Often, boundaries that had been established formerly are maintained for many years. Usually little conflict is observed on these except when the male or pair are first establishing it. After establishment it seems that little effort is necessary to maintain it. Territory around the roaming young follows the birds and varies in area, location, even in size, according to where the family is located.

All cranes show certain behavior. Some show much more severe territorial defense than others. For example, *G. vipio* and *G. japonensis* are much more defensive than *G. monachus* even though there are greater numbers of the latter. Following is the method used by the usual crane against one of its own species when trespassing. The displays are:

1. *Pecking at the back.* Most cranes, including *G. japonensis*, do this rather deliberately, as if preening the back or scapular regions. *G. leucogeranus* does it almost with a jerk, most often pecking itself in the mid-back. Often when it brings its head forward, it again does so with a jerky motion.

2. *Preening. False Preening.* Apparently all cranes do this prior to attack, and especially when showing territorial defense.

3. *Wing-flapping.* Some birds do this violently; some only moderately; others not all.

4. *The defense stance.* Bill pointing downward, neck arched, swanlike, the bird faces and begins swiftly approaching its opponent. If the invading crane has not left by now, he does so quickly, unless he wants to fight.

5. *Stiff-legged, goose-step approach.* This is not always displayed but usually follows 4. The crane moves directly toward its opponent.

6. *Wings raised slightly.* This is not always done but may make the bird appear larger and more fearful, causing its opponent to "escape" rather than "attack."

7. *Running.* Following the above steps, the bird begins to run toward its opponent. Most invading birds leave rapidly at this maneuver.

8. *Flying at opponent.* If the opponent is some distance away, the attacker often flies directly toward it without doing any of the above. I have never seen

Japanese Cranes in night roosting spot, Akan River, March 8, 1969.

any bird remain on another's nesting territory when it saw the rightful owner flying toward it.

9. *Attack*. Using the bill, feet and legs are weapons, strongly beating wings waving back and forth, definite attack is often quite severe. Pecking and clawing are the most deadly of attack methods. A young male *Grus canadensis*, pecked on the back of the head by a larger and stronger male, was killed immediately. The skeletal material was saved and in the base of the occipital bone was an opening showing where the skull had been fractured. Downy chicks at times show this same attitude. It is not necessarily the oldest one. The weaker bird shows such extreme fear at times that it tries to "escape," running a long distance from its parents or nest mate.

It is not known whether one egg of a set produces a male bird, the second egg a female, as some investigators have theorized. On two occasions this proved to be the case with *G. canadensis*. At times the eggs could be both males, both females or one of each. If they are the same sex, or if one is more belligerent, a fight between them might ensue. But there are many times when both chicks are reared to maturity side by side without showing any animosity toward each other. In some families one parent takes one chick, the other parent the other chick, and they wander a few meters apart so the chicks have no contact. By this method two chicks are sometimes reared to full growth. I have found two-thirds-grown chicks at Haehnle Sanctuary in July all alone, with no parent anywhere near them. Possibly in regions of adequate food and few enemies, a chick may reach maturity without parental care. But evidence is strong that on many occasions one chick attacks his sibling as soon as a few hours after birth. I even talked with a man in Florida who stated that he saw parent *Grus canadensis* kill one of their offspring by attacking it with their bills. I have never seen this happen myself.

Recent Japanese Records

In Hokkaido, Tancho was found during 1972 in additional regions from where we found it in 1968. At that time it was known to nest at (1) Ôhtu, (2) Onbetsu, (3) Otanoshike, (4) Tsuru Koen, (5) Yamahana, (6) Shimoninishibetsu (Akan Town), (7) Hokuto, (8) Kushiro Shitsugen, (9) Onneai Gawa, (10) Miyajima, (11) Setsuri Gawa, (12) Kirokotan, (13) Watanabe Gawa, (14) Kothutaro Gawa, (15) Kayanuma Station, (16) Shirarutoro Ko, (17) Toro Ko, (18) Eoruto Numa (19) Omishiron Gawa (20) Takobu Ko, (21) Shimochanbetsu, (22) Baito Gawa, (23) Hichirippo, (24) Biwase Gawa, (25) Furen Ko, and around the Nemuro region. All of these regions were within 60 km of Kushiro, Akan or Nemuro. Discovery of these regions, some published, were made by Hiroyuki Masatomi (1970, 1971), Tsuneo Hayashida (1973), Takeo Iwamatsu (1963, 1967), Ito and Kamada (1964), R. Y. Takahashi and Akio Yoshida, many of whom recorded it in print (as above). They also recorded wintering regions as: (1) Ôhtu, (2) Akan, (3) Hororo, (4) Shimosetsuri, (5) Shimohororo, (6) Tsuru Koen and (7) Nemuro region.

Annual December counts made by the Japanese Crane Clubs, children from the Middle Schools, were as follows: 1952 (33), 1953 (42), 1954 (52), 1955 (61), 1956 (76), 1957 (92), 1958 (125), 1959 (139), 1960 (172), 1961 (175), 1962 (184), 1963 (147), 1964 (154), 1965 (172), 1966 (170), 1967 (200), 1968 (171), 1969 (212), 1970 (179), 1971 (147), 1972, (222), with 24, 26, 33 and 26 of these young birds, 1965-68.

Chapter Six

THE WHOOPING CRANE

(Grus americana)

Ardea americana, Linnaeus, *Syst. Nat.*, 10th ed., 1, 1758, p. 142.
Type locality: North America, i.e. Hudson's Bay, *ex*.Edwards.
Vernacular names: The Whooping Crane, Whooper, Big White Crane
(English); la Grue de Amérique (French); der Weisse Amerikanische
Kranich, Trompeterkranich (German); de Amerikaanse Kraanvogel
(Dutch); Grulla Blanca (Mexican); viejo del agua (Mexican cowhands);
Wapo Oocheechawk (Cree); Tutteeghuk (West Coast Hudson Bay Es-
kimo); Trumpetar Trana (Swedish).

The Whooping Crane is a symbol of many things: of conservation, of survival
under odds, of regal beauty, of wilderness. This great bird is an example of
wildlife preferring complete isolation to contact with other species, especially
man. Back in 1941 only fifteen Whooping Cranes returned to Aransas Wildlife
Refuge, Texas, having survived the onslaughts of civilization and the encroachment of men to the edges of and even into this last refuge. These were
the forebears of the present (and growing) population of fifty-five or more wild
birds and twenty captive birds.

I am glad to have seen the Whooping Crane, in captivity at Aransas and in
the wild. I am glad my children have seen the bird; I hope that my grandchildren and succeeding generations of Americans will see this great bird,
which has survived on the North American continent for millions of years.

From the Pliocene fossils of the Snake River, Idaho, come the remains of a
crane classified as a Whooping Crane (Miller, 1944). From the Pleistocene of
Rancho la Brea (Miller, 1925) and McKittrick, California (DeMay, 1941) come

Adult and young Whooping Cranes on feeding grounds, Aransas National Wildlife Refuge, Austwell, Texas, Feb. 3, 1971.

a very limited representation of a large crane ascribed with some reservations to *G. americana* (Miller, 1944). From the Pleistocene of Seminole Field, Itchtucknee River and Melbourne, Florida, other remains of the Whooping Crane were found (1931 A.O.U. Check List).

During historic times Linnaeus (1758) first described the bird from two types: One from Catesby and his description of a white crane from Carolina; the second from Edwards, who painted one taken along the west coast of Hudson Bay. When Lewis and Clark made their historic trip across Western America, in what is now McLean County, North Dakota, they noted some very large cranes, pure white with black wing tips. Audubon and his contemporaries confused first-year Whooping Cranes with Sandhill Cranes, and so many of their records lose value.

Robert P. Allen in his masterful work (1952) on the Whooping Crane summarized that the most rapid decrease...[in Nebraska migration numbers] took place between 1890 and 1910. The year 1910 also approximates the beginning of serious decline on the wintering grounds in Louisiana. But prior to this, about 1800 the Whooping Crane was no longer observed along the Atlantic seaboard and by 1900, except a small region in Louisiana, it was gone from wintering regions east of the Mississippi. Soon it reached the lowest numbers of any known crane. In late 1941, the U.S. Fish and Wildlife Service, the Canadian Wildlife Service, and the National Audubon Society, realizing its plight, began quick and drastic action to try and save it. The weak spots were the winter home, the long migration route and the fact no one knew where the small population spent their summers. Winter habitat along the

Texas coastline was purchased and named the Aransas National Wildlife Refuge. Whooping Cranes had wintered here as long as man had known them. This region, 47,261 acres with a coastline of 45 miles, bordered San Antonio, Ayres, Mesquite, Aransas, and St. Charles Bays. The few remaining cranes wintered almost exclusively on this new refuge, occasionally on adjacent St. Joseph and Matagorda Islands, rarely as far away as King Ranch or south to northern Tamaulipas, northeastern Mexico. A stepped-up publicity program to aid the species began in the 1940's and has continued to this day all over North America.

Another program to study the biology of the species was begun, while its past and present distribution was mapped and a search for its unknown breeding grounds was begun. The last known breeding locality had been in south-central Saskatchewan in 1922. The remaining birds nested to the north, somewhere in the vast Canadian wilderness. No one knew whether the few birds were scattered over this immense wilderness or if the entire group remained somewhat loosely intact on their summer nesting grounds. At times from 1945 to 1948, Fred Bard, Olin S. Pettingill, Jr., Robert P. Allen, Robert Smith Walter Tholen, I and many others searched by air through this wilderness. These searches were unsuccessful.

On June 30, 1954, a fire started in the northwest corner of Wood Buffalo Park, Northwest Territories, Canada. Helicopters were used to take in fire-fighting equipment. In one craft en route to Fort Smith, Don Landalls, the pilot, and M. G. Wilson, Superintendent of Forestry, passed over an immense region of small lakes bordered by muskeg and spruces. Suddenly, below them, they spotted two adult Whooping Cranes and their week-old chick. The report to the Canadian Wildlife Service mammalogist at Fort Smith, William A. Fuller, brought word to Ottawa and spread throughout the world. After ten years of searching, the nesting region of this nearly extinct bird was discovered in an impassable wilderness in the most extensive Canadian National Park. The Canadian Wildlife Service began, and has continued until this day, regular reconnaissance flights over the nesting grounds of this rare bird, continuing from spring to fall.

During the summer of 1955, after several weeks of trial and error, Robert P. Allen and Robert and Raymond C. Stewart reached the nest pond. They traveled first by canoe and on foot amid hordes of mosquitoes and flies. They found the region impassable and returned to Fort Smith. Then, later they flew by helicopter, to an area from which they could walk to the nesting site. They studied the nesting pond of one pair, found their old nest and later observed from the air the pair with two chicks.

That same year the Canadian Wildlife Service located four nests or family groups throughout the region; by 1967 to 1970, they found ten to 14 nests annually. Thus the region, limited in area, limited in access, has been discovered, nests mapped and studied mostly from the air (Novakowski, 1966). The majority of Whooping Cranes were found to nest in the potholes region of Wood Buffalo Park. Occasionally a lone bird or two has been seen farther north or in Saskatchewan.

The Whooping Crane survives today primarily because of four things:

(1) the creation of Wood Buffalo National Park, Canada; (2) the fact the bird nested in an impenetrable wilderness, far from enemies like man; (3) the creation of Aransas National Wildlife Refuge; (4) the educational program begun by the National Audubon Society and carried on by both the Canadian Wildlife Service and the U.S. Fish and Wildlife Service to convince the public that the Whooping Crane was in danger of extinction and that the bird was and is worthy of saving. Many poachers are city dwellers and young boys, ignorant of wildlife identification. Although a few have an indifferent attitude, the majority want to learn. In the school educational programs teen-agers have learned about the rarity of this bird and the need for its preservation. This effort in turn aided other conservation programs. Those who cared used the knowledge; those who did not care possibly were made more fearful, if not of the law, then at least of public opinion. Hunters, farmers and scientists alike have participated in the educational program. Jerome J. Pratt (January 1965) wrote: "It was pointed out by some of the Canadian and U.S. Wildlife officials I had talked with that most of the whoopers that leave Aransas in the spring and fail

to return the next fall are killed with a gun, accidentally or otherwise. Folders with a "Memorandum to all Sportsmen" were enclosed urging sportsmen's groups to join in the educational program to stop the needless killing of these valuable birds. The response was gratifying, for many of the sportsmen's organizations passed the information on through their official publications...For the first time every bird that left Aransas in the spring of 1964 returned to the refuge in the fall. This is a great improvement over such years as 1941, when 26 went north and only 13 came back."

This also was the real beginning of the uptrend in the Whooping Crane population. It brings home the fact that a continuous educational program is essential if this and other rare birds and wildlife are going to be preserved. If the population of several thousand Whooping Cranes could not compete with 19th-century civilization, what chance is the small surviving group going to have against 20th-century sprawl unless humans change their thinking. This difference of thinking is strongly evident in Japan, where every crane is of great importance to everyone. People do not come there to shoot them, they come with cameras to photograph them. Imagine nearly 100 Americans rushing out to Aransas Refuge, as I saw in Kyushu, to see the departure of the cranes flying northward in the spring.

DESCRIPTION

Adult. (Sexes alike, male slightly larger). All the plumage is white except the alula, primaries, and their greater coverts, which are uniform slaty black. Not as glossy, satiny-white as with the White Pelican (Allen, 1952:197). Allen stated that one individual showed some white at the base of some of the primaries, a brownish cast on others and considerable white-brown in the five smaller feathers of the greater coverts. The last two coverts were completely white except for a few minute black spots near the tip of the smaller. Of the four feathers of the false wing, three were slaty-black toward the terminal end and one was washed with gray. The age of this bird was not known and it was presumed to be a female. There is a wedge-shaped patch of dark plumbeous feathers on the nape or post-occipital region (Ridgway and Friedmann, 1941).

The forehead, crown and anterior part of the occiput are bare, except for sparse, black, hair-like feathers, heavier on the forehead than anteriorly. The skin is warty or granulated carmine reddish. The lores and the cheeks (malar regions), including a narrow angular strip extending from the latter down each side of the throat, also naked, are carmine, and similarly bristled, the bristles denser anteriorly (Ridgway and Friedmann). There is some

Whooping Cranes in flight, western Saskatchewan. (Photo by Fred G. Bard and F. W. Lahrman, Sask. Museum of Natural History.)

variation in the shades of color in the bare portions and some variation in the size of the dark spot on the nape (Allen). There is apparently considerable difference in the deepness of the red color as with other cranes. Often unhealthy birds show much lighter color than well-fed, healthy birds.

Stevenson and Griffith (1946) stated "The bill is olive-gray, tipped with dark gray. In certain lights it appears light yellow." It also varies according to health conditions (Allen, 1952). The base of the bill is pink or rosaceous which is more extensive on the upper mandible. The small bare area between the rami is also red. Ridgway and Friedmann (1941) described the bill as "Wax Yellow, tipped with dull greenish or yellowish." Allen (1952,198) reported the lining of the bill as seen through the nostrils was dark flesh-color. The eye is surrounded except behind with bare skin more or less covered with black hair-like feathers.

The inner secondaries are longer than the primaries as in most cranes and are down curved. These can be raised above the back, at will, when certain displays are desired (as with many other cranes). When standing, the black primaries and alula do not show, the bird appearing pure white.

Juvenal Plumage

Predominantly white but covered with brownish or buffy-tipped feathers. The belly, lower breast, and back are predominantly white. Wings, head (feathered) and neck show quite a bit of brown, which Bent (1926) wrote was "pinkish cinnamon," "cinnamon buff" or "sayal brown," in an October bird. By February the same bird may be almost white (Allen). By the time it reaches Canada in May it appears entirely white. There is some variation in individuals, some acquiring the white much sooner than others, some even acquiring the bare face region quicker. Ridgway and Friedmann (1941) report that the head may be colored "sayal brown." Allen (1952) reported the color may vary between a rather dark russet brown or sayal brown to a light buff, either yellowish, saffron, or orange-tinged or pinkish-buff on the head. The primaries, alula and greater upper coverts are dull blackish. In at least

some birds the base of the bill is somewhat flesh-colored (Allen, 1952).

A young bird that remained at Aransas Refuge in 1941 retained a few brown coverts and a few cinnamon-tipped inner secondaries, as well as some brown-tipped tail feathers (Stevenson and Griffith, 1946).

Downy chick. Ridgway and Friedmann (1941) said: "General color of upper parts dull cinnamon to sayal brown, deepening into mikado brown or russet on rump, where still darker (liver brown or bay) along median line, continued along the median line of back, paler and grayer on neck, still paler behind wings; underparts pale dull grayish buffy or dull brownish whitish, tipped or suffused with pale cinnamon; bill pale buffy-brown, flesh color basally, with a small whitish spot on the upper mandible; tarsi and toes, light brownish." Fred Bradshaw, as quoted by Bent (1926) described the downy chick as buff colored from the neck to rump on the back it was somewhat darker, while the underparts were much paler. The white spot described on the tip of the upper mandible was the egg-tooth.

Robert Allen (1952:200-201) described the molts, but much more is now known by the U. S. Fish and Wildlife Service, which has reared many birds in captivity, and this information should be published shortly. Harvey Fisher and Donald C. Goodman (1955) gave a thorough report on the myology and summarized anatomical literature at that time. Berger (1956) has since recorded the appendicular myology of the Greater Sandhill Crane with comparative remarks on the Whooping Crane.

Measurements. Adult male: 9 specimens (CNHM, 2;MCZ,7). Wing, 626.4 (583-694) mm.; exposed culmen, 144.75 (126-153) mm.; from base of nostril, 98.5 (95-102) mm.; tarsus, 286.3 (279-299) mm.; bare tibia, 132 (119-146) mm.; middle toe with claw, 130 (124-139) mm.; length (1), 1,295 mm. Weight (1), 18 lbs (8,164.8 grams).

Adult female: 10 specimens (CNHM,1;U. of Kansas,1; LSU,1; MCZ,4; USNM,3). Wing, 611.9 (576-652) mm.; exposed culmen, 142.6 (132-161) mm.; from posterior base of nostril to tip of upper mandible, 89.2 (79-100) mm.; tarsus, 281.5 (234-312.5) mm.; tail (1), 309 mm.; bare tibia, 127.7 (115-139) mm.; middle toe with claw, 113.5 (113-114) mm.

Whooping Crane at Aransas National Wildlife Refuge, Feb. 3, 1971.

DISTRIBUTION

Although never common, this crane formerly summered over central North America. At one time it was found as far east as Cape May, New Jersey, and as far west as Great Salt Lake, Utah, northward through Yellowstone National Park to the mouth of the Mackenzie River, Northwest Territories, Canada, east to Hudson Bay and south to coastal Louisiana. In winter it was found in southern Louisiana and Texas southward into central Mexico.

During Pleistocene times it occurred near Los Angeles and in three Florida regions, and during Pliocene times in Idaho (Howard, 1930; Wetmore, 1931; Miller, 1944; Feduccia, 1967). During the 1800's the breeding ground extended in a narrow region from northern Illinois, across Iowa, southern Minnesota, North Dakota, across southern Manitoba, over much of Saskatchewan and east central Alberta northward into southern Mackenzie (Allen, 1952).

Migration

Normal departure from Aransas Wildlife Refuge is given in Table 14. Ordinarily Whooping Cranes leave in family groups, or groups of one or two families, sometimes in much larger groups. The average departure date is usually April 15 to 22, sometimes as early as March 24, as late as May 9. Birds usually leave in good weather with a tail wind. Robert H. Shields and Earl Benham (1968) watched a mass departure on April 6, 1966. The weather was clear, with an 18-20 mph southeast wind blowing. Twenty birds from a flock of thirty-two rose at 9:00 A.M. and began spiraling clockwise up and up to gain elevation. In twelve minutes they were visible only as tiny airborn specks and in a few minutes were no longer discernible in 7 x 50 binoculars.

The cranes left the ground in a group but began the ascent in groups of 3, 3, 2, 7 and 5, with a horizontal and vertical separation of the (probably family or non-breeders) groups from about 400 to 1,200 feet in a circle approximately a quarter-mile across. The birds maintained this position throughout their ascent. At 9:14 A.M. Benham noted a group of three beginning a similar ascent. In about five minutes they too were following the other twenty. As they ascended they continued to call, making a terrific din, while the twelve birds still on the ground were completely silent. A group observed leaving Saskatchewan by Fred Bard rose to a mile or so of elevation before leaving, thus indicating why many cranes in migration are never seen. They ordinarily fly about 35 miles per hour and probably fly for many hours before stopping. Otherwise they would be seen on the ground more often. For a detailed account of sightings around the United States see pp. 182-183.

NESTING

Nesting biotopes. Allen (1952:178) has recorded former nesting communities from Louisiana and other states and provinces. In Louisiana, a woman born in 1873, Mrs. Gaspard, observed a number of Whooping Crane's nests around 1883 near her childhood home on Pine Island, Vermillion Parish. The region was near White Lake, the most common growth, a bulrush (*Scirpus californicus*) and paille-fine (*Panicum hemitomum*). The birds broke down the rushes and put them into a huge pile that was capable of floating when strong south winds raised the water level.

In Iowa, where prairie is dominant, most nests were apparently found along the borders of lakes or in huge marshes with or without some woodlands encircling. All were regions of complete isolation at that time. Water usually was a few inches to a few feet in depth. Several nests were found in the heart of the marsh, a mile from shore but conspicuous because of their color. The nests were firm heaps of dead surrounding grass, placed on firm sod just out of water, about one and one-half feet high, each with a slight depression in the top for the eggs. In 1894 R. M. Anderson (1907) visited the Eagle Lake marsh: "as we came over a low ridge on one side of the marsh, two great white birds rose up several hundred yards away, and flew with slow, heavy flaps to the further side, where they stalked along with stately strides as fast as a man could walk. Occasionally one would utter a loud, ringing, resonant "whoop" that could be heard for a long distance. Near one end of the slough, in a small branch or inlet, several old Crane's nests, or muskrat houses, were found only a few rods apart. On one of these were two large greenish-brown eggs, spotted quite thickly over the whole surface with brown and buff spots and purplish shell markings. Both eggs were perfectly fresh and measured 4.06x2.38 and 4.03x 2.50. The nest was a mass of grass, rushes and reeds, about two feet across and rose eight to ten inches above the water, which was about eighteen inches deep. The nest was so solidly built that I sat down on it without sinking it into the water. The water was open for a few feet around the nest, but in most places was grown up with rushes and sawgrass... (The birds) approached within about twenty rods and would stand perfectly still for a minute at a time, with the wings widespread and held out from the body, making a beautiful picture with their graceful snowy-white bodies and great black-tipped wings. On moving towards them, they flew a short distance and alighted again, but defied closer approach."

The two last Saskatchewan nests described by Bent (1926) and Allen (1952) were both in very extensive marshy regions. The one found May 19, 1922 near Baliol, 20 miles north of Davidson, by Neil Gilmour was located in a marsh approximately 3 miles long and 1 to 2 miles wide, comprising upwards of 3,000 acres, nowhere more than 3 feet deep, most of it about knee-depth. It was grown to last year's dead grass about 2 feet above the water surface. The nest was in an open sheet of water about 30 feet across, a mound of the same coarse grass and reeds, flat with a slight concavity on top. On May 28, 1922, Fred Bradshaw found a nest in an open region, made of grass, three-cornered sedges, pulled up by the roots. The diameter was 4.5 feet, the height 15-18 inches above water level with a very slight depression in the center. This was at Muddy Lake, 7 miles south of Unity, Saskatchewan.

Allen (1952) wrote that "nearly all of the Canadian nesting sites of the Whooping Crane were in aspen parkland of the transitional zone lying between that type and the true prairie. All U. S. sites were in prairie habitats.... Much of the area occupied by aspen parkland is covered by sloughs, the majority of which are grown to willows (*Salix petiolaris* Sm.), but this willow is absent if the soil shows a high percentage of alkaline salts, as at Quill Lake and elsewhere in Saskatchewan, in which case the succession is direct to prairie. This variety is the rosemary willow (*S. longifolia* Muhl. *S. interior* Rowlee), on the other hand, develops if there is an abundant water supply and denuded soil (sometimes running water)."

The year after the Whooping Cranes were located in 1954 in Wood-Buffalo Park, Allen and others were dispatched to the region. The Park consists

A pair of Whooping Cranes (in foreground) in photo taken from Canadian Wildlife Service helicopter, June 3, 1964, Wood-Buffalo Park, N. W. T., Canada.

of 11,072,000 acres, he wrote (1956), including many regions never before visited by man. It lies some 270 miles south of the nearest tundra, 2,400 miles north of the limit of frost. It is in the sub-Arctic region between Transition and Arctic. Raup (Allen, 1956) listed 461 plants from the region, of which 449 were distinct species. Soper (1942) listed 46 mammal and 216 bird species.

The Sass and Klewi River regions occupied by the Whooping Crane have many pot-hole lakes, some only a few acres in size. Allen (1956) wrote: "From the air one sees a bewildering patchwork of ponds, irregular in shape and varying from an acre or two in size to a few lakes that must total 50 or 60.... All of them are extremely shallow...and are separated ...by narrow ridges, some two or three feet in height, which support the dense thickets of dwarf birch, willows, black spruce and occasional tamaracks. Here and there the pattern is broken by areas of higher ground, rising like islands, some five or six feet or more above the surrounding confusion of ponds. Most of these have evidently supported stands of black spruce and tamarack at one time or another, but fires have swept over them and the only live trees that remain are clustered about wet depressions in the uneven terrain, or along the course of the river. The island on which we camped...is perhaps 50 acres in size and away from the river (Sass) it seemed almost lifeless and infinitely dreary. ...A map of the park...shows an elevation of 925 feet in the vicinity of the upper Sass, and 780 to 640 feet along the last escarpment just west of the Little Buffalo, near Lobstick Creek...From the vicinity of the crane ponds to its junction with the Little Buffalo, the Sass drops some 240 feet over a straight line distance of 16 miles, or about 15 feet in every mile. But the actual course of the Sass twists and turns so many times for every mile of airline distance, that in reality it covers a distance of approximately 70 miles from the limestone escarpment upriver from our campsite to its mouth...

"The river lies at a somewhat higher elevation than the pond areas on either side, thus explaining, in part, the poor drainage of those sectors... Perhaps the chief source of water for these ponds is the melting snow and ice...

"The weather during our stay was hot and dry...

92°Fahr. at 6 P.M. on the 23rd (June), and frequently starting the day in the low 80's."

They collected northern pike, three species of dace in the streams, but later found in the shallow ponds (1) brook stickleback (*Eucalia inconstans*); (2) finescale dace (*Chrosomus neogaeus*); (3) northern pearl dace (*Semotilus margarita nechtriebi*); and (4) fathead minnow (*Pimephales promelas*). None were abundant.

Wood frogs (*Rana sylvatica*), chorus frogs (*Pseudacris nigrita septentrionalis*) a common garter snake (*Thamnophis sirtalis*) were found, while mollusks were very abundant, nine species being found in the crane ponds, including bladder snail (*Physa jennessi* Dall), pond snail (*Stagnicola palustris* (Müller)), great pond snail (*Lymnaea stagnalis* (Linnaeus)), wheel snail (*Helisoma trivolvis macrostomum* (Whiteaves)), wheel snail (*Gyraulus circumstriatus* (Tryon)), wheel snail (*Gyraulus parvus* (Say)), *Promenetus exacuous* (Say), *Pisidium liljeborgi* Clessin (pill clam) and *Oxyloma haydeni* (W. G. Binney).

Probable food insects of the Whooping Crane included:
Orthoptera (grasshoppers, crickets, etc.)
1. (*Acrididae*) *Nomotettix* (?) (short-horned grasshopper?).
Ephemeroptera (mayflies).
1. (*Baetidae*) *Siphlonurus* sp.
Odonata (dragonflies and damselflies)
Anisoptera (dragonflies)
1. *Libellula* sp.
2. *Aeschna* sp.
Zygoptera (damselflies)
1. *Enallagma* (?).

When I visited the region during early June 1964, the young Whooping and Sandhill Cranes were hatching simultaneously with the emergence of myriads of dragonflies. A young Sandhill Crane I captured, devoured many of these avidly and soon dropped off to sleep, lying as though dead on the ground in the warm sun.

I saw my first Whooping Crane nest in the rushes of a shallow lake surrounded by spruce and willow. The nest was placed well out amongst rushes, and a place about five meters in every direction from the nest was bare, showing where the birds had pulled

Nest and eggs of Whooping Crane, Wood Buffalo Park, June 3, 1964.

nearly all the rushes in the vicinity and piled them into a haphazard heap in the center. It was about 4 x 5 feet (122 x 153 cm) wide and 12-15 cm high. The water appeared a foot or less in depth. Beneath was typical marl bottom. The tracks of the birds' movements were plainly visible. The nest was slightly hollowed in the center for the eggs and was somewhat circular in shape, wider at the base, as usual. The two eggs could have passed for Sandhill Crane eggs I have always been unable to differentiate definitely between eggs of the two species

unless they are labeled. The bird, that left the nest spread its wings, demonstrating distraction display, while the second stood motionless, watching us. We had already gone circling to the soutwest, where a Sandhill Crane pair began demonstrating also. Now we circled to the north and east, and on swinging back southward we saw a second pair with their nest. This nest was a much larger pile of rushes, somewhat longer, about 5 x 7 feet across, one direction and was also located in an immense patch of rushes well out from surrounding spruce shorelines.

Here the parents demonstrated, not only by spreading their wings but by opening their mouths. One could imagine how loudly they were whooping at our presence. Here too were two beautiful, rather elliptical, ovate-shaped typical crane eggs in a slight depression in the pile of rushes. Now we were gone, and as we passed over the bison corral some distance to the east, a pair of Sandhill Cranes behaved as though they had a nest, too. Since I had a few more days before my plane departed northward, I decided to return to the corral region, where there was a small cabin. Part of the time there I operated mist-nets, capturing birds, and part of the time I searched for Sandhill Crane nests. At the place where we had seen the Sandhill pair, I found a nest with two newly hatched chicks. This nest, too, was a pile of rushes — (*Scirpus validus*), *Carex trichocarpa, Calamagrostris inexpansa, Triglochin palustre* and other less common plants. Wood frogs were rather common, and dragonflies were everywhere. Birds netted in the region were Traill's Flycatcher (*Empidonax traillii*), Swainson Thrush (*Hylocichla ustulata*), Orange-crowned Warbler (*Vermivora celata*), Myrtle Warbler (*Dendroica coronata*), Savannah Sparrow (*Passerculus sandwichensis*) and Lincoln's Sparrow (*Melospiza lincolnii*). Farther out in the marsh were American Bittern, Wilson Snipe, several species of ducks and Nelson's Sparrow (*Ammospiza caudacuta*). While flying over the Whooping Crane ponds we had noted Bufflehead, Raven and a small falcon, besides the Sandhills and Whoopers.

The Eggs

The eggs of the Whooping Crane are elliptical ovate, ovate, at times approaching elliptical. The ground color as described by Bent (1926) is "cream buff" to "olive-buff." Like other crane eggs, some have a greenish tinge, some brownish. They are heavily marked along the long axis with varying sizes spots of brown or shades of brown, "dull brown," "wood brown," "buffy brown," sometimes "gray," a few "lavender," and at times very dark brown. More spots are found on the larger ends of eggs. There is little point in measuring more eggs

than have been measured, for the only ones in existence are the same ones every one will measure. Bent gave the average of 38 eggs, 98.4 x 62.4 mm, with the extremes 108.0 by 59.3, 98.0 by 67.5, 87.0 by 59.0 and 87.4 by 50.2 mm. Robert Allen (1952) wrote that of 94 possible eggs, only 41 had the state or province of origin listed. Eleven were from Manitoba, 2 from Saskatchewan, 2 from Northwest Territories, 1 from North Dakota, 2 from Minnesota and 23 from Iowa. These were taken between 1864 and 1900, eleven of them in 1871, four in 1877 and the remainder, one or two per year, mostly in the 1870's and 1880's.

The Schönwetter weight, given by Allen was 20.75 for 14 eggs. One egg reached as high as 24.7 grams. Allen estimated the weight of a normal fresh egg as about 212 grams, which would compare with other crane eggs.

Many of the early sets probably were divided for economical reasons. But Novakowski (1966) in his study noted during 12 years in one nesting site they found eleven nests in 11 of the 12 years, and each contained two eggs. In fact, all nests he observed, except one that contained one egg, contained two eggs. During the past three years thirty-four nests were found, of which only one contained a single egg.

Incubation is performed by both birds. I summarized the observations (1965) (see also Table 15) Crip and Jo, two captive Whooping Cranes that nested during 1950 at Aransas National Wildlife Refuge. The United States Fish and Wildlife Service allowed me to make notes for seven days. The Whooping Cranes nesting in a much hotter region than Sandhill Cranes in Michigan changed places an average of 7 (6-8) times per day, while the Sandhills in Michigan averaged 3.6 times (29 observation days). The female did much more night incubating than the male. The average of 23 attentive periods during daytime for the male was 126 (60-207) minutes; for 19 female attentive periods, the average was 125 (53-215) minutes. The period between the average times of the last nightly change (6:47 P.M.) and the first morning change (6:11 A.M.) was 684 minutes. On three of seven occasions the same bird was on in the morning that had been there the evening before. The average period during these three nights was 683 minutes. During the seven days, the eggs were incubated by one or the other bird 92.7 percent of the time; the male was responsible for 52.9 percent of daytime incubation.

Conway (1957) watched these same two birds in the Audubon Park Zoo, New Orleans. During 1955 Jo laid an egg May 29, but it was broken. During 1956 she laid eggs April 28 and May 2, which hatched May 29 and June 1, but both youngsters died shortly. During 1957 she built her nest in exactly the same spot and laid eggs April 18 and 21. George Scott, the Bronx Zoo's Head Keeper of Birds, was dispatched to the Whooper aid. He stayed with them for weeks. Conway wrote concerning this watch:

The nest was formed by Josephine lying down on the site and drawing the nest material to and under her with her long beak. Crip was never seen to offer her nest material, but he frequently pulled sticks about in the typical graceful building fashion of other cranes.

Both Crip and Jo took turns incubating the eggs... Josephine had the heavy duty; Crip did much of his incubation at night, when it was cool and breezy, leaving Josephine to struggle through most of the day's heat. Completely unshaded (always the case) in the direct semi-tropical sun, both birds panted with half-closed eyes during their day shifts...

During a normal nest relief, the female might arise, reach down, delicately roll the two eggs with her bill and look about. At this point she was usually joined by Crip. As Jo walked away to preen, feed, or drink, Crip would take a position over the eggs, peer down, roll them anew, arrange them a slight distance apart, and gingerly settle

An adult with young Whooping Crane feeding in saline region along Aransas National Wildlife Refuge, March 1968.

down to his shift. Usually the eggs were incubated high-up, on either side of the breast. Crip…required many adjustments and attempts to get settled in a satisfactory position…After he had incubated for awhile, he would stand up carefully turn the eggs, and Josephine …assumed her shift, once again rolling the eggs. This rolling process is extremely important to the proper development of most bird embryos…

The eggs were rarely left uncovered for any length of time. Surprisingly there was no special direction which the incubating birds faced at the nest (which I have observed with all cranes) and the egg orientation was often changed.

From 7:00 A.M. to 4:00 P.M., the day before the first egg hatched, the incubating parents changed shifts 21 times …may have been caused by the terrific heat.

At 9:25 A.M., on May 18, Mr. Douglass reported the pipping of the first egg. By 10:40 A.M. a small hole was apparent at one side of the thick end of the egg (all pipped Crane eggs, I have ever seen were pipped at the larger end). It was extremely hot; Josephine had been sitting all morning. 12:05 P.M., Crip relieved Josephine at the nest for two minutes. Both birds rolled the eggs as usual, despite the pipping. The hole did appear to end uppermost, however. At 2:30 P.M., Josephine rose and turned the eggs again. Crip made three awkward attempts to settle on the eggs, but Jo finally drove him away, again sitting on the nest herself. The hole was much larger and the chick could be seen moving within the egg. Mr. Scott reported the chick completely free of the shell at 11:30 P.M.

At 6:40 A.M., May 19, Crip came over and coaxed the chick from the nest while Josephine continued incubating the remaining egg. Seven hours and ten minutes from the time it was first seen free of the shell, the young one took its first steps outside of the actual nest. It did not, however, wander more than a foot or two from the site. The chick stayed out, unbrooded, the first time, for twenty minutes."

After incubating the second egg and brooding the chick for another hour, Josephine rose, turned the egg, and was relieved by Crip. The chick followed Josephine about for two and a half hours before being brooded when Josephine took over nest duty again. After a short time the chick attempted to leave the brooding hen, but Jo nudged it back with her bill.

On May 21, 25 hours and 30 minutes after the beginning of pipping, the second youngster emerged, dried rapidly, left the nest completely dry within an hour after it was completely free of the shell. The shells were pushed to one side. The second youngster was even more agile than the first and wandered away six feet on its first excursion. Thirty hours after hatching, shortly before 6 A.M. May 20 the first chick took its first food; the second chick took its first food much sooner. A feeding parent constantly battered food in its bill, then offered it to the chicks. If the chick did not accept it, the adult dropped it on the ground then did this several times. In this fashion the chick began picking up food. The chicks are offered food almost constantly and may accept or reject it. Both Crip and Jo dug with their bills for the good supply of earthworms and together with dragonflies and grasshoppers made up the large share of the youngsters food although the parents seldom ate these items themselves. When brooding the young, both birds often had a ritual of tramping down the grass prior to when Jo sat down and the youngsters pushed their way beneath. This tramping was first noted when the first egg was pipped and was apparently for the purpose of knocking down taller vegetation so that the parent could sit down and the chicks work their way beneath.

At times the two youngsters would grasp each others bills and twist, some of which might be caused by feeding. One youngster might grab a food particle the other already had. Both Crip and Jo put their heads down and sounded their low rattling calls. Josephine was the most aggressive of the pair and advanced in a menacing fashion in case of some unfavorable object, person or other, made its presence. Crip was not observed to sleep during the entire nesting procedure. Even at night he was on guard, watching silently.

Conway's description of the chicks follows:

Four days after the second hatching, the oldest chick stood nearly seven inches tall. Covered except for their pale orange, brown-tipped bills and sturdy legs with soft down, the baby cranes very much resembled over-sized barnyard chicks. Face and forehead were yellowish-brown and their color graded to a darker, rusty, buffy brown on back and thighs. Breast and belly and a prominent spot on each humerus were a soft grayish-white washed with buffy ochraceous. The heavy legs were encased with down to the tibia, where the bare gray scales contrasted with the dark brown of the tarsus set off by a pale orange tarsal joint and foot. In contrast to the adult's yellow eyes, the eyes of the young were warm dark brown."

In my observations at Aransas of Crip and Jo, Crip was noted chasing Great Blue Herons, American Egrets, Snowy Egrets, Louisiana Herons, Reddish Egrets, White Pelicans, Mottled Ducks and even on one occasion some Barn Swallows flying by. Both Crip and Jo chased deer, but once Crip showed fear of a group of deer approaching his direction.

This nest was in water, as are most nests in the wild. The water was sea water, or at least brackish. When the wind blew from the bay side, it definitely must have been much more saline, so the birds seldom drank any of it. They rinsed their bills in it regularly but came to two freshwater pools on the adjoining knoll to drink. Here they were fed fowl pellets daily, which they ate regularly, especially Jo. Crip was more fearful than she and so did not

The commercial boat that has taken thousands of people close to Whooping Cranes at Aransas, near Rockport, Texas.

come as often. A few other notes taken at or near the nest follow:

May 9, 1950, 7:22 A.M. Crip leaves nest; Jo onto eggs, as usual she turned the eggs several times, then worked with nest material. Crip began pulling grass about 4 feet from edge of nest. As he pulled it with his bill, he rotated sidewise and threw it back toward nest. He did not move his feet at all, but kept pulling for 5 minutes then worked away 12 feet, where he stopped and preened. Jo sat with her head tucked into scapular feathers. (Sometimes she pulled adjacent grass without rising and piled it onto the nest beside her. Much of this was also grass that Crip had pulled. Sometimes she pulled grass when leaving, the same as he, and tossed it back toward the nest.).

11:51 A.M. As Jo reached the nest pool, she preened, then scratched the top of her head with her middle right toe.

2:45 P.M. Huge Man-of-War bird circling over nest marsh from south. Crip, some distance from nest, ran on the double to it. Both birds were stand-ing, one on one side, the other on opposite side of nest, both with heads turned sidewise looking up. The Man-of-War bird circled closer, noting now the nest and birds. As he passed over he dropped to 100 feet above them. Both adults spread their wings slightly; both pointed their bills in his direction and screamed their defiance. As they began calling, the Man-of-War bird circled farther away and soon disappeared. Crip took over incubation duties at 2:50 P.M. Jo came to feed dish, which was empty, so I filled it. She hissed a *"Husssh"* slightly, then went right after it. She must have eaten ¾ of a teacup full, then went to freshwater pool to drink. A turtle swam 6 inches from her, but she did not touch it.

5:19 P.M. Crip circled an American Egret 35 feet north of nest, but the egret flew before he reached it. Crip danced, jumping with legs half bent, hanging limp and motionless below his body. He hopped 6-9 feet and had spread wings. When he dropped back, he bowed his head several times, fanned the air with his outspread wings. He had fanned air when at peak of jump.

May 10, 1950, 11:07 A.M. Jo went to feed dish, found it empty, then went to far side of second freshwater pool. Here she drank, then began eating grasshoppers. She fed for some time.

May 12, 1950, 5:35 A.M. Jo left nest as Crip climbed up. She headed 40 feet from nest, preened. In 2 minutes headed for food dish, which was empty. She went to pool, drank 7 times, then began eating small lethargic grasshoppers on surrounding grass. During next 75 minutes she swallowed 828 objects, most of which were grasshoppers. She did not always get each grasshopper at which she stabbed.

May 13, 1950, 4:06 P.M. Jo fed, then went to drink from freshwater pool #1, then went to pool #2, where she waded in up to her leg joints. She began dipping her head into water, first shaking it from side to side both under and above water. Then she wiped side of her head on her back. Now lowering her breast into the water and vibrating her wings slowly, threw water over her back. Next she lowered her body into the pool until it was almost submerged —her head was all that really was visible. She vibrated her wings several times, raised up and laid down, rolling from side to side with vibrating wings, threw more water over the wings and back as well as beneath the wings. Then she left the pool rapidly, shaking her wings, then her tail. She went to Valentine Island. As a flock of gulls came over she jumped crazily into the air, but was so soaked she could do little. Now she started preening. The bath required about five minutes, but the drying process was much longer even though the sun was hot and a stiff breeze was blowing. At first she shivered terrifically, even though it was the warmest day since I had been there. It was also the first day she had bathed. Two days later at about the same time, 4:04 P.M., she bathed again in a similar manner. Crip did not bathe during the entire week.

Vocalizations

The call of the downy young is similar to that of other baby cranes, a shrill piping whistle, similar to the 'Peep' of a baby chicken but with more trill to it. At times, when excited, this is even more shrill and it or a close rendition is maintained until the birds

reach the spring following birth. Then they acquire the adult call. This call can be heard at least two miles normally (Stevenson, 1943a).

Robert P. Allen (1952:87) wrote: "The sight of the Whooping Crane in the air is an experience packed with beauty and drama. We see the broad sweep of the great wings in their stiff, almost ponderous motion...as we drive down the narrow trail that borders the low salt flats close to Mullet Bay, a trio of the big fellows may appear, quite suddenly, in the waist-high oak brush, where they have been feeding on acorns. Their heads come up and the shrill, bugle-like notes *Kerloo! Ker-lee-oo!* send a shiver along the length of your spine. They are up at once, leaning forward, running a few steps, and then lifting their heavy bodies in straight-away, horizontal flight. Neck and head are extended forward, like the spear of a lance, and slightly down. The long black legs stretch out behind. The wing stroke is like that of the other cranes, and of the limpkins as well. The complete arc of the stroke is narrow and there is a powerful *flick* on the upbeat. Normal flight produces about two beats per second and there is ease and competence in the way these giants skim low over the salt grass towards the shore of the bay."

Prior to take-off, the birds raise their head and quickly arch their neck forward. They appear to lean forward considerably. But often they give the above call as they do so. Allen (1952:142) wrote that the same call is given when a bird challenges another on his territory, for the birds maintain a winter territory the same as a summer territory, unlike the majority of cranes, which have only summer territories.

This *Ker-lee-oo*, often repeated four to seven times, is the regular call. It is much more penetrating than the Sandhill call. Allen described the approach of two families, in each case a pair and one full-grown youngster on the salt grass (*Monanthochloe littoralis*) flats. The two males walked forward from the family group until they were standing face to face. As they approached they strutted, legs raised stiffly, wings dragging slightly, the tibiae raised higher than usual. When they were 1 meter apart, one dropped his head as though feeding. So did the other. Both retreated a few feet, then came right back again. This time the females came up. Their

A Whooping Crane family at Aransas, Feb. 3, 1971.

heads came up, bills pointing skyward, wings drooping, plumes raised over their backs, heads almost together, and uttered a loud blast. They continued this show for nearly 50 minutes, then slowly separated, each family resuming normal feeding. The location of this display was on the exact boundary of their territories. Sometimes there is no such display. One male will quickly eject the entire family, especially if they are on his territory. Allen (p.146) commented that the birds roosted in the shallow ponds at night and often drank the brackish water. But as noted above they did prefer freshwater. Crip

and Jo walked a good half-mile each day to drink from the freshwater ponds.

Crip and Jo were heard to utter a number of other calls. The normal Unison Call, given when they changed places occasionally, was a shrill, buglelike *Kronk-kronk-kronk-kronk-kronk*, usually five to eight syllables in length. Both birds gave this call or some rendition of it—*Kronka* was used at times. They used a similar call when the Man-of-war bird came over the nest on May 9, 1950. It was strong defiance. To me Jo had a higher-pitched call than Crip. Sometimes they gave only a one-syllable call.

Sometimes they called a gooselike *Graaaw*, again they uttered a low hissing call when approaching a human near their feeding dish. They used a purring call near their young.

When giving the "Unison Call," the male holds his secondaries above his back, the primaries stiffly displayed on each side. The female stands with wings tightly held against her sides.

Territory, Food and Flocking

Most Nearctic and Palearctic cranes winter in flocks. Although the family groups of three or four (where there are young) may break away during the daytime, they most often roost at night in shallow water only a few feet from others of their kind. As with most species, the parents will defend their progeny with extreme viciousness. Their territories may be no less than a few feet in every direction from the family group, but no other bird is supposed to wander into this small space. Usually he is evacuated from the region with a few strong jabs of the bill or a running attack by the father, more rarely by the mother, crane. As Bob Allen pointed out, the father's job is one of guarding. The mother's job is to aid the youngster in getting food—a learning process of what to find and where. The father helps some, but he is ever watchful. He knows that his size and brilliant white color make him and family very vulnerable. He prefers to keep them away from brush and trees where people are in evidence. Yet on their nesting ground, where there are no people they work right in amongst the bushes and trees.

In 1966 Novakowski pointed out that for twelve years in Wood Buffalo Park cranes had used the same territories in most cases continuously each summer. (I found this to be the case at Phyllis Haehnle Memorial Sanctuary, Michigan with Sandhill Cranes over a thirteen-year period.) Probably little defense was necessary here, for the birds had established their territory years ago, as had the Sandhills at Haehnle. When the cranes return in spring, they immediately land in their nesting regions, without fanfare, without any sign of necessary territorial boundary dispute—except when young non-breeders wander in. They generally pay little attention to each other, but live throughout the summer in the domain of their own, a region of about 640 acres (one square mile). They arrive in early May, at times in late April, and remain throughout the nesting season. If they are successful in hatching and rearing young, they stay throughout the summer and early fall. Their domain is this network of ponds, well isolated by bordering spruces, willows and dwarf birches. They cannot see their neighbors, may never see them all summer, yet they can hear them when they vocalize. They know when all is in order, and when others are in trouble, by this vocalization. When fall and cold weather arrive, they may become more closely knit, grouping together without the strong desire to chase away other cranes. Yet even at this point they will not tolerate any really close approach to the family. They may begin the southward trip in a family unit; they may go in larger groups of several families; non-breeders also group together, and this is probably where the young birds acquire their mates.

When they reach Aransas, they again require a territory, this time about 400 acres (Allen: 1952). But here as populations increase, as they have in recent years, these territories may become "crowded," and birds may be forced to search out other wintering regions. The pairs defend their territories almost as strongly as or stronger than in the summertime. The pairs with young do so more than those without. Here they remain, as long as food is available, on their winter domain, until spring. So the average family lives on less than one square mile of the earth's surface from about October 25 until April 15-20 in Texas, then from early May until early October in Wood Buffalo National Park, Canada. For a period of one or two weeks each spring and fall they are on the move between these two regions.

Food is the strongest reason for territories. Bob Allen pointed out (1952) the following:

1. The original winter range had been confined to a coastal strip extending from Marsh Island, etc. in Louisiana, southwestward across the Gulf Coast of Texas to the vicinity of Matamoros, Tamaulipas, Mexico with smaller wintering regions along the Atlantic seaboard, prior to 1858, and on the interior

tablelands near San Angelo and San Antonio, Texas, and in central Mexico, the last prior to 1904.

2. Approximately 10,000 acres of salt flats and brackish water areas are used by cranes. The salinity varies with rainfall (1.4°/oo-28.5°/oo) and water temperature varies (0°C.-34.5°C.). Air temperature varies between freezing or lower, up to over 90°F. during the stay of the cranes. In Wood Buffalo Park the water is strongly alkaline, more so in the feeding ponds, 7.6 to 8.3 pH as compared to unused ponds, 7.2-7.3 (Novakowski, 1966). In Wood Buffalo Park air temperatures vary between −3° and 92°F. during the season cranes are there while sometimes (May 1955-2.3 in.; May 1959-5.6 in.; May 1960-1.8 in.; May 1962-3.0 in.; June 1965-1.6 in.) considerable snow falls. In 1952 85 percent of the Whooping Cranes used the Aransas Refuge in winter.

3. The present Whooping Crane habitat, geologically, has been duplicated with only slight variations, from the Pleistocene Ingleside, and with only slight variations differs little today from then.

4. The vegetation of the higher ground is chiefly live oak (*Quercus virginiana*), pin oak (*Q. myrtifolia*) and blackjack oak (*Q. marilandica*) the former which produces groves or mottes, especially valuable in that the acorns are eaten by Whooping Cranes at times. Below the 5-foot level salt-loving plants are most common. Those with widest distribution, Allen wrote, were salt grass (*Distichlis spicata*), salt flat grass (*Monanthochloe littoralis*), saltwort (*Batis maritima*), sea ox-eye (*Borrichia frutescens*), salicornias (*S. bigelovii, S. europaea, S. perennis*) and *Spartina alterniflora*.

The ecological relationship of animals and plants

Jo, semi-captive Whooping Crane, nesting at Aransas, May 15, 1950, taking her daily bath in fresh-water pool.

in the salt flat environment is probably the most important survival factor for the Whooping Crane. The amount of grasses could be dependent even on the number of grazing ducks, on the rainfall, the height of incoming tides (much heavier when strong winds blow from offshore), etc. Few animals cause damage to Whooping Cranes at Aransas, for the bird is strong enough to battle for its own interest. It feeds by day in brackish pools far out toward the water-front; it roosts at night in shallow ponds some distance from solid land. If freshwater is unavailable near the coast, it goes inland to get it at flowing wells or freshwater ponds. It does drink brackish water but definitely must have fresh water at least once and often twice daily.

5. The food of the bird is important. Probably the most important belong to Arthropoda and include the Crustacea:

Shrimp (*Peneus aztecus*), common edible shrimp (*Peneus setiferus*), pistol shrimp (*Crangon hetero-chaelis*), grass shrimp (*Palaemonetes* sp.), river shrimp (*Macrobrachium onionis*), mud shrimp (*Callianassa jamaicense* var. *louisianensis*), hermit crab (*Clibinarius vittatus*), blue crab (*Callinectes sapidus*), Pinnixid crab (*Pinnixa cylindrica*), mud crab (*Sesarina cinereum*), fiddler crab (*Uca pugnax*) and common fiddler crab (*Uca pugilator*). Which insects are eaten is not known, but I noted that the semi-captive crippled Whooping Cranes devoured many grasshoppers at times and at certain times of the year these may fill in a great gap. Three Pelecypoda are in the Aransas feeding region: *Tagellus gibbus*, *Solen (viridis?)* and *Rangia cuneata*. Three species of Gastropoda, *Littorina irrorata*, *Melampus coffeus* and *Cerithiidea* sp. the latter found in droppings.

Gunther (Allen, 1952: 150) reported the mullet (*Mugil cephalus*) and the cyprinodontid (*Cyprinodon v. variegatus*) made up over 50 percent of the entire catch, which consisted of 29 species in the two bay stations and 17 species in the salt flat ponds. Amphibia occurred in the tension zone between salt flats and high land, 5 species, cricket frog (*Acris crepitans*), leopard frog (*Rana pipiens berlandieri*), green tree frog (*Hyla c. cinerea*), tree frog (*Hyla squirella*) and the toad (*Bufo* sp.).

Repitilia included 27 species, of which the small skinks and lizards might at times be used for food. I watched one of the captive Whooping Cranes in May 1949 capture a 3-foot unidentified snake some 100 m from where I stood. After threshing it over the hard ground for some time the crane devoured it.

Allen listed 62 species of birds observed on a sample one-day count, October 26, 1947. Of course, many more are found throughout the winter. During the Christmas Bird Count there, December 20, 1969 (Audubon Field Notes, 1970,24:373-374), 142 species were listed from the refuge.

Mammalia included besides pasturing cattle, most detrimental to the Whooping Crane, 4 other forms raccoon (*Procyon lotor*), coyote (*Canas nebraceneis texanus*), red wolf (*Canis rufus*) and Texas white-tailed deer (*Odocoileus virginianus texanus*)., with several other less important species.

Allen (1952: 153) listed four types of ponds: (1) Permanent pond, lake, ditch or bayou open to bay tides at all seasons, flow depending on wind force and direction. Water source natural. Including such regions as: Mustang Lake, Dunham Pond, Dunham Bayou and Mullet Bayou. (2) Semi-permanent ponds connected by narrow bayous to permanent water, changing with rise and fall of natural water and occupying the trough of a Pleistocene inter-beach ridge depression, including Long Pond, Middle Pond and Camp Pond. (3) Yellow ponds or sloughs, with no connection to other pond systems or bays except during extremely high tides, with red and yellow algae and after flooding filled with trapped organisms. Dunham Ponds, Fence Pond, and 1080 Pond. (4) Former Type 1 pond cut off by artificial structure, such as Redfish Slough. (5) Former Type 3 ponds now open to by by means of borrow ditches, improved. Example, Rattlesnake Ponds.

Allen concluded the blue crab was the preferred food in winter. Since then, some of the shrimps have been found equal if not better during certain years. Whooping Cranes, like many other cranes, feed on the food available, and do not depend on one form entirely. Allen discussed the management of the blue crab so that food of this type would be available when the birds arrived from the north each fall.

More recently Fish & Wildlife personnel have developed regions of grain plantings, which are somewhat successful at times when other foods are less available. Corn, sorghum and possibly other grains might be successful, especially if planted near the freshwater drinking holes. In the past Whooping Cranes were noted for their raids on sweet potato patches, indicating that they may eat roots of some plants — as do many other cranes.

Both Stevenson and Griffith (1946) and Allen (1952) presented decimating factors affecting the species and factors aiding the species. One of the favorable factors is the longevity of cranes, the Whooping Crane being no exception. If shooting can be stopped completely, the population should grow to favorable size in a few years even if each pair was not able to produce a single young each year, but did so every second or third year. If one examines the production of young in Table 13, it becomes evident that breeding pairs at Wood Buffalo Park increased either three, four or five years after a good reproductive year. Probably most young birds begin breeding either four or five years after birth. Although they apparently do not return to Canada's Sass River region for the first years, when the time comes to breed they apparently have a homing instinct to return to the region of their birth.

NESTING RECORDS

The Whooping Crane is known now to nest only in the District of Mackenzie, Northwest Territories, Canada in Wood Buffalo National Park. Here the first nests were found during 1954, and as the bird has increased in numbers, ten nests were found during both 1967 and 1968; twelve during 1969; fourteen in 1972 (Canadian Wildlife Service records) (See also R. P. Allen, 1956; Novakowski, 1965, 1966 : Walkinshaw, 1965). Except for some recent Louisiana records all other records were in the past. Two of these earlier records came from Mackenzie: (1) Big Island. (2) Great Slave Lake. Both, single eggs in USNM. All Mackenzie records were eggs found in May or early June, all hatching in June.

In Alberta nests were found near: (1) Killam (1904-1905). (2) Edmonton (1906-1907). (3) Whitford Lake (1909). (4) Buffalo Park, Wainwright (1914) (all listed by Allen, 1952; Farley, 1932). Eggs were found in Saskatchewan near: (1) Moose Mt. (1881?). (2) Battleford, 1884, 2 eggs. (3) Yorkton, May 16, 1900, 2 eggs. (4) Davidson, 1911. (5) Unity, May 28, 1922, 2 hatching eggs. (6) Baliol, May 19, 1922, 2

eggs. (7) Bradwell, 1911-1912 (Bard; Allen, 1952; Bent, 1926; Cooke, 1914; Bradshaw, 1956; Macoun, 1882, 1900; Mitchell, 1924; Raine, 1892). In Manitoba eggs were found near: (1) Winnipeg, August 1871, 2 eggs. (2) Lake Winnipeg, 1877, 2 eggs. (3) Red River mouth, 1891, 2 eggs. (4) Lake Winnipegosis, May 9, 1885, 2 eggs. (5) Oak Lake, June 17, 1891, 2 eggs; May 21, 1893, 1 egg; May 13, 1894, 2 eggs; May 16, 1900, 2 eggs; May 18, 1900, 2 eggs. (6) Dufferine County (?), May 30, 1906, 2 eggs. Possibly also at Shoal Lake (1886-1924); Westbourne (1890); Margaret (1909-1913); Benito (1948) (Fred Bard; Allen, 1932).

In North Dakota eggs were found at (1) Ina, Rolette County, June 3, 1871, 1 egg. (2) Adams, Walsh County, 1 egg. (3) McHenry County (?), (Allen, 1952), and in Minnesota near: (1) Brainerd, Morrison County, 1873. (2) Elbow Lake, Grant County, May 21, 1876, 2 eggs. (3) Thief Lake, Marshall County, June 19, 1889, 2 eggs, (Allen, 1952; Coues, 1874; Deane, 1923; Nute, 1945; Roberts, 1932).

Many eggs were taken in Iowa as follows: (1) Northwest Iowa, June 1886, 1 egg; June 1867, 2 eggs. (2) Sac County, 1868, 1869. (3) Dubuque County, April 25, 1868, 2 eggs. (4) Western Iowa, May 10, 1871, 2 eggs. (5) Blackhawk County, May 12, 1871, 2 eggs; May 15, 1871, 2 eggs. (6) Lake Mills, Winnebago County, May 12, 1879, 2 eggs. (7) Oakland Valley, May 6, 1874, 1 egg. (8) Cherokee County, May 8, 1877, 2 eggs. (9) Franklin County, May 2, 1880, 2 eggs. (10) Wright County, May 8, 1881, 2 eggs. (11) Kossuth County, May 14, 1881, 2 eggs. (12) Hancock County, Eagle Lake, May 4, 1883, 1 egg; May 26, 1894 2 eggs (last Iowa nest — R. M. Anderson, 1907) also a pair observed June 5, 1897. (13) Midway, 1883 (Allen, 1952; Cooke, 1914; Spurrell, 1917; Krider, 1879).

Nesting was reported in central Illinois in 1870 by Nelson (1877) where a number of specimens were taken while there seems to be only specimen records from Indiana, March 28, 1881 in LaPorte County (MCZ, No. 205536) and near Bloomington (Cuvier Club, Cincinnati) (Allen, 1952; Butler, 1898) while it was observed in Porter County about 1905 (Backowski, 1955).

A long overlooked nesting colony existed in Vermillion and Cameron parishes, coastal Louisiana, where 11 birds were found resident in 1938, 13 in

1939, when a nest with hatching chicks was found May 15. This flock dwindled one by one until the last bird disappeared in December 1949. The famous Audubon Park Zoo female, Jo, who reared the first chicks to adulthood in captivity, came from this colony. She has just died recently.

WINTER

In Winter, Whooping Cranes are now found only along the Texas coastline, mostly at Aransas National Wildlife Refuge, and neighboring islands, rarely as far south as Tamaulipas, Mexico and northwest to King Ranch. One specimen was taken in Durango at Lerdo in 1889 (Dresden Mus.); another was shot at Bolson del Mapima about 1894 while in Guanajuato, on the Plains of Silao another was taken in 1869, and several live specimens were observed by Jouy (1894) at Hacienda el Molina, near La Barca and at Hacienda de Buena Vista in 1903 and birds were observed in the wild near Lago de Chapala and La Barca (Allen, 1952; Nelson, 1929). Dresser (1866) reported birds in June, 1863 possibly nesting in Tamaulipas at Boca del Rio Grande, SW of Bagdad and at Metamoros, where Evenden (1952) observed a pair, February 23, 1951.

Allen (1952) also reported wintering formerly on Dauphin Island, near Millwood and near Prattville, Alabama (1899), once at Bay St. Louis, Mississippi, and in 1722-23 at the mouths of the Savannah and Aratamaha rivers, Georgia, with a sternum and trachea (Acad. Nat. Sci.), a humerus (USNM) and a specimen taken, November 12, 1885 (Ga. State Mus.) (Griffen and McLean, 1957). In Florida it was found from the Pleistocene of Brevard, Pinellas and Columbia counties and was observed by Catesby (1722-23?), along rivers near St. Augustine while specimens were taken in Florida (MCZ, Nos. 46872, 46873). It was found on the Waccamaw River, South Carolina about 1850 (Charleston Mus.) and formerly occurred at Cape May (1810?) and Great Egg Bay (1857) in New Jersey (Allen, 1952). There were two records—Fort Thorn (1853-54), Portales (1938) from New Mexico while in Texas it was found near San Antonio (Nov. 1845), Corpus Christi, Cameron County (lower Rio Grande, Brownsville, Padre Island, Galveston Island, Brazos River mouth,

Houston, Tom Green, Williamson, Comal, Aransas, Cooke, Fannin, McLennan, Hidalgo, Refugio, Willacy, Cameron, Clay, Jefferson, Nueces, Kleberg, Wilbarger, Caldwell, Calhoun, Chambers and Wharton counties as well as at Beaumont, Matagorda Island, Dallas, Laguna Larga, St. Joseph Island, and Dewberry Island.

RECENT SPRING RECORDS

During spring migration it was reported in Audubon Field Notes by Baumgartner (1959, 1961, 1962, 1963, 1965) and by Boeker (1960, 1961, 1962, 1963) from Oklahoma at Bartlesville, May 18, 1961, May 21, 1963 (1 each); at Salt Plains, NWR, May 5, 1963 (1); and in Kansas at Quivira NWR, April 26, 1961 (2) and Dorrance, April 13, 1968 (1-killed by flying into power line). In Nebraska it is more regularly noted in spring indicating the normal first stop from Aransas. Records were Adams, March 16, 1957; Brady, March 8, 1949; Halsey, March 25, 1954; Hastings, March 29, 1939, March 31, 1936; Keya Paha, April 16, 1957; Lincoln, April 24, 1958; Logan, April 12, 1965; North Platte, March 18, 1939, May 3, 1937, April 14 and 19, 1965; Stapleton, March 16, 1934, March 21, 1943; Valentine, May 1, 1959 (6 ad.); Webster, March 22, 1960; in South Dakota at La Creek NWR, May 18, 1962, Huron, April 17, 1964 (5); Rapid City, April 20, 1964 (Lister, 1964). It was observed at Medicine Lake NWR, April 24, 1962 (2) in Montana and in North Dakota, at Foxholm, May 1, 1959 (4 ad.), Kenmare, April 14, 19, 1954 (3); April 20, 1960 (2); at Langdon, May 10, 1961 (1); Medora, April 19, 1961 (5), Sherwood, April 12-20, 1954 (3); Bowbells, Burke County, April 12, 1968 (2). In Alberta it was observed east of Edmonton, April 19, 1957 (Gammell, 1957) while more records pertain to Saskatchewan than anywhere else in spring (all recorded by Fred G. Bard: 1953, 1956, 1957, 1958, 1959, Lister, 1964, 1965. Hatch, 1966, 1968. Boeker, *loc. cit.*): Arbury, April 13, 1958 (3); Benson, April 27, 1958 (2); Blaine Lake, April 21, 1958 (3); Brier Crest, May 4, 1959 (4); Duck Lake, April 25, 1962 (2); Goodwater, April 14, 1959 (4); Govan, April 8, 1958 (3); Katepwa Beach, April 17, 1958 (3); Langhan, April 26, 1960, 1966; Luseland, May 28, 1959 (1); Marcelin, April 18-21,

1968 (3); Milestone, April 19, 1960 (2); Penn, April 19, 1958 (3); Pierceland, April 25, 1958 (5); Perdue, May 2-4, 1966 (2); Pittman, April 29, 1960 (4); Prince Albert, May 9, 1964 (2); Saskatoon, April 22, 1966 (2); Simpson, May 6-30, 1958 (1).

In Northwest Territories, at Wood-Buffalo Park, conditions vary, year by year. Apparently if winter continues too long, the Whooping Cranes may not nest similar to what William Taylor and I found in northern Michigan with Sandhill Cranes during the 1972 spring. Novakowski reported Whooping Cranes arrived in pairs on the nesting grounds at Wood-Buffalo Park, the past seasons young apparently having been deserted in southern Saskatchewan. Indications show that normally very few return there but they must return when they are older because nesting pairs increase there regularly.

Boeker (1960) wrote about the 1959 spring: "The spring 'break-up' in the Sass River area of Wood Buffalo Park...occurred approximately 3 weeks later than normal...on May 22...birds were on the move and even at that late date showed no signs of nesting...Subsequent observations...indicated a very poor nesting success during 1959."

Boeker (1961) reported the first observation at Ft. Smith, N.W.T., Canada May 4, 1960 (2), with 5 observed the next day.

FALL MIGRATION

Boeker (1960) reported 10 Whooping Cranes were still present on the Wood-Buffalo nesting grounds on September 30, 1959 but also that 10 were observed 30 mi SE of Edmonton on August 10, 1960; 4 at Rocky Mt. House, Alberta September 19, 1960; two at Richmond Park, October 4; four at Alberta Beach, October 6; five the next day at Rocky Mt. House and seven SE of Hanna, November 2, 1960.

In Saskatchewan, Fred Bard (1953, 1956, 1957, 1958, 1959, 1960) reported one was shot at Weyburn, in October 1952; three were observed November 3, 1953 at Herbert; two adults and one young, at Osage, October 24-27, 1956; three adults and one young at Pierceland, October 13, 1957 then during the 1958 fall, from September 30 until October 31, mostly single birds or pairs and twice, a pair with two young, at Buffalo Pound Lake, Ceepee, Corning, Creelman, Cymric, Gibbs, Govan, Imperial, Khe-

dive, Langham, Last Mt. Lake, North Battleford, Strasbourg, Wadena and Weyburn. One was observed at Eyebrow, September 8, 1959 (Boeker, 1959) and one or two at Simpson, Govan, Meota, Lockwood, or Ambassador between September 15 and October 1, 1960 then two birds between September 22 and October 10, 1961 around Last Mt. Lake, Imperial, Craven, Glaslyn (Boeker, 1961; Fred Lahrman). Four were seen at Moose Jaw, 18-30 October 1965 (Hatch, 1966); two at Saskatoon, September 22, 1968; four October 10, 1968 at Goose Lake and three at Radisson, October 13-14, 1968 (Hatch, 1969).

Two adult and one young Whooping Cranes were found on Medicine Lake NWR, Montana, September 25 until October 18, 1967 (Hatch, 1968) while three were noted at Sherwood, North Dakota, October 21, 1954 and a lone bird was seen at Lostwood NWR, October 19, 1955 and others including a pair and one young were noted in October 1960 between 11th and 27th, at Dunn Center, Wiseton, Caron, Ft. Clark, Horsehead Lake. Another was seen September 21, 1962 at Snake River NWR and the same year at Williston, eight on October 18 and four on October 26. October 2-17, 1964 a pair with one young were seen at Des Lac NWR (Gammell, 1960; Gammell, Gammell and Huenecke, 1954; Gammell and Huenecke, 1955, 1956; Hatch, 1966, 1968, 1969; Lister, 1964, 1965; Boeker, *loc cit.*). One was observed at Quincy, Illinois, October 15 – 4 November, 1958 (Mumford, 1959) and one at Mound City, Squaw Creek Ref., October 13, 1958, another at Mingo Refuge, Puxico, up until December 6, 1958. Lone birds were observed at Reva South Dakota, October 13, 1967 and one at Mobridge, September 19, 1958.

At Sutherland, Nebraska two were seen with one young October 19, 1960 and two at Wilcox October 16, 1960.

In Kansas, at Hoisington a pair were seen October 28, 1961 and a pair at Concordia October 20, 1962, a lone one the same day at Hill City; three at Kirwin Refuge, Phillips County, October 19, 1964 and a pair with one young there 30-31 October 1965. At Kiowa it was reported November 6, 1964 and on November 4, 1965 one young male was killed by flying into a power line, the second to have this happen, a similar fate to what has happened to many cranes throughout the world.

Chapter Seven

THE WHITE-NAPED CRANE

(Grus vipio)

Grus Vipio, Pallas, *Zoographia Rosso-Asiatica,* 2, 1811, p. 102.
Type locality: Transbaikalia.
Vernacular names: The White-naped Crane, The White-necked Crane
(English); der Weissnackige Kranich (German); la Grue à cou blanc
(French); de Witnek Kraan (Dutch); Vithalsad Trana (Swedish);
даурисн журавль (Russian); Manazuru フナヅ*V* (Japa-
nese).

This beautiful crane is found in summer in eastern Asia, nesting in remote
marshy valleys chiefly in southeastern Siberia, northwestern Mongolia, some
in northern Manchuria. Here the families are raised. When autumn begins,
they fly by stages to Korea and eastern China, a small group eventually ending
up on the Japanese island of Kyushu. Here in a rather localized region, a few
years ago at Akune, more recently at Arasaki, around 200 to 250 of these
birds spend the colder winter months. Some do not show up until January and
some begin leaving shortly after mid-February, while all are usually gone by
March first even though Hooded Cranes stay several weeks longer.

White-naped Cranes flying from feeding ground, Arasaki, Kagoshima Prefecture, Japan, January 1968. Photograph by Eizi Takabayashi.

When I reached Izumi-shi the mid-afternoon of February 11, 1969, I was rushed to Arasaki, a few miles away, to watch the nightly return of both the Hooded and White-naped Cranes to their roost, some little distance out on the flat rice fields all well drenched with a few inches of standing water. Here, in typical crane fashion, the groups, each species separated from the other, spent the dark of night. Although the Hooded Cranes flew some distance for food in the morning, the White-naped species moved less than one kilometer to where food had been thrown during the night or early morning for their consumption. Because they allowed this procedure, the people appreciated them much more than the former. The Hooded Cranes did much more crop damage.

Several older people reported both species of cranes had come to Arasaki during the past forty-five years and that prior to that they wintered in the valley at Akune. Now, with the exception of a few hundred *G. monachus*, all wintering cranes in southern Japan stay in this wide extensive valley at Arasaki, Kagoshima Prefecture. Uchinda (1930) described the behavior of these cranes in winter here. He photographed both *Grus vipio* and *G. monachus*. The region is adjacent to the sea with a fine view of Amajusa Island on the north and mountainlike hills on most other sides. The valley consists of rice, wheat and other cultivated fields or regions of grass and weeds—all favorite feeding sites for cranes. Uchinda (1930) also wrote that the *Grus vipio* does not congregate in as large flocks as does the Hooded Crane, remaining in families of two, three or four individuals, which drove other White-naped Cranes from their respective territories. They fed then on bulbous roots, grain and other foods given them by local residents.

The birds now have changed considerably. They feed almost entirely on wheat and crucian fish (carp) thrown to them by the local Crane Warden, S. Matano, and his helpers. They do not leave their night roost until all, or nearly all, Hooded Cranes have flown away in the morning. The majority come about sunrise and in one flock begin systematically devouring the food, like a domestic flock of chickens. On occasion a small group flies early in the morning to some neighboring field, but usually they all remain eating wheat and fish. The birds seldom fly farther. Many times a male attacks another bird or birds if they come within ten feet or even less of him, his mate or family. More often they feed a few feet apart until the food is all, or nearly all, gone. Then certain individuals show dominance so that as the day wears on family groups become separated from other families, but the members of each family remain in fairly close proximity to each other.

Prior to attack, the male runs towards his opponent, wings slightly raised. He then arches his neck, bill pointing forward and downward. The attacked bird usually retreats hurriedly. If he does not, he is attacked with fury and leaves invariably. Seldom do they have actual dual combat, and even if they do, it lasts only a few seconds when the attacked bird retreats a few feet and the fight ends. Birds often display the "false preening" act prior to attack. This is often either before or after the arched neck display.

The birds feed for hours, more or less, during the early morning, at times during midday, again about 4 P.M., until nearly dark when they retreat by family groups or more to their roosting field, an old rice field covered with a few centimeters of shallow water. Here, during the winter of 1968-1969, a maximum of 203 spent their nights, a few fields from roosting Hooded Cranes.

In Table 2, under the Hooded Crane, arrival records are given both for that species and for *Grus vipio*, for the fall of 1964. Although three White-naped Cranes arrived at Arasaki on October 17, and

thirteen on October 25, most arrived after November 1. A total of 121 arrivals had come by January 1, 1965. During the fall of 1968, the first White-naped Cranes arrived after November 1 and a total of 121 arrivals was reached by January 1, but the final total of 203 birds did not arrive until January 12, 1969.

Spring departure during 1965 from the Arasaki region is given under Hooded Cranes in Table 3. On February 12, seventy White-naped Cranes left, while the last ones departed March 1. During 1969, forty-six birds left on February 9, ninety on February 21, about sixty-five on February 25, and the last two on March 2.

After eight days of rainy weather, February 21 dawned clear and cool (sunrise, 6:56 A.M., temperatures: high, 15.5°C., low, −8.1°C.). A light northeasterly wind was blowing. At 9:30 A.M., 167 White-naped Cranes fed steadily on wheat and fish placed that morning in the usual field. As they fed, a few flew back to the roost region, drank, preened and loafed. At 10:15 A.M., several groups of four and three and larger groups of eight flew into the air, joining into a large flock of about forty-five birds, making one big circle which brought them to the same elevation as the coastal hills; some three hundred meters above the sea they began drifting northwestward. Three or four more circles took them up another 300 to 500 meters in great circles; they now became smaller and smaller specks in the sky, their voices dwindling beyond reality, and they slowly disappeared from sight. Another group of similar size followed close behind. A third group of about twenty-three rose from the roost, began the great ascent until they were even with the top of the mountain, but they suddenly changed their minds and returned to the ground in three great spirals. Ninety birds had gone to Siberia, only seventy-seven remained.

Before the birds had reached the top of the mountain, however, forty to seventy-five local senior citizens, all warmly dressed, arrived around the Crane Warden's headquarters, some little distance from their homes, all with faces toward the northwest, watching silently as the last specks disappeared from view. Then for some time they stood conversing about the flight with their friends and neighbors. How oblivious they were to anything else at the time! How much interest they showed in their favorite cranes! And how much the episode related to me without words how significant cranes were and had been in the lives of these friendly people!

On February 25, 1969, about sixty-five more left for Siberia at 8:30 A.M., followed by sixteen other cranes (the latter probably *Grus monachus*) at 10 A.M. The first group was purely *Grus vipio*. Again it was a clear day, after three rainy days (temperatures: high, 13.6° C., low, —.03° C. Sunrise, 6:51 A.M., sunset, 6:12 P.M., wind, very light). The last days of February were again cloudy, some rainy, but on March 1 it was again clear and cool. I did not see any *Grus vipio* at all that day, but the next morning there were still two present. These were not seen again, but scarcely any *Grus monachus* had departed. Each morning they continued to fly to their fields and at times fed in crops which reached up to their necks as the new growth flourished from the rains and warmer weather.

MIGRATION

Dementiev and Gladkov (1951) wrote: In Siberia "*Nesting and migratory bird.* In the Maritime Province, it arrived early in the second half of March. In 1868, on the upper reaches of the Sungachi, first flocks were flying 27 February, when snow lay in deep layers with no thawed patches anywhere. night temperatures reaching —20° C. A heavy migration was observed in mid-April when small flocks of three to eleven individuals were flying. In 1869 first flocks were observed on 15 and 16 March, migration lasting until 12 April when a flock of thirteen individuals was encountered flying northward (Przhevalsky). In 1928, on 25 April, at the mouth of the Lefu (at the south edge of Lake Khanka, Lat. 44.5° N., Long. 132°-133° E.) five were seen and at Troitkosavsk (Kyakhta) on the Chikoy River on 26 April 1896 a flight of Daurian Cranes was seen, and one of the flock was taken (Molleson). During migration and the first days of arrival, it keeps to open marshy valleys.

"The return flight is gradual, covering the entire months of September and October, in the southern Maritime Province, even up to the end of November. The first migrating flocks of the Daurian Crane were observed flying southward along the Sungachi River 4 September 1859 (Maak). In 1867 migration was observed 15 September on the Suyfun River (Lat. 44° N., Long. 132° E.) (Near Chakhuzu), 13 and 18 October in small numbers near Novgoradsk harbour on 22, 23, and 28 November, when a few flocks were observed at Pos'yet Bay (Przhevalsky).

"*Wanderings.* Often migrations of the Daurian Crane are observed in spring, summer, and autumn,

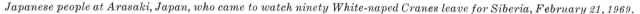

Japanese people at Arasaki, Japan, who came to watch ninety White-naped Cranes leave for Siberia, February 21, 1969.

most often in flocks of other species of cranes, mostly the Gray Crane (*Grus grus*), sometimes far from nesting and wintering regions. It has been encountered in summer on the western shore of Baikal (Radde), during the fall migration in the valley of the Khara River (Lat. 48°-49° N., Long. 106° E.) (foothills of Kenteya, Koslova) mixed with flocks of Gray Cranes. Records of more distant wanderings are very doubtful; the majority were observed at great distances, even when birds were taken, identification was not made by specialists and collected specimens were not preserved. Distant flight of the Daurian Crane has been observed in central Asia—two specimens were taken from a flock of five on the Syr-Darya in the environs of Kzyl-Orda (Lat. 45° N., Long. 66° E.) in mid-April and a specimen from Lake Kamishli-bashi on 10 October 1913 (Zarudniy), on the steppes of the eastern littoral of the Caspian, on the lower Ural, west of Rostova-on-Don. A specimen was taken 16 May 1876 in the southern part of Lenkoransk District and one on 5 March 1892 in the environs of Kumbasha Station (In both cases the cranes were taken from a flock of Gray Cranes; Tizengauzen, Satunin); it was observed at Makhach-Kala. Determination was doubtful in this case. The entire issue as to which cranes are found along the Caspian Sea is not clear. Everman called these the Daurian Crane *G. antigone* but described their plumage as being like that of *G. vipio*. A specimen taken 16 May 1976 was not preserved."

C. M. Fennell (Letter, January 13, 1966) reported this crane as a common winter visitor in southern Korea.

ECOLOGY

Dementiev and Gladkov (1951) wrote: "Monogamous. On arrival they are already broken up into pairs, sometimes they arrive in pairs, but for the first period of arrival they remain in flocks in open places; only after the thawing of marshes, i.e. in southern Ussuri region, approximately in mid-April the flocks break up into pairs occupied definitely with nesting, remaining thus until fall. They select an impassable marsh amidst seclusion in a narrow mountain valley.

"In the courting period and even at hatching time, the cranes often get into a dance resembling the Demoiselle Crane dance (Przhevalsky, 1870,

1876). It happens that they are very alert in the morning and evening. Usually several pairs living in one neighborhood gather together on a dry spot in a drier marsh where there are no available bushes, ravines, or any cover, where they are able to watch for enemies. With much clamor the cranes fly to this spot for the 'Dance' . . . one or two birds jump out and lead off, jumping, bowing heads, curtsying and more jumping . . . tumbling back with spread wings and uttering a trumpeting sound. The rest watch them and later dance while the others rest. The dance continues about two hours, then the birds with loud calls begin scattering to their nesting ponds (a pond at Lake Khanka—Przhevalsky, 1870). Independent from the dance, the male roams with the female through the marsh often bowing in front of her, half jumping and sailing, bowing as does the Demoiselle Crane."

ABUNDANCE

Almost customary to abundant on the Argun, Onon and Tarey-Nor (Tachanovsky, 1875) at the time of the first investigations of eastern Siberia and the Maritime Province, it was observed more frequently than any other crane in the Khanka Lake basin, along the mountain streams in the southern extremity of the Ussuri Region and particularly in the Sungachinskikh Swamp (Przhevalsky, 1876). At present it is rare and in places has disappeared completely; thus, on the Tarey-Nor it probably does not nest any more now, but on the Daurian Steppes among the lakes in the basin of the Onon and Borza and other rivers it is abundant (Dolgushin, 1941). It is rare at Lake Khanka, on the Daubikha and on the rivers which empty into the Sea of Japan (Shul'pin, 1936). On the lower courses of the Ussuri River it was always rare and much scarcer than on the Argun and Onon (Tachanovsky, 1875), while farther to the south, along the valley of this river, it probably did not nest at all. Simultaneously with the decrease in numbers of the Daurian Crane, the extent of the nesting range has been reduced.

NESTING

Przhevalsky (1877) wrote that this crane is usually found amongst the foothill moraines in the less extensive marshes. Koslova (1935) found it breeding in brush-covered situations. Dementiev and

Gladkov (1951) wrote the Biotope used was narrow mountain chains and marsh-ridden valleys with rivers flowing through them.

Blaauw (1897) reported (according to Dr. Dybowski): The nest of this crane is placed in the marshy parts of steppes. The birds select an islet elevated a few inches above the surrounding marsh and on this form a nest of dead dry grass. The structure is flat with a small depression in the middle. The birds, like all cranes, are apt to foresake their eggs if repeatedly disturbed.

The White-naped Crane often has nested in captivity in aviaries, zoos, etc. Here it most often builds its nest of a mass of grass which becomes haylike, on dry ground. I reported (1951) on such a nest in the Detroit Zoological Park where a pair of birds nested during 1945, 1946 and 1947. The species has also bred in the Zoological Garden in Amsterdam, Holland; when a pair nested the first year they were brought from Japan to Germany in 1933 (Hagenbeck, 1940) and raised two young, then one each year in 1935, 1936 and 1937, and hatched four young (two killed by hail) in 1938 and two in 1939. It has bred at the New York Zoological Park where one young was raised during 1916, another in 1943 (Crandall, 1944). The first successful nesting in the Detroit Zoological Park was in 1946 as described by Keith Kreag (1946). The birds bred here also in June 1945. In 1946, one egg hatched June 24, indicating the eggs were laid about May 25. During 1947 one young was observed for the first time on June 19, only a few days old, indicating the eggs were laid about May 16. In 1948, the birds were released into the en-

White-naped Crane dancing, Arasaki, Japan. Photograph by Eizi Takabayashi; January 1968.

closure in mid-April. Both eggs hatched June 1 (Keith Kreag, letter), indicating the first egg must have been laid about April 30.

The birds also have bred in the Philadelphia Zoological Gardens (John Griswold, 1962) and in the Honolulu Zoo (Paul Breeze, letter). It also has bred several times in Tokyo, Japan.

In the wild, Przhevalsky (1877) took the earliest young of May 19 at Lake Khanka, and Grote (1943) stated the eggs hatched toward the end of May.

EGGS

The eggs are similar to Sandhill Cranes' eggs, ovate, at times elongate-ovate in shape, a rather dull shell, pitted finely as other crane eggs, not perceptible on many except with a magnifying glass. The color is buffy-brown to smoke gray. The marks are often confluent at the larger ends or in striations along the long axis, buffy-brown, brownish-olive, olive, some even light gray. Many markings are 12 to 18 mm long, 4 to 6 mm wide.

Dementiev and Gladkov wrote (1951), "In a set, two eggs. Measuring: 103.0 and 62.0, and 96.0 and 61.8 (mm). Weight, 22.0 and 18.0 grams (Harbin-Johansen, 1930)," They wrote that eggs resemble those of *Grus grus* and that eggs from Harbin were greenish-brown with dark cinnamon brown spots,

Theodor Schroeder with White-naped Crane chick, five weeks old, July 4, 1946, Detroit Zoological Park, Royal Oak, Michigan.

smeared and speckled. One egg in the British Museum (Natural History) was taken at Lake Baikal by Parrea and Dobrowski in 1872. The average measurements of six eggs was: 99.3 (92.7—103.0) x 61.46 (58.5—62.7) mm. Two eggs taken after they failed to hatch at the Honolulu Zoo in 1957 were smaller, possibly because the female was young or lacked essential foods. They measured 85.5 x 57.8 and 84.7 x 59.9 mm. They were laid on May 8 and May 12, 1957, respectively.

Przhevalsky observed, at the end of April 1868, that these birds were already flying singly to feeding regions in southern Ussuri. Ivanov, *et al.* (1951) gave the incubation period as thirty to thirty-one days. John Griswold (letter, February 19, 1963) wrote it was between thirty and thirty-three days, averaging thirty-one at the Philadelphia Zoological Gardens, while Blaauw (1897) and Hagenbeck (1940) gave it as thirty days.

INCUBATION

At the Detroit Zoological Park, I watched the nesting birds from daylight until dark, May 28, 1948, and from daylight until 12:30 P.M., May 29, 1948.

On May 28, the temperature varied between 53° F. (6 A.M.) and 82° F. (4 P.M.). On May 29, the high was 68° F. On May 28 the sky was clear almost all day, but on May 29 it was cloudy until near noon. There was no rain.

When settling onto the eggs, the White-naped Crane, as other cranes do, placed one foot on each side of the eggs, lowered the breast, then by shaking some, positioning the eggs beneath the breast feathers, the bird settled down, usually raising its head and neck to peer all around. Later it often sat in a sleeping position, head tucked beneath scapular feathers on one side.

The bird stood up and turned the eggs with its bill, often several times before settling down. Sometimes it required several trials before it appeared comfortable.

The female was on the eggs from dark on May 27 until 8:20 A.M., May 28, probably more than twelve hours, and 230 daylight minutes on May 28. She also sat during the day for periods of 57, 58, 55 and 63 minutes and one period on May 29 of 73 minutes, totaling 536 minutes on the nest between 4:30 A.M., May 28 and 12:30 P.M., May 29.

The male incubated for periods of 113, 112, 74 and 65 minutes on May 28, 16 hours and 36 minutes during the evening, night and morning of May 28 and 29, and began incubating in the afternoon of May 29 at 12:17 P.M., so was on the nest for a total of 903 daylight minutes and 470 minutes of darkness.

Thus, on two successive nights the female incubated one night, the male the next. During thirty-two hours of observation, the parents remained on the nest all but eleven minutes. The female (the smaller and less aggressive bird) stood up, preened and worked with the nest and eggs for 25 minutes; the male for 33 minutes, so the eggs were attended by one or the other for 30 hours and 51 minutes, or 96.4 per cent of the time. The female roosted all night in exactly the same spot, not having moved in the morning from where she was at night.

On May 28 the female fed chiefly between 8:25 A.M. and 9:20 A.M. and from 6:45 P.M. until 8:40 P.M. on May 29 from 4:30 A.M. until 10:29 A.M. The male fed on May 28 between 5:25 A.M. and 7:45 A.M. and from 5:28 P.M. until 5:45 P.M.; on May 29 from 11:10 A.M. to 11:35 A.M., a total of 197 minutes for the female and 117 for the male for the whole day of May 28 and the morning of May 29.

Most feeding was on grain thrown in by the caretaker. Fish were also thrown in, but the cranes did not eat many of these, even though some landed only ten meters from the nest. The pelicans and storks, working in swift dashes, got most of these before the cranes chased them away. Then there followed more raids and chases until the fish were gone.

Much of the crane feeding time was spent probing with their bills in the ground. Some time was spent capturing grasshoppers and other insects amongst the taller grasses. Once one White-naped Crane captured what appeared to be a crayfish from the lake bank, threshed it back and forth against some stones, then swallowed it whole.

They drank much like chickens, lowering the bill into the water, shovelling it forward to get water, then raising it rapidly and swallowing.

They bathed once or twice daily, lowering themselves into the water breast first, the entire body next, so that the head and neck alone protruded from the water. Vibrating some under water they remained only a few seconds, then rose swiftly, shook their feathers and spent many minutes preening.

The male roosted at night in shallow water twenty to thirty centimeters deep, with his head tucked underneath his scapular feathers. The next night the female did the same and both were only a few meters from the nest.

THE YOUNG

Dementiev and Gladkov (1951) wrote: "In the valley of the Siyankhe River (southern Ussuri region), 1 June 1869 a downy young was taken, hatched two or three days earlier. First young were encountered in a basin of Lake Khanka on 30 May; in the valley of the Lefu River, parents with young were encountered in mid-June 1869 (Przhevalsky, 1876)."

The call of the downy young in the Detroit zoo was a shrill plaintive *Peeep* or *Peeer*. This call was retained until the following spring when the adult call was acquired. Young birds at Arasaki, Japan, were still giving this call in late February when they departed for Siberia.

In the Detroit zoo parents fed the young bird the following day after hatching. In only a few days it was picking up objects by itself at times while the parents continued to feed it periodically, even up until the following winter. But in general it picked up its own food a few days after hatching. When it was ten to ten-and-a-half-months old the parents evicted it from their presence, the male being the aggressor, repeatedly driving the young bird away, when and if it came near the female bird. He also did this with other cranes during the late winter.

At Arasaki, Japan, young birds were with their parents in late February 1969 and departed with them, probably at least as far as Korea. During the winter they fed along with their parents regularly and remained in family groups.

Griswold (1962) gave weights of two newly hatched *Grus vipio* at the Zoological Society of Philadelphia. They weighed respectively, at one day of age, 112 and 127 g; at two days, 96 and 116; at three days, 92 and 109; at four days, 96

A pair of White-naped Cranes in display. Arasaki, Japan, January 1968. Photograph by Eizi Takabayashi.

and 124; at five days, 97 and 160; at six days, 114 and 182; and at seven days, 118 and 200 g.

The tawny-colored downy chick grows rapidly, the legs becoming large and awkward, the plumage, a lighter tawny color. In 1945 nesting occurred in June; in 1946 one egg hatched June 24 and in 1947 about June 19. These young began to show the juvenal plumage by six weeks of age, the tips of the flight and tail feathers still tipped with beautiful plumes, or down. These feathers were retained throughout the first winter on the wing, possibly on the tail. All the rest were molted from late August into late October, the bird acquiring a plumage somewhat similar to that of the adult. The young birds are not as dark gray as the adults even into the first winter, nor do they molt again as far

as is known until the following August to October. The face becomes bare during the first winter.

TERRITORY

Grus vipio is strongly territorial both in winter and during the breeding season, probably even more so during spring, and some in the fall. Birds with young are prone to attack quicker than those without. Whereas, Uchinda (1930) remarked that these birds were strongly territorial and families fed apart from other families. Nowadays in Japan they have changed so that they feed side by side for some time, day after day, usually all strung out in a long line. But even here they maintain a territory around each family and even around the individual. The male usually guards this much more than the female. This is maintained in both the roosting and feeding regions.

In the Detroit zoo, the birds had to contend with two of their own kind, and six other crane species, as well as storks, pelicans, flamingos, turkeys, African vultures, two species of geese, black ducks, mallards, peacocks and guinea fowl. The nest was on dry ground near the small lake. The birds easily kept most birds away from there by force showing a strong "attack" action. Attack was at times preceded by "false preening," twice by lying down on the ground in front of larger Sarus Cranes (*G. a. antigone*), the "lying pose" following this. On one occasion the Sarus Cranes pressed them even more, attacking the female bird which was lying near the territorial edge in front of them. The male dashed off the nest and both male and female *G. vipio* chased the Sarus Cranes from the neighborhood. Following this they uttered the unison call; this time actually it was a victory call.

In winter and more into late February, they maintained a territory a few feet from each pair. Here they went through the usual crane procedure: (1) false preening; (2) arching the neck, bill pointing groundward; (3) attack, and at times they used the "fluffed feather" display after the preening, but many times they did not. I saw twenty-five to thirty encounters where birds were driven away. At no time did the opponent remain to be attacked nor show signs of returned attack. The "escape" tendency was always the rule.

Dancing was performed by both young birds and adults. Adults jumped, catapulted, spread their wings, and sometimes called while dancing. I never saw them bob their heads nor twist. At times they had synchronized jumping, and at others they picked up objects.

VOICE

Often while in a flock the birds give the unison call. Once they gave it when changing places at the nest, and once when driving away a pair of Sarus Cranes in the zoo. In the wild they give this regularly all winter in Japan. The male sometimes holds his head straight up, again slightly forward, but quite often with the neck arched, bill pointing over his back upward. He also holds his primaries stiffly at his side, the secondaries arched prettily over his back; the female simultaneously keeps her bill pointing upward or slightly forward, with no feather display. The male commences the call with a shrill, penetrating *Gar-oooo---gar--oooo----gar-oooo----gar-oooo----gar-oooo*, often giving five to twelve syllables. The female utters a less penetrating call, producing each syllable immediately following the male's call, *Tuk-tuk---tuk-tuk---tuk-tuk---tuk-tuk*. She continues to call, usually as long as he calls. Sometimes the birds face each other, but as often they may have their backs together or be standing side by side. Many times females initiate this call (George Archibald, verbal).

The young bird at hatching gives the usual *Peeep* and continues to give a similar call into the first winter. By the following spring it acquires the adult call.

When flying, often one bird or more in the flock gives a low guttural *Garraw* call and they give a low snoring *Purr* when calling the young or reassuring each other.

FOOD

Dementiev and Gladkov (1951) wrote: "Not studied . . . apparently . . . it constitutes chiefly of vegetable matter with sufficient small amounts of animal food."

In the Detroit zoo, the birds ate wheat, fish, grasshoppers, probably earthworms, other insects and, at one time, apparently a crayfish. At Arasaki, Japan, they ate wheat and crucian fish (carp) mostly, but at times returned to open fields where they worked over the land, thoroughly searching, digging, etc. There were some frogs here and no doubt they make use of them at times, as do other cranes.

DISTRIBUTION

It breeds in southeastern Siberia from Transbaykalia and northwestern Mongolia east through Manchuria to the Amur and Ussuri rivers. It winters in middle China to the Yangtse Valley in the east; in southern Korea; and in southern Kyushu, Japan, while a few have been found in Ussuriland.

Summer distribution—U.S.S.R. Dementiev and Gladkov (1951) wrote: "Range. Daurian steppes. Rivers Onon and Argun; Lake Torey-Nor perhaps visiting somewhat farther up to Troitskosavska (at Kyakhta), and northern Mongolia (taken on the Chikoy River and on the Bureya River south of Troitskosavaka—Molleson), lower reaches of the Bureya River (Shul'pin), it may nest in the southeastern part of Mongolia (Przhevalsky); in the summertime on Lake Dalay Nor and in the region from the lake up to Kalgan (Changkaikow, Lat. 41° N.; Long. 115° E.) (Johansen, 1930); a bird taken 115 km northwest from Tsitsihar (Lat. 47° N.; Long. 123° E.) (Meyze); southwestern Primorya Oblast (Maritime Province); Daubikhe River, Khanka Lake, Sungayi, Lefu, Mo, Siyankha (Lat. 43° N.; Long. 131-132° E.); and other little rivers in the Lake Khanka Basin, the Ussuri up to the lower course."

Years ago Przhevalsky (1877) wrote that this was the most common crane about Lake Khanka, arriving early in March. Koslova (1932) in her travels through Mongolia, 1924-1926, once observed several pairs in the valley of the Khara River only. She judged there were young nearby from their behavior.

China. In China this crane winters chiefly along the Yangtze (Kiang) River. La Touche (1933) wrote that the collecting of a specimen by Rickett in February (1893) at Foochow (Lat. 26° N.; Long. 119.7° E.) was no doubt accidental. Styan mentioned one was shot near Shanghai in January, and La Touche had one sent to him from Chinwangtao (Lat. 40° N.; Long. 119.7° E.) dated October 10 (probably in migration), as were those reported by Wilder and Hubbard; at Peitaiho when they saw flocks of from twenty to several hundred flying south October 8th and 9th.

There are specimens from China: N. E. Chihli, an adult male taken in winter (La Touche, 1933); Foochow, an adult female, February 1893 (BMNH, *ex* C. B. Rickett); N. E. Chihli, Chinwangtao, male taken October 10, 1918 (MCZ *ex* J. D. La Touche).

It is possible that a few remain in winter, or at times, in the southern part of the Maritime Province on the Suyfun (Lat. 44° N.; Long. 132° E.) (Przhevalsky).

Korea. The White-naped Crane used to winter here in large numbers and is still found in favorable localities in fair-sized flocks. Ben King (verbal) reported a flock of 2,300 on a mud flat at the confluence of the Han and Imjin Rivers, in November 1961. He reported that the establishment of the demilitarized zone may have saved the few remaining wintering birds near Panmunjom. C. Fennell (letter, January 13, 1966) wrote that *G. vipio* was still fairly common in South Korea in some regions.

Korean museum specimens are: Giseifu, adult female, 1916, Kuroda (1918); Keiki District, Keiki do Province, Anjo, adult male, February 1933, (YIOZ); Keiki-do, Risen, adult female, January 7, 1919 (YIOZ); Keiki-do Province, adult female, February 23, 1938 (CNHM); Mokpho, immature female, January 29, 1930 (YIOZ *ex* H. Oru), immature female, January 20, 1940 (CNHM); adult male, April 1940 (CNHM); Pusan, immature female, December 6, 1883 (USNM *ex* P. L. Jouy); Chongi-do, adult males, March 12, 1918, February 25, 1919 (NR); Keikido, adult male and female, March 10, 1940 (MCZ *ex* Chosen Christian Coll.); "Korea" adult male, December 1908 (CNHM).

Taiwan. Horikawa (1942) reported this species here.

Bonin Island (Lat. 27.5° N.; Long. 142° E.). There is a female specimen (MCZ) from here taken by A. Owston in January 1883.

See Kuroda ("The Measurements of *Grus vipio* in Korea." *Tori*, 9 (41) December 1935, pp. 84-85—in Japanese). (See Hand-List of the Japanese Birds, 1958).

DESCRIPTION

Adult. Face and forehead are devoid of feathers to about 25 or 30 mm behind the eye. A region, somewhat oval-shaped, just below the level of the eye and posterior to it, 20 to 25 mm horizontally, 18 to 24 mm vertically, is covered with ashy-gray feathers. The bare face region is red, but covered with dark bristly, hair-like feathers. The back of the neck, from the mantle to the bare red skin, the throat, and the front and sides of the neck above, are white. The remainder of the plumage is generally dark slaty-gray extending up the sides of the neck as well as in front. This comes to a point within about 30 mm of the gray ear patch. Primaries are black with white shafts, the basal portion of the inner webs is white. Secondaries are blackish with white bases becoming mottled about the fourth inward. The innermost secondaries are white falcated, lengthened and pendant. Wing co-

A pair of White-naped Cranes giving 'Unison Call' at Arasaki, Kagoshima Prefecture, Japan, January 1963. Photograph by Toshiaki Harada.

verts are lighter gray; the greater coverts, white at the ends. The lower portion of the neck anteriorly, the sides up to the point on each side, the breast and lower part of the body are dark slaty-gray. The tail is dark gray tipped with black, with lighter gray on the under tail-coverts. Primaries, 11; third, longest, second, and fourth somewhat shorter. Rectrices, 12.

The iris is orange-yellow; bill, greenish-yellow; legs and feet described as bluish-pink in live birds by Blaauw; by La Touche as crimson-lake.

Sub-adult. The head is covered entirely with soft downy feathers. The upper part of head, occiput and the upper parts are light cinnamon–brown,

lightest on the neck with an almost whitish line up the back of the neck by three months of age. The mantle and wing-coverts are darker. The cinnamon-brown feathers of the head and neck have light bases. The brown is dominant because the outer portion is brown while the inner portion of the same feathers is concealed gray similar to the adult color. The throat is yellowish-white; the lower neck in front, grayish-yellow. The breast and underparts are gray with slightly yellowish margins. In younger birds the yellow predominates, but as the birds get older the gray is more evident. The tail and wings are blackish-gray (described by Blaauw, 1897, from a bird reared in captivity in the Zoological Garden of Amsterdam, which died at eighty-five days, and some from a bird raised in the Detroit Zoological Gardens, Detroit, Michigan).

Downy chick. Tawny-yellow. Somewhat white below, but brownish above, with darker spots extending onto the upper parts of the wings, the rump and lower back. It becomes more tawny-yellow as it gets a few weeks older.

MEASUREMENTS

Adult male. (Nine specimens, AMNH, 3; BMNH, 1; CNHM, 2; MCZ, 2; YIOZ, 1). Exposed culmen, 145.1 (128-155); from base of nostril (2), 106; wing, 562.9 (510-585); tail (2), 213; tarsus, 253.7 (242-262); bare tibia, 107.8 (67-126); middle toe with claw, 112.75 (104-118) mm.

Adult female. (Six specimens, BMNH, 2; CNHM, 1; MCZ, 2; YIOZ, 1). Exposed culmen, 137.8 (128-148); from base of nostril (2), 100.5; wing, 546.8 (521-560); tail, 204.7 (196-216); tarsus, 242.3 (230-263); bare tibia, 120.4 (103-140); middle toe and claw, 107.3 (105-113) mm.

Chapter Eight

THE SARUS CRANE

(*Grus antigone*)

THE INDIAN SARUS CRANE

(*Grus antigone antigone*)

Ardea Antigone, Linnaeus, *Syst. Nat.,* 10th ed., *1,* 1758, p. 142.
Type locality: Asia. Farther India (as restricted by Hartert, 1921, 1820). This, the typical form, differs from the Eastern Sarus Crane in that the former has a white collar below the bare neck, and has the inner secondaries almost pure white, whereas the eastern form has both of these similar to the gray color of the body.
Vernacular names: The Indian Sarus Crane, the Sarus Crane of India (English); Halsbandkranich (German); la Grue a collier (French); el blanco cuello Grulla (Spanish); de Ringkraan (Dutch); O-O zuru オオヅル (Japanese); белый журавль (Russian); Saras, Sirhans (Hind.); Khur-sang (Assam); Korchan (Assam).

This tremendous crane is found almost entirely inside India, spreading out slightly to the west, east and north. It never has been found in the extreme southern portion of India but has been found rarely in Burma, Nepal, Bangla Desh, and Pakistan.

BEHAVIOR

I saw my first wild Sarus Cranes from a speeding train south of New Delhi. There were a few scattered ponds and jheels along the way, the only remaining water in a drought-stricken land. The cranes were feeding either along their margins or very nearby. At times they continued feeding, but nearly always raised their heads and watched the train rush by. There were five pairs and three lone birds, all miles apart. After the train pulled into Bharatpur, I was driven behind a horse and driver in a buggylike *tanga* to the Keoladeo Ghana Bird Sanctuary. This pastured forestry region with many isolated openings was the place Dr. Salim Ali had suggested would be the ideal place for my studies of the Sarus Crane.

The afternoon of that same day, September 1, 1965, I finally reached the only spot in this very dry forest region where there was water. Here was a treeless marshy region of about 450 acres, with several parallel rows of six- to eight-foot mounds that ran nearly the entire width and were immersed in about a foot of water. For the next four hours I sat at the edge of this region watching no less than forty-five groups of one and two cranes, an almost unbelievable sight. Some pairs were only slightly over 100 feet apart, others were separated by up to 1,200 feet or more; the average was approximately 467 feet. Some were only slightly over 100 feet from me as I sat at the edge of the highway, on which a good many people were walking.

Since they seemed to remain within a small designated spot, with almost regular spacing, I assumed that each pair maintained a position, probably not a permanent territory, but out of reach of neighboring birds. Side by side, only three to five feet apart, feeding, preening and periodically uttering their ringing resonant unison call, each pair roamed its specified area.

In giving the unison call, the male held his neck erect, his head so that the bill was pointed slightly backward, raised his wings above and out from his sides and back, and displayed his white secondaries above the stiffened primaries, which were held down toward the ground like those of a strutting turkey gobbler. The female stood with wings close-

Indian Sarus Crane dancing, Keoladeo Ghana Bird Sanctuary, Bharatpur, Rajasthan, India, February 1969.

ly held against her side, head and bill pointing straight up, or nearly so, but did not raise her secondaries. Both birds vibrated all over when they called. Often when one pair called, others entered the symphony. Again only one pair trumpeted. The male called, "*Krrrr-kweerrrr-Krrrr-krrrr, krrrr-krrrr,*" the female, "*Tuk-tuk-tuk-tuk-tuk-tuk-tuk,*" continuing as long as the male called. The cranes remained the entire night, each pair roosting in the shallow water of its own domain.

For the remainder of the month all my spare time was spent watching these Sarus Cranes. The groups of birds observed at Ghana Sanctuary are given in Table 16. The next three days brought the monsoons, during which nineteen inches (48.3 cm) of rain deluged the region. Since the sanctuary lies in a closed basin, the water began rising in the upper impoundments immediately. On September 8 the roosting marsh was flooded with seven to twelve feet of water. Even the main highway to Agra was under seven feet of water in places. I could walk the roads and bunds in the sanctuary, or wade waist-deep in the crane-inhabited regions. Because of the extreme heat I wore light trousers and tennis shoes. These were often temporarily soaked, but usually dried a short time after leaving the water.

Shortly after the monsoon, the birds scattered widely, even beyond the sanctuary. (I found only twenty-seven pairs within its boundaries.) Although many nests have been found, showing that Sarus Cranes often nested as early as July and August, there was no evidence during 1965 of any pre-monsoon nesting (apparently monsoons come earlier some years). On September 8 the first territorial battles and nest building were seen. I began to observe four rather interesting pairs of cranes: Pair A, relatively submissive; Pair B, the dominant pair, but not as aggressive as Pair C, whose male was a bit of a bully; Pair D, much like Pair A.

Pair A was the first to nest. The female worked adjacent to the nest, pulling wads of debris and vegetation from the water and piling it onto the nest site with a sideways motion. The male stood about fifteen feet from the nest, pulling material from the water, then dropping it near the nest, but just out of the female's reach. She worked thirty-three minutes on the nest, her mate, twenty-five.

At this point Pair B invaded their territory. Both A's leaped to action, and the B's stopped seven to eight feet away. The males faced each other and false-preened furiously. The females stayed a few feet behind their respective mates, but also preened. Male D came rushing up with his female close behind. A went into a defense pose, arched his neck, pointed his bill towards the ground, and with outspread wings and rigid legs, jumped at Male D. The B's walked away, apparently disinterested in asserting their dominance. The situation cooled off then, and Pairs A and D fed for some time only six to eight feet apart. After about twenty minutes, Pair A walked back to their nest and the D's departed.

On September 10, I went to watch Pair A, who were busy on their nest, even though their neighbors—B, C and D—showed no signs of nest building. Female A sat down twice on the now huge pile, once for an entire minute. The nest was in the shallowest spot in the vicinity. The water appeared to be about one to one-and-a-half feet deep. Both birds were six to fifteen feet from the nest, pulling wads of debris and green vegetation up and piling it on the nest which now showed well above the water. Twice they took time out to give the unison call. Pair C, slowly roaming around their territory, responded with one of their own. Then the male began walking swiftly directly toward Pair A, sometimes through three feet of water. The female followed, a few feet behind. The nesting pair saw them coming and moved fifty feet in their direction, then stopped. The C's came on, stopping about nine feet from them. Both pairs began preening furiously. Male C started toward Male A, who retreated to another fixed spot where he and his mate (still three feet away) stopped and began preening again. Male C kept coming. The nesting pair arrived at the nest and climbed onto it. Male C then jumped directly at Male A, causing both A's to half-run, half-fly twenty feet away. Pair C climbed onto the nest and began calling. The female started tearing the nest to pieces, tossing wads of material out into the water. For seventy-five minutes they remained on the nest, the female frantically throwing pieces of the nest into the water, the male standing at attention. Pair A stood dejectedly and silent nearby, up to their breasts in water. The C's withdrew about twenty-five feet. then thirty minutes later, about 2:45 P.M., flew 600 feet back into their own territory.

Female A came back immediately, however, and swiftly began picking up wads of nest material to carry back onto the nest. Finally, at 3 P.M., the male came back, and by 3:07 P.M. both birds were working silently on the nest. Later, when they left, they came near another pair northeast of the site, and all four birds began preening. At times they fluffed out their feathers, often shaking all over.

On September 11, on a circuit of the eleven miles around the sanctuary, I found no other birds engaged in nesting. On September 13 I again observed Pairs A, B, C and D. At 10:12 A.M. the busy B's entered A territory again, causing the A's to call in unison and rush to meet the invaders. Male A showed more spunk today, and the B's withdrew.

The morning was filled with many unison calls (Pair B, for instance, at 8:42, 8:50, 9:00, 9:45, 10:12, 10:38, 11:35, 11:40, 11:42 A.M.) and minor skirmishes. Pair C squabbled with Pair B shortly after eleven o'clock. At noon Pair D started walking toward Pairs C and B. The C's stopped calling, and the D's stopped walking (in shallow water about 30 cm deep). They preened awhile, then almost simultaneously began bathing. They dropped breast first, swished around so their entire bodies were under water, with just their heads and part of their necks protruding above. They flapped their wings up and down, even dropping their

Indian Sarus Crane at nest in Lincoln Park Zoo, Chicago, Illinois, September 1, 1946.

heads under water at times. At 12:43 P.M. the female stood up; three minutes later, the male. They were drenched, shook some, and then began to preen until 2:10 P.M., when they wandered away, feeding.

At 1:30 P.M., Pair A gave the unison call when they spotted Pair C coming within about sixty-five meters of their nest. They were evidently a bit afraid, but managed to keep the C's on the opposite side of a group of dead trees. Soon Pair A went to work on their nest with a good deal of fever. They pulled vegetation within two to five meters of the nest and threw it sidewise toward it. At 3:45 P.M. Pair C walked away, Pair A following a short distance behind, feeding.

No pair controlled less than 100 acres (40.47 hectares) and not over 150 acres (60.7 hectares). I observed dancing four times. Once the male started it, once the female; twice I was not sure. The first dance observed was September 13 (11:07-11:10 A.M.); the next, Pair A, September 15 (12:55-12:57 P.M.); the third, Pair B, September 17; the fourth time Pair D on September 27. At first the instigator began bowing, head almost touching the ground several times in succession. Then the bird jumped stiff-legged into the air ten or twelve feet with wings spread. The second bird always responded with similar hops, bows and jumps. They did not call while dancing.

On September 13 I observed Pair A copulate. The female was the aggressor. Both birds were feeding about 300 feet apart and 500 feet from their new nest. At 9:17 A.M. both birds started towards each other. The female suddenly stopped, turned her back to the male and raised her head and neck, with her bill pointing upward and forward. The male hurried forward, and when he arrived, stepped slowly and carefully onto her lower back. Then with wings slowly beating, he copulated with her. The act required only about thirty seconds. When leaving he hopped over her head.

I saw no distraction displays at Ghana nor at Baroda, but when the train on which I was riding stopped just north of Gangapur, Rajasthan, on September 28, a pair of seemingly dejected Sarus Cranes ran by. I rushed to the opposite window to see their nest, with two eggs, in a small pond. All of the employees had dashed off the train, and two young men stood beside the nest. One picked up one of the eggs. Both cranes, in crouched positions, ran with outspread wings directly away from them. Neither bird called. The men replaced the egg and climbed back onto the train. When it started away a minute or two later, both cranes hurried back to the nest.

DESCRIPTION

Adult. Head, throat and upper neck are bare. Crown is smooth and pale ashy-green; the remainder of the bare portion is covered with coarse granulations, orange-red in color, much deeper and brighter during the breeding season. The upper throat and some of the neck are covered with long, black hairlike bristles. A small patch of bluish-gray feathers is found over the ears. A ring of white feathers about 7.5 cm wide stretches between the bare neck and the gray feathers farther down. The primaries, primary coverts and alulu are black or dark gray. The innermost secondaries are lengthened, lanceolate but not decomposed; outer secondaries are darker gray on the outer webs, lighter on the inner. The remainder of the plumage is bluish-gray or light gray. The iris is yellowish-brown or orange. The bill has a pale greenish-horn color with a darker tip. Legs and feet are red, fleshy-red, to bluish-pink.

The bare portion extends about 18 cm from the top of the head, while the bare portion beneath the dark bristles is about 2.5 cm wide.

Sub-adult. The entire head and neck are feathered, buffy in color. Younger birds have feathers edged with brownish-gray—those on the upper part are cinnamon-brown—all with the down adhering to the tips as with other young cranes.

Downy chick. Except for the bill and legs, it is entirely covered with down. The head, neck and throat are pale isabelline. Lower neck, sides of breast and belly, vent and thighs are darker isabelline. Center of breast and belly are white. Two broad lines of dark brown extend from the base of the neck, enclosing a paler brown median stripe, down the back to the rump. A large buffy-white spot is opposite the base of both wings. Wings are cinnamon-brown with buffy-white tips (Ticehurst, 1926).

MEASUREMENTS

Adult male. (Thirteen specimens, AMNH, 1; BMNH, 2; CNHM, 2; MCZ, 4; UMMZ, 4): Exposed culmen, 171.2 (156-187); from base of nostril (2), 120.5; wing (chord), 631.2 (590-675); tail, 242.5 (240-245); tarsus, 329.3 (278-352); bare tibia, 197.3 (170-220); middle toe and claw, 135.6 (121-152) mm.

Adult female. (Eight specimens, BMNH, 3; CNHM, 4; UMMZ, 1): Exposed culmen, 163.6 (157-169); from base of nostril, 108.7 (95-114); wing (chord), 623.3 (580-671); tail, 253 (234-265); tarsus, 304.4 (272-350); bare tibia, 180.7 (113-218); middle toe and claw, 134.0 (129-147) mm.

HABITAT AND NESTS

The area in which the Sarus Crane nests at Keoladeo Ghana Bird Sanctuary is a forestry region where many Indian trees are found on the impoundments and in higher regions. Some trees have died, and the stubs add to the solitude of the flooded marsh. The entire region is pastured to cattle and water buffalo, which do not disturb the birds. The pH of the water is about 9.0, but very basic. When rains come there is no vegetation protruding above the water, but in only a few days there is extensive growth, which shortly grows well above the water, producing good cover.

There are many kinds of trees, some of which are Babul (*Acacia arabica*), Kandi (*Prosopis spicigera*), Keli-kadamb (*Stephegyne parvifolia*). Average rainfall is about twenty-seven inches, usually coming in the monsoons. Temperatures are very high in August and September, but ranged between —1° and 20° C. February 4, 1969.

The cranes nest back amongst the trees, in open marshy regions where dead stubs are found, and at times on the flooded embankments. Usually they place the nest on the highest spot in the vicinity, or where several old stubs help to support it. In 1965, at nesting time, the water was waist-deep in many places, but only about one meter deep directly around the nest.

At Ghangapur, the nest was a foot from shore in three or four centimeters of water, with practically no vegetation around it. It was very conspicuous, whereas the ones at Keoladeo Ghana were in isolated regions, often far from roads, trails and people.

Indian Sarus Crane pair at evening rest, Keoladeo Ghana Bird Sanctuary, Rajasthan, India, February 6, 1969.

Near Baroda, there was no rain in 1965. Many of the marshes, ponds and shallow lakes were dry. A few had some water. In one dry region which usually flooded each year, a pair of Sarus Cranes had built a nest, but it remained dry and they never laid any eggs. The birds remained in the territory all season. They could find little food and were stripping matured rice from the stalks with their bills, as well as grass seeds from nearby plants. In another region a pair built a nest on a thirty-foot-long island about two meters from water. Another nest was built amidst scattered fine grasses in a sewer pond. It must have been used for years from the size of it, and it floated about at the end of the pool. Many of the plants growing in the vicinity of these nests were:

Indian Sarus Crane, Keoladeo Ghana Bird Sanctuary, India, September 1965.

Grasses	Gramineae:	*Oryza sativa* Var. *Fatua*
		Paspalum distichum
		Echinochloa colonum
Sedges	Cyperaceae:	*Scirpus maritimus*
	Cyanophyceae:	*Lyngliya* sp.
Water lilies	Nymphaeaceae:	*Nymphaea lotus*
Pulse	Leguminosae:	*Aeschyomene indica*
Large water lily	Gentianaceae:	*Limnanthemum indicum*
	Scrophulariaceae:	*Limnophylla heterophylla*
	Steruliaceae:	*Melochia corchorifolia* *

*Thanks to MS University of Baroda, Botany Division.

Most nests rested on the mud beneath the water; some were placed on higher spots where the water was more shallow; others were among a group of dead stubs, which made them sturdier. At Ghana Bird Sanctuary the birds continued to add to their nests as long as the water rose. At Baroda this was not necessary for there the water in 1965 was continually receding. In the sewer inside Baroda at Bapot, the immense nest floated as apparently it had for years. It supported the weight of the crane and was out of reach of people on shore. By using a stick a person could move it about to examine it. At Timbi the water pH was 9.0; in the sewer region it was 7.2. Except for the island nest and the unused one on dry land, all other nests were built in water. The average height above water to the nest rim was 17.36 (3-25.4) cm and the average water depth adjacent to nests was 33.4 cm. Nine nests averaged at water level 150.7 (94-277) x 167.7 (119-308) cm across and were narrower at the top, usually about 90 to 130 cm. Most nests were in remote isolated regions where few people bother them.

Nests were built of the most available materials—mostly plants and loose debris in the vicinity—including cow dung. At one nest a large snail (*Pila globosa*) was found beside the two eggs the female was incubating.

EGGS

Hume (Blaauw, 1897) reported that in over 100 sets of eggs he found, only 2 consisted of three; the remainder consisted of two eggs. Many museums have sets that apparently were divided by collectors, for there are many one-egg sets. The five complete sets I observed in 1965 all contained two eggs. Of 132 sets, of which the egg number is given, there were 4 sets of one; 126 of two; 2 sets of three; average, 1.985 eggs.

Earlier writers have said most eggs were laid in June, July, August and more rarely in September. And then in recent years there are more of the latter dates. Monsoons may have come earlier in past years, for the birds definitely nest right after the rains. During 1965 they were building nests as early as five days after the end of the monsoons, though the majority of birds waited about three to four weeks.

Nest and eggs of Indian Sarus Crane, Keoladeo Ghana Bird Sanctuary, India, September 25, 1965

There are two definite records of eggs laid in June: one, a set of two eggs (BMNH) taken June 14, 1903 at Dibrugarh, Assam, by E. C. S. Baker; the second, recorded by Blaauw (1897) as found by Irby. There are nine eggs (probably five sets) taken by A. O. Hume (BMNH) at Zillah, Etawah in July (1866,1869); one taken at Nr. Chotta Bheel, Cachar, Assam, in July 1899, while Blaauw (1897) recorded another egg set found July 25 at Bolundshahr by G. F. L. Marshall. There are eight records for August and twelve for September, but Salim Ali, more recently (1940), recorded a nest (C/2) from Central India September 11, 1940. I found these nests: One (one egg), September 25; two days later, two eggs; two others with two eggs, September 25 and September 27. At Ghangapur, a nest had two eggs September 28, while two nests each with two eggs were observed at Baroda September 29 and 30 (all in 1965). I find one October record, two for November, five for December, one for January, five for February and three for March, but none for April or May, so one can say only that the date each year varies depending on the date of the monsoons.

The eggs are rather long, somewhat pointed at times at the small end, but chiefly oval-shaped. The ground color is white, very light blue, light green, even pinkish at times, and nearly always lightly spotted with various sized spots of brown, yellow, dark pink and purple, or combinations of these colors, usually more at the larger ends. Some eggs have been reported without spots, but all I have seen were spotted. The egg surface is very hard, somewhat pitted, at times quite glossy, at times with only a little gloss.

Baker (1928) gave the average measurements of 100 eggs as 104.4 (93.2-113.2) x 64.3 (53.8-69.8) mm. Blaauw (1897) gave records of 51 eggs as 101.5 x 65.0 mm. Seventy-three eggs of which I have measurements (including those in the British Museum [Natural History] averaged 101.35 (88.3-112.7) x 64.27 (58.7-70.1) mm. During 1965 I measured and weighed ten eggs averaging 101.1 (93.2-112.3) x 62.76 (58.7-65.6) mm, and 212.56 (183.4-247.6) g when fresh.

INCUBATION

Both Sarus Cranes incubate their eggs and care for the young. On September 26, 1965, I watched a pair which were setting on two eggs at the Keoladeo Ghana Bird Sanctuary. Following are notes taken that day as I sat beneath a tree 125 meters away.

Very hot, clear. Nest well out in the open with no shade of any kind. Male roosted very near nest in shallow water; female stayed on eggs all night. Sunrise about 6:15 A.M.; sunset, 6:25 P.M. (Asterisks denote nest changes.)

6:30 A.M.* Male went to nest on foot; female left on foot and fed. When changing, they gave unison call.

9:07 A.M.* Female came back on foot. Again they gave unison call. Male walked away and fed west of nest as had the female.

10:20 A.M.* Male came within 2 m of nest. Female rose and silently walked away. Male rearranged eggs one minute, then set. Female again fed west of nest.

12:58 P.M. Male stood up, walked three steps off nest, drank two sips of water, came right back and sat down.

1:45 P.M.* Female came back on foot within 100 m of nest. As usual she waded in about 1 m of water. Male stood, raised his secondaries again and initiated unison call. Immediately joined by female. As he stepped from the nest he reached down, picked up several wads of material and tossed them back toward the nest. Female hastened onto nest, wings half-spread, and sat right down. Soon she stood and worked with eggs. Then she sat down. Male shook all over, preened, then fed westward again. Female stood three times, then became satisfied and sat.

2:14- 2:15 P.M. Female rose and worked with eggs.

2:17 P.M. Three cranes flew over, calling. Male, feeding some 300 m from the nest, flew back to within 125 m of it, watched.

2:21 P.M.*	Male walked to nest; birds gave the unison call and changed. Female walked away a short distance.
2:38 P.M.	Female, 100 m from nest, walked towards it, but went right by, then turned and came back. Male did not get up, so after a short time she went on.
3:28 P.M.	Male stood over eggs 1½ minutes.
3:50 P.M.	Pair of cranes across trail gave unison call.
3:52 P.M.*	Female flew back to within 33 m of nest; male rose, and they silently changed places. Male pulled and tossed wads of debris back towards the nest.
4:40-4:46; 4:52-4:53; 4:58-5:01 P.M.	Female stood, looked around, preened. Male preened nearby.
5:21-5:29 P.M.	Female stood, preened. They did not change places again. Male roosted 100 m from the nest, where he stood the night before, in water 45 to 48 cm deep. Both birds easily discernible from trail, for there was little vegetation (region had been completely dry on September 2).

When I passed at noon the next day, the female was incubating. On September 26 these birds changed places six times; gave the unison call four times; flew only about 150 m between each, once during the day, but walked long distances.

THE YOUNG

At hatching, the young Sarus Crane is a ball of rusty-buff down, is very weak and may remain in the nest up to two days. When the parents are disturbed, the young sit or stand on their weak haunches on the nest, at first unable to stand on their wobbly legs. Even then they sometimes try to escape and are good swimmers. By two days they are much stronger, can walk well and swim very well.

The parents watch over them continuously, helping to feed them, guarding them, walking with them as they go. The young freeze motionless at a single call by one of the parents and do not come out until the parents call them again. At first the parents offer them food, but at about two days they begin picking up some things themselves. In a few days the young get much of their own food. They grow rapidly. Often, where there are two young at hatching, one disappears. The pair seldom raise more than one. (During February 1969 I saw

Indian Sarus Crane at nest, Keoladeo Ghana Bird Sanctuary, India. Photograph by E. P. Gee.

only three pairs with young; one pair had two, the others had but one.) Jack Kiracofe (1964) found that two chicks raised by his captive pair in Pennsylvania did not attack each other as do many young cranes.

The young remain with their parents at least ten months. I watched one pair with a full-grown youngster at Keoladeo, all feeding together in a compact trio. This pair was apprehensive when I was near, whereas the usual pair paid little attention to me at the same distance. Finally they rose and flew away. The young birds join together when their parents begin breeding again and roam the vicinity in groups.

There are a number of records of flocks up to as many as 200 birds (Acharya, 1936: 831, for one). However, many observers mention that birds remain in family groups or pairs, in these flocks, isolated a short distance from each other. I observed this at Keoladeo in both 1965 and 1969.

WINTER

In early February 1969 I visited Keoladeo Ghana Bird Sanctuary for the second time. The ponds were drying rapidly, but six still had some water—the mound pond (now grown to one or two eight-to-twelve-foot-tall trees per mound) the most. The Sarus Cranes roosted in three of these ponds—two being especial favorites—but not in the mound pond. Some birds remained in the ponds all day and all night, feeding, drinking and sleeping. Others flew out around daylight to neighboring fields or meadows (for flight times see Table 17). Some birds returned to the roost ponds shortly after 10:00 A.M. to drink, and after a while returned again to nearby meadows, fields and grain fields. Others came later, so there was a continual turnover during the day. The birds remaining in the ponds during the entire day appeared to be the dominant individuals, for they did not allow others to remain very long. Those with young were the most dominant, especially the males. Sometimes they went completely out of their way to drive other birds away. Since the pairs with young were widely separated, I observed no conflicts among males with young.

At night the remaining cranes divided about evenly amongst the three ponds. There were con-siderable skirmishes amongst groups so that most family groups or pairs ended up from 3 to 100 meters from each other. Yet as darkness approached, they all seemed to work into a certain region where they roosted in shallow water throughout the night. They seldom called at night, but in the morning they began calling loudly at, or shortly after, daylight. The dominant birds did not pick on one cripple I observed on February 3rd. This bird had a swollen foot; later, when it was caught in a net, a large leech was found on the under-wing surface. Possibly its foot had become swollen from continual scratching on this wing (as stated by men from the Bombay Natural History Survey). The leech was removed, the bird released. It was very weak now, often setting down during the day in some dry spot. Occasionally it rose and fed, often eating snails or other available food. On February 6 I watched it roam away during the afternoon onto nearby dry land, feeding as it went. When the crane was about 200 meters from the water, a jackal passed within ten meters of it. Neither paid any attention to the other as far as one could see, but the next morning the crane could not be found. Two days later I found its half-devoured, headless body a short distance from where this meeting had taken place. This is probably the chief reason this and many cranes roost in water while sleeping, and why they take their young at night back to wet regions.

Here the birds roost at night, departing shortly after daylight and making considerable noise at daybreak both winter and summer. Dominance is evident amongst birds although few actual battles are seen. In showing the defense pose, the male usually goes through certain behaviors: (1) Often the bird picks at the water or beneath it aimlessly as though feeding, but not feeding; (2) Preening begins, often on the back or shoulders—false preening; (3) the bird arches its neck, bill pointing groundward; (4) it dashes at its offender, which always moves away a few meters or, if the attack continues, flies to another more remote spot. Sometimes fluffing or shaking of feathers enters the display.

Most pairs roosted farther apart than did groups of birds; pairs with young maintained clearance for some distance.

Often pairs, or even groups, dashed madly about, a form of "play" initiated when a bird picked up a stick or piece of grass or a clod. It jumped around, holding it in its bill, or tossed it into the air as it jumped into the air beside the stick. Sometimes one bird of a pair danced; again, both birds did so, often each dancing a circle or part circle about the other. The dance consisted of bows, hops, jumps and dashes. Usually the bird jumped five to ten feet upward, with wings half-spread and legs held stiffly or slightly bent below. Often the two birds came close together and "billed," or touched their bills gently together. Often, prior to this, they bobbed their heads up and down. Sometimes they were so close to each other that their necks were swung back and forth, not always in complete synchrony, then their bills touched. Again they just touched bills, one or both dashed away for a few more jumps, then returned and touched bills again and again.

Once, one of a pair seemed out of sympathy with the other, which was jumping around crazily, and when it came back to bill, he pecked at her severely. She dashed away and discontinued her frivolities.

Unlike the Australian Crane, which walks much of the time from the night roost, the Sarus Crane more often flies away. Although the birds resemble each other very much, the downy young are definitely not at all alike. The young Sarus is more tawny; the Brolga chick is dark gray.

When flying from the roost, the Sarus Crane most often leaves silently, family groups all going together, often several families simultaneously. They fly directly away toward their feeding grounds, often just clearing the surrounding trees. They do not circle as do the Siberian Cranes. They fly much closer to the ground and are much quieter at this time. Occasionally one will utter a low guttural *Garraw*. They come back the same way, but once on the home roosting grounds often become very noisy, more so in the early morning or late evening.

The dance is given both in winter and during the breeding season. It follows much the pattern of the Australian Crane and usually lasts only a few minutes. The birds do not appear to whirl, as do the Wattled Cranes I have observed. Jumps and bows are straight up and down, but when on the ground they often run in circles.

Sometimes the dance is used as a distraction display, especially when a person walks near their nest, eggs or young. Again they use a definite distraction display with outspread wings, running around in a crouched position.

VOICE

The downy chick has a shrill *Peeep* with a trill to it, very similar to that of other crane chicks. When the parents call the chick, they use a guttural *Purrr*, resembling a snore at times.

The regular call is a loud, trumpeting *Krrr-kwerrr-krrrr-krrrr-krrrr-krrrr-krrrr* or *Garrrroooa-garrrooa-garrrooa-garrrooa*, uttered at times in many more syllables than this. The former call is often given by the male when the pair gives the unison call. The female simultaneously calls *Tuk-tuk-tuk-tuk-tuk-tuk-tuk*. These birds called an average of 7.8 syllables (4-12) on February 4, 1969, as compared to 23 syllables uttered by *G. leucogeranus* the same day. Although they make much more noise—their call is easily heard two to three miles away—they do not call nearly so often.

These calls are given at all seasons, during the entire day, more often during the morning hours, less often later in the day, and at times, especially on moonlit nights, during the night. During the breeding season they sometimes call on their own, but often respond to a chorus of peacock calls. During the winter peacocks are usually silent. When on territory, the pairs often respond with the unison call given by other pairs, often several pairs calling simultaneously by day and often at night.

Dharmakumarsinhji (1955: 143) reported the call to be similar to that of *Grus grus lilfordi* but said it is deeper, more drawn out and more resonant.

A single-syllable call given when birds are flying is a guttural *Graauw*, often the only clue that a pair is flying somewhere overhead. The alarm or distrust note is often a single blast, much shriller than the normal call.

FOOD

The birds are quite omnivorous. During the har-

Indian Sarus Crane pair giving 'Unison Call.' Male on right shows secondaries above back with primaries held stiffly below; female with wings held against sides. February 1969.

vest season, they feed considerably on wheat and gram (*Cicer arietinum*) fields, devouring grain lost in the harvest. I watched a pair in a ripened rice field September 29, 1965, stripping rice from the stalks with their bills. They walked along the edge of the patch taking one stalk at a time and deftly removing all the rice with one sweep of the bill.

At Ghana Bird Sanctuary, in very dry regions, they fed at times where there must have been few seeds. Here they must eat grasshoppers and other insects, as well as bulbs, for which they often dig. After rains they often dig in the water for food with their bills.

Baker (1929) wrote: "Their food consists of all kinds of grain, shoots, aquatic plants, frogs, lizards, insects, etc. and they feed alike in shallow water up to 18 inches deep and in cultivated fields

and open plains. Two or three pairs in a field of young wheat or rice are said [to be] capable of doing considerable damage, though this is never to be compared with the destruction of crops by the mighty flocks of Common or Demoiselle Cranes."

Law (1930) showed that they also like fish when available, but prefer green vegetation, tubers and insects. Dharmakumarsinhji (1955) added, "Water-plants, lotus or nymphae bulbs, water-snails, insects, and frogs. . . . during the breeding season it lives almost entirely upon plant and water-life."

On February 4, 1969, I watched a pair of Sarus Cranes with two young (about two-thirds grown), one a little larger than the second. I arrived just in time to see the male completely threshing a two-foot-long common water snake (*Natrix piscator*), and place it in front of the larger young. This bird picked it up by the tail and after three trials—each time dropping it on the ground—managed to swallow it whole, two minutes later. Ten minutes later he still gaped now and then. In thirty minutes he sat, dazed, on his haunches on a dry piece of ground, quite oblivious of happenings about him, but when I passed the next day, he was as active as before.

While he was swallowing this snake, his father rushed back thirty or forty feet into two-foot-deep water, reached into some thick vegetation and pulled out another snake of about the same size. He gave it a quick sidewise twist and dropped it immediately into the water. He repeated this ten or twelve times in rapid succession, working closer to shore until finally he had it on dry land. After twenty-eight minutes of threshing this snake around, pinching it, dragging it, swallowing it until only three to four inches of the head and neck showed from his bill, and dropping it back on the ground sixteen times, he dropped the lifeless snake in front of the smaller youngster. The female, who had tried repeatedly to get it away from him, even one time getting pecked for her effort, now grabbed it and offered it to her youngster, who tried five or six times to swallow it, without success. In the meantime, the male, acting oblivious to what was going on, came quickly up beside the female, reached around, and took the snake from her and immediately swallowed it, tail first.

Another Sarus Crane was observed pulling snails from the water. I could not be sure whether it ate the complete snail, but feel sure it did.

DISTRIBUTION

Migrating only in times of extreme drought, the Sarus Crane is a typically Indian bird. Fossils have been found in Europe and in modern times have been reported from Caspian Sea shores, more recently from southern Kashmir and southern Nepal, to Assam, then south into western Burma, Bangla Desh, west to West Pakistan and south to the Bombay region (rarely), and in the east to the Godaveri River. Observations have been made:

U.S.S.R.. Blaauw (1897) reported that Nordmann and Radde both regarded it as exceptional on the western shores of the Caspian Sea and Komarow observed it at Derbent. Dement'ev *et al.* (1951) considered these early records questionable.

Nepal. Rand and Fleming (1957) reported it from Dhangarhi (spec.) at 900 feet and said pairs were observed in western Nepal.

Burma. At Arakan and Myahaung, Hopwood (1912) reported one shot which proved to be *G. antigone.*

Assam. Two eggs were taken June 14, 1903. (BMNH) at Dibrugarh by E. C. S. Baker and two eggs in July 1899 (BMNH) at Nr. Chotta Bheel, Cacher and another pair was observed in 1894 at Haiakandy by E. C. S. Baker (1899: 494).

Kashmir and Jammu. In the valley of the Kashmir, Ward (1907: 945) reported the bird on two occasions.

West Pakistan. At Hardoi, N.W.P., Pershouse (1911: 854) found a nest with one egg on December 23, 1901 and Baker (1929) wrote it was found eastward from the Indus while Ali (1945) said it was resident but not common.

India. In Punjab, Whistler (1918) reported the bird was found rarely near Ambala and Jagadhri and Chamkaur. Hingston (1921) reported it as common in places below 3,500 feet near Dharmsala while Walter Koelz took several specimens (AMNH, UMMZ) during the winters of 1931 and 1933.

In Rajasthan at Keoladeo Ghana Bird Sanctuary, Bharatpur, the species is abundant. It was reported here by Bates (1925), Ali (1953) and Gee (1964). Bates found nests on February 7 and in November; Ali photographed birds at their nests; Gee showed a photograph of birds at a nest. Here I observed up to 103 birds during one day (early September 1965) and 308 (average 171) in February 1969 during eight days of observation. I found nests with eggs: (1) September 25, 1965 (one egg—the second laid September 27); (2) September 27, 1965 (two eggs); (3) September 27, 1965 (two eggs), and observed others not yet ready for eggs.

I also observed a nest (two eggs) at Gangapur on September 28, 1965. O'Brien (1909) found a nest (hatching) February 12, 1909, and Mosse (1910) a nest (two eggs) February 12, 1903 at Mahi Kantha Agency, Mahisa District. Hume said (Whistler, 1938: 231) it was common at Jodhpur, and Barnes (1885, 1886) reported the species bred in August and September, but he found a nest February 5,

Indian Sarus Crane pair in flight, Keoladeo Ghana Bird Sanctuary, February 1969.

1885 with two eggs sixty miles from Neemuch and another March 30, 1885 with two eggs at Jeerun.

In Gujarat the bird is a common resident (Barnes, 1885), (Acharya, 1936). At Baroda Drs. John George and R. M. Naik (verbal) consider the bird rather common. Dr. A. J. Berger (letter, October 17, 1964) found two nests: (1) September 6, 1964; (2) October 16, 1964 (both with two eggs). Drs. George and Naik showed me two nests September 29 and 30, 1965 (both empty), another (two eggs) at Bapot, and we found a nest at Timbi (two eggs), September 29, 1965. A two-egg set (BMNH) was taken at Kharagoda, August 21, 1904. Dharmakumarsinhji (1955: 142) and Ali (1945) reported it from Kutch and Saurashtra, while Ali and Abdulali (1939) reported it at Bombay as an aberrant straggler during severe cold and

drought in 1900 and 1908. Two two-egg sets (BMNH) were taken in Guzarat, one at Kharagora, the other at Sial, December 16, 1892. Other two-egg sets were taken at Dwarka, Bombay (BMNH), at Godra, Pancha Mahals on September 15, 1878, and at Malao, November 14, 1878.

Law (1930) found it in Uttar Pradesh at Bareilly and Bates (1935) photographed two nests (one and two eggs, respectively) on August 20 and found another pair building a nest August 9th. At Delhi there is a specimen (BMNH) and Basil-Edwardes (1926) reported it common. I saw my first Sarus from the train on September 1, 1965 thirty-four miles south of Delhi and rather regularly thereafter until we reached Bharatpur. Again in this same region I saw twenty-eight Sarus Cranes on February 2, 1969, also in pairs, one pair with a nearly full-grown young. At Dhanari a two-egg set (BMNH) was taken August 28, 1903 and at Zillah, Etawah, several sets (BMNH): (1) August 1857 (one egg); August 1865 (one egg); (3) July 1966 (one egg); (4) August 16, 1867 (three eggs); (5) August 20, 1867 (three eggs); (6) August 27, 1867 (one egg); (7) August 1967 (two eggs); and at Zillah, Etawah sixteen eggs (probably eight sets) were taken July 15, 1869 (Hume), while Brookes took a specimen (BMNH) in 1865. A. Andersen took one egg (BMNH) at Futtegurh on August 18, 1871 and Osmaston (1913) wrote the species was found at Gorakhpur on the Gondak River. A specimen (CNHM) was taken in April 1877 on the River Jumna and both Lowther (1949) and Frome (1947) reported it common east of this river. At Kanpur, A. J. R. Hill (1930) found a nest (one egg) October 5 (probably 1929), and a specimen (CNHM) was taken at Nichlaul, February 3, 1947 by Koelz.

At Oudh two specimens (BMNH), one in February 1874, were taken by A. O. Hume and egg sets (BMNH) were taken on August 8, 1870 (two eggs); September 2, 1876 (one egg—Rothschild Collection); September 10, 1876 (one egg) by W. Brookes. In Bihar, at Kamla, Inglis (1903) observed the bird. Two specimens (CNHM) were taken May 30, 1946 at Breraghat, Madhya Pradesh by Koelz. D'Abreu (1912 and 1935) reported it breeding in July, August and March at Paraswara. Young (1905) observed it May 9 at Mhow. There is an egg (BMNH) taken September 2, 1880 at Morar and two nests were observed (two eggs each) December 28 by Whitehead (1911). King (1911) reported it nesting about August, also two years running in March at Saugor Lake.

The species has been noted at: Bhopal, Bhopal Lake, Sanchi (Gulgaon Tank); Gwalior: Harsi Lake (Narwar District); Surwaya, Chanderi: Indore; Choral (Balwada Tank), Mandleshwar (Choli Tank); Dhar; Mandu, and at the latter place a two-egg nest was observed on September 11 (Ali, 1940).

Barnes (1885) reported the species common throughout Rajputana and Guzarat, very rare in Sing and missing from Deccan, while Baker (1929) reported it present in northern India from the Indus to western Assam (Gowhati, south to the Bombay Presidency on the west as far as Khandesh Godaveri River on the east.

B. THE BURMESE SARUS CRANE, *Grus antigone sharpii*

Grus (Antigone) sharpii, Blanford, *Bull. British Ornithological Club*, 5, 1895, p. 7 (Burma).
Type locality. Burma.
Vernacular names. The Burmese Sarus Crane, The Eastern Sarus Crane (English); Der Burmeisische Saruskranich (German); la Grus antigone orientale (French); Gyogya (Burmese); Hur-Sang (Assamese); Wolnu, Woinuren (Manipuri); The Sarus Crane (Australian).

DESCRIPTION

Adult. Plumage is almost exactly as *Grus antigone antigone*, except darker. It has no white collar below the bare neck. The inner secondaries are darker, differing little in color from the outer secondaries and back. The head, neck, bill, legs and feet are colored as in the former bird. This bird is slightly smaller than the nominate form. The inner secondaries seem somewhat lighter-colored than those of *Grus rubicundus*, and the bare region extends some distance down the neck, whereas it extends only to the back of the head or throat in that bird. The three forms—*G.a. antigone*, *G.a. sharpii*, and *G. rubicundus*—are closely related forms. Their color, size, voice, nesting habits and even much of their behavior are similar, but the chicks of *G. rubicundus* are gray, as compared to tawny with *G. antigone antigone* and probably *G.a. sharpii*.

MEASUREMENTS

Adult male. (Three specimens: AMNH, 2; BMNH, 1). Exposed culmen, 162.3 (158-174); wing (chord), 569.6 (514-640); tail 248 (1); tarsus, 296 (269-330); bare tibia, 180.6 (152-205); middle toe with claw, 125.5 (112-139) mm.

(Two specimens, Atherton Tableland—Willett's Swamp, Australia, October 24, 1967, Queensland Museum. Both birds non-breeding adults). Exposed culmen, 155 and 171 mm; wing (chord), 632, 582 mm; tail, 292, ——mm; tarsus, 310, 287 mm; tip of body to tip of bill, 116.6, 111.2 cm; weight, 18.5 lbs. (8,406.4 g), 17,25 lbs. (7,838.4 g). (Thanks to

Eastern Sarus Crane, on Croydon Road, near Normanton, Queensland, Australia, 1967. Photograph by Bruce Cook.

Dr. Hugh Lavery, Dept. of Primary Industries, Townsville, Queensland.)

Adult female. (Three specimens: BMNH, 2; USNM, 1). Exposed culmen, 155.5 (155-156); wing, 584 (557-605); tail, 221 (220-222); tarsus, 303.3 (289-320); bare tibia, 193.3 (187-213); middle toe with claw, 120 (119-121) mm.

A female specimen taken at Mataas, North Cahoy, near Cabanatuan, Nueva Ecija, Philippines, September 21, 1908, by R. C. McGregor (USNM) had recorded on its label: weight 11 lbs. (4,989.6 g); length, 127 cm; extent, 220 cm. Bill and forehead pale dirty green. Tip of bill, gray. Iris, yellow. Legs, rose pink, brown along tarsus. Papillose part of head and neck red, darker behind ears.

OTHER BEHAVIOR

This crane is apparently migratory in certain regions. Deignan (1945: 102) found it thus at Chiang Mai, Burma, coming only during the cold weather, December 8 to March 23, often in flocks of eight to forty birds. At times they flew over, giving their clarion call. On the Chiang Rai savannas they were often seen stalking about the marshes in family groups or pairs. Usually they are very hard to approach, much more so than the western form.

Baker (1928: 5) wrote: "In 1902-3 Coltart noticed a pair of these birds constantly frequenting a wide-open space in the forest on the Dehing River. This place, perhaps half mile across or a little more, was entirely surrounded by virgin forest and in the cold weather was dry and covered with short grass a foot or so high with a deep swamp in the centre much frequented by Wood Duck. In the rains practically the whole area was under water except for small islands of rather high land. On one of these the Cranes had constructed their cone-shaped nest and on June 19 when I went to see if they had thoughts of nesting, I found it completed and containing two hard-set eggs. Wardlaw Ramsay and Oates found it breeding in Burma during August and September and its early breeding in Assam may have been due to the early breaking of the rains in that province and to the naturally wet and marshy nature of the country. The eleven eggs I have seen average 101.1 x 63.8 mm., maxima 106.8 x 63.8 and 103.6 x 68.0 mm; minima 97.3 x 64.8 and 98.5 x 58.5 mm. I have seen no pure white eggs of this race. The birds from whom I took the eggs in Margherita made no defence of the nest and no protest beyond trumpeting as they flew away."

Most writers report this as a much wilder bird than the Indian Sarus Crane, using more isolated marshes and swamps. Livesey (1937: 420) wrote that the birds in Burma (Karenni) join together in flocks at certain seasons.

In general the nest is quite similar to that of the western form; the eggs are similar too, but slightly smaller. Eight eggs in the British Museum (Natural History) averaged in measurements 98.06 (96.7-101.2) x 64.5 (63.3-68.0)mm.

Delacour, Jabouille and Lowe (1928: 37) wrote that this bird was found in pairs or small parties on the low plains as well as the high plateaus.

McGregor (1905: 29) wrote: "Although this species has been recorded from Luzon, the record was based upon a mounted specimen and a bird in confinement. Therefore it is not superfluous to note that Mr. Worcester observed five individuals ...in the Cagayan Valley, northern Luzon, in January 1905."

There is a female specimen (USNM) taken by McGregor at Mataas, North Cohoy, near Cabanatuan, Nueva Ecija Province, Luzon, the Philippines, September 21, 1908.

The flock of three birds we saw near Atherton, Australia, was close to the highway, but when we stopped they moved rather swiftly on foot along a grass-grown fence row until they were some distance away. The flock of Brolgas on a peanut field one mile away was just as wild. During the two hours we spent watching these groups, they showed no signs of joining together.

At Normanton these birds fed in small groups of two to four, in long-grass prairies. The grass was about knee-high, dead, but in places flooded by recent monsoons. The birds seemed to be feeding on the many grasshoppers in the tall grass. They fed from shortly after daylight until 8:00-9:30 A.M., then went to nearby pools to drink. One breeding bird fed and drank while its mate incubated. Again they did not associate with the Brolgas. The latter stayed more on the tidal flats, closer to Normanton, where they roosted and probably nested on nearby flooded regions, where I found them in the daytime, as well as along the Little Bynoe.

DISTRIBUTION

Found in Assam, east to Kamrup, Burma, formerly Thailand, parts of Malay Peninsula, Cambodia, southern Laos, southern Viet Nam, formerly parts of Luzon and recently in Queensland, Australia. Regions where the species has been found are:

Assam. Baker (1928) reported this bird east of Kamrup.

Burma. In the British Museum (Natural History) there are the following specimens: from Pegu (March) taken by E. W. Oates; Tounghoo (two) September 21, 1875 taken by R. G. W. Ramsay; Ataran, Amherst (South Burma), taken by W. Davidson; Sinang, taken by Dr. Cantor. There is a two-egg set (BMNH) from Pegu (17° N.; 96° E.) taken by Oates, August 15, 1879 and another (one egg) taken by H. Coltart, September 5, 1904; a third set (one egg) taken at Martaban (16.5° N.; 97.5° E.) by R. C. Beavan; another from Lower Burma (two eggs) taken August 3, 1904. J. P. Cook (1913) added Kalaw; Wickham (1930) also added Chin, Kachin and Shan Hills and MacDonald (1906) added Myingyan (21° N.; 96° E.) as regions where the birds are found. Blaauw added between Salwell and Sitang Rivers, Upper Burma, on the lower Pegu and from Tounghoo, Arakan and Thaton. Roseveare (1949) added Shwebo at Kadu Lake (22.5° N.; 96° E.).

Thailand. Deignan (1945) reported it as common in Chiang Rai Province, on Chiang Mai plains during cold weather (December 8 to March 23), and found a one-egg set from Muang Fang probably in July 1914. DeSchauensee (1929) reported it from Ban Chong, and there is a Siamese specimen (BMNH) taken by L. C. Bulkley.

Dr. Boonsong Lekagul of Bangkok (verbal and letter) reported the few recent records from Thailand as: North of Songkhla Lake, Province of Patalung, 1965; Phitsanilok National Park, four to six birds in 1958, by Dr. Lekagul; Sariburi, a pair observed by Dr. Nicholson; Dat Phai Lorm Sanctuary (40 kilometers north of Bangkok), four birds in 1964, but one was shot.

Cambodia. Dr. Boonsong Lekagul, Joe Marshall and Ben King (verbal) reported this bird present north of Cambodia Lake.

Viet Nam. Delacour and Jabouille (1931) reported this bird was found in Cochinchina (South Viet Nam) and at Anbinh, Baclieu (9° N.; 106° E.).

Laos. Delacour and Jabouille (1931) wrote, as did Delacour, Jabouille and Lowe (1928), the bird was present in small parties.

The Philippines. McGregor (1905: 29) reported this bird from Aparri and the Candaba Swamp, Luzon (specimen) and five individuals were observed by Worcester in Cagayan Valley, northern Luzon in January 1905.

Malaya. Occurs (Baker, 1929: 56); (Blaauw, 1897).

Australia. Queensland. E. E. Zillmann and Fred Smith (letter, July 18, 1967) found twenty-one of these birds at Norman River and another pair at Burketown in 1967, the first Australian records. During early 1968, Hugh Lavery and Gavin Blackman took photographs and two male specimens on the Atherton Tableland, near Atherton (Willett's Swamp). Bruce Cook (verbal), Billie Gill (1969) and Jim Bravery (1969) found the bird on the Atherton Tableland and Cook photographed the bird near Normanton in August 1967. My wife and I found a family of three (the youngster about two-thirds grown) near Atherton, November 10, 1968 (Bravery saw the same group until late November 1968). These birds fed on grassy margins of plowed fields while we watched. Meanwhile a neighboring flock of nineteen Brolgas fed in the middle of a plowed field where unharvested peanuts had come to the surface after plowing. Later (January 26, 1969), I found thirteen between ten and fifteen miles from Normanton. That same day I found a two-egg nest seven miles out along the Croydon Road from Normanton and noted another pair which might have had a nest judging from their behavior. Blackman (1971) added other regions where the species was found: Archer River and Mt. Isa, even to Ingham. The largest flock observed was one of seventy-five at Willett's Swamp. During 1972 Sarus Carnes were found on Townsville Common (Franz Breuer).

The first Sarus Cranes I observed near Normanton, January 26, 1969, were at Magowra Station, where they came from a nearby roost along the Little Bynoe River. They flew out shortly after daybreak onto the open grass-grown plains where they fed for several hours. Since there were no seeds apparent, no roots available, they must have been feeding mostly on grasshoppers, which were very abundant. About 8:30 A.M. to 9:30 A.M. they retreated to bathe and drink in monsoon pools abounding near the meadow. The weather was extremely hot. Dogs, horses, cows and birds were sitting in watery roadside pools or drinking, adjacent to many smaller birds.

As we drove later the same day along the Croydon Road, we observed a mixed herd of horses and cows drinking and bathing in a roadside ditch. Amongst them was a lone Sarus Crane, easily identified as *Grus antigone sharpii*, getting a drink. As we approached, the bird wandered away to the east into some long grass, eventually fading among some scattered trees. Its behavior made me think there might be a nest nearby, so I left the car and started in the direction it had gone. About 450 meters from the highway, where the meadow and trees met, a second crane, previously unobserved,

rose from the grass and flew directly away towards where the other bird had gone. Later both birds were drinking at the pool by the highway.

On a slight mound, on completely dry ground, was a makeshift nest. Only half the mound was covered with nest material; the remainder was bare. Probably when the nest had been built, it had completely covered the mound, but as incubation advanced, one side became bare. It was built of grasses and sedges adjacent to it, and measured 212 x 212 cm across. If rains continued after this time, water soon would surround the nest region. In the nest were two beautiful eggs, almost glossy white, with a tinge of blue, which measured 99.8 x 61.5 and 100.6 x 62.7 mm and weighed 181.8 and 204.8 grams respectively.

Chapter Nine

THE BROLGA OR AUSTRALIAN CRANE

(Grus rubicundus)

Ardea rubicunda, Perry, *Arcana,* Pt. 6, 1810, pl. 22.
Type locality: Botany Bay, New South Wales.
 (Formerly this species was separated into two subspecies, now only one is recognized.)
Synonym: Mathewsia rubicunda argentea, Mathews, *Nov. Zool.,* 18, 1912, p. 227.
Type locality: Derby, Northwest Australia.
Vernacular names: The Brolga, The Australian Crane, Native Companion (English); der Australische Kranich (German); la Grue d'Australie (French); de Australische Kraanvogel (Dutch); Gōshū zuru (Japanese); Австралийка журавль (Russian).

 This is another very large crane, equaled only by the Sarus and Wattled Cranes undoubtedly. It, too, is a slow deliberate bird, preferring to walk wherever it can without flying. Still it is very adept on the wing and may be seen at times circling so high in the air it is barely visible. In fact some undoubtedly go beyond sight. Possibly they do this during the hot days, in mid-day to climb into the upper cooler thermals, again when frightened.

Before the discovery in 1967 of a small group of Burmese Sarus Cranes in northern Queensland, the only crane in Australia was the Brolga, whose name was derived from the aborigine term *Buralga*. Buralga was a fair aborigine maiden, who feared she was going to be forced to marry an old tribal chieftain. She managed to escape to the open country, where she found her young lover. As the tribal chieftains came to capture them, they were both encircled, and disappeared into a tornadolike funnel of dust, reappearing as two large birds.

Early explorers of the vast continent "Down Under" did not distinguish between the Brolga and the Indian Sarus Crane. Actually the big birds are quite similar, but the Indian bird has the bare region extending much farther down the neck; the Brolga has a bare dewlap hanging from the upper throat near the base of the lower mandible, and is somewhat darker than the Sarus.

Brolgas are resident on the open plains and in the larger marshes, both inland and near the sea. During the dry season, generally from June to December, they remain in wetter regions—ponds, lakes, marshes and tidal flats, at night feeding on nearby dry tubers of bulkuru sedge. During intensive droughts they migrate to wetter portions of the country. One bird has been found in New Zealand. When food becomes scarce, these normally shy birds often wander into farms or even villages in search of sustenance.

A good many years ago this trust they had in people got them into trouble in Victoria. The local farmers, angered at the damage they were doing to their crops, poisoned large, unsuspecting flocks during the winter. Brolgas are now very rare in this region, though they are still quite abundant in Queensland, along the coast, in some interior regions, and in the northern portion of Northern Territory. Here they live where they can secure their favorite food, bulkuru sedge. Curiously, two separate actions by man are at one and the same time improving their future and making it doubtful. The construction of water impoundments has greatly increased the acreage of suitable crane breeding grounds. The increased growth of grain, rice, corn and wheat makes good fodder in drought years. But, as farms take up more and more land formerly overgrown with bulkuru sedge, the cranes virtually will be forced to raid the farmers' planted fields. This development, if carried too far, eventually will give these big birds an implacable, perhaps an unbeatable, foe. Conservation requirements are being reevaluated, however, and the Brolgas' future seems to be assured, at least for the present.

DESCRIPTION

Adult. The general color is light bluish-gray, and the back and wing-coverts have lighter margins. The primaries are darker, almost black; the secondaries are gray, the inner ones somewhat elongated and hanging over the tail. The small ear-patch and rump are light gray. The crown is bare, covered with greenish-gray skin. Face, cheeks, occiput and gular pouch are bare, covered on the occiput with papillae, coral-red or bright orange up to and slightly forward of the ear. An orange tint is found above and below the eye, and less brilliant on the sides of the face. The remainder of the bare regions, except the crown, is covered with fine black hairlike feathers. The upper bare regions, as well as below the lower mandible, are olive-green. In some large males the gular pouch approaches the wattle. The long, large, straight beak is greenish-gray. The legs and feet are dark gray to black. The eye is orange, yellow or yellow-orange.

Downy chick. Mostly gray, darker gray above, lighter below, with the down on the neck and head changing to buff-color. Iris is dark brown, and the bill, pink-tipped with greenish-gray. Legs are pinkish-gray. As the bird becomes older, the gray becomes lighter. The head is still feathered and buffy-gray. Each feather on the wings and tail is tipped with a beautiful plume.

Lavery and Blackman (1969) wrote: "Birds-of-the-year have buff/grey fully-feathered heads, legs dark grey and irises dark brown. In yearlings (that is, from the second to the third wet season of life), irises assume adult coloration, greenish-gray skin appears on the crown and light orange skin on the comb; adult size is reached. Between yearling and the next period of reproductive opportunity, the birds (sub-adults) have orange combs with some grey feathers still noticeably interspersed.

"There is no difference in plumage appearance between sexes but there may be a considerable dif-

Feeding Brolgas on Pallarenda Town Common, Townsville, Queensland, Australia, October 1968.

ference in size. Where birds are paired the sexes are readily differentiated.

"Adult males on the average weigh 15 lb. (ranging from 10½ lb. to 17½ lbs.) and measure approximately 45 in. from tip of bill to base of tail. Adult females average 12½ lb. in weight (range 9½ lb. to 15½ lb.) and measure 42 in. in body length."

MEASUREMENTS

J. G. Blackman (unpublished master's thesis) sent me measurements and weights of ten known males and females (all pairs) taken between June and December 1968 near Townsville, Queensland, Australia. The records of these twenty birds are in Table 18 and those of three chicks in Table 19.

Rand and Gilliard (1967: 106) gave measurements: Male, wing, 578 mm; tail, 241 mm; tarsus, 289 mm. Female, wing, 542 mm.

Mathews and Iredale (1921) gave: Length, 1,220 mm; culmen, 163 mm; wing, 580 mm; tarsus, 290 mm, for adult males.

Tom House and I captured a bird at Lake Buchanan, Yarrowmere, Queensland, January 4, 1969, which had the following measurements: wing,, 564 mm; exposed culmen, 155 mm; tarsus, 292 mm; bare tibia, 190 mm; tail, 178 mm; expanse, 213.4 cm.

MIGRATIONS

The "Buralga" of the aborigines, Brolga of present-day Australians, is usually a non-migratory bird, but large numbers must migrate yearly judging by the increased concentrations along the regions adjacent to the sea. Each dry season at Townsville, Pallarenda, Cromarty, Giru, Clevedon and other regions in Queensland, Brolga concentrations feed on their favorite bulkuru sedge marshes recently dried up following the wet season. Some concentrations occur as far north as Ingham, some as far south as Ayr. These birds cannot all nest in the immediate vicinities of these concentrations, and must come from the interior, where food and water have disappeared with the coming of the dry season. With the increase of water during the annual rainy season, they return to their respective inland marshes, ponds or dams to nest. If the rains fail, as they did in the summer of 1968-1969, the birds remain in the bulkuru sedge regions, but very few nest. At this time, many die, for the bulkuru sedge tubers are very hard to dig out of the baked soil. As a result the birds probably do considerable damage to such crops as rice, which is grown in many places where bulkuru formerly grew, and which cranes find quite palatable.

According to Lavery (1964), peaks are reached during mid-dry seasons, usually between June and November.

There may be other types of migrations, too, but the search for water and food is the main reason. Austin (1907) reported fairly large flocks coming to Talbragar River, N. S. W., during May and June to feed on cultivated paddocks of newly-planted wheat. At other times hundreds drink and roost in dams, making them so filthy that livestock cannot use the water. Le Souëf (1903) described large flocks arriving between Balranald and Swan Hill, Victoria, June 12 (1903?), all flying in a southwesterly direction, a good height from the ground, in distinctive V-formations. Flight was first observed in early afternoon up until sunset. Simpson (1903) also reported a similar flight in November 1902 near Echuca, Victoria. In this case the birds flew westward towards the lakes at the mouth of the Murray River, coming from the lake regions farther north where hundreds spent the winter. He attributed the flight to a sudden spell of hot weather. Barnard and Barnard (1925) described a pair of Brolgas that appeared near a house during a drought. Here they picked up scraps of meat and other food thrown out.

Lavery (1964) wrote: "Clearly the largest populations occurred on the bulkuru sedge swamps of the Cape Pallarenda Town Common.

"During the wet season the small scattered populations were generally as pairs or as single birds. Immediately after the rains the brolgas congregated on the swamps [marshes] at Cape Pallarenda; few, if any, were seen around deeper waters [Belgian Gardens Town Common, Mt. St. John] or on adjacent grasslands. Numbers increased rapidly to a peak, but as the season progressed, water and vegetation disappeared, the swamp floor became parched and hard, dead brolgas were not uncommon, and small flocks moved to the slightly deeper depressions such as Belgian Gardens Town Common. As these wetlands dried out brolgas became more common at Mt. St. John, although the deeper water there supported little vegetation: the birds, however, during this, the driest part of the year, moved widely over adjacent grasslands to feed on grass seeds and probably insects. With the first rains they quickly left this type of habitat.

"Concurrent with these studies in the Bohle River basin, observations were made in the Ayr-Brandon district . . . where brolga populations were of a similar order and seasonal dispersal followed the same pattern. In this district, and in some other northen areas, attacks on crops, mostly sorghum (Sorghum vulgare Pers.) and maize (Zea mays L.), have been recorded on lands adjacent to extensive bulkuru sedge swamps: these were usually in October and November during 1960 and 1961, but some occurred as early as June in the latter year."

Although during the dry period the majority of Brolgas congregate and feed on the dried or nearly dried-up bulkuru marshes throughout Queensland and Northern Australia, smaller groups spend this time on whatever wet regions are available farther inland. These include many dams created throughout these regions for watering cattle; lakes, such as Lake Buchanan and small adjoining lakes, even though some are slightly saline; large swamps (marshes) near this lake such as Cauckingburra Swamp at Yarrowmere; large Atherton Tableland marshes such as Bromfield Swamp, Willett's Swamp, Arraga Dam, and many others, all of which produce scattered nesting and concentration regions. These are probably used the entire year unless water disappears completely during extra-dry years. During October 1968 we found Brolgas using small marshes and dams near Charters Towers, Pajingo, etc., usually a pair, a pair and their young, or a small group in each region, while we found forty or more birds around Lake Buchanan, scattered pairs around Cauckingburra Swamp in late October and early November 1968, up to around 700 in early January 1969. During early November and mid-December 1968 we found small groups, usually several pairs, or pairs and families, mixed on the Atherton Tableland. These latter birds were feeding on plowed lands where loose peanuts, corn, wheat and other good food came to the surface. At Lake Buchanan cranes fed on a grass that had a small tuber beneath the sandy soil. These birds, although drinking some saline water from Lake Buchanan, periodically went back to Cauckingburra Swamp for fresh water. Later, when Lake Buchanan began to dry up and become more saline, the birds resorted to a little nearby lake for fresh water entirely.

DRY SEASON BEHAVIOR

During the rainy season bulkuru sedge protrudes in thick masses in flooded marshes, so thick that Brolgas are unable to get much for food, since they feed on the tubers three to five inches beneath the ground. When the water has disappeared from the marshes during the dry season, dead stalks are all over the ground, but as cattle pasture over them

A Brolga family, parents giving 'Unison Call'; male on right; female between two young. December 1967, Kynuna, Queensland. Photograph by Hugh Lavery and J. G. Blackman.

they disappear. However the bulbs or tubers beneath the surface are still moist and palatable. The Brolgas dig for them with their long, strong bills, which sometimes become covered with mud. As soon as their hunger is satisfied, each family walks or flies back to its roosting spot and each bird immediately washes off its bill. Some regions on tidal flats have saline water. At times I observed Brolgas sipping some of this, but not often. Once as I watched they flew up, circling one to three times for elevation, then flew three to seven miles away for fresh water at some dam or pond. Two small ponds on the Pallarenda Town Common were also used. These were only about a mile from where the Brolgas fed. During hot days, and during the driest periods, when no other water was available, there was a continual stream of families going to this water from midday until about 5:00 P.M. Then they returned to feed again. Many of the families walked to the water, flew over the fence and drank when they could find an opening. Some of the birds that were feeding farther away flew low (six to twenty feet) over the common, usually landing outside of the fence, then flying over it.

When leaving their watery or muddy roost site—the tidal flat was most often covered with a few inches of salt water but occasionally was just a flat of sticky mud—the Brolgas in early mornings most often walked onto dry land. If their food was half a mile or less away they walked to it; at times they walked even farther. A group occasionally flew, but usually there was a gray mass of Brolgas moving along the ground shortly after daylight.

Most Brolgas remain in families of one to four birds, and less often in larger groups. Flocks of up to several hundred birds or even more are often found along the coastal regions, but they do not feed or roost in a compact mass. Each bird in a family group stands or feeds five to seven feet from the others, while each family group feeds or roosts seven to twenty-five feet from their closest neighbors. There appears to be a definite hierarchy in the flocks, with the males of each family vying for dominance. They show only protection toward their mates and young, but if a single foreign individual or group comes too close, they show immediate concern. Most often a male attacks the individual or group immediately, running with

spread wings towards them, usually with head and neck arched upward and forward. The other bird or group departs at once, usually running or flying a short distance away. Less often I have seen birds chase others twenty to fifty feet or more, but usually they do not press the issue as long as the interlopers leave. On his return the defending male often stands erect, neck arched swanlike, bill pointing groundward. Sometimes he calls, but as often is quiet. Sometimes both he and his mate give the unison call.

At Cape Pallarenda Town Common, Townsville, Queensland, I spent many mornings and some evenings watching the behavior of Brolgas. Following are observations made the morning of December 2, 1968 (4:45 to 10:00 A.M.):

The morning was clear—no fog and no dew. The temperature was 77° F. (the low for the day) and the high was 90° F.

4:45 Into blind. All Brolgas standing in 3-4 inches of water on tidal flat, spread about a quarter mile. They began calling at 4:40, usually in pairs, giving the unison call. Group of 4 cranes flew to bulkuru sedge region about ¼ mile away.

5:08 Groups of 6, 3, 3 walking out, and 1 flew to sedge. Birds were now strung over extensive front, 138 counted walking to the muddy border, strung out in lines from water to mud to land.

5:11 4 more flew to sedge region. Still 881 in water.

5:20 5 more flew out, but a big mass, moving on foot, passed on both sides of blind—family groups, 2s, 3s, 4s, occasionally a larger group. Hundreds were walking.

5:25 3 more flew out as sun began showing above horizon, then 1, 3 and 4. In families walking closer I noted 1 pair with 2 young; 2 pairs with 1 young; 4 pairs without young. All took 60-90 steps per minute (measured steps ranged 52.1-71.1 cm, averaging about 52.6 cm). Flying birds ranged between 112 and 129 beats per minute. Occasionally a bird or pair danced as they went; sometimes a lone bird called a single *Graaaw*; one bird uttered a guttural *Purrr*; at times a pair gave the unison call; but the general business was getting to food immediately.

5:40 Only about 50 cranes remain in water. Most on food region.

5:45 Only 10 cranes in water now.

5:50 The last (one of 2 on shore), 3, 3, 2, 2, 2 individuals in separate groups, flew to food region.

7:50- Tide coming in. Groups of cranes flying up
8:30 and out to fresh water about 3 miles away. I counted 19 groups of 2; 7 of 3; 3 of 4; a group of 6; followed by a big mass of about 500. The latter group went into the tidal flat for a short time, then gradually small groups flew away to fresh water.

The total morning count was 1,035 Brolgas. Of these, 37 flew out, and the remaining 998

Adult Brolga showing dewlap beneath chin. Taken at Kynuna, December 1967. Photograph by Lavery and Blackman.

walked to the food. None walked back and by 10:00 A.M. the Common was nearly deserted by the birds.

A different pattern followed the morning of October 21, 1968.

5:39 Sunrise. Clear. No dew, no wind. Brolgas roosted in same region as above.

5:00 Four pairs of Blue-winged Kookaburras called in nearby woodland. Brolgas were scattered over saline water tidal flat. Many birds walked out, but more flew out. Favorite feeding region at this time was ¼ mile away; another was 1½ miles. They flew very low— usually just a few feet above ground. Birds flying to food went in the following groups at the following times:

		TOTAL
5:32	3, 4 cranes flew east to food	7
5:36	2 x *1*, 3 x *2*, 7 x *3*, 4 x *4*, 2 x *5*, 3 x *6*, 1 x *7*, 1 x *8*	88
5:40	6 x *2*, 5 x *3*, 8 x *4*, 3 x *5*, 1 x *6*	80
5:45	3 x *1*, 10 x *2*, 6 x *3*, 3 x *4*, flocks of 5, 6, 7, 9	80
5:47	5 x *2*, 2 x *3*, flocks of 7, 33, 10	66
5:50	3 x *1*, 16 x *2*, 6 x *3*, flocks of 4, 28, 34	119
5:55	49 still in water; 113 on mud beside water; 22 walking NE	184
6:05	Groups flying out, 5, 5, 3, 2, 2, 2	
6:07	Groups flying out, 3, 3, 2, 2, 2, many walked away so that only 50 remained in water region. There was much calling all morning. Total count, 624 Brolgas.	

Evening arrival at the tidal flat was different. The birds were widely scattered, but the majority moved into a nearby feeding region about a half-mile from the roost site. The weather was clear; temperature about 30° F; sunset at 6 P.M. I was in one of the small cement bomb shelters beside the roost region:

November 6, 1968 (4:00-8:00 P.M.)

5:50 Groups of cranes began flying into tidal salt-water flat or onto mud beside it. Some landed on grass-grown land nearby, then walked in. Counts were 2, 3, 4, 16, 2, 3, 4, 2, 2, 4 (3 flew away).

6:11 3 in from SW; 1, 3 flew in; 1 walked in.

6:21 Sunset, 2, 3 flew in.

6:27 2 flew in from N; 1 bird stuck bill into water; shook it.

6:31 3 in from N (a few birds flew out, so I counted those in water. Total: 44
                                    TOTAL

6:35 Venus visible. 2 into water, followed by 4, 4, 1   11

6:40 55 birds now in water.

6:42 Groups flying into water (often one bird in each group calling): 9 x 2, 5 x 3, 4 x 4, 2 x 5, 7, 8, 9, 9   92

6:46 Many calling and flying in, 3, 86, then 346   435

6:47 Groups flying in, some only a short distance: 3, 5, 6, 38, 6, 2, 250, 7, 4, 2, 7, 10, 2, 3. Often they pecked at the bottom; then shook heads.   345

6:52 Groups flying in, 3, 13, 3, 3, 8, 13, 4, 2, 2, 3, 2, 3   59

6:55 Groups flying in: 3, 3, 2, 2, 2. Flock strung out about ¼ mile.   12

7:02 4 birds flew in almost darkness from ENE and 2 from SW. As I walked   6 back to the woodland in the darkness, not one crane called, nor did I hear any all the time I walked back 4 miles to Townsville, about an hour. Total evening count, 1,004 individuals

On November 12, 1968, I counted Brolgas going to roost at Cape Pallarenda Town Common, 4:00-8:00 P.M. It was clear, hot and dry, with some wind. High temperature during the day was 92° F. (There had been only .24 inches of rain in September; .53 inches in October, and now only .16 inches in November.) Since the cranes called the usual anxious *Graaauw* when I was near them, I went into the old cement bomb shelter as a blind.

Between 6:16 and 7:01 P.M., I counted 1,033 individuals. A few birds called that night even after I reached the woods. Usually they gave the unison call, by pairs. At 7:15 P.M., all became quiet, except for blue-winged kookaburras which delighted to call as I passed beneath them in the dark.

Behavior at Atherton Tableland was different. Here a few individuals banded together in small groups, which at times joined together in one con-

centration. They roosted amongst grasses in a marsh in shallow fresh water, well away from shore in an extinct volcano. Four Brolgas were observed feeding in a plowed cornfield near Willett's Swamp. They flew at 5:53 P.M. towards Bromfield Swamp, December 14, 1968, crossing dry Willett's Swamp. We found twenty-one Brolgas roosting in the former swamp when we drove there. The next morning six birds came again over Willett's Swamp at 6:02 A.M., from the direction of Bromfield, and we could find none there at midday at any time. These birds behaved much like other cranes—they fed on plowed grainfields by day and roosted in shallow fresh water by night.

At Lake Buchanan, Queensland, I watched a group of Brolgas all day November 1, 1968 (5:00 A.M.-6:30 P.M.). I managed to get into a blind at 8:40 A.M., then left it at sundown. It was very hot and clear with some wind. Sunrise was at 5:33 A.M.

At 8:30 A.M. there were three groups of Brolgas feeding along a sandy shore. One group (a pair and one young) flew away. All were digging up bulbous roots of *Cyperus* aff. *rotundus*. At 9:01 A.M., a group of three and another of two flew away, and at 9:07 a group of three came back, then continued south out of sight. At 9:45 A.M. nineteen Brolgas were strung out along the dune. There was no bulkuru sedge here and no grain; only water at practically the same salinity as the ocean. At 9:58 two groups (two and three) walked to the lake, dipped their heads into the water and each took its turn to drink this saline water. One bird drank five times. When they walked back to the ridge, one hopped, skipped and danced, all over the ridge. Other groups continued to drink this saline water periodically all during the day. Usually they were feeding or preening, but at times a few small groups flew away, apparently to Cauckingburra Swamp where there was fresh water. At one time a crane chased several stilts from his neighborhood. After 5:21 P.M. they all fed seriously, some as far as 400 to 500 feet from the lake shore. At times they fed even amongst trees. After sundown they worked gradually back to the lake, where they ended up at dark roosting in shallow water.

During the day, a dominant male, as always, demonstrated a certain defense procedure: (1) he

Brolga preening. Kynuna, December 1967. Photograph by Lavery and Blackman.

flapped his wings violently, two or three times; (2) he arched his neck upward and forward, and the opponent walked swiftly away; (3) he walked swiftly toward the interloper or group and they moved faster; (4) he ran towards them with wings slightly spread and they ran away faster; (5) he returned silently to his mate who had stood watching, and at times they gave the unison call.

On January 4, 1969, I watched Brolgas from a blind at a small fresh-water lake only about one kilometer from saline Lake Buchanan. I am sure the birds roosted at night in Lake Buchanan. It abounded with ducks and black swans but there were no Brolgas there when I arrived at 8:00 A.M. The first ones (five) arrived at 9:01 A.M. and immediately began drinking, as did the next group (a family of three) which arrived at 9:20 A.M. Groups came from then on, reaching a peak betwen 9:50

and 10:10 A.M., when 211 birds came in family groups. Prior to this 125 birds had arrived, and another 111 came later. The total was 447, most of which were there until 10:35 A.M., when the first flew away, followed shortly by many more.

Alexander (1923) wrote that near Alice Downs, central Queensland, Brolgas frequently appeared, especially at the edges of open downs, generally in flocks of about eight individuals. Trumpeting was heard chiefly in early morning and late evening. If disturbed, one or both birds often danced. They often walked to water where they drank much like domestic hens.

Berney (1907) wrote that Brolgas in North Queensland soared so high they often passed unnoticed, unless they called. Crossman (1910) reported that birds were found in parties of seven or eight on plains, and that they often danced and played. Mrs. Mayo (1931) wrote that while boating along the Queensland coast, down Pumice Stone Channel, they saw Brolgas fly to a sandbank where they began dancing. "On very 'light fantastic toe' they sprang high into the air extending their wings slightly and seeming to float gently back to the ground. They passed in and out in a dignified way, bowing gracefully, then took flight. . . . Their dance was repeated with all birds taking part. Finally they dispersed and fed in twos and threes about the banks. . . . Mrs. Curtis tells me that she disturbed a pair of nesting Brolgas a while back on Stradbroke Island and they showed their annoyance by dancing—with many high kicks—in front of her."

Mathews (1914) wrote that this crane often danced and jumped, then tumbled upon the ground, at times with the feet uppermost, and finished by rolling like a dog.

Campbell (1902) wrote that back of the Murray, in northeastern Victoria, cranes frequented the adjacent plains, undulating country where the ridges, clothed with pine and bull-oak, were interspersed with excellent sheep-raising regions. Here and there were large plains where storm waters collected during the wet seasons.

Stone (1913) wrote that the Brolga was considered a pest in wheatlands, and was poisoned wholesale with strychnined wheat. Once he found that a fox caught one. MacGillivray (1910, 1914) reported two cranes digging rhizomes so that the ground appeared as though rooted by pigs. He reported a nest found in the Gulf country of northern Queensland on March 26, 1910. On a trip from Croydon to Cairns, 200 were counted, while toward evening flocks of seven, eight or more kept flying in until there were over a thousand birds.

Russell (1921) wrote that a pet crane spent the entire day with a favorite horse. Each day they fed away and at night returned with the mob. Eventually another horse killed the bird.

Church (1925) reported the native head rainmaker told him he never had any weather success unless he consulted the Brolgas. Early explorers used the bird regularly for food, and Dickison (1932) reported the meat, when boiled, resembled beef in both texture and flavor, except that there was no fat.

I observed dancing from September to January. Sometimes many birds did it, again only one. As the wet weather began, birds danced more than during the dry period. Sometimes one bird of a pair danced around its mate for several minutes. It tossed objects into the air again and again. Sometimes both birds danced. Sometimes they brought their throat regions close together, moving their necks sidewise as does *Grus antigone*. Sometimes they were stimulated to dance when I approached a flock, and when I went to a nest, the birds often danced as well as running around with drooping-spread wings in distraction display.

NESTING

Usually the Brolgas go back to their nesting marshes only when the rainy season arrives. At times during the dry season, or even during dry years, a pair will nest, but usually it is in the wet season. Apparently they use the same marsh for years. Dennis (1933) wrote that Mathews, Iredale and Caley stated the Brolga made no nest, but he found a very substantial one at Terang, Victoria, built of tussock grass pulled in the vicinity, the space being more or less denuded around their shallow water nest. Mud adhering to roots of the grasses used made it more solid. Le Souëf (1903) also reported that nests were raised knolls in shallow swamps, composed of coarse grass, sticks and leaves, but at times there was practically no nest at

all. McGilp (1924) described a nest on a small islet at Teatree Lake, South Australia, placed on the ground among cane grass. A similar nest was described by Barrett (1925) at McLaughlin's Swamp (Queensland), an islet almost in the center of a big marsh. A nest pictured by Caley (1967: 260) was a large pile of vegetation.

At times the birds nest far from water. Barnard (1914) reported such nests on the plains, one fully a mile from water at Brunette Downs, N.T. In January 1969 I found two nests away from water, but had heavy rains come, both would have been surrounded by water at least. This was at Pallarenda Town Common, Townsville, Queensland.

McLennan (1908) found a remarkable nest containing seven emu eggs and two Brolga eggs. The emus incubated the eggs while the cranes fed nearby. Astley (1900) described the nesting of this bird in captivity in England; losing her eggs, she laid another set and finally laid four sets, but all were lost to predatory birds.

Elliott (1938) wrote that ". . . a pair of Brolgas frequented a dried-up lagoon on a neighboring property, close to the Dingadee boundary [Moonie River, N. S. W., near Queensland border], and they would vigorously attack any dogs that approached the spot—a sure sign of nesting. Next morning (October 15, 1937) . . . we saw the Brolgas driving a group of horses away from the vicinity by menacing them with half-open wings, at the same time uttering loud, deep, trumpetlike calls. As we approached, the birds withdrew toward the top end of the lagoon, which was dried up and very rough from the hoof-marks of horses made when the mud was soft.

"A nest was found near an old one of the previous season. It was ten to twelve inches in height, two to three feet across the top, and about twenty yards from what would be the edges of the lagoon when full of water—as it undoubtedly had been when the Brolgas started to breed. It held one egg very much water-stained, but which obviously had originally been with indistinct markings at the larger end. The egg was chipped and the chick could be distinctly heard calling weakly from within. Some broken egg-shells were in the nest also, whilst nearby the chick which . . . hatched from this second egg was located."

A pair of Brolgas in foreground, other Brolgas in background, at a fresh-water lake, Yarrowmere Station, Queensland, January 4, 1969.

Church (1925) wrote: "The nest itself in every case consisted of dried grass piled about 10 inches above ground. No sort of covering was used when the parent birds left the nest; but though apparently easily distinguished, I often had difficulty in observing the eggs. This I believe, is due to the faint brownish markings."

Franz Breuer (verbal) found a nest at Cape Pallarenda Town Common, Townsville, in February 1967, well out on an island in the salt tidal flats, but remote from the roosting region. Grass and vegetation at that time was nearly shoulder-high. Andrée Griffin (verbal) described a nest placed on a small island in a small pond near Mt. St. John, Townsville, February 27, 1968 and she and Bruce Cook (letter) found a similar nest February 15,

1969 on the same island. It was built of Para grass (*Brachiaria miliiformis*), the main plant on the nesting island. Gavin Blackman showed me a nest he found in September 1968 at Pajingo in thick bulkuru sedge (*Eleocharis dulcis*) in a few inches of standing water in a drying-up pond. It was made completely of bulkuru sedge. Other nests found by Blackman (unpublished master's thesis) were made of *Sporobolus virginicus* (L.) Kunth, *Cyperus scariosus* R. Br., *Cyperus exaltatus*, and, in one case, even some water hyacinth (*Eichhornia crassipes*). The two nests I found at Cape Pallarenda Town Common were made entirely of *Sporobolus virginicus*.

Measurements of seven nests varied between 57 and 142 cm across. The first nest I found at the

Town Common on dry land (January 8, 1969) measured 68.6 x 68.6 cm at the widest spots in opposite directions; nest two (January 22, 1969) was 89 x 75 cm across. These nests were only about five to six centimeters thick, hollowed in the center for the eggs. The central portion of both measured about eighty centimeters across. The nest found at Mt. St. John (Dr. George Heinsohn) measured 142 cm across the base, 73 cm at the top and about 20 cm in the depressed portion. The average widest measurement of seven nests was 86 cm.

Lavery and Blackman (1969) wrote: "Brolgas nest on or beside moist areas, often islands, or swamps; frequently these are water impoundments for stock watering. Nests are isolated, simple, low structures averaging 4 ft. in diameter and constructed predominantly of grasses (sand couch [*Sporobolus virginicus* (L.) Kunth]) or sedges (*Cyperus scariosus* R.Br.). There is little or no lining of down or other feathers. Occasionally a nest may be floating in the centre of the area which birds clear in the course of construction."

The species is also found in Willett's Swamp, Atherton, and Lavery and Blackman (1969) described this: "Vegetation . . . at 'Willett's Swamp' near Atherton . . . consists mainly of sedges (for example, *Rhynchospora brownii* R. and S., *Cladium glomeratum* R.Br., *Juncus* sp.), grasses (for example, *Schoenus yarrabensis* Domin) and herbs (for example, *Eriocaulon australe* R.Br., *Melastoma polyanthum* Bl., *Philydrum lanuginosum* Banks and Sol. ex Gaertn.)."

THE EGGS

Campbell (1913) wrote in the Commonwealth Collection that examples of the Native Companion usually consisted of two eggs, but there was one set of three.

I find records of twenty-seven complete sets of Brolga eggs (6 x 1; 20 x 2; 1 x 3), averaging 1.815 eggs per set. Eggs are minutely pitted all over, slightly lustrous, and varying between dull white and clear cream or creamy-buff ground color, which is dotted and blotched with shades of chestnut and dull purplish-brown, the latter often appearing beneath the surface. In some there are irregular patches, even streaks; most often markings

are confined to the larger end. Some eggs become very dirt-stained before hatching. Makatsch (1959) gave measurements of twenty-six eggs as 92.0 x 60.5 mm and shell weights as 19.5 g. The average measurements of sixty-three eggs, recorded by me, others, and those in the British Museum (Natural History) were 90.62 (85.0-99.8) x 60.89 (56.38-67.3) mm, and the average weight of five eggs was 190.9 (185-195) g.

Wolstenholme wrote (1925) that two eggs of a set may have different shapes and the markings may vary. North wrote (1913) that the usual shape is oval or elongated oval. The index (division of length by width) as classified by Preston (1962, 1968, 1969) extends from 1.26 to 1.77, but the average is 1.48. Eggs of *Grus antigone sharpii* are generally larger with fewer markings, and the index for eleven eggs was 1.58. Brolga eggs in general are shorter and thicker than many eggs of similar-sized cranes.

Both birds incubate. According to Makatsch, under authority of Moody, the incubation period is thirty-two days. I watched a pair at their nest all day January 13, 1969 at Pallarenda Town Common, Townsville, Queensland (summarized in Table 2).

Dates. Most Brolga eggs have been found in Queensland. Of twenty-seven recorded, they were spread over the wet season, with a few during the dry season. They were: September, 3; October, 2; November, 1; December, 2; January, 4; February, 7; March, 6; April, 1; and June, 1. From about the same latitude in Northern Territory, nine recorded

Nest and eggs of Brolga, Pallarenda Town Common, Queensland, January 23, 1969.

Adult and young Brolga, Pallarenda Town Common, Townsville, Queensland, October 26, 1968.

were: January, 1; February, 1; March, 5; April, 1; and June, 1. In Western Australia one nest was found in February; in New South Wales, one in October and three in November, while in Victoria nests were discovered between August and November. Many people were searching for Brolga nests during the summer of 1968-1969, but it was very dry. At Townsville first eggs were found in four nests between January 2-5, January 22, between January 27 and February 15 and late February.

THE YOUNG

At hatching, young Brolgas are bundles of soft gray down, except for the tawny-colored heads. They can run around in just a few hours and, if necessary, swim. The parents guard them assiduously for ten to eleven months and may keep them another year if they do not renest then.

FOOD

Lavery and Blackman (1969) wrote: "The two species (*G. a. sharpii, G. rubicundus*) gather food by grazing and digging, preferably on moist ground. Feeding takes place during the day with intensive searching until mid-morning and extensive searching during late afternoon.

"Brolgas feed for the most part at swamps on bulkuru sedge tubers and on insects such as grasshoppers (for example, *Atractomorpha crenaticeps* [Blanch.]) and leafhoppers (for example, *Melampsalta* sp.). Foods eaten at other habitat types include a wide variety of insects of all age stages (dragonflies, mantids, beetles, moths), freshwater and saltwater mollusks, crustaceans, spiders and frogs, and on wetland and dryland plants (all parts) including agricultural crops and improved pastures. Stomachs may contain items such as teeth, bones, and barbed wire. Indirect evidence suggests that downy chicks are fed on insect material by the parents whose attention is attracted by soft purring calls.

"Food of those eastern Sarus Cranes examined included maize seeds and native grasses."

Bulkuru sedge (*Eleocharis dulcis* [Burm. f.] Trin.) is definitely the chief food. The region of greatest abundance of this plant is from Darwin around to Brisbane (Lavery), and this is the region of greatest abundance of the Brolga. During the entire dry period Brolgas dig these tubers in the early mornings and late afternoons, going down at times 4-6 inches so that some soils are pitted with small holes about the same size in diameter. I also found they were eating corn, wheat, rice, peanuts, some grasshoppers, and apparently at times considerable numbers of mud skippers (*Periophthlmus vulgaris*—Eggert, 1935), fiddler crabs (*Uca* sp.) and freshwater crayfish (*Cherax depressus*—Rich, 1951) where these occurred in waters where Brolgas fed.

Two authors, D'Ombrain (1921: 62) and Morse (1922:27), reported Brolgas at that time retired during drought periods to the prickly pear country, living on the fruit of that plant. According to entomologists, insects introduced for the purpose of eliminating this plant have, by now, just about completed their mission. In many regions the bulkuru sedge marshes are being drained and put into cultivation. So the chief foods of the Brolga found before white people settled Australia possibly will be eliminated. In many regions the bird has become a nuisance, destroying large quantities of rice, wheat and corn. In many world crane regions the original foods are not known. But now in Australia, with the work of Lavery and Blackman, the food of the Brolga is known. Man still has time to save some of these original foods; if he doesn't do so these cranes will have to depend entirely on farm crops for food, a situation that often makes for open warfare against the birds.

At Lake Buchanan there was no bulkuru sedge. Here another plant, *Cyperus aff. rotundus*, was dug out with equal zeal, the birds feeding off and on nearly all day. But here, as everywhere, water is essential. Although I saw Brolgas drink some saline water, the majority of water taken has to be fresh. Usually the birds feed until nine or ten o'clock in the morning, then come to water, where they spend a half-hour or more. Often huge concentrations occur at waterholes, dams, ponds and lakes at these times, and frequently make considerable noise while there.

Lavery and Blackman (1969) wrote: "In the early wet season (December-February) birds of both species (*G. rubicundus* and *G. a. sharpii*) ex-hibit mating displays, which, like alarm warnings, involve repeated stretching, bowing, jumping, and walking. Birds are dispersed widely during and immediately after the wet season, when nesting mostly occurs. Unseasonal nesting happens sometimes. Movements of brolgas are primarily dispersals from principal food sources to and from suitable breeding grounds and supplementary feeding sites which, particularly nowadays, may be widespread. . . .

"Brolgas in captivity have been known to live for up to 33 years. . . .

"Parasites of brolgas include one species of feather mite, three of lice, and three of flukes. . . .

"The only parasite recorded from the eastern Sarus crane in Australia is a body louse, *Heleonomus* sp. . . .

"Red-backed sea-eagles, *Haliastur indus* (Boddaert), are predators of brolga eggs; dingoes (*Canis dingo*—Meyer) and foxes (*Vulpes vulpes* L.) prey on young birds.

"Brolgas invade sorghum, maize, improved pasture grasses such as *Cynodon* species, and occasionally other agricultural crops, particularly during the period of grain maturation which coincides normally with dispersion of birds on habitat types other than swamps.

"Control measures presently recommended are to patrol farms prone to infestation, that is, situation near brolga concentration areas (all well known), during early mornings before harvesting and to frighten any birds by loud noises and general disturbance. Scarecrows are effective for awhile.

"Conservation. Cranes are protected in Queensland; populations are relatively small and distribution is restricted mainly to a few large swamps. The increase in remote country that has been made suitable for breeding by the construction of water impoundments is in contrast to a declining situation for cranes of other countries. Moreover, increasing grain-crop growth acts as drought-fodder for birds as well as stock. Nevertheless, the few principal food sources of the Brolga are being used increasingly by man for his purposes and attempts need to be made now to preserve some of this environment for conservation requirements."

VOICE

When a man approaches a pair or a flock of Brolgas, the nearest birds begin to utter a gooselike *Garraw*. As the birds retreat, more and more of them give this call, though it seems as if one bird in each family utters it, not the entire group. When flying, one bird in a group periodically gives a low, guttural *Graaaw*, not nearly as loud as the shrill alarm note.

Occasionally birds give a single trumpet call, a shrill *Garoooo*, but the outstanding call of the adults is that given by a pair in unison. It resembles the call of the Sarus Crane. When giving this, the male stands with head erect, neck stretched full length upward, bill pointing slightly backward. He raises his secondaries over his back, holds the primaries stiffly at his side and commences the call. The first note is not as loud as the second and thereafter they taper down. The second syllable is much the shrillest. His call goes, *Kaweee-kreee-kurr-kurr-kurr-kurr-kurr-kurr*. Simultaneously, immediately following each syllable of the male's call, the female utters her call, *Kuk-kuk-kuk-kuk-kuk-kuk-kuk-kuk*. Usually she calls as long as he. She does not raise her wings, but keeps them tightly against her side and holds her head and neck straight up. Often a unison call given by one pair brings a simple response from one or more pairs.

The call of the downy chick is a chickenlike *Peeep* similar to that of other downy cranes. Adults give a low, guttural *Purr* when calling the chick to them or reassuring each other.

DISTRIBUTION

Brolgas are resident in western and northern Australia, Queensland, parts of New South Wales, Victoria and South Australia, and in New Guinea from Frederik-Hendrik Island to Fly River, Sepik River basin. They were found once on Willis Island and once in New Zealand. They migrate during the dry season and drought periods to regions of fresh water. Additional records are:

AUSTRALIA: *Western Australia.* Campbell (1901), Kilgour (1904), Mathews (1909, 1910), Crossman (1910), Hill (1911), Whitlock (1925), Jenkins (1947), Shilling (1948), Glover (1956) and Serventy and Whittell (1962) gave specific re-

gions where Brolgas were observed as: Anna Plains, Ashburton, Argyle, Beacon, Bohemia Downs (19° S.; 126° E.) (a nest with two eggs), Broome (18° S.; 122° E.), Drysdale Mission, Eucla, Fitzroy River (18° S.; 124° E.), Flora Valley, Gogo (18° S.; 125° E.), Hills Camp, Ivanhoe, Kimberley, Langrey's Crossing, Noonbanbah, Onslow, Ord River, Parry's Creek, Shark Bay, Sturt Creek, Upper Liveringa Station, and Wyndham. There was an invading influx during 1951-1952. Andrée Griffin (letter) observed Brolgas at Police Lagoon between Kununurra and Wyndham.

Northern Australia. Le Souëf (1903), Ashby (1906), Barnard (1914), H. L. White (1917), S. A. White (1923), Chalmers (1934), Rhodes (1944), Humphries (1947), Sedgwick (1947), Francis (1949) and Storr (1967) reported Brolgas had been found at Adelaide River (13° 5′S.; 131° E.), Alexandria (19° 03′S.; 135° 57′E.), Anthony's Lagoon (17° 58′S.; 135° 32′E.), Banka Banka Station (18° 47′S.; 134° 03′E.), Batavia River, Brunette Downs (18° 38′ 135° 57′E.) (also a nest and one egg), Daly Waters (16° 15′S.; 133° 20′E.), Darwin (12° 28′S.; 130° 51′E.) (also four clutches in March and one in June), Elliott, Glyde River (12° 20′S.; 135° E.), Groote Eylandt (14° S.; 136° 40′E.), Howard Island Channel, King River Camp, Koolpinyah Station (24 mi. E. of Darwin), MacDonald Downs (22° 27′S.; 135° 13′E.), Melville Bay (12° 10′S.; 136° 40′E.), Melville Island (11° 35′S.; 131° E.), Newcastle Waters (17° 22′S.; 133° 22′E.), Port Bradshaw, Port Keats (14° 14′S.; 129° 32′E.), Red Lily Lagoon, Roper Downs, Roper River (14° 43′S.; 135° 23′E.), Warlock Ponds (15° 06′S.; 133° 10′E.) and Wycliffe Creek. Also recorded as a rare visitor (presumably from Lake Eyre basin) to the Finke.

More recently Billy Gill (letter) recorded Brolgas at Alligator River (12° 12′S.; 132° 23′E.), Anthony's Lagoon, Avon Downs (20° 02′S.; 137° 30′E.), Fog Dam (thousands), Elliott (17° 34′S.; 133° 21′E.), Goose Camp, Jandidgee Bore, Jin Jin Crossing, Lake Woods (17° 50′S.; 133° 30′E.), Oenpelli (12° 20′S.; 133° 03′E.) and at Leaches Swamp.

Andrée Griffin (letter) observed two to three hundred at Fog Dam, July 5, 1966 and others at Elsey (14° 58′S.; 133° 20′E.) June 29, 1966, with still others at Red Lily Lagoon.

Brolgas coming to Pallarenda Town Common, Townsville, Queensland, January 1969.

I observed the species at Humpty Doo and Yarrawanga (near Darwin) on January 31, 1969.

Queensland. The following specimens and eggs have been deposited in the British Museum (Natural History); Two-egg sets— one taken in 1899 by A. S. Meek; another from Hariman Park, September 3, 1909 by S. Robinson; one taken at Norman River marshes by R. Kemp; two taken by A. J. North, one at Coomooboolaroo, Dawson River, the other at Dawson River; two taken February 17 and March 16, 1916 by T. B. Sheckleton at Infracombe, Wellshot Station; Specimens—an adult (no data) taken in northern Queensland by E. M. Crookshank and a female taken May 6, 1923 at Thomby Station by Capt. G. Wilkins.

The following persons have made other recordings of observations and nests from Queensland:

Berney (1907), Cornwall (1910), Wm. MacGillivray (1910, 1914, 1918, 1924), Broadbent (1910), Barnard (1911), Campbell and Barnard (1917), Le Souëf (1918), Agnew (1921), H. L. White (1922, 1923), S. A. White (1923), Alexander (1923), Wolstenholme (1925), Barrett (1925), Barnard and Barnard (1925), Church (1925), Barnard (1926), W. D. K. MacGillivray (1929), Mayo (1931), Bryant (1931), Bourke and Austin (1947), Storr (1953), Binns (1954), Lord (1956), Wheeler (1959), Lavery and Hopkins (1963) and Lavery and Blackman (1969).

These cover the following regions:

Atherton, Atherton Tableland (17.5° S.; 145° E.); Archer River (13.5° S.; 142° E.), Balkaldena Station (76 mi. from Winton), along the Barrier Reef region, Bellenden Plains towards Tully River, (Upper) Barcoo (25° S.; 144° E.), Bulloo (28° S.; 143° E.), Burketown (17.5° S.; 139° E.) (several nests—November 1924-January 1925), Cairns (20 mi. S.W.), Caldwell, Cardwell (18° S.; 146° E.), Cape York (11-15° S.; 142-145° E.), Cobham Lake, Comongin Station (near the Bulloo), Cooktown (Laura Dist., 15° S.; 145° E.), Coomooboolaroo Station (Dauringa Dist.—24° S.; 150° E.), Dawson River, Gulf Country, Herbert River (18° S.; 146° E.), Lake Barrine (Atherton Tableland), Longreach (W. of Tambo—25° S.; 144° E.), Mackay (Thompson's Creek, 70 mi. from Mackay), Mitchell Plains (near Burketown), Moreton Bay, Murphy's Creek District, Murray River, Newry (40 mi. N.), Noosa Lake, Peel Island (Moreton Bay, Stradbroke Island), Pumice Stone Channel (22 mi. from Brisbane River), Richmond (21° S.; 143° E.) (eggs observed—September 28, two nests in October, one each in December and January, three in February), Rocky Creek, Rockhampton (23.5° S.; 151° E.) (nest with two eggs), Rockingham Bay District, Stradbroke Island, Tambo (25° S.; 146° E.), Tewantin, Thomby Station, Toorilla (23° S.; 149° E.), Townsville (many regions), Upper

Barcoo, Whitula Creek, Willis Island (16.5° S.; 150° E.), Wilson River, Windorah and Yungaburra (Atherton Tableland).

Lavery and Hopkins (1963) and Lavery (1968) gave several regions near Townsville where Brolgas are found: Mt. St. John, West Mt. St. John, Thornley Park (near Garbutt), Belgian Gardens (now drained) and Cape Pallarenda Town Common, for a total of 1,180 acres, of which a considerable amount grew to bulkuru sedge, *Eleocharis dulcis* (Burm. f.) Trin. Brolga counts (1959-1963) gave maximum and minimum populations of 2,650 ± 50 to 2,000 ± 50 and 265 ± 5 to 17 ± 5, with seasonal appearances remarkably consistent, the highest and lowest counts both coming during 1961, a drought year. They said birds were found from St. Lawrence to Rocky River (near Princess Charlotte Bay) and the largest Queensland concentration was at Cromarty (12,000).

J. G. Blackman (unpublished master's thesis) observed nests at Pajingo (21° S.; 146° E.)—one egg, late September 1968 (nest was empty when I saw it October 14); Bonanaba near Inkerman—two nests (two eggs, one egg), March 30, 1967 and at Cromarty, (two eggs), June 1968.

While with Hugh Lavery I saw twelve Brolgas October 23, 1968 at Giru, and groups of one and three near Pajingo. Then Lavery, Blackman, J. Grimes and I saw 1,257 at Cromarty, 3,000 at Billy Birds and 136 at Serpentine, all on October 23, 1968.

Billie Gill (letter), a strenuous field person in Australia, has seen Brolgas on Atherton Tableland, at Kaban (17° 30′S.; 145° 25′E.), Willett's Swamp, Bromfield Swamp, Innisfail (rare), Gillus River, Burketown, Normanton, Norman River at Glencoe Crossing (17.5° S.; 141° 10′E.), the salt flats along Karumba Road, Leichardt River (17° 45′S.; 139° 45′E.), Georgia River, black sand plains along Burketown Road, Georgetown (18° 45′S.; 143° 30′E.), Prosperpine (20° 45′S.; 148° 30′E.), Thoedonia Station, Townsville, valley of Lagoons, Gunnawarra, Walters Lake, Clevedon, Gin-gin (25° S.; 152° 30′E.), Clermont (23° S.; 147.5° E.), Mackay (21.5° S.; 149.5° E.), E. Leichardt River, St. Lawrence Plain, Karumba (17.5° S.; 140° 50′E.), Julia Creek (21° S.; 142° E.), 54 miles east of Max Welton.

Franz Breuer found and photographed a two-egg nest at Pig Island, near Pallarenda during February 1967. Andrée Griffin and Bruce Cook found two-eggs nests at Mt. St. John on February 27, 1968 and February 15, 1969.

My wife and I observed Brolgas at Atherton Tableland in several regions (thanks to Bruce Cook and Andrée Griffin): Arraga Dam, December 15, 1968 (9); Kairi, December 15, 1968 (4); Atherton, November 10, 1968 (19). Other sightings were: Willett's Swamp and Hastie's Swamp, December 14 (10) and December 15, 1968 (6); Malanda (4 mi. N.W.), December 13 and 14, 1968 and Bromfield Swamp, December 14, 1968 (21).

We also saw Brolgas at Ingham (18.5° S.; 146.5° E.) October 5, 1968 (1); November 10, 1968 (12), January 10, 1969 (5) and January 11, 1969 (42—and a young bird unable to fly). George Heinsohn took me there the last two times. R. G. S. Allingham and H. R. Bosworth both have found nests east of Ingham regularly.

At Lake Buchanan (22° S.; 146° E.) Hugh Lavery, J. G. Blackman, John Grimes and I observed Brolgas October 30 (47), October 31 (35); November 1 (41) in 1968; at Cauckingburra Swamp, Yarrowmere Station the same year we saw more October 29 (21), October 30 (4), October 31 (16), November 1 (2). At little Lake Constart, Tom

Young Brolga begging for food from parent, December 1967. Kynuna, Queensland. Photograph by Lavery and Blackman.

House and I found 309 Brolgas January 2, 427 on January 3, 571 on January 4, 1969. Tom House, manager of Yarrowmere, estimated 1,000 during November and December 1968, then reported (letter June 20, 1969) that 100 remained, even though they had had only eighteen wet days with 626 points of rainfall, as compared to twenty-five wet days and 2,536 points during 1968. Lake Constart, Lake Buchanan and Cauckingburra Swamps all were dry by May 1969. We observed four cranes at their outstation, Thirlestone, January 4, 1969. That summer of 1968-1969 I observed three Brolgas at Mingela (20° S.; 146° E.) October 14 and 29 and November 2 and January 5.

From September 1968 to January 1969 I observed Brolgas at Pallarenda Town Common, Townsville, as follows: September—two hours (500); October—fifteen field trips, 42 hours (7,000); November—fourteen field trips, 68 hours (7,977); December—ten trips, 35½ hours (5,547); January—fifteen trips, 82½ hours (5,075).

On January 8 I found a nest with two eggs and another with one egg on January 22. Thus, during five months of observation there I observed 26,099 Brolgas on fifty-five field trips and spent 230 hours in the field. Sample counts during this period were: September 30, 1968 (500 estimated); October 8 (521); October 11 (632); October 18 (731); October 26 (754); November 6 (1,004); November 12 (1,033); November 16 (633); November 24 (915); December 2 (1,035); December 9 (734); December 20 (666); December 27 (875); December 29 (1,050); January 7, 1969 (397); January 10 (285); January 13 (518); January 17 (267); January 19 (25); January 21 (700) and January 22 (396).

During eight days at Yarrowmere Station and vicinity I observed 1,473 Brolgas during seventy-nine field hours and while at Normanton during fourteen field hours, forty Brolgas and fifteen Sarus Cranes were noted. During forty field hours on Atherton Tableland, eighty-six Brolgas and three Sarus Cranes were seen.

Actually, the greatest concentration of Brolgas in Queensland occurs south of Townsville near Clevedon, Giru, Cromarty, Paralko and St. Heleis with fewer at Serpentine and many other neighboring stations.

New South Wales. In the British Museum (Natural History) there are egg sets taken at Tumut (two eggs, November 1 and 3, 1884) by A. J. North and a set (one egg) from Maitlands (32.5° S.; 151.5° E.) by J. Gould. Other observations have been recorded by Austin (1907), Barrett (1916), Jackson (1912), D'Ombrain (1921), Morse (1922), Chisholm (1929), Sullivan (1931), Lansell (1933), Bryant (1934), Elliott (1938), Hindwood (1940) Hindwood and McGill (1951) and Sefton (1958). They recorded the birds from Barwon and MacIntyre Rivers (29° S.; 149° E.), Berrigan (35.5° S.; 146° E.), Cambo Cambo Station (near Queensland border), Coocalla, Derra Derra (N.W. of Bingara—30° S.; 150° E.), East Bogan District, County of Flinders (45 mi. S. of Nyngan), Illawara District, Garah, Moree (29° S.; 150° E.). Here, both D'Ombrain and Morse wrote that Brolgas retired to the prickley pear country to eat the fruit during drought times. Other sightings were made at Moonie River near Goondublui (29.5° S.; 149° E.), Moulamein District (35° S.; 144° E.), Murrumbidgee Irrigation Area (34° S.; 147° E.), Talbragar River, Tocumwal and Yanko Creek (34° S.; 148° E.).

A downy chick was reared at Yanko Creek. Eggs were found October-November 1933 at Moree and two eggs near Goondublui October 15, 1937.

Victoria. Brolgas have been recorded by: Campbell (1902), Le Souëf (1903), Simpson (1903), Pawsey (1906), Batey (1907), Hill (1907), Stone (1912, 1913), Cole (1920), Barrett (1924), Cohn (1926), Wilson (1928), Howe (1928), Dickison (1932), Dennis (1933), Brown (1950), Jones (1952), Binns (1953), Wood (1955, 1959) and Bedggood (1959).

Regions where birds were found were: Ararat (37.5° S.; 143° E.), Balranald to Swan Hill, Boorhamen, Bendigo (37° S.; 145° E.) (nests every year), Corop, Echuca (36° S.; 145° E.), Geelong (adults with chick December 28, 1953), Karradoc, Lake Boga, Kulkyne State Forest, lake region, Lockie (34° S.; 142° E.), Melton Plains (1907), Murray River (36° S.; 146° E.), Raywood, Rivenina (Jerilderie—400 Brolgas poisoned), Stawell District near Grampians, Terand (Lake Bolac), Turkeith (38° S.; 143° E.) (nests found in August prior to 1930; since then in October and November), Victoria (after crossing the Murray below the Mitta

Mitta, but now gone), Yarraberb (36.5°S.; 144°E.) and many nests in western Victoria (1933).

Billie Gill (letter) observed Brolgas recently at Geelong and at Weber Lake in the Grampians near Dunkeld.

South Australia. Lyons (1901-02), Nicholls (1924) and McGilp (1924) found these birds in the Lake Eyre District at Kooperananna, at Lake Frome (31°S.; 140°E.) where a nest was found on a small islet in Teatree Lake, and at Munderanie (27°S.; 140°E.) and also June 15-20, 1937, Etulileluli, near Abminga, Blood Creek and Mt. Daer Station (Condon, 1938).

NEW GUINEA. On the south coast of Frederik-Hendrik Island to Fly River, Mayr (1941) reported this species, and from the middle of the Sepik north of Timbunke at 4°N.

NEW ZEALAND. *South Island.* The species was recorded here only once.

Table 18—Measurements of 20 adult Brolgas taken by J. G. Blackman. Table 19—Measurements of three Brolga chicks taken by Blackman.

Chapter Ten

THE SIBERIAN WHITE CRANE

(Grus leucogeranus)

Grus Leucogeranus, Pallas, *Reise Versch. Prov. Russ. Reichs, 2:* 1773, p. 714.
Type locality: Marshes bordering the Ischim, Irtysh and Ob rivers.
Vernacular names: The Siberian Crane, The Siberian White Crane, The Asiatic White Crane (English); стерх (Russian); ソデグロヅル (Japanese); der weisse indische Kranich, der Nun Kranich (German); la Grue blanche d'Asie (French); de Witte Aziatische Kraanvogel (Dutch); Karo-Khar (in North West Province, India); Tunhi (Oudh); Chini Kulang (Hind, Hansi); Burmuch (Behari).

This bird has the most outstanding voice of any crane. It is much less of a bugle, more of a whistling sound, quite un-crane-like. It carries a much shorter distance and is less penetrating than with other *Grus.* The birds call considerably on their wintering grounds, often pairs calling in unison. While giving these calls they have a more jerky motion, at times, than do other cranes and it appeared as though both birds raised their wings above their backs, the females much the least.

Siberian White Crane pairs in flight, Keoladeo Ghana Bird Sanctuary, Bharatpur, Rajasthan, India, February 4, 1969.

The large White, or Siberian Crane, nests only in Arctic Siberia. Formerly it was found from the Caspian Sea to the Yangtse in winter, from the Ob to the Kolyma in summer, and in several small isolated localities in between. The birds from the more southerly breeding grounds have disappeared gradually. Probably only the northern population now survives. This region has been described recently by Uspenski (1961):

"The Nuncrane was [formerly] comparatively widespread in Siberia and Kazakhstan, but recently . . . has significantly declined. Today this species has a divided range nesting in isolated regions in the river valleys, Ob, Indigirka, possibly the Lena. Their greatest numbers occur in northeast Jakutien, the valley of the lower Indigirka, and bordering regions of the Yana-Indigirka lowlands.

"In the summer of 1960, while spending some time on the lower Indigirka, we had the opportunity to gather material concerning the biology and population. . . . Our observations secured by hikes on foot, by boat, and by aeroplane, also by inquiries, proved that the nesting area of the Nuncrane is the territory bordered on the west by the

Yana and in the east possibly to the Alaseja. The northern border of the nesting region coincides with the north border of the Moos-Fletcher Tundra. In the south, in the river valley of the Indigirka, the Nuncrane is present only up to the 69th parallel. . . . It nests only in the territory between the Yana and Alsei in the Moos-Fletchen-Strauch Tundra and also in the open places in the Forest Tundra and in the north of the Tiaga. In these areas this bird may be considered a breeding species. The greatest density is attained in the Tundra, especially in the lowlands of deep marshy regions, which have large bodies of water. Counting from an aeroplane showed distances between nesting pairs in the Moos-Fletchen Tundra (in the river valleys of the Indigirka and the Jelona) was 12 to 14 km up to 30 or 35 km, averaging about 20 km. Or in a region of 100 km² 25 pairs nested. Based on this information and presuming the main nesting territory was in northeast Jakutien which is 2,500 to 3,000 km², and that pairs are more or less evenly scattered over this region, their numbers can only be estimated, about 500 to 700 nesting pairs. We were not actually able to see nests of the crane, but judging by observations from the air and local inquiries, the birds nest chiefly near large bodies of water, along lake shores and on lake islands.

"The arrival of the birds occurs in the end of May or early June, a period of intensive thaw, also when the geese come (*Anser fabalis, Anser albifrons*). During the year 1912, the first cranes were observed on 3 June at the Russkoje Ustje. In 1929 the first birds were observed at the mouth of the River Moma (two flights with 7 and 9 birds) and in 1930 one lone Nuncrane was seen at Allaicha on 20 May. In 1960 in the district of Tschokurdach arrival of pairs of cranes began on 24 May. In the region of Schamanow cranes were first observed on 28, 29 and 30 May. The Nuncrane apparently arrives in spring along the river valley of the Indigirka alone, in pairs, or in small flocks. According to local hunters and breeders, in early spring the mutual dancing of the pair of cranes is accompanied by loud and varied calls. In general the call of the Nuncrane somewhat resembles that of the Gray Heron but is more sonorous. Shortly after their arrival they start nesting. The prenesting period is so short that, according to K. A. Worobjew, in the

year 1960 on 30 June they found a nest which was already abandoned by chicks. The nest itself, according to local people, is a large structure one meter in diameter and 50 cm tall, made of grass blades (reed and wool grass). The nest contains two eggs. The immature birds have a partially brown plumage (straw-yellow, brown, or gray-brown), live mostly in flocks numbering eight to 10 and may be sighted in the summer near the breeding regions even north to the Arctic Tundra. The departure takes place in the beginning of September and coincides with the first snow and the departure of geese. On 15 September 1929, at Russkoje Ustje, a very small Nuncrane was captured, which had the size of a full-grown bird, except the wings (length of wings 467 mm according to Mikhel, 1935).

"Until recently it was uncertain what their food consisted of. The majority of authors were inclined to believe the Nuncrane fed on animal matter although Baker (1929) reported this particular species fed more on vegetable matter than any other crane in India. As a morphological study particularly, the Nuncrane has deep notches on the upper and lower beak. Perhaps they are helpful in securing live prey or other animal food. . . . Recently Sludski published for the first time parts of the diaries of the explorer G. S. Karelin in the Kaspi region written during the last century. Karelin examined stomachs of three cranes taken on the northeast banks of the Caspian Sea outside of the nesting period (24 September 1854 and 5 May 1855). The contents consisted only of roots and sprouts from *Butomus umbellatus*. The stomach contents of a crane captured 14 March 1928 on the west banks of the Caspian revealed also remains of vegetable food (Djukow, 1928). Sludski pointed out in the far north and in the river valleys of the Ob and Indigirka, animal food is scarce.

"With the help of local hunters four Nuncranes were captured during the nesting season . . . in the lowlands of the Khroma and Indigirka in the year 1960.

"The stomach contents were as follows:

"Number 1. Adult female. Moist contents: 95.5 g., ground-up roots of *Veratrum Misae*, 50 per cent volume; Gastrolites—smooth fragments of hard minerals and rocks (quartz, granite, and pebbles, in sizes of small gravel, seven to nine mm long and five to six mm high, 50 per cent of volume. Total weight, gastrolites, 50.5 g., also seven whole roots of *Veratrum Misae*.

"Number 2. Female, subadult. Moist weight content, 59.5 g. Chopped vegetable food residue, mostly buds, roots of reed grass (20 per cent by volume), various grasses, buds of shave grass, seeds of *Empetrum nigrum* 50 per cent volume. Gastrolites—smooth parts of the same hard minerals and rocks—10 to 12 mm in length and 8 to 10 mm in width (total weight of gastrolites, 28.5 g.).

"Number 3. Female, subadult. Weight, moist content, 99.0 g. Contents —chopped vegetable matter with large amounts of *Eriophorum* (20 per cent volume), buds of grasses (20 per cent volume), insignificant amounts of seeds and gastrolites—smooth pieces of same rocks 10-12 mm long, 6-8 mm wide, 60 per cent volume (Total weight, gastrolites, 58.5 g.).

"Number 4. Male, subadult. Moist content 80 g. Shave grass buds (5 per cent volume). Hide and bones of *Lemmus obensis* about 20 specimens. Two specimens of *Microtus gregalis*, *M. oeconomus*, *M. hyperboreus* (80 per cent volume). Gastrolites, same rocks, 13-14 mm long, 8-10 mm wide (25 per cent volume). Total weight gastrolites, 21.0 g.

"This shows that the Nuncrane feeds chiefly on vegetable matter, except for small mammals. The stomach much resembles that of a goose and weighed 280 to 300 g., had a very thick wall and was filled with a large amount of gastrolites. The notches on the beak are similar to those of the goose and assist in pulling and securing deep roots and vegetable matter."

DISTRIBUTION

This crane breeds only in northern Siberia. It migrates through the Tomsk region, Transbaikalia, Manchuria, Turgay, the upper Ob, Turkestan, west to southeast European Russia and Asia Minor. It winters in northern India, parts of western Pakistan, and China. Accidental migration into Sweden and as far east in winter as Japan (five specimens) is known.

Summer distribution. The Siberian Crane is found in arctic Siberia in summer, chiefly between 68° and 72° N. Latitude. Dementiev and Gladkov (1951) summarized the breeding and summer records. Uspenski (1961) added much more detail to our knowledge of the northeastern breeding region. One nesting locality is in the northwest; another is in the northeast of Siberia. The western region extends along the lower Ob, in the Konda and Sos'va basins northward to Berezovo (Lat. 64°, possibly even to 64° 30'), then southward to Station Samarsk. Several have been found in the north depression of the Irtysh at the Ob. They are also reported as nesting in the marsh bordering the Barabinsk Steppes (Lat. 56° N.; Long. 79° E.), in all likelihood, according to Ruzskiy (1940).

The bird also has been reported in eastern Siberia in the Indigirka Basin, from the mouth of the spread of the River Moma, to the westward to the River Khroma (Mikhel), on the lower course of the Yana and at Syvatoi Cape (Birulya; Bunge). It is possible that it stops on the eastern Lena between 68° and 72° N. Lat. (Argentov), on the Kolyma, apparently reaching its mouth, and in the environs of Yakutsk at Lake Taboga (Middendorf, Ivanov). In the valley of the Vilyoya it is established during nesting time (Maak) and on the Vitimsk flats (Polyskovim).

Uspenski (1961) reported the main breeding grounds were just south of the southern edge of the Arctic Tundra, along the northern edge of the Waldtundra and the Landschaften bergiger Tundra, from the Yana (Ust Yansk) on the west across the Indigirka in the region of Nakirdakh and eastward to the Alaseja River from about 68° N. Lat., 135° to 155° E. Long.

Dementiev and Gladkov (1951) reported Siberian Cranes in the summer, apparently as single birds, far from nesting regions (similar to the Whooping Crane). The regions of flight are two: the first, from the lower Volga and Ural in central Asia, in the south to northern Priural (middle course of the Kama below 58° 06' N. Lat., Cherdyn), and the lower course of the Ob in the north up to the Barabinsk Steppes in the east; second from Transbaikalia, northern Mongolia, and the Maritime Province to Yakutsk, Yana, Indigirka and Kolyma. In central Siberia the bird is not found during summer or migration periods.

It is doubtful that it occurred in Karelia during

Siberian White Cranes on feeding ground, Keoladeo Ghana Bird Sanctuary, February 4, 1969.

nesting times, and cranes have been observed near Gur'ev only in the summer of 1907. A single flight was noted over Syr-Darya in the region of Kazalinsk Bischarna—apparently a single wandering bird. In the last century it may have nested in Kazakhstan at Lakes Dzhity-Kul, Ayk, Chalkar-igya-kar, and at the source of the Tobol, but in 1894 this lake was dry. In the latter part of the last century the bird nested at the watershed lakes of the Irgiz (48° N.; 60-61° E.) and at Tobol, on the Turgay (47° N.) and possibly at Naurzuma (Sushkin, 1908). Now it does not nest in these places. It has been known to nest at Bernaul (53° N.; 84° E.), and on the Barbinsk steppe (female specimen taken June 22, 1876, by O. Finsch—BMNH), at Chenakh, on Lake Sartian. During the last three-quarters of the nineteenth century, according to natives, this crane occurred in the Chelyabinsk region (55° N.; 61° E.), but by 1898 it had gone. During the same period it may have nested at Lake Severn near Tyumen (a pair was observed in the course during three different years).

Dementiev and Gladkov (1951) doubted that it bred in the southeast in Transbaikalia and northeastern Mongolia, by authority of Molleson and Radde. There is a specimen in the Troitskosavsk Museum labeled "Northern Mongolia" (Molleson, 1906), and another in the Chitinsk Museum taken in the environs of Chita, with no other data (Stegman, 1928). Dementiev and Gladkov (1951) thought that possibly the bird nested on the Argun and Onon, but it has not been reported from there.

They also said there was no indication the bird ever had nested in the Primor'ye territory, as has the Manchurian Crane. Possibly some of the early records were cases of mistaken identity.

Summer wanderings. Some non-breeding birds collect in flocks, sometimes in two's, or even single birds, and wander throughout the summer. These far-reaching wanderings have been observed on the lower reaches of the Ural (Ruzskiy), on the lower Syr-Darya in the territory of Kazalinsk at Bishartu (July 1858), on Lake Kurgal'dzhin, May 13, 1946 (Derevyagin, 1947), at Chanakhin in July (Kots, 1910), at Kainsk, May 30, 1909 (Johansen), in the neighborhood of Semipalatinska on May 19 (Khakhlov and Selevin, 1928), in Abakan near the village of Izikh in June 1877, at Nazyvayevka, Omsk territory in the summer of 1927 and in the southern parts of the Omsk vicinity between Cherlak and Urlyotyop in summer, 1928. It also has been found near Ufa on the Kama below Chardyn'yo.

One individual was taken at Altae near Station Katon-Karagai (49° N.; 86° E.) in December 1882 and another was taken near Rostov-on-Don in the spring. The Siberian Crane was encountered in Turkmen (Dementiev) and has been observed at Sakhalin. A large flight was observed at Koko Nor on October 20, 1872.

Winter. The winter region is disconnected. One part is in southeast China on the lower Yangtse; another is in northern India east from Bikhar; others are in Iran at Seistan, Khurasan, Mazanderan and Gilan. It is possible the Siberian Crane winters at Zakharkaz (in February 1925 four were encountered at Lankoran by E. P. Spangenberg, but in his opinion these were migrating birds).

JAPAN. Amadon (1949) summarized the Japanese records. The first three birds were recorded by Temminck and Schlegel (1849), including one immature specimen, and taken at Nagasaki, Kyushu and sent to the Leiden Museum, Holland. According to Dr. G. C. A. Junge these birds were still there in 1949. Amadon found a fourth bird mounted and labeled "Japan," which is now located in the American Museum of Natural History, having been obtained from the Verreaux brothers of Paris about 1870. There is a fifth specimen, male, in the British Museum (Natural History) labeled "Naga-saki, Japan, 18 January 1880," from the collection of F. Ringer. Seebohm (1890) listed the species as a spring and autumn visitor to Japan.

In the *Hand-List of Japanese Birds*, it was reported from Sakhalin by Nikolsky and according to old Japanese literature it migrated to Kyushu in the past as well.

CHINA. The Siberian Crane winters in the Shanghai region and along the lower Yangtse Valley. It is a migrant in Chihli (La Touche, 1933). There are two specimens from Shanghai (BMNH): one a winter male, the second a head and neck only, bought in a market by F. W. Styan in January 1895.

David and Oustelat (1877) included this bird from China. La Touche (1933) wrote: "It probably keeps to the coast when migrating through Chihli, avoiding the interior, as Wilder and Hubbard at Peitaiho and I at Chinwangtao recorded great numbers passing over in March, April, October and November."

WEST PAKISTAN. Butler (1879) and Barnes (1885) recorded this species as rare in Sind.

INDIA. In Rajasthan, at what is now the Keoladeo Ghana Bird Sanctuary, Siberian Cranes were found up until winter, 1880. Then they disappeared until 1960 when three birds reappeared. Since then the birds have been present each winter, Maharaja of Bharatpur, verbal).

There are specimens (BMNH) from Etawah (26° 05'N.; 79° E.): three without sexes registered, taken by A. O. Hume (two in 1865), and three taken by W. B. Brooks at Tuman Jhil (a male and a female February 4, 1871, and a female February 22, 1871). At Futtehghur, A. Anderson (BMNH) took three specimens—a male, February 15, 1873, and two females, December 6, 1874 and December 31, 1876.

In Gwalior State (26° N.; 78° 05' E.), Maries (1897) listed the species and a specimen is in the Gwalior State Museum. From Central Provinces at Kuhi near Nagpur (21° 05' N.; 79° E.), D'Abreu (1935) reported a straggler was shot. At Delhi Frohme (1947) recorded the bird.

In a chaur near Beerpur Fty, not far from Jainagar, Darbhanga District (26° N.; 86° 05' E.), Inglis (1903) saw White Cranes during the winter of 1898, while the *mir-shikars* knew the bird and called it *Burmuch*.

At Rampur (32° N.; 77° 30′ E.), Donald (1952) observed this bird migrating over the Himalayas 762 to 914 m above his location at an elevation of 3,657 to 3,972 m.

Near Hissar, Kamauli (28° 05′ N.; 76° E.), Walter Koelz collected a male specimen (UMMZ) on March 12, 1933 (probably migrating).

OTHER LOCATIONS: The White Crane also winters along the coasts of the Caspian Sea, where it has been recorded by Pallas and Nordmann, and in Asia Minor where it has been seen in a flock of a hundred in a field bordering the Kisil Irmak River by Danford (Blaauw, 1897). Probably few, if any, birds use this region now.

MIGRATIONS

La Touche (1933) wrote: "Amongst the flocks that I saw [in China] were parties of Grey Cranes, the variegated V's formed by the birds flying in grey and white patches being very noticeable. Probably not many stay to rest in North China."

Dementiev and Gladkov (1951) wrote: "Migrating small flocks, pairs or individuals in autumn reach favorable locations for resting and feeding. Formerly they were observed in migration in large flocks up to 300 (Zarudniy . . . ; Bostanzhoglo . . .). First birds appear in the south of our country early. For instance, at Lenkoran (on the west side of the Caspian Sea) flying flocks were observed in the second half of February, on the delta of the Volga in the very beginning of April. At Emba (48° N.; 58° E.) in the middle of April, in the environs of Chkalov (52° N.; 55° E.) in the middle and in the end of the first half of April. On the shores of the Aralskoe Sea at Kamyshli-Basha it was observed April 5, 1858, near Karamakchi, the 16th of April, 1858 (Severtsov, Bostanzhoglo . . .), in Solo-Tyube, 14 April 1927 (Spangenberg and Feygin . . .), in late March 1891, on the shores of Sary-Kamysha, in late April, near Kazalinsk (Zarudniy . . .).

"In the Primorye Territory the Siberian Crane is met in flight only in the southern parts of the territory. The flight begins in the first half of April. In 1868 the first birds made their appearance on the upper reaches of the Sungacha on 4 April. In 1869

on 1 April heavy flight was observed in the middle of April. . . . By the end of the month it had vanished completely (Przhevalsky). At Yakutsk first Siberian Cranes were migrating on 10 April 1843 (Middendorf), in Verhoyanske on the Yana River (67° 05′ N.; 134° E.) a flying flock was observed on May 12 (Bunge) . . . At the mouth of the Moma River (a tributary of the Indigirka) first birds were observed 18 May 1929 (Mikhel).

"After conclusion of nesting (when young are in flight) in late July and the beginning of August, the Siberian Crane collects in small flocks, young together with the old, and they begin wandering. At first they roam near their nesting place, then gradually fly away farther and farther. The dates and places where these wandering groups have been observed are: early August 1884—near Chelyabinsk (55° N.; 61° E.), on 7 August 1936—on the River Tartas, a tributary of the Om, Omsk Territory (Ruzkiy); on Lake Tavolzhan—8-10 August 1896 (Ruzkiy); on Lake Terma-kul—14 August 1923 and near Karachi 27 July 1938 (Ruzkiy); 14 August 1915 at Lake Kara, Pavlodarskogo Territory (Shukhov, 1930); on 7 August on the road between Borovogo and Azby (Slovtsov); 6 August 1936 at Naurzuma (Mikheev); 12 August—in the Vilyoya Valley at the source of the Chiili River, 65° Lat. (Maak); 28 August on the Vitimskoe Plateau (Polyakov).

"The return migration began in September and lasted into the middle of October. On the Indigirka on 15 September 1929, a young crane was still taken (Mikhel). On the lower Ob (in the region of KondoSosva) they fly in the beginning of the second half of September (19 September 1941, Raevskiy). At Naurzuma flight was observed in the second half of September and to the end of that month. Usually it flies in flocks of 7 to 25 individuals, stopping for water and food at lakes—in particular, at Ak-Suata—collecting there in a few, separated, large flocks of 40 to 60 (Mikheev). At Mugodzhar flying flocks were encountered on 30 August 1857 at Lake Khodzha-Kul near the northern part of B. Barsukov 17 October 1857 (Bostanzhoglo) on the lower reaches of the Angrena—in the last of September and at . . . Arys on 6 October 1908 (Zarudniy). In late September 1913 near Dzaudzhikau."

Siberian White Cranes flying, Keoladeo Ghana Bird Sanctuary, India, February 4, 1969.

Other regions in which they mentioned that Siberian Cranes had been encountered during migration were on the southwest shores of the Caspian Sea, around Derbenta and to the south of Apsheronskogo, on the lower reaches of the Ural, and Volga, at Cerdyni and Kama (58° 30′ N.), at Ili, on the south shores of Balkhasha and to the Kara-talu River, on the Irtysh and Kurchum, in Troitsko-savska Territory on the Chikoy River, in Dauria in the environs of Tsurukhaytul, on Lake Tarey-Nor and near cities in Bureya Mts.

Taczanowski reported this crane from Dauria during migration; Radde collected four specimens in northern Mongolia; Przhevalsky observed it at Koko Nor in October. An adult specimen (CNHM) was taken April 12, 1937 at Harbin, North Manchuria, by W. A. Weymarn (CNHM).

NESTING

Reproduction. Dementiev and Gladkov (1951) wrote: "There is almost no information. The Siberian Crane usually comes north already paired. After arrival at the nesting locality, the birds soon set about nesting while some remain in a nomadic form of living (the young non-breeding birds). The Crane male, with half-spread wings, lowered head, and outstretched neck with beak parallel to the ground, utters a melodious trumpeting sound (Kondo-Zosvinsky Preserve, Raevsky). The nest placed on an eminence in a dry spot, amidst a remote marsh . . . was loose and slipshod, thrown into a heap, the materials of reeds and sedges. At the nest the male and female are very protective, guarding it in sequence.

"The egg set consists of two; the basic tone in color is yellowish-green with dark stains (Pallas), or dark green (Birulya). The duration of the embryonic development and postembryonic growth of the young is not known. As soon as the young grow up, the Siberian Cranes collect in a flock and spend the days on the steppes."

Baker (1929) wrote: "There is very little known of the breeding of this fine Crane. It is said by Godlowski to arrive at the breeding haunts in April, leaving again in September. . . . As regards its nesting Kuschel when forwarding me two eggs writes: 'From nests of rushes and reeds on the ground in a lake.' The eggs are not distinguishable from those of the Common Crane, though they may average larger. Four measure, 98.9 X 54.6; 95.0 X 62.0; 92.7 X 61.7; and 101.3 X 63.2 mm. Two eggs only are laid and the breeding season seems to be in June."

Pallas, in 1773 (Blaauw, 1897), reported a nest composed of grass and placed amongst reeds and rushes in which two eggs were laid in May. The male defended the nest and mate against enemies of all kinds.

The birds nested in the Zoological Gardens of Amsterdam without success and there is an egg (BMNH) taken from the aviaries of Lord Lilford, June 10, 1900. There are two more eggs in the British Museum taken May 10, 1919, without other data.

Seven eggs averaged in measurements: 98.48 (92.7-107.4) X 61.67 (54.6-65.7) mm.

The shape of an egg described by Blaauw (1897) was long oval. The color was a deep olive, with spots smaller than on many crane eggs concentrated near the larger end, a few over the entire egg, consisting of dark shades of brown, olive and some shades of gray.

WINTER BEHAVIOR

Hume (1868) wrote: "In 1859, I succeeded in shooting one out of a flock of some five and twenty, which I found in a large jheel or shallow rain-water lake, about halfway between Agra and Cawnpore. During the winters of 1865-6 and 1866-7, I procured and preserved a number of specimens in the same neighbourhood, and have had many opportunities of watching them pretty closely."

Hume added (Blyth and Tegetmeier, 1881): "They are very probably to be found during the cold weather in suitable localities throughout the plains of the north of India; but the only places where I have observed them, out of the Himalaya, is in a tract of country lying to the north of the Etawah, and south of the Mynpooree districts, in the middle of the Duab, or Mesopotamia, of the Ganges and Jumna, and, as I said before, about halfway between Agra and Cawnpore. That they themselves are rare, and that localities suited to their tastes are not numerous, may be inferred from the fact that, apparently, Dr. Jerdon, when he published his work, had never seen one; while, as far as I know, until I last year sent a pair to Madras, there were no specimens in any of our (Indian) museums. The locality in which, during these last two winters, I have seen and procured, comparatively, so many of these beautiful birds is somewhat peculiar. A broad straggling belt of *dhak* (*Butea frondosa*) jungle, some ten miles in width —at one time doubtless continuous, but now much encroached upon, and intersected in many places by cultivated lands—runs down through nearly the whole of the Duab, marking, I suspect, an ancient river course. Just where the northern and southern boundaries of the Etawah and Mynpooree districts lie within this belt, the latter incloses a number of large shallow ponds or lakes ("jheels," as we here term them), which, covering from two hundred acres to many square miles of country each at the close of the rainy season, are many of them still somewhat imposing sheets of water early in January, and some few of them of considerable extent even as late as the commencement of March. . . . Many of them abound with rushes and sedges, and as the waters gradually dry up, or are drawn off for irrigation purposes, become successively the favourite haunts of the White Crane.

"There will always be at any particular time two or three "jheels" that for the moment they particularly affect, and these are, as a rule, just those that then happen to average 18 in. to 2 ft. in depth, and that have a great deal of rush (*Scirpus carinatus* amongst others) somewhere in the shallower parts.

"To this tract of country they make their way as

early as the 25th October (and possibly sooner, though this is the earliest date on which I have observed them); and there they remain at least as late as the end of March, or perhaps a week or two longer. During the whole of our cold season they stay in this neighbourhood, and, though growing more and more wary (if possible) each time they are fired at, and disappearing for a day or two from any jheel where an attempt has been made to kill or capture them, they never seem to foresake the locality until the change of temperature warns them to retreat to their cool northern homes. Week after week, I have noticed, and repeatedly fired at, sometimes even slightly wounded, particular birds, which have nevertheless remained about the place their full time; nay, I have twice now killed the young birds early in the season, and the parents, one by one, at intervals of nearly a couple of months."

Hume also reported that the natives said the crane returned to this region every year and had for fifty years as far back as they could remember. Usually they returned in pairs or with a single young one. At first on return, the young bird was a strong contrast to the white parents, but as the season progressed it lost much of the buff color.

Siberian White Cranes at night roost, in typical single-file formation, during early-morning feeding before flying to regular daytime feeding region, Keoladeo Ghana Bird Sanctuary, India, February 4, 1969.

Out of over a hundred pairs with young, only one youngster per pair was ever observed. He also wrote: "The watchful care and tender solicitude evinced by the old birds . . . is most noticeable. They never suffer the young one to stray from their side, and while they themselves are seldom more than thirty yards apart, and generally much closer, the young, I think, is invariably somewhere between them. If either bird finds a particularly promising rush-tuft, it will call the little one to its side by a faint creaking cry, and watch it eating, every now and then affectionally running its long bill through the young one's feathers."

He told how the birds must pair for life like other cranes, mentioning a pair which had their legs crippled by shot one year. They returned the next year with their newly nearly-grown chick, and:

"Each year small parties of birds are noticeable unaccompanied by any young ones, and never separating into pairs. These, when they first come, still show a few buff feathers, and have a dingy patch on the tarsus; and though before they leave us they become almost as purely white, and have almost as well-coloured faces and legs as the old ones that are in pairs, they never seem to attain to the full weight of these latter. From these facts I am disposed to infer that these parties, which include individuals of both sexes, consist of birds of the second year, that our birds do not either breed or assume their perfect plumage till just at the close of the second year, and that . . . they do not attain their full weight until they have bred once at least.

"Unlike the four other species of crane with which I am acquainted, *G. leucogeranus* never seems to resort, during any part of the day or night, to dry plains or fields in which to feed; and unlike them too, it is exclusively a vegetable-eater. I have never found the slightest traces of insects or reptiles (so common in those of the other species) in any of the twenty odd stomachs of these White Cranes that I have myself examined. Day and night they are to be seen, if undisturbed, standing in the shallow water. Asleep, they rest on one leg, with the head and neck somehow nestled into the back; or they will stand like marble statues, contemplating the water with curved necks, not a little resembling some White Egret on a gigantic scale; or, again, we see them marching to and fro, slowly

and gracefully, feeding among the low rushes. Other cranes, and notably the Common and the Demoiselle, daily pay visits in large numbers to our fields, where they commit great havoc, devouring grain of all descriptions, flower shoots, and even some kinds of vegetables. The White Crane, however, seeks no such dainties, but finds its frugal food—rush seeds, bulbs, corms, and even leaves of various aquatic plants—in the cool waters where it spends its whole time. Without preparations by me for comparison, I hardly like to be too positive on this score; but I am impressed with the idea that the stomach in this species is much less muscular than in any of the others with which I am acquainted. The enormous number of small pebbles that their stomachs contain is remarkable. Out of an old male I took sufficient very nearly to fill an ordinary wineglass, and that, too, after they had been thoroughly cleaned and freed from the macerated vegetable matter which clung to them. These pebbles were mostly quartz (amorphous and crystalline), green-stone, and some kind of porphyritic rock; the largest scarcely exceeded in size an ordinary pea, while the majority were not bigger than large pins' heads. Perhaps, in the hands of some abler mineralogist than myself, these tiny fragments (of which I have a small bag full) may prove to contain as yet unnoticed mineral forms from Central Asia. I have found similar pebbles in the stomachs of the Grey and Demoiselle Cranes, but never in anything like such numbers as in those of the present species. . . .

At Keoladeo Ghana Bird Sanctuary the first three Siberian Cranes in eighty years arrived in December 1960. During the 1964-1965 winter there were about 200 birds, from mid-December until early March. On December 23, 1967, six pairs were found, eleven pairs on January 11, 1968, and 100 birds (including fifteen pairs, each with one young) on January 28, 1968. On January 30 an unsuccessful attempt was made to capture some of these birds and they disappeared toward Delhi or other parts of the sanctuary. On February 3, 1968, two pairs with one young returned, then six pairs and three young on February 5. The cranes increased again in early March so that on March 7 there were fifty and eighty on March 8. But all

Siberian White Crane pair showing typical head and wing, display (male right) while giving 'Unison Call.' This pair may have had two young.

went north by March 10. There had been a sudden rise in temperature on March 2. (See Tables 20, 21.)

The next winter, first birds appeared on January 13 (3); January 14 (6); January 20 (80); January 23 (120); and on January 25 sixteen circled up and up as though leaving, but came back (Virenda Sahai Saxena, Divisional Forestry Officer and Pamey Simgh, Resident Game Warden-verbal).

At night the birds roosted in shallow water, usually in one of two regions. One region was about one kilometer, the other about three kilometers, from the feeding territories. The birds roosted in only one group as a rule, often strung out in a long line and removed from the Sarus Cranes, which also roosted in the same ponds. Sometimes a few Sarus Cranes roosted adjacent to them in prefer-

ence to roosting with their own kind. But only once during the ten days I was there did Siberian Cranes (two on February 3, 1969) roost with Sarus Cranes. They roosted in water from one to six inches deep (2.5-15 cm).

The birds usually fed in one or two loosely connected groups in a pond overgrown in that region with water hyacinth. Each pair or family fed slightly removed from other groups, from about fifteen up to several hundred feet apart (five to 100 or more meters). They fed beneath the surface of the water, so that often their heads were entirely submerged as they probed for food. Numbers observed are given in Table 1; arrival and departure times from the night roost in Tables 2 and 3.

VOICE

W. E. Brooks (1869) wrote: With regards to the notes of *Grus leucogeranus*, how the natives can imagine that their name *karekhur* or as I shall call it, *care-cur*, expresses any one of them, I cannot conceive. The notes are all simple whistles, from a mellow one to a peculiar feeble shrill shivering whistle, if I may so express it."

Blaauw (1897) wrote: "This bird has a very peculiar and rather melodius cry, and a very original movement of its body whilst putting it forth. It moves its head and neck backwards and forwards and the wings up and down at the same time, and the more excited it gets, the quicker those curious movements become. Generally both sexes join in this exercise." He wrote they also have a rather melodious, harsh trumpet call similar to that given by other cranes.

My notes on birds heard on the wintering grounds in India indicate that the voice of the Siberian White Crane differs much from that of other cranes. It is the most musical of any, not nearly so loud, but still it can be heard from one-half to one mile (.8-1.6 km), depending on weather conditions. When calling, the birds jerk their heads forward and backward, the forward jerk going much lower. Simultaneously they jerk their wings up and down. When giving the call the bird seems to bob up and down somewhat as though it were jerked in the direction it faces, and simultaneously becomes very active. The call given by the male, and at times by the female, resembles *A-hooya—A-hooya—A-hooya—A-hooya—A-hooya*, again more like *Tooya—tooya—tooya—tooya—tooya*. The male gives many more of these calls than the majority of cranes. Often he gives more than fifty. The average of forty records was 23 (4-86) syllables, on February 3, 1969. Often the female, following very closely behind the call of the male, utters *Ahuya—ahuya—ahuya—ahuya— — —* or a different call *Pucha—pucha—pucha—pucha— — —*. The male raises his secondaries above his back, primaries held stiffly beside him, not as high as *Grus antigone, G. japonensis, G. rubicundus* and *G. grus*, but much higher than *G. canadensis*. The female also raises her secondaries, much higher than most female cranes. Often the birds face each other, and quite

often the female calls as many times as the male; sometimes she stops before he has finished.

Another call given by both birds, especially the male, is quite *grus*-like—*Grooya—grooya—grooya—grooya— — —*, repeated many times also. One bird, February 4, 1969, called a single call, *Grooya*, off and on all afternoon. Another time two males calling near each other, gave series of calls between thirty and fifty times, uttering during the afternoon some 800-1,200 syllables, while others made no sound at all.

A very pleasing call, *Ahooya* or *Toya*, murmurs through a flock when the birds are at roost. Often this is given even until dark; occasionally it is given in the early morning. When the birds prepare to fly they give it more often and many times one or more give it when flying to the feeding grounds.

A young bird in India also was heard giving a normal cranelike *Peeer* call in early February.

The alarm call, also rather pleasing, is a shriller *Turrrr* or *Turra*. Often when the birds give this call, they stand erect and soon fly away if danger persists.

Birds seemed to call more in the afternoons than mornings, while others seldom make any noise at all.

FOOD

The best information was given by Hume (Baker, 1929) and by Uspenski (1961). Dementiev and Gladkov (1951) said it was poorly known, but composed of small fish, lizards, serpents and small rodents. These cranes do not damage cultivated plants as do many cranes, but they apparently do feed very much on vegetable food (see above).

DESCRIPTION

Adult. The primaries, primary coverts and alula are black; the remainder of the plumage, pure white. The forecrown, forehead, face and sides of the head, extending back from the base of the bill to just posterior to the eye are bare, covered in front with a few white or yellowish-white hairlike feathers, and with black ones where the naked skin meets the white feathers of the crown or lower mandible. The bare face, the beak and legs are brick-red (Uspenski, 1961). The legs and feet are reddish-pink (Hume, from Baker, 1929). The iris is red or pale yellow. Hume added (1868): "The colour does not vary with age; but in some birds the iris is almost silvery, and in others there is a pinkish tinge."

Sub-adult. In the young there is no bare face. The entire head and upper part of the neck are somewhat rusty-buff. Hume (1868) added that the future bare spot is well defined in the youngest winter specimens, the feathers browner or dingier in hue than those of the remainder of the head and clinging much closer to the skin. The buff is clearest and deepest on the cheeks, top and back of the head, but very pale on the throat and chin. The rest of the plumage in the fall (except the primaries, greater coverts and alula) is buff, in some places more rufous, in others duller and sandier, with white everywhere beginning to show. In February, the white begins to predominate and by the end of March, when the birds are about nine months old, the face begins to become bare, with the remaining buff much duller.

Downy chick. Ticehurst (1926) wrote: "Entirely covered. Underparts dirty buff, belly white. Head and neck dark isabelline; creamy streak on each scapular, rest of upper parts pale chestnut, darker on mid-dorsum (captivity bred)." The eyes probably are dark brown.

MEASUREMENTS

Adult male. Eight specimens: AMNH, 1; BMNH, 3; CNHM, 1; UMMZ, 1; La Touche (1922), 1; Uspenski (1961), 1 (excluding the sub-adult from USSR). Exposed culmen, 188.16 (182-199); wing (chord), 607.1 (563-625); tail, 204.0 (190-208); tarsus, 264.0 (241-285); bare tibia, 122.5 (109-130); middle toe with claw, 147.3 (122-180) mm. Uspenski (1961) gave the following measurements for the sub-adult male, taken at the mouth of the Khroma in early June 1960: Body length, 1,080 mm; wing span, 2,210 mm; weight, 6,750 g. This bird had skin fat up to 3mm thick and intestinal fat 9 mm thick. The rose-colored testes measured 20 X 4 and 22 X 5 mm.

Adult female. Seven specimens: AMNH, 1; BMNH, 4; USNM, 1; Uspenski (1961), 1. Exposed culmen, 178.4 (162-186); wing (chord), 571.0 (538-597); tail, 200.0 (190-212); tarsus, 258.5 (254-262); bare tibia, 117.2 (112-125), middle toe with claw, 120.6 (117-125) mm. Uspenski also gave total lengths for three females: adult, 1,220, sub-adult, 1,230 and 1,200 mm. For wing expanse he gave: adult, 1,971, sub-adult, 2,096 and 2,060 mm. They had skin fat at the widest place of 2 mm on the adult, 3 mm on the sub-adults; intestinal fat 3-4 mm on the adult and 6-10 mm on the sub-adults. The adult female weighed 5,250 g on May 28, 1960 and was taken in the valley of the Jelona. The two sub-adults weighed 4,750 and 5,200 g respectively, both taken in late May 1960 at the mouth of the Markowa, all in Siberia.

Hume reported female weights up to sixteen pounds (7,270 g), male weights up to nineteen pounds (8,622.6 g) and for sub-adults, about ten pounds (4,544 g).

Chapter Eleven

THE WATTLED CRANE

(Bugeranus carunculatus)

Ardea carunculata, Gmelin, *Syst. Nat., 1,* Pt. 2, 1789, p. 643.
Type locality: Africa – Cape of Good Hope, *ex.* Latham.
Vernacular names: The Wattled Crane (English); der Glocken-Kranich, Klunkerkranich (German); la Grue caronculée (French); The Caffree Crane, Lelkraan (South Africans); i-Quqolo, i-Gwampi (Xhosa); Mothlathomo (Sotho, Sesuto); Makalanga (Zambian at Lake Benguela); Hooka zuru (Japanese).

The Wattled Crane is a bird of the wilderness but in some regions is quite conspicuous in farming regions. It, like most other cranes, is a bird of the great open spaces, except in Zambia where, even there, it seldom is found near the forest regions. It is a rather good flier but, like most of the larger cranes often walks where smaller cranes might take to the air. It must consume hundreds of grasshoppers, other insects, and at times, grass and grain seeds in its relentless search for food. It, like other long-billed cranes, often digs in the soil for food as well as procuring it from above ground.

This large, slow, deliberate crane is found in certain widely separated African regions. I saw my first one in Southern Rhodesia in the vicinity of Rainham Dam, Salisbury, but it remained only a few minutes, then vanished. In Natal, South Africa, in early December 1961, I found a flock of non-breeding birds near Nottingham Road; later, a few widely separated pairs right up to the base of the foothills of the Drakensberg Mountains. None was found in the foothills nor in the bergveld. Like the Crowned Cranes they remain at slightly lower altitudes but are not found in the really low-lying regions along the Indian Ocean. Since the bird most often nests during the winter months, I was fearful I would not see one of their nests. On December 21, as I drove along a small branch of the Hlatikulu River, I noted a lone Wattled Crane feeding in a pasture sloping up from this stream, which was

Adult Wattled Crane at Lochinvar Ranch, Monze, Zambia, January 21, 1962.

bordered by a nice marsh. As the car stopped, the bird moved farther back from the highway; simultaneously a white head came up quickly above the hip-high vegetation along the stream. This crane moved deliberately to the opposite side, joined the second bird and slowly paced back and forth across the shallower marsh in that region.

I entered the marsh and found their nest with its one egg. It was built well above the surrounding water, which under heavy rains must have run all around the nest. It was hollowed on top and well packed down by the heavy birds. Once the male spread his wings in a distraction display, the female walking, half-crouched, beside and behind him. Suddenly he jumped into the air, whirling as he did so, then dropped back to the ground. After two or three of these dances he joined his mate and both birds, half-crouched, paced deliberately back and forth without making a sound. These birds would not tolerate photography, so after one attempt I did not disturb them any further. They hatched their single egg late in January after I had left the region (according to William Barnes).

In Zambia, at Lochinvar Ranch, pairs and families of this species were prevalant. This region is really their stronghold. During a ten-mile hike from the ranch to the Kafue River we counted thirty-three, while returning, twenty-two. Three pairs had feathered-headed youngsters which could fly. In the same vicinity we counted fourteen Crowned Cranes on the way out and seven on return. In addition, a tame pair greeted us when we arrived at ranch headquarters. The region between Zambia and Ethiopia appears to be devoid of Wattled Cranes, but in the highlands of central Ethiopia the species is quite abundant, roaming the extensive wet meadows, roosting and nesting in the equally extensive marshes. We found the species near Tefki, southwest of Addis Ababa, where large flocks were feeding near the road, not too far from the local villages. We found fewer birds north of Addis Ababa, and they gradually diminished as we neared Lake Tana, so that none were to be found in that vicinity.

PRENESTING BEHAVIOR

Since the Wattled Crane has such a widespread distribution, the nesting season is spread throughout most of the year. Some birds are nesting; others are in the pre-nesting cycle. Still others show no signs of nesting and some may be roaming around with nearly full-grown chicks. In Ethiopia, Emil K. Urban and I found all Wattled Cranes in small flocks, rarely in pairs, in late August 1965. They roosted in a large marsh near Tefki, flew shortly after daylight to a nearby damp meadow, fed there for hours in groups of two to ten or eleven. During January 1962, Rudyerd Boulton and I found this species at Lochinvar Ranch, also in pairs, a few of which had nearly full-grown chicks that could fly. They still showed territorial behavior, the mates roaming side by side, separated from adjoining pairs by one to two kilometers.

In Rhodesia, Boulton found a nest in April 1961. During December 1961 a pair of Crowned Cranes took over the territory, even using the same nest, and although I observed a single Wattled Crane here one day, it remained only a few minutes and was not seen again for some time. In Natal, South Africa, during December 1961, several birds were paired on territory, only one pair with eggs. Yet, simultaneously, ten birds roosted in the nearby pond, grouped separately from the Stanley and Crowned Cranes. This pond was several miles from the territorial marshes of all three nesting species. These non-breeding individuals roosted some ten to forty meters from the others and often fed about the same distance apart, but sometimes much closer.

When nesting time arrived the birds moved onto their territories and proceeded to maintain complete control over all cranes, chiefly because they were larger and stronger.

West (1963) wrote: "In contrast to the records of non-breeding birds congregating socially in flocks, the record from Grasslands (Rhodesia) shows that although the locality surrounding the nesting site occupied by the breeding pair was visited occasionally by strange cranes, these visits usually gave rise to fighting and ended in the departure of the visitors; the breeding pair remained in sole possession of the whole vlei. In this connection the records for 1956 are the most important and they are as follows:

"16 April: After a period of absence two cranes were seen on the vlei.

"17 April: Two birds present.

"18 April: Four birds present.

"19 April: Three birds.

"20 April: Three birds on the vlei. At 10 A.M. two were fighting while the other stood by. Eventually one of the fighting birds gave in and flew off. The victor flew after it, seeing it off. The victor, after pursuing the vanquished for about 200 yards, emitted a hoarse croak, and returned to the third bird still waiting on the ground, while the bird that had been seen off, pitched some hundreds of yards further up the vlei and remained where it had landed. In the afternoon only one bird was on the vlei (the vanquished?).

"21 April: In the early morning only one bird. A pair (the victor?) arrived at about 11 A.M. In the afternoon the third bird had gone and the vlei was occupied by the pair.

"22 April: The two cranes on the vlei remained near the clover beds all morning. At 12:30 P.M. they were dancing. In this dance one of the two was much more active than the other. Both participated, the one very actively, the other in a more restrained fashion. Dancing they assumed a weird heraldic attitude, wings held high, beak open and legs often right off the ground. In the evening at 5:30 both birds were at the old nesting site.

"23 April: In the morning a third bird came again, which was chased off by one of the pair. In the afternoon the paired birds had left. No birds on the vlei. They were not seen again until the afternoon of the 28th, when at 4 P.M. a pair was seen at the clover beds. At 5 P.M. they had gone.

"29 April: At 4 P.M. two birds were seen at the nesting site. One crouching and apparently stacking bits of grass. At 6 P.M. both birds were at the clover beds.

"30 April: At 7 A.M. no birds on the vlei, not seen again until

"9 May: One pair present on the vlei."

From then until May 15 the pair was there only a day now and then. On May 15, 16 and 17 one bird was observed for short periods of time. On May 20 and 21 both birds were at the nesting site, one sitting, and the first egg was observed May 22.

BREEDING

Nesting habitat. Open grass and sedge marshes

bordered with drier flat or sloping grassland meadows, with vegetation usually knee- to shoulder-high, water up to one meter deep, form ideal nesting regions for this species. Most often the surrounding meadows are pastured by cattle or some form of wildlife, so that vegetation is only a few centimeters high. Where the Wattled and Crowned Cranes use the same marshes, the former nests during the cold dry season, the latter during the wet summer period. But I did find one region where a pair of Wattled Cranes was on eggs simultaneously with two Crowned Crane pairs on adjacent territories.

In the Tefki Marsh, thirty kilometers southwest of Addis Ababa, Ethiopia, some vegetation consisted of species of *Cyperus* (4 sp.), *Eleocharis* (1 sp.), *Scirpus* (1 sp.), *Setaria* (1 sp.), *Cynodon* (1 sp), along with some legumes and rosaceous plants which were scattered throughout the marsh.

At Lochinvar Ranch, Kafue River region, Zambia, the vegetation included *Panicum, Sporobolis, Chloris, Eragrostis, Hyporrhinia, Setaria, Brachiaria, Digitoria* and *Echinochloa*. Some trees along the border included *Acacia sieberiana* (Walkinshaw, 1965).

West (1963) described plants from Wattled Crane marshes at Marandellas, Rhodesia, as grasses (*Leersia hexandra*) and sedges (*Eleocharis, Cyperus* and *Juncus*). *Cyperus* and *Juncus* are also found in marshes at Rainham Dam, Salisbury, Rhodesia.

In Natal, South Africa, nearby sedges consisted of *Cyperus denudatus, C. fastigiatus, Scirpus inclinatus, Pycreus unioloides, Pycreus oakfortnesis, Ascolepsis capensis* and *Carex* sp., while grasses were *Pennisetum thunbergii, Andropogon appendiculatus* and *Miscanthidium* (sp.).

All nesting regions were covered with shallow water maintained by sufficient rainfall, while usually a small stream passed through the region.

Nest and Nest Site. One of the first known Wattled Crane's nests, described by Graham Hutchinson, was found on a tributary of the Mooi River, Natal. Built on top of a large submerged rock in the middle of a running stream, it since has proven rather atypical. Most nests are large piles of grasses, sedges—anything close by—pulled up by the birds' bills, tossed into a haphazard heap over which the birds walk many times, packed down so that eventually they become much neater and strong enough to hold the birds' weight. Some are placed on natural mounds, knobs, old spur-winged geese nests, while many are built entirely by the birds themselves.

On December 21, 1961, I found a nest twenty miles west of Rosetta, Natal, along a tributary of the Hlatikulu River. Built by the birds in the deepest portion of a long narrow treeless marsh, it was flat-topped and consisted of dead grasses, sedges and other nearby plants, all pulled in from the region from as far as four meters away so that the immediate nest region appeared almost devoid of vegetation. Much of the sedge was almost shoulder-high, while a pastured vlei covered with grass extended for about one kilometer on one side; long sloping meadows extended back to the Drakensberg foothills on another; the marsh was on a third side and a small meadow between the marsh and the highway on the fourth. The nest measured 136 by 139 centimeters across at the water's edge and was thirteen centimeters above the water, which was twenty-six centimeters deep. The marsh elevation was 1,827 m (6,000 ft.).

David Adler (letter, September 1954) reported three nests directly west of Pietermaritzburg, Natal, from 1952 to 1954, where only one pair of birds was resident. They built on a small marshy mound one summer, then a few meters from it during the second and third.

A. W. Vincent (1945) described two nests in (Southern) Rhodesia built in open treeless pools near small running streams, behind which broad strips of rough grasslands sloped gradually up to soft woodlands. The nests were quite in the open, but rather isolated. One nest was placed in thirty centimeters of water, protruding fifteen centimeters above the surface. It was a solid circular mound of water-weeds, rushes, dry grass and bits of reed blades, 122 centimeters in diameter, almost flat-topped, with the slightest hollow in the center for the eggs. The second nest was merely a natural hollow on an islet, lined with a little dry grass. The islet was only a little larger than the nest.

West (1963) described six nests at Grasslands Research Station near Marandellas (18° 11'S.; 31° 33'E.), Rhodesia. A 1954 nest was placed in the "Big Vlei" below the Mess Block, and the birds

Nesting pair of Wattled Cranes, partly distraction display, 20 miles west of Rosetta, Natal, South Africa, December 21, 1961.

lived in the vlei most of the year. The 1955 nest was in a marshy patch at the bottom of the vlei. This new nest consisted of a great mass of grass and sedge piled into a platform about 183 centimeters across, in standing water about 61 centimeters deep. The vegetation had been trampled down or pulled close to the nest, but beyond this, dense grass (*Leersia hexandra*) and sedges (*Eleocharis variegata, Cyperus* [sp.], and *Juncus oxycarpus*) were prominent. Immediately behind this, eleven meters away, was an old nest platform. The new nest had two eggs on June 15 and one chick on June 19, which disappeared August 21. On September 2 the parents were crouching and digging at the nest. On September 24 the same pair (presumably) had a new nest 200 meters from the old one. It was placed on a submerged islet, completely surrounded by fairly deep water. This nest was surrounded by *Leersia hexandra* grass. On October 26 a single young hatched from one of two eggs; he swam across on October 28 and disappeared on November 10.

Near the first 1955 nesting site they again built a large nest in May 1956. On May 20 at 10:30 A.M., the bird was first observed setting. Although there were still two eggs June 26, there was only one chick by June 28 at 2:50 P.M. This flightless chick, observed on October 8, could not be found on October 10.

The pair used the first 1955 nest again in 1957, having two eggs on May 19 and a newly-hatched chick in early June, which began flying October 9. He remained with the parents at least until April 26, 1958, when all three disappeared.

The birds were setting on the same nest May 19, 1958. One chick hatched June 27 and was flying with the parents on November 21. The entire region and marsh were very dry in 1959. The birds built three nests at the edge of the remaining water, abandoned them for new sites, but produced no eggs. During an even drier year, 1960, the birds, although present, did not even attempt to nest, nor did they in 1961. During 1962 they moved to another site.

Hulett (1953) described a nest at Himeville, Natal, South Africa, as "... a trampled grassy mound some nine inches above water level ... all round, rushes and grasses had been stripped to leave a protecting expanse of water."

Benson (1960) reported that in Zambia eggs were laid on mounds of vegetation in shallow pans of water. A nest described by W. Krienze (So. Rhodesia Nest File Card) was a hugh pile of dry grass, bulrushes, reeds, etc., with an almost flat top, measuring 76.2 x 108 centimeters across. The nest found by Rudyerd Boulton in April 1961 at Rainham Dam, Salisbury, Rhodesia, was a pile of *Scirpus* sp., *Juncus* sp., etc., and was definitely the same nest used the next December by a pair of Crowned Cranes. (I found the latter nest in December and later showed it to Boulton, who said the Wattled Crane had nested there in April. We could find no other mound in the vicinity.) The nest in January 1962 measured 81.3 x 85.4 centimeters on the day the young Crowned Cranes hatched, and was located in twelve centimeters of standing water, while the top was fifteen centimeters above the water surface.

Belcher (1927) described a nest on the Vipya Plateau, Malawi, from the high uplands (5,000 feet) in a belt of short-grass country dotted with forest clumps. A small stream flowed into the center of a pond dotted here and there with long reedy grass, adjacent to a circular pool, perhaps ten meters across, in which stood a small islet some two meters across. In the center of the islet a mere handful of flattened grass had been placed, and on it rested a single large spotted egg.

Cooper (1969) described a Rainham Dam, Salisbury, Rhodesia nest 97 x 115 cm across, 5 cm thick, and constructed of uprooted *Scirpus muricinux* and some grass (*Echinochloe* sp.).

THE EGGS

Eggs are ovate, long ovate or subelliptical in shape, usually without much gloss. They have a few nodules at times on both ends, a ground color of olive-buff, deep cream, reddish-fawn or dirty bluish-white, and are spotted, at times heavily, with reddish-brown, yellowish-brown and other shades of brown, buff or pale mauve, sometimes with some larger chocolate-colored spots.

Forty-eight eggs averaged in measurement: 102.4 ± 12.8 x 65.3 ± 6.36 mm (standard deviation given). The actual average of fifty-five eggs was 101.9 x 65.3 mm. Sixteen eggs from one-egg sets averaged 103.5 x 66.4 mm, while eighteen eggs from two-egg sets averaged 101.3 x 64.6 mm. The largest egg measured 116.5 x 68.5 mm. One egg measured 106 x 71.5 mm, while the smallest measured 91.0 x 60.9 mm and 95.2 x 59.6 mm (the last two from the same set). One fresh egg, December 21, 1961 (near Rosetta, Natal, South Africa), weighed 265.3 grams and measured 102.0 x 68.4 mm. Cooper (1969) gave for two eggs from Rhodesia (Rainham Dam), 112.7 x 65.7 mm; weight, 251.2 grams and 102.9 x 62.8 mm; weight, 215.8 grams.

Eggs have been observed every month of the year. The majority of egg dates occurs between May and August, with another fairly large group in October. Of 90 recorded sets 55 contained two eggs, and 35, one egg. Egg records by month for Zambia, Rhodesia, Malawi and South Africa, were: January, 3; February, 4; March, 2; April, 4; May, 16; June, 17; July, 14; August, 12; September, 2; October, 7; November, 3; December, 6.

At Himesville, Natal, Mr. Turner watched a pair of cranes building a nest from January 1-3, 1963. There was one egg on January 5 and 6, and two on January 7, indicating a two-day interval between the laying of two eggs.

Incubation. According to West (1963) both birds remained near the nest during the first week of incubation and sat very close, never leaving the eggs uncovered. From about the seventh day the parent not engaged in setting began foraging further afield, and was often found several hundred yards to a quarter of a mile from the nest, usually on the drier portion of the vlei where the cover was dominated by *Hyparrhenia filipendula.* From about the eighteenth day, both birds occasionally were away from the nest simultaneously. At hatching time, however, both birds concentrated on the nest again, and after the chick hatched the pair attended it very closely.

West wrote: "In 1956, incubation began as nearly as could be observed on Sunday 20 May. Both birds kept together near the nesting site, one sitting and the other feeding or preening near by, until 26

Wattled Crane chick and egg, Dartmoor Forestry Reserve, Natal, South Africa, September 2, 1963. **Photograph by William Barnes.**

May. On that day one of the pair was noticed for the first time to have left the immediate vicinity of the nest and to be feeding by itself near the clover beds, several hundred yards away from the nest but still on the vlei. Later . . . about a mile downstream, one of the two flew down over the dam and then back to the nest. In the evening both birds were at the nest, the one sitting, the other standing nearby. On 6 June in the early morning one was sitting, the other standing nearby. After breakfast there was only one bird at the nest, standing or sitting; at 10:30 A.M., one bird sitting; at 12:15 P.M. one sitting, the other near the nest. After my car had passed both flew off and fed in the vlei leaving the nest unattended, one returned 10 to 15 minutes later and sat. In the afternoon one was sitting while the other fed out on the vlei. In the evening one was sitting, the other nowhere to be seen.

"On 15 June I noted that both birds were quite frequently off the nest together, though the two were always together at the nest in the early morning.

"On 27 June, I noted that the birds were sitting closely again. I did not approach the nest. On 28 June at 2:50 P.M. I saw a chick in the nest with one unhatched egg."

The behavior of this pair at the nest in Marandellas, Rhodesia was quite similar to one I watched in Natal, South Africa.

West noted the birds changed places at the nest June 1, 1958 (fourteenth day of incubation) at 8:40 and 10:55 A.M. while he watched from 8:00

to 11:25 A.M. On May 31, 1958, at the same nest (2:15-4:17 P.M.), they changed places once at 2:58 P.M. One bird sat, the other stood nearby preening or was away feeding. They showed concern if someone passed near the nest and the sitting bird often rose, stood and preened, until the person or persons passed by.

At a two-day watch at the Natal, South Africa, nest, I found that the larger bird (the male) incubated at night. On December 22, 1961, he incubated a single egg less than one week old throughout the night until 6:15 A.M., again between 10:34 A.M. and 1:17 P.M. and between 4:36 and 5:28 P.M., when he rose and fed for a few minutes only ten to fifteen feet from the nest. He came right back and sat until dark. The female fed most of the daylight hours, incubating between 6:28 and 10:34 A.M., again from 1:17 to 4:36 P.M. The first change was between 6:15 and 6:28 A.M.; other changes came at 10:34 A.M., 1:17 and 4:36 P.M. On December 31, at the same nest, the male incubated until 6:08 A.M., from 1:27 until 3:58 and from 5:19 P.M. until dark. The female was there from 6:08 A.M. to 1:27 P.M. and from 4:10 to 5:19 P.M. Thus changes that day occurred at 6:08 A.M., 1:27, 3:58-4:10 (the male left twelve minutes before the female arrived), and at 5:19 P.M.

Four changes were made daily. The male daytime attentive periods averaged 157 (151-163) minutes; the female attentive periods, 238 (69-439) minutes. The average of six daytime attentive periods (both birds) was 211 minutes. The first morning incubation change averaged 6:12 A.M. (6:15, 6:08 A.M.) and the last evening change, 4:17 P.M. (4:36, 5:19 P.M.). During 1,552 minutes of observation, the two cranes incubated 1,473 minutes or 94.9 per cent of the time—546 daytime minutes (35 per cent) by the male, and 927 daytime minutes (59.5 per cent) by the female.

Although inconspicuous while they sat, if some disturbing factor became evident the conspicuous white head of the setting crane appeared above the surrounding vegetation. Occasionally the setting crane rose to work with nest or egg, or just stood and preened. If someone walked along the roadway nearby, the setting bird usually moved a few meters from the nest, then stopped and preened, returning to the nest as soon as the person passed by.

Sometimes the bird not incubating fed near the nest, but often it fed one or more kilometers away. When leaving, these Wattled Cranes walked away to feed seven times, but the eighth time a bird flew out into the neighboring field after walking thirty meters away. On returning they always walked to the nest, often stopping to preen and feed. Except once, when the birds called a goose-like *Kronk-kronk-kronk* in unison, they were silent when changing places. West (1963) observed that the birds usually walked from the nest, but on several occasions they did fly.

In the New York Zoological Park, incubation of eggs required thirty-six days (Crandall, 1945), but West (1963) gave two periods: forty and thirty-eight days. At the nest I found in Natal, South Africa, on December 21, 1961, the egg hatched either January 22 or 23, 1962 (William Barnes), thirty-two or thirty-three days after I found it.

THE YOUNG

West wrote (1963): "28 June, 1956. I visited the hide at 2:50 P.M. As I came into sight one of the birds flew from the nest out into the vlei. The sitting bird crouched and left the nest as I approached the hide, whereupon its mate, out in the vlei, flew back towards the nest. Both birds remained near the nest. They were agitated and walked about conspicuously. I saw a newly hatched chick on the nest with an unhatched egg. The chick scrambled off the nest and over water and weeds to about ten feet from the nest. I observed from the hide for about an hour. The parent birds returned very quickly and stood behind the chick without making any demonstration. They then began to retreat slowly into the taller vegetation away from the flattened area around the nest and away from the hide. The chick followed. After it entered the taller vegetation I could see it no longer. Then the parent birds acting together began to paddle a circle, lifting their feet high and plunging their beaks into the water after the manner of a Wood Ibis feeding. At intervals one of the birds would stand stand still and appeared to be feeding the chick, which I could not see. . . . As soon as we left, the birds returned to the nest and one was seen to be sitting within five minutes of our departure."

During the next three weeks the cranes kept the chick close to the nest, returning near evening to spend the night on the old nest with the chick. One bird always slept in the marsh nearby. During the day they favored a small seepage zone where several tiny streams came into the vlei. At first both parents stayed with the chick, but later one often fed away on the vlei.

West tried to locate this chick July 8 and 18, but it was too well hidden. On July 8 the parents flew to the opposite side of the marsh, picked up old dried maize leaves which they threw into the air with their bills, periodically dancing for some time. When West left, they returned to the chick and continued feeding with him.

On October 29, 1955, West searched for the newly hatched chick from that nest. This time the cranes walked awkwardly along the water's edge nearby. They became very perturbed when he went to where they had originally been, spreading their wings and screaming. Most often they spread their wings only, or did this and danced, but seldom did they call.

During the 1956 hatching, the chick was taken to the *Hyparrhenia* field for two days. After this they foraged over the entire vlei, one adult always near the chick, the other not too far away, but they returned at sundown, with the chick, to the old nest.

On September 15, when the chick was eighty days old, the parent hid it, now about about half as big as they, in the long grass. Then at 10:30 A.M. they went into the maize field 300 to 400 meters away to feed. When they were disturbed, they flew over the chick to the opposite side, and he walked to them.

The chick was brooded at the nest until 103 days old. As evening approached the family began feeding back toward the nest, arriving there about sundown. When encountering a nearby fence, the chick usually went under first, followed by the female. Finally, when the female and chick reached the nest neighborhood, the male flew to a nearby spot where he spent the night. The female brooded the chick.

Wattled Crane male in distraction display near nest, along Hlatikulu River, Natal, South Africa, December 21, 1961.

West wrote (1963) that during the first five or six days, he could go to the spot where the parents had been feeding and here find the chick by its 'chirruping,' but thereafter it was very hard to locate because it lay very quiet and did not move. It could swim almost immediately after hatching.

Adults seldom go far from the nest or young when a human visits them. They walk back and forth nearby, sometimes dancing, less often protesting by calling. But often they show much agitation. Sometimes they pick up clods of dirt or pieces of vegetation to throw into the air. They always remain in the neighborhood. But when the chick becomes older, the parents often walk swiftly away when they see someone approaching, hide the chick in tall vegetation if available, then leave it while they either fly or walk some distance. If surprised, the chick will get up and run away.

West (1963) reported the 1956 chick was unable to fly when ninety days old, although it stretched its wings and tried to get off the ground. This chick, apparently still unable to fly, disappeared when 103 days of age. The 1957 chick was flying on October 9 when 131 days old; the 1958 chick could not fly at 100 days, but could fly well at 148 days.

The 1957 chick remained with the parents within the breeding region from the time of hatching in early June until at least February 19, when all three birds disappeared from the vlei. The three appeared on the vlei again on March 14, remaining until April 21, 1958, and were not seen again until May 16, when eight birds reappeared, but two (obviously the pair), remained apart from the others. By May 19, 1958 they were again on eggs.

West (1963) also wrote of five hatched chicks from five different nests that only two survived until they could fly. During 1955, when the chick disappeared at sixty-four days of age, the birds renested thirty-five days later and had a new chick in thirty-two days which disappeared in about two weeks (November 10). After this, the birds did not nest until the following May 20.

Guy Hardingham (letter, January 25, 1963) wrote that during fourteen years he observed twenty Wattled Crane nests at Himeville, Natal, but only two young were reared until they could fly. Here the parents led the chicks onto fields bordering marshes, walking several miles a day until the youngster was almost full grown, yet unable to fly. At this stage natives often captured them for food. He observed parents drive a full-grown flying chick away on December 15, 1962, just prior to their new nesting.

At Lochinvar Ranch, Monze, Zambia, three pairs I observed had flying young, all with feathered heads. One day we observed twelve groups of two, six of three, and three of four, indicating that at times, under favorable conditions, two young are reared.

FLOCKING

Many species of cranes flock, especially when too young to breed or when none of the birds is nesting. West (1963) described flocks of fifty-two on 20 September, 1950 up to sixty-three on December 2, which disappeared during mid-December, through January and February 1951. Thereafter, from March until the following December, he observed flocks of varying sizes, from six to eighty-two individuals. Probably Wattled Cranes, like other cranes, do not breed until four years old and possibly even much later, while all pairs may not nest each year. These birds constitute the non-breeding flocks roaming through favorable African regions.

Urban and I found flocks ranging from two to forty-three individuals, near Tefki, Shoa Province, Ethiopia (8,169 feet) between August 23 and October 10, and others (Urban and Walkinshaw, 1967) saw groups of up to sixty-three on October 30 and seventeen on November 2, 1965. We noted pairs or groups of three in Gojjam Province, between 8,500 and 9,000 feet at Cima, north of Dejem and found no birds below 7,000 feet. I also found a flock of ten Wattled Cranes (where they are scarcer) at Nottingham Road, Natal, South Africa, and on several occasions in December 1961.

Yet in January 1962 most cranes in Zambia were in family groups of two to four.

VOICE

West described (1963) the call of the downy chick as a thin, piping chirrup. Probably it resembles the chickenlike peep with a cranelike burr to it. These calls vary little, except acquiring a little more burr, until most cranes are ten to twelve months of age. Probably Wattled Cranes do not acquire the adult call until they are over one year old.

Adult Wattled Cranes are extremely quiet compared to other cranes. The only call I heard was a gooselike *Kronk*. Mackworth-Praed and Grant (1952) reported it as a grating but rather bell-like *Kronk*, with occasional low-voiced jabberings when in a group. They seldom repeat the call over and over, but just give the one syllable. Once I heard a pair repeat the *Kronk* three times rapidly when changing places at the nest. Once a bird uttered a shrill *Kah-eee— — — kah-eee*. When reassuring each other at the nest or the chick as they wander, they often give a guttural *Purrr* similar to that of other cranes.

During my field experiences with the Wattled Crane in Africa (including Ethiopia, Zambia, Rhodesia, and Natal, South Africa), I had heard this bird vocalize only about three times. On a visit to Busch Gardens, Tampa, Florida in December 1969, I noted they had about nine in their life displays, the largest number anywhere in the world. I wrote their veterinarian to ask if it were possible to take some of the definite pairs to some nearby ranch where they might be given some freedom and induced to nest. He wrote that this was impossible. In correspondence I also asked him if he had ever heard the birds call and he wrote me he never had. About that time George Archibald was beginning his doctoral work at Cornell University and obtained a pair of these same cranes from Busch Gardens on loan. Archibald slept very close to the crane pens. In September 1971 he separated the birds (a pair). For four days nothing happened. Then they began giving extensive flight intention calls and paced about as though they intended to take flight. The next morning at about 3 A.M. he bounced out of bed because of a terrific screaming nearby. It was *Bugeranus carunculatus*. It was a uniform unbroken scream. The female instigated the call and was followed a microsecond later by the male, who was not in visual contact by his mate. He sent me these calls on tape and they differ from those of any other crane. They are terrific in intensity—very high pitched—and if one listens carefully he can detect a cranelike rhythm to them.

FOOD

A strong vegetarian and insect eater, this bird digs for hours in the soil, using its long bill to extract tubers, insects and the like. It eats grasshoppers, crickets and other insects, snakes or frogs when available. In South Africa it eats wheat and mealies at times and some grass seeds, but not as much as the other two South African cranes. It wanders on foot through its feeding territory, gleaning visible materials, often for many hours. It apparently is not abundant enough to damage crops greatly in most regions, and in many areas is certainly beneficial to the ecology.

DISTRIBUTION

The Wattled Crane is a resident of central (somewhat southwestern) Ethiopia, eastern Congo, Zambia, Rhodesia, Benguela, Malawi, Bechuanaland Protectorate, Tanzania, southwestern South Africa, Southern Angola, and possibly the Somali Republic.

SOMALI REPUBLIC. Roberts (1951) reported the Wattled Crane here (there apparently are no records from Uganda and Kenya).

ETHIOPIA. Mackworth-Praed and Grant (1952) wrote that this species breeds here from May to August. Cheeseman and Sclater (1935) found a nest (two eggs) August 21, 1928 at Dangila, Gojjam Province at 7,000 feet (2,134 m). They saw forty individuals between May 19, 1929 and May 25, 1930 at Wahasa Abo, Gojjam Province at 8,340 feet (2,542 m). Guichard (1950) observed scattered flocks at Tefki Marsh, Shoa Province (8,169 feet) from July to October, while Urban and I (1967) found the species but no nest here August 23, 1965 (19); August 24 (16); August 25 (19); August 29 (20); and Urban saw forty-three on September 29 and fifty-eight on October 10, 1965.

Dr. E. Gilbert and Miss P. Allen saw sixty-three here on October 30 and seventeen on November 2, 1965. In the Haile Selassie I University Natural History Museum there are two male specimens: One was taken January 14, 1940 at Tefki, Shoa Province—the second, at Arussi Province, Tiggio on January 20, 1940.

Of three specimens in the British Museum (Natural History), one was recorded from Ethiopia without data, the other two from Jimma: a male, May 22, 1905 and a female, May 23, 1905. Toschi (1959) observed thirty individuals between Bocoggi and Bonga (in Arussi, Shoa or Kaffa Province?) in March 1941. Moltoni and Ruscone (1944) recorded the species at Wahasa Abo and Dangila (Gojjam Province), Lake Abiata (Shoa Province) and Lake Chamo (Gemu Gofa Province). Mr. L. Brown (personal communication) observed two adults and a half-grown young at Adoba, Bale Provice at 11,700 feet (3,566 m) between November 26 and December 1, 1963. He also found Wattled Cranes from 9,500 to 10,000 feet between Wondo and Adola, Sidamo Province, and in early February 1964, a pair between Debros Marcos and Dangila, Gojjam Province. In February 1966 he observed seven Wattled Cranes thirty to thirty-five kilometers southeast of Adoba, Bale Province: February 14 (1); February 18 (3); February 19 (2); February 21 (1)—all between 11,000 and 12,000 feet. Urban and I (1967) observed the species in Gojjam Province between 8,500 and 9,000 feet: one kilometer north of Cima, August 25, 1965, two groups of three; August 28, one group of three; and sixteen kilometers north of Dejam, two on August 25. We did not find this bird north of here near Bahar Dar and Lak Tana where Crowned Cranes were abundant.

CONGO. Blaauw (1897) recorded the species from Banana (there are apparently no recent records from this region). Chapin (1939) wrote there are specimens from Nieuwdorp in the upper Katanga, from Kinda in the Lulua District, Elisabethville; from Malambwe and sixty-five kilometers northeast of the Mwati River. He also reported birds from Banda, western Kasai and from Kindu on the Lualaba.

TANZANIA. Shelley (1899) reported a specimen and Jackson (1938) reported this species occurred at Burungi and Uhehe.

ZAMBIA. At Abercorn (8½° S.; 31¼° E.) a chick hatched March 2, 1959 (West). In the Balovale District (13° S.; 23° E.) it is sparingly distributed (White, 1945). In the Lake Bangweula District (12° S.; 30° E.), Neave (1910) wrote it was not uncommon, with five birds observed at times. Pitman (1935) records a nest (one egg) October 1, 1934, while Brelsford (1947) counted two hundred one morning. The largest concentration was south of Chafye Island and on Itili Plain.

It was recorded at Boma by Clay (1953); at Busango Swamp as "plentiful" (Benson and White, 1957); on Western Plateau, Isoka District (Clay, 1953); and in the Chambezi River Valley at 4,000 feet (1,219 m) two specimens, male and female, were taken April 19, 1905 (Neave, 1910).

At Kafue National Park, Kafue Flats, Kasempa Section (15° S.; 26° E.), Benson and Pitman (1959) wrote that Ansell found a downy chick and one large one on November 10, 1955 and another downy chick August 15, 1957. Benson and White (1957) wrote "Plentiful and a set (two eggs) just hatched found in June by Carr." Benson (1960 and letter, February 19, 1963) added for Kafue National Park: "1958: 2 eggs hatching, 27 June (Mitchell); two sets (both 2 eggs), 22 August (Uys); 28 September (2 eggs), Grimwood.

"1959: 15 May, 3 July, 26 July, 20 August nests with 1 egg, the last hatching and 2 eggs 30 July and 4 August in different nests.

Wattled Crane pair at nest site, Dartmoor Forestry Reserve, Natal, South Africa. Photograph by William Barnes.

"1960: 1 egg, 20 June (collected; could have been 2); 2 eggs, 30 May, 2 July (the last hatching) (For this same period young less than 1 week old were found 5 July, 7 and 18 August (2 places), and 18 September.).

"1961: 1 egg, 18 December.

"1962: 1 egg, 5 July. Others with 2 eggs, 8 June, 18 June, 6 August, 19 August, 26 August (the 6 August nest had only one egg hatch, about 20 August.)."

On June 13, 1951, Ansell found a downy chick in a nest in the Kasempa sector and on June 9, 1957, Uys found a large chick near the Musa River. Carr and Uys found a nest with two eggs at Ngoma, May 4, 1958 (Benson and Pitman, 1959).

There are three specimens in the British Museum (Natural History)—two taken in the Chambezi Valley April 19, 1908 (male and female), the other marked simply "Zambia."

At Kasha Dambo, J. Shenton took a two-egg set June 20, 1960 (BMNH), while at Lochinvar Ranch, Kafue River sector (16° S; 27½° E.) R. Boulton and I observed fifty-two (1 X 1; 12 X 2; 5 X 3; 3 X 4) Wattled Cranes January 22, 1962. Three pairs had full-grown flying young which still had feathered heads.

Thirty miles east of Lusaka (15° S.; 29° E.) Mrs. Critchley (Benson and White, 1957) found a nest (two eggs) November 4 and observed the bird at Nyika. Groups of four to ten were observed at Mwinilunga (White, 1945).

RHODESIA (SOUTHERN). At Beatrice, two nests (both two eggs) were found by W. Krienke May 25, 1932 and July 16, 1932 (SRNFC). At Kingswood Farm, Darwendale, A. D. Gosling found two-egg nests May 23, 1954, June 21, 1954 and July 11, 1955 and a one-egg nest September 12, 1954 (SRNFC). At Dett, a pair raised one young during 1959 and another pair was observed with one young September 2, 1960, by Mrs. H. R. Gillett (SRNFC). She also observed one young September 21, 1960 at Gokwe, Dandande Pan (18° S., 29° E.) and at Cewali Pan, a one-egg nest in which the egg hatched July 31, 1961 (R. Brooke, letter, May 13, 1963).

On the Rhodes Estate, Inyanga (el. 6,000 ft.), Purdon found a nest (one egg) October 2, 1935 (Salisbury Museum), while Rankine found a nest (one egg) at Nyamarora Reserve, April 10, 1956 (SRNFC). K. W. Grenhow found a nest (one egg) on the Duru River October 14, 1953. Mrs. D. Wheeler found one-egg nests January 8, 1962, December 28, 1961-January 3, 1962 and saw one chick in gray-fluff with its parents, along the Haerizi River in January 1962 (R. K. Brooke, letter, March 14, 1963).

At Shiota Pans, Marandellas, a nest (two eggs) was found October 5, 1930 by C. D. Priest (SRNFC), while at Shiota Reserve a nest (two eggs) was found May 15, 1960 (R. K. Brooke, loc. cit.). At Marandellas, the Grassland Research Station (18° 11′S.; 31° 33′E.) West (1963) reported a nest during 1954 and several two-egg nests (one from which a chick hatched June 15, 1955 [chick died]) and October 10, 1955, May 30, 1956, May 19, 1957 and May 19, 1958, while a nest was built but not used in 1959 and no nests were built during the drier years of 1961 and 1962. A two-egg nest was also found here by B. V. Neuby-Varty on June 12, 1956 (SRNFC).

At Salisbury (17° 30′S.; 31° 30′E.) on the Nyarakuru Farm, a nest (one egg) was found June 12, 1957 by R. K. Brooke and C. J. Vernon (SRNFC), while R. Boulton found nests at Rainham Dam April 12, 1962 (one egg) and October 12, 1961 (contents ?) (Letters, April and October 20, 1961).

Brooke and Tarboton (1964) reported two birds at Sinoia (17° 17′S.; 30° 07′E.) in December 1961. At Umvuma (19° S.; 31° E.) A. W. Vincent (1945) observed one one-third grown chick July 19, 1938, another half-grown August 28, 1937 and found nests (both two eggs) August 17, 1940 and July 15, 1941. A male specimen was taken at Chirinda, May 23, 1899 (BMNH). At Rubenheimer's Farm (locality ?) a one-egg nest was found by K. W. Grenhow on August 3, 1951 (SRNFC-Southern Rhodesia Nest File Cards).

ANGOLA. Benguela Layard wrote (1875): "Common in the interior of Benguela and procured near Humbe on the Cunene River," while Bocage (1881) and Blaauw (1897) listed the species from here. Traylor (1963) recorded it as widespread in the south, north to Cuanza Sul and southern Lunda, but not found on the coast. Downy chicks were taken in August and nearly-grown sub-adults

September 14, 1931 and July 11, 1934 at Andula, Chitau, District Bihe (CNHM).

MALAWI. Benson (1940, 1942, 1953) and Belcher (1927, 1950) have the following localities between 1,252 and 2,333 meters where Wattled Cranes occurred: Bembeke, Chitara, Edingeni, Lake Nderendere, Lake Kasuni, Nyika Plateau, South Rukuru, Vipya Plateau and Zomba, and below 611 meters at Chirome, Chilwa and lower Songwe. Apparently they do not breed in the latter regions. Belcher (1950) listed two-egg nests from Chitara May 29, June 21 and July 17, 1945 and on the Vipya Plateau (one egg) in 1926. There are two specimens, male and female, taken on Shirwa Plain in October 1895 (BMNH), while another adult male was taken at North Angioland, Lake Kazuni, September 18, 1906.

BECHUANALAND PROTECTORATE. West (1963) listed the species from Chobe, Seroddela and at Makarakari Pan. Traylor (1965) reported it widespread in Kalabo, common on Liuwa Plain and that others had seen the species in Ngamiland. Smithers (1964) recorded it from Linyanti, Okavango, Lake Ngami and Lake Dow. Three specimens have been taken on the Mochabe River (19° 59′S.; 23° 25′E.). One was taken May 21, 1930 (adult female, Transvaal Museum), an adult female and an immature male (CNHM), June 1, 1930.

SOUTHWEST AFRICA. Andersson (Blaauw, 1897) recorded this species from Damaraland on the rivers Okavango, Tioge and Drongo, and Lake Ngami (some of which fall in Bechuanaland). Winterbottom (1965) also listed the species here.

MOZAMBIQUE. Haagner (1948) listed the species from the Beira marshes and tandos (open spaces) and found it breeding at the mouth of the Sabi River south of Sofalo. There is a specimen, probably from Mozambique, (BMNH) from Chinde.

SOUTH AFRICA. *Cape Province.* The Wattled Crane has always been rare in the Cape region. Latham (1785), who first described the species, declared it was rare at the Cape of Good Hope, while more recently Hewitt (1931) added it is now extremely rare. Stark and Sclater (1906) gave records from Somerset West in the Stellenbosch division, Caledon, Cradock and East London. Hewitt (1931) added Lusikisiki, Sterkstroom, Kabusi and Matatiele.

At Amanzi, Uitenhage District, Niven and Niven (1966) gave one record only: two birds in 1935. Courtenay-Latimer (1964) gave only one record at East London, May 22, 1929 (R. Godfrey), while Skead (1964) recorded four birds on December 9, 1955 at King William's Town District. Two were reported at Blauwfontein, Swartberg District, September 20, 1957 by Shephard (1962) and Winterbottom (1962) added they had been reported in the Worcester District.

Natal. There are three specimens labeled Natal (BMNH, 1; Pietermaritzburg Museum, 2) as well as one in the Transvaal Museum, Pretoria (a female) taken July 28, 1919 at Karkloof, and another female taken on the Symons farm, Mooi River (Durban Museum).

The species is more common here, especially amongst the vleis (elevations 1,524 to 1,829 m), immediately below the low berg regions. The following breeding records give some idea as to its abundance:

Dartmoor Forestry Reserve—A nest (two eggs) was found August 5, 1963, from which one chick hatched September 2 (William Barnes, letter, June 21, 1964); another nest (two eggs) was found August 24, 1965 (SANFC)

Greytown, near the Karkloof Mountains—G. Jackson (SANFC) observed a nest (one egg) in June 1964.

Himeville (Underberg)—Guy Hardinham (letter, January 25, 1963) observed twenty Wattled Cranes' nests over a period of many years and during every season of the year. He wrote the birds preferred nesting when the grass was just turning brown and that all nests contained either one or two eggs. Here at Himeville, P. Turner (SANFC) watched a Wattled Crane building a nest January 1-3, 1963. This nest contained one egg January 5, but at 10 A.M. January 7, a second was laid.

Hlatikulu River region (a tributary of the Mooi, about 28° S.; 29° E.)—I found a nest (one egg) December 21, 1961, which still contained one egg on January 8, 1962, but William Barnes (letter) found the egg hatched January 22 or 23. In the region between here, Mooi River and Nottingham Road, I observed fifty-five Wattled Cranes during 282 field hours in December 1961 and January 1962.

Howick, Sarsdon Hill—A two-egg nest (SANFC)

was found October 14, 1962 by N. H. S. Michaelhouse.

Mooi River, "Forleigh"—V. L. Pringle (SANFC) found a nest (two eggs) from which one egg hatched June 22, 1947, and a set of two eggs was taken here June 21, 1948 by R. G. Symons (G. Symons coll.) and another (two eggs) June 15, 1949 (Chas. Jerome coll.). At Hidcot a set (one egg) was taken May 2, 1904 (Sparrow, 1935) and there is an egg in the Pietermaritzburg Museum from here (date ?). Another set (one egg) was taken on the Upper Mooi River tributary (Hutchinson [in Stark and Sclater], 1906), while another set (one egg) was taken at Mooi River January 1, 1913 (Transvaal Museum, Pretoria).

Newcastle—There is a set (two eggs) taken here in 1895 (Pietermaritzburg Museum), while a set (one egg) was reported by Sparrow (1935) from Nodete.

Nottingham Road—Of two sets taken here, one was dated November 27, 1921 (one egg, B. Symons Coll.); the second (two eggs) was found by R. E. Berney (SANFC) March 26, 1922.

Pietermaritzburg, 64 km west—Here David Alder (letter to author) observed nests on his farm between 1948 and 1954. One nest (one egg) in December 1952 was a small mound in a marsh surrounded by beads. The young was fledged. On December 26, 1953 the birds used the same nest (one egg), but it was later destroyed by predators. On February 2, 1954 they had a new nest (two eggs) only a few feet away.

Tugula River—Dr. Slanger took a set (one egg) here (BMNH).

There are two sets (both one egg) taken in Natal by Thomas Ayres (BMNH) (Jourdain, 1935) and he described three sets taken from Natal: December 12, 1920 (one egg), February 11, 1922 (one egg) and February 12, 1922 (two eggs).

Weenen County—West, Wright and Symons (1964) reported Wattled Cranes at the Pasture Research Station, Tabamhlope Vlei from 1938 through April 1945, and they were observed with chicks in July 1939, October 1941, January 1942 and in 1943. They were also seen at Udine near Rietvlei December 7, 1942; at Orton's Dam, March 10, 1943; at Kamberg Nature Reserve where a nest (one egg) was found November 22, 1955 and from

which a chick was observed on March 11, 1956. They also reported the species nested at Southdowns.

ORANGE FREE STATE. At Harrismith a set (two eggs) was taken (Pietermaritzburg Museum) and van der Plaat (1961) reported the species from Harrismith and Kroonstad. Van Ee (letter) reported it as very rare in the Free State.

TRANSVAAL. At Belfast a set of two eggs (date ?) were taken (Transvaal Museum), while de V. Little (1962) listed the species from the Caolina District and Gurney (1864, 1868) described a nest (two eggs) found by G. A. Phillips in a large lagoon on the Vaal River.

MEASUREMENTS

Adult male. Seven specimens. Exposed culmen, 174.0 (150-185); wing (chord), 669.7 (613-717); tail, 257.0 (233-270); tarsus, 321.6 (298-342); bare tibia, 183.8 (148-204); middle toe with claw, 124.2 (117-127) mm.

Adult female. Seven specimens. Exposed culmen, 161.4 (124-183); wing (chord), 634.1 (619-687); tail, 261.3 (227-295); tarsus, 309.8 (232-330); bare tibia, 177.5 (153-200); middle toe with claw, 118.7 (108-135) mm.

Both sexes. Twenty-one specimens, including above fourteen (BMNH, 13; CNHM, 2; Natural History Museum, Haile Selassie I University, 2; Pietermaritzburg Museum, 1; Transvaal Museum, 1; Durban Museum, 1; USNM, 1). Exposed culmen, 166.9 (124-188); wing (chord), 661.9 (613-717); tail, 259.0 (227-295); tarsus, 315.9 (232-342); bare tibia, 180.1 (148-204); middle toe with claw, 122.0 (108-135) mm.

DESCRIPTION

Breeding adult. Wattled Cranes are among the largest cranes. The bare-face coloration in the male is darker red than in the female. The bare region anterior to the wattles is covered with small rounded excrescences. The feathered crown is dark slaty-gray. The remainder of the head, the wattles (except the anterior edge) and the neck, extending down onto the upper breast, are white. The mantle, breast, primaries, secondaries, tail-coverts and tail are black. The remainder of the back and wings are ashy-gray. The inner secondaries are elongated, extending far beyond the tail. The bill is light reddish-brown. The legs and feet are black or dark gray. The eye is dark orange or reddish. The two prominent white wattles, almost fully feathered and extending down from the upper throat region, are certainly the method by which to make a quick identification of this species.

Sub-adult. Sub-adult birds do not have the bare face. The lappets are less prominent than in adults.

The plumage is more tawny—not the contrasting black and white.

Downy chick. The chick was first described by West (1956): "Head and neck, pale buff with the last half-inch of the back and neck as well as the middle of the back, the back of the wings, the thighs, dark brown, the remainder buffy. The bill is horn-colored, the legs and feet, blue-black. Wattles, slightly evident, covered with pale buff down. The eye is brown."

Approximate measurements of a newly-hatched chick were: wing, 42.5 mm; tarsus, 44.1 mm; exposed culmen, 21.1 mm.

Chapter Twelve

THE DEMOISELLE CRANE

(Anthropoides virgo)

Ardea Virgo, Linnaeus, *Syst. Nat.,* 10th ed., 1, 1758, p. 141.
Anthropoides virgo, Vieillot, *Analyse,* 1816, p. 59. *Nouv. Dict.,* vol. ii, p. 163.
Type locality: "In Oriente," = India (Peters, 1934, p. 153).
Vernacular names: The Demoiselle Crane (English); Jungfernkranich (German); de Jufferkraan (Dutch); la Demoiselle de Numidie (French); Aneha zuru (Autonous, Older-sister-feathered crane) (Japanese); Журавль-Красавка (Russian); Karchira-Togoru (The Screaming Crane of the Burjates of the Upper Irkut); Karkarra (Hindi); Ghanto (Nepalese); Kallam (Deccan); Garara (Uriya); Rahokarkarra (Arabic); Damigella (Maltese).

This small crane is one of the most common in the world, yet it is little known for it nests in remote Siberian regions, less often in European Russia, at times in Rumania and even in Algiers in northern Africa. Although widely scattered in summer, it occurs in huge flocks in winter, especially along the Nile River in Sudan, south of Khartoum, in central Ethiopia at times, and again in portions of India. These immense flocks behave much like Lesser Sandhill Cranes in winter in southern United States and Mexico. This bird, most often, builds its nest on dry ground, and many times of small pebbles.

DISTRIBUTION

The Demoiselle Crane breeds in Algiers, possibly more extensively in north central Africa; in Rumania, southern Russia, scattered localities across central Asia to Mongolia and adjacent southern Siberia. Stragglers have been taken in England, Sweden and Japan. It winters, or has wintered, in southern Spain, Morocco, Algiers, Tunisia, central Sudan and Ethiopia, and rarely in northern Nigeria, Iraq, Iran, northern India, Burma and southeastern China.

Breeding distribution. ALGIERS. Many authors have reported this species breeding in Algiers and other parts of northern Africa. There is a single egg taken in 1885 by Captain Loch at Zahrez (35° N.; 3° E.) (BMNH), and there are five eggs (BMNH) taken from a female which was caught when yet a downy chick on the high plateau south of Boghari (36° N.; 3° E.). Many points in this area reach an elevation of 1,922 m.

RUMANIA. Dr. A. S. Cullen (1869) reported on the breeding of this bird in what was then Turkey at Kustendje (now Constanta) and at Dobrudscha (Medjici), Dobrogea. Of the many nests with eggs he observed, six eggs are now in the British Museum (Natural History), all taken at Kustendje. Some are listed as two-egg sets, while others are recorded as separate eggs. The dates are May 20 and 22, 1864 and May 10 and 15, 1865. Another set was taken at Dobrudscha by H. Seebohm in May 1883 (BMNH), and another set (BMNH) between Kustendje and Tchernavoda by Seebohm. Both of these regions are recorded as from the Medzidge Steppe. Quoting Dr. Cullen, E. C. S. Baker (1928) published the following:

"This bird arrives in the Dobrudscha in about the second week of April. It makes its appearance in flocks of from twenty to thirty birds and upwards, and the form of these flocks very much resemble those of the Common Crane, and they almost always fly very high, especially when passing wooded country; but when crossing the plains they fly lower, and occasionally come within gunshot. For the first week after their arrival, flocks of these birds mingle with those of the Common Crane, and resort to any fields of newly-sown grain that they can find, and to these they often do great damage. Regularly once or twice during the day they repair to some lake or pond of fresh water to drink. In the evening the fields are deserted, all the birds going to the nearest lakes and marshes . . . soon the flocks break up into pairs, which disperse themselves all over the country. Very soon after the birds have paired they begin to lay. Eggs may be found from about the third week in April to very nearly the end of May; but much depends on the state of the weather. The nest of the Demoiselle Crane is, without exception, made on the ground usually amidst some kind of young grain, but often amongst grass and fallow land, and now and then, though more rarely, amongst stubble. The nest—if indeed such it can be called—is made by the birds pulling up or treading down the grain, grass, or stubble for the space of about two feet, and scratching the shallowest possible hollow in the middle of the bare patch thus formed. A few small straws and stones are often found in and about this hollow, but whether they are brought there by the birds, or found there by them, which is very probable, I cannot say with any certainty.

"I believe myself, however, that they are placed there by the birds. The eggs, which are never more or less than two in number, are always placed side by side, in the hollow already described, with their small ends pointing in the same direction. The male assists the female in hatching the eggs; indeed, I have every reason to think that he sits as much as the female. To the uninitiated in the habits of this bird, its eggs are very difficult to find. When an intruder approaches the spot where the eggs lie, he at first sees nothing except perhaps a solitary bird standing on one leg as if sleeping. Should he not be a very good observer, as he draws nearer he will probably only notice a pair of birds walking rapidly away, plucking the grass as they go apparently feeding eagerly, and he will most likely account for the sudden appearance of the second bird by concluding that it had been sitting on the ground resting, and will not think anything about the matter, and pass on. Very few persons indeed would at all suspect that the birds had a nest. Often, nay, almost always, when the birds have placed some distance between them and their nest, they will take flight, and to all appearance desert the spot altogether, but no sooner is the intruder's back turned, than there they are again in a wonderfully short . . . time. One of the birds, I believe the male,

Demoiselle Crane at Detroit Zoological Park, May 28, 1948.

always keeps watch over the other, except in the middle of the day in very hot weather, when the bird, which acts as sentinel, deserts its post and goes to the nearest pond or lake to drink. It does not, however, remain away very long.

"Should the bird whose place it is to watch while the other sits be absent, the sitting bird when disturbed is not quite so guarded in its movements, and will allow a much nearer approach. When the eggs are first laid the birds will leave them as soon as an intruder comes in sight, but as the incubation advances they become less shy, and will not leave their eggs so readily.

"I cannot say whether the bird which watches stands close to or a little distance from the nest. I rather incline to the latter opinion. If a crane be observed chasing other birds away from any particular spot, it is a sure sign that it has a nest not far off. This bird will give chase to eagles and great bustards without the least fear, should they venture near the nest. For all kinds of harriers and seagulls it has a great dislike. I have been told by the Tartars that should a dog chance near the nest of this bird, both of the birds will attack him, striking him with their beaks and wings, and making a great noise all the time. I myself have never had an opportunity of witnessing such a interesting encounter, but I am certain that this bird has sufficient courage for one. The Demoiselle Crane is easily domesticated when young."

MESOPOTAMIA. A two-egg set was taken here (no date) (BMNH).

U.S.S.R. Dementiev and Gladkov (1951) wrote: "Beautiful or Little Crane . . . the greater portion of its nesting range extends inside our boundaries and much of this is not established. Found in Ukraine, Crimea, where is known up to the Black Sea littoral, in the north to Kherson and Dnepropetrovsk Oblasts. It is found in the southern portion of Kiev Oblast, in southern Poltav Oblast, it nested during the 90 years of the past century in the Izyum and Starobelsk districts . . . but more recently only in the southern parts of these Oblasts. It is not in Podoli but found in North Kavhas-Manichskie Steppe, at Mozdokski and Nogaysk Steppes and in territory about Lake Sevan. It nests in the Astrakhan region, but is not found on the delta of the Volga on the north coast of the Caspian Sea nor the mouth of the Ural. It is found northward along the Volga up to Stalingrad, possibly even somewhat northward. On the Volga-Ural Steppes, northward to 49° N. Lat., it is possible to 50° N. Lat., on the middle course of the Ilek, but it is likely it does not reach Chkalov (. . . indications are that it nested there in 1888 on Donguzsk Steppe, 15 km from Chkalov) . . . , found in Kurgal'dzhinsk region, Barabinsk Steppe (it is possible at present it is found only in the southern parts), Kainsk, Barnaul, Biysk, Altay, with the exception of northeast and southeast Altay, southern parts of the Minusinsk region, PriBaikal and southwest Transbaikalia, Dauriya to the Amur but in Primorya regions it is not found.

"In the southern part of Asia it goes to the lower reaches of the Ural to Uyla (48° N. Lat.), upper reaches of the Emba, Mugodzhari to the north coast of the Aral Sea and the valley of the Syr-Dar'ya River, Sari-su, Lake Teli-kul . . . , Chu, Ili, it is possible in northern Tadzhikistan, Leninabad territory (it does not nest in Turkmen), Zaysan, Tarbagatay, Tannu-tuva, Mongolia, except central and southern; it is possible that it occurs in northern Chzhili in northwest China."

In the British Museum (Natural History) there are specimens from the Volga River, southern Russia (two eggs), taken by Bidwell, from Sarepta (on the Volga River, in Astrakhan), four sets, three of which are of one egg and one of two, one only with the date, April 29, 1899. All of these were taken by W. R. Saunders. There are also seven eggs without data from Sarepta (Rothschild Collection). Three other two-egg sets were taken by Dr. Stader and O. Moller in southern Russia (no dates given). There are three two-egg sets in the Rothschild Collection taken on the Sarpa Steppes, one set on May 14, 1907, and two two-egg sets taken in May 1909 on the Kalmuk Steppe (46° N.), Astrakhan (Rothschild Coll., BMNH). One two-egg set (BMNH) was taken at Charbonniere; another set (one egg) (BMNH) was taken on the Amur by Radde.

CHINA. La Touche (1933) wrote: "Abundant in Mongolia, and . . . Pére David, in *Les Oiseaux de la Chine*, reports it to be common in summer on the western boundaries of China on both sides of the Great Wall, unknown on the Chihle plain. I have never seen it, neither have Wilder and Hubbard met with it at Peitaiho or near Peking; but Wilder writes, in his *List of Chihli Birds*, that hunters of Changli (between Chinwantao and Tongshan) reported having shot them there."

Winter distribution. NIGERIA. Elgood (1964) and Elgood, Sharland and Ward (1966) produced evidence that this bird is found rarely on savannas near Lake Chad and occasionally in the Chad Republic. A flight of ten was seen March 3, 1961 at Gajibo, twenty miles south of Lake Chad and a single bird was seen several times at the same place between March 7 and 12, 1961.

SUDAN. Berg wrote (1930); "We came upon such crane resorts at intervals of three to six miles or more along the White Nile from the desert region south of Omdurman and throughout the Kordofan scrub country as far as Abu Seid, where the river becomes constricted between rocks and the woods reach down to the banks. But there the numbers of our gray cranes began to fall off. Their favorite winter quarters appear to lie between the uncultivated plain at about 13° North Latitude and the region where wooded islands first began to split the river. Beyond this territory the demoiselle cranes were always more predominant and eventually the flocks consisted of them alone, together with larger contingents of crowned cranes."

Mathiasson (1963) wrote that *Anthropoides virgo* with *Grus grus* winters south of Khartoum in flocks numbering up to 20,000. W. P. Lowe (BMNH) took two specimens, male and female, five miles from the mouth of the Sobat River, January 30, 1914. I saw a small group of six near Khor Adar, eighty miles north of Malakal, February 4, 1962.

INDIA. Baker (1928) wrote: "The Demoiselle Crane arrives in India in October and the first flocks which arrive seem to fly straight down to their southern limits as it is said to arrive in the Deccan in the middle of October, whilst in the north few birds seem to settle until the end of that month, though they must pass over on their way south. They return north in March or April. Whistler records numerous flocks from the Jhang District between March 8 and April 7. Both coming and going they assemble in vast multitudes, and a most interesting letter from A. A. Phillips, quoted by Whistler, gives a graphic account of one of these assemblies:

"On March 25, C. and I went out after them. They were a sight worth seeing and hearing. There seemed to be vast divisions of them about, but we only *shikared* one division; while they were feeding on the ground there was a broad band of them for about 1½ miles. When alarmed they bunched together and looked just like a white pebble beach about 100 by 500 yards in extent, and when they rose the noise was like the roaring of the sea. We shot three which were all Demoiselles."

Baker adds: "They are extremely wary, clever birds and, whether it is desired to shoot or trap them, they are very difficult to bring to bag. They are, however, sometimes caught in nets and, less often, in nooses, and when once caught soon become affectionate pets, but they are very jealous of other pets and jealous and irritable with small children."

In the British Museum (Natural History) are six specimens taken December 8-22, 1872 by R. M. Adam at Sambhur, Rajputana; one from Marwar, October 10, 1868 by G. King; two from Delhi by A. O. Hume, December 27, 1867 and two on February 21, 1881, by W. N. Chill; several from

Bareilly, Etawah and Oudh by Hume in the winters from 1865 to 1873; two taken by J. Davidson, February 12, 1884 (male) from Nandurbar, Khandesh and the other a female, January 31, 1892, at Bijapur. In Rajasthan this bird was reported to me only as a migrant.

KASHMIR. One specimen (BMNH) was taken at 5,000 feet at Gilgit, September 1876, by J. Biddulph.

SIKKIM. L. Mandelli took a specimen April 1874 (BMNH) (no other data).

NEPAL. In BMNH are several specimens labeled Nepal and taken by B. H. Hodgson. There is another specimen taken October 20, 1960 from the Kathmandu Valley by J. Fleming.

Summer distribution and migration. MANCHURIA. In Greater Khingan, Djalantun an adult male was taken May 10, 1939. From the same region, a female was taken June 7, 1939. A sub-adult specimen was taken at Barga Lake, Dalai Nor, July 11, 1940, and a downy chick in the same region June 28, 1940 (CNHM).

CHINA. A female specimen was taken in Ordos Suiyuan on April 22 by Przevalsky (BMNH). In Kansu, Kingnsia (thirty miles west), a female was taken June 1, 1923 for the National Geographic Society Expedition (USNM). Another specimen was taken at Shansi, Kweiwbating, November 12, 1921 (MCZ).

SPAIN. A female was taken at Seville April 1869 by H. Saunders (BMNH).

SAUDI ARABIA. J. W. Wall (BMNH) took a bird at Jedda, November 6, 1941.

IRAQ. A specimen was taken by P. Cox and R. E. Cheeseman at Mosul (no other data).

CYPRUS. A specimen was taken by Lord Lilford (sex and date unknown).

U.S.S.R. A male specimen is known from Volga (MCZ).

DESCRIPTION

Breeding adult. Both sexes are alike. From forecrown to nape it is light gray. A line over the ear coverts, a patch below the eye and a long aigrette behind the coverts are pure white. The remainder of the head and neck are black. The feathers of the lower foreneck are long and lanceolate, falling over

Demoiselle Crane at nest in Ostrova Zoo, Czechoslovakia. Photograph by Dagmar Hruskova.

the breast. Alula, greater coverts and primaries are black. The inner secondaries are extremely long, some measuring 134mm or more beyond the ends of the primaries. There is no bare spot on face or head. The bill is short, sea-green at the base, yellowish in the center and pinkish at the tip. Legs and feet are black with some plumbeous. The eye is red, crimson or red-brown (probably the latter in young birds).

Sub-adult. The general plumage is dark gray; primaries and tail, black. Head and neck are black and gray mixed. The top of the head is white, extending back onto occiput. The plumes which develop on the ends of the feathers disappear as with other sub-adult cranes. These, when the bird is about one-and-a-half months old, are about fourteen millimeters long on many feathers. The legs and feet are grayish. As the birds become older they resemble the adult more, but the entire head is grayish; the neck is brown behind, more gray in front and there are no lengthened plumes. The wing is as in the adult, but the inner secondaries are only slightly lengthened.

Downy chick. (From a downy chick taken at Barga, Lake Dalai Nor, Manchuria): The top of the head and occiput are light buff. The face and throat are also buff, but much lighter than the top of the head. At the base of the occiput, as though a line were drawn, the color changes to medium gray and buff, mixed. The buff on the throat extends down farther than on the back of the neck. The neck (posterior), back, rump, wings and sides are shades of gray, either medium, light or dark. A darker median stripe along the back narrows near the insertion of the wings. The wings are also darker. Below is light gray, darker than the chest. The egg tooth is white to pale gray. The legs and feet are dark blue as in *A. paradisea.* This chick resembles that one, but is smaller. This specimen was 45.0 grams in weight (CNHM).

MEASUREMENTS

Adult male (fifteen specimens: BMNH, 13; CNHM, 1; MCZ, 1). Exposed culmen, 66.35 (63-71) mm; from posterior of nostril, 50 mm (one specimen only); wing, 484.4 (453-508) mm; tail, 174.53 (164-184) mm; tarsus, 180.1 (168-201) mm; bare tibia, 84.06 (59-96) mm; middle toe, 78.78 (71-86) mm.

Adult female (twelve specimens: BMNH, 7; CNHM, 3; MCZ, 1; USNM, 1). Exposed culmen, 65.11 (60-68) mm; wing, 469.8 (449-490) mm; tail, 168.8 (158-177) mm; tarsus, 170.4 (152-186) mm; bare tibia, 78.7 (72-85) mm; middle toe, 78.14 (66-88) mm.

Both sexes (forty specimens: BMNH, 33; CNHM, 4; MCZ, 2, USNM, 1). Exposed culmen, 65.24 (60-71) mm; wing, 480.74 (449-508) mm; tail, 170.9 (152-184); tarsus, 175.75 (152-201) mm; bare tibia, 82.5 (59-96) mm; middle toe, 77.77 (66-88) mm.

Downy chick (CNHM, 16640). The measurements of the downy chick taken at Barga, Dalai Nor, Manchuria, June 28, 1940 were: spread wings, 168 mm; length, 177 mm; exposed culmen, 18 mm; from tip of bill to posterior edge of nostril, 13 mm; wing, 30 mm; tarsus, 31 mm; bare tibia, 16 mm.

MIGRATIONS

Dementiev and Gladkov (1951) wrote:

"Nesting and migratory bird. It flies like the gray crane "wedge-shaped," flying ordinarily with one side of the line shorter than the other. They fly very high, so they are more often heard than seen. They fly a little later than the gray crane. In springtime they fly in small flocks, sometimes even by pairs ... The beginning of the flight coincides with the gross flight of the gray crane. The winter regions in Africa they abandon in February to March. In Bessarabia they migrate in the second half of March and in cold springs, only in April. In the Ukraine (Dnepropetrovsk Oblast), in late March and the first of April. At Kavkaze the last third of March up to the second half of April.

"In Turkmen the flight is rare, from late March up to early April at Tedzhene on the 26 of March until the 3 April 1886 at Chemen-i-bida and Kushka—4 April 1887 (Radde and Val'ter). It was encountered in flight at Kyzyl-Kum, especially in the eastern part.

"In Tadzhikistan the flight comes the first half of April (7-16 April, Gissarsk Valley, Ivanov, 1940). On the lower Syr-Darya (near Karauzyak), the second third of April at the Aral Sea [and] at Lake Kamishli-bash, the end of April. At Embe, near Kok'dzhidi the first birds appear at the end of April; on the lower reaches of the Irgiz, the second half of April. At Ili the flight begins in the middle of the first half of April (9 April 1913), intensified during the second half (17-25 April 1913). A detached flight of pairs is encountered to the end of April and in early May (Shestopervov, 1929). In Altai they fly in the beginning and middle of April (in the Chul-ishman Valley—in mid-April). ... In the environs of Troitskosavak, the little crane flies in late April (30 April, Molleson, 1897). In northern Mongolia flight goes in late April to early May (in southwest Kenteya gross flight was observed on 28 April, on Lake Orok-Nor first cranes appear in April, Koslova, 1930). In eastern Mongolia migration was first seen on 16 April (Bianki, 1906).

"On the first of August, detachments in flocks are already withdrawing; some still remain on the nesting sites; some depart to flood plains and steppes. Soon a nomadic life begins and the range becomes greater and greater until the birds gradually fly away. This return flight begins nearly imperceptibly. The birds of passage make their appearance in new flocks ... autumn flocks reaching large scale at Ili, flocks up to 400 and more (Shestoperov, 1929). At Dauria (Lake Tarei-Nor), the greatest number of birds were flying on 27-28 August and late birds had vanished by 12 September (Radde, 1863). At Altay flight occurred the second half of August (17 August at Biysk ... Sushkin, 1938) and lasted to mid-September (in the valley of the Chulyshman in the beginning of September, Folitarek and Dementiev, 1938), in the lower reaches of the Chernogo-Irtysh on 7 September a large flying flock was seen (Sushkin, 1938). At Ili the returning flight of the Demoiselle Crane was observed throughout September, but some flocks were observed the very first of August (2 August, Shestoperov, 1929); in the lower reaches of the Irgiz, returning flight begins in late August; at the mouth of the Ural, in late August until late

September. In Turkmen, at Akhal-Tekinskoy Plains, the flight went in mid-September (16 September 1884, Zarydniy, 1896). In the Ukraine (Dnepropetrovsk Oblast) it was observed in the first of September. In the Nile valley it occurs the first days to the end of September."

This species has been observed repeatedly during times of migration in different regions in Europe, including the Scandinavian countries and the Orkneys (Dementiev and Gladkov, 1951), and like flights of birds were observed at Podolsk, in the southern portion of Chernigovsk Oblast, in Poltavsk Oblast, Smolensk Oblast, in the northern

A pair of Demoiselle Cranes giving 'Unison Call' at Ostrova Zoo, Czechoslovakia. Photograph by Dagmar Hruskova.

parts of Chkalovsk Oblast, in the environs of Kustanay, at Krasnoyarsk, in the valley of the Lena at 61° 20′ N. Latitude, below Verkhoyansk and in the environs of Vladivostok.

HABITAT

This crane prefers semi-desert land and steppes, although it avoids steppes covered with low forests or those settled by man (Dementiev and Gladkov, 1951). It also occupies wasteland, or land which is grassy, brushy, stony, clay-salty and sometimes stony or metallic ground, as well as river valley steppes.

ABUNDANCE

The species is found chiefly in the Crimea and to the south in Russia. In the Ukraine it is more abundant on the Volga, especially below Stalingrad at Manich. Here E. P. Spangenberg (Dementiev and Gladkov, 1951) found ten nests within ten kilometers, some of which were no more than 200 to 300 meters apart. This region was a thick-forested steppe with regions of salt and ravines lying between. It is also common in Kazakhstan, but farther to the east it becomes rare, although it occurs in the present desert in Armenia.

ECOLOGY

The Demoiselle Crane is monogamous. When it pairs, the birds go immediately to their nesting territories. Occasionally they collect in large numbers on some level dry region where they dance. They bow, jump up and down with half-spread wings, neck stretched out, spread the feathers of the throat region and utter a guttural noise at the same time. This dance is most often observed in spring, but at times has been seen in autumn or summer. It was observed between August 30 and September 8, 1905 in the Dnepropetrovsk Oblast and at Altay, on Lake Teniga, from August 1 to 3. They roam throughout late summer (Abakansk Steppes, June 30, 1930 [flock of thirty]); at Lake Teniga, Altay, August 1-3 [flock of twenty birds which appeared to be adults [Dementiev and Gladkov, 1951]).

NESTING

Prenesting behavior. E. C. S. Baker (1928), quoting Nordmann's description of the dance of this crane, states:

"They arrive in the south of Russia about the beginning of March, in flocks of between two and three hundred individuals. Arriving at the end of their journey, the flock keeps together for some time; and even when they have dispersed in couples, they reassemble every morning and evening, preferring in calm weather to exercise themselves together, and amuse themselves by dancing. For this purpose they choose a convenient place, generally the flat shore of a stream. There they stand in a line or in many rows, and begin their games and extraordinary dances, which are not a little surprising to the spectator. They dance and jump around each other, bowing in a burlesque manner, advancing their necks, raising the feathers of the neck-tufts, and half unfolding the wings. In the meantime another set are disputing in a race the prize for swiftness. Arriving at the winning-post they turn back, and walk slowly, and with gravity; all the rest of the company saluting them with reiterated cries, inclinations of the head, and other demonstrations, which are reciprocated. After having done this for some time, they all rise in the air, where slowly sailing, they describe circles, like the swan and other cranes. After some weeks these assemblies cease, and from that time they are constantly seen walking in pairs together. . . ."

Baker (1928) continues:

"Drybowski says that in Dauria 'it nests on the rocky banks of rivers and rarely on bare mountains. The nest is made of small stones fitting close to each other, the surface of the nest is flat or deepened somewhat towards the centre; it chooses sometimes a place which is a few inches higher than the surrounding ground, and fills up all the crevices and openings with stones.'

"The breeding season lasts from the middle of May to the middle of July, a month earlier in its most southern breeding haunts, even later in the more northern. The normal clutch is two only, small replicas of those of the Common Crane but they are still longer and more narrow in proportion to their size. The ground colour varies from a pale olive yellow to a warm olive brown or olive green whilst the marking consists of large primary blotches of purplish-lavender. In most eggs these

are fairly numerous over the whole surface, but in some they are confined to the larger and where they form an indefinite ring or cap. One hundred and twenty eggs average 83.3 X 53.1 mm., maxima 91.4 X 55.1 and 84.2 X 56.6 mm.; minima 74.1 X 48.5 and 78.0 X 47.0 mm."

Fifty-three eggs in the British Museum (Natural History) averaged in measurement 83.56 (72.0-91.5) X 53.81 (48.9-56.65) mm.

Dementiev and Gladkov (1951) gave measurements of a set of two eggs recorded by Johansen as 94.0 X 59.0 and 92.0 X 59.0 mm; a set from Barabinsk Steppe and another from Akbulak, Kazakhstan recorded by Spangenberg measured 83.2 X 53.8 and 81.0 X 54.2 mm. The sets consist of two eggs, rarely one or three.

D. I. Chekmenev (1960, *Biology of the Demoiselle Crane in Central Kazakhstan*, Trudy Inst. Zool. Akad. Nauk, SSR, Alma Ata, 13: 142-147), wrote concerning a study he made during 1957 and 1958 in the western part of the Akmolinsk region near the central River Tersakkan, west of central Shoindykul and Zharkul, 60 km west of the central flow.

"In the desert region the cranes are distributed widely although their numbers are not high. The form of the relief as well as the vegetation apparently do not influence the distribution . . . for they are even found in hilly steppes. The essential condition is the proximity of water—lakes, rivers, small streams. Beyond 1.3 km from water no nests were found. The nesting area is partly or entirely free of vegetation (the majority of nests were 200-500 m from water). Nests are always composed of small stones. The contour within the nest is barely defined but a slight bed is made of little stones 1 to 5 cm in length, pieces of grass and rootlets, while in none was there a concavity. They harmonize in the best possible way with the surroundings . . ."

Four nests were found near the River Kokpekty during 1957, May 19, 21, and 26. Three contained two eggs, the fourth, three eggs. These nine eggs averaged in measurements 83.02 (81-87) X 56.4 (51-57.3) mm and in weight, 120.1 (102-142) grams. The May 19 eggs contained fully developed embryos which weighed 86 and 88 grams respectively, exactly the same as the first May 21 nest (which hatched June 1 and 2). One egg in the other May 21 nest was apparently infertile. In the May 26 eggs, embryos had developed from one-fourth to one-third. Eggs were 8 to 10 cm apart and parallel (which is normal for cranes). They were circular oval in shape.

Once an old nest of stones was found two or three meters from the new one (as we found with *A. paradisea* in South Africa in the Drakensberg Mountains).

Chekmenev continues: "These birds are very deliberate. They do not feed closer to each other than 300 m. The female looks around with head held high and even if it is above surrounding grass, she is hard to see. If she senses danger she rises, walks away some distance, takes flight, anxiously calling, and flies to her mate. Then they both fly, circling the small area. From time to time they alight, walk around the nest area. . . . When they are convinced danger is past, they approach the nest, look around, and the female resumes incubation. Sometimes the male walks by the nest looking it over. Only when convinced all is quiet does he wander away. The female does not allow raptors to come close . . . she is tolerant of domestic animals, ignoring sheep pasturing up to 100 m from the nest, but if they came within 40 or 50 m, she left the nest and returned when they passed by. If flushed from the nest the bird will not return very quickly. In the morning when the temperature is 6° C. the bird will return in one hour, while later when the temperature is 20° C. she may stay away two or three hours.

"Chicks in central Kzakhstan hatched during mid-June, in one nest on May 21, in another on June 2. . . . Apparently parents take them away as soon as they are dry. When approached they lie on the ground like downy balls. Parents are very uneasy when chicks are near; they lurk around, then fly around calling. The chicks awkwardly hide under grass and when put together are very quarrelsome, standing on their haunches and fighting. In a few days the chicks are able to walk better. The swelling leaves their feet and they are able to straighten out their toes. In June, near Lake Sasykkul (70-80 km N. of Zhanarka), two quite large young were captured (weights, 70 and 80 grams). Only the head and neck were still downy. Feathers were longest on the shoulders. Adults often do not hide, but run and often run along with their large chicks to guard them."

The major role in food is vegetable matter. In stomachs of two adults were grain, seeds and a few beetles. Since they were collected during the nesting period the grain came from the previous year probably. First birds arrived on April 14 (flock) and last in the fall on October 4 (11) flying southwest 30-70 meters above the ground.

Nesting season. The nesting season (Dementiev and Gladkov, 1951) often extends over several months. In one region one can observe beginning nesting, laying of eggs and large young at the same time. In the Crimea and the Ukraine egg-laying usually occurs between mid- to late April and the middle of May. They gave egg records as follows:

"Yevpatorii 23 May 1901 (two eggs with dead embryos [Molchanov]).

"Dnepropetrovsk Oblast 1 May 1906; 11 May 1898, 2 May 1899 (the first two sets freshly laid; the latter slightly incubated [Borobikov]).

"Manyche. 20 and 24 May 1950. Two sets heavily incubated eggs with young peeping inside. 28 May 1950, a half incubated set. 25 May 1950, egg shells from which young had just hatched (Spangenberg).

"In Ak-Bulake, Kazakhstan, laying was in the middle of May to the end of June. 22 May 1931 (two eggs just hatching), 31 May and 2 July (well-incubated eggs [Spangenberg]).

"Lake Telikul'. 22 May 1927 (two well-incubated eggs—one egg pipped slightly [Spangenberg]).

"In Iliysk territory sets were found from early May to the beginning of June. A female was killed with an egg still not quite developed on April 10, and a set of two perfectly fresh eggs was found May 15 (Shestoperov).

"At Barabinsk Steppe near Kainsk, 11 May 1903 (unincubated set [Johansen]).

"At Altay (Lake Teniga), 4 June [a nest] with heavily incubated eggs (Sushkin).

"Northern Mongolia on the River Tol, first set taken 27 May; the last set in late June (Kozlova)."

Behavior at the nest. Both parents incubate, but the male much the least. He sometimes diverts danger by dancing nearby, often giving advance notice by calling. The female walks about 100 meters from a man near the nest, often rises from the nest at some distance, then lands on the ground. Some-

*Nest of Demoiselle Crane, Anthropoides virgo, Ostrova Zoo,
Czechoslovakia.* Photograph by Dagmar Hruskova.

times the birds bend over, going through distraction displays. Incubation apparently requires
about a month. As soon as the young are dry they
set out with their parents. Hatching begins from
late May or the beginning of June and usually lasts
until mid-June. In Bessarabia, three-day-old young
were taken June 10, 1899 (Osterman). Downy
chicks (age unknown) were encountered at Altay
(the lower reaches of the Chulyshmana) June 8 and
23 (Sushkin); at Tarbagatae (Chiliktinsk Steppe)
May 26 (Finch); a downy young was taken June 8,
1936 at Sari-su (Coll. Zool. Museum Moscow
Univ.); in northern Mongolia fresh eggs and downy
young were both found at the very end of June.

Feathers begin to appear on the young in June
and early July as they did on the young at Ongu-
day in Altay July 2, while two young seemed fully
feathered on July 27, but could not fly (Kashenko,
Sushkin) and on August 3 poorly flying young
were observed by Sushkin. In early August many
young cranes were already flying in northern
Kazakhstan (Dementiev and Gladkov, 1951).

Even after they fly, the young cranes remain
closely attached to their parents, the families remaining intact throughout day and night on
steppes, meadows, grain fields and roosting

marshes. Soon they begin to collect in flocks. In
Dnepropetrovsk Oblast, as well as in the Iliysk re-
gion cranes began organizing in mid-July; in
Abakan, in mid-August.

THE MOULT

Dementiev and Gladkov (1951) wrote: "A study
is inadequate and, apparently, it happens chiefly in
winter. Primary replacement goes from the inner
and extreme primaries to the middle, with the last
next change the 3-e or 2-e. The primaries are lost in
late July and it goes on until December, requiring
4-5 months. Thus specimens taken in September in
northern Tsaydem always have fresh primaries, except 2 and 4, which are still old; a specimen from
northern Tibet in October had old primaries only
3-e; 2 specimens on 9 December at Begun River (a
tributary of the Syr-Dar'i) in one case only secondaries; the other with 3-e. From data of Sushkin the
moult of the primaries from Altay began in late
July. The small feathers, the tail, secondaries and
tertials, apparently, as is observed in dried specimens, moult late, notwithstanding a very shabby
plumage with no trace of moult. Migrating spring
birds have a fresh plumage like specimens taken in
early April on the Begun River. The plan of moult
is similar to that of the Gray Crane."

NUTRITION

Little is known about the food eaten by this
species of crane. It appears to be chiefly vegetable
matter and, in very small amounts, animal matter—
chiefly insects. In the second half of summer and
in the fall these cranes usually feed on various
ripened grains. Later families fly to grain fields
daily, causing considerable damage. They alleviate
the good they do when they eat the heads of the
grain.

VOICE

The ordinary flight and ground calls of this
crane resemble those of the Common Crane very
much, but are not as strong. When I saw them at
Khor Adar, Sudan, their *Garrooo* calls seemed very
much like that of the Common Crane in February
1962.

The voice of both *Anthropoides virgo* and *A.*

276

paradisea differs from that of *Grus. Anthropoides* has fewer and shorter syllables. Dr. George Archibald (letter, October 10, 1971) brought this out when he wrote, "The Unison Call of *Anthropoides* differs from *Grus.* Whereas several *Grus* species call up to two or three minutes, with an average of about 12 seconds, *Anthropoides* varies only between three and four seconds depending on the pair calling (captive birds)." I found this to be the case with *A. paradisea* in the wild in Natal, South Africa. Archibald also added: "The loudness is around 78-82 decibels whereas in *Grus* it is 88-104 decibels."

Both Archibald and I feel that this weaker call may have something to do with territorial size. Birds with larger territories may have the strongest voices. Territory may vary in size according to availability, abundance and types of food. Both *Anthropoides* and *Balearica* are chiefly vegetarians, as is *Grus leucogeranus.* All of these species have either weaker of shorter vociferations, and all (except *G. leucogeranus*) live where vegetable food is fairly abundant in fields or plains. Other *Grus* and *Bugeranus* eat vegetable foods but they are strong on animal matter. They also feed in marshes as well as fields.

Chapter Thirteen

THE BLUE OR STANLEY CRANE

(Anthropoides paradisea)

Ardea paradisea, Lichtenstein, *Catalogue Rerum Naturalium Rarissimarum,* Hamburg, October 21, 1793, p. 28.

Tetrapteryx capensis, Thunberg, K. *Vertensk. Akad. Forh.,* 1818 p. 242.

Anthropoides paradisea, Blaauw, *Monograph of the Cranes,* 1897, pp. 41-43.

Tetrapteryx paradisea, Walkinshaw, "Some life history studies of the Stanley Crane, *Proc. XIIIth International Ornith. Congress, 1963,* pp. 344-353.

Van Ee, "Notes on the breeding behaviour of the Blue Crane, *Tetrapteryx paradisea.*" *Ostrich,* 37 pp. 23-29, 1966.

Type locality: Inner South Africa.

Vernacular names: The Stanley Crane, The Blue Crane (English); de Paradijskraan (Dutch); Groote Sprinkhaan-vogel (Boers, Transvaal); Great Locust Bird, Bloukraan (South Africans); i-Ndwe (Xhosa); i-Ndwa (Zulu); Mokhokoli (Sotho, Sesuto); Paradieskranich (German); la Grue de Paradis (French); Hagoromo zuru, (Japanese).

During the early 1960's the Stanley Crane was made the national bird of South Africa. Visually recorded once or twice in Rhodesia, all other recorded sightings have been confined to South Africa, their range extending through all the provinces and to Southwest Africa. I traveled many miles through this country, but never saw any cranes; in other regions, however, there were many, and this crane was the most plentiful. Spectacular because of its blue-gray color, it was one of the outstanding characteristics in these favorable localities from late November until early January. During the winter months everyone reported it from lower altitudes.

At first I found many scattered pairs feeding in fields on the veld, but as time wore on, single birds began appearing where there had been two. Searching through the nearest small vleis I then found their nests and the second bird of the pairs. Usually nests were located in very shallow water, but some eggs were laid in short grass without any nest proper, some distance from water. Farther up in the Drakensberg Mountains, around Giants Castle, William Barnes showed me some nests and we found others, placed on some isolated foothill, the big bergs looming above, the foothills extending for miles in all other directions with deep valleys winding between. A few were partially wooded; others were covered with short grass only.

The Mooi, the Little Mooi, the Bushman, the Hlatikulu Rivers and farther to the east the Umzimkulu and Umkomaas Rivers originate.

Above the valleys on the highest, or near the highest, portion of these foothills, the birds built open nests of little pebbles, placing them similarly to stones in a cobblestone road in a little circular region some three feet or less across. Often the remains of several old nests were placed a few feet from the occupied one. Here Barnes reported the birds had increased during recent years since they encountered little or no human interference. Few large mammals, except for a few wandering baboons, roamed at this 2,000-meter elevation. Convectional rains produced damage at times when accompanied by hail, but in general the region was ideal. Farther down in the veld (elevation 1,372 to 1,829 meters), there were Stanley Cranes, but here Colonel Jack Vincent reported a decrease in the

species where there had been an increase in human activity in recent years and nearly all the regions had been heavily pastured to cattle.

When the young cranes hatched, they were led out onto the pastured veld or the bergveld of the Drakensbergs, the family groups feeding and roaming for several months in their respective territories. With March came prospects of future snowstorms, especially in the higher regions, so the birds departed to lower elevations. Often in September and October, when spring came again, the young cranes formed in flocks at lower elevations, remaining throughout the summer months, the pairs returning to their nesting territories above them. These flocks cause damage to wheat and mealies (corn) both winter and summer.

PAIR FORMATION

Van Ee (1966) worked with a flock of Blue Cranes in a zoo at Bloemfontein, Orange Free State, South Africa. Four were two-year-old birds (sexes unknown), and six were full-grown, three of each sex. They were given freedom on a thirty-five-acre enclosure during July, when wild birds are in flocks. In a few days they moved to an alfalfa field. Dominance was shown from early September on, when the six birds formed three pairs. On September 25 they began attacking the young birds, one of which was killed on September 30th. The others escaped to the zoo grounds. Using only one attack method the pairs jumped onto the younger birds, pecking them on the back of the head, while kicking them above the tail. After the young left on September 30th, the paired adults rested until October 8th, when they began running in circles about their mates. It was not ascertained whether the males or females started this. It lasted one to five minutes and became intensified during the next four days, followed by calling. On October 13th one male picked up bunches of grass, branches, dried donkey dung—anything that was available—and tossed it into the air, each time jumping with flapping wings above the ground. He then ran around the others and stopped in front of his chosen female, following which he ran away from all of them. They all followed suit. After he had run 150 meters away, he stopped and began calling. Two days later, the selected female joined in throwing objects, jumping and running around in the field. The other four followed half-heartedly. On October 18th a definite breakup of the group was evident, and on the 20th a pair began chasing the others. On the 24th the other four birds left the field, going to the zoo grounds. Territorial attack followed a typical pattern. One of the paired-off birds bowed its head to the ground, shook its wings and raised its head, stood in an erect position wagging its tail and sometimes calling. The other four birds then retreated. Sometimes, after calling, the male attacked the other four birds. Usually the dominant male was the aggressor, but on two occasions the female was.

When I worked over the highland sourveld in Natal in December 1961, each pair was separated by at least 400 meters from its nearest neighbor. In one locality, nine pairs averaged 1,711 meters between nests. The hilly topography aided pair isolation, but in one long vlei three pairs nested within sight and sound of each other, while their feeding grounds were contiguous. In early December the cranes did not appear on definite territories, but in only a few days scattered pairs began taking up stations near some vlei. At first they stood or fed on the dry ground above the vlei; then, in about ten days they moved into the vlei, where they often stood, fed or worked. Each day they remained there for lengthened periods. In only a few days one could often be seen setting on some mound. Each pair had its own territory and in that territory showed dominance over other pairs who showed respect to them, as they did to other pairs' surrounding territories. The rightful male walked in the direction of any trespassing birds and they left immediately, either flying or, if from a nearby territory, walking.

COURTSHIP AND MATING

Van Ee (1966) wrote: "Courtship of the blue crane can best be described as a 'dance.' This 'dancing' can take from one to four hours. It starts with the running in circles and gives the impression that the male is chasing the female. There is no contact at all between the birds and there is a distance of approximately 10 feet between two danc-

ing birds. All of a sudden they stop and loud calls follow.

"The following phase is characterised by the picking up of bunches of grass, which are thrown into the air, both birds performing this ritual simultaneously. They jump high in the air, run in circles, again pick up grass bunches and throw them in the air, kicking them when they come down and then again they run in small circles. This ritual sometimes lasts half an hour. Now the birds stop very near to each other, resuming their call. Then they run straight across the field calling, again very near to each other. The last phase is again the throwing up of bunches of grass. The birds now face each other; sometimes one of the birds snaps up the bunches of grass thrown up by the other and throws it up also. This phase never lasts longer than 10 minutes. All of these phases are repeated time and again and after every phase there is calling. The shortest time recorded is 28 minutes for the whole ritual, the longest lasted four hours, uninterrupted. This goes on for nearly a fortnight, no mating following.

"During November 1959/1960/1961 the behaviour of a lone female was studied in a very large camp. She was approached by the Curator, who started calling and she reacted immediately, calling back and coming up to him. He started to play the role of the male running around in circles and she followed suit. When he started throwing bunches of grass into the air, she picked them up and kicked at them and started to dance. When he carefully imitated the male bird and stopped at times, she faced him and started calling with him. This experiment was repeated twice daily for half an hour and she reacted each day in a more responsive manner. As soon as the Curator entered the camp and started calling she ran up to him and the dance started, taking her through all the phases. This continued for nearly a month . . . After a month the Curator started looking for a nesting site imitating the *kworr* call. Picking up different objects, she walked with him and after 7 days she picked up the cow-dung offered to her. After calling and inspecting the nesting-site she started cleaning it. After two days an egg was laid and a second egg a day later. From this moment she broke-off the contact with the Curator and did not start breeding. No crouching movements, calling or dancing ever followed again. The next year the test was repeated and she responded exactly in the same manner up to the egg-laying stage when she again became disinterested."

COPULATION

Van Ee (1966) wrote further: "As the 'dancing' increases in intensity after the first 14 days, copulation follows, the female crouches low on her legs, wings a little spread, tail high up, the neck a little bent and stretched forward. The male mounts, gripping her neck feathers just behind the head, his claws in her elbows, flipping his wings at the start of the copulation, but at the end he brings his wingtips to the ground so as to have an extra pivot. When he dismounts both birds start calling again. In all the phases starting with the pairing off, the calling follows the pattern as described during the pairing-off.

"An exception in the copulation-pattern was observed in pair Z3. During the copulation, the female stood erect on her legs and the male did not bring his wings down at the end but kept on flapping his wings to keep his balance. During the day a maximum of 3 copulations was seen."

Stanley Crane pair near nest, west of Mooi River, Natal, South Africa, December 15, 1961. There is a newly hatched chick and one egg in the nest.

NESTING

Selection of site. According to Van Ee (1966): "A week before the first egg is laid the male starts selecting a nesting-site. After copulation he wanders off slowly accompanied by the female and starts picking up objects, but dropping them again immediately in front of the female. At the same time he utters a low call, best described as *kworrr*. She looks at him but acts as if she is not interested and wanders off, the male staying behind and repeating the same ritual three or four times. If she does not return he follows her and starts again on another spot. This is repeated for some days until she responds to his picking up by inspecting the site, lifting and putting down the objects he has gathered and answering his *kworrr* by the same call but in a higher tone. After accepting the site, she starts cleaning it, and both birds repeatedly call at the nesting site. No copulation was ever seen on the actual nesting-site. The nesting-site was usually a bare spot of ground, a little bit higher than the surroundings. The selected site was guarded against anything coming near it. The calling at the nesting-site is now intensified, up to 13 times per 10 minutes."

Habitats. I have listed (1963) several plants collected from Blue Crane nesting vleis. Most were grasses and sedges. Few plants were more than one meter tall, most were knee-high. The shallow water was neutral or slightly acid (pH 7.0 to 6.0). Probably these vleis dry up in winter, for the rains come during the summer. In this region 82 per cent of the annual thirty-four inches of rainfall comes during the summer months (Thorrington-Smith, 1960). Severe storms take their toll of eggs, some by water, others by hail.

Construction of nests varies. There are four types:

1. In the vleis, nests are most often placed on a mound amongst the short grasses and sedges, where surrounding water is one to ten centimeters deep. Often the first egg is laid on the mound when there is no nest material there at all. Shortly after the second egg is laid, a few wisps of vegetation from immediately around the site are placed alongside the eggs. This may help to prevent the eggs from rolling off the mound, for they still remain on the very black dirt, which eventually stains them considerably. The mounds are usually damp.

2. Blue Cranes sometimes lay their eggs in the short green grass of some pastured hillside, there being no evidence of a nest at all. Large herds of cattle roam in close proximity, but the cranes keep them at a safe distance and the cattle show great respect for them.

3. One nest was placed in the rush-grown border of a man-made damsite. This was a typical rush and sedge crane-made island 61.5 X 84 cm across, the largest of all the Blue Crane nests I observed. Amongst some water lilies only ten meters from it was the nest of an African Dabchick. But even here the rushes were only sixty centimeters tall.

4. On the high dry bergveld, shaded at times by the high peaks which towered above them and isolated by peaks and valleys, the cranes built nests of small pebbles which abounded in the region. ranging between one and two-and-one-half centimeters across, the stones were neatly placed on a flat site, some so well placed they were as smooth as a crushed-rock pavement, some thirty square centimeters or more, with very short grass surrounding them.

Season. At the Zoological Gardens, Bloemfontein, O.F.S., South Africa, Van Ee (1966) recorded several nests in fairly natural conditions, giving the laying time and the date of the two eggs in each set and the hatching date as follows: Z1 Paddock, 1959, November 29—6:20-6:39 A.M., bird on nest and first egg laid; November 30—6:50-7:27 A.M., second egg laid; both hatched December 30 in the early morning.

In Z2 Paddock in 1961 the first egg was laid between 7:21 and 9:00 A.M. on January 17; the second the following day between 7:27 and 8:15 A.M.; both hatched on February 17 in the early morning.

In Z3 Paddock during 1961 the bird laid the first egg November 2 between 6:50 and 6:59 A.M.; the second the next day between 6:50 and 7:55 A.M.; both hatched during the early morning of December 3.

In Z4, a public area, in 1962 the first egg was laid between 6:47 and 8:45 A.M. on November 16; the second egg was laid the next day between 6:15

and 8:06 A.M.; both hatched December 17, again in the early morning.

In Z5, in the alfalfa field, the first egg was laid between 7:10 and 7:26 A.M., December 1, 1963; the second egg was laid the next day between 7:15 and 7:39 A.M.; both hatched in the early morning of January 1, 1964.

The results were very similar at a sixth nest. Yet I found a somewhat different behavior near the Drakensberg Mountains, Natal at Nest 5, twenty miles west of the Mooi River. Here I observed seventeen Blue Cranes in a future nesting vlei. On December 13 the first egg was laid before noon. On December 14 there was still but one egg, but the next day the second egg was laid in the morning. At Nest 9, twenty-two miles west of the Mooi River, I found a nest at 4:30 P.M. December 16, with one egg. There was still only one egg the next two days, but on December 19 at noon there were two. The eggs in Nest 5 hatched January 14, 1962 (William Barnes, John and Jack Vincent), but those in Nest 9 were washed out by high water.

William Barnes (South African Nest File Cards) found two Blue Crane nests—each with one egg—during 1962. The first had one egg November 20, and a second egg on November 22. One hatched December 20, the second by 10:00 A.M., December 21. The second nest had one egg November 24 at 11:00 A.M., but two eggs the same time the next day. On December 22 at 10:00 A.M. there were two eggs, one pipped considerably, and the next morning there were two young.

In the zoo nests studied by Van Ee, five incubation periods were all thirty days, as in the one nest I observed. The incubation period was twenty-nine days in the two nests studied by William Barnes and Plath (1943) gave it as thirty-three days in the Brookfield Zoo, Oak Park, Illinois.

Allowing an incubation period of thirty days, and from known laying dates, first eggs were laid during 1961 on November 9, 16, 20, 24, 26 and 28 and December 2, 7, 8, 11, 14 and 16, with the average November 30.

In collections, and from other egg records, earliest eggs were found on October 3, 1962 (2), October 14, 1962 and October 17, 1939, while the latest record was March 1, 1917 (two fresh eggs).

From records sent to me or found in museums and the literature, nine egg records were made in October, sixteen in November, twenty-four in December, seven in January, four in February and one in March.

THE EGGS

Blue Crane eggs are ovate to long ovate in shape, lack any gloss, have a few nodules over the entire surface at times and are darker in color than most crane eggs. The ground color is buffy-brown or smoky-gray, spotted heavily over the entire surface with varying-sized markings of shades of olive, brownish-olive, dusky-brown and, at times, even black. The irregularly-shaped markings are often arranged in wavy striations along the long axis of the egg with more near the larger end. The average measurements of fifty-two eggs with standard deviations were 92.4 (80.6-101.0) ± 4.35 mm X 59.63 (55.1-65.5) ± 2.11 mm.

Van Ee (1966) and I (1963) listed measurements of first- and second-laid eggs in twelve different sets, showing little difference in average sizes. Twelve first-laid eggs averaged 93.2 X 59.05 mm, while twelve second-laid eggs averaged 94.15 X 59.05 mm. However, the twelve eggs laid by the zoo birds averaged 95.94 X 58.87 mm, longer than thirty-eight I measured in Natal, which averaged 91.69 X 59.96 mm.

The average weight of twenty-seven eggs in Natal was 171.4 g, with extremes of 141.8 and 201.8 g. The average weight of six newly-laid eggs was 185.3 (168.2-201.8) g; for twelve eggs during mid-incubation, 167.4 (150.4-187.5) g; for nine eggs at hatching time, 156.4 (141.8-183.2) g.

The average size of sixty-one clutches was 1.901 (7 X 1; 53 X 2; 1 X 3) eggs.

INCUBATION

Observing the Blue Cranes in the zoo at Bloemfontain, Van Ee found that the male birds seldom incubated eggs, and that the females often left the eggs for periods of time ranging from seven minutes to 4.07 hours. This varies greatly from the habits of the birds in the wild in Natal and other cranes in the wild. Van Ee (1966) wrote that there was a constant watch at the nest but, "in ZI, the eggs were covered 83 per cent of the time. In Z2 the eggs were covered 76 per cent, Z3 42 per cent, Z4 89 per cent and Z5 41 per cent of the time (daylight)," while Z6 incubated 56 per cent of the observed time. Yet all eggs had the same thirty-day incubation period. From thermocouples in nests, where not torn out by the birds, the maximum temperature reached in Z2 was 103.5° F., no day-temperature being higher than 93° F. during incubation, and a minimum of 45.5° F. being recorded when the minimum night temperature went to 43° F. In Z5 the maximum recorded was 107.9° F. and the minimum, 55.7° F., the last the night of December 16, when the air temperature went to 52° F. This fluctuation apparently had no effect upon the embryos.

I (1963) reviewed two-and-a-half days' observations on birds near the Drakensberg Mountains in Natal.

"Incubation commenced immediately after the first egg was laid. It was performed by both parents, and during 2 complete days of observation one pair changed places at least 9 times on the first day and 10 on the other. At one nest the male incubated at night; at the other the female. During nearly 3 days' observation (1,927 minutes), the male incubated 823 minutes (42.6 percent) of the time while the female incubated 1,047 minutes (54.3 percent) of the time. Eggs were unattended for only 57 minutes (3 percent of the time) and usually then when some man came near to a nest. The first morning change on 2 days was at about 0530 and at 0612. Last changes on three nights were 1815, 1830 and 1812. Sunrise was just prior to 0500 and sunset, 1900.

"On 14, 27, and 30 December, 12 periods of incubation by the male averaged 64.25 (18-89) minutes; 11 periods by the female, 93.8 (56-190) minutes. Actual incubation during the average day of 766 minutes consisted of 674 minutes (87.9 percent). During the remainder of the time the incubating bird stood on the nest gazing about, preening, etc.

"In the early morning, after the first change, the bird that had been incubating left the nest vicinity for some time and fed some distance from the nest. After the second change, the second bird did the same. Thereafter, they usually remained close to the nest. They often fed on grasshoppers and other insects, but more often on the seeds from the heads of nearby grasses and sedges. At times they ate crabs, parts of which they fed their young.

"Usually the bird leaving the nest walked to its regular feeding ground, pecking at morsels as it went, stopping to drink at times, occasionally stopping to preen, but always on the alert. Sometimes they walked over a nearby hill out of sight, at times more than a kilometer from the nest. But soon they returned slowly to the nest. Then the second bird repeated the performance. Seldom did they fly."

BEHAVIOR TOWARD OTHER BIRDS AND MAMMALS

Van Ee (1966) wrote: "Any bird or mammal approaching the nesting-site was relentlessly attacked by the male. Even in the case of Z3, which shared its nest in the paddock with cows, the latter did not at the end of the breeding period cross an imaginary line half-way through the paddock, out of fear of being kicked in the face by the male. The wounds inflicted by the kicking of the male are serious and blood was drawn on several occasions. Tortoises nearing the nest were attacked with the beak and by hitting the head and the legs of the tortoise, the animal was made to turn around and put to flight. Guinea-fowls, plovers and even sparrows were chased away. A stuffed guinea-fowl was put at the edge of the nest and was torn to pieces in less than 5 minutes by both birds. This was the only instance in which the female took part in an attack (Z5). Calling followed after these attacks. An area with a diameter of 50 feet was in this way kept clear of any approaching bird or mammal."

He also wrote that behavior toward persons was as follows:

"As soon as a human entered the breeding grounds he was attacked by the male. First there was a threatening attitude, wings spread open, body was erect, beak pointing at the person. If the latter turned around, attack followed immediately by picking and kicking at any spot the bird could reach. This continued until the person left the breeding area. If he was not frightened by the threatening attitude of the male and still approached the nest, the attack would start in all its ferocity, being so heavy at times that the kicking birds' legs stuck with their nails in the clothes and arms of the approaching person, clothes being torn to pieces at times. Immediately after dislodging the nails the attack continued. Waving a stick or hat did not make the slightest impression on the bird. On the contrary, it aroused more ferocity. The female was then crouching very low around the person and the fighting male bird, wings spread, giving the impression of being wounded, if the person approached her he could come as near as to five feet from her, the male always trying to be between her and him. She kept this position up to nearly 250 feet from the nest, the measured distance in Z6 being 287 feet from the eggs. The attitude of the female was very panicky if the nest was really approached as had to be done to take the temperature measurements. She sometimes, as in the case of Z5, fell over on her side, lying motionless with outspread wings. When the person turned away from the nest and was far away enough for the male to stop his attacks, both birds joined in calling and repeated this several times before returning to the nest." These, of course, were in zoo grounds.

I wrote (1963): "Because of their size and prominent blue color, Stanley Cranes were quite conspicuous. Since the majority of nests were located in situations where the surrounding vegetation was short, they were conspicuous on the nest. Their chief concern was man. When anyone appeared in close proximity to their nest, they walked away. In two cases where the surrounding vegetation was taller, the incubating bird remained on the nest with its head extended in front of it, well hidden from view.

"When the incubating bird left the nest, it was almost immediately joined by its mate which was always feeding nearby. Walking a few meters apart, they circled the man near or at the nest—sometimes with wings outspread, sometimes dancing, sometimes calling, sometimes silent. As soon as the man left the nest region, the bird that had been incubating usually returned to the eggs.

"Seldom did they pay any attention to other birds, only occasionally chasing one of the larger ones if it came too near their nest. They chased other Blue Cranes immediately if they came into their territory, driving them out by air.

"All nests were located where cattle, sheep, sometimes wild mammals, such as eland, grazed. I never saw any of these mammals come very near to a nest. The mammals avoided the nest site. No nests that I found were trampled down by cattle even though there were large herds in some of the fields."

THE YOUNG

I wrote (1963): "In the 17 nests that I observed, 34 eggs were laid. Four of these were deserted because of some human interference. The outcome of two was unknown. From the remaining 28 eggs, 25 hatched (89 percent). Two eggs from one nest were washed out by heavy rains; 1 egg was infertile. At Giant's Castle, several of the park men reported that eggs and young were lost because of heavy hail at times. Others reported that half-grown young were captured at times for food. These seemed to be the chief limiting factors.

"Young could be heard peeping inside the eggs about 24 hours before these were pipped. They hatched 12-24 hours after the eggs were first pipped. After hatching, they remained wet and bedraggled in the nest for several hours. As they dried off, their down acquired a fine sheen, and they became much more stable on their legs. They remained in the nest about 12 hours. When the birds in a nest hatched on successive days, the older youngster remained longer. The parents then led them to higher land, feeding as they went. On these higher short-grass, pastured fields they were raised.

"Newly hatched young tried repeatedly to pick up objects. If they were with a nest mate, they often pecked at each other's face and bill, sometimes severely. But on several occasions I observed a pair of adults with two young one-third grown, indicating that they did bring both young through the posthatching period."

Van Ee (1966) wrote: "After the chicks hatched, the drying usually took 3-4 hours after which they started to get up and look around. The first walking movements were noticed 6-8 hours after hatching.

"Both parents were extremely interested in the

youngsters and called regularly. The first day was spent in the nest and around it not farther than five yards away from it. The behaviour of the male and the female was still the same on the first day, the male fiercely attacking, the female crouching away from the nest with the chicks. No flattening movements were seen from the chicks in Z1-Z5, though in Z6 when the danger in the form of a person came too near, both chicks flattened. This could be called an 'intruder reaction,' as it was performed only when the person was very close to them and as soon as he retreated both chicks stood erect to look around.

"The second day the chicks started walking around with the parents and the behaviour of the female now totally altered. She became as aggressive as the male and an intruder was attacked by both birds. The chicks did not flatten when an attack was going on, but stood looking around. There was little rest for the chicks during the day as both parents were always on the move. When the sun was very hot the chicks walked or stood in the shadow of the parents. There was only a definite period of rest during the hottest time of the day, mostly between 2-4 P.M. The chicks were lying down in the shadow of the old birds. When the chicks lie down they flatten their necks onto the ground and give the impression of being dead.

"On the first day after hatching no feeding was seen. The second day the female started lifting up pieces of food and brought them to the beak of the youngster, touching it several times before the youngster accepted it. There was never a begging movement from the youngster. The male bird did not take part in the feeding at all. Food-offering was done nearly every five minutes the first two days, after this the tempo increased. The first two days are critical in the life of a young crane.

"The way the female begged the youngsters to take the food is remarkable. She touched the beak of the youngster from left to right very softly and sometimes as often as twelve times, before the youngster accepted the food offered. During the offering of the food a very low and soft *urrrrrrrr* could be heard. This the mother bird did until the third day. After the first two days the youngster took food more readily and after the sixth day the female just offered the food and it was taken by the youngster at once. She kept on offering food not longer than 10 days. After that she only pointed her beak to the food and the youngster started taking it from the ground. After 15 days the youngsters picked up their food without the aid of the female."

He added that when the youngsters began moving about, parent birds did not go around anything they were able to walk over, so the chicks often had a rather hard task going over objects such as stones, tree stumps, etc. Sometimes it took the chicks five to ten minutes to mount these obstacles from which they fell to the opposite side. They, like other downy cranes, were good swimmers, swimming at times up to thirty-five feet.

Van Ee continued: "The care of the young birds lasts until the next breeding season when they are chased away from the breeding ground. In the case of Z1 the youngsters were still seen with their parents after eight months.

"Flying movements of the youngsters start very late after hatching (this might start earlier if the parents could fly). In the case of Z1 the youngsters could fly after five months and in Z5 only after six months. In the case of Z6 the youngsters were able to fly after three months and three weeks. The voice of youngsters was heard after four days when a soft peep-peep accompanied their movements.

Stanley Crane chicks, one just hatched, the second less than one day old, 20 miles west of Mooi River, Natal, South Africa, December 28, 1961.

This sound was still heard when they were more than a year old. The real calling started only after 16 months. The attacking of the old birds lost its impetuosity after three months and ceased after five months (Z5) when they were approached by a human being. Instead they took flight with the youngsters following their parents."

He wrote that hand-reared birds grew more slowly than those raised by their parents.

Just prior to the new nesting season, parents drive last year's young away from them. The youngsters join with other similar young, forming varying-sized flocks, feeding on velds and fields, roosting at night in some shallow pond or river bar, most often some distance from shore.

Blaauw (1897) wrote: "Mr. Ayres informs us . . . about twenty miles below Bloemhof (on the Vaal River) are favourite places of assembly for the bird during migration in winter. He saw them here amusing themselves by dancing and by soaring at immense heights in the air. Barratt observed as many as fifty birds in one of these hibernating flocks. These assemblies generally sleep standing in water in company with Crowned Cranes, Flamingoes and Storks, and Holub observed that they always try to reach the middle of the pool for the safety, and that if the troop is numerous (as many as 300 birds being sometimes assembled in a large pool) the voices of the birds are heard all through the night. . . . One night the experiment was made to approach a sleeping flock of these Cranes in a pool, but, although all possible pains were taken to come near to them unnoticed under cover of the reeds, the disturbance was signalled when the invaders were some fifty paces distant and soon all the birds flew away. During the day these flocks often mix with the heads of Springbok Antelopes, and all feed together in perfect harmony. The Cranes often warn the Antelopes of coming dangers, being very watchful and flying off as soon as they see anything unusual, when the Antelopes follow their example and run away also. The Cranes do not fly high on these occasions, seldom mounting into the air above a few yards. When migrating they often fly at a great height."

THE VOICE

Blaauw (1897) wrote: "The voice of this Crane is guttural and although much louder than that of *Anthropoides virgo* has in some of its notes much resemblance to it."

It also resembles the call of *Grus canadensis*, but is not as loud and shorter. The alarm call of the adult is a shrill *Karrooo*, and a similar call, the unison call, is often given by birds at the nest when they change places. Calling also is given from the roosting flocks, and this increases in intensity in the early evening or early morning. When birds become paired, they often increase their calling during the two weeks prior to egg-laying. Van Ee also has shown this to be the case. When calling the downy chicks to them or reassuring each other they often give a low guttural *purrr*. By imitating this call, I was able to call the downy chicks to me from their hiding places in the surrounding vegetation.

The young give a shrill *peeep*, at times even from the egg before they hatch, and thereafter. Sometimes it has a strong burr to it, more a *peeer*. Van Ee reported the change from this to the adult voice came when about sixteen months old, but I did not hear wild birds giving it from the non-breeding flocks when the youngest birds must have been ten to twelve months of age. All birds were giving the adult call at that time.

When giving the 'Unison Call' the male raises his inner secondaries with some pointing even higher than others, so they are all well above his back and tail with the primaries drooping stiffly below them. The female holds her wings against her sides. The male arches his neck over his back and calls with the bill pointing upward and often backward. The female raises her neck upward and has the bill pointing normally straight up.

FOOD

Blaauw (1897) wrote: "These Cranes are stated to feed a great deal on locusts and in the years that locusts are abundant they become very useful. . . . Besides locusts, these Cranes feed on all kinds of insects, worms, reptiles, fishes and small mammals, also on different bulbs and other vegetable matter, animal food, however, forming the greater part of the diet."

The birds I watched often fed from the ground, capturing insects, including grasshoppers, frogs and crabs. They also pecked seeds from the surrounding grasses and sedges. During grain-planting time they can cause damage to wheat, corn and other farm crops. They also dig up roots, some of which they eat. Van Ee wrote that they liked nearly any kind of food.

DISTRIBUTION

The Blue Crane is found south of the Zambezi, confined chiefly to eastern South Africa, from the grasslands to Karoo. It has also been recorded from Mashonaland.

Blaauw (1897) wrote: "During the annual dry season this species migrates in some places." Roberts (1951) wrote that the migrations remained to be mapped. From the Drakensberg Mountain region, migrations are chiefly altitudinal, up in September, down in March. Up to 200 birds concentrate winters in the Swartberg District, East Griquland (Shephard, 1962); pairs or parties up to twenty remain the entire year in Weenan County, Natal (West, Wright and Symons, 1964); while 300 congregate commonly in winter in the Orange Free State (Van Ee, letter, December 19, 1966). Here the elevation is 1,428 m. Concentrations were reported to me from Transvaal. Hewitt (1931) reported flocks from twenty to three hundred near Bedford, Cradock and Tarka.

SOUTH AFRICA. *Cape Province.* This crane has been reported in Beaufort West, Berg River, Colesberg, Deelfontein (common), Hope Town, Knysna, Nelsport, Port Elizabeth and King Williams Town.

Jourdain (1935) collected a set of two eggs (BMNH) labeled Cape Colony, while another set of two eggs was taken by W. de Klerk de Klerk, December 3, 1941 at Kingsdale, Adelaide.

Winterbottom (1966) did not include the Blue Crane from Arid Karoo and Namaqua Broken Veld of Cape Province, and rarely from Central Upper Karoo, but he did report it abundantly in False Upper Karoo. His percentage of occurrence in these four communities was 2, 0, 0 and 41.

Blue Crane nests have been recorded (South African Nest Cards and recent literature, Percy Fitzpatrick Institute of African Ornithology) from Cape Province at Adelaide (two eggs) October 1939 by W. de Klerk de Klerk. J. S. Taylor (1964)

said the species nests in October. In the drier Karroid open veld at Albany (32° S.; 27° E.) Skead (1965) recorded the species. At Amanzi (32° 26′S.; 25° 30′E.) and Bathurst (32° S.; 27° E.) single birds and pairs were observed in July, September, November and January to April, with young in February (C. K. and P. N. F. Niven, 1966; E. M. Jones, 1965). At Bedford a two-egg nest was found October 21, 1947 by V. L. Pringle; at Bradesdorp, a two-egg nest December 27, 1958 by C. J. Uys and another with two eggs was found in wheat stubble by Mrs. Martin November 25, 1965. At Colesberg (31° S.; 25° E.) Dott found a nest (two eggs) March 1, 1917; at DeAar (31°S.), S. F. Townsend found nests October 1883 (one egg) and February 1894 (two eggs). At Swartberg, East Griqualand, Shepard (1962) reported winter flocks up to 200 or more, while at Fort Jackson (East London) (32°S; 27.5° E.) Miss Courtenay-Latimer (1964) reported it as resident, as did Winterbottom (1962a, 1962b) at Worcester District, Brandvlei and Whitesands.

Blaauw (1897) wrote that Holub and Pelzeln claimed this species bred in West Griqualand, in southern Bechuana country and the more open parts of the bushveld of the Kalahari Desert.

Orange Free State. Van der Plaat (1961) reported the Blue Crane as widespread here. Stark and Sclater (1906) recorded it at Bloemfontein (el. 1,428 m), while F. A. Barratt took an egg set (one egg, BMNH) December 5, 1874. Van Ee reported it common with flocks of up to 300 in July. At Dewetsdorp an egg set (two eggs, SANFC) was taken February 25, 1906. It was recorded at Lindley (Stark and Sclater, 1906) and two egg sets were recorded by Sparrow (1935): two eggs, December 8, 1901 and one egg taken December 13, 1901. At Kirklington (el. 1,615 m) Boddam-Whetham (1965) said the species was an unusual visitor, while an egg set (one egg, SANFC) was taken January 19, 1951 by R. E. Skamon at Viljoensdrif. In the Rothschild Collection (BMNH) one egg was taken November 3, 1916 at Lofter, while Van Ee (letter) reported Blue Cranes bred in nearly all districts of the Orange Free State.

Transvaal. Blaauw (1897) wrote that the Blue Crane was generally distributed here. I crossed Transvaal by train in both December 1961 and January 1962 but saw no birds.

At Belfast (26° S.; 30° E.) eggs were reported December 9, 1901 (SANFC), while two sets, both two eggs, were found at Bloemhof (27.5° S.; 25° E.) February 26, 1942 (late because of drought—D. C. H. Plowes). Blaauw (1897), Stark and Sclater (1906) and Skead (1965) also recorded the species from here. J. de V. Little (1963) reported it common in the high veld (el. over 1,219 m) in the Caroline District, P. le S. Milstein (1962) noted it at Groblersdal and Markus (1964) reported it not uncommon at Pretoria. An egg set (two eggs, BMNH) was taken by Col. Stephenson Clark December 10, 1902 at Ermelo at Kaffir Spruit; another (one egg) on October 25, 1900 at Middelburg.

Natal. I was in Natal from December 6, 1961 until January 10, 1962. I neither heard of nor saw any cranes around Durban, Pietersmaritzburg, nor until I reached Nottingham Road from the east. Here there was a flock (up to sixty-three) on land owned by Sir George Usher. There were none close to the Mooi River, nor at Rosetta, but two pairs nested on the Godfrey Symons farm near Estcourt and one pair on the Price Moor farm near Lowlands. Jack Vincent (verbal) reported cranes usually nested on the plateau and upwards, above 1,524 meters. Birds nested up to 2,134 meters in the Drankensberg Mountains.

Concerning this region I wrote (1963): "Some Blue Cranes have been found nesting in the dry thornveld (el. 914-1,219 m) in the region of streams and dams. But the chief breeding grounds are the highland sourveld (6,395 km², el. 1,372-1,829 m) and the lower portion of the bergveld (el. 2,000 m). These are mostly pastured grass-covered hills, valleys, and plains with a few scattered tree plantings. Besides the Mooi River uplands and a narrow belt along the Drakensberg Mountains, the highland sourveld has an eastward and southward extension into the Orange Free State plateau (Thornington-Smith, 1960)."

I observed seventeen nests, as well as observations by others, as follows:

Estcourt: A nest was found November 11, 1961 by Barry Symons. On his farm I observed it December 11. It had two eggs, one of which hatched

that day, the second the next. Godfrey Symons found another nest which was deserted later in December 1961. The Symons' and Charles Jerome had in their collections these egg sets: three eggs, November 3, 1933 and two eggs, November 24, 1955. D. C. H. Plowes recorded a nest (two eggs) twenty miles southwest of Estcourt December 3, 1941 (SANFC), and two sets (one egg, two eggs) were recorded as having been found by Mr. Turner October 3, 1963 and October 4, 1964.

Giant's Castle, in the Little Berg Region. William Barnes showed me a nest (two eggs) December 12, 1961; a second nest (two eggs) January 1, 1962; another in early December 1961. We also found a nest with two newly-hatched chicks January 2, 1962 and another pair with a one-third- grown chick on the same day. William Barnes has found many nests during recent years in this region. Two nests, each with one egg, were found November 20 and November 24, 1962. Both later contained two eggs. D. M. Skead (SANFC) reported two nests (both two eggs) November 16, 1960 and January 5, 1961.

Lowlands, east of Estcourt. A two-egg nest was found by Price Moor on his farm December 23, 1961 and on December 28th I observed a pair about two kilometers from here with two chicks about one-third grown. Moor reported these birds nested again during December 1966 as they had for many years (letter).

Mooi River. About 26 to 30 kilometers west on the reaches of the Hlatikulu and Little Mooi Rivers, I found several nests (all two eggs) December 11, 13 (two nests), 14, 16, and 21, 1961 and January 7, 1962. R. Dean discovered a nest (two eggs) near this river in December 1957 (SANFC). In the Charles Jerome and Godfrey Symons collections are two sets (both two eggs) taken December 4, 1948 and November 14, 1951. Another set (two eggs, Transvaal Museum, Pretoria) was taken here October 17, 1939.

Rockmount, near Drakensberg foothills. William Barnes and I found a nest (two eggs) January 7, 1962. During early January that year I observed several pairs with small chicks throughout this region.

Some other Natal observations are:

Hilton, just outside of Pietermaritzburg. Guy Hardingham (letter, January 25, 1963) reported seeing a nest here. There is another record of a nest (two eggs, SANFC) from here by D. A. Calder, October 19, 1941.

Himesville. Hardingham (*loc. cit.*) reported Blue Cranes nesting here every year near the end of September up until the end of October.

Ladysmith. Sparrow (1935) recorded a two-egg set November 29, 1903 and another set from Natal without more data.

Greytown. One set of two eggs (Pietermaritzburg Museum) was taken here in 1897 and another labeled Natal (two eggs) was taken January 19, 1915.

Nottingham Road. N. H. S. Michaelhouse (SANFC) discovered a nest (two eggs) October 14, 1962. I observed many cranes in this region during December 1961 and January 1962.

Pietermaritzburg (el. 1,828 m and 64 km west). David Alder (letter, September 1954) reported Blue Cranes nested on his farm annually.

Qudeni (Zululand). W. J. Lawson (SANFC) discovered two nests November 17, 1965 (one egg, two eggs).

SOUTH-WEST AFRICA. Blaauw (1897) reported this bird as migrating here during the rainy season and that it bred in both Damaraland and Great Namaqualand. During dry weather it congregated in favorable places. Winterbottom (1965) listed it from here too. Smithers (1964) did not include it from Bechuanaland Protectorate nor from the Caprivi Strip. I find no records from Mozambique.

LESOTHO (Basutoland). Winterbottom (1964) reported that J. P. Murray saw this species fly across Mafeteng.

DESCRIPTION

Breeding adult. The sexes are similar in appearance. The most prominent color is blue, pearly-gray, somewhat darker on the upper neck and back of the head, where the feathers are thick, dense and decomposed. Primaries are black or slaty-gray with coverts darker than the back. Secondaries, especially the innermost ones, are much elongated, extending so far beyond the tail that they often drag on the ground. These become nearly black or pearly-black near the tips. The crown, forehead,

lores and the anterior part of the cheeks have varying amounts of white. The tail is black, or nearly so. Cheeks, ear-coverts and nape are dark ashy-gray, the feathers lengthened, disintegrated and loose, giving a cobralike puffiness to the head. The feathers of the foreneck are elongated and pointed. The eye is dark brown; the bill, pale ochre with a strong tinge of pink. The legs and feet are dark gray or black.

Sub-adult. These birds are much more tawny than the downy chick and have darker legs and feet. The down on the head and upper neck is yellowish-tawny changing to tawny. As the sub-adult becomes older it acquires a lighter blue-gray color than in adults, but the top of the head still remains somewhat tawny. When about three months old it acquires the post-juvenal plumage slightly lighter gray than the adult.

Downy chick. Newly-hatched chicks are covered with short buffy-yellow down over the entire head and most of the neck. The shoulders, upper portion of the wings, back, rump, and some on the sides, are pearly gray with scattered regions of buff along the sides. The lower portion of the anterior part of the throat, the breast and the undersides of the wings are nearly white. The eye is dark brown. At first the legs and feet are very swollen, bluish-gray in color, with the undersides of the feet and toes buffy-yellow. When one day old, the legs and tops of the toes become much darker gray. The pale bluish-gray bill has a flesh-colored base and a white egg-tooth at the tip. There are two small claws on each wing—one at the tip, the second at the bend.

Five Blue Crane chicks at hatching averaged 103.1 g in weight, varying between 97.1 and 109.2 g. Their wing measurements averaged 31.7 (30.3-33) mm; tarsi, 42.5 (40-45) mm; exposed culmen, 19.5 (19.3-20) mm; middle toe (34.3 (33-37.2) mm.

Four one-day-old chicks averaged 120.1 (111.4-134.2) g in weight. Their average measurements were: wing, 33.3 (30-35) mm; tarsi, 43.1 (41.4-49) mm; exposed culmen, 19.6 (19-21) mm; middle toe, 35.2 (33.5-36.5) mm.

MEASUREMENTS

Adult specimens. Two males in the South African

Museum measured: wings, 570 and 550 mm; tail, 265 and 229 mm; exposed culmen, 88 and 81 mm; tarsus, 215 and 205 mm. Two females (BMNH, 1903.3.9.880; Chicago Natural History Museum, 297054), the first taken March 19 at Deelfontein, C.P. and the second from the Brookfield Zoo, Oak Park, Illinois, measured: wing, 550 mm; tail, 243 mm; exposed culmen, 94 and 87 mm; tarsus, 243 and 252 mm; bare tibia, 120 and 105 mm; middle toe with claw, 98 and 85 mm. The average measurements of ten specimens (two male, two female, others—sexes unknown) were: wing, 552.6 (514-590) mm; tail, 237.5 (202-265) mm; exposed culmen, 88.8 (81-98) mm; tarsus, 235.2 (205-252) mm; bare tibia, 119.7 (105-130) mm; middle toe with claw, 97.3 (85-113) mm (So. Af. Mus., 2; BMNH, 6; CNHM, 1; MCZ, 1).

Blaauw (1897) gave these measurements: total length, about 101.6 cm; exposed culmen, 101 mm; wing, 584 mm; tail, 216 mm; tarsus, 254 mm; middle toe and claw, 89 mm.

Roberts (1940) gave: length, 1,067 mm; wing, 560 mm, with the long secondaries projecting about 445 mm beyond the primaries; tail, 228 mm; tarsus, 235 mm; culmen, 76 mm.

Stanley Crane near nest, west of Mooi River, Natal, South Africa, December 15, 1961.

Chapter Fourteen

THE WEST AFRICAN CROWNED CRANE

(*Balearica pavonina pavonina*)

Ardea pavonina, Linnaeus, *Syst. Nat.,* 10th ed., i, 1758, p. 141.
Type locality: Cape Verde, Senegal (Willoughby, *Orn,* 1667, p. 201, plate 48).
Vernacular names: The West African Crowned Crane, The Dark Crowned Crane (English); l'Oiseau royal le Grue couronnée (French); Pfauenkranich (German); de Kroonkraan, de Kroonvogel (Dutch); Guaraka (Hausa).

The West African Crowned Crane is slightly larger and has more white in the cheek than the Sudan Crowned Crane. Both are much darker than either of the two southern forms, The East African and South African Crowned Cranes. The West African Crowned Crane has a very small red chin wattle but has a slight bare region there. The bare cheek-patch is white above with the lower portion reddish or pinkish and much wider than the white portion.

On July 23, 1965, as I checked out my luggage in the Jos, Nigeria, airport, a man approached me and introduced himself as Dr. Victor W. Smith, with whom I had corresponded for some time. He, his wife June, and son Roger, who had just arrived on another plane from England, and I, headed for the Smith house at Vom. This was my home for the next month. This region is the home of the West African Crowned Crane, and also the home of the Hausa and Fulani people. Here the people and cranes live in close proximity. The first day I saw many people, but no cranes. The next day Victor Smith took me out to Kafo and here I saw my first West African Crowned Cranes, three pairs of these beautiful stately birds. Two pairs were trudging across the plains; in a third pair, one bird was lying on the ground sunning and resting, its mate standing beside it. During the month I found many other pairs in the same region, at times a large flock up to twenty-eight or more birds. These birds fed, drank and danced as they roamed through the region, but as the month of August wore on the flock dwindled to six and the breeding pairs increased in numbers. Pairs began showing up in certain definite regions near and beyond Kafo, a few near Jos, Kurra Falls and one pair at Barikin Ladi.

One day I had the opportunity to ride with a lorry driver on his daily eighty-five-mile milk route. We passed through Tenti, Daffo, Bokkos and Mbar to Kuba. Many cans of milk were picked up in each village and vicinity. We left at 10 A.M. and arrived home after dark. The country was rolling, the roads good and bad and it rained some of the time. During this trip we saw only two pairs of cranes. People reported many of the birds had been shot.

On July 30 I hiked from Vom and circled a sugar cane patch where I had seen a lone Crowned Crane fly into a thick field of grass. As I approached, I found two women working in a cocoa yam patch only a short distance from a pair of cranes which stood watching them and me. I found the nest with one immaculate light blue egg. The women did not know I found it, so I left immediately. But the birds, fearful of the women close by, did not return. Two days later, when Victor Smith and I again visited the nest, some predator had eaten the egg, apparently along with a second one, leaving only broken shells strewn over the nest. A second nest incurred a similar fate.

Here women worked even closer. But soon I found four nests farther afield, far enough from working agriculturists to have better success. I found another nest in the clearing adjacent to Sacred Grove, sacred for many generations and consequently untouched and seldom disturbed. Only herds of pasturing cattle roamed through here in quest of water, and the cranes enjoyed better isolation. On August 9 this nest had two eggs; two days later there were three, while on September 6 June Smith found all three eggs pipped, so they should have hatched that day or the next. Another nest at Barikin Ladi was also built far out amongst rushes in a larger marsh, well removed from normal thoroughfares of traffic, so these, too, should have been successful.

Many things favor these birds. The residents like them and admire them for their beauty. They often capture the chicks or take the eggs to raise

Typical nest and eggs of West Africa Crowned Crane at Vom, Northern Nigeria, August 17, 1965.

the young in captivity. They are sometimes sought for food, and present-day laws do not protect them, even during the nesting season. We saw one man hunting right through the region of the greatest crane population during the height of the nesting season. The country is being defoliated of protective trees, more land is being put into agriculture and more land is drained annually. However, birds nest during the rainy season so they are somewhat protected by deeper water and greener, taller vegetation.

NESTING

Biotope. Small marshes, damp meadows, low spots on open plains, borders of lakes and stream, or even large open marshes, are used for nesting. In nearly all cases the birds require nearby dry open meadows for feeding. The elevations vary. In Gambia it must be close to sea level; at Lake Chad, around 922 feet (283 m); on the Nigerian Plateau it is between 3,600 and 4,500 feet (1,107-1,385 m).

Water, up to several inches deep, immediately surrounding the nest or in some manner aiding its isolation, is also essential, as is some vegetation to provide isolation, preferably complete. The pH of occupied Nigerian marshes varied between 6.64 and 6.8. The vegetation was knee- to shoulder-high, most often grasses, sedges or round rushes. Often the cranes nested in flooded fields where some crop was raised, such as rice, atcha or yams. The marshes were surrounded by treeless, or almost treeless, plains. From their nests, the birds had visibility, often for miles, and watched streams of humans daily as they moved to and from fields, farms and villages.

Nesting sites. Dr. Serle (Bannerman, 1951) wrote: "The surroundings of both nests were similar—water a foot deep interspersed with tufts of reed and coarse grass. Raised but a few inches above the level of the surrounding water the nest was a haphazard accumulation of grasses. A minimum of constructive effort had been made in building the nests, one of which was roughly circular, 30 ins. (76.2 cm) across; the other was oval 40 X 30 ins. (101.6 X 76.2 cm)."

Seven of the eight nests I found on the Jos Plateau, August 1965, were on dry land, yet all within three meters of water and all positioned so that in case of extreme rains the cranes could build them higher to keep the eggs above water. Six of the eight nests were built amongst farm crops, two so close that people kept the birds away long enough so that crows or other predators took the eggs from one and the other pair finally deserted. One nest was placed in two feet (61 cm) of water. All nests were less than one hundred meters from higher drier land where the birds fed.

Prenesting behavior. When I arrived at Vom, in northern Nigeria, July 22, 1965, many cranes were in flocks of from four to twenty-eight. In a few days these flocks dispersed. On August 17 a small flock of six was observed, but all other birds were then in pairs, located on nesting territories.

The birds in each pair remained close to each other, continuously roaming only a few feet apart over the great stretches of plains. They roosted side by side nights in some remote trees. Mornings they flew back to their feeding plains and often danced during the morning. The male usually instigated the dance. After he had jumped around the female for several minutes, she often entered the cooperative display and both danced, hopped, bowed and jumped about crazily. On completion of this activity they resumed feeding on nearby grass seeds. Thus they passed the time, stopping to preen for long periods. But as the rainy season progressed and the valleys began accumulating water, the birds moved into marshy places. In one place where a pair had fed for many days in late July, the female suddenly raised her head upward and forward on August 2 at 1:00 P.M. She stood quietly thus for about one minute. The male, ten feet away, came quickly, mounted her as she squatted slightly and they copulated, he standing on her back with his wings slowly waving. Then they fed again. Still, they showed no signs of nest-building. On August 5 one of them chased a marsh owl from the water-soaked yam patch, but shortly they flew to the plains a mile away and fed. At 1:35 P.M. the female flew from the male, who remained feeding, into a rice patch three or four hundred feet east of the yam patch. She called mournfully as she came, dropping immediately onto one of the dry narrow ridges extending parallel across the water-soaked rice field. She stood, calling mournfully periodically for about half an hour; then suddenly she flew back to feed with her mate. On August 11 these birds were in the yam patch. For some time they fed aimlessly between the yam patch and the rice field. At 8:50 A.M. they stopped feeding, worked up onto a slightly raised piece of ground, then alternately began trampling down the vegetation with their feet. Part of the time they scratched. This lasted twenty minutes. They pulled grass with their bills, tossing it sideways onto this spot, trampling and scratching some more. At 9:30 A.M. they resumed feeding. Later they flew out of sight and I did not see them again until 3:00 P.M. On another territory, the same day, I flushed a standing crane from a huge pile of vegetation on a raised mound in an atcha field. This bird flew away, calling mournfully.

On August 13, V. W. Smith stopped and observed a lone crane in the yam patch site. On August 14 I returned. A large crane fed five hundred feet from a smaller one, which was setting on the ridge where she had stood alone nine days earlier. The nest contained one egg, apparently laid the day before. On August 17 at 9:00 A.M. it contained three eggs.

The nest. Usually the nest is a haphazard pile of the nearest vegetation. After it is completed it is much neater because it has been trampled down and walked over so much. Both birds pull up vegetation and throw it on, or if too far away, towards,

West Africa Crowned Crane at nest, Vom, Nigeria, August 15, 1965.

the nest with a slight sidewise action. If it lands several meters away it is picked up later and tossed onto the nest. They scratch at times with their feet, moving all loose material in the vicinity towards the nest, but their chief mass of material is pulled up or off with the bills, then swung onto the nest.

Where I watched, if water was deep at the site the cranes built a larger nest, neater and much wider at the base with a narrower top. Grasses, sedges, rushes—anything with bulk—was used. One such nest was built in rushes. The majority of nests were in drier locations. Three were in atcha fields, one in a grassy field, one in grass in a cocoa-yam patch, one in a grass-sedge marsh, one in a rice patch and only the one in an immense rush-grown marsh.

The average measurements of eight nests were 88.2 (68.6-109.2) X 105.9 (71.1-139.7) cm across. The deep-water nest measured at water level 94 X 121.9 cm across, but at the top, which was 33 cm above water level, it was 35.6 X 38 cm.

Dr. V. W. Smith (1962, 1964) described several nests near Vom. All were similar to those I found. Cawkell and Moreau (1963) wrote that this species nests along the middle river only in Gambia from September to October.

When building dry-land nests, the birds often build two or more. Sometimes an extra nest is only a few meters from the occupied one, but in one territory it was three hundred meters away.

TERRITORY

Size. The size of territory maintained by each Crowned Crane pair varied between 86 and 388 hectares (some pairs had much more than a square kilometer under domination; others were compressed between neighboring territories into less than half a square kilometer). Usually, however, each pair lacked any close neighbors. The nesting territory was guarded much more closely than the more distant feeding territory to which the cranes paid little attention. Here they allowed both cranes and other birds species to feed without disturbance. Usually cranes fed from one-half to one mile from the actual nest. Most often they flew to the feeding grounds from the nest, but on occasion they walked, feeding as they went.

Defense. Both male and female chased other birds and cranes from the nesting territory— spur-winged geese, white-faced ducks, black-bellied bustards and marsh owls. If these birds came near the nest, one of the cranes flew toward them until they departed swiftly. Non-breeding cranes were chased in a similar manner, but when breeding pairs or one member of a pair came near, behavior was different. On two occasions a pair landed near another pair's nest (both had eggs). The defending incubating crane left its eggs, was joined immediately by its mate, and both pairs—the birds of each pair only a few feet apart—walked into a defense position opposite the other pair. This required only a short time, and as they came up the other cranes moved into a similar position only a few meters away. Here they both stopped. The male arched his neck, neck and head in a curve, bill pointing groundward, and stood almost motionless for ten to thirty minutes. Often both males went into the same pose. Once a male shook himself after fifteen minutes, spread his feathers, shook some more, preened (false preening), while the other did the same. On no occasions did I see actual bodily contact or evidence of attack, but in two cases all four birds were extremely alert. After all four cranes preened for several minutes, all began feeding; the tension was broken and they worked back into their territorial centers, one bird of each pair going to the eggs.

The steps in this procedure were: (1) the birds noted a trespassing intruder; (2) they approached the intruder; (3) they assumed the defense pose; (4) they false-preened. A fifth step would have been attack, but in these cases it was not necessary and possibly the false-preening pose is substituted for attack in many cases.

THE EGGS

Eggs, when fresh, are immaculate, light blue or pink, with a rather rough shell, some with a slight gloss, ovate-shaped or subelliptical. Even when one day old they become stained and when ready to hatch are so badly stained the original ground color is not discernible. Fifteen eggs, not more than two days old, averaged in weight 140 (122.0-168.1) grams. At hatching time three eggs averaged 115.3 (the last weights taken by Mrs. V. W. Smith).

Twenty-one eggs averaged in measurements 80.1 (76.3-86.8) × 57.9 (55.0-61.4) mm, slightly larger than eggs of the Sudan Crowned Crane. I observed five complete sets in 1965, one of two eggs, four of three. In thirteen complete egg sets at Vom, ten had three eggs, three had two.

J. B. Welman found a nest in August 1924 with three eggs at Gashua, Northern Bornu, and observed many other cranes apparently on eggs near the the River Yo during the last week in August (Bannerman, 1931). Bannerman (1951) gave one record for September 22. V. W. Smith (1962, 1964) gave egg set dates as: July 10, 1960 (three eggs); July 27, 1961 (first of three eggs); July 5, 1962 (three eggs); August 30, 1963 (first of three eggs).

Nests I found at Vom, Nigeria, in 1965 had eggs laid as follows: July 30 (one egg, later broken, probably by pied crows); August 2 and 4 (two eggs laid, later deserted); August 6, 8 and 10 (eggs laid on each of these dates, all of which were pipped the early morning of September 6 and must have hatched that day and the next); August 13, 14 and 16 (eggs laid on each of these dates, but destroyed by predator on August 20); August 16 (complete set of three eggs found); August 17 (another complete set of three eggs and one of two eggs found, and another nest with no eggs, even the next day).

Incubation. Incubation, performed by both birds, begins when the first egg is laid. One bird remains on the nest all night; the other roosts one-half to one mile away in a small tree, which is usually well-leafed out. On one occasion a bird roosted in a leafless tree. The smaller bird, probably the female, incubated at night. During two complete days of observation, the first was somewhat interrupted by cattle herds watering near the nest site; the second day there were no interruptions.

On August 12, two days after the third egg was laid, the female incubated 330 daylight minutes all night to 7:29, 9:25-10:14 11:27-11:57 A.M., 1:00-2:12 P.M. and 5:15 P.M. through the night). The male was on the nest 260 minutes (7:29-8:03, 10:14-11:27 A.M. and 2:12-4:45 P.M.). Three periods were spent away from the nest (8:03-9:25 A.M., 11:57 A.M.-1:00 P.M. and 4:45-5:15 P.M., totaling 175 minutes), the first by the birds' own

Blind at Crowned Crane nest, Vom, Nigeria, August 15, 1965.

volition. Thus, between 6:00 A.M. and 6:45 P.M., daylight to dark, the eggs were attended by one or the other parent for 75.7 per cent of the time (36.1 per cent by the male). The female remained on the nest the night of August 12 from 5:15 until 6:30 A.M. on August 13. At the same nest, August 13, between 6:00 A.M. and 6:45 P.M., the female was on the eggs 376 minutes (all night to 6:30 A.M., 7:31-9:15, 10:57-11:58 A.M., 12-17-2:02, 2:45-3:36 and 6:20 P.M. on through the night) for 49.15 per cent of observed time; the male incubated for 362 minutes (6:30-7:31, 9:15-10:30 A.M., 11:58 A.M.-12:17 P.M., 2:02-2:45 and 3:36-6:20 P.M.) for 47.32 per cent of daylight time. Both birds were away from the nest twenty-seven minutes (10:30-10:57 A.M.). Thus, both birds attended the eggs a total of 96.47 per cent of the time, but the male, while there, stood over the eggs forty-two minutes without incubating and the female stood seventy-three minutes, during the day. Consequently, the eggs were incubated only 81.4 per cent of the daylight time.

The first change in the morning at Vom on four different days was at 6:36, 6:37, 7:29 and 6:30 A.M. The last changes occurred on two days at 5:15 and 6:20 P.M.

Although the eggs were laid August 6, 8 and 10 at Nest 3 at Vom, they were all pipped September 6 and the third certainly would have hatched only a few hours after the first, as I have observed with South African Crowned Cranes and V. W. Smith has observed with other Nigerian Crowned Cranes. The last egg in this case required twenty-eight days of incubation while the first was laid thirty-one days before it hatched.

THE YOUNG

Since the eggs hatch within a few hours of each other, not more than one day apart, the young are similar in age and remain with the incubating parent, especially if the weather is rainy. They probably require little food the first day, but the second day they begin to wander away with their parents in search of food. They remain near the nest for several days and may, like South African Crowned Cranes, return to the nest at night for a short period of time. Thereafter they roam with their parents over the drier portions of their nesting territory. According to V. W. Smith and others who have raised Crowned Cranes in Nigeria, the young are not able to fly until four months old.

Their voice changes from the *Peeep* of the downy young to the *Ka-wonk* of the adult when about one year old. The cheek patch becomes pink when between ten and twelve months of age. Apparently they do not breed until they are four years old.

VOICE

Young West African Crowned Cranes, like the other cranes, utter a low plaintive *Peeep* with a purr to it. Acquisition of the adult call is gradual. Adults call their chicks with a low guttural *Purrr*. Sometimes this sounds like a snort (Smith, 1964) or a snorelike noise. The characteristic adult call is a double-syllabled *Ka-wonk*, often repeated several times. Although mournful, it is much more gooselike than the calls of the South and East African Crowned Cranes. Bannerman described the call as *Oyak-oyak* or *Quack-Quack*. Regardless of in-

Downy South African Crowned Cranes, Rainham Dam, Salisbury, (Southern) Rhodesia, January 14, 1962.

terpretations, the call is strongly accented on the second syllable. A pet crane at Jos, Nigeria, also gave a low clucking while feeding, much like the clucking of a mother hen.

FOOD

Food consists of many grass seeds and, at times, grain. The birds may do some crop damage. They also eat millipedes (*Spirostreptus* sp.) and crabs (*Potamon* sp.) which are found rather abundantly in Northern Nigeria. They do much digging for roots and eat other insects too.

DISTRIBUTION

This crane is found predominantly in West Africa between 8° and 15° N. Latitude, from Cape Verde to Lake Chad and the Cameroons.

The type came from Cape Verde, Senegal (Willoughby, *Orn.*, 1667, p. 201, plate 48). Blyth and Tegetmeier (1881) wrote that it was common at the river Ponny in Cape Verde, in Guinea, Gambia, on the Gold Coast, in Fida and in Whida. Many birds were brought to Europe during the fifteenth century. Little has been written about their presence in Senegal since then.

Bannerman (1931) wrote that the species was common in certain places and bred especially in Niamina, Gambia, with flocks of hundreds occurring at Sallikenni and nearby places; that the first and only records on the Little Scarcies River in Sierra Leone were during April 1930; and its numbers had increased during the past fifty years in the northern portion of the Gold Coast, but it was not abundant in most parts of that country.

There is a specimen in the British Museum (Natural History) from North Tamale, Gold Coast (sex and date not given) and a male speciman taken July 21, 1909 at Gunnal, Portuguese Guinea. Another specimen (sex unknown) was taken in July 1872 at Accra, Ghana. In the same museum there are also three specimens from Northern Nigeria (two without other data), one of which was taken in either 1939 or 1940, eleven miles north of Kafanchan, Zaria. Two eggs from the above mentioned deserted nest were taken in August 1965 at Vom, Northern Nigeria, and are in the British Museum (Natural History).

Bannerman (1951) reported the species from French Sudan (present-day Mali), as well as Nigeria. More recently, Cawkell and Moreau (1963) reported it bred along the middle Gambia River and flocks numbering three hundred or more were found during the dry season.

NIGERIA. This species is generally and plentifully distributed in Northern Nigeria (Bannerman, 1931), especially north of 10° North Latitude. Since western and eastern Nigeria are, in general, heavily wooded, the species is probably only a straggler here. But on the open plateau of the north it is found in a favorable habitat. In Bornu it occurs in huge flocks as it does at Lake Chad (Bannerman, 1951) and its nests have been found at Gashua, Northern Bornu (Bannerman, 1931). Tony Hopson (letter) reported flocks in the Lake Chad region during the non-breeding season which dispersed during the rainy season to favorable nesting regions. On the Jos Plateau, Plateau Province, it is rare at Zaria (Fry, 1962). It was reported as present at Kaduna (Skilleter, 1963), but it is much more abundant and breeds at Vom (Smith, 1962, 1964). During 1965, when I stayed with the Victor Smith family at Vom, we found nests at Kafo, Kato, Vom, Makafo and Barikin Ladi and observed birds at Jos, Bukuru, Kurra Falls, Hoss Station, Machi, Kassa, Ropp, Kurra Dam, Tenti Dam, Mbar and north of Bokkos.

CAMEROON. The Crowned Crane is very abundant in the northern portion and occurs in large flocks in April during the non-breeding season (V. W. Smith, C. H. Fry and Dave Godfrey, verbal).

DESCRIPTION

Breeding adult. This form is very similar to *B. p. ceciliae,* but the latter is a little smaller and has slightly more red in the lower portion of the cheek patch.

As with other cranes the male is slightly larger, but both sexes are colored alike. The general color is dark slaty-gray passing into black, especially on the upperparts, where the feathers are pointed and more or less falcated. Wing coverts are white; the inner greater coverts straw-colored and composed of disintegrated plumes; primary coverts and alula are white. Primaries are black, the secondaries maroon-chestnut, the innermost ones a little broadened and lengthened and slightly decomposed. The tail is black. The crown is covered with velvety-black short feathers. The occiput has a tuft of strawlike bristles. Each bristle is a spiral, white on one side, brown on the other and black at the tip. These bristles all radiate from a small spot and spread out in all directions from the back of the head. Lores, sides of the face and cheeks are bare; the upper third is white, the lower part, pink. The throat is covered with black down; the middle portion is bare, covered with red skin with two very small wattles about two centimeters long with a fold between. The neck feathers, especially those of the lower portion in front, are elongated and lanceolate, slightly lighter in color than those on the back. The bill and legs are black. The iris of the eye is white or a very pale blue.

Sub-adult. The general color, above and below, is blackish-gray. The upper parts are edged with rufous, the underparts with sandy buff. The primaries are black and the secondaries are darker at the tips. Head and neck are rufous. The crown is chestnut with dark bases to the feathers. The lore is bare and the remainder of the sides of the face and ear coverts are covered with yellowish-white down. The crest is small and chestnut-colored. Legs are black; eyes, light ash-colored.

Downy chick. Newly-hatched cranes are covered over the entire body, neck and head with down. The young of *Balearica pavonina* are very similar to those of *B. regulorum*, but may have a more buffy or yellowish cast.

B. *Balearica ceciliae,* Mitchell, *Abstracts of Proc. Zool. Soc. London,* Nov. 15, 1904, No. 10, p. 13; Mitchell, P. C., "On the Species of Crowned Cranes," *Proc. Zool. Soc. London,* 2: pp. 200-205.

Type locality. Khartoum, Sudan.

In Sudan I visited the Khartoum Zoo on November 29, 1961. Here I studied a group of rather tame Sudan Crowned Cranes in a very large enclosure. I also worked up and down the Blue and White Nile Rivers in a fruitless search for wild cranes. Unable to acquire the necessary permit travel for the closed Southern District, I continued into Kenya and Southern Rhodesia, getting the necessary

papers for the Sudan entrance from the south. We obtained these at Kampala, Uganda, and flew January 31, 1962 to Juba, landing on a clear hot and dry day, typical of that region. Since there was no evidence of cranes here, we moved northward and from our Malakal resthouse room heard and observed our first wild Sudan Crowned Cranes. Out along the Nile I approached and studied these rather tame cranes daily. We photographed them, made voice recordings and tried to discover what they were eating. We watched their flights from along the Nile River to the dry parched plains adjoining. We noted how they disappeared at night, possibly roosting in trees in the vicinity. We heard their gooselike voices, most often early in the morning, some during the day, a little more towards evening and even heard two birds flying along the Nile in the dark one night.

On February 4, 1962 my wife and I drove eighty miles northward from Malakal to Khor Adar with a native taxi driver who spoke only his own language, his mechanic who spoke another and Mannoah, our interpreter, who spoke those two languages, his own and English. We stopped at a narrow flood region from the Nile to eat lunch and found a group of boys who could understand none of these languages, nor could we understand them. We noted a pair of Crowned Cranes a short distance away. As we approached them they flew around and around us, dropped to the ground, ran around us with drooping wings and in general became quite agitated. Soon we saw the reason—two half-grown chicks which had dashed out into the deep water to a central reed-grown center two hundred feet from shore. We could not get close to them so we returned to Malakal that hot afternoon, and we saw more Sudan Crowned Cranes as well as my first and only flock of Demoiselle Cranes.

During 1965 Dr. Emil K. Urban and I visited the little town of Tefki, southwest of Addis Ababa, Ethiopia on August 24. Here we found a new nest of this Crowned Crane. Giving their mournful call, they flew to a distant spot. In another portion of the marsh Wattled Cranes fed leisurely on somewhat drier ground. On September 29 Emil Urban found three eggs in this nest and apparently these hatched later. On August 25 Dr. and Mrs. Urban

Sudan Crowned Cranes in flight over Nile River, Malakal, Sudan, February 7, 1962.

took me to Bahar Dam on Lake Tana. In one marsh adjacent to the road a lone Crowned Crane stood not too far away. We stopped to watch it for a few minutes. It suddenly began walking toward us for a few meters, when a second bird rose from a nest and began walking away as the first bird settled down onto the three eggs which we soon observed. They were placed on a well-built grass pile, were a rich light blue in color, ovate-shaped and slightly smaller than those of the Nigerian race, but much smaller than South African Crowned Crane eggs. At Lake Tana Crowned Crane pairs and groups (as many as seventy-one birds) were found on the Gondar Road along the east side of the lake to the edge of the escarpment some sixty-nine miles from Bahar Adar. There were no Wattled Cranes in Begemder Province, but there were some scattered pairs north to Dejem and Cima, Gojjam Province.

At present this beautiful bird is in no danger. It lives close to people and nests in rather remote marshes which are still fairly numerous. It feeds in remote places, in fields near houses, along high-ways, often not too far from villages. It shows little fear of people, indicating it is not shot at or disturbed very often.

NESTING

Biotope. As a rule this crane uses larger marshes than those in Nigeria. In the fresh-water cotton marsh, Tefki, 30 kilometers southwest of Addis Ababa, Shoa Province, Ethiopia, most of the vegetation includes unidentified species of *Cyperus* (4 sp.), *Eleocharis* (1 sp.), *Scirpus* (1 sp.), *Setaria* (1 sp.), *Cynodon* (1 sp.), legumes (subfamily *Papilionideae*) and rosaceous plants (*Alchemilla?*) (Urban and Walkinshaw, 1966). Some of these plants were also found in the nesting marsh twelve kilometers west by northwest by Debros Marcos, Gojjam Province, Ethiopia. Both nesting marshes, the Tefki up to one meter, the Debros Marcos with only a few centimeters, were covered with water. The vegetation was between knee- to hip-high, while there were very few shrubs in either marsh. The marshes along the Nile and its tributaries near

Sudan Crowned Crane nest and eggs, 10 miles north of Debros, Marcos, Gojam Province, Ethiopia, August 25, 1965.

Malakal, Sudan, were somewhat similar with probable plant variations.

The nest. Similar to those of *B. p. pavonina*, the nest is placed on a hummock, a rise of ground or a little island surrounded by wet marsh. The Debros Marcos nest measured 76.2 X 91.4 cm across the base and 45.7 X 50.8 cm at the top. It was well concealed amongst vegetation so that we did not see it until only a few meters separated us from the setting bird. The nest was built of surrounding vegetation and was slightly depressed in the top for the eggs.

Incubation. The male and female both incubate and their changeover at the Debros Marcos nest aided us in finding it. Periods of attentiveness of parents and incubation periods have not been recorded.

THE EGGS

Eggs are light blue when laid, immaculate and unstained. By two or three days of age they be-

come stained, often streaked with brown or green. Sudanese eggs are the same as Ethiopian ones. The Debros Marcos eggs measured (probably number as laid, determined by the amount of stain on each): (1) 78.4 X 58.7; (2) 78.4 X 58.8 and (3) 76.8 X 56.3 mm. They weighed respectively 131.5, 138.2 and 126.6 grams. The average measurements of ten eggs from Ethiopia and Sudan (Urban and Walkinshaw, 1966) were 75.36 (70.4-78.4) X 55.24 (52.0-58.8) mm, showing they are the smallest of the Crowned Crane eggs.

VOICE

The voice resembles that of *B. p. pavonina* very much. It is rather musical, somewhat gooselike in sound, yet there is a note of sadness to it, especially when heard in the distance. It resembles *Ka-wonk, Ka-wonk, Ka-wonk*, often repeated many times. It is quite pleasing when several birds call simultaneously. It can be heard at least a mile away on a quiet day and is unmistakable.

FOOD

During winter in Sudan, when there is no rain, these birds feed from the dry baked soil near the Nile River. Often they work for hours trying to find grass and other seeds. Certainly there are few insects available at that time. After several hours of feeding they fly to pool adjacent to the Nile to drink. Here they remain for some time, preening, loafing and occasionally bathing. Late in the afternoon they go back to search the parched soil again for seeds. Although some may roost in the Nile marshes, most spend the night in trees, probably as they do in Ethiopia. In Ethiopia they have much more favorable conditions. Here they feed on ripened grass and other plant seeds, probably some animal foods similar to other cranes and, at times, grains which they sometimes damage. In general they feed on grass seeds and insects.

DISTRIBUTION

This crane is found in southern Sudan, southwestern and central Ethiopia and rarely in extreme northern Uganda and Kenya. Formerly it ranged along the White Nile to Khartoum. Following are more detailed records:

SUDAN. *Darfur Province, Zalingei* (12° 54′ N.; 23° 29′E.). Two downy chicks were taken October 27, 1921 by Admiral Lynes (British Museum, Natural History). It breeds in September in Darfur (Mackworth-Praed and Grant, 1952).

Khartoum Province, Khartoum (15° 36′N.; 32° 31′E.). One female was taken March 14, 1900 by S. S. Flower (BMNH). It was reported breeding at Kosti (13°10′ N.; 32° 40′ E.) by Cave and Macdonald (1955). A downy male specimen (BMNH) was taken by S. S. Flower in November 1910 at Singa (13° 09′ N.; 33° 56′ E.). At Kaka (10° 38′ N.; 32°12′ E.) two female specimens were taken January 23, 1914 by W. P. Lowe (BMNH). One male (BMNH) was taken June 3, 1909 by A. L. Butler. W. P. Lowe took two female specimens (BMNH) March 6, 1914 at Kodok (09°55′N.; 32°10′E.). At Khor Adar (09° 40′ N.; 32° 45′E.) I observed a pair with two six-week-old young on February 4, 1962. At Fathworo, just north of Malakal, I observed two individuals February 4, 1962. Early in February 1962 I observed the species daily at Malakal (09° 32′ N.; 31° 39′ E.). Two female specimens

have been taken: one, December 5, 1960 (Chicago Natural History Museum), the other February 22, 1962 (University of Michigan Museum of Zoology) from the last seven miles out Nasir Road. Both the last specimens were taken by H. Hoogestrall or his party. From Fashoda, just southwest of Kodok, two specimens (BMNH) were taken, one without data; the second, a male, taken March 22, 1901 by R. M. Hawks. One male (BMNH) was taken by W. P. Lowe from Tonga (09° 30′ N.; 31° 05′ E.).

Bahr el Ghazal Province, Yirol, 06° 34′ N.; 30° 30′ E.). Two fresh eggs (BMNH) were taken early in October 1939 by J. G. Myers. He also took at least two other sets of eggs (Sudan Natural History Museum) which now lack other data.

Equatoria Province, twenty miles north of Torit (04° 24′ N.; 32° 33′ E.). Three specimens exist (CNHM)—two females taken January 12, 1946 and one sub-adult male taken January 27, 1946 by A. B. Anderson.

ETHIOPIA. *Begemder Province, Lake Tana, Dak Island*. The species is recorded as numerous and as nesting in August and September (Moltoni and Ruscone, 1944). Urban and I (1966) observed fifty-seven birds on August 26 and seventy-one on the 27th along the Gondar Road, from fifty to seventy kilometers northeast of Bahar Dar in 1965. Cheeseman and Sclater (1935) reported the species here and said it probably nested on Dak Island.

Gojjam Province, Zeghie and Bahar Dar (11° 40′ N.; 37° 25′E.). Cheeseman and Sclater (1935) and Moltoni and Ruscone (1944) both reported cranes here. Urban and I found two cranes August 26, 1965, fifteen kilometers southeast of Bahar Dar near the Tissisat or Blue Nile Falls. L. Brown (personal communication) found flocks of five to twenty in February and March 1964 between Debros Marcos and Bahar Dar. At twelve kilometers west by northwest of Debros Marcos, Urban and I (1966) found a pair and their nest (three eggs) August 25, 1965. Three days later we observed a pair seventy-one kilometers south of Bahar Dar and another pair nineteen kilometers southeast of Debros Marcos (10° 20′ N.; 37° 40′ E.).

Shoa Province, Tefki (09° 50′ N.; 38° 30′ E.). Moltoni and Ruscone (1944) recorded the species here and at Lake Cheleleka, near Bishoftu and Lake Abiata. Urban and I (1966) found two

Crowned Cranes August 23, 24 and 29, 1965, and the beginning of a nest on the 19th. Urban observed the pair September 29, 1965 and found their nest containing three eggs. Guichard (1950) recorded the birds from temporary marshes west of Bishoftu and at Bishoftu Lakes and Toschi (1959) reported it very common in the lake regions, as did Pohlstrand (personal communication). In August 1964, Dr. J. Birket-Smith (personal communication) saw three Crowned Cranes three or four kilometers from Lake Metahara. Dr. E. Beals and Emil Urban found three individuals at Koka Reservoir, one hundred kilometers south of Addis Ababa.

Illubabor Province, at the Baro River (08° 20′ N.; 34°-35° E.). Moltoni and Ruscone (1944) observed the species here.

Kaffa Province, Jimma. Toschi wrote (1959) it occurs here sporadically. Neumann (1904) records it from Anderatscha.

Gemu Gofa Province, Nargi. Moltoni and Ruscone (1944) listed the species from here. J. R. Swart (Urban and Walkinshaw, 1966) observed two Crowned Cranes (species?) 100 meters from the Omo River, ten kilometers north of Lake Rudolph (04° 40′ N.; 36° E.).

Arussi Province. One of two specimens of this crane in the Natural History Museum of Haile Selassie I University lacks data; the other was taken April 30, 1939 at some lake, probably in this province. A specimen in the British Museum (Natural History) taken in 1912 from Ethiopia gives no other locality. Moltoni and Ruscone (1944) mentioned the species was found along the Awash River near Djille and near Barachet in the central Awash valley (province?).

UGANDA, *Nimule* (03° 40′ N.; 32° 10′ E.). This species has been found here (Jackson, 1958).

KENYA, *northeast corner of Lake Rudolph.* An adult male specimen collected by Oscar T. Owre (1966) is now in the University of Miami Department of Zoology. Owre (personal communication) believes, because marshes were more abundant and earlier writers publicized the fact, that there are more cranes here, especially on the Ethiopian side.

DESCRIPTION

This crane is slightly smaller than *B. p. pavonina* (see Table 22). It is supposed to have less white in the cheek and a darker bill tip. Apparently neither characteristic holds true. If there are specimens available from the Republic of Chad, they should be intermediate in size between the two forms. All plumage is apparently exactly alike between these two forms.

Chapter Fifteen

THE SOUTH AFRICAN CROWNED CRANE

(Balearica regulorum regulorum)

Anthropoides Regulorum, Bennett, *Proc. Zool. Soc. London,* 1833 (1834), p. 118.
Type locality: South Africa.

The Gray Crowned Cranes are as spectacular as their northern relatives. To see a flock roaming the open veld in South Africa, or the plains of Zambia, or a pair working carefully along the edge of some marsh, is so outstanding that a bird observer from far away, will stop immediately to watch. Even local residents will often stop. Most of their feeding is done on open dry fields. Their color is so spectacular, they are so easily observed, no one can miss them as they pass along some neighboring highway.

The Crowned Cranes are different from other cranes in that they roost at night as often in some neighboring tree-top as in a marsh, where other cranes normally spend the night. They also lay three eggs about as often as two, which other cranes lay. The eggs are a clear bluish similar, when laid, to those of herons. But the chicks are precocial as are other baby cranes. The typical call of the chick is almost exactly as those given by other baby cranes. The call of reassurance given by a member of a pair to either its chick or mate, is a similar snore or *Purrr* given by other cranes but their normal notes, to me, have a sound of sadness, especially the call of four notes, *Ya-oooou-goo-lung.*

The South African and East African Crowned Cranes are larger than their northern relatives and are much lighter gray, a pearl gray instead of slate gray, especially on the back and neck. The bare cheek patch of this bird is white with a narrow half-moon upper portion, carmine red. The bare cheek patch of the East African Crowned Crane has a rounded extension up into the black velvety crown feathers. The red chin wattle of both forms is much larger than in the Central African Crowned Crane.

Vernacular names. The South African Crowned Crane (English); de Kroonkraan van Zuid-Afrika (Dutch); Ma-hem (South African); i-hem (Xhosa); u-Nohemu (Zulu); le-Hehemu, le-Hemu (Sesuto); la Frue ronnée du Cap (French); der Konigskranich (German); Minima Kanmuri-zuru, (Japanese); Маковка журавль , (Russian).

When Rudyerd Boulton took me to Rainham Dam, Salisbury, (Southern) Rhodesia, I expected to see my first Wattled Crane. I only saw one of these, but late in the evening of December 3, 1961 a lone Crowned Crane flew from a pasture field to roost in the top of a nearby tree at 6:25 P.M. At 5:35 A.M. the next morning he flew back to the same field. In a neighboring tree two others left at 5:45 A.M., also landing in the same field. They maintained their distance from the lone bird; in fact, they repeatedly chased him away from them. He possibly was their youngster from the previous year.

On December 8, 1961, just north of Nottingham Road, Natal, South Africa, I saw a lone Crowned Crane, but no others for several days. On December 11 a lone bird flew into a small marsh as I watched and walked up to where another bird rose from a nest. This nest, my first, contained three eggs. This was half-way between Mooi River and the Drakensberg Mountains, Natal. The same day I found my first Stanley Crane nest a few miles closer to the Drakensbergs. During the ensuing days two more Crowned Crane nests were found in South Africa. Clara, my wife, joined me at Johannesburg and on January 11, 1962 we again flew into Salisbury, (Southern) Rhodesia. On January 12, Clara and I collected plants all day until rain drove us away in the late afternoon. The next morning I worked in the same Rainham Dam marsh all morning, eventually coming back to the spot where Boulton had shown me the old Wattled Crane's nest in December. To my utter surprise, a lone Crowned Crane flew from that same nest which now contained three eggs, two of which were pipped. Indications showed these eggs must have been laid December 13-17, 1961. Showers again drove me out and the next day, between harassing intermittent showers, we went to the nest and found all three young hatched. Many notes and many photographs paid us rich dividends. On January 20, 1962, the Boultons and we left for Lochinvar Ranch, Northern Rhodesia (now Zambia). A Land Rover carried our many supplies, a touring car, others. Having generator trouble at Mazabuka, we stayed overnight, reaching Lochinvar the next morning, January 21. Boulton and I hiked over twenty miles from the ranch the next day back to the Kafue River. The day was warm, with much mud underfoot—so much that the Land Rover had to be left behind.

My tennis shoes wore out on the trip so that I had to finish the return trip barefooted. We arrived back at the ranch well after dark. But the expansive marshes between the Kafue and the ranch headquarters were a delight to see, as well as large numbers of black lechwe, nine pairs and three single Crowned Cranes and larger numbers of Wattled Cranes. Although we were tired that night, the next morning Clara and I explored a nearby large marsh and soon came to a Crowned Crane nest with three eggs. There was no bird at this nest, so we returned later during the day, hoping it was all right. A bird now was setting. On the second visit we took a blind with us and worked with 100 feet of the nest, photographing and taking notes the following day.

At first the birds did not return, wading around the nest in the tall grass, with only their heads visible. But periodically they came near the nest, close enough so that they could examine the eggs. Between two of these visits a large snake crawled from the surrounding vegetation up onto the nest and repeatedly tried to swallow one of the eggs. He was still attempting this when the cranes returned. They observed him and began walking side by side to the nest, their wings spread so that one's wing was spread beneath the other's. The snake slowly

South African Crowned Crane standing on nest, Lochinvar Ranch, near Monze, Zambia, January 24, 1962.

crawled away into the grass; one of the birds remained and we photographed it. The same morning Clara and I found this nest, we found a second with two eggs and a hatched chick. That afternoon all three eggs were hatched, all three young remaining in the nest.

The morning of January 25 I carefully approached the photographed crane nest, fearing the birds might have deserted. With relief I noted a crowned head rise carefully above surrounding grasses. I hurriedly departed. That afternoon and the next day we were at Kafue Pilot Polder, an experimental region for black African farmers. Here we found a family with a very beautiful Crowned Crane pet. He was one year old. When released from his night pen, he danced all over the yard, jumping at times as high as fifteen feet into the air. As usual, he was completely devoted to the person who cared for him.

NESTS

Biotope. The preferred regions for nesting are marshes, some only a few acres in area, others extending for many miles. Water is preferred, from a few centimeters deep to a meter or more, with vegetation extending about one meter, more or less, above the water. In the small marshes there is only one pair, but in the larger ones, which extend through valley after valley, pairs are spaced about a mile part. Although the birds feed considerably in the nesting marshes, they often fly to neighboring drier meadows, vleis and velds. Since the Wattled Cranes use the same marshes, the plants are described earlier in the chapter about that species.

Most South African marshes have few or no trees around them. A few trees grew near Rainham Dam, (Southern) Rhodesia, but at Lochinvar Ranch near Monze, Zambia, bordering the great Kafue River marshes, many trees encircled the region. The night we returned after dark we frightened a Crowned Crane from an acacia (*Acacia sieberiana*) tree.

Prenesting behavior. In South Africa these cranes roost at night during the winter months in a group, but by October and November they begin to break away and take up their respective territories. By early December some are nesting and others are well established on territories; but a few remain in groups (probably non-breeding birds). They often roost in the same pond or marsh as Stanley and Wattled Cranes with some in nearby trees. The latter two species never roost in trees. While roosting, each group remains apart from the other species. Some birds begin nesting before December, others later. When arriving on territory, the birds often feed, work or loaf near the new nest. At times they dance, both in the marsh and on adjoining fields. In South African regions there are few adjoining trees, so the birds most often roost in marshes or ponds; only occasionally do they roost in a nearby tree. In Southern Rhodesia night roosting is usually in a tree; in Zambia it is regular, even during nesting time. Sometimes birds roost adjacent to the setting birds by the nest, standing only a few feet away in shallow water. When feeding, the birds remain only a few feet apart all day; at night they roost side by side.

Very close to the Hlatikulu River, Natal, South Africa, a pair of Wattled Cranes built a nest and laid an egg in mid-December 1961. On December 18 a pair of Crowned Cranes moved between that and the territory of another Wattled Crane pair in the opposite direction. The pair that had the nest was separated from the Crowned Cranes by a fence, but because of their more terrestrial behavior never flew all day, so did not go over the fence. The Crowned Cranes fed on the opposite side of the fence and were very conscious of the larger birds. If the Wattled Crane fed a half-mile or more away, they flew over the fence at times onto his territory to feed. However, the Wattled Crane was dominant. At times the male advanced towards the fence beyond which stood one or both Crowned Cranes. When he reached the barrier he strutted back and forth, rather stiff-legged. Usually at this time the Crowned Cranes worked farther away. Once, however, the male Crowned Crane lay down on the ground with his head erect, about 100 meters in front of the Wattled Crane. Once I noted such behavior when both White-naped Cranes were on eggs in the Detroit Zoological Park, Michigan. They sat down in front of a much larger pair of Indian Sarus Cranes. In neither case did the larger birds advance any closer.

This one pair of Crowned Cranes spent their entire breeding season in this marsh and on a neighboring field. They seldom flew, usually walking from the marsh into the field, a hundred or two hundred meters away. Eggs were laid between December 23 and 30. Another pair, closer to Rosetta, flew regularly from their marsh to feed, sometimes 1,500 meters away. A third pair also flew some distance away.

Defense of territory. Crowned Cranes maintain their territories the same as other cranes. They drive away other Crowned Cranes, Stanley Cranes and spur-winged geese easily, by force or merely by the advance of one of the Crowned Cranes toward intruders. At other times they pay little attention to other species. With the dominant Wattled Crane, the Crowned Cranes at times advanced with spread wings just parallel and inside the territorial boundary, always on the safe side of the fence, some twenty-five to fifty feet away. They definitely feared this bird. Once a steer came to the edge of a clearing around a Crowned Crane nest. Without hesitation the setting bird rose, uttered several *Ya-oou-goo-lung* calls, spread its wings and slowly advanced towards the animal. Its mate quickly joined it, flying in from the nearby field, and the two birds walked towards the steer side by side, both with wings spread. It retreated quickly. One bird then settled onto the eggs; the other returned to the neighboring field to feed. When a snake tried to eat one of the Crowned Crane eggs in Zambia, the behavior was almost identical. As the birds neared the snake, it slithered away into the surrounding grasses.

Nest sites. Six nests in South Africa, Rhodesia and Zambia were located in shallow marshes, the vegetation knee- to shoulder-high, in water eight to eighteen centimeters deep (average twelve centimeters)—usually the wettest portion of the marsh and in the region of tallest vegetation. But even here the bird could peer in every direction, setting or standing, with only its head visible above the vegetation. Stanley Cranes sometimes nest up to 7,000 feet (2,132 m) and at times down to 3,000 feet (914 m), but Crowned Cranes preferred regions 3,000-5,000 feet in elevation (914-1,523 m). The pH of water in Crowned Crane marshes in Natal, South Africa was 6.0 to 6.3; at Rainham Dam, Salisbury, (Southern) Rhodesia, it was 7.0, while at the dam it was 8.0; at Lochinvar Ranch, Monze, Zambia, it was 7.5.

Construction. Both birds, pulling up vegetation with their bills, build the nest. They trample down much vegetation in the process, so that a region five or more meters in every direction is somewhat flattened, at times a ten- to fifteen-meter circle. Into the center of this circle they toss grasses and sedges into a haphazard pile over which they tramp, at times sitting down on the mass so that it gradually becomes flattened. The center of this mass becomes somewhat depressed, and into this depression the eggs are laid. The six nests I observed averaged 70.2 X 77.6 cm in diameter, varying from 50.8 X 52.3 to 76 X 86 cm. After completion they were rather neat piles of grasses. The average height above water level was 12.2 (8-18) cm to the rim.

Wyndham (1940) described a nest almost two meters across at the base with a cupped top portion twenty-three centimeters across.

THE EGGS

Newly-laid eggs are a beautiful light blue and immaculate. They soon acquire stains and spots, lose the blue color and become a dirty white, streaked with dirty brown or green. Wyndham wrote (1940); "The ground color of the shell is a pale greenish-blue of a shade practically identical with that of the normal heron type, but differing from the latter in being thinly incrusted over almost the entire surface with a dull-white chalky deposit similar to that found on the eggs of the various species of cormorants."

Thirty eggs from South Africa measured 85.0 (75.9-93.4) X 56.82 (50.4-61.5) mm and fifteen eggs from Zambia and Rhodesia averaged 86.41 (77.0-93.9) X 57.7 (56.9-59.0) mm. The forty-five eggs averaged 85.43 X 57.1 mm. The average

weight of thirteen eggs was 149.66 g varying between 126.1 (at hatching) and 182.0 (when fresh).

In seventeen sets from Zambia and Rhodesia, ten contained three eggs, three contained two and four contained one, averaging 2.35 eggs per set. Of thirty-four South African sets, five contained four eggs, sixteen had three, ten had two and three had one, averaging 2.67 eggs per set. The fifty-one South African Crowned Crane sets from South Africa, (Southern) Rhodesia and Zambia averaged 2.57 eggs per set, with strong indications that egg sets farther south were larger.

Beginning in October, egg sets varied per month as follows: October, 2.0 (1 X 1, 1 X 2, 1 X 3); November, 3.66 (1 X 3, 2 X 4); December, 3.25 (1 X 2, 4 X 3, 3 X 4); January, 2.4 (1 X 1, 1 X 2, 3 X 3); February, 2.5 (5 X 2, 5 X 3); March, 3.0 (1 X 3); April, 2.0 (1 X 2); May, 2.0 (1 X 1, 1 X 3).

Benson and White (1957) gave nesting records for December and January. Smithers, Irwin and Paterson (1957) gave ten breeding records for Rhodesia for January and one for February, while Roberts, McLachlan and Liversidge (1958) recorded the nesting season in South Africa as December to February. Actually, in South Africa there is evidence of nesting from October 15 to May 22 from present available records. Benson (1940, 1953) gave two breeding records for January, one for April and one for May in Malawi.

Wyndham (1940) found that the first egg of a set was laid four days prior to the second egg, while the third egg was laid three days after the second. All three eggs in one South African nest I observed were laid during the period of one week.

Benson (1960) wrote of the Rhodesias and Nyasaland: "The few data in the check list . . . point to this species being a rainy season breeder (as in South Africa). . . ." The percent of nesting records given by him were: December, 27 per cent; January, 47 per cent; March, 8 per cent; and April, 12 per cent.

Incubation. Both sexes incubate the eggs, but my records show the non-incubating bird remained closer at night to the nest than did the West African Crowned Crane. This bird usually roosted in shallow water a few meters from the nest in South Africa, probably because there were no nearby trees, while in (Southern) Rhodesia and Zambia

Eggs and newly hatched chick, South African Crowned Crane west of Mooi River, Natal, South Africa, December 21, 1961.

they roosted in nearby trees, thereby indicating their preference.

At one nest in South Africa the female incubated the eggs three of four nights. First morning changes occurred at 5:31 A.M. (December 12), 6:36 A.M. (December 18) and 6:15 A.M. (December 31), while last changes occurred at 6:01 P.M. (December 18) and 5:42 P.M. (December 31). On December 18, three days before the young hatched, the female incubated between 6:36 and 9:38 A.M., 1:17 and 3:07, 4:49 and 5:03 and 6:01 P.M. into the night, a total of 324 daylight minutes. The male was on the nest all night until 6:36 A.M. 9:42 A.M. to 12:47 P.M., 3:07 to 4:03 and 5:03 to 6:01 P.M., for a total of 335 daylight minutes.

At another nest, December 31, the day after the last egg was laid, the female incubated for 295 daylight minutes, all night until 6:15 A.M., 9:38 A.M. to 12:01 P.M., 2:21 to 3:50 and 5:42 P.M. through the night, while the male incubated 455 minutes: 6:15-9:38 A.M., 12:01-2:21 and 3:50-5:42 P.M.

The eggs were incubated an average of 90.5 (85.3-95.6) per cent of the time on these two days, while the male incubated for 56.0 (50.9-60.1) per cent of the time. Eggs were unattended 79 minutes on December 18 and 33 minutes, December 31 (see Walkinshaw, 1965b).

Young South African Crowned Cranes usually hatch within a twenty-four hour period of each other. Two to four days elapse between the laying of the eggs and they hatch twenty-nine to thirty-one days after the last egg is laid. One pair of Crowned Cranes (subsp.) in the Providence, Rhode Island, Zoo, hatched the last egg twenty-nine days after it was laid. In South Africa the young in one nest all hatched December 21-22; one egg hatched in another nest January 28, 1962, while all three eggs hatched between the afternoon of January 13 and noon the next day at Salisbury, Rhodesia. All three eggs in a nest at Lochinvar Ranch, Monze, Zambia, hatched January 23, 1962, while a nearby nest had three fresh eggs and Mr. Robinette found eggs in still another nest a full month later.

THE YOUNG

Crowned Cranes are very weak at hatching, but in case of danger they will leave the nest when only a few hours old. At hatching time they are wet and bedraggled. The beautiful down dries in a few hours, the youngster, at the same time, gaining strength so he can raise his head above the body, then sit on his tarsi and gaze around. When twelve hours old they can stumble off the nest on bent legs and enter the water and are capable of swimming very well, for they float like little balls, and can propel themselves well with their swollen feet and legs. They repeatedly try to escape any human who comes to their nest when they are ten to twelve hours old. About this same time—twelve hours of age—they will peck at objects offered them, but really begin eating when twenty-four hours old. The light flesh-colored legs are a real contrast to the dark-colored legs of downy Stanley and Wattled Cranes. Weights and measurements of seven downy chicks were given by the author (1965b). All were less than twenty-four hours old; several were still somewhat wet.

At several nests parents led the chicks back to the nest at night for at least two weeks. In the daytime chicks fed with their parents only a few hundred meters from the site; towards evening they always worked slowly and carefully back to the nest where they were brooded overnight. Parents did not lead them out onto the neighboring veld or plains as do Stanley and Wattled Cranes. As a result the chicks continued to work through much heavier cover than the other two species of cranes nearby and were able to hide much more effectively. They remained with their parents about ten months. Often they are driven away at that time. Departing from parental care they join with others of similar age to form flocks which forage across favorable plains and marshes removed from breeding cranes. Sometimes they resort to grain fields, eating and damaging crops to some extent. Fortunately, they do not form flocks of thousands as do some cranes farther north.

VOICE

Downy chicks call very much like other cranes—a sharp, shrill *Peeep* with a burr to it. Parents call the chicks to them the same as other cranes do, by using a low guttural *Purrr*. This call is often used as a signal of reassurance between parent birds. The outstanding normal call of both South African and East African Crowned Cranes is at times a single-syllabled *Oouuw*, but much more often a very sad, *Ya-oou-goo-lung*, accented on the last syllable. Sometimes they give a double-syllabled sad call too, which probably has been responsible for their acquiring the name of *Ma-hem*. All their calls are much more mournful, much less gooselike, than calls of either the Sudan or West African Crowned Cranes. Young do not acquire these calls until between eleven and twelve months of age in captivity, and probably about the same in the wild.

FOOD

At three different nests I found parents fed chicks, when about twenty-four hours old, with pieces of crabs (*Potamon* sp.), which abounded in nesting regions. The birds fed less on insects than many other cranes do, but definitely did capture some grasshoppers and other insects as I watched. But they fed chiefly on seeds from grasses, often pecking them right off the stalks as they worked from one plant to another. At times they fed from the ground. They did not dig as much as many of the longer-billed cranes do. I did not see them digging for roots and bulbs at all.

DISTRIBUTION

The southernmost of the Crowned Cranes, this bird is found in favorable localities from southeastern Congo to Tanzania, south of Ngamiland on the west to eastern Cape Province and Natal on the east. Following are some distributional records:

ANGOLA. Found only at Humbe on the Cunene River (Layard, 1875); found along the lower Cunene River in the district of Huila (Traylor, 1963).

CONGO. This is the form found in southeastern Congo (Chapin, 1939).

ZAMBIA. Nesting records for December and January (Benson and White, 1957): Benson (1960, 1963) wrote that this species nests in the Rhodesias (including Zambia) and Nyasaland during the rainy season. He gave the percentages of records as: December, 27 per cent; January, 47 per cent; March, 8 per cent and April, 12 per cent. Benson also listed breeding localities as Kasempa District, Kafue National Park, Monze: June 1, 1959 (full-grown young able to fly with parents), Uys; July 20, 1959 (young bird, two-thirds grown), Ansell. At Lochinvar Ranch, Zambia, my wife and I found two nests January 23, 1962 (one nest with three eggs, the other with two eggs and one chick) and W. L. Robinette found a nest February 18, 1962 with three eggs.

Liuwa Plain, Kalabo (15° S.; 22°15′ E.) Barotseland. Traylor (1965) called it common. A male specimen from Kafue Flats taken by S. Clarke, September 1, 1920 and another specimen taken in the Zambezi River Valley are in the British Museum (Natural History).

RHODESIA, *Bulawauo* (20° S.; 28° E.), Criterion Farm. A nest with two eggs was found February 23, 1962 by A. Masterson (So. African Nest File Cards).

Gwelo District, Guinea Fowl. Nests were found January 1, 1955 (two eggs), January 26, 1955 (two eggs) and February 15, 1953 (three eggs) by Mr. Salmon (Southern Rhodesia Nest Record File Cards—SRNRFC).

Metapos Research Station. Three records of nests (all three eggs) found during early January 1950, 1951 and 1952 are given by D. C. H. Plowes (SRNRFC).

Nala. A nest of two eggs was found January 13, 1954 by I. Cannell (SRNRFC).

Sabi Valley (20°16′ S.). This crane is a rare irregular visitor (Brooke and Cackett, 1965).

Salisbury (5,000 ft.—1,538 m) (17°45′ S.; 30°52.5′ E.). A specimen (BMNH) was taken August 6, 1899 by G. G. Marshall. At Rainham Dam, a nest was found (three eggs) January 11, 1951 by H. M. Miles and R. M. Henderson. A pair was observed with a full-grown young December 1959; a nest (three eggs) was found January 9, 1960; another nest (one egg) was found January 8, 1961 by C. J. Vernon and G. Hopkinson (all SRNRFC). I found a three-egg nest with hatching young January 13, 1962.

Victoria Falls National Park. Jensen (1966) lists this crane as occasional.

Wankie National Park, Ngama, Robins. Nests were found in January and February (Davison, 1965).

BECHUANALAND. The Crowned Crane has been found from the Chobe River (18° S.; 24° E.), the Linyanti Swamp, Okavango Swamp (21°40′ S.; 18°15′ E.), Marari kari and Lake Dow (21°15′ S.; 24°40′ E.) regions (Smithers, 1964). Two male specimens were taken here (BMNH) by R. B. Woosnam, July 30, 1909.

MALAWI, *Lake Shirwa.* A specimen (BMNH) was taken February 1894 by H. Johnson. A male specimen (BMNH) was taken August 29, 1921 by C. C. Roberts. At Karonga (el. 1,700 ft.—518 m) C. W. Benson took a male specimen (BMNH). Benson (1940) wrote that his bird was widely distributed in the northern region. He also wrote (1953) that an intermediate form was present below 5,000 feet in the larger dambos and swamps. Sometimes flocks of over one hundred were found. Wilkes (1928) reported the species from around Lake Nyasa.

PORTUGUESE EAST AFRICA, *Beira.* Occasion the Crowned Crane is seen, but it is much more common further north and also is found on the Sabi River south of Beira where it breeds (Haagner, 1948). Jack Vincent (1934) wrote that it was fairly common on inland vleis, but he found no nests.

SOUTH-WEST AFRICA. It is found up to the northern part (Stark and Sclater, 1906) and is listed from here by Winterbottom (1965).

SOUTH AFRICA, *Cape Province.* Courtenay-Latimer (1964) recorded this species as resident in the border region, East London. At King William's Town, C. J. Skead (1964) reported nests of this bird as far west as Debe Nek. Skead (SANFC) reported three nests, two on February 12, 1955 (both two eggs) and the third on February 18, 1962 (two eggs).

East Cape Region, Fort Beaufort, Hogsback, Stockenstroom, Victoria East. Taylor (1964) recorded the species here.

Griqualand East, Franklin District. Two three-egg nests were recorded by H. W. Bell-Marley (SANFC) February 22, 1931 and March 17, 1931. From this same place three-egg sets were taken February 19, 1931 and May 22, 1931 (Transvaal Museum). In Mount Currie Division, Swartberg,

Shephard (1962) recorded this species as a common breeder.

Tembuland, Elliotdale Division, Nkamya. Here V. L. Pringle (SANFC) reported a nest of three eggs January 14, 1956.

Transkei. C. Wyndham (SANFC) recorded nests October 15-23, 1939 (three eggs); October 20, 1939 (two eggs).

Kentani. Three-egg nests were taken here December 24, 1946, January 26, 1947 and November 1, 1947 by Pitt Fennell and are now in the collections of Charles Jerome and Godfrey Symons (Estcourt).

Kobonqaba. Pike (1965) reported this bird as resident and nesting.

Ngamakwe, Blythswood. Nests were found by E. Pike (SANFC) January 6, 1943 (three eggs), April 3, 1955 (two eggs) by R. Godfrey, and eggs were recorded here January 31, 1929. On the west bank of the Kei River, approximately four miles from the coast, one pair was seen (Page, 1948).

Natal, Dannhauser, Newcastle District. A nest was found (two eggs) by Sparrow (1935).

Himeville. R. Turner (SANFC) found a nest December 16, 1953 (four eggs), and in the same nest in 1964 and 1965 he found four eggs again.

Hlatikulu River region (20 mi W of Mooi River). Two nests (three eggs) were found December 31, 1961 and January 6, 1962 and one with one egg on January 6, 1962 by L. H. Walkinshaw.

Howick, Shafton House. R. E. Symons (G. Symons Collection) found a nest (one egg) October 19, 1931.

Newcastle. The species was recorded from here by Layard (1875).

Nottingham Road. I observed this bird regularly here during December 1961 and January 1962.

Rosetta (about 5 mi W). J. Vincent (verbal) observed this species regularly here during the early 1960's. Eight miles west William Barnes and Godfrey Symons (letters) found a nest (three eggs) February 24, 1962 and twenty miles west I found a nest (three eggs) December 11, 1961. I found the species right up to the foothills of the Drakensberg Mountains.

Vryheid. Two nests were found by W. J. Lawson (SANFC) (both four eggs) December 1 and 3, 1964.

South African Crowned Crane pair at nest, near Monze

Weenan County. West, Wright and Symons (1964) reported this species as occasional in the highveld grassland and noted that a pair spent the summer of 1941-42 at Tabamhlope Pasture Research Station.

Orange Free State. The species was sparsely distributed here (Layard, 1875). It has been reported from Bloemfontein, Harrismith, Kestell, Kroonstad and Olivierskoekpas (van der Platt, 1961 S. J. Townsend found a nest (one egg) at Kimberley, Warrentown in the center of a vlei formed by the Vaal River in May 1891 (SANFC).

Transvaal, Belfast. A set of two eggs was taken January 1, 1908 by H. C. Risch (Transvaal Museum, Pretoria). Miss E. B. Cusack (1943) found a downy chick at Bloemhof March 20, 1938 and a nest (one egg, two on January 13) January 10, 1941 and observed two large young April 13, 1940. D. C. H. Plowes (D. M. Skead, 1965) found a nest (two eggs) February 4, 1946, probably the set in the Transvaal Museum. Jeanne de V. Little (1963) recorded the birds from the highveld of the Carolina District, but not as common. A set of three eggs was taken at Matlagas December 7, 1934 (Traansvaal Museum). A sub-adult specimen (BMNH) in the Sharpe Collection was taken at Potchefstroom, and two specimens were taken from Transvaal (location not specified) by F. A. Barratt.

Lesotha. Winterbottom (1964) recorded that J. P. Murray had observed this bird on several occasions and five were seen at Teyateyaneng, 1895-1897.

DESCRIPTION

Breeding adult. The sexes are alike, but the male is slightly larger. This bird is very similar to *B. regulorum gibbericeps.* The feathers of the neck are much more pearl gray than the slate gray of *B. p. pavonina* and *B. p. ceciliae.* The crest and the greater wing coverts are generally a paler yellow than in that species also. Each bristle in the crest has a black tip and is ringed with white and yellow or brown. The throat is naked with a large red pendant wattle, the base of which is black and continuous, with black velvety feathers around the bare cheek patch. The majority of the bare cheek patch is white. Sometimes there is a small half-moon-shaped bright carmine-red upper border; sometimes this seems to be lacking. This red border is ten to twelve millimeters wide at its widest point. Bill and legs are black; the eye, grayish-white.

Sub-adult. The general color is gray, with upper parts broadly edged with rufous and those of the underparts with sandy buff margins. The ends of the maroon secondaries are darker than in the adult. Head and neck are rufous; the crown, chestnut with dark bases on the feathers. The lores are bare and the remainder of the sides of the face and ear coverts are covered with yellowish-white down. The crest is small and chestnut. Legs are black; eyes, light ash color.

Downy chick. Downy young, when first hatched, are rather pot-bellied, but they are covered all over with beautiful down ten or more millimeters long, except on the face and cheeks where it is shorter—about five millimeters. The

front of the head is pale umber; back of head, darker. Forehead, superciliary region, cheeks and throat are pale ivory, shading into light buff. The skin of the eyelid is pale greenish-yellow. Back and dorsal stripe are umber with flank spots darker and a shield-shaped and darker caudal spot. The shoulders also are darker. The general color is pale buff. Distal edge of wing is light umber, the anterior edge, buffy, with a dark spot at the bend. Belly is very pale buff; chest, darker buff. Bare skin above the eyelid is slaty, tinged with pink. Bill is slate gray with buffy flesh color at base of lower mandible. Base of bill and skin of lower mandible are light horn color. Egg tooth is pale ivory. Legs are generally flesh color, brightest at the joints. Soles of feet are pale yellow; each scale on the tarsus has a dark base and an outer edge of pale flesh. Nails are pale horn color; eyes are dark brown.

B. *Balearica gibbericeps,* Reichenow, *Journ. für Ornith.,* 40, 1892, p. 126.

Type locality. Lake Jipe, near Mt. Kilimanjaro, in East Africa.

The East African Crowned Crane is very much like the South African Crowned Crane, but the bare cheek patch extends upward, rather knoblike in shape, into the velvety black feathers of the top of the head, farther than in any of the other Crowned Cranes. This bird also is slightly larger than the others.

Mr. J. W. English and I drove the sunshiny morning of December 2, 1961 from Nairobi, Kenya across the beautiful Rift Valley to Lake Niavashi. Cloudless skies greeted us and continued well into the afternoon, but by mid-afternoon there appeared across the mountains to the west of us an immense white cumulus cloud. In a short time there were several, then, by late afternoon, a complete cloud cover. By the time of our return journey just before evening, a severe thunderstorm was drenching the land.

However, during the beautiful morning of ideal temperature and sun, we watched herds of zebra near the highway or far away on the plains. Thompson's gazelles grazed nearby and at Lake Niavashi, white pelicans (*Pelecanus onocrotalus*), white storks (*Ciconia ciconia ciconia*), Egyptian

Nest and eggs of South African Crowned Crane.

vultures (*Neophron percnopterus percnopterus*), black-breasted harrier eagles (*Circaetus pectoralis*), red-knobbed coots (*Fulica cristata*), African jacanas (*Actophilus africanus*), blacksmith plovers (*Hoplopterus armatus*), spur-winged plovers (*Hoplopterus spinosus*), little African swifts (*Apus affinis abessynicus*), white-rumped swifts (*Apus caffer streubelii*) and Horus swifts (*Apus horus*) were observed. We found the nest of a shrike near a ranch house, then walked towards a potato field where the English farmer said there had been some cranes.

Suddenly from a distance came the mournful unmistakable call, *Ya-oou-goo-lung*, and as I peered in that direction, a group of three East African Crowned Cranes flew from the potato fields, circled the end of Lake Niavashi twice, then landed far out in a marshy corner far from any human beings. The beautiful creatures remained in the region the entire morning, feeding between the marsh and the potato patch. As we left in the late afternoon for Nairobi, sheets of water pelting our car, we realized these storms were what produced the rich green vegetation that greeted each sunny

315

morning—one of the reasons Kenya is one of the most beautiful countries in the world.

THE NEST

Most Crowned Cranes apparently prefer nesting during the rainy season. Benson (1960) commented on this in Zambia; Smith (1962) and I found this the case in northern Nigeria and I found it to be the case in South Africa and Ethiopia. In East Africa the rainy season is often spread over or consists of two more extreme periods. Here Crowned Cranes nest over a much wider season. For example, five sets of eggs in the British Museum (Natural History) and the Rothschild Collection from Uganda and Kenya were taken January 11, 1939; May 30, 1903; June 23, 1938; October 6, 1906 and November 22, 1920. In the Museum of Comparative Zoology, Harvard College, one set was taken November 11, 1938 in Belgian Congo and a downy chick was taken there at the foot of Mt. Mikeno (el. 7,250 ft.) March 22, 1927.

Biotope. Shores of lakes, large marshes grown to reeds, rushes, sedges and papyrus, where the cover is extremely dense—places were the birds are actually well hidden by tall vegetation—are the chief sites. Sometimes these are also rather deep with some floating islands of vegetation, regions often quite impassable to humans; again they may use a smaller, shallower marsh similar to other cranes.

Construction. The nest differs little from that of other Crowned Cranes. A region of shallow water is used where marsh vegetation is dragged into a haphazard pile which, after use, becomes packed down and neater, slightly hollowed in the top for the eggs. Jackson (1938) wrote that the birds bred in Uganda and Kenya between May and July in water a foot or more deep. Chapin (1939) wrote that Dr. van Someren reported nests in Kenya in June and July built amongst reeds in marshes. The territory of the pair I watched at Lake Niavashi varied in water depth and amount of vegetation, but there were many spots where the vegetation was extremely tall. At Entebbe, Uganda, another Crowned Crane region was present beside Lake Victoria, where the entire marsh was grown to nearly shoulder-high reeds.

THE EGGS

They are exactly like the eggs of other Crowned Cranes, light blue when newly laid, a dirty brownish or greenish in a few days, often streaked with darker shades. The color near hatching time becomes a dirty white with the acquired shades of brown or green still strongly evident. Of the available records of full complements of eggs, I find eleven sets of two eggs and one set of three, averaging 2.08 eggs per set. Ten eggs in the British Museum (Natural History) averaged 85.53 (82.3-89.5) X 57.46 (55.8-58.9) mm. Makatsch (1959) gave the average of fourteen eggs as 83.0 X 57.5 mm, and the Schönwetter weight as 15.5 g.

VOICE

To me this bird sounded identical to the ones in South Africa, Rhodesia and Zambia, but much different from those in Sudan and West Africa.

FOOD

Jackson (1938) wrote that food consisted of crawling insects, grasshoppers, seeds and grain. Mackworth-Praed and Grant (1952) described Jackson's observation that these birds often stamped their feet as they advanced through the grass, frightening up insects, which they ate. The birds I watched fed above the surface of the ground and did not dig as many longer-billed cranes do.

Although very shy in the wild these birds make good pets, as do most cranes, and in zoological collections they prove to be among the most attractive larger birds displayed. They are easily kept when given proper diet, but on occasion, when some disease is caught by one it may spread to more of the flock. Thus, chicken cholera took several birds in the Detroit Zoological Park.

DISTRIBUTION

This subspecies is found in Eastern Congo, Uganda, Kenya, Tanzania and north of the Pangani River to Uganda, including Albert Nyanza and Lake George.

Benson wrote (1940) that a specimen attributable to this form came from Lake Chilwa, while one farther north was from Karona and was

South African Crowned Crane in defense pose against snake trying to eat one of its eggs. Note bill and primary of second bird on right of picture as both birds came up side by side with spread wings. Lochinvar Ranch, Zambia, January 24, 1962.

B. r. regulorum. Mackworth-Praed and Grant (1952) listed this bird from northeastern Zambia to Mozambique. Sclater (1930) reported it from the Pangani River to Albert Nyanza and Lake George. Owre (1966) and Keith (1968) both have shown that there is a region of some distance between the range of this bird and the Sudan Crowned Crane in Kenya, possibly in Uganda. In Uganda Keith wrote (1968) that Smart observed two Sudan Crowned Cranes on the Victoria Nile in 1963 and two more on subsequent visits until the spring of 1964, while two birds were observed by Smart and Pakwatch in March 1964 on the Albert Nile, in the northwest corner of Murchison Park. Jackson gave (1938) a record from Difule near Nimule on the Uganda-Sudan border just inside the Uganda boundary, while Owre reported (1966) this bird from northern Lake Rudolf, Kenya, in 1959. He wrote that during the same expedition Dennis Paulson observed *B. regulorum gibbericeps* near Maralal, about eighty miles south of Lake Rudolf, on January 4, 1959 and that since the lake is about

145 miles long, a distance of about 225 miles separated points where the two species are known to occur at present.

Specimens in the British Museum (Natural History) are from:

KENYA, Gilgil (two specimens, October 9, 1903); Kiboka Swamp (August 14, 1899); Loita Plains (November 6, 1909); Sattima (two specimens, January 30, 1903) and Thika (August 25, 1914).

UGANDA, Ihunga, SW Ankole (December 10, 1910); Kigezi, Mfumbiro (November 17, 1910); Lake Albert Edward Nyanza (no data); south end of Lake George (three specimens, December 4, 5 and 6, 1910); Lake Ruaketenge, Ankole (November 1903) and two specimens labeled only "Uganda."

TANZANIA. One specimen is labeled "Tanganyika," while another was labeled "Iringa Uplands," Southern Tanganyika, February 16, 1932.

In the United States National Museum there are labeled specimens from:

BRITISH EAST AFRICA, Sotex, Telex River (May 13, 1911); Solik, Kabalot Hill (July 5, 1911); South Guaso, Nigiro, Nigara Marsh (February 6, 1911); Jekyundu River, Maru (no data); Thika (January 11, 1909) and Lake Nyanza, Tanzania (February 28, 1920).

In the Museum of Comparative Zoology, Harvard, there are specimens from Unyanganyi, Tanzania (four specimens, December 6, 1929); Nygaza, Lake Victoria (March 4, 1910); Sindam Goma, Rutshura, Congo (male, female and eggs, November 11, 1938); Nyakabande, Rouerda, Uganda (January 27, 1939) and Labago, Kenya near Nairoba (October 17, 1922).

In the Coryndon Museum, Nairobi, Kenya, there are four Kenya specimens: Kabete, near Nairobi (July 1, 1944); Nairobi (February 17, 1961); Nakuru Rift Valley (January 12, 1958) and Limuru (January 17, 1957). In the University of Michigan Museum of Zoology there are two female specimens taken at Lake Manyara, Tanzania (el. 3,000 ft. or 914 m) in June 1939. In the Chicago Natural History Museum there are two specimens, male and female, taken near Entebbe, Uganda on January 1, 1912.

Chapin (1939) wrote that Emin had found the Crowned Cranes of Wadelai in the Bahr el Jebel, to have light ashy-gray long neck feathers and their bare cheek patches were pure white with an upper red border. He also reported Crowned Cranes common around Lake Albert and at Mahagi, while *B. p. ceciliae* apparently does not occur south of Lake No. *B. r. gibbericeps* has been found at the eastern base of Ruwenzori, Lake Edward, throughout the Kivu Highland, to Lake Bunyoni (el. 6,700 ft. or 2,042 m) and in a small marsh on the western slope of Mt. Mikeno (el. 7,200 ft. or 2,195 m).

Allan Brooks, Jr. (verbal communication) reported the Crowned Cranes of northern Uganda often had color intergradations between the two forms, but I have not been able to find specimens of any birds from this northern region. This region is probably the only place where the southern forms meet the northern ones.

Jackson (1938) wrote that *B. r. gibbericeps* avoided localities above 7,500 feet in elevation. I found this the case with *B. r. regulorum* in South Africa. Jackson also gave localities where the East African Crowned Crane had been found as: Ankole, Athi River, Bombo, Buddu, Elmenteita, Entebbe, Gilgil, Il-polossat, Jinga, Juju, Kendu, Kigezi, Kisumu, Kyagwe, Lakiundu River, Mt. Elgon, Mpumu, Mumias, Nairobi, Naivasha, Nakuru, Nandi, Njoro, Pesi Swamp, Rombo, Ruatenge, Ruibale, Thika, Toro and Tsavo. Dean Murray (verbal) found the species common at Arusha, Tanzania. I found it at Lake Naivasha, Kenya December 2, 1961 and at Entebbe, Uganda in January 1962.

DESCRIPTION

Breeding adult. This crane is colored almost identically to the South African Crowned Crane. However, in measurement it is slightly larger (see Table 22). These birds are pearly gray above and below. The alula and primary coverts are white; the inner great coverts are straw-colored, composed of disintegrated plumes. The bird is generally much paler than *B. p. ceciliae*. The primaries are black; the secondaries, maroon-chestnut. The inner secondaries are broad, long and slightly decomposed. The tail is black. The crown is covered with short velvety-black feathers. On the occiput is the usual tuft of strawlike white and yellow spiraled feathers with black tips. The upper portion of the white cheek patch is carmine red.

The bare cheek patch extends upward, forming a bony knoblike protuberance so it is much closer to the opposite bare patch than in any of the other Crowned Cranes. Although the width of the skulls of *B. r. regulorum* and *B. r. gibbericeps* measures almost the same, the distances between the bare spots in the latter measured 23.8 (18-32) mm for twenty specimens (both sexes), while the entire skull width was 40.7 (37-48 mm). In fourteen specimens (both sexes) of *B. r. regulorum* the narrowest region between the bare cheek patches averaged 31.6 (25-36) mm and the width of the skulls averaged 41.6 (37-49) mm. These same measurements averaged 25.7 (23-28) mm for *B. p. pavonina*, (six birds, both sexes), while the widest portion of the skull averaged 45.1 (42-47) mm. In fourteen specimens of both sexes of *B. p. ceciliae* these same distances measured 28.8 (26-34) mm and the widest portion of the skull, 40.5 (37-44) mm.

The longest feathers of the crest in four birds representing all four forms averaged: *B. p. pavonina*, 114.1 (100-126) mm; *B. p. ceciliae*, 94.1 (71-113) mm; *B. regulorum regulorum*, 107.5 (91-118) mm and *B. r. gibbericeps*, 119.9 (97-132) mm. Male crests averaged a little longer than those of the females.

TABLE 1

NESTING DATA OF COMMON CRANE AT SKANSEN ZOOLOGICAL GARDENS, STOCKHOLM, SWEDEN*

Year	Eggs Laid	Days Between Egg Laying	Eggs Hatched	Days Between Hatching Of Eggs	Number Of Eggs	Of Young	Days of Incubation for Last Egg
1895	17-21 May	4	——	—	2	0	—
1896	10-13 May	3	8-9 June	1	2	2	27
1897	6-7 May	1	8 June	0	2	2	32
1898	5-7 May	2	13-15 June	2	2	2	39
1899	30 April—2 May	2	31 May—1 June	1	2	2	30
1900	5-9 May	4	5 June	—	2	1	27 or 31
1901	7-9 May	2	4-5 June	1	2	2	27
1902	9 May	—	6 June	—	1	1	28
1903	25-27 April	2	30 May—1 June	2	2	2	35
1904	5-7 May	2	3-4 June	1	2	2	28
1905	8-10 May	2	5 June	—	2	1	26 or 28
1906	19 April—3 May	14	30 May	—	2	1	(27)
1907	4-5 May	1	2-4 June	2	2	2	30
1908	3-7 May	4	——	—	2	0	—
14 Yrs.	4-7 May	3.2	4-6 June	1.43	27	20	30.3

*(From Behm, 1908.)

TABLE 2

1964 ARRIVAL OF CRANES AT ARASAKI, NEAR IZUMI CITY, KAGOSHIMA PREFECTURE, KYUSHU, JAPAN

Arrival Dates	Grus vipio White-Naped Crane	Grus monachus Hooded Crane	Grus grus Common Crane	Total Arrivals	Total Count
October 17	3	—	—	3	3
October 20	—	4	—	4	7
October 21	—	6	—	6	13
October 25	13	115	—	128	141
October 27	—	35	—	35	176
October 31	—	290	—	290	466
November 1	6	150	2	158	624
November 9	8	270	—	278	902
November 16	2	13	—	15	917
November 23	13	—	—	13	930
December 1	31	60	—	91	1021
December 4	9	—	1	10	1031
December 27	20	180	—	200	1231
January 1, 1965	16	4	—	20	1251
Total	121	1127	3	1251	1251

TABLE 3

1965 DEPARTURE OF CRANES FROM ARASAKI (NEAR IZUMI CITY),
KAGOSHIMA PREFECTURE, KYUSHU, JAPAN

Departure	*Grus vipio* White-Naped Crane	*Grus monachus* Hooded Crane	*Grus grus* Common Crane		Total Departures	Total Count
February 12	70	1127	3	WNC	51	1200
February 15	25	1127	3	WNC	45	1155
February 26	21	1097	3	WNC HC	4 30	1121
February 27	21	1064	3	HC	33	1088
February 28	2	953	3	WNC HC	19 111	958
March 1	1	653	3	WNC HC	1 300	657
March 3	1	509	3	WNC HC	1 144	512
March 4	0	404	3	HC	105	407
March 7	0	384	3	HC	20	387
March 8	0	195	1	HC CC	189 2	196
March 9	0	10	0	HC CC	185 1	10
March 15	0	3	0	HC	7	3
March 17	0	2	0	HC	1	2
Total Departures	121	1125	3			1251

Table 4

Total Crane Counts at Arasaki, Kagoshima Prefecture, Kyushu, Japan

Year	*Grus monachus* Hooded Crane	*Grus vipio* White-Naped Crane	*Grus grus* Common Crane	*Grus japonensis* Japanese Crane	*Grus leucogernaus* Siberian Crane	Total Cranes
1938	2550	211	2	1		2764
1939	3217	347	3			3567
1940	3435	467	3	1		3906
1947	250	25				275
1948	300	50				350
1949	245	30				275
1950	265	28				293
1951	218	23				241
1952	243	20				263
1953	259	20				279
1954	255	22				277
1955	274	25				299
1956	318	27				345
1957	356	31				387
1958	350	34				384
1959	375	45			1	421
1960	376	60			1	437
1961	723	71				794
1962	811	96				907
1963	1053	95				1149*
1964	1127	121	3			1251
1965	1442	129	2			1573
1966	1467	181	6			1654
1967	1450	221	5	1		1677
1968	1452	203	5			1661**

*1 *Grus canadensis* (Sandhill Crane); **1 hybrid—*Grus monachus*—*Grus grus*.

TABLE 5
NESTING OF THE SANDHILL CRANE (*Grus canadensis*)

Subspecies	Locality	Latitude North	Nesting Dates	Average Nesting Date	Number of Records
G.c.canadensis	Banks Island	72-73°	10 June—10 July (Estimated)	16 June (Actual)	6
" " "	Alaska	60-67°	23 May—6 August (May, 4; June, 64; July, 1; August, 1)	15 June	70
G.c.rowani	Saskatchewan, Alberta, British Columbia, Manitoba	50-60°	11 April—1 July (April, 1; May, 24; June, 17; July, 1)	26 May	43
G.c.tabida	Oregon	42-45°	7 April—4 July	1 May	112
" " "	Idaho	42-45°	6 May—20 June	26 May	13
" " "	Iowa (old)	41-43.5°	4-29 May	19 May	7
" " "	Michigan (Upper Peninsula)	46-47°	28 April—1 July (April, 1; May, 22; June, 1; July, 1)	19 May	25
" " "	Michigan (Lower Peninsula)	41.5-43°	1 April—1 July (April, 102; May, 45; June, 1; July, 1)	25 April	149
G.c.pulla	Mississippi	30.5-31°	29 March—10 June (March, 1; April, 10; May, 17)	2 May	28
G.c.pratensis	Georgia	30.5-31°	2 March—12 April	29 March	8
" " "	Florida	26-30°	10 December—June (December, 2; January, 5; February, 26; March, 54; April, 17; May, 3; June, 1)	13 March	108
G.c.nesiotes	Isle of Pines	21.5-22°	23 March—10 June (March, 1; April, 5; May, 2; June, 1)	30 April	9

323

TABLE 6

NESTING OF THE SANDHILL CRANE (*Grus canadensis*)

Subspecies	Locality	Average Egg Measurements (Extremes Below)	Number	Average Egg Weight (Extremes Below)	Number	Average Egg Set Size	Number of Sets
G.c.canadensis	Banks Island	86.23 × 54.9 (82.4-90.0) (52.1-57.1)	8	123.1 (120.0-126.2)	2	2.00	6
" "	Alaska	90.82 × 57.52 (77.4-101.0) (44-63.2)	91	139.7 (118.3-155)	7	1.883 (9×1; 68×2)	77
G.c.rowani	Saskatchewan, Alberta, Manitoba, British Columbia	91.69 × 59.27 (85.3-102) (54.6-65)	22	173.0 (159.1-190)	3	1.943 (5×1; 48×2)	53
G.c.tabida	Oregon	97.5 × 62.7 (92.0-102) (60.0-66)	8	178.9 (173.2-190.2)	6	1.938 (9×1; 120×2; 1×3)	130
" "	Idaho	97.9 × 62.3 (88.9-105.9) (57.5-66)	19	167.9 (160-175)	4	1.900 (1×1; 9×2)	10
" "	Iowa	99.0 × 61.4 (98.3-100.6) (59.4-63)	5	—	—	—	—
" "	Michigan (Northern)	94.81 × 61.20 (76.0-104.0) (58-65.0)	22	196.6 (175.0-216.3)	3	1.905 (2×1; 19×2)	21
" "	Michigan (Southern)	94.96 × 60.84 (86.0-108.0) (54.5-65.7)	264	196.19 (fresh) 156.9 (hatching)	143 6	1.975 (6×1; 155×2; 1×3)	162
G.c.pulla	Mississippi	95.96 × 58.56 (89-104) (56.2-59)	16	147.9 (121.1-162.2)	6	1.839 (6×1; 24×2. 1×3)	31
G.c.pratensis	Georgia	93.02 × 59.02 (86-97.3) (56.5-63.1)	9	161.6 (138.4-207.1)	6	1.850 (1×1; 5×2)	6
" "	Florida	92.77 × 59.56 (85-104) (56-67)	119	164.69 (138.9-185.4)	8	1.941 (6×1; 60×2; 2×3)	68
G.c.nesiotes	Isle of Pines	87.94 × 57.13 (82.6-89.5) (53-60)	5	133.2 (108.1-158.2)	2	2.00 (10×2)	10
Totals and Averages		93.73 × 59.89 93.55 × 59.53 mm.	(588) (12)	186.8 grams 161.64	(196) (12)	1.9303	574 sets

Table 7

Measurements and Weights of Chicks

Subspecies	Locality	Wing Chord	Exposed Culmen	Tarsus	Bare Tibia	Weight in Grams
				In Millimeters		
G.c.canadensis (2)	Alaska Hooper Bay	34.5 (34-35)	19.0	39.0 (38-40)		
G.c.rowani probable (4)	N.W.T., Ft. Smith, Alberta Fawcett	37.5 (30-46)	22.8 (21-24.8)	43.2 (37-49)		107.7 (96.7-125.0)
G.c.tabida (28)	Oregon, Malheur. Idaho, Caribou Co. Southern Michigan	34.5 (25.8-42)	23.3 (21-26.6)	46.3 (40-52.4)	24.5 (20-30)	115.2 (98.5-133.5)
G.c.tabida (day of hatching) (15)	Michigan (Southern)	33.7 (25.8-38)	22.7 (21-25)	44.2 (40-49.6)		114.2 (98.5-132.3)
G.c.tabida (one to 1½ days) (13)	Southern Michigan	35.4 (26.6-42)	23.9 (22.5-26.6)	47.9 (42.5-52.4)		116.1 (102.2-125.6)
G.c.pratensis, pulla (6)	Mississippi Georgia Florida	35.5 (31-40)	24.6 (21-25)	43.6 (38-49)		101.1 (98.5-120.3)
G.c.nesiotes (3)	Isle of Pines	38.5 (36-42.5)	31.1 (26-37.6)	54.3 (51-60.5)		

Table 7A

Territory	Number of Eggs	Elongation Length/Breadth	Extremes	Years
A-1	17	1.573	1.503-1.646	1948-1969
B-2	18	1.518	1.416-1.595	1960-1969
C-3	21	1.527	1.432-1.638	1959-1969
D-4	17	1.499	1.461-1.572	1961-1969
E-5	19	1.529	1.410-1.629	1959-1967
F-6	3	1.722	1.688-1.763	1968-1969
G-7	23	1.610	1.522-1.688	1948-1969
Average	17 (118)	1.549	1.410-1.763	

TABLE 8
SURVIVAL OF SANDHILL CRANE CHICKS UNTIL AUTUMN, 1947-1968
SOUTHERN MICHIGAN

Year	Breeding Pairs Known	Number of Pairs Without Young	Number of Pairs With One Young	Number of Pairs With Two Young	Total Young	Average Number of Young Per Pair	Total Non-Breeders Observed
1947	8	5	2	1	4	0.50	
1948	4	1	1	2	5	1.25	
1949	16	10	4	2	8	0.50	
1950	8	3	4	1	6	0.75	
1951	9	7	1	1	3	0.33	
1952	48	15	27	6	39	0.812	60
1953	47	17	21	9	39	0.829	60
1954	43	15	17	11	39	0.907	48
1955	44	12	20	12	44	1.000	72
1956	48	22	16	10	36	0.750	92
1957	42	15	16	11	38	0.905	68
1958	50	20	25	5	35	0.700	81
1959	2	0	1	1	3	1.500	
1960	7	3	3	1	5	0.714	
1961	2	1	1	0	1	0.500	
1962	22	12	7	3	13	0.591	32
1963	41	23	14	4	22	0.537	65
1964	46	35	7	4	15	0.326	60
1966	27	18	7	2	11	0.407	100+
1967	54	26	20	8	36	0.667	100+
1968	30	14	8	8	24	0.758	
Total	598	274	222	102	426	0.712	828
Average	28.5	13.0	10.5	4.85	20.3		69

TABLE 9

Localities surveyed and total number of Cranes found in successive years

	1948	1949	1950	1951	1952	1953
Big Valley, Lassen County	6*	9	0	2	14*	9*
Fall River Valley, Shasta County	0	0	0	2	2	0
Goose Lake, Modoc County	7	0	0	2	4*	0
Honey Lake Valley, Lassen County	0	0	0	0	2*	4*
Horse Lake, Lassen County	0	0	Not Surv.	Not Surv.	2	2*
Jess Valley, Modoc County	5	9	0	13*	29*	22*
Pit River Valley, Modoc County	9*	8	0	10*	14*	15*
Steele Swamp, Modoc County	2	4*	0	2	4*	0
Surprise Valley, Modoc County	22*	20*	24*	2	22*	6
Boles Meadow, Modoc County	0	0	0	2	0	0
Willow Creek Valley, Lassen County	0	0	0	2	0	0
Upper Roberts Reservoir, Modoc County	0	0	0	0	2*	0
Grasshopper Valley, Lassen County	0	0	0	0	2	0
Cowhead Lake, Modoc County	Not Surv.	Not Surv.	Not Surv.	Not Surv.	3*	Not Surv.
Wood Valley, Modoc County	"	"	"	0	4	0
Meiss Lake, Siskiyou County	"	"	"	0	3*	0
Ash Valley, Modoc County	"	"	"	Not Surv.	Not Surv.	2
Dixie Valley, Lassen County	"	"	"	0	0	2*
Total	51	50	24	37	107	62

*Nests found or young observed; latter included in estimate of total cranes present.
(From Naylor, *et al*, 1954.)

TABLE 10

Summary of yearly observations on the Sandhill Crane in northeastern California

	1948	1949	1950	1951	1952	1953
Pairs	12	17	9	14	39	16
Singles	—	—	—	4	3	10
Groups	22	16	3	—	10	18
Young	5	—	3	5	16	2
Nests	4	3	—	—	5	5
Total Cranes	51	50	24	37	107	62

TABLE 11

Location	Pairs	Pairs/ Broods	Single Cranes	Grouped Cranes	Total
Idaho					
Grays Lake Area	115	45	38	160	577
Blackfoot River	28	11	9	—	105
Bear Lake Area	25	13	11	12	112
Bear River Valley	4	4	2	17	41
Teton Basin	9	1	2	26	50
Henry's Fork of Snake River Area	67	9	16	232	412
Camas NWR[1]	2	1	—	10	18
Wyoming					
Lincoln County	22	9	11	104	188
TOTAL	272	93	89	561	1,503

[1]Data provided by R. Twist, Refuge Manager, other records from Rod Drewien, Mss.

TABLE 12

Summary of Greater Sandhill Crane staging area
aerial survey, August 28-29, 1969
(from Rod Drewien, Mss, Idaho Coop. Research)

Location	Total Cranes
Grays Lake Area	1,153
Bear Lake Area	168
Teton Basin	1,343
Henry's Fork of the Snake River	127
TOTAL	2,791

TABLE 13

PROBABLE GAINS AND LOSSES OF WHOOPING CRANES BETWEEN 1938 AND 1972 AT ARANSAS NATIONAL WILDLIFE REFUGE, TEXAS, AND PROBABLE OR KNOWN BREEDING PAIRS AT WOOD BUFFALO NATIONAL PARK, NORTHWEST TERRITORIES, CANADA

Year	Total Adults	Total Young	Total Cranes	Gain	Loss	Percent Of Flock Adults	Percent Of Flock Young	Known Or Probable Pairs	Known Or Probable Eggs
1937	12 ?		12 ?						
1938	12	4	16	4		75.0	25.0	4	8
1939	16	6	22	6		72.7	27.3	4	8
1940	21	5	26	4	1	80.8	19.2	4	8
1941	13	2	15		13	86.7	13.3	2	4
1942	15	4	19	4		78.9	21.0	3	6
1943	16	5	21	2	3	76.2	23.8	5	10
1944	15(16)	3	18(19)		5	84.2	15.8	3	6
1945	14(19)	3	17(22)	(3)		87.3	12.7	3	6
1946	22	3	25	3		88.0	12.0	3	6
1947	25	6	31	6		80.6	19.3	5	10
1948	27	3	30		4	90.0	10.0	3	6
1949	30	4	34	4		88.2	11.7	4	8
1950	26	5	31		8	83.9	16.1	4	8
1951	20	5	25		11	80.0	20.0	5	10
1952	19	2	21		6	90.5	9.5	2	4
1953	21	3	24			87.5	12.5	3	6
1954	21	0	21		3	100.0	00.0	3	6#
1955	20	8	28	7	1	71.4	28.5	6	12
1956	22	2	24		6	91.3	8.7	5	9
1957	22	4	26	2	2	84.6	15.4	5	10
1958	23	9	32	6	3	71.9	28.1	5	10
1959	31	2	33	1	1	93.9	6.1	6	6
1960	30	6	36	3	3	83.3	16.7	6	12
1961	33	5	38	2	3	86.8	13.2	6	12
1962	32	0	32		6	100.0	00.0	0	0
1963	26	7	33	1	6	78.8	21.2	7	14
1964	32	10	42	9	1	76.2	23.8	8	16
1965	36	8	44	2	6	82.8	18.2	8	16
1966	38	5	43		6	88.4	11.6	8	16
1967	39	9	48	5	4	81.2	18.7	10	20
1968	43	6	49	1	5	87.7	12.3	11	21
1969	48	8	56	7	1	85.7	14.3	12	24
1970	51	6	57	1	5	89.4	10.6	13	24
1971	54	5	59	2	3	90.1	9.9	14	28
1972	45	5	50		14	90.0	10.0	?	?
Total	976	168	1144		130	85.3	14.8		app. 400

From this table it is indicated that 85.3 percent of the long time group consisted of adult birds, 14.8 percent, young birds, at Aransas Refuge. It also indicates that about 42 percent of eggs laid produced young which survived until fall. It shows how close the species was to extinction especially during 1941, 1944 and 1952. If losses, probably from shooting, such as occurred during 1941, 1951 and 1972, came every year, the species would not survive. These figures are from the United States Fish and Wildlife Service and the Canadian Wildlife Service, together with my figures of what was happening. Cranes do not breed normally until four or five years old. The number of young brought to Aransas per pair in the fall, was also used. In addition to the above six eggs were taken during 1967, ten during 1968 and ten during 1969, a similar number during 1970 and 1972. From these a captive flock of twenty captive birds now exists at Patuxent Research Station under supervision by the U. S. Fish and Wildlife Service and the Canadian Wildlife Service.

TABLE 14
WHOOPING CRANE STATISTICS
SHOWING TEXAS ARRIVAL AND DEPARTURE

Winter	Autumn Arrival	Total Arrivals	Total Adults	Number of Young Per Family	Spring Departure	Total
1949-50	4 October	34*	30	1, 1, 1, 1	*Pete died; Jo and Crip new captive. Migrants only in 34.	
1950-51	5 October	31*	26	2, 1, 1, 1	*One of young in twin family died in winter. One adult stayed and died during summer.	
1951-52	27 October (None) 3 November (18 Counted)	25	20	1, 1, 1, 1, 1	Two died near Refuge. Only 23 went North.	
1952-53	14 October	21	19	1, 1	Loss: 1 in Canada; 1 in Kansas on migration.	
1953-54	27 October	24	21	1, 1, 1	Summer '53 began intensive public appeal. All adults returned.	
1954-55	17 October	21	21	None	Nesting ground discovered.	
1955-56	18 October (2 Ad., 1 Yg.) 4 November (28)	28	20	2, 2, 1, 1, 1, 1	One bird died December; one injured in Lampasas County—to San Antonio Zoo. 26 went N.	
1956-57	13 October	24	22	1, 1	Three remained all summer. When captured one died.	
1957-58	20 October (1 Ad.); 25 October (4 Ad., 1 Yg.); 26 October (1 Ad.); 29 October (2 Ad.); 5 November (4 Ad., 2 Yg.); 6 November (5 Ad.); 14 November (3 Ad., 1 Yg.).	26	22	1, 1, 1, 1	3 April (3 left); 7 April (5 left); 11 April (6 left); 15 April (4 left); 21 April (3 left); 29 April (4 left); 6 or 7 May (1 left).	
1958-59	19 October (2 Ad.); 20 October (3 Ad.); 21 October (2 Ad., 1 Yg.); 23 October (4 Ad., 4 Yg.); 1 November (7 Ad., 4 Yg.); 12 November (5 Ad.)	32	23	2, 2, 2, 2, 1 (9)	3 April (7 Ad., 4 Yg.); 14 April (4 Ad.); 27 April (12 Ad., 5 Yg.).	32
1959-60	12 October—13 November	33	31	1, 1 (2)	23 March (1 Ad.); 30 March (3 Ad.); 8 April (1 Ad.); 12 April (2 Ad.); 19 April (8 Ad.); 26 April (5 Ad.); 9 May (9 Ad., 2 Yg.). (2 stayed all summer)	33
1960-61	19 October (1 Ad.); 21 October (3 Ad., 1 Yg.); 22 October (2 Ad., 1 Yg.); 28 October (4 Ad.); 29 October (1 Ad.); 31 October (10 Ad., 4 Yg.); 4 November (6 Ad.); 15 November (1 Ad.).	36	30	1, 1, 1, 1, 1, 1 (6)	31 March (3 Ad., 1 Yg.); 4 April (2); 7 April (3); 14 April (24, inc. 5 Yg.); 2 May (3 Ad.).	36
1961-62	14 October (1 Ad.); 17 October (3 Ad.); 20 October (8 Ad., 2 Yg.); 24 October (7 Ad.); 27 October (7 Ad., 2 Yg.); 31 October (4 Ad.); 9 November (1 Ad., 1 Yg.); 29-30 January (2 Ad.).	38	33	1, 1, 1, 1, 1	2 April (5); 11 April (3); 19 April (21); 25 April (4); 2 May (4); 16 May 1).	38
1962-63	19 October (2 Ad.); 22 October (1 Ad.); 25 October (13 Ad.); 27 October (4 Ad.); 31 October (6 Ad.); 5 November (4 Ad.); 7 December (2 Ad.).	32	32	0	20 December (3); 28 February (1); 25 March (2); 28 March 2); 8 April (4); 12 April (4); 15 April (8); 18 April (2); 22 April (3); 13 May (1); 16 May (2).	32

TABLE 15
ATTENTIVE PERIODS OF WHOOPING CRANES AT THE NEST
AT ARANSAS WILDLIFE REFUGE, TEXAS, IN 1950

Date	Number of incubation changes[1]	Length of each period on the nest		First morning change		Last daily change	
		Male	Female	Time	Bird leaving nest	Time	Bird going onto nest
9 May	8 (0)	74, 152, 119, 62	137, 132, 90	0608	♀	1921	♀
10 May	8 (0)	193, 194, 118, 75	89, 127, 109	0600	♀	1935	♀
11 May	6 (1)	126, 119, 109	90, 185	0545	♀	1614	♀
12 May	7 (1)	122, 106, 108, +	215, 122, 149	0535	♀	1917	♂
13 May	6 (0)	159, 129, 194	88, 176	0536	♀	1811	♀
14 May	6 (1)	207, 111	132, 136, 57	0757	♂	1846	♂
15 May	8[2]	112, 188, 159, 60	53, 215, 84	0534	♀	2005	♀
16 May				0700	♂		
Averages and Totals	7.0	126 Minutes	125 Minutes	0611		1847	
					6 ♀ ♀		5 ♀ ♀
					2 ♂ ♂		2 ♂ ♂

[1]Number in parentheses is the number of times the birds called when changing places at the nest.

[2]Both birds called at 0759, 33 minutes after the second change.

Note: Both birds left the nest 27 minutes, 9 May; 9 minutes, 13 May; 7 minutes, 14 May because of men and boats nearby.

Table 16

SARUS CRANE GROUPS ON ROOSTING AND BREEDING REGIONS
ON THE KEOLADEO GHANA BIRD SANCTUARY, BHARATPUR,
RAJASTHAN, INDIA, SEPTEMBER 1965

Date in September	Weather	Region Worked	1	2	3	4	5	6	7	9	Total
1	Clear	Roost Pond	8	43	3						103
2	Rain	" "	7	35					1		84
3	"	" "	5	33	1	2	1				87
4	"	" "		12	1						27
5	Cloudy	" "	11	17			1			2	68
6	Clear	" "	2	9	2		1				31
7	"	West Region		1							2
8	"	" "		10							20
9	"	" "	2	11	2				1		37
10	"	" "	1	17							35
11	"	11 Mi. Circuit		15			1				35
12	"	Near Rest House	1	7	1						18
13	"	" " "		12							24
14	"	Southeast	2	17				1			42
15	"	"	2	16							34
16	"	Near Rest House		8							16
17	"	" " "		11							22
18	"	11 Mi. Circuit	1	20							41
19	"	Near Rest House		7							14
20	"	11 Mi. Circuit		27							54
21	"	Rest House & SE		14							28
22	"	Rest House & SE		7							14
		To Agra	1	1							3
23	"	Rest House Area		15							30
24	"	East & Southeast		15							30
25	"	" " "		22							44
26	"	" " "		14	1						31
27	"	" " "		15							30
28	"	" " "		7							14
Total Groups			43	438	11	2	4	1	2	2	(503)
Total Cranes			43	876	33	8	20	6	14	18	1,018

TABLE 17

DEPARTURE OF INDIAN SARUS CRANES FROM NIGHT ROOST AT KEOLADEO GHANA
BIRD SANCTUARY, BHARATPUR, RAJASTHAN, INDIA
3 FEBRUARY 1969

Time In Hours	*Sizes of Groups Flying Out*	*Total*

Sarus Cranes called much more in early morning than *G.leucogeranus*.
In general they flew at an earlier hour.

0705—First Sarus Cranes flew from roost, 14, 12, 4	30
0710—2 Sarus Cranes flew (132 beats of wing per min.)	2
0716—Groups flying, 6, 7, 3 (a pair with 1 young), 34 x 2	84
0719—Groups flying, 3, 2, 1, 1, 1	8
0945—Three pairs and 1 crippled bird feeding yet in pond; they never flew away.	

7 FEBRUARY 1969

TOTAL FLYING	124

0615—Went in dark to pool to watch	
0630—Many Sarus Cranes calling.	
0649—First Sarus Cranes flying out to feed, 5, 3, 3, 3, 1, 1	16
0654—Sarus Cranes flying out from roost, 12, 5, 7, 3, 1, 1	29
0700—Sarus Cranes flying out just over trees, 5, 2, 2	9
0706—Sarus Cranes flying out from roost, 9, 2, 2 (0707 sunrise)	13
0712—Sarus Cranes flying from roost, 2; those walking away, 2, 2, 2, 2	10
0715—Sarus Cranes flying from roost, 2	2
0720—Sarus Cranes flying from roost, 2	2
0750—Sarus Cranes flying from roost, 2	2
0830—28 Sarus Cranes still feeding throughout pond	28

TOTAL (THE PREVIOUS NIGHT 171 Sarus Cranes came to roost) (Human activity near roost must have frightened some away)	111

TABLE 18

MEASUREMENTS AND WEIGHTS OF TEN MALE AND TEN FEMALE
BROLGAS (ALL PAIRS) TAKEN BETWEEN JUNE AND DECEMBER 1968
BY J. G. BLACKMAN

	Ten Males		Ten Females	
	Average	*Extremes*	*Average*	*Extremes*
Weight in grams	6,996.8	(6,265.3-8,278.2)	5,721	(5,244.7-6,350)
Length (from bill tip to tail base) (Centimeters)	112.5	(104.7-134.0)	101.3	(97.2-106.0)
Forearm (Wing chord minus primary) (Millimeters)	239.8	(226-250)	223.7	(212-235)
Head length (mm.)	257.0	(245-276)	241.4	(230-250) (9)
Head depth (mm.)	60.5	(57.5-65.0)	56.45	(53.5-60.0)
Head width (mm.)	49.8	(48.0-51.7)	46.75	(44.5-49.5)
Exposed culmen (mm.)	164.4	(157-170)	156.1	(145-163)
Tarsus (mm.)	304.9	(295-317)	278.4	(258-299)
Middle toe (mm.) with claw	113.0	(108-118)	109.8	(102-116)

TABLE 19

MEASUREMENTS OF THREE BROLGA CHICKS TAKEN BY J. G. BLACKMAN

Bird Hatched	Date Measured	Body Length	Wing Length	Tarsus	Exposed Culmen	Weight In Grams
April 5, 1968	(same)	190.0	65.6	38.4	24.5	102.0
June 25, 1968	June 28, 1968	190.0	60.0	40.0	26.0	90.8
March 10, 1969	March 12, 1969	210.0	68.0	41.0	23.0	114.0

Measurements in millimeters.

TABLE 20

SIBERIAN CRANES OBSERVED AT KEOLADEO GHANA BIRD SANCTUARY, RAJASTHAN, INDIA IN FEBRUARY 1969 BY AUTHOR

February Date	Total Birds Observed	Evident Pairs	Young Birds With Parents
2	58	6	3
3	65	26	7
4	52	21	6
5	86	25	6
6	70	17	7
7	53	12	6
8 (A.M.)	54	6	1
8 (P.M.)	74	14	7
9	76	14	7
AVERAGE	65	15.4	5.5

TABLE 21

DEPARTURE OF SIBERIAN CRANES FROM NIGHT ROOST
KEOLADEO GHANA BIRD SANCTUARY, RAJASTHAN, INDIA

FEBRUARY 9, 1969

Time in Hours	Departing Flocks Showing Grouping of Individuals	Total Birds Out
0600	Sarus Cranes calling as well as Owl from woods	
0635	One Sarus chasing others	
0650	First Siberian Cranes flew (4, 3, 2)	9
0652	Groups of 4, 3, 3, 2	12
0655	Groups of 3, 2, 2	7
0700	Groups of 3, 1	4
0701	Calling a low *Toy, Toy* 3, 3 flew out (0706 Sunrise)	6
0704	Calling gently, 4, 2	6
0707	One group (3)	3
0708	Siberian Cranes, 5, 6	11
	Many Bar-headed Geese	
0717	Three birds called *Put-tock—put-tock—* 19, 8, 12 syllables	
0720	They called again 8-20 times	
0732	Groups of 2, 1	3
0751	Last ones, 7, 3, 5	15
TOTAL		76

TABLE 22

MEASUREMENTS OF CROWNED CRANES

Number Measured	Sex	Wing	Tail	Tarsus	Bare tibia	Middle toe	Exposed culmen	Crest	Weight
				Balearica pavonina pavonina					
1	Male	585	275	203	156	116	64	112	
1	Female	506	241	196	156	107	53	113	
6	Both	547.5	244.3	196	146.5	115.3	56.5	114.1	
	Extremes	506–585	233–275	190–203	123–156	107–122	53–64	100–126	
				Balearica pavonina ceciliae					
4	Male	511.7	220	192.5	156.7	113.6	56.2	97 mm	3628.8 g
9	Female	491.1	222.5	187.8	132.1	118.1	54.8	94	3628.8 g
17	Both	496.7	224.3	188.0	134.5	116.4	56.1	94.1	
	Extremes	470–565	207–252	172–205	100–161	100–129	49–62	71–113	
				Balearica regulorum regulorum					
9	Male	560.7	241	205.1	128.6	115.6	63.3	111	
2	Female	523		223		116	62	105	
22	Both	565.2	238.7	207.1	121.2	115.2	61.9	107.5	
	Extremes	523–642	212–256	183–234	104–142	109–120	57–68	91–118	
				Balearica regulorum gibbericeps					
16	Male	565.4	258.6	205.4	133.6	120.5	60.9	123	
14	Female	543.5	250.1	196.8	129.1	120.6	59.7	122	
44	Both	559.4	250.1	201.1	133.8	117.6	59.4	119.9	
	Extremes	458–615	224–270	170–234	113–161	100–126	52–71	79–132	

TABLE 23

AMOUNT OF TRACHAEL CONVOLUTIONS, VOICE, AND DISPLAY
DURING UNISON CALL PERIOD OF CRANE PAIRS

Species	Degree of Trachael Convolutions in Sternum	Degree of Loudness of Voice	Male with Secondaries Over Back When Calling	Male with Stiff Primaries by Side Like Turkey Gobbler	Birds Holding Wings Tight Against Body When Calling
5. *Grus japonensis*	Extensive	Very penetrating *Karrooo* or whoop	Yes	Over back also	Female, yes Male, no
6. *Grus americana*	"	" " "	"	By side	Female, yes Male, no
1. *Grus grus*	"	" " "	"	" "	Female, yes Male, no
2. *Grus nigricollis*	"	" " "	?	?	?
7. *Grus vipio*	Moderate	" " "	Yes	By side	Female, yes Male, no
8. *Grus antigone*	"	" " "	Yes	By side	Female, yes Male, no
9. *Grus rubicundus*	"	" " "	Yes	By side	Female, yes Male, no
10. *Grus monachus*	Extensive to moderate	Higher pitch Loud but less penetrating *Karrooo* or *Garrooo*	Not as much	Not as much	Female, yes Male, no
4. *Grus canadensis*	Moderate	" " "	Practically none	No	Female, yes Male, yes
11. *Bugeranus carunculatus*	Along edge	A scream or *Kronk* call	Seldom call	?	Female, yes Male, ?
12. *Anthropoides virgo*	" "	Less penetrating fewer syllables higher pitch	Yes	Yes	Female, yes Male, no
13. *A.paradisea*	" "	" "	Yes	Yes	Female, yes Male, no
10. *Grus leucogeranus*	Looped close by	Less penetrating *Toy-oy-ya*	Yes	Yes	Female, some Male, no
14. *Balearica pavonina*	None	Goose-like *Ka-wonk*	Seldom call in unison	No	Female, yes Male, yes
15. *B.regulorum*	"	*Ah-ooyu* or *Ya-oo-goo-lung*	" "	"	Female, yes Male, yes

APPENDIX

APPENDIX

PLANTS

Acacia arabica (Mimosoideae), Babul, *A. sieberiana.*

A coelorraphe Wrightii, Everglades Palm.

Acer rubrum L. (Aceraceae), Red Maple.

Aeschynomene indica (L.) (Leguminosae), Pulse.

Agropyron Smithii Rydb. (Gramineae), Blue Joint Grass.

Alfalfa (Leguminosae), *Medicago sativa* L., (Browse).

Alder (Betulaceae), *Alnus glutinosa* L., *Alnus incana* (L.) Moench., Speckled Alder.

Andromeda glaucophylla Link. (Ericaceae), Rosemary.

A. polifolia.

Andropogon appendiculatus Nees (Gramineae); *A. scoparius* Michx., Little Blue Stem Grass; *A. virginicus* L., Broom Sedge.

Arbutus, Trailing (Ericaceae), *Epigaea repens* L.

Aristida spp. Needlegrass, Wiregrass.

Arrowhead, (Alismataceae), *Sagittaria lancifolia* L.; *S. latifolia* Willd., Broad-leaved Arrowhead.

Arum (Araceae), *Peltandra virginica* (L.) Kunth.

Ascolepsis capensis Ridley (Cyperaceae).

Aspen (Salicaceae), *Populus tremuloides* Michx.

Avena sativa L. (Gramineae), Oats. (Food).

Babul (Mimosiudeae), *Acacia arabica.*

Barley (Gramineae), *Hordeum vulgare* L. (Food).

Batis maritima (Chenopodiaceae), Saltwort.

Bay, Red (Lauraceae), *PerseaBorbonia* (L.) Spreng.

Bay, Swamp, *Persea palustris* (Raf.) Sarg.

Beak-rush, *Rhynchospora* spp.

Beauty, Meadow (Melastomataceae), *Rhexia* spp.

Beech (Fagaceae), *Fagus grandifolia* Ehrh.

Betula alba L. (Betulaceae), White Birch; *Betula alba papyrifera* Marsh, Paper Birch; *B. glandulosa* Michx., Dwarf Birch; *B. lutea* Michx. f., Yellow Birch; *B. nana; B. pubescens; B. pumila* L. Swamp Birch.

Bouteloua curtipendula (Michx.) Torr., Grama; *B. eriopoda* (Torr.), Black Grama; *B. gracilis* (HBK) Lag., Blue Grama.

Blackberry (Rosaceae), *Rubus* spp.

Bladderwort (Lentibulariaceae), *Utricularia inflata* Walt.

Blueberry (Ericaceae), *Vaccinium* spp.

Brachiaria miliiformis, Para Grass.

Buckbean (Gentianaceae), *Menyanthes trifoliata* L.

Buchloe dactyloides (Nutt.) Engelm. Buffalo Grass.

Bulrush (Cyperaceae), *Scirpus acutus* Muhl.; *Scirpus validus* Vahl.

Bur-reed (Sparganiaceae), *Sparganium eurycarpum* Engelm.

Burro Brush, *Salicornia Bigelovii* Torr.

Butea frondosa, Dhak.

Butomus umbellatus L., Flowering Rush.

Butterwort (Lentibulariaceae), *Pinguicula lutea* Yellow; *P. caerulea,* Blue.

Buttonbush (Rubiaceae), *Cephalanthus occidentalis* L.

Byrosonima verbascifolia.

Calamagrostis inexpansa Gray (Gramineae), Reed Grass.

Calopogon neglecta (Ehrh.), Grass-pink;

C. tuberosus (L.) BSP.

Caltha palustris L. (Ranunculaceae), Marsh Marigold.

Carex nigra (acuta) (L.) Reich; *C. acuta; C. trichocarpa* Muhl., Sedges (Cyperaceae).

Cattail (Typhaceae), *Typha angustifolia* L., *T. latifolia* L., Common Cattail.

Centella asiatica (Umbelliferae), Pennywort.

Cephalanthus occidentalis L., Buttonbush.

Chamaedaphne calyculata (L.) Moench (Ericaceae), Leatherleaf.

Cicer arietinum L., Gram, Chick-pea.

Cladium glomeratum R. Br. (Cyperaceae); *C. jamaicense* Crantz, Sawgrass.

Cliftonia monophylla, Buckwheat Tree.

Colpothrinax Wrightii Griseb. and Wendl., Bottle Palm.

Comarum palustre (L.) Scop (*Potentilla*) (Rosaceae).

Corn (Gramineae), *Zea mays* L. (Important food).

Cornus amomum Mill. (Cornaceae), Gray Dogwood; *C. stolonifera* Michx. Red-osier Dogwood.

Cotton-grass (Cyperaceae), *Eriophorum polystachion; E. spissum* Fern.; (*E. callitrix* Cham.)

Cranberry (Ericaceae), *Vaccinium oxycoccos* L.; *V. macrocarpon* Ait.; *V. Vitis-idaea* L.

Crowberry (Empetraceae), *Empetrum nigrum* L.

Ctenium aromaticum (Walt.) Wood., Toothache Grass.

Cynodon Dactylon (L.) (Graminae), Bermuda Grass.

Cyperus denudatus Linn. f.; *C. esculentus* L.; *C. exaltatus, C. fastigiatus* Rottb.; *C. rotundus* L; *C. scariosus* R. Br. (Cyperaceae), Nut Grass (Food).

Cypress (Taxodiaceae), *Taxodium distichum* (L.) Rich.

Cyrilla racemiflora L., Leatherwood.

Decodon verticillatus (L.) Ell. (Lythraceae), Water-willow.

Digitaria spp. (Gramineae).

Distichlis spicata (L.) Greene (Gramineae), Salt Grass.

Drosera brevifolia Pursh. (Droseraceae), Sundew.

Echinochloa colonum (L.) Link.; *Echinochloa* spp.

Eichhornia crassipes (Mart.) Solms., Water Hyacinth.

Elderberry, (Caprifoliaceae), *Sambucus.*

Eleocharis dulcis, Bulkuru Sedge; *E. variegata* (Cyperaceae).

Empetrum nigrum L. (Empetraceae), Crowberry.

Epigaea repens L. (Ericaceae), Trailing Arbutus.

Equisetum limosum; E. palustre L.; *E. sylvaticum* L., (Equisetaceae), Horsetails.

Eragrostis spp., Meadow Grass (Gramineae).

Eriocaulon compressum Lam.; *E. australe* R. Br.; *E. decangulare* L., Pipeworts (Eriocaulaceae).

E. decangulare L., Pipeworts (Eriocaulaceae).

Eriophorum callitrix Cham; *E. polystachyum; E. spissum* Fern., Cotton-grass (Cyperaceae).

Fagus grandifolia Ehrh., Beech (Fagaceae).

Fern, Bracken (Polypodiaceae), *Pteridium aquilinum* (L.)

Fernwort (Scrophulariaceae), *Pedicularis verticillata.*

Filipendula ulmaria (L.) Maxim., Spiraea (Rosaceae).

Gale, Sweet (Myricaceae), *Myrica gale* L.

Gaultheria procumbens L. Wintergreen (Ericaceae).

Goldencrest, *Lophiola americana* (Pursh) Wood.

Gordonia Lasianthus Ell. (Theaceae), Loblolly Bay.

Gram, *Cicer arietinum* L.

Grass, Arrow (Juncaginaceae), *Triglochin maritima* L.; *T. palustris* L.

Grass, Bluestem (Gramineae), *Andropogon scoparius* Michx.; *A. appendiculatus; A. smithii; A. virginicus* L.

Grass, Dropseed (Gramineae), *Sporobulus* spp.

Grass, Meadow, *Eragrostis ciliarus* (L.) R. Br.

Grass, Para, *Brachiaria miliiformis.*

Grass, Salt, *Distichlis spicata* (L.) Greene.

Grass, Saw (Cyperaceae), *Cladium jamaicense* Crantz.

Grass, Yellow-eyed (Xyridaceae), *Xyris Smalliana* Nash.

Grass (Gramineae), *Paspalum distichum* L.

Hypericum fasciculatum; H. stypheloides (Hypericaceae), St. John's Wort.

Hyperrhenia filipendua.

Ilex spp. (Aquifoliaceae), Holly.

Iris (Iridaceae), *Iris Orientalis* Mill.; *I. Pseudacarus* L.; *I. savannarum; I. versicolor* L., Blue.

Juncus effusus L.; *J. oxycarpus; Juncus* spp., (Juncaceae), Juncus, Rushes.

Kalmia angustifolia L.; *K. polifolia* Wang., (Ericaceae), Laurels.

Kandi, *Prosopis spicigera.*

Keli-kadomb, *Stephegyne parvifolia.*

Kitayoshi, Reed, *Phragmites communis* Trin.; *P. lingivalois* (Gramineae).

Lachnanthes tinctoria (Walt.) Ell., Redroot, (Food).

Lachnocaulon anceps (Walt.) Morong, Bog-button.

Larix laricina (Du Roi) Koch., American Tamarack.

Ledum groenlandicum Oeder; *L. palustre* L., Laurel (Ericaceae).

Leatherleaf, *Chamaedaphne calyculata* (L.) Moench.
Leersia hexandra Sw. (Gramineae).
Limnanthemum indicum (Gentianaceae).
Limnophylla heterophylla (Scrophulariaceae).
Liquidambar styraciflua L. (Hamamalidaceae), Sweet Gum.
Lobelia spp. (Lobeliaceae).
Lyngliya spp. (Cyanophyceae).
Magnolia grandiflora, Magnolia; *M. virginiana* L., Sweet Bay (Magnoliaceae).
Maiden-cane (Paniceae), *Panicum hemitomum* Schultes.
Marigold, Marsh (Ranunculaceae), *Caltha palustris* L.
Melastoma polyanthum Bl.
Melochia corchorifolia (Sterculiaceae).
Menyanthes trifoliata (L.) (Gentianaceae), Buckbean.
Miscanthus spp. (Gramineae).
Molinia caerulea (L.) Moench. (Gramineae).
Monanthocloe littoralis Engelm., Salt Grass.
Moss, Spanish, *Tillandsia usneoides* L. (Bromelieceae).
Myrica cerifera L. (Wax Myrtle); *M. gale* L., Sweet Gale, (Myricaceae).
Nymphaea lotus, Water Lily; *N. odorata* Ait., White Water Lily (Nymphaeaceae).
Nymphoides aquatica (Walt.) Kuntze., Floating Heart, (Gentianaceae).
Orontium aquaticum L., Never-wet (Araceae).
Oryza sativa L. (Gramineae).
Palmaceae: Bottle Palm, *Colpothrinax Wrightii* Griseb. & Wendl.
Palm, Cabbage, *Sabal Palmetto* R. & S.
Palmetto, Saw, *Serenoa repens*.
Panicum hemitomum Schultes (Gramineae), Maiden-cane.
Panicum spp. Switchgrass.
Paspalum distichum L. (Gramineae), Knot-grass.
Peanut, *Arachis hypogaea* L. (Fabaceae) (Food).
Peltandra virginica (L.) Kunth. (Araceae), Green Arum.
Pennisetum thunbergii Kunth. (Gramineae).
Persea Borbonia (L.) Spreng. Red Bay (Lauraceae).
Philydrum lanuginosum Banks & Scl. ex Gaerth.
Picea canadensis (Mill.) BSP. (Pinaceae), White Spruce (*glauca*); *P. excelsa* L., Spruce; *P. mariana* BSP., Black Spruce.
Pickerelweed (Pontederiaceae), *Pontedaria cordata* L., *P. lanceolata* Nutt.
Pinguicula caeruluea, Blue Butterwort; *Pinguicula lutea*, Yellow Butterwort (Lentibulariaceae).
Pines (Pinaceae); *Pinus caribaea* Morelet; *P. elliotii*, Slash Pine; *P. palustris* Mill., Long-leaf Pine; *P. silvestris* L., European Pine; *P. Strobus* L., White Pine; *P. taeda* L., Loblolly Pine; *P. tropicalis*, Tropical Pine; *P. resinosa* Ait., Red Pine.
Plantain, Water (Alismataceae), *Sagittaria latifolia* Willd.
Prosopis spicigera, Kandi.
Psedra (*Parthenocissus*) (Vitaceae), Woodbine.
Pteridium aquilinum (L.) Kunth., Bracken Fern.
Pycreus unioloides (R. Br.) Urban (Cyperaceae), *P. oakfortensis* C. B. Cl.
Quercus (Fagaceae), Oaks: *Q. alba* L., White Oak; *Q. laevis*, Turkey Oak; *Q. marilandica* Muench. Black Jack Oak; *Q. nigra* L., Water Oak; *Q. robur* L., European Oak; *Q. rubra* L., Red Oak; *Q. velutina* Lam., Black Oak; *Q. virginiana* Mill., Live Oak (Often used for food).
Red-root, *Lachnanthes tinctoria* (Walt.) Ell.
Rheixa spp. (Melastomataceae), Meadow Beauty.
Rhus Toxicodendron L. (Anacardiaceae), Poison Ivy.
Rhynchospora brownii R. & S.; *Rhynchospora* ssp. Beakrush.
Rompe Ropa, *Tabebuia lepidophylla* (Bignoniaceae).
Rosemary, Bog, *Andromeda glaucophylla* Link.
Rubus spp.; *R. arcticus*, *R. chamaemorus* (Rosaceae).
Rush, Baltic, *Juncus balticus*; Rushes, *J. effusus* L.; *J. effus solutus*; *J. oxycarpus*.
Rush, Spike, *Eleocharis*.
Sabal Palmetto R. & S. (Palmaceae), Cabbage Palm.
Sagebrush, *Artemesia tridentata*.
Sagittaria lancifolia L.; *S. latifolia* Wild. (Alismataceae), Arrowleaf.

St. John's Wort, *Hypericum fasciculatium*; *H. stypheloides*.
Salicornia europeaea L.; *S. Bigelovii* Torr.; *S. perennis*, Salicornia (Chenopodiaceae).
Salix caroliniana Michx.; *S. interior* Rowlee; *S. longifolia* Muhl.; *S. petiolaris* Sm. (Salicaceae), Willows.
Sambucus canadensis L.; *S. (pubens)* Michx.; *S. racemosa* L.; *S. simpsonii* (Caprifoliaceae), Elderberry.
Sarracenia purpurea L. (Sarraceniaceae), Pitcher Plant.
Schoenus yarrabensis Domin.
Scirpus acutus Muhl.; *S. cespitosus* L.; *S. inclinatus* Del.; *S. maritimus*; *S. muricinux*; *S. validus* Vahl. (Cyperaceae).
Scleria ciliata Michx.; *S. nitida* Willd.; *S. oligantha* Michx.; *S. pauciflora* Muhl.; *S. reticularis* Michx.; *S. triglomerata*, Nut-rush (Cyperaceae).
Sedge, Bulkuru, *Eleocharis dulcis*.
Serenoa repens (Palmaceae), Saw Palmetto.
Setaria (Gramineae), Foxtail Grass.
Smilax rotundifolia L.; *S. laurifolia* L. (Liliaceae), Greenbrier.
Sorghastrum spp., Indian Grass.
Sorghum vulgare Pers., Sorghum; *S. v.* var. *durra* (Forsk.) Hubb. & Rehder, Durra; *S. v.* var. *caffrorum* (Retz.) Hubb. & Rehder, Kafir (Important crane foods).
Sparganium eurycarpum Engelm. (Sparganiaceae), Bur-reed.
Sporobolus cryptandrus (Torr.) A. Gray, Dropseed; *S. virginicus* (L.) Kunth. Sand Couch (Gramineae).
Spruce, *Picea excelsa* L.; *P. canadensis* Mill. BSP; *P. mariana* (Mill.) BSP. (Pinaceae).
Stephegyne parvifolia, Keli-kadamb.
Sundew, *Drosera brevifolia* Pursh.; *Drosera* spp.
Sweetbay, *Magnolia virginiana* L.
Switchgrass, *Panicum* spp.
Tabebuia lepidophylla (Bignoniaceae), Rompe Ropa.
Tamarack, *Larix laricina* (Du Roi) Koch.
Taxodium distichum (L.) Rich. (Taxodiaceae), Cypress.
Tea, Labrador, *Ledum groenlandicum* Oeder.
Tillandsia usneoides L. (Bromeliaceae), Spanish Moss.
Triglochin palustris L. (Juncaginaceae), Arrow Grass.
Typha angustifolia L.; *T. latifolia* L., (Typhaceae), Narrow-leafed and Broad-leafed Cattails.
Utricularia inflata Walt. (Lentibulariaceae), Bladderwort.
Vaccinium oxycoccos L.; *V. ulginosum* L.; *V. Vitis idaea* L., (Ericaceae), Cranberry; Foxberry.
Veratrum Misae.
Vitis aestivalis Michx.; *V. munsoniana* (Vitaceae), Grapes.
Wheat, *Triticum aestivum* L.
Willow, *Salix* spp.; *Salix caroliniana* Michx.
Willow, Water, *Decodon verticillatus* (L.) Ell.
Wintergreen, *Gaultheria procumbens* L.
Wiregrass, *Aristida* spp.
Wort, St. John's, *Hypericum fasciculatum*; *H. stypheloides*.
Xyris Smalliana Nash. (Xyridaceae), Yellow-eyed Grass.
Zea mays L., Maize.

ANIMALS
INVERTEBRATA

ANNELIDA
Earthworms.
Leech spp.

ARTHROPODA
Crustacea
Crab, Blue, *Callinectes sapidus* Rathbun.
Crab, Common Fiddler, *Uca pugilator* (Bosc.).
Crab, Fiddler, *Uca pugnax* (Smith).
Crab, Hermit, *Clibinarius vittatus* (Bosc.).
Crab, Mud, *Sesarina cinereum* (Bosc.).
Crab, Pinnixid, *Pinnixa cylindrica* (Say).
Crab, *Potamon* spp.

Shrimp, *Peneus aztecus* (Ives).
Shrimp, Edible, *Peneus setiferus* (Linn.).
Shrimp, Grass, *Palaemonetes* spp.
Shrimp, Mud, *Callianassa jamaicense* var. *louisianensis* Schmitt.
Crayfish, *Cambarus* spp.
Crayfish, Freshwater, *Cherax depressus* Rich.

Insects
Beetles, Coleoptera.
Dragonflies, Odonata.
Long-horned Grasshoppers (Tettigoniidae) Sub-families:
Phaneropterinae, False Katydids. (Crane food).
Pseudophyllinae, True Katydids. (Crane food).
Conocephalinae, Meadow Grasshoppers. (Crane food).
Copiphorinae, Cone-headed Grasshoppers. (Crane food).
Grasshopper, *Atractomorpha crenaticeps* (Blanch).
Gyrllinae (*Gryllus*), Field Crickets. (Crane food).
Locustinae, Spur-throated Locust. (Crane food).
Mantidae, Praying Mantis (Listed by Allen, 1952).
Blattidae, Cockroaches (Rarely eaten).
Mosquitoes, Flies, Diptera, *Tipula* larvae.

ARANEIDA
Spiders (Occasional crane food).

MOLLUSCA
Pelecypoda
Clam, *Solen* spp.
Clam, Short Razor, *Tagellus gibbus* (Spengler).
Rangia cuneata (Gray).

Gastropoda
Snail, Disc Pond, *Helisoma trivolvis; H. anceps; H. campanulatum* (Apparent crane food).
Snail, Ear, *Melampus lineatus* Say.
Snail, *Pila globosa.*
Periwinkle, Common, *Littorina irrorata* Say.

CHORDATA
VERTEBRATA

Pisces
Cobitis spp. (*Grus japonensis* food?).
Lefua spp. (*Grus japonensis* food?).
Misgurunus anguillicaudatus (Mud Fish in *G. japonensis* waters);
Periophthalmus vulgaris Eggert, Mud skipper.

Amphibia
Toad, American, *Bufo americanus.*
Toad, Rocky Mt., *Bufo w. woodhousei* Girard.
Frog, Bull, *Rana catesbeiana* Shaw.
Frog, Leopard, *Rana pipiens; Rana sphenocephala.*
Frog, Green Tree, *Hyla cinerea cinerea.*
Frog, Squirrel Tree, *Hyla squirella.*
Peeper, Spring, *Hyla crucifer.*
Frog, *Pseudaoris triseriata* Wied.
Frog, Cricket, *Acris crepitans* Baird.
Frog, Southern Cricket, *Acris g. gryllus.*

Reptilia
Alligator, *Alligator mississippiensis* (Daudin).
Anone, Green, *Anolis carolinensis* Voigt.
Moccasin, Cotton-mouth, Agkistrodon piscivorus (Lacépède).
Racer, Blue, *Coluber constrictor flaviventris* (Say).
Rattlesnake, *Crotalus horridus.*
Rattlesnake, Western, *Crotalus atrox atrox* (Baird and Girard).
Rattlesnake, Pigmy (Massasauga), *Sistrurus catenatus.*
Snake, Hog-nosed, *Heterodon platyrhinos.*
Snake, Common Water, *Natrix sipedon sipedon* (Linnaeus).

Snake, Common Water, *Natrix piscator* (India).
Snake, Rat, *Elaphe obsoleta.*
Snake, Garter, *Thamnophis ordinatus.*
Snake, Checkered, *Thamnophis marcianus* (Baird and Girard).
Snake, Eastern Garter, *Thamnophis sirtalis sirtalis.*
Turtle, Painted, *Chrysemys picta marginata.*
Turtle, Snapping, *Chelydra serpentina* (Linnaeus).
Turtle, Box, *Terrapene carolina.*

Aves
Podiceps ruficollis capensis Salvadori, African Dabchick.
Pelecanus onocrotalus Linnaeus, African White Pelican.
Fregata magnificens Matthews, Frigate Bird.
Ardea herodias Linnaeus, Great Blue Heron.
Ciconia ciconia (Linnaeus), European White Stork.
Phoenicopterus ruber roseus Pallas, Greater Flamingo.
P. minor Geoffrey, Lesser Flamingo.
Branta canadensis (Linnaeus), Canada Goose.
Anser fabalis.
Anser albifrons (Scopoli), White-fronted Goose.
Chen hyperborea (Pallas), Lesser Snow Goose.
Chen caerulescens (Linnaeus), Blue Goose.
Plectropterus gambensis (Linnaeus), Spur-winged Goose.
Neophron prenopterus (Linnaues), Egyptian Vulture.
Circaetus pectoralis Smith, Black-breasted Harrier Eagle.
Lyrurus tetrix Linnaeus, Black Grouse.
Lagopus lagopus Linnaeus, Willow Ptarmigan.
Pavo cristalus Linnaeus, Peacock.
Fulica cristata Gmelin (Rallidae), Red-knobbed Coot.
Otis tarda Linnaeus (Otididae), Great Bustard.
Actophilornis africanus (Gmelin), African Jacana.
Hoplopterus spinosus Linnaeus, Spurwing Plover.
H. armatus (Burchell), Blacksmith Plover.
Lymnocryptes minimus (Brünnich), Jacksnipe.
Capella gallinago delicata (Ord), Common Snipe.
Numenius arquata (Linnaeus), Curlew.
Numenius phaeopus (Linnaeus), Whimbrel.
Stercorarius longicaudus Vieillot, Long-tailed Jaeger.
Columba palumbus, Wood Pigeon.
Cuculus canorus Linnaeus, European Cuckoo.
Dacelo leachi, Blue-winged Kookaburra.
Apus affinis abessynicus, Little African Swift.
Apus caffer streubelii (Hartlaub), White-rumped Swift.
Apus horus (Heuglin), Horus Swift.
Empidonax traillii traillii (Audubon), Traill's Flycatcher.
Garrulus glandarius, Jay.
Corvus corax principalis Ridgway, Raven.
Corvus brachyrhynchos Brehm, Common Crow.
Turdus musicus (Turdidae), Redwing.
Hylocichla ustulata swainsoni (Tschudi), Swainson's Thrush.
Phylloscopus trochilus, Willow Warbler.
Acrocephalus paludicola, Aquatic Warbler.
Vermivora celata celata Say, Orange-crowned Warbler.
Dendroica coronata (Linnaeus), Myrtle Warbler.
Agelaius phoeniceus phoeniceus (Linnaeus), Redwinged Blackbird.
Passerculus sandwichensis, Savannah Sparrow.
Ammospiza caudacuta (Gmelin), Nelson's Sparrow.
Melospiza lincolnii lincolnii (Audubon), Lincoln's Sparrow.

Mammalia
Blarina brevicauda kirtlandi Bole & Moulthrop, Short-tailed Shrew (Soricidae) (M. D. Pirnie observed one eaten by *G. c. tabida*).
Canidae: *Canis aureus,* Jackal (Apparently one ate a crippled *G. a. antigone*—L. Walkinshaw); *C. dingo* Meyer, Dingo (Enemy of *G. rubicundus*); *C. latrans* (Say), Coyote (Enemy of young *G. c. tabida*); *C. lupus, C. rufus,* Wolves (Possible enemy of young *Grus*).
Homo sapiens, Man (Worst enemy of all Gruidae).
Microtus spp. *M. gregalis, M. hyperboreus, M. oenconomus,* (Cricetidae) (Used by *G. canadensis* and *G. leucogeranus* for food.)

Mus musculus Linnaeus (Muridae), House Mouse (Food).

Odocoileus virgianus (Boddaert), (Cervidae), White-tailed Deer (May frighten *G. c. tabida* at night from nest.)

Ondatra zibethica (Linnaeus), Muskrat (*G. c. tabida* sometimes uses their houses on which to nest.)

Papio mormon, Baboon (May take eggs of *A. paradisea.*).

Peromyscus spp. (Critcetidae), Deer Mouse (Food?)

Procyon lotor Linnaeus (Procyonidae), Raccoon (Takes eggs of *G. canadensis.*).

Synaptomys cooperi Baird (Cricetidae), Bog Lemming (Food).

Vulpes vulpes Linnaeus (Canidae), Fox (Enemy of *G. Grus,* but often controlled by birds, Franden, 1958.)

Vulpes fulva (Desmarest), Red Fox (Possible enemy of young *Grus canadensis.*)

BIBLIOGRAPHY

BIBLIOGRAPHY

Grus grus grus and *Grus grus lilfordi*

Acharya, Hari Narayan G. 1936. Sarus flocks. *J. Bombay Nat. Hist. Soc.*, 38: 831.

Adams, A. Leith. 1864. Notes and observations of the birds of Egypt and Nubia. *Ibis*, 6: 1-36.

Agardi, E. 1962. Passing of Cranes above Pecsvarad. *Aquila*, 67-68: 247.

Alexander, H. G. 1929. Some birds seen in the Indian Ocean and the Mediterranean. *Ibis*, 12th ser., 5: 41-53.

Ali, Salim. 1927a. The Moghul Emperors of India as Naturalists and Sportsmen. Pt. 2. *J.. Bombay Nat. Hist. Soc.*, 32: 34-63.

———. 1927b. A Sind Lake. *J. Bombay Nat. Hist. Soc.*, 32: 460-471.

———. 1934. The Hyderabad State Ornithological Survey. Pt. 5. *J. Bombay Nat. Hist. Soc.*, 37: 425-454.

———. 1940. The birds of Central India. Pt. 2. *J. Bombay Nat. Hist. Soc.*, 41: 470-488.

———. 1941. The birds of Bāhalwalpūr (Punjāb). *J. Bombay Nat. Hist. Soc.*, 42: 704-747.

———. 1945. *The birds of Kutch.* Oxford Univ. Press., Brit. Indian Press, Bombay. xviii + 175 pp.

———. 1953. The Keoladeo Ghana Bird Sanctuary of Bharatpur (Rajasthan). *J. Bombay Nat. Hist. Soc.*, 51: 531-536.

———. 1961. The book of Indian birds. 6. Bombay.

Allouse, Bashir, E. 1953. The avifauna of Iraq. College of Arts and Science, Iraq Nat. Hist. Mus., Al-Tafayyudh Press, Baghdad. vii + 1-63 pp., map.

Austin, Oliver L., Jr. 1948a. The birds of Korea. *Bull. Mus. Comp. Zool.*, 101 (1): 1-301.

———. 1948b. Japanese Ornithology and Mammalogy during World War II. Nat. Res. Sect. Rept. No. 102HQ, SCAP, Tokyo, 1-47.

———. 1951. Review. *Wilson Bulletin*, 63: 352-353.

———. 1961. *Birds of the World.* 318 pp.

Austin, Oliver L., Jr. and Nagahisa Kuroda. 1953. The birds of Japan, their status and distribution. *Bull. Mus. Comp. Zool.*, 109 (4): 279-637.

Baker, E. C. Stuart. 1899. The birds of North Cachar. Pt. 10. *J. Bombay Nat. Hist. Soc.*, 12: 486-510.

———. 1922. Hand-list of the 'Birds of India.' Pt. 7. *J. Bombay Nat. Hist. Soc.*, 28: 830-873.

———. 1928. *The Game Birds of the Indian Empire.* Vol. 5. The waders and other semi-sporting birds. Part 7, with a coloured plate (*Antigone antigone antigone*). *J. Bombay Nat. Hist. Soc.*, 33: 1-6.

———. 1929. The Fauna of British India, including Ceylon and Burma. 2 ed., London. Vol. 6, xxxv + 499 pp.

———. 1935a. Bird notes on Lapland trips. *Oologist Record*, IX.

———. 1935b. The nidification of birds of the Indian Empire. Vol. IV, pp. 330, London.

Balfour, E. 1956. Crane in Orkney. *British birds*, 49: 38.

Barnes, Lt. H. Edwin. 1885. *Handbook to the Birds of the Bombay Presidency.* Calcutta, Central Press Co., Ltd. xxiv + 1-449 + xi.

———. 1886. Birds nesting in Rajpootana. *J. Bombay Nat. Hist. Soc.*, 1 (1): 38-62.

Basil-Edwards, S. 1926. A Contribution to the ornithology of Delhi. *J. Bombay Nat. Hist. Soc.*, 31: 567-578.

Bates, R. S. P. 1925. Bird-nesting with a camera in India. Pt. 3. *J. Bombay Nat. Hist. Soc.*, 30: 306-313.

Benson, C. B. G. 1950. Crane in Suffolk. *Brit. Birds*, 43:192-193.

Berg, Bengt. 1930. *To Africa with the migratory birds.* G. P. Putnam's Sons, N.Y. 274 pp.

Bernis, F. 1960. About wintering and migration of the Common Crane (*Grus grus*) in Spain. *Proc. XIIIth Int. Ornith. Cong. Helsinki*, 5.12. VI. 1958. 1:110-117.

Blaauw, F. E. 1897. *A monograph of the Cranes.* E. J. Brill, Leiden and London. viii + 64 pp., 22 col. plates.

Blakiston, T. and H. Pryer. 1878. A Catalogue of the Birds of Japan. *Ibis*, 1878: 209-250.

———. 1880. Catalogue of the Birds of Japan. *Trans. As. Soc. Japan*, 8: 172-241.

———. 1882. Birds of Japan. *Trans. As. Soc. Japan*, 10: 84-186.

Blyth, E., and W. B. Tegetmeier. 1881. *The Natural History of the Cranes.* Horace Cox Co., London. 92 pp.

Bolam, H. G. 1940. Common Crane in Rutland. *Brit. Birds*, 34: 20.

Brown, G. J. 1955. Crane in Yorkshire. *Brit. Birds*, 48: 87.

Burton, J. F. 1970. Birds of the World. IPC Magazines, Ltd., London, England. pp. 739-742.

Butler, E. A. 1880. Birds of the southern portion of the Bombay Presidency. Govt. Cent. Press, Bombay. 113 pp., map.

Caldwell, Harry R., and John C. Caldwell. 1931. South China birds. Hester May Vanderburgh, Shanghai. iv + 447 pp.

Campbell, James W. 1956. Crane in Outer Hebrides. *Brit. Birds*, 49: 281-282.

Cave, F. O., and J. D. MacDonald. 1955. *Birds of the Sudan.* Edinburgh and London, Oliver & Boyd. xxvii + 444 pp., map, illus.

Chapman, A. and W. J. Buck. 1893. *Wild Spain.* London.

Chapman, E. A., and J. A. McGeoch. 1956. Recent field observations from Iraq. *Ibis*, 98 (4): 577-594.

Cheeseman, R. E., and W. L. Sclater. 1935. On a collection of birds from North-western Abyssinia. Pt. 2, *Ibis*, 77: 297-329.

Christison, A. F. P., Assisted by C. B. Ticehurst. 1942. Some additional notes on the distribution of the avifauna of Northern Baluchistan. *J. Bombay Nat. Hist. Soc.*, 43: 478-487.

Christison, Philip, A. Buxton, A. M. Emmet, and Dillon Ripley. 1946. Field notes on the birds of coastal Arakan and the foothills of the Yomas. *J. Bombay Nat. Hist. Soc.*, 46: 13-32.

Collman, J. R. and J. P. Croxall. 1956. Spring migration at the Bosporus. *Ibis*, 109 (3): 359-372.

Cott, Hugh B. 1953. The exploitation of wild birds for their eggs. Pt. 1. *Ibis*, 95: 643-675. Pt. 2. *Ibis*, 96: 129-149.

Currie, A. J. 1916. The birds of Lahore and the Vicinity. *J. Bombay Nat. Hist. Soc.*, 24: 561-577.

Curry-Lindahl, Kai. 1960. Ecological studies . . . in the eastern Belgian Congo. Part II (Report No. 1 of the Swedish Congo Expeditions 1951-1952 and 1958-1959). Ann. Mus. Roy. du Congo Belge (neuer Name: de l'Afrique Centrale), Tervuren, 87, 1960. 170 pp.

D'Abreu, E. A. 1912. Notes on the bird collecting trip in the Balaghat District of the Central Provinces (India). *J. Bombay Nat. Hist. Soc.*, 21: 1158-1169.

———. 1935. A list of birds of the Central Provinces. *J. Bombay Nat. Hist. Soc.* 38: 95-116.

Delacour, Jean. 1929. On the birds collected during the fourth expedition to French Indo-China. *Ibis*, 12th ser., Vol. 5, No. 2: 193-220.

———. 1939. The birds of Clères in 1939. *Aviculture Magazine*, 5th ser. 4: 347-350.

Delacour, Jean, P. Jabouille and W. P. Lowe. 1928. On the birds collected during the third expedition to French Indo-China. *Ibis*, 12th ser., Vol. 4, 23-51, pt. 1.

Dharmakumarsinhju, R. S. 1955. *Birds of Saurashtra, India.* Times of India Press, Bombay. liii + 561 pp.

Dolgushin, I. A. 1960. *Birds of Kazakhstan.* Vol. 1. Acad. of Science Kazakhskoi S.S.R., Alma-Ata. 471 pp.

Donald, C. H. 1952. Bird Migration across the Himalayas. *J. Bombay Nat. Hist. Soc.*, 51: 269-271.

Dorst, Jean. 1962. The Migration of birds. Houghton-Mifflin and Co., Boston.

Dresser, H. E. 1905. An oological journey to Russia. *Ibis*, 8th ser., 5: 149-158.

————. 1908. On the Russian Arctic Expeditions of 1900-1903. Pt. 2. *Ibis*, 9th ser., 2: 593-599.

Drost, R. 1951. Study of bird migration 1938-1950. *Proc. Xth Int. Ornith. Cong. Uppsala, June 1950,* Almquist & Wiksell, Uppsala 216-340.

Edelstam, Carl. 1951. The Ottenby Bird Station. *Proc. Xth Int. Ornith. Cong., Uppsala, June 1950,* Almquist & Wiksell, Uppsala. 259-309.

————. 1963. The Capri Bird Observatory and its activities in 1956-61. *Var Fagelvärld,* 22 (4): 267-270.

England, M., and others. 1956. Photographic studies of some less familiar birds. LXXV. Crane. *British Birds,* 49: 435-437, 8 pls.

Engström, Boris. 1963. The Capri Bird Observatory and its activities in 1956-61. Verksamheten 1960. *Vår Fågelvärld,* 22 (4): 267-270.

Evans, WIlliam. 1961. On the periods occupied by birds in the incubation of their eggs. *Ibis,* Ser. 6., Vol. 3, pp. 52-93.

Feeny, P. P., R. W. Arnold and R. S. Bailey. 1968. Autumn migration in the South Caspian Sea region. *Ibis,* 110 (1): 35-86.

Fennell, Chester M. 1951. Akune, winter home of the Cranes of Japan. *Elepaio,* 12(5): 33-35, (6): 38-39.

————. 1952. Some observations on birds of southern Korea. *Condor,* 54 (2): 101-110.

Finnis, R. G. 1952. Some observations on the movements of birds in So. Italy . . . . *Revista Ital. di Orn.,* 22: 89-108.

Flower, S. S. 1925. Contributions to our knowledge of the duration of life in Vertebrate Animals. IV. Birds. *Proc. Zool. Soc. London,* 1925, pp. 1365-1422.

————. 1938. Further notes on the duration of life in animals. IV. Birds. *Proc. Zool. Soc. London,* Vol. 108, Ser. A, pp. 195-235.

Friedrich II. 1943. The art of Falconry . . . , trans. and ed. by Casey A. Wood and Marjorie Fyfe. Book Iv. Stanford Univ. Press, London, Oxford Univ. Pres.

Frome, N. F. 1947. The birds of Delhi and district. *J. Bombay Nat. Hist. Soc.,* 47: 277-300, map.

Ganyushkin, M. A. and A. E. Luguvoy. 1963. An experience of the Ringing of Moulted ducks in the Astrakhan Wildlife Preserve. *Trans. Astrakhan Wildlife State Preserve,* Vol. 8, Astrakhan (in Russian with English titles, *In* K. A. Worobjew, *The Fauna and Ecology of birds of the Volga-Delta and Caspian Sea shores*).

Gavrin, V. R. and D. I. Chekmenev. 1968. The mass moult of the Common Cranes on the Lake Salety Teniz. *Trudy Inst. Zool. Akad. Nauk Kazakh S.S.R.,* 24: 59-64.

Godfrey, W. Earl. 1966. The birds of Canada. Natl. Mus. Canada. Bull. No. 203, Biol. Ser. No. 73, Queen's Printer, Ottawa. 428 pp., 69 col. pls., 71 line drawings, 2 maps.

Grant, C. H. B. 1948. On the Genus for the Common Crane. *Ibis,* 90: 602-603.

Gray, Annie P. 1958. Bird Hybrids.

Guichard, K. M. 1950. A summary of the birds of Addis Abeba region, Ethiopia. *J. E. African Nat. Hist. Soc.,* 19: 154-178.

————. 1956. Observations on wintering birds near Tripoli, Libya. *Ibis,* 98 (2): 311-316.

Hand-List of the Japanese Birds. 1958. 4th and rev. ed., Orn. Soc. Japan, Yamashina Inst. for Orn. and Zool., Tokyo. 264 pp.

Harber, D. D. 1955. Special Review. The birds of the Soviet Union. G. P. Dementiev and N. A. Gladkov, eds., *British Birds,* 48 (6): 268-276.

————. 1965. Report on rare birds in Great Britain in 1964 (with 1963 additions) *British Birds,* 58: 353-372.

Harington, H. H. 1909. A list of the birds of the Bhamo District, Upper Burma. Pt. 2. *J. Bombay Nat. Hist. Soc.,* 19: 299-313.

Harrison, C. J. O. 1967. Sideways-throwing and sideways building in birds. *Ibis,* 109 (4): 539-551.

Hartert, E. 1907. Notes on African birds. *Novit. Zool.,* 14: 484-503.

Hendrickson, H. T. 1969. A comparative study of the egg white proteins of some species in the Avian Order Gruiformes. *Ibis,* 111 (1): 80-91.

Higgins, J. C. 1921. Manipuri names of certain birds. *J. Bombay Nat. Hist. Soc.,* 28: 288-290.

————. 1934. The game birds and animals of the Manipur State with notes of their numbers, migration and habits. *J. Bombay Nat. Hist. Soc.,* 37: 81-95 (Part 4).

Hopkinson, Emilius. 1926. Records of birds bred in captivity. H. F. & G. Witherby. xii + 330 pp.

Hume, A. O. 1868. Stray notes on Ornithology in India. II. *Ibis,* 28-40.

Inglis, C. M. 1903. The birds of the Madhubani sub-division of the Darbhanga district, Tirhut, with notes on species noticed elsewhere in the district. *J. Bombay Nat. Hist. Soc.,* 14: 764-771.

Irby, L. H. L. 1895. The Ornithology of the Straits of Gibraltar. 2nd ed., London.

Ivanov, A. I., E. B. Koslova, L. A. Portenko, and A. Ya. Tugarinov. 1951. Birds of the USSR. Vol. 1, Acad. of Sciences USSR, Moscow.

Jenkins, David. 1953. Migration in late September and early October 1951. *Brit. Birds,* 46: 78.

Jögi, A. 1967. New data on the Ornithofauna of Saaremaa Island. Lääna-Eesti Meresaarte Linnustik, Ornitoloogiline Kogumik IV. *Tartu:* 8-28 (English 28-31).

Johansen, Hans. 1961. Revised list of the birds of the Commander Islands. *Auk,* 78: 44-56.

Journal Bombay Natural History Society. Waters of Western India. *J. Bombay Nat. Hist. Soc.,* 3 (1): 1-17.

Kereso, F. 1948-1951. Migrating cranes, *Grus grus* in the county of Békés. *Aquila,* 55-58: 268.

Kessell, Brina, and Robert W. Kelly. 1958. First North American sighting and photographic record of Common Crane, *Grus grus. Auk,* 75: 465.

Keve, A., and M. D. F. von Udvardy. 1951. Increase and decrease of the breeding range of some birds in Hungary. *Proc. Xth Int. Orn. Cong.,* Uppsala, June 1950. Almquist & Wiksell, Uppsala, 468-476.

————. 1951. Increase and decrease of the breeding range of some birds in Hungary. *Proc. Xth Int. Orn. Cong.* op. cit.

Koslova, E. V. 1932. The birds of South-West Transbaikalia, Northern Mongolia and Central Gobi. *Ibis,* 74: 567.

Lack, D. 1933. Nesting conditions as a factor controlling breeding time in birds. *Proc. Zool. Soc. London.* 231-237.

Lack, David, and Elizabeth Lack. 1953. Visible migration through the Pyrenees; an Autumn Reconnaissance. *Ibis,* 95 (2): 271-309.

Lambert, Anthony. 1957. A Specific check list of the birds in Greece. *Ibis,* 99 (1): 43-68.

————. 1961. Spring migration of raptores in Bulgaria. *Ibis,* 103a (1): 130-131.

Lathbury, Sir Gerald. 1970. A Review of the birds of Gibraltar and its surrounding waters. *Ibis,* 112 (1): 25-43.

La Touche, J. D. 1924. On the birds of South-east Yunnan, S. W. China. Pt. 4. *Ibis,* 11th ser., 6: 284-307.

————. 1933. A Handbook of the birds of eastern China. Vol. 2, Pt. 4, pp. 229-400, 3 pls., Taylor and Francis, Fleet Street, London.

Lebret, T. 1947. The migration of the Teal, *Anas crecca crecca* L., in western Europe. *Ardea,* 35: 79-131.

Lehrman, Daniel S. 1959. Hormonal responses to external stimuli in birds. *Ibis,* 101 (3/4): 478-496.

Linné, Carl von. 1792. The Animal Kingdom, or Zoological System of the Celebrated Sit Charles Linnaeus. Class II, Birds. 644 pp.

Linné, Charles. 1758. Systema Naturae, 10th ed. Vol. 1. Stockholm, 824 pp.

———. 1758. Systema Naturae, 10th ed. Vol. 1 Stockholm, 824 pp.

Littlefield, Carroll D. 1970. Flightlessness in Sandhill Cranes. *Auk*, 87: 157.

Luard, C. E. 1927. Ornithology in the Bible.   32: 553-570.

Ludlow, F. 1917. Notes on the bird life of Ahwaz, Persia. *J. Bombay Nat. Hist. Soc.*, 25: 303-306.

Lundberg, Stig. 1963. The Capri Bird Observatory and its activities in 1956-1961. Verksamheten 1961. *Vår Fågelvärld*, 22 (4): 267-270.

Mackworth-Praed, C. W., and C. H. B. Grant. 1952. Birds of Eastern and North Eastern Africa. African Handbook of Birds. Ser. 1 Vol. 1 Longmans, Green and Co., London. xxv + 836 pp.

———. 1957. Birds of Eastern and Northeastern Africa. 2 ed. London, Longmans, Green and Co.

Marchant, S. 1941. Notes on the birds of the Gulf of Suez. Pt. 1. *Ibis*, 14th ser., 5: 265-295.

———. 1963. Migration of water-birds and raptors. *Ibis*, 105: 396-398.

Mascher, J. W., Bengt-Olov Stolt and Lars Wallin. 1962. Migration in spring recorded by radar and field observations in Sweden. *Ibis*, 104 (2): 205-215.

Mathiasson, S. 1963. Visible diurnal migration in the Sudan. *Proc. XIIIth Int. Orn. Cong., Ithaca, June 1962*. La. State Univ. Press, Baton Rouge, 430-435.

Meinertzhagen, R. 1920. Some preliminary remarks on the altitude of Migratory flight of birds, with special reference to the Palearctic Region. *Ibis*, Ser. XI, 2: 920-936.

———. 1927. Systematic results of birds collected at high altitudes in Ladak and Sikkim. Pt. 2, *Ibis*, 12th ser., 3: 571-633.

———. 1928. Some Biological problems connected with the Himalaya. *Ibis*, 12th ser., 4: 480-533.

———. 1938. On the birds of Northern Afghanistan. Pt. 2. *Ibis*, ser. 4, 2: 671-717.

———. 1949. Notes on Saudi Arabian birds. *Ibis*, 91: 465-482.

———. 1955. The speed and altitude of bird flight (with notes on other animals). *Ibis*, 97 (1): 81-117.

Meise, W., and E. Stresemann. 1950. Notes on South African birds described in A. Lichtenstein's Catlogue 1793. *Ibis*, 92: 22-26.

Mitchell, P. Chalmers. 1911. On longevity and relative viability in mammals and birds; with a note on the theory of longevity. *Proc. Zool. Soc. London*, 1911. 425-548.

Monson, Gale. 1961. Regional Report, Southwest Region. *Audubon Field Notes*, 15 (3): 348-351.

Moody, A. F. 1937. Common Cranes in Northamptonshire. *Brit. Birds*, 31: 91-92.

Moreau, R. E. 1928. Some further notes from Egyptian deserts. *Ibis*, 12th ser., 4: 453-475.

———. 1953. Migration in the Mediterranean Area. *Ibis*, 95: 329-364.

———. 1954. The main vicissitudes of the European Avifauna since the Pliocene. *Ibis*, 96 (3): 411-431.

———. 1961. Problems of Mediterranean-Saharan migration. (Pt. 1). *Ibis*, 103a (3): 373-427.

———. 1966. *The bird faunas of Africa and Its Islands*. New York, Academic Press.

———. 1967. Water birds over the Sahara. *Ibis*, 109 (2): 232-259.

Mountfort, G. R. 1957. Distraction display of the Crane. *Brit. Birds*, 50: 166-168.

Mountfort, Guy, and I. J. Ferguson-Lees. 1961. Observations on the birds of Bulgaria. *Ibis*, 103a (3): 443-471.

Mrugasiewicz, A., and J. Witowski. 1962. An Ornithological sketch of the Barycz Valley in Poland. *Brit. Birds*, 55: 245-272.

Müller, G. 1944-47. Crane migrating in the country Bihar from autumn 1946 till autumn 1948. *Aquila*, LI-LIV: 125-126.

Munn, P. W. 1932. Further notes on the birds of the Balearic Isles. *Ibis*, 13th ser., 2: 262-266.

Nielsen, Bent Pors, and Hans-Jørgen Speyer. 1967. Some observations of birds in northern Iran. *Dansk Orn. For. Tid.*, 61: 30-39.

Nisbet, I. C. T., P. R. Evans and P. P. Feeny. 1961. Migration from Morocco into southwest Spain in relation to weather. *Ibis*, 103a (3): 349-372.

Nisbet, I. C. T., and T. C. Smout. 1957. Autumn observations on the Bosphorus and Dardanelles. *Ibis*, 99 (3): 483-499.

Oates, Eugene W. 1902. Catalogue of the collection of Birds' eggs in the British Museum (Natural History). Vol. 2. Carinatae (Charadriiformes-Strigiformes). London, 8 vo., pp. 1-xx.

Ogawa, Minori. 1908. A Hand-List of the Birds of Japan. *Ann. Zool. Jap.*, 6: 337-420.

Okada, N. 1891. Catalogue of the Vertebrated Animals of Japan. *Aves*. Tokyo, pp. 73-114.

Ornithological Society of Japan, Special Committee of. 1922. A Hand-List of Japanese Birds. 1st ed., Tokyo.

———. 1932. A Hand-List of Japanese Birds. 2nd ed. Tokyo.

———. 1942. A Hand-List of Japanese Birds. 3rd ed. Tokyo.

Osmaston, B. B. 1925. The Birds of Ladakh. *Ibis*, 12th ser., 1: 663-719.

———. 1927. Notes on the Birds of Kashmir. Pt. 2. *J. Bombay Nat. Hist. Soc.*, 32: 134-135.

Passburg, R. E. 1959. Bird notes from northern Iran. *Ibis*, 101 (2): 153-169.

Pateff, P. 1950. The birds of Bulgaria. Illus. (English summary).

Payn, W. A. 1938. Spring migration at Tangier. *Ibis*, Ser. 14, Vol. 2: 33-38.

———. 1948. Notes from Tunisia and eastern Algeria: February 1943 to April 1944. *Ibis*, 90: 1-25.

Pease, H. J. R. 1938. Birds of Hailuoto, Finland. *Ibis*, Ser. 14, No. 2: 38-65.

Peters, James L. 1934. Check-list of the birds of the World. Harvard Univ. Press, Cambridge, Mass., Vol. II.

Peterson, Roger T., Guy Mountfort, and P. A. D. Hollom. 1954. A field guide to the birds of Britain and Europe. Collins, London.

Pitt, Frances. 1929. Notes on the effect of temperature upon the breeding behavior of birds, with especial reference to the Northern Golden Plover (*Charadrius apricarius altifrons*) and the Fieldfare (*Turdus pilaris*). *Ibis*, 12th ser., Vol. 5, (1): 53-71.

Pleske, Theodore. 1928. Birds of the Eurasian Tundra. *Mem. Boston. Soc. Nat. Hist.*, 6: 109-485.

Porter, Richard, and Jan Willis. 1968. The autumn migration of soaring birds at the Bosphorus. *Ibis*, 110 (4): 520-536.

Przevalsky, N. 1870. Journey in the Ussuri region in 1867-1869.

———. 1877. The birds of Mongolia, the Tangut Country and the solitudes of Northern Tibet. Pt. 3. In Rowley's Ornithological Miscellany, Vol. 2: 417-438.

———. 1888. Fourth journey into Central Asia (from Kyahkti to source of Zhelgoi River).

Radcliffe, H. De Lame. 1915. List of the birds of Baluchistan. Part 2. *J. Bombay Nat. Hist. Soc.*, 24: 156-169.

Rand, Austin L., and Robert L. Fleming. 1957. Birds of Nepal. Fieldiana. *Chicago Nat. Hist. Mus.*, Vol. 41.

Rattray, R. H. 1899. Birds collected and observed at Thull during five months in 1898, and notes on their nidification. *J. Bombay Nat. Hist. Soc.*, 12: 337-348.

Riddell, W. H. 1945. Field notes from observations in Spain on birds in the British list. *Ibis*, 87: 408-422.

Riley, J. H., and C. W. Richmond. 1922. A partial bibliography of Chinese birds. *J. North China Branch of the Royal Asiatic Society*, 53: 196-237.

Ripley, S. Dillon II. 1961. A Synopsis of the birds of India and Pakistan. *J. Bombay Nat. Hist. Soc.*, The Diocesan Press, Madras.

Safriel, U. 1968. Bird migration at Elat, Israel. *Ibis*, 110 (3): 283-320.

Sage, Bryan L. 1958. Field notes on autumn migration in the Khanaqin Area in 1958. *Iraq Nat. Hist. Mus. Publ. No. 16*, 33-48.

Saunders, Howard. 1869. Ornithological rambles in Spain. *Ibis*, 5th ser., 2: 170-186.

———. 1871. A list of birds of So. Spain. *Ibis*, 3rd Ser., 1: 384-402.

Seebohm, Henry. 1890. The birds of the Japanese Empire. 8 vo. London.

Sharpe, R. Bowdler. 1893. *Bull. Brit. Orn. Club*, 1: 43 (in text).

Sharpe, R. Bowdler, *et al.* 1874-1898. Catalogue of the birds in the British Museum. London, Vols. I-XXVII (XII-*Gruidae*).

Smith, K. D. 1957. Annotated Check List of the birds of Eritrea. *Ibis*, 99 (1): 1-26.

———. 1960. The passage of Palaearctic migrants through Eritrea. *Ibis*, 102 (4): 536-544.

———. 1965. On the birds of Morocco. *Ibis*, 107 (4): 493-526.

Smythies, B. E. 1953. The birds of Burma. Edinburgh and London.

Snow, D. W. 1952. A Contribution to the Ornithology of North West Africa. *Ibis*, 94 (3): 473-498.

Spence, T., *et al.* Cranes in Fife, Inverness and Lanarkshire. *Scot. Birds*, 2: 422-425.

Stanford, J. K. and Ernst Mayr. 1941. The Vernay-Cutting Expedition to Northern Burma. Pt. 5. *Ibis*, 14th ser., 5: 479-518.

Stanford, J. K. and Claud B. Ticehurst. 1939. On the birds of Northern Burma. *Ibis*, 14th ser., 3: 211-258.

Stevens, H. 1930. (Account of a recent trip to China). *Bull. Brit. Orn. Club*, 50: 46-54.

Stresemann, Erwin. 1963. Taxonomic significance of wing molt. *Proc. XIIIth Int. Orn. Cong., Ithaca, N.Y. June 1962.* La. State Univ. Press, Baton Route, p. 171.

Suregi, J. 1955. A great number of Cranes at Nádudvar, Bee-eaters near the River Bodrog. *Aquila*, 59-62: 438.

Svärdson, Gunnar, and Sigfrid Durango. 1951. Spring weather and population fluctuations. *Proc. Xth Int. Orn. Cong., Uppsala, June 1950.* Almquist & Wiksell, Uppsala, 497-501.

Swinhoe, Robert. 1861. Letter. *Ibis*, 3: 408-409.

————. 1870. On the Ornithology of Hainan. *Ibis*, 6: 342-367.

Tait, William C. 1924. The birds of Portugal. H. F. & G. Witherby, London.

Taka-Tsukasa, Prince N. 1932-1943. The birds of Nippon, 4to, Tokyo.

———. 1935. Birds of Jehol. Rept. of the first Scientific Expedition to Manchoukuo. Sec. v, div. ii, part iii (also rev. *Emu*, 1935: 35: 186-187).

———. 1967. The birds of Nippon. Maruzen, Tokyo.

Taka-Tsukasa, Prince N., and Hon. M. U. Hachisuka. 1925. A contribution to Japanese ornithology. *Ibis*, 12th ser., 1: 898-908.

Thompson, A. Landsborough. 1953. The study of visible migration of birds. An introductory review. *Ibis*, 95 (2): 165-180.

Thornbill, C. M. 1918. Some notes on game birds in Mesopotamia. *J. Bombay Nat. Hist. Soc.*, 25: 486-490.

Ticehurst, Claud B. 1926. On the downy plumages of Indian birds. *J. Bombay Nat. Hist. Soc.*, 31: 368-378.

———. 1927. The birds of British Baluchistan. Pt. 3. *J. Bombay Nat. Hist. Soc.*, 32: 63-97.

Ticehurst, Claud B., P. A. Buxton, and R. E. Cheeseman. 1922. The birds of Mesopotamia. *J. Bombay Nat. Hist. Soc.*, 28: 650-674.

Ticehurst, Claud B., Percy Cox, and R. E. Cheesman. 1926. Additional notes on the avifauna of Iraq. *J. Bombay Nat. Hist. Soc.*, 31: 91-119.

Tinbergen, N. 1948. Social releasers and the experimental method required for their study. *Wilson Bulletin*, 60: 6-51.

Trott, A. C. 1947. Notes on birds seen and collected at Jedda and in Arabia during 1937, 1938, 1939, and 1940. *Ibis*, 89: 77-98.

Tristam, Rev. H. B. 1868. On the Ornithology of Palestine. Pt. VIII. *Ibis*, Ser. 2, 4: 321-335.

Tucker, B. W. 1950. Crane in Suffolk. *Brit. Birds*, 45: 193.

Wadley, N. J. P. 1951. Notes on the birds of Central Anatolia. *Ibis*, 93 (1): 63-89.

Waite, H. W. 1948. The birds of the Punjab Salt Range (Pakistan), *J. Bombay Nat. Hist. Soc.*, 48: 93-117.

Whistler, Hugh. 1916. A note on some birds of the Gujranwala district, Punjab. *J. Bombay Nat. Hist. Soc.*, 24: 689-710.

———. 1918. Notes on the birds of the Ambala district, Punjab. Pt. 2. *J. Bombay Nat. Hist. Soc.*, 26: 172-191.

———. 1936. The Verney Scientific Survey of eastern Ghats. *J. Bombay Nat. Hist. Soc.*, 38: 695.

———. 1938. The Ornithological Survey of Jodhpur State. *J. Bombay Nat. Hist. Soc.*, 40: 213-235.

———. 1945. Materials for the Ornithology of Afghanistan. Pt. 5. *J. Bombay Nat. Hist. Soc.*, 45: 462-485.

Whitehead, C. H. T. 1911. Notes on the birds of Sehore, Central India, with special reference to migration. *J. Bombay Nat. Hist. Soc.*, 21: 153-170.

———. 1911. On the birds of Kohat and the Kurram Valley, Northern India. *J. Bombay Nat. Hist. Soc.*, 20: 954-980.

Wickham, P. F. 1930. Notes on the birds of the Upper Burma Hills. Pt. 3. *J. Bombay Nat. Hist. Soc.*, 34: 337-349.

Wildash, Philip. 1968. Birds of South Viet Nam. Chas. E. Tuttle Co., Rutland, Vt. & Tokyo.

Wishart, William, and Fred Sharp. 1959. Earlier photographic records of the Common Crane (*Grus grus*) for North America—in Alberta, Canada. *Auk*, 76: 358.

Witherby, H. F. On the birds of central Spain, with some notes on those of South-East Spain. Pt. 2. *Ibis*, 12th ser., 4 (4): 587-663.

Witherby, H. F., F. C. R. Jourdain, N. F. Ticehurst, and B. W. Tucker. 1940. The Handbook of British Birds. Vol. 4. H. F. Witherby, Ltd., London.

Wolfendale, R. 1956. Crane in Suffolk. *Brit. Birds*, 49: 38-39.

Wolley, John, Jr. 1859. On the Breeding of the crane (*Grus cinerea*) in Lapland. *Ibis*, 1 (2): 191-198.

Wolley, John, and Alfred Newton. 1905-1907. Ootheca Wooleyani. Illustrated catalogue of the Collection of birds' eggs. Vol. 2, R. H. Porter, London.

Grus nigricollis

Ali, Salim. 1946. An Ornithological pilgrimage to Lake Mānāsārowār and Mount Kailas. Map, 7 pls. *J. Bombay Nat. Hist. Soc.*, 46: 286-308.

Austin, Oliver L., Jr. 1948. The Birds of Korea. *Bull. Mus. Comp. Zool.* Harvard Coll., Vol. 101 (No. 1), pp. 1-301, 1 map.

Bailey, F. M. 1909. The Nesting of the Bar-headed Goose (*Anser indicus*) in Tibet. *J. Bombay Nat. Hist. Soc.*, 19: 367-369.

———. 1911. Some notes on Birds from Gyantse and Chumbi in Tibet, with a list of the Game Birds killed during the four years, 1906-1909. *J. Bombay Nat. Hist. Soc.*, 21: 178-186.

Baker, E. C. Stuart. 1922. Hand-List of Birds of India. Pt. 7. *J. Bombay Nat. Hist. Soc.*, 28: 830-873.

———. 1928. The Game Birds of the Indian Empire. Vol. 5, Pt. 6. *J. Bombay Nat. Hist. Soc.*, 32: 617-618.

———. 1929. The Fauna of British India, including Ceylon and Burma. 2nd ed. London. Vol. 6, xxxv + pp. 1-499.

Battye, R. K. M. 1935. Notes on some Birds observed between Yatung and Gyantse, Tibet. *J. Bombay Nat. Hist. Soc.*, 38: 406-408.

Blaauw, F. E. 1897. A Monograph of the Cranes. E. J. Brill, Leiden. viii + 64 pp., 22 col. pls.

Blyth, Edward, and W. B. Tegetmeier. 1881. *The Natural History of the Cranes.* Horace Cox, London. viii + 92 pp., 20 illus.

Delacour, M. J. 1924. Letter from Indo-China. *Ibis*, 11th ser., 6: 398.

Delacour, Jean, and Pierre Jabouille. 1925. On the birds of Quangtri, Central Annam; with notes on other parts of French Indo China. *Ibis*, 12th ser., 1: 209-260, pls. 6-7.

Delacour, Jean, P. Jabouille, and W. P. Lowe. 1928. On the Birds collected during the Third Expedition to French Indo-China. Pt. 1. *Ibis*, 12th ser., 4: 23-51, 4 pls.

Dresser, H. E. 1905. An oological journey to Russia. *Ibis*, 8th ser., 5: 149-158.

———. 1906. On some Palaearctic bird's eggs from Tibet. *Ibis*, 8th ser., 6: 337-347.

Hingston, R. W. G. 1927. Bird notes from Mount Everest Expedition of 1924. *J. Bombay Nat. Hist. Soc.*, 32: 320-329, pl. 1.

La Touche, J. D. 1924. On the birds of south-east Yunnan, S.W. China. Pt. 4. *Ibis*, 11th ser., 6: 284-307.

Ludlow, F. 1920. Notes on the nidification of certain birds in Ladak. *J. Bombay Nat. Hist. Soc.*, 27: 141-147.

———. 1927. Birds of the Gyantse Neighborhood, southern Tibet. Pts. 1, 2, 3. *Ibis*, 12th ser., 3: 644-659, pls. 16-17. (1928) 4: 51-73; 211-232.

———. 1928b. Dongtse or stray bird notes from Tibet. *J. Bombay Nat. Hist. Soc.*, 33: 78-83.

———. 1937. The Birds of Bhutan and adjacent territories of Sikkim and Tibet. Pt. 3. *Ibis*, ser. 14, 1: 467-504.

———. 1944. The birds of southeastern Tibet. Pt. 3. *Ibis*, 86: 348-389.

———. 1950. The birds of Lhasa. *Ibis*, 92: 34-45.

———. 1951. The birds of Kongpo and Pome, southeast Tibet. *Ibis*, 93: 547-578.

MacLaren, P. I. R. 1947. Notes on the birds of the Gyantse Road, Southern Tibet, May 1946. *J. Bombay Nat. Hist. Soc.*, 47: 301-308; *Ibis*, 90: 199-205.

Meinertzhagen, R. 1927. Systematic results of birds collected at high altitudes in Ladak and Sikkim. Pt. 2. *Ibis*, 12th ser., 3: 571-633.

———. 1928. Some biological problems connected with the Himalaya. *Ibis*, 12th ser., 4: 480-533.

Mori, Tamezo. 1917. A rare crane collected in Korea (in Japanese). *Tori*, 1: 43-44.

Ogilvie Grant, W. R. 1900. On the birds collected ... in South China. *Ibis*, 7th ser., 6: 573-606.

Osmaston, B. B. 1925. The birds of Ladakh. *Ibis*, 12th ser., 1: 663-719, map.

———. 1927. Notes on the birds of Kashmir. Pt. 2. *J. Bombay Nat. Hist. Soc.*, 32: 134-153.

Peters, James L. 1934. *Check-list of Birds of the World*. Vol. 2. Harvard University Press, Cambridge, Mass. xvii + 401 pp.

Riley, J. H. 1931. A second collection of birds from the Provinces of Yunnan and Szechwan, China .... *Proc. U.S. Natl. Mus.*, 80 (article 7): 1-91.

Rowley. 1877. Ornithological Miscellany. Vol. 2, p. 436.

Sharpe, R. Bowdler. 1894. *Catalogue of the birds in the British Museum.* Vol. 23. xiii + 354 pp., pls. 9.

Stevens, H. 1930. (Account of a recent trip to China). *Bull. Brit. Orn. Club.*, 50: 46-54.

Taka-Tsukasa, Prince N., and Hon. M. U. Hachisuka. 1925. A contribution to Japanese Ornithology. *Ibis*, 12th ser., 1: 898-908.

Walton, H. J. 1906. On the birds of southern Tibet. *Ibis*, 8th ser., 6 (pt. 1): 57-84, pl. 1, map; (pt. 2): 225-256.

Grus monachus

Austin, Oliver L., Jr. and Nagahisa Kuroda. 1953. The Birds of Japan, their status and Distribution. *Bull. Mus. Comp. Zool.*, Cambridge, Mass. Vol. 109 (4:) 279-637.

Baker, E. C. S. 1928. The Game Birds of the Indian Empire. The waders and other semi-sporting birds. Vol. 5, Pt. 6, *J. Bombay Nat. Hist. Soc.*, 32: 620-621.

Blaauw, F. E. 1897. *A Monograph of the Cranes*. E. J. Brill, Leiden and London, viii + 64 pp.

Dementiev, G. P., and N. A. Gladkov. 1951. The Birds of the Soviet Union. State Publishers, "Soviet Science," Moscow.

Hand List of Japanese Birds. 1958. 4th & Rev. Ed. Ornith. Soc. of Japan. Yamashina Inst. of Ornith. and Zoology. Tokyo. viii + 264 pp.

Ivanov, A. I., E. B. Koslova, L. A. Portenko and A. Y. Tugarinov. 1951. *Birds of the USSR*. Vol. 1. Academy of Sciences USSR, Moscow. 361 pp.

La Touche, J. D. D. 1933. *A Handbook of the Birds of Eastern China*. Vol. 2. xxiii + 566 pp.

Vorobiev, K. A. 1954. *The Birds of the Ussuri Region*. Acad. Sciences USSR, Moscow. 361 pp.

Grus canadensis

Allen, A. A. 1932. The Sandhill Crane. *Bird-Lore*, 34: 414-424.

———. 1945. Some changes in the bird life of Churchill, Manitoba. *Auk*, 62 (1): 129-134.

Allen, A. A., *et al.* 1944. Report of the A.O.U. Committee on Bird Protection for 1943. *Auk*, 61 (4): 622-635.

Allin, A.E. 1943. Sandhill Cranes (*Grus canadensis*) in the Lake Superior region of western Ontario. *Canadian Field-Naturalist*, 57: 13-14.

———. The Canadian Lakehead. *Flicker*, 1959, 31 (3): 77-81; 1962, 34 (2): 58-60; 1965, 37 (4): 145-148; 1966, 38 (2): 65-69.

Annabel, Russell. 1966. Sandhill Crane adventure. *Sports Afield*, 156 (5): 61-62, 113.

Arthur, Stanley C. 1931. The birds of Louisiana. *La. Dept. Cons. Bull. No. 20*.

Bagg, Aaron M., and Ruth P. Emery. 1961. Regional Reports, Northeastern Maritime. *Audubon Field Notes*, 15 (4): 390-394; 1962, 16 (1): 7-12; 1964, 18 (1): 7-17; 1965, 19 (1): 7-18.

Bailey, Alfred M. 1918. Louisiana bird-refuges. *Wilson Bull.*, 30:11-15.

Bailey, A. M. 1927. Notes on the birds of southeastern Alaska. *Auk*, 44: 1-23.

Bailey, A. M., and H. B. Conover. 1935. Notes from the state of Durango, Mexico. *Auk*, 52: 421-424.

Bailey, A. M., and R. J. Niedrach. 1965. Birds of Colorado. Denver Mus. Nat. Hist., Denver.

Bailey, Alfred M., and Earl G. Wright. 1931. Birds of southern Louisiana. (Pt. 2). *Wilson Bull.*, 43:190-219.

Bailey, H. H. 1930. Bailey Mus. and Libr. Nat. Hist., Bull. No. 4, 1930, p. 2.

Baillie, James L. 1951, Regional Reports, Ontario-Western New York. *Audubon Field Notes*, 5 (1): 12-14; 1953, 7 (1): 13-15; 1955, 9 (4): 328-329.

———. 1958. Six old yet new Ontario Breeding birds. *Ontario Field Biologist*, No. 12 (May): 1-7.

Baines, Fred S. 1957. My experience with the Sandhill Crane. *Blue-Jay*, 15 (2): 59-60.

Baird, Spencer F. 1876. Ornithology. List of birds collected by Charles S. McCarthy, taxidermist. *In* J. H. Simpson, Report of Explorations across ... Utah ... 1859. U. S. Army Eng. Dept., Washington, D.C., Appendix K., pp. 377-381.

Baker, Bernard W., and L. H. Walkinshaw. 1946. Bird notes from Fawcett, Alberta. *Canadian Field-Naturalist*, 60: 5-10.

Baldridge, Alan, and J. B. Crowell. 1966. Regional Reports, No. Pacific Coast. *Audubon Field Notes*, 20 (1): 81-86.

Bangs, O., and W. R. Zappey. 1905. Birds of the Isle of Pines. *Amer. Naturalist*, 39: 179-215.

Barbour, T. 1923. The birds of Cuba. Mem. Nuttall Orn. Club, No. 6.

———. 1943. Cuban Ornithology. Mem. Nuttall Orn. Club, No. 9.

Bard, F. G. 1959. Museum notes. *Blue Jay*, 17 (2): 80.

Bard, F. G., and F. W. Lahrman. 1965. Sandhill Cranes flying with feet drawn up. *Blue Jay*, 23 (3): 121.

Barger, N. R. 1941. Field Notes. *Passenger Pigeon*, 3: 18-20; 37-39; 92-93.

———. 1943. The spring season (southwest area). *Passenger Pigeon*, 5: 45-47.

———. 1944. The spring season. *ibid*, 6: 69-71.

———. 1946. The autumn season. *ibid*, 8 (1): 31-33.

———. 1946b. The spring season. *ibid*, 8 (3): 88-94.

———. 1956. Sandhill Cranes feeding on cutworms. *ibid.*, 18 (4): 174.

Barnes, C. T. 1943. Spring migration on Farmington Bay, Utah. *Auk*, 60 (1): 102-103.

Barrett, L. L. 1946. Spring migration of Sandhill Cranes. *Flicker*, 18 (2): 43-44.

Baumgartner, F. M. 1950. Spring migration . . . . *Audubon Field Notes*, 4: 248-251.

_____. 1951. Regional Reports, Southern Great Plains. *Audubon Field Notes*, 5 (1): 25-17; 1952, 6 (1): 25-26; 1954, 8 (1): 27-28; 1959, 13 (1): 43-45, 304-306; 1961, 15 (1): 54-56; 15 (4): 422-424; 1962, 16 (1): 50-52; (3): 345-347; 1963, 17 (1): 45-46; (4): 414-415; 1964, 18 (1): 50-52; 1965, 19 (1): 53-56; (3): 395-398.

Baynard, O. E. 1913. Two months in the Everglades. *Oologist*, 30: 287-294.

_____. 1945. Check list of the birds of the Hillsborough River State Park. *Florida Naturalist*, 18 (4): 64-67.

Beard, D. B., F. C. Lincoln, V. H. Cahalane, H. H. T. Jackson, and B. H. Thompson. 1942. Fading Trails. Macmillan Co., New York.

Beckie, P. L. 1950. 1950 Spring Migration records. *Blue Jay*, 8 (2): 10.

Bee, R. G., and J. Hutchings. 1942. Breeding Records of Utah Birds. *Great Basin Nat.*, 3: 61-85.

Bennett, G. M., M. Mitchell, and W. W. H. Gunn. 1958. Regional Reports, Ontario-western New York. *Audubon Field Notes*, 12 (1): 26-30.

Bent, A. C. 1927. Life Histories of North American Marsh Birds. U. S. Natl. Mus. Bull., no. 135: 1-490.

Bent, A. C., and Manton Copeland. 1927, Notes on Florida Birds. *Auk*, 44: 371-386.

Besadny, C. D. 1953. By the Wayside. *Passenger Pigeon*, 15 (1): 38-40.

_____. 1953b. The early Spring season, Feb.-Apr. 1953. *Passenger Pigeon*, 15 (3): 135-141; (4): 174-181.

_____. The Seasons. *Passenger Pigeon*, 1954, 16 (1): 33-41; (2): 76-81; (3): 33-41; (4): 151-160; 1955, 17 (1): 36-45.

Beyer, George E., Andrew Allison and H. H. Kopman. 1908. List of birds of Louisiana. (Pt. 4). *Auk*, 25:173-180.

Boeker, E. L., W. S. Huey, and John W. Aldrich. 1961. Study of the experimental Sandhill Crane hunting season in New Mexico . . . . U. S. Fish & Wildlife Service, Spec. Scientific Rep.—Wildlife No. 63.

Boeker, Erwin L., William S. Huey, and Pierce B. Uzzell. 1962. Study of Texas-New Mexico Lesser Sandhill Crane hunting season—November 4-December 3, 1961. (Mimeo.) U. S. Bureau of Sport Fisheries & Wildlife.

Boggs, Bob, and Elsie Boggs. 1960. Regional Reports, Northern Pacific Coast. *Audubon Field Notes*, 14 (1): 65-67; (3): 414-416; (4): 472-474; 1961, 15 (1): 68-70; (4): 433-434; (5): 487-489; 1962, 16 (1): 66-69; (4): 440-442; (5): 500-502; 1963, 17 (1): 58-61; (4): 427-429.

Bond, James. 1947. Field Guide of birds of the West Indies. Macmillan Co., New York.

Boulware, Charles, and Malcolm G. Edwards. 1963. From the Field. *Oriole*, 27: 35.

Brandt, Herbert. 1943. Alaska Bird Trails. Bird Research Foundation, Cleveland, Ohio.

Breckenridge, Walter J. 1932. Field notes. *In* Thomas S. Roberts, Birds of Minnesota. Univ. Minn. Press, Minneapolis, Vol. 1, 437-438.

Breckenridge, Walter J., and David Cline. 1967. Sandhill Cranes and other birds from Bering Strait, Alaska. *Auk*, 84: 277-278.

Brewster, W. 1901. Bell's Vireo and the Sandhill Crane in New Hampshire. *Auk*, 18: 274.

Brodkorb, Pierce. 1955. The type locality of the Florida Sandhill Crane. *Auk*, 72: 207.

Brooks, Maurice. 1944. A Check-list of West Virginia birds. Agric. Expt. Stat. W. Va. Univ. Bull. 316.

Brooks, W. Sprague. 1915. Notes on birds from east Siberia and Arctic Alaska. *Bull. Mus. Comp. Zool.*, 59: 361-413.

Brown, Harold, and Louis Vogel. 1936. Christmas Census, Soledad Plantation, near Cienfeuges, Cuba. *Bird-Lore*, 38 (1): 85.

Brown, R. C. 1942. The Sandhill Crane. *Wyoming Wildlife*, 7 (8): 21-23.

Browne, W. E. 1937. A visit to 'Manywings.' *Bird-Lore*, 39: 358-361.

Bull, John L. 1959. The changing seasons. A summary of the nesting season. *Audubon Field Notes*, 13 (5): 408-413.

Buller, Raymond J. 1967. Sandhill Crane study in the central flyway. U. S. Fish & Wildlife Service, Spec. Scientific Rept., Wildlife, No. 113.

Buller, Raymond J., and E. J. Boeker. 1965. Coordinated Sandhill Crane study in the central flyway. Trans. 13th North American Wildl. and Nat. Res. Conf.

Burleigh, Thomas D. 1952. Regional reports, Palouse-northern Rocky Mountain. *Audubon Field Notes*, 6 (1): 29-31.

_____. 1958. Georgia Birds. Univ. Oklahoma Press, Norman, Oklahoma.

Butts, W. K. 1936. A Florida (Sandhill) Crane at Chattanooga. *Migrant*, 7: 24.

Carleton, Geoffrey. 1962. Regional Reports, Hudson-St. Lawrence. *Audubon Field Notes*, 16 (1): 12-15; 1963, 17 (1): 15-18; 1964, 18 (3): 340-343; 1965, 19 (4): 454-457; 1967, 21 (3): 399-401.

Caslick, James W. 1955. Sandhill Cranes in Yellowstone Park. *Auk*, 72: 82-83.

Chamberlain, B. Rhett. 1961. Regional Reports, So. Atlantic. *Audubon Field Notes*, 15 (3): 317-320.

Chase, Theodore, Jr., and Robert O. Paxton. 1965. Regional Reports, Middle Pacific Coast. *Audubon Field Notes*, 19 (5): 574-576.

Choate, E. A. 1959. Reports from Regional editors, Region No. 5. *New Jersey Nature News*, 14: 19.

Christmas Bird Counts, *Audubon Field Notes*, Vols. 1-22 (Nos. 2), 1949-1967.

Conover, H. B. 1926. Game birds of the Hooper Bay region, Alaska. *Auk*, 43: 162-180; 303-318.

Cooke, W. W. 1897. The birds of Colorado. (Colo.) State Agric. Coll. Bull. No. 37 (Tech. Ser. No. 2).

_____. 1914. Distribution and migration of North American rails and their allies. U. S. Dept. Agric. Bull. No. 128.

Cottam, C. 1936. Notes on the birds of Nevada. *Condor*, 38: 122-123.

Coues, Elliott. 1874. Birds of the Northwest. U. S. Geol. Surv. Terr. Misc. Publ. No. 3.

_____. 1878. Field notes on birds observed in Dakota and Montana along the Forty-ninth Parallel during the seasons of 1873 and 1874. F. V. Heyden, in charge, Bull. U. S. Geol. Geog. Surv. Terr. 4 (No. 3): 545-661.

_____. 1883. New England Bird Life . . . Lee and Shephard, Publ. Boston, Pt. 2.

_____. 1893. History of the expedition under the command of Lewis and Clark, Vols. 2 and 3, Francis P. Harper, New York.

Craven, Earl W., George Williams, Joe Heiser, Everett Beaty. 1942. Christmas Bird Count, Aransas Natl. Wildlife Refuge, Austwell, Texas. *Audubon Magazine*, 44 (No. 1, Supp.): 1-76.

Crowell, John B., Jr., and Harry B. Nehls. 1966. Regional Reports, Northern Pacific Coast. *Audubon Field Notes*, 20 (4): 539-542; 1967, 21 (1): 67-72; (3): 532-535; 1968, 22 (1): 78-83.

Danforth, Stuart. 1935. Investigations concerning Cuban birds. *Puerto Rico Journ. Agric.*, 19: 425.

Daugherty, Mrs. C. H. 1941. Season Reports (Southern California Region). *Audubon Magazine*, 43 (No. 3, Sect. 2): 318-319.

Davids, Richard C. 1966. Summer birds of Clearwater County (Minn.). *Flicker*, 38 (1): 21-24.

Davis, Harry T. 1958. Cranes in North Carolina: old reports confirmed. *Chat*, 22 (2): 45-46.

deLaubenfels, Max W. 1954. A second flock of Whooping Cranes. *Wilson Bulletin*, 66 (2): 149.

Dementiev, G. P., and N. A. Gladkov. 1951. Birds of the Soviet

Union, Moscow. Vol. 2, pp. 114-116.

Denis, Keith. 1967. The Canadian Lakehead. *Flicker,* 39 (4): 132-134.

Devitt, Otto E. 1962. Further additions to the birds of Simcoe County, Ontario. *Canadian Field-Naturalist,* 76 (3): 153-158.

Dice, L. R. 1918. The birds of Walla Walla and Columbia Counties, southeastern Washington. *Auk,* 35: 40-51.

Dick, John H. 1967. Sandhill Cranes in South Carolina. *Chat,* 31: 24-25.

Drew, Frank M. 1881. Field notes on the birds of San Juan County, Colorado. (Pt. 2). *Bull. Nuttall Ornith. Club,* 6: 138-143.

Drewein, Roderick C. 1969. Ecology of the Greater Sandhill Crane, *Grus canadensis tabida,* in southeastern Idaho. Project WU-78. *Idaho Coop. Wildlife Research Unit,* Univ. Idaho. 24-32.

Edney, J. M. 1940. The Sandhill Crane in Middle Tennessee. *Journ. Tenn. Acad. Sci.* 15 (4): 401.

Edwards, George. 1750. A natural history of uncommon birds. Pt. 3, London. pp. cvi-clvii, 106-157; pls. 106-157.

Edwards, Malcolm G. 1963. From the field. *Oriole,* 28 (3): 35.

Ellis, R. 1935. Bird Records from northeastern Nevada. *Condor,* 37: 86-87.

Farley, Frank L. 1944. Saskatchewan records of the Whooping Crane. *Canadian Field-Naturalist,* 58 (4): 142.

Farner, D. S. 1952. The birds of Crater Lake National Park. Univ. of Kansas Press, Lawrence.

Felger, A. H. 1910. Birds and mammals of northwestern Colorado. *Univ. Colo. studies,* 7 (No. 2): 132-146.

Ferry, J. F. 1908. Notes from the diary of a naturalist in northern California. *Condor,* 10: 30-44.

Figgins, J. D. 1923. The breeding birds of the vicinity of Black Bayou and Bird Island, Cameron Parish, Louisiana. *Auk,* 40:666-677.

Fink, Louis C. 1965. Sandhill Cranes definitely on Atlanta list. *Oriole,* 30: 96-97.

Flahaut, Martha R. 1950. Regional Reports, North Pacific Coast. *Audubon Field Notes,* 4 (1): 30-32; (4): 257-258; 1952, 6 (1): 33-35; 6 (4): 263-265.

Flahaut, Martha R., and Zella M. Schultz. 1954. Regional Reports, North Pacific Coast. *Audubon Field Notes,* 8 (4): 324-326; 1956, 10: 47-50.

Forster, J. R. 1772. An account of the birds sent from Hudson's Bay. . . . *Phil. Trans. Roy. Soc.* Vol. 62, pp. 382-433.

Gabrielson, Ira N. 1944. Some Alaskan notes. *Auk,* 61: 105-130 (Pt. 1).

Gabrielson, Ira N., and Stanley G. Jewett. 1940. Birds of Oregon. Oregon State Coll., Corvallis.

Gabrielson, Ira N., and Frederick C. Lincoln. 1959. The Birds of Alaska. Stackpole Co., Harrisburg, Pa., and Wildlife Management Institute, Washington, D. C.

Gammell, Dr. and Mrs. R. T. 1949. Spring Migration April 1 to May 31, 1949. Northern Great Plains Region. *Audubon Field Notes,* 3 (3): 213-214.

———. Regional Reports, Northern Great Plains Region. *Audubon Field Notes,* 1950, 4 (1): 21-22; (4): 247-248; 1951, 5 (1): 24-25; 1952, 6 (1): 23-25.

Gammell, Ann M., and Howard S. Huencke. 1954. Regional Reports, Northern Great Plains. *Audubon Field Notes,* 8 (5): 350-352; 1955, 9 (4): 338-340.

Gavin, Angus. 1947. Birds of Perry River District, N.W. Terr. *Wilson Bulletin,* 59 (4): 195-203.

Gibson, Daniel D. 1967. Regional Reports, Alaska. *Audubon Field Notes,* 21 (4): 530-531.

Goldman, E. A. 1908. Summer birds of the Tulare Lake region. *Condor,* 10: 200-205.

Goldman, Luther C. 1954. Regional Reports. South Texas. *Audubon Field Notes,* 8 (1): 28-32.

Goldman, Luther C., James Murdock, Frank F. Chuman. 1941. Forty-first Christmas Bird Census. Salton Sea Natl. Wildlife Refuge, Brawley, Calif. *Audubon Magazine,* 43 (No. 1 Sup.): 146.

Goldman, Luther C., and Capt. James H. Sikes. 1943. Christmas Bird Census. Bitter Lakes Natl. Wildlife Refuge, Roswell, N. M. *Audubon Magazine,* 45: 51-52.

Goldman, Luther C., and Frank Watson. 1952. Regional Reports, South Texas. *Audubon Field Notes,* 6 (1): 26-29; 1953, 7 (1): 39-40; (3): 223-225; (4): 282-285.

Goldman, Luther C., *et al.* 1955a. Christmas Bird Count. Laguna Atacosa Natl. Wildlife Refuge, San Bebito, Texas. *Audubon Field Notes,* 9 (2): 203-204.

———. 1955b. Christmas Bird Count. Santa Ana Natl. Wildlife Refuge, Alamo, Texas. *Audubon Field Notes,* 9 (2): 205.

Gollop, J. B., J. F. Roy, and R. V. Folker. 1963. Some 1962 bird records from the Saskatoon District (Sask.). *Blue Jay,* 21 (1): 12-13.

Goodwin, Clive E. 1966. Regional Reports, Ontario, Western New York. *Audubon Field Notes,* 20 (1): 35-38; 1967, 21 (1): 25-29; (4): 500-503.

Gould, F. W. 1962. Texas Plants. A Checklist and ecological summary. Agric. and Mech. College of Texas, Texas Expt. Station, College Station, Texas.

Greene, Janet C. 1964. Regional Reports, Western Great Lakes. *Audubon Field Notes,* 18 (1): 33-34, 39-42; (4): 450-454.

Greene, Earle R. 1938. Christmas Census. Okefenokee Wildlife Refuge, Fargo, Georgia. *Bird-Lore,* 40 (1): 44-45.

Gregory, Robert S. 1967. Sandhill Cranes in Morgan County. *Indiana Audubon Quarterly,* 45 (1): 16-17.

Grewe, Al. 1958. A new birding area. *Flicker,* 30 (2): 50-52.

———. 1958b. Sandhill Cranes in Morrison County (Minn.). *Flicker,* 30 (4): 159.

Grey, John. 1963. Cranes in North Carolina in 1957, a correction. *Chat,* 27: 78.

Grimes, S. A. 1944. The birds of Duval County (Cont.). *Florida Naturalist,* 17 (4): 57-68.

Grinnell, Joseph. 1900. Birds of the Kotzebue Sound Region. *Pacific Coast Avifauna.* No. 1.

Grinnell, Joseph, Harold Child Bryant, and Tracy Irwin Storer. 1918. The Game birds of California. University of California Press, Berkeley.

Grinnell, Joseph, and Alden H. Miller. 1944. The Distribution of the birds of California. *Cooper Ornithological Club,* No. 27.

Grinnell, Lawrence I., and Ralph S. Palmer. 1941. Notes on bird-life of Churchill, Manitoba. *Can. Field Nat.,* 45 (4): 47-54.

Griscom, Ludlow, and M. S. Crosby. 1925. Birds of the Brownsville region, southern Texas. *Auk,* 24: 519-537.

Griswold, J. A. 1962. Proven methods of keeping and rearing Cranes in captivity. Spec. Rept., Int. Wild Waterfowl Association, Inc.

Grow, Raymond. 1953. Fall migration report. Northern Indiana. *Indiana Audubon Quarterly,* 31 (1): 2-7.

———. 1954. Regional Reports. Northern: Spring, 1953. *Indiana Audubon Quarterly,* 32 (2): 30-33.

Gullion, Gordon W. 1947. Additional notes on Cranes in the Cascade Mountains of Oregon. *Condor,* 49 (3): 128.

———. 1948. Crane migration in the Willamette Valley, Oregon. *Condor,* 50 (4): 165.

———. 1951. Birds of the southern Willamette Valley, Oregon. *Condor,* 53 (3): 129-149.

Gunn, William W. H. 1958. Regional Reports, Ontario, Western New York. *Audubon Field Notes* 12 (4): 348-352.

Hall, George A. 1960. Regional Reports, Appalachian. *Audubon Field Notes,* 14 (1): 35-38; (3): 309-311; 1961, 15 (3): 328-331; 1963, 17 (1): 31-34; 1965, 19 (3): 377-380; 1966, 20 (3): 422-425; 1968, 22 (1): 37-40.

Hamerstrom, F. N., Jr. 1938. Central Wisconsin Crane Study. *Wilson Bulletin,* 50 (3): 175-184.

Hamilton, Mrs. R. E. 1965. From the field. *Oriole,* 30: 71.

Hart, John A. 1967. Summer Sandhill Crane at Salt Lake (Minn.). *Flicker,* 39 (4): 138-139.

Harvey, J. M., B. C. Lieff, C. D. MacInnes, and J. P. Prevett. 1968. Observations of Sandhill Cranes. *Wilson Bulletin,* 80 (4): 421-425.

Hatch, David R. M. 1966. Regional Reports, Northern Great Plains. *Audubon Field Notes*, 20 (4): 519-522.

Henika, Franklin S. 1936. Sand-Hill Cranes in Wisconsin and other Lake States. *Proc. No. Amer. Wildl. Conf.*, 1936: 644-646.

Henshaw, Henry Wetherbee. 1875. Report upon the ornithological collections made in portions of Nevada, Utah, California, Colorado, New Mexico, and Arizona during the years, 1871, 1872, 1873, and 1874. *In* Wheeler's Report Exploration Survey West 100th Meridian, Vol. 5: 131-507.

Hesse, Werner, and Hilde Hesse. 1965. Regional Reports, Northern Pacific Coast. *Audubon Field Notes*, 21 (1): 68-71; (4): 505-507.

Hinde, R. A. 1956. The Biological significance of Territories of Birds. *Ibis*, 98: 340-369.

Hines, John. Birds of the Noatak River, Alaska. *Condor*, 65 (5): 410-425.

Hoffman, Ralph. 1927. Nesting of the Sandhill Crane in Modoc County, Calif. *Condor*, 24 (2): 118.

Hoffman, W. J. 1881. Annotated list of the birds of Nevada. *Bull. U. S. Geol. Geog. Surv. Terr.*, 6: 203-256.

Höhn, E. Otto. 1959. Birds of the mouth of the Anderson River and Liverpool Bay, Northwest Territories. *Canadian Field-Naturalist*, 73: (2): 93-114.

Höhn, E. O., and D. L. Robinson. 1951. Some supplementary bird notes from the general area of MacKenzie Delta and Great Slave Lake. *Canadian Field-Naturalist*, 65 (3): 115-118.

Hollister, N. 1919. Some changes in the summer bird life at Delavan, Wisconsin. *Wilson Bulletin*, 31 (4): 103-108.

Holmes, Charles F. 1945. A 1936 Saskatchewan record of the Whooping Crane. *Canadian Field-Naturalist*, 59: 69.

Holt, Ernest G. 1930. Nesting of the Sandhill Crane in Florida. *Wilson Bulletin*, 42 (3): 162-182.

Hooper, Ronald R. 1962. Birds of Lynn Lake, Manitoba. *Blue Jay*, 20 (4): 158.

Hopkins, Milton. 1959. From the field. *Oriole*, 24:44; 1960, 25:10; 1962, 27:9; 1964, 29:21; 1965, 30:71.

Hopkins, Mary, and Milton Hopkins. 1964. From the field. *Oriole*, 29: 21.

Houston, C. Stuart. 1947. *Blue Jay*, 6 (No. 1): 4-5.

———. 1949. The birds of the Yorkton District, Sask. *Canadian Field-Naturalist*, 63: 215-241.

———. 1955. Sandhill Crane nesting at Rokeby Marsh. *Blue Jay*, 13: 9.

Houston, Mary and C. Stuart Houston. 1966. F. C. Gilchrist's Diary —Fort Qu'Appelle 1883-1896. *Blue Jay*, 24 (4): 169-170.

Howell, Arthur H. 1932. Florida bird life. Fla. Dept. of Game & Fresh Water Fish, Tallahassee.

Hoy, P. R. 1853. Notes on the ornithology of Wisconsin (with concluding part). *Proc. Acad. Nat. Sci. Phila.*, 6: 425-429.

Huber, Ronald L. 1962. The . . . Season. *Flicker*, 34 (3): 80-85; (4): 114-121; 1963, 35 (2): 49-59; (4): 121-129. *Loon*, 1964, 36 (2): 45-53; (3): 83-91; (4): 119-127; 1965, 37 (4): 136-144; 1966, 38 (1): 8-21; (2): 48-55; 1967, (3): 84-96; (4): 118-129; 1967, 39 (1): 9-18; (3): 86-99. (after 1964 *Loon*)

———. 1967. The . . . Season. *Loon* 39 (4): 122-131; 1968, 40: 7-17.

Huey, W. S. 1959. Weights of Sandhill Cranes. *Auk*, 76: 96-97.

———. 1960. Waterfowl Studies. Sandhill Crane Investigations. Federal Aid Project W-91-R-3, Job. 14. New Mexico Dept. of Game and Fish.

———. 1965. Sight records of color-marked Sandhill Cranes. *Auk*, 82: 640-643.

Hyde, Dayton O. 1957. Crane notes. *Blue Jay*, 15 (1): 19-21.

———. 1957b. Problems of raising young Sandhill Cranes. *Blue Jay*, 15 (3): 114.

———. 1957c. My Greater Sandhill Cranes. *Audubon Magazine*, 59: 264-267.

———. 1968. Sandy, The Sandhill Crane. Dial Press, Inc., New York.

Imhof, Thomas A. 1962. Alabama Birds. Alabama Dept. of Cons., Game and Fish Div. Univ. of Alabama Press.

Inglis, J. W. 1964. Sandhill Crane nesting record for southern Saskatchewan. *Blue Jay*, 22 (3): 109.

Jahn, Laurence R., *et al.* 1963. Annual report of the Conservation Committee. *Wilson Bulletin*, 75 (3): 295-325.

James, Douglas. 1963. Regional Reports, Central Southern. *Audubon Field Notes*, 17 (1): 37-40.

Jewett, S. A., W. P. Taylor, W. T. Shaw, and J. W. Aldrich. 1953. Birds of Washington State. Univ. Wash. Press, Seattle.

Jollie, M. 1955. New records for Idaho. *Condor*, 57: 189.

Kelso, J. E. H. 1926. Birds of Arrow Lake, West Kootenay District, British Columbia. *Ibis*, 67: 689-723.

Kenyon, Karl W. 1961. Birds of Amchitka Island, Alaska. *Auk*, 78: 305-326.

Kenyon, Karl W., and James W. Brooks. 1960. Birds of Little Diomede Island, Alaska. *Condor*, 62 (6): 457-463.

Kumlien, L., and N. Hollister. 1903. The birds of Wisconsin. *Bull. Wis. Nat. Hist. Soc.*, 3 (new ser.).

———. 1951. The birds of Wisconsin, Wis. Soc. for Orn. (with revisions by A. W. Schorger).

Laing, H. M. 1915. Garoo, Scout of the Prairie. *Outing*, 66: 699-710.

Linsdale, Jean M. 1936. The Birds of Nevada. Cooper Ornith. Club., No. 23.

———. 1947. Regional Reports, San Francisco. *Audubon Field Notes*, 1 (3): 141-142.

———. 1950. Regional Reports, Middle Pacific Coast. *Audubon Field Notes*, 4 (3): 218-219.

Littlefield, Carroll D. 1966. An Ecological study of the Greater Sandhill Crane at Malheur National Wildlife Refuge, Oregon. College of Forestry and Nat. Res., Dept. of Fisheries and Wildlife Biology, Colo. State Univ., Fort Collins.

Littlefield, Carroll D., and Ronald A. Ryder. 1968. Breeding biology of the Greater Sandhill Crane on Malheur National Wildlife Refuge, Oregon. Colo. State Univ., Fort Collins.

Lockerbie, C. W. 1943. The Season (Utah Region). *Audubon Magazine*, 45 (4, sect. 2): 12-13; 1944, 46 (2, sect. 2): 75-76; (3, sect. 2): 90-92; (4, sect. 2): 108-110.

———. 1945. Spring migration (Utah Region). *Audubon Magazine*, 47 (July-Aug., sect. 2): 39-40; 1946, 48 (July-Aug., sect. 2): 116.

———. 1947. Regional Notes, Utah. *Audubon Field Notes*, 1: 14-17.

———. 1948. Fall migration (Aug. 1-Nov. 30, 1947) (Utah Region). *Audubon Field Notes*, 2 (1): 20-22.

Low, Jessop B. 1952. Regional Reports. Great Basin, Central Rocky Mountains. *Audubon Field Notes*, 6 (4): 260-261; (5): 292-293.

Lumsden, Harry G. 1971. The status of the Sandhill Crane in northern Ontario. *Can. Field-Nat.*, 85 (4):285-293.

Lupient, Mary. 1947. Seasonal bird report. *Flicker*, 19 (2): 50-51; 1950, 22: 105-107; 1951, 23: 50-53; 1953, 25 (4): 273-275; 1957, 29 (2): 77-79; 1959, 31 (2): 42-44, (4): 109-111.

———. 1961. Regional Reports. Western Great Lakes Region. *Audubon Field Notes*, 15 (1): 42-44, (5): 469-471; 1962, 16 (1): 34-35, (4): 411-413; 1963, 17 (1): 34-36.

McAllister, Thomas H., and David B. Marshall. 1945. Summer birds of the Fremont National Forest, Ore. *Auk*, 62 (2): 177-189, pl. 9.

McBriar, Wallace N., Jr. 1958. Spring season. *Passenger Pigeon*, 20 (3): 121-136; 1959, 21 (4): 152-171; 1960, 22 (4): 192-212.

McCaskie, Guy. 1966. Regional Reports. South Pacific Coast. *Audubon Field Notes*, 20 (3): 458-461; 1967, 21 (3): 456-460.

McCaskie, R. Guy, and Eleanor A. Pugh. 1964. Regional Reports. South Pacific Coast. *Audubon Field Notes*, 18 (3): 385-390; 1965, 19 (3): 416.

McIlhenny, Edward A. 1897. A list of the species of Anseres, Paludicolae and Limicolae occurring in the state of Louisiana. *Auk*, 14:285-289.

McIlhenny, Edward A. 1938. Florida Crane a resident of Mississippi. *Auk*, 55: 582-602, pls. 21-22.

McIllwraith, Thomas. 1894. The birds of Ontario. 2nd ed. William Briggs, Toronto.

McLeod. Edith Rutenic. 1954. Sandhill Cranes at Meiss Lake, northern Calif. *Condor*, 56: 227.

Madsen, Carl R. 1967. Food and Habitat selection by fall migrant Sandhill Cranes in Kidder County, N.D. Thesis, Mich. State Univ.

Mahar, William J. 1959. Habitat distribution of birds breeding along the Upper Kaolak River, northern Alaska. *Condor*, 61 (5): 351-368.

Mailliard, Joseph. 1921. Notes on some specimens in the Ornithological collection of the Calif. Academy of Sciences. *Condor*, 23: 28-32.

Manning, T. H. 1948. Notes on the country, birds, and mammals west of Hudson Bay between Reindeer and Baker Lakes. *Canadian Field-Naturalist*, 62 (1): 1-28.

Manning, T. H., E. O. Höhn, and A. H. McPherson. 1956. The birds of Banks Island. Natl. Mus. Canada, Bull. No. 143.

Marshall, William H., and Lee Kay. 1938. Notes on the Sandhill Crane near Tremonton, Utah. *Utah Acad. Sci., Arts, and Letters*, 15: 89-90.

Merriam, C. Hart. 1873. Birds. *In* F. V. Hayden, 6th Annual Report of the U. S. Geo. Sur. of the Territories. Part III, Zoology and Botany. Dept. of Interior, Washington, D. C., pp. 670-715.

Merriam, C. Hart, and Leonard Stejneger. 1891. Results of a biological reconnoissance of south central Idaho. *No. American Fauna*, No. 5.

Merrill, George W. 1961. Loss of 1,000 Lesser Sandhill Cranes. *Auk*, 78: 641-642.

Monson, Gale W. 1934. The birds of Berlin and Harwood Townships, Cass County, N.D. *Wilson Bulletin*, 46 (1): 37-58.

———. 1949. Fall Migration. Southwest Region. *Audubon Field Notes*, 3 (1): 26-28.

———. 1950. Regional Reports, Southwest. *Audubon Field Notes*, 4 (1): 28-30, (3): 214-216; 1952, 6 (3): 208-210; 1953, 7 (1): 29-31, (3): 229; 1954, (3): 262-264; 1955, 9 (1): 46-47, (3): 275-277, (4): 348-350; 1956, 10 (1): 44-47, (3): 271-275; 1957, 11 (1): 47-50, (3): 285-287; 1958, 12 (3): 298-301; 1959, 13 (1): 53-55, (3): 312-315; 1960, 14 (1): 60-63, (3): 329-332; 1961, 15 (1): 62-66, (3): 348-351; (4): 429-431.

Mowat, Farley M., and Andrew H. Laurie. 1955. Bird observations from southern Keewatin and the Interior of Northern Manitoba. *Canadian Field-Naturalist*, 69 (3): 93-116.

Mumford, Russell E. 1950. And the Sandhills dance. *Indiana Audubon Quarterly*, 28 (4): 82-86.

———. 1961. Regional Report, Middlewestern Prairie. *Audubon Field Notes*, 15 (1): 44-46, (4): 413-416.

Munro, D. A. 1950. The economic status of Sandhill Cranes in Saskatchewan. *Journal Wildlife Management*, 14: 276-284.

Munro, J. A., and I. Mct. Cowan. 1947. A review of the bird Fauna of British Columbia. Spec. Publ. No. 2, Brit. Col. Prov. Mus., Dept. of Educ., Victoria, B.C.

Naylor, A. E., A. W. Miller, and M. E. Forster. 1954. Observations on the Sandhill Crane in N.E. Calif. *Condor*, 56: 224-226.

Nero, Robert W. 1961. Regional Reports, Northern Great Plains. *Audubon Field Notes*, 15 (3): 337-341, (4): 419-422; 1962, 16 (1): 47-50, (4): 423-426, (5): 486-488; 1963, 17 (1): 40-44.

———. 1967. Additional bird notes for Little Gull Lake, Sask. *Blue Jay*, 25: 11-14.

Newman, Robert J. 1957. Regional Reports, Central Southern. *Audubon Field Notes*, 11 (1): 30-34; 1958, 12 (1): 36-39, (3): 284-287, (5): 417-421.

Nord, W. H., and W. J. Breckenridge. 1941. Record flight of Sandhill Cranes. *Flicker*, 13 (1): 2-4.

Oberholser, H. C. 1921. Notes on North American birds. *Auk*, 38: 79-82.

Packard, Fred Mallery. 1945. The birds of Rocky Mt. Ntl. Park, Colo. *Auk*, 62: 371-394.

Parnell, James F. 1966. Regional Reports, South Atlantic Coast. *Audubon Field Notes*, 20 (1): 27-30.

Paul, W. Adrian B. 1959. The birds of Klenna Klenna, Chilcotin District, B. C. 1947-1958. *Canadian Field-Naturalist*, 73 (2): 83-93.

Peters, Harold S. 1952. Sandhill Crane taken in Fulton County. *Oriole*, 17: 31.

———. 1953. Sandhill Crane over Atlanta. *Oriole*, 18: 45.

———. 1961. Spring migration of Sandhill Cranes. *Oriole*, 27: 29-30.

Peters, James Lee. 1925. Notes on the Taxonomy of *Ardea canadensis*, Linné. *Auk*, 42:120-122.

Petersen, Peter C., Jr. 1966. Regional Reports, Middlewestern Prairie. *Audubon Field Notes*, 20 (3): 429-431, (4): 513-515; 1963, 17 (1): 36-37, (4): 407-409.

Phelps, Frank Miles. 1914. The resident bird life of the Big Cypress Swamp region. *Wilson Bulletin*, 26: 86-101.

Pittman, H. H. 1957. Saving the Cranes. *Blue Jay*, 15 (2): 58-59.

Porsild, A. E. 1943. Birds of the Mackenzie Delta. *Canadian Field-Naturalist*, 57 (2-3): 19-35.

Potter, Julian K. 1959. Regional Reports, Middle Atlantic Coast. *Audubon Field Notes*, 13 (1): 17-19.

Pratt, Jerome J. 1963. Whooping Crane Conservation Association Items. Dec.

Preble, Edward A. 1908. A Biological Investigation of the Athabaska-Mackenzie region. *No. Amer. Fauna No. 27*. U. S. Dept. of Agric.

Preston, F. W. 1953. The shapes of birds eggs. *Auk*, 70: 100-182.

Pugh, Eleanor. 1962. Regional Reports, Middle Pacific Coast. *Audubon Field Notes*, 16 (3): 359-362.

Rand, A. L. 1944. Birds of the Alaska Highway in British Columbia. *Canadian Field-Naturalist*, 58 (4): 111-125.

———. 1946. List of Yukon Birds and those of the Canol Road. *Natl. Museum Canada, Bull. No. 105* (Biol. Ser. 33).

———. 1950. H. B. Conover's bird work in the Yukon. *Canadian Field-Naturalist*, 64: 214-220.

Randall, T. E. 1946. Birds of the eastern irrigation district, Brooks, Alberta. *Canadian Field-Naturalist*, 66: 123-131.

———. 1962. Birds of the Kazan Lake Region, Sask. *Blue Jay*, 20 (2): 60-72.

Rapp, William F., Jr. 1951. Twenty-five year summary of Bird Migration in Nebraska. Pt. 5, Grouse to Coots. *Nebraska Bird Review*, 19 (2): 26-28.

Read, A.C. 1911. Sundry trips. *Oologist*, 28: 5-7, 113.

———. 1913. Birds observed on the Isle of Pines, Cuba, 1912. *Oologist*, 30: 123-125, 130.

Reed, Edward B. 1956. Notes on some birds and mammals of the Colville River, Alaska. *Canadian Field-Naturalist*, 70 (3): 130-136.

Reese, Staber. 1944. Nest and eggs of the Sandhill Crane. Sandhill Crane habitat. *Passenger Pigeon*, 6: cover photo and p. 34.

Rehn, James A. G. 1930. An unpublished letter of John K. Townsend. *Auk*, 47 (1): 101-102.

Ridgway, Robert. 1877. Ornithology. *In* Clarence King. Report of the Geological Exploration of the 40th Parallel. U. S. Army Eng. Dept. Prof. Papers No. 18, Vol. 4, Pt. 3: 303-643, 652-669.

Ridgway, Robert, and Herbert Friedmann. 1941. The birds of North and middle America. *U. S. Ntl. Mus. Bull. 50*, Pt. 9.

Robbins, Sam. 1946. The . . . season. *Passenger Pigeon*, 8 (4): 125-128; 1947, 9 (1): 29-34, (3): 112-118, (4): 147-151; 1948, 10 (1): 33-39. (3): 116-123; 1949, 11 (2): 66-72, (2): 80-91, (3): 133-139, (4): 183-190; 1950, 12 (1): 40-50, (3): 136-143, (4): 171-183; 1951, 13 (1): 37-46, (2): 75-82.

———. 1960. Wisconsin's favorite bird haunts. Leola Marsh. *Passenger Pigeon*, 22 (1): 45-47.

———. 1966. Wisconsin's Summer bird count: 1961-1965. *Passenger Pigeon*, 28 (2): 47-62.

———. 1966b. Regional Reports, Western Great Lakes. *Audubon Field Notes*, 20 (5): 570-574; 1967, 21 (1): 36-38, 42-44; 1968, 22 (1): 40-44, 47-48.

Roberts, Hal and Nancy Roberts. 1964. Summer season *Passenger Pigeon*, 26 (1): 63-67; 1965, 27 (2): 81-87; 1966, 28 (2): 79-83.

Roberts, Thomas S. 1932. The birds of Minnesota. Vol. 1. Univ. of Minn. Press, Minneapolis.

Roest, Aryan I. 1957. Observations on birds of central Oregon.

Condor, 59: 141-142.

Rogers, Thomas H. 1955. Regional Reports, Palouse-Northern Rocky Mountains. *Audubon Field Notes*, 9 (5): 389-392; 1958, 12 (4): 370-372.

———. 1959. Regional Reports. Northern Rocky Mountain-intermountain. *Audubon Field Notes*, 13 (1): 49-51, (4): 388-390, (5): 443-446; 1960, 14 (1): 56-58, (4): 407-409, (5): 465-467; 1961, 15 (4): 427-429; 1962, 16 (1): 58-61, (4): 433-435, (5): 493-495; 1963, 17 (1): 51-53, (4): 419-422; 1964, 18 (1): 57-60; 1965, 19 (1): 60-63, (4): 497-500; (5): 564-567; 1966, 20 (1): 72-76, (4): 532-535, (5): 585-588; 1967, 21 (4): 524-527, (5): 587-590; 1968, 22 (1): 69-73.

Ronning, Rudolph. 1966. Whooping Cranes in 1938. *Blue Jay*, 24 (2): 100.

Rooke, R. P. 1947. Bird Life in the Yorkton District in the 1890's. *Blue Jay*, 5 (3 & 4): 26-27.

Ross, Bernard Rogan to Spencer Fullerton Baird. 1859. Letter, reprinted. *Canadian Field-Naturalist*, 1942: 120-122.

Rowan, William. 1927. Details of the release of the Hungarian Partridge (*Perdix perdix*) in central Alberta. *Canadian Field-Naturalist*, 41: 98-101.

Salt, W. Ray, and A. L. Wilk. 1966. The Birds of Alberta. Rev. ed. The Queen's Printer, Edmonton.

Sauer, E. G. Franz and Emil K. Urban. 1964. Bird notes from St. Lawrence Island, Alaska. *Bonner Zoologische Beitr.* 1/2, pp. 45-58.

Schoenebeck, A. J. 1939. The birds of Oconto County (Pt. 1). *Passenger Pigeon*, 1: 79-88.

Scott, F. R., and David A. Cutler. 1962. Regional Reports, Middle Atlantic Coast. *Audubon Field Notes*, 16 (1): 15-18; 1963, 17 (1): 18-22, (4): 394-397.

Scott, F. R., and J. K. Potter. 1959. Regional Reports, Middle Atlantic Coast. *Audubon Field Notes*, 13 (1): 17-19.

Scott, Oliver K. 1955. Regional Reports, Great Basin, Central Rocky Mountains. *Audubon Field Notes*, 9 (1): 44-46, (3): 274-275, (5): 392-393; 1956, 10 (1): 43-44; 1957, 11 (1): 45-47, (3): 283-285, (4): 421-422; 1959, 13 (4): 390-391; 1960, 14 (1): 58-60; (5): 467-468; 1962, 16 (4): 435-436, (5): 495-496; 1964, 18 (3): 374-376; (4): 474-476; (5): 526; 1965, 19 (1): 63-64; (3): 404-406; 1967, 21 (3): 443-444; (4): 527-528; (5): 590-592; 1968, 22 (1): 73-74; 1969 (1): 86-87.

Scott, W. E. (Editor). 1940. By the wayside. *Passenger Pigeon*, 2: 84: 1941 (3): 84-85.

———. 1953. Sandhill Cranes nesting in numbers. *Passenger Pigeon*, 15 (1): 41.

Sennett, George B. 1878. Notes on the Ornithology of the Lower Rio Grande, Texas during the season of 1877. *Bull. U. S. Geol. and Geog. Surv. of the Territories*, 4 (1): 61.

———. 1879. Further notes . . ., *ibid.*, 5: 371-440.

Seton, Ernest E. T. 1886. The birds of western Manitoba. *Auk*, 3: 145-156.

———. 1891. The birds of Manitoba. *Proc. U. S. Natl. Mus.*, 13: 841: 457-643.

Small, Arnold. 1953. Regional Reports, Southern Pacific Coast. *Audubon Field Notes*, 7 (3): 235; 1954, (1): 40-43, 268-272; 1955 9 (4): 358-360; 1956,, 10 (1): 54-59, (3): 280-285; 1957, 11 (1): 58-63, (3): 289-291; 1958, 12 (1): 57-60, (3): 304-306, (4): 384-387; 1959, 13 (1): 60-67, (3): 319-325, (4): 398-400; 1960, 14 (1): 70-74, (3): 340-344, (4): 419-421; 1961, 15 (1): 73-78, (3): 356-357; 1962, 16 (4): 446-449; 1963, 17 (1): 66-72, (3): 356-360.

Small, Arnold, and Robert L. Pyle. 1951. Regional Reports, Southern Pacific Coast. *Audubon Field Notes*, 5 (3): 225-228; 1952, 6 (3): 212-214; 1953, 7 (1): 36-39.

Smith, Mary A. 1957. Regional Reports, Cohoe, Alaska. *Audubon Field Notes*, 11 (4): 370-372, (5): 423-425; 1958, 12 (1): 51-52, (5): 433-435; 1959, 13 (1): 55-57, (4): 393-395; 1960, 14 (1): 63-65, (4): 412-414; 1961, 15 (4): 431-432; 1963, 17 (4): 425-427; 1964, 18 (1): 64-65; 1966, 20 (1): 80-81.

Smith, Parker B. 1960. From the field. *Oriole*, 25 (1): 10.

Sooter, Clarence A. 1943. Canada Geese perching at Malheur Refuge. *Auk*, 60 (1): 96-97.

Soper, J. Dewey. 1946. . . . Baffin Island Expeditions of 1928-1929 and 1930-1931 . . . . Pt. 2. *Auk*, 63 (2): 223-239.

Soulen, Thomas. 1961. Spring Season, . . . *Passenger Pigeon*, 23 (4): 146-165; 1962, 24 (4): 134-150; 1963, 25 (4): 159-179; 1965, 27 (1): 24-47; 1966, 28 (1): 21-43; 1967, 29 (1): 37-51.

Spencer, Haven H. 1948. Sandhill Crane observed in southwestern Ohio. *Wilson Bulletin*, 60: 187.

Sprunt, Alexander, Jr. 1954. Florida Bird Life. Coward McCann, and Natl. Aud. Soc., New York.

———. 1963. Addendum to Florida Bird-Life, 24 pp.

Sprunt, Alexander, Jr., and B. E. Chamberlain. 1949. South Carolina Bird Life. Cont. Charleston Museum.

Stamm, A. L. 1957. A fall record of the Sandhill Crane. *Kentucky Warbler*, 33: 15.

Stansbury, Howard. 1852. Exploration and survey of the valley of the Great Salt Lake of Utah. (*U. S. Senate Ex. Doc. No. 3*). Lippincott, Grambo & Co., Phila.

Stephen, W. J. D. 1960. The use of exploders in protecting crops against Sandhill Crane depradations. *Blue Jay*, 18 (1): 23-24.

———. 1967. Bionomics of the Sandhill Crane. Can. Wildlife Serv. Rept. No. 2.

Stephen, W. J. D., R. S. Miller, and J. P. Hatfield. 1966. Demographic factors affecting management of Sandhill Cranes. *J. Wildlife Management*, 30 (3): 581-589.

Sterling, Tom. 1958. Young Sandhill Cranes banded near Dafoe, July 17, 1957. *Blue Jay*, 16 (1): 15.

Stevenson, Henry M. 1955. Regional Reports, Florida. *Audubon Field Notes*, 9 (3): 250-254; 1956, 10 (1): 18-22, (3): 244-248; 1959, 13 (3): 285-289, (4): 426-429; 1960, 14 (1): 25-29, (3): 301-305; 1962, 16 (1): 21-25; 1964, 18 (3): 346-351; 1966, 20 (1): 30-35; 1967, 21 (1): 22-25, (5): 558-561.

Stewart, James R. 1964. Regional Reports, Central Southern. *Audubon Field Notes*, 18 (5): 512-515.

Stewart, Robert E. 1966. Notes on birds N. W. T. *Blue Jay*, 24 (1): 22-32.

Stimson, Louis A. 1942. Notes on occurrence of some less common birds in south Florida. *Florida Naturalist*, 15 (4): 55.

Stone, Norman R. 1953. Wisconsin's favorite bird haunts. Crex Meadows. *Passenger Pigeon*, 15 (2): 71-72.

Stone, Witmer. 1937. Bird studies at Old Cape May. *Del. Valley Orn. Club*, Phila.

Strelitzer, Carl L. 1951. The . . . Season. *Passenger Pigeon*, 13 (3): 109-112; 1952, 14 (4): 162-165; 1953, 15 (1): 41-45.

———. 1952. The . . . May Day Counts. *Passenger Pigeon*, 14 (1): 30. (3): 109-110.

———. 1952b. By the Wayside. *Passenger Pigeon*, 14 (1): 42.

Strelitzer, Carl L., and Norbert E. Damaske. 1952. By the Wayside. Possible nesting of Sandhill Cranes. *Passenger Pigeon*, 14 (1): 42.

Stueck, Ralph. 1961. Capturing Sandhills at Last Mountain Lake. *Blue Jay*, 19 (4): 157-164.

Sugden, John W. 1938. The Status of the Sandhill Crane in Utah and southern Idaho. *Condor*, 40: 18-22.

Sutton, George Miksch. 1946. A baby Florida Sandhill Crane. *Auk*, 63: 100-101.

———. 1967. Oklahoma Birds. Univ. of Okla. Press, Norman.

Tanner, D. 1941. Autumn food habits of the Sandhill Crane. *Flicker*, 13: 21.

Taylor, Robert R. 1966. Summary of the first eight years of the Prairie Nest Records scheme. *Blue Jay*, 24 (4): 180-181.

Thatcher, Vernon E. 1947. Cranes and egrets in Dougals County, Ore. *Condor*, 49 (1): 42.

Thompson, Charles F. 1967. Notes on the birds of the northeast Cape of St. Lawrence Island and of the Punuk Islands, Alaska. *Condor*, 69 (4): 411-419.

Thomas, Harriet P. 1957. Cooper Society Meetings, Northern Division. *Condor*, 59: 272.

Todd, W. E. Clyde. 1916. The birds of the Isle of Pines. *Ann. Carnegie Museum*, 10: 146-296, pls. 22-27, map.

———. 1940. Birds of western Pennsylvania.

Toner, G. C., W. E. Edwards and Murray W. Curtis. 1942. Birds of Leeds County, Ontario. *Canadian Field-Naturalist*, 56: 34-44.

Trammer, Elliot J. 1965. Notes from Athens, Georgia. *Oriole*, 30: 112-113.

Turner, Lucien M. 1886. Contributions to the Natural History of Alaska. Pt. V. Birds. U. S. Army Sig.Serv. Arctic,Ser. Publ. No. 2: 115-196.

Valentine, Jacob M., and Robert E. Noble. 1970. A Colony of Sandhill Cranes in Miss. *J. Wild. Man.*, 34 (4): 761-768.

Van den Akker, John B. 1949. Winter Season . . . Central Rocky Mountain Region. *Audubon Field Notes*, 3: 178-180.

Van den Akker, John B., and Vanez T. Wilson. 1949. Spring Migration . . . Central Rocky Mountain Region. *Audubon Field Notes*, 3: 217-218.

Walker, A. 1917. Some birds of central Oregon. *Condor*, 19: 131-140.

Walkinshaw, Lawrence H. 1931. Nesting of the Sandhill Crane in Calhoun County, Mich. *Auk*, 48 (4): 594-595.

———. 1933. The Sandhill Crane in a Michigan Marsh. *Wilson Bulletin*, 45 (3): 99-106.

———. 1941. The Bernard W. Baker Sanctuary of the Mich. Audubon Society. *Jack-Pine Warbler*, 19 (4): 98-103.

———. 1941b. A list of birds which have been observed on the Bernard W. Baker Sanctuary area. *Jack-Pine Warbler*, 19 (4): 106-128.

———. 1947. A week in the Okefenokee. *Oriole*, 12 (1): 1-5.

———. 1947b. Exploring Chippewa County, Mich. Sandhill Crane Marshes. *Jack-Pine Warbler*, 25: 130-139.

———. 1949. The Sandhill Cranes. Bull. 29, Cranbrook Institute of Science.

———. 1950. The Sandhill Crane in the Bernard W. Baker Sanctuary, Mich. *Auk*, 67 (1): 38-51.

———. 1950b. Sizes of spring flocks of the Sandhill Crane at Jasper-Pulaski Game Preserve, Indiana. *Indiana Audubon quarterly*, 28 (4): 78-82.

———. 1950c. Some bird observations at Chevak, Alaska. *Auk*, 67: 249.

———. 1950d. Incubation period of the Sandhill Crane, *Grus canadensis tabida. Auk*, 67: 513.

———. 1950e. Nesting of the Sandhill Crane at Parr (Indiana). *Indiana Audubon Quarterly*, 28 (4): 86.

———. 1953. Nesting and abundance of the Cuban Sandhill Crane on the Isle of Pines. *Auk*, 70: 1-10, 3 pls., 1 map.

———. 1953b. The Greater Sandhill Crane in Georgia. *Oriole*, 18: 13-15.

———. 1953c. Some bird observations on the Isle of Pines, *Papers Mich. Acad. Sci. Arts and Letters*, 38: 261-263.

———. 1953d. Notes on the Greater Sandhill Crane. *Auk*, 70: 204-205.

———. 1955. The Sandhill Crane on the Phyllis Haehnle Sanctuary Area. *Jack-Pine Warbler*, 33 (3): 77-82.

———. 1956. Two visits to the Platte River and their Sandhill Crane migration. *Nebraska Bird Review*, 24 (2): 18-21.

———. 1956b. Sandhill Crane observations at Jasper-Pulaski Game Preserve, Indiana. *Indiana Audubon Quarterly*, 34 (2): 22-30.

———. 1956c. Sandhill Cranes killed by flying into power line. *Wilson Bulletin*, 68 (4): 325-326.

———. 1960. Some Mississippi Crane notes. *Migrant*, 31: 41-43.

———. 1960b. Summer records of the Sandhill Crane in Saskatchewan. *Blue Jay*, 18 (1): 20-23, map.

———. 1960c. Some Saskatchewan bird observations. *Blue Jay*, 18 (3): 125-127.

———. 1960d. Migration of the Sandhill Crane east of the Mississippi River. *Wilson Bulletin*, 72 (4): 358-384, 4 maps.

———. 1960e. My second Okefenokee visit, 1960. *Oriole*, 25: 24-25.

———. 1961. Addition to the list of birds observed on the Bernard W. Baker Sanctuary. *Jack-Pine Warbler*, 39 (3): 100-124.

———. 1961b. The problem of the Lesser Sandhill Crane. *Blue Jay*, 19 (1): 8-13.

———. 1962. Kiwanis Lake at Baker Sanctuary. *Jack-Pine Warbler*, 40 (4): 134-135.

———. 1965. Territories of Cranes. *Mich. Acad. of Sciences, Arts, and Letters*, L: 75-88.

———. 1965b. Sandhill Crane studies on Banks Island, N. W. T. *Blue Jay*, 23 (2): 66-72.

———. 1965c. The dispersion of Sandhill Cranes from the Baker Sanctuary area. *Jack-Pine Warbler*, 43 (2): 96-99.

———. 1965d. One hundred thirty-three Michigan Sandhill Crane nests. *Jack-Pine Warbler*, 43 (3): 136-143.

———. 1965e. Why the decrease of young cranes? *Jack-Pine Warbler*, 43 (3): 148.

———. 1965f. A new Sandhill Crane from central Canada. *Canadian Field-Naturalist*, 79 (3): 181-184.

———. 1965g. Attentiveness of Cranes at their nests. *Auk*, 82 (4): 465-476.

Walkinshaw, Lawrence H., and Bernard W. Baker. 1946. Notes on the birds of the Isla of Pines, Cuba. *Wilson Bulletin*, 58: 133-142, pls. 3-6.

Walkinshaw, Lawrence H., W. Powell Cottrille, and Betty Darling Cottrille. 1960. Southern Michigan Sandhill Crane Survey, 1952-1958. *Jack-Pine Warbler*, 38 (1): 25-28.

Walkinshaw, Lawrence H., and John J. Stophlet. 1949. Bird observations at Johnson River, Alaska. *Condor*, 51 (1): 29-34.

Walkinshaw, Lawrence H., and Harold F. Wing. 1955. Censusing southern Michigan Sandhill Cranes. *Auk*, 72: 374-384.

Wallace, George J. Seasonal records of Michigan birds. *Jack-Pine Warbler*, 23 (3): 106, 122, 165-176; 1946, 24 (1): 23-27, (4): 154-167.

———. 1962. Michigan Bird Survey. *Jack-Pine Warbler*, 40 (1): 18-22; 1965, 43 (1): 26-38.

Wallace, G. J., and C. T. Black. 1948. Seasonal records of Michigan birds. *Jack-Pine Warbler*, 26 (1): 22-34, 161-176; 1949, 27 (1): 13-31.

Warren, Edward R. 1904. A Sandhill Crane's nest. *Condor*, 6: 39-40.

Wayne, Arthur Trezevant. 1910. Birds of South Carolina.

Weaver, Katherine. 1962. From the field. *Oriole*, 27 (1): 9.

Webster, Fred S., Jr. 1956. Regional Reports, South Texas. *Audubon Field Notes*, 10 (1): 37-40; 1958, 12 (1): 41-44, (3): 365-370; 1959, 13 (1): 45-49; 1960, 14 (1): 52-56, (4): 401-407; 1962, 16 (3): 347-350; 1965, 19 (1): 56-60, (4): 490-497; 1966, 20 (1): 66-72, (4): 525-532; 1967, 21 (4): 520-524; 1968, 22 (1): 61-69.

Webster, J. Dan. 1950. Notes on the birds of Wrangell and Vicinity, southeastern Alaska. *Condor*, 52 (1): 32-38.

Weeden, Robert B. 1960. The birds of Chilkat Pass, British Columbia. *Canadian Field-Naturalist*, 74: 119-129.

Weston, Francis Marion. 1965. A survey of birdlife of Northwestern Florida. *Bull. Tall Timbers Research Station*, No. 5, Sept. 1965.

Wheeler, Robert H., and James C. Lewis. 1970. Observations on behavior and development of trapping techniques for Sandhill Cranes in the Platte River, Nebraska. Bur. Sport Fisheries and Wildlife.

Williams, Frances. 1968. Regional Reports, Southern Great Plains. *Audubon Field Notes*, 22 (1): 57-60.

Wickstrom, George. 1950. Seasonal Records. *Jack-Pine Warbler*, 28: 114-126; 1951, 29 (3): 91-101, 143-153; 1952, 30 (1): 7-19, (4): 125-131; 1953, 31 (1): 28-38, (3): 79-95; 1954, 32 (1): 3-14.

Williams, George G. 1938. Notes on waterbirds of the Upper Texas coast. *Auk*, 55 (1): 62-70.

———. 1941. The Season (Texas Coastal Region). *Audubon Magazine*, 41 (2, sect. 2): 233-234.

———. 1948 Winter Season, Texas Coastal Region. *Audubon Field Notes*, 2 (1): 19-20, (3): 145-146.

———. 1949. Winter Season, South Texas Region. *Audubon Field*

Notes, 3: 176-177.

_____. 1950. Regional Reports, South Texas. *Audubon Field Notes*, 4 (1): 24-25; 1951, 5 (1): 27-29.

Williams, Laidlaw. 1958. Regional Reports, Middle Pacific Coast. *Audubon Field Notes*, 12 (3): 303-304.

Williams, Lovett E., Jr., and Robert W. Phillips. 1972. North Florida Sandhill Crane populations. *Auk*, 89 (3):541-548.

Williams, M. Y. 1922. Biological notes along 1400 miles of the Mackenzie River system. *Canadian Field-Naturalist* 26 (40: 61-66.

Williamson, Francis S. L. 1957. Ecological distribution of birds in the Napaskiak area of the Kuskokwim River Delta, Alaska. *Condor*, 59: 317-338.

Wilson, Gordon. 1923. Birds of Calloway County, Ky. *Wilson Bulletin*, 35 (3): 129-136.

Wilson, Vanez T., and Ross H. Norr. 1949. Nesting season . . . Central Rocky Mountain Region. *Audubon Field Notes*, 3: 246-247.

_____. 1950. Regional Reports, Great Basin, Central Rocky Mountains. *Audubon Field Notes*, 4 (1): 26-28, (3): 212-214, (4): 253-255; 1951, 5 (1): 30-32, (3): 218-219, (5): 301-303.

Wing, Harold F. 1943. Capturing a Sandhill Crane. *Jack-Pine Warbler*, 21 (4): 122-124.

Wing, Leonard W. 1950. Size of summer bird grouping, Texas to the Yukon. *Canadian Field-Naturalist*, 64: 163-169.

Woodard, Donald W. 1966. Regional Reports, Central Southern. *Audubon Field Notes*, 20 (3): 431-433.

Woodford, James. 1962. Regional Reports, Ontario-western New York. *Audubon Field Notes*, 16 (4): 404-408; 1963, 17 (5): 457-459.

Woodford, James, and Donald E. Burton. 1961. Regional Reports, Ontario-western New York. *Audubon Field Notes*, 15 (4): 405-409.

Woodford, James, and John Lunn. 1962. Regional Reports, Ontario-western New York. *Audubon Field Notes*, 16 (1): 25-31.

Woodruff, Robert E., and Ruth P. Emery. 1967. Regional Reports, Northeastern Maritime. *Audubon Field Notes*, 21 (1): 7-13, (3): 397-399, (4): 487-488; 1968, 22 (1): 9-13.

Wright, J. B. 1961. The Sandhill Cranes of Big Grass Marsh. *Blue Jay*, 19 (1): 14-15.

Zimmerman, Dale A. 1962. Regional Reports, Southwest. *Audubon Field Notes*, 16 (1): 62-65; 1963, 17 (1): 54-57, (3): 347-349.

Zimmerman, F. R. 1961. Sandhill Crane nest in Marquette County (Wisc.). *Passenger Pigeon*, 23 (3): 95, photos, 96.

Grus japonensis

Austin, Oliver L., Jr. 1948. The Birds of Korea. *Bull. Mus. Comp. Zool.* 101 (1): 1-301, map.

Austin, Oliver L., and Nagahisa Kuroda. 1953. The Birds of Japan, their status and distribution. *Bull. Mus. Comp. Zool.*, 109 (4): 279-637, 1 map.

Blakiston, T., and H. Pryer. 1882. Birds of Japan. Trans. as. Soc. Japan, 10: 84-186.

Hand-List of Japanese Birds. 1958. 4th rev. ed., Orn. Soc. Japan, Yamashina Inst. for Orn. and Zool., Tokyo.

Ivanov, A. I., E. B. Koslova, L. A. Portenko, and A. Y. Tugarinov. 1951. Birds of the USSR. Vol. 1. Acad. of Sciences USSR, Moscow, p. 262.

Iwamatsu, Takeo. 1963. Tancho-zuru. 61 pp., many photos.

_____. 1967. The Japanese Crane. 86 plates, 18 pp.

Ito, Hiromichi, and Tsutoma Kamada. 1964. With The Japanese Cranes. The Akan Junior High School. 34 pp., map, many photos.

Keith, G. Stuart, and M. Yoshii. 1962. A Short survey of Winter Birdlife in eastern Hokkaido. *Tori*, 79-80: 54-65.

La Touche, J. D. D. 1933. A Handbook of the Birds of Eastern China. Vol. 2.

Masatomi, Hiroyaki. 1970. Ecological Studies of the Japanese Crane. *Grus japonensis* I: 37-45; 1971. II: 1-19.

Seebohm, Henry. 1884. The Birds of the Japanese Empire. 8vo. London.

Takahashi, R. Y. 1967. Leaflet about Tsuru Koen. 4 pp.

Grus americana

A. A. M. 1886. Spirit and Okoboji Lakes, Attraction offered to Sportsmen in the Lake Region of Iowa. *Western Sportsman*, 1 (1): 5.

Abbott, William L. 1880. List of Birds taken at Pembina, Dakota, July, 1879. *Forest and Stream*, 13 (24): 984-985.

Addison, Richard. 1931. Curious Creatures. *Nature Magazine*, 17 (4): 217.

Agersborg, G. S. 1885. The Birds of southeastern Dakota. *Auk*, 2 (3): 287.

Aiken, C. E. 1873. Notes on the birds of Wyo. and Colo. *Proc. Boston Soc. Nat. Hist.*, 15: 209.

Aldrich, John W. 1963. Meeting of Whooping Crane Cons. Assoc., Detroit, Mich. 5 March 1963. Status of the Whooping Crane and conservation efforts—1962.

_____. 1967. Review N. S. Novakowski, Whooping Crane population dynamics. *Arctic*, 20 (4): 276.

Alexander, W. B., B. A. Southgate, and R. Bassindale. 1932. The salinity of water retained in the Muddy Foreshore of an Estuary. *J. Marine Biol. Assoc.*, 18 (1): 297-298.

Allen, Arthur A. 1937. The Shore birds, Cranes . . . their relatives Deserve Protection. The Book of birds. Vol. 1, 261, 194-295. Ntl. Geog. Soc., Washington, D. C.

Allen, Arthur A., and others. 1950. Report of the Committee on bird protection. American Orn. Union. *Auk*, 67 (4): 316-324.

Allen, Francis H. 1941. Conservation notes. *Auk*, 58 (2): 288.

Allen, Joel Asaph. 1871. On the mammals and winter birds of east Florida, etc. *Bull. Mus. Comp. Zool.*, 3 (3): 357.

_____. 1876. Decrease of birds in Mass. *Bull. Nutt. Orn. Club*, 1 (3): 53,58.

_____. 1886. A revised list of the birds of Mass. *Bull. Am. Mus. Nat. Hist.*, 1: 7: 263.

Allen, Robert Porter. 1947. Status of the Whooping Crane. *Wilson Bulletin*, 59 (2): 127-128.

_____. 1947b. The Whooping Cranes still dance. *Audubon Magazine*, 49 (3): 136-139.

_____. 1947c. . . . Field Reports . . . North Platte, Neb. *Audubon Magazine*, 49 (3): 174-175.

_____. 1948. Lost· Part of a continent. *Audubon Magazine*, 50 (1): 28-35.

_____. 1948b. An Editorial Comment. *Audubon Magazine*, 50 (4): 231.

_____. 1948c. Field notes. *Audubon Magazine*, 50 (5): 296-298.

_____. 1950. The Whooping Crane and its environment. *Audubon Magazine*, 52 (2): 92-95.

_____. 1950b. The unique drama of a wild Whooper. *Audubon Magazine*, 52 (3): 194-195.

_____. 1952. The Whooping Crane. Research Report No. 2, New York., Nat. Aud. Soc.

_____. 1953. Whooping Crane. Leaflet No. 148, Nat. Aud. Soc.

_____. 1953b. Help wanted for the Whooping Crane. *Audubon Magazine*, 55 (5): 210-213, 224, 225.

_____. 1954. Additional data on the food of the Whooping Crane. *Auk*, 71 (2): 198.

_____. 1954b. Whooping Cranes face another test. *Audubon Magazine*, 56 (5): 221.

_____. 1956. The Whooping Crane. *Our Endangered Wildlife*. Nat. Wildlife Federation, Washington, D. C.

_____. 1956b. A report on the Whooping Crane's northern breeding grounds. Suppl. Res. Rept. No. 2, Nat. Aud. Soc., pp. 1-60.

Allen, Robert P., and Frederick Hamerstrom, Jr. 1947. Status of the Whooping Crane. *Wilson Bulletin*, 59 (2): 127-128.

Allen, Robert P., and F. K. Truslow. 1959. Whooping Cranes fight for survival. *Nat. Geog. Mag.*, 116: 650-669.

Amadon, Dean. 1953. Migratory birds of relict distribution: some inferences. *Auk*, 70 (4): 460-469.

American Game Protective and Propagation Association. 1916. Whooping Cranes might be saved. *Bull.* 5 (2): 2.

———. 1918. Game in the Province of Sask. *Bull.* 7, (1): 22.

American Ornithologists' Union. 1886. The code of Nomenclature and Check-list of North American Birds.

———. 1895. Check-list of North American Birds, 2nd rev. ed.

———. 1910. Check-list of North American Birds, 3rd rev. ed.

———. 1931. Check-list of North American Birds, 4th ed.

———. 1957. Check-list of North American Birds, 5th ed.

American Ornithologists' Union, Committee for Bird Protection. 1939. Report for 1938. *Auk*, 56: 212-219.

———. 1940. Report for 1939. *Auk*, 57 (2): 279-291 (Victor Cahalane, Chmn.).

———. 1941. Report for 1940. *Auk*, 58 (2): 292-298 (Victor Cahalane, Chmn.).

———. 1942. Report for 1941. *Auk*, 59 (2): 286-299 (Victor Cahalane, Chmn.).

———. 1943. Report for 1942. *Auk*, 60 (1): 152-162 (Victor Cahalane, Chmn.).

———. 1944. Report for 1943. *Auk*, 61 (4): 622-635.

———. 1950. Report for 1949. *Auk*, 67 (3): 321-322 (Ira N. Gabrielson, Chmn.).

———. 1954. Report for 1953. *Auk*, 71 (2): 186-190 (Ira N. Gabrielson, Chmn.).

———. 1956. Report for 1955. *Auk*, 73 (1): 119-123 (Ira N. Gabrielson, Chmn.).

———. 1957. Report for 1956. *Auk*, 74 (1): 90-93 (Ira N. Gabrielson, Chmn.).

———. 1962. Report for 1961. *Auk*, 79: 463-478 (Clarence Cottam, Chmn.).

———. 1963. Report for 1962. *Auk*, 80 (2): 352-364 (Clarence Cottam, Chmn.).

———. 1964. Report for 1963. *Auk*, 81 (2): 417-425 (Victor Cahalane, Chmn.).

American Sportsman. 1873. Some western birds. 2 (4): 51.

Anderson, R. M. 1894. Nesting of the Whooping Crane. *Oologist*, 11 (8): 263-264.

———. 1907. The birds of Iowa. *Proc. Davenport Acad. Sci.*, 11: 125-417.

Anonymous. 1913. Bird migration at Lincoln, Neb., spring of 1913. *Proc. Nebr. Orn. Union*, 6 (3): 55-68.

———. 1944. Bird notes. *Blue Jay*, 2 (4): 31.

———. 1951. Howard the Crane succumbs. *Blue Jay*, 9 (4): 18.

———. 1952. Whooping Cranes head north. *Fla. Nat.*, 25 (3): 100.

———. 1953. Whooping Cranes return to Arkansas (Aransas). *Blue Jay*, 11 (1): 8.

———. 1956. The Whooping Crane problem. *Blue Jay*, 14 (4): 111-113.

———. 1957. Whooping Cranes photographed in the Aransas Refuge. *Blue Jay*, 15 (1): 16-17.

———. 1963. U. S. Dept. Interior, Fish and Wildlife Service Release, 7, April 1963.

———. 1965. Injured Whooping Crane. *Blue Jay*, 23 (1): 52.

———. 1966. Endangered species report. Whooping Crane and Trumpeter Swan. *Natl. Park Magazine*, 40: 21.

———. 1967. Cover Photo. *Blue Jay*, 25.

———. 1967b. U. S. Dept. Interior, Bureau of Sport Fisheries and Wildlife Memorandum No. 13, Whooping Crane advisory group, April 1967.

———. 1967c. Back from the brink. Breeding Whooping Cranes in captivity. *Science N.*, 91: 592.

———. 1967d. Wildlife exploitation and the Sandhill Crane. *Audubon Magazine*, 69: 5.

———. 1968. Scientific egg hunt: Whooping Cranes. *Science Digest*, 63: 42-43.

———. 1969. Whooping Crane population grows to record 49. *Modern Game Breeding*, 5 (3): 22.

———. 1969b. Whooping Cranes. Resource Publ. 75., U. S. Dept. Interior, Fish and Wildlife Service.

———. 1969c. It's time to halt taking of wild Whooping Crane eggs. *Audubon Magazine*, 71: 122.

Anthony, A. W. 1886. Field notes on the birds of Washington County, Ore. *Auk*, 3 (2): 161-172.

Anweiler, Gary G. 1970. The birds of the Last Mountain Lake Wildlife Area, Sask. *Blue Jay*, 29 (2): 74-83.

Armstrong, Edward A. 1942. Bird display: An introduction to the study of bird psychology. London, Cambridge Univ. Press.

Arthur, Stanley C. 1918. Birds of Louisiana. Bull. No. 5, La. Dept. of Conservation, pp. 1-80.

———. 1929. Winter requirements of migratory waterfowl. *Trans. 16th Am. Game Conf.*, p. 101.

———. 1931. The birds of Louisiana. Bull. No. 20, La. Dept. of Conservation.

Astley, Hubert D. 1901. Cranes in captivity. *Aviculture Magazine*, 7 (4): 65-69.

———. 1907. The Cranes. *Aviculture Magazine*, New Series 5 (12): 347-353.

Audubon, John James. 1827-1838. The birds of America. 4 vols. (double elephant folio). Pl. CCXXVI, London, author.

———. 1835. Ornithological Biography. III: 202-213, 441. Edinburgh, A. and C. Black.

———. 1839. A Synopsis of the birds of North America. Edinburgh, A. and C. Black.

———. 1941. The birds of America. Edited by William Vogt, New York, Macmillan.

Audubon Magazine. 1953. Twenty-two Whooping Cranes return to Aransas. 55 (1): 47.

———. 1953b. Don't shoot Whooping Cranes (reprinted from Houston *Post*, Sept. 18, 1953), 55 (6): 263.

———. 1955. Whooping Crane count. 57 (1): 45.

Aughey, Samuel. 1878. Notes on the nature of the food of the birds of Nebraska. *First Rep. U. S. Entom. Comm. for 1877.* app. 2: 13-62.

Avery, W. C. 1890. Birds observed in Alabama. *American Field*, 34: 25: 584.

Baczkowski, Frank. 1955. Whooping Cranes in Porter County 50 years ago. *Indiana Audubon Quarterly*, 33: 43-44.

Baerg, W. J. 1931. Birds of Arkansas. Bull. 258. Ark. Agr. Exp. Station, p. 56.

Bailey, Alfred M. 1928. Notes on the winter birds of Chenier au Tigre, La. *Auk*, 45: 277.

——— 1934. Additional notes on the wintering birds of Chenier au Tigre, La. *Auk*, 51: 398-400.

Bailey, Alfred M., and E. G. Wright. 1931. Birds of southern Louisiana. *Wilson Bulletin*, 43 (3): 190-219 (Pt. 2).

Bailey, Florence Merriam. 1928. Birds of New Mexico. N. M. Dept. of Game and Fish.

Bailey, Harold H. 1925. The birds of Florida. Baltimore, author.

Baily, William L. 1869. Our own birds. Phila., Lippincott.

Baird, S. F., J. Cassin, and G. N. Lawrence. 1858. U. S. War Dept. reports of explorations and surveys . . . in 1853-56. Vol. 9, Pt. 2, General report upon the zoology of the several Pacific Railroad routes. *Birds. U. S. Senate Ex. Doc. No. 78.*

Baker, John H. 1945. The President Reports to You. *Audubon Magazine*, 47 (3): 179-180, (4): 245, 246; 1946, 48 (1): 55, (5): 311; 1947, 49 (1): 55-56, (2): 115-116, (3): 173-175; 1948, 50 (3): 177-178, (5): 303; 1949, 51 (3): 178-180, (4): 251-252; 1950, 52 (1): 50, (4): 256; 1951, 53 (2): 127; 1952, 54 (1): 50, (3): 178, (6): 380; 1954, 56 (5): 220; 1956, 58 (1): 22.

Bard, Fred G. 1948. Whooping Cranes. *Blue Jay*, 6 (2): 27.

———. 1953. A memorable experience. *Blue Jay*, 11 (4): 4-7, 10.

———. 1954. Lending a helping hand. *Blue Jay*, 12: 29-31.

———. 1956. Whooping Crane in migration. *Blue Jay*, 14 (2): 39-42.

———. 1956b. Whooping Cranes in southern Saskatchewan in 1956. *Blue Jay*, 14 (3): 81.

———. 1957. Give the Whooping Crane "safe Passage." *Blue Jay*, 15 (3): 115-116.

_____. 1958. Whooping Cranes, 1958. *Blue Jay*, 16 (1): 11-14.

_____. 1959. Annual report of Whooping Cranes in Saskatchewan, 1958. *Blue Jay*, 17 (1): 9-11.

_____. 1959b. Museum notes. *Blue Jay*, 17 (2): 80.

_____. 1960. A visit to the Wildlife Refuges on the Gulf of Mexico. *Blue Jay*, 18: 64-69.

_____. 1962. Annual report on the Whooping Crane population. *Blue Jay*, 20 (1): 6-7.

_____. 1963. Whooping Crane winter count, 1962-63. *Blue Jay*, 21 (1): 11.

_____. 1966. Whooping Crane population report. *Blue Jay*, 24 (1): 21.

_____. 1968. Whooping Crane survival. *Blue Jay*, 26 (3): 143-144.

_____. 1969. Whooping Crane Conservation Association. *Modern Game Breeding.*, 5 (7): 22-23, (9): 18-20, 28, illus, 2 maps.

Bard, Fred G., and Fred W. Lahrman. 1965. Sandhill Cranes flying with feet drawn in. *Blue Jay*, 23 (3): 121.

Barnard, Vincent. 1861. A catalogue of the birds of Chester County, Pa. *Ann. Rept. Smithsonian Inst. for 1860*, p. 438.

Barrows, W. B. 1912. Michigan bird life. *Spec. Bull. of Mich. Agr. College, Lansing, Dept. of Zool. Phys.*

Bartram, William. 1791. Travels through N. C., S. C., Ga., E. and W. Fla., etc. Phila., James and Johnson.

Bartsch, Paul. 1900. A trip to the Zoological park. *Osprey*, 5 (2): 20.

Bates, Frank A. 1896. The game birds of North America. Boston, Whidden.

Beckham, Charles W. 1885. Observations on the Birds of southwest Texas. *Proc. U. S. Natl. Mus.*, 10: 633-696.

Bedford, Duchess of. 1907. Cranes of Woburn Park. *Aviculture Magazine*, New Series, 6: 1: 26.

Beebe, William C. 1902. Rare birds in the Zoological Park. *N. Y. Zool. Soc. Bull.*, 7: 38.

_____. 1906. The bird, its form and function. New York, Holt.

Belding, L. 1891. Notice of some California birds. *Zoe*, 2: 99.

Benners, G. B. 1887. A collecting trip to Texas. *Ornith.. and Oologist*, 12 (6): 83.

Bennitt, Rudolf. 1932. Check-list of the birds of Missouri. *Univ. Mo. Studies*, 7 (3): 27.

_____. 1938. Whooping Cranes in southwestern Missouri, 1937. *Wilson Bulletin*, 50 (1): 61-63.

Bent, Arthur Cleveland. 1926. Life histories of North American marsh birds. *Bull. 135, U. S. Natl. Mus.*

Bertgold, W. H. 1931. The season, Denver region. *Bird-Lore*, 33 (5): 339.

Beverly, Fred. 1874. The Okeechobee expedition. *Forest and Stream*, 2 (4): 50.

Beyer, George Eugene. 1900. The avifauna of Lousiana. Reprinted from *Proc. La. Soc. Nat. Hist. for 1897-99.*, p. 19.

Beyer, George Eugene, A. Allison, and H. H. Kopman. 1908. List of the Birds of Louisiana. Part IV. *Auk*, 25 (2): 176.

Blaauw, Frans Ernest. 1897. A monograph of the Cranes. Leiden & London, E. J. Brill, R. H. Porter.

Black, Cyrus A. 1922. Some bird notes from central and western Nebraska. *Wilson Bulletin* 34 (1): 43.

_____. 1933. Nebraska records of the Whooping Crane for 1932 and 1933. *Nebr. Bird Review*, 1 (3): 61-62.

_____. 1934. A Nebraska record of the Whooping Crane for the fall of 1933. *Nebr. Bird Review*, 2 (1): 6-7.

_____. 1934b. The Whooping Crane in the spring of 1934. *Neb. Bird Review*, 2 (3): 117-118.

_____. 1935. Whooping Cranes seen in the fall of 1934. *Nebr. Bird Review*, 3 (1): 26.

_____. 1936. Records of the Whooping Crane for the spring of 1936. *Nebr. Bird Review*, 4 (4): 81.

_____. 1937. Whooping Cranes and Whistling Swans seen in the fall of 1936. *Nebr. Bird Review*, 5 (1): 10.

_____. 1937b. Some Observations of the Whooping Crane in the spring of 1937. *Nebr. Bird Review*, 5 (2): 33.

_____. 1937c. The Whooping Crane near Kearney, Buffalo County. *Nebr. Bird Review*, 5 (4): 106.

_____. 1938. Some 1937 notes on Whooping Cranes and other birds. *Nebr. Bird Review*, 6 (1): 12.

Blackly, C. P. 1884. Whooping Crane (correspondence). *Orn. and Oologist*, 9 (2): 24.

Blakiston, Thomas. 1863. On the birds of the interior of British North America. *Ibis*, 5 (17): 128.

Blanchan, Neltje. 1902. Birds that hunt and are hunted. New York, Doubleday and Page.

Blincoe, Benedict J. 1925. Birds of Bardstown, Nelson County, Ky. *Auk*, 42 (3): 404-420.

Blyth, Edward, and W. B. Tegetmeier. 1881. The natural history of the Cranes. Horace Cox, London.

Boeker, E. L. 1960. Whooping Cranes in 1959. Bureau of Sport Fisheries and Wildlife, Denver Res. Center.

_____. 1961. Whooping Cranes in 1960. *ibid.*

_____. 1961. Whooping Cranes in 1961. *ibid.*

_____. 1963. Whooping Cranes in 1962-1963. *ibid.*

Bonaparte, Charles Lucien Jules Laurent, Prince de Canino. 1825. Observations on the Nomenclature of Wilson's Ornithology. *J. Acad. Nat. Sci., Phila.* 5 (Part 1): 66.

_____. 1827. Contributions of the Maclurian Lyceum to the Arts and Sciences, 1: 24.

Bradshaw, Fred. 1923. Saskatchewan. Report of the Chief Game Warden for 1923, pp. 14-15.

_____. 1956. The home of the Whooping Crane. *Blue Jay*, 14 (3): 76-78.

Brooking, A. M. 1934. The Whooping Crane in the spring of 1934. *Nebr. Bird Review*, 2 (4): 117-118.

_____. 1942. The vanishing bird life of Nebraska. *Nebr. Bird Review*, 10 (2): 45.

_____. 1943. The present status of the Whooping Crane. *Nebr. Bird Review*, 11 (1): 5-8.

_____. 1943. Additional records of the Whooping Crane. *Nebr. Bird Review*, 11 (2): 47; 1944, 12 (1): 7.

Brooking, A. M., and J. J. Hickey. 1944. Status of the Whooping Crane. *Wilson Bulletin*, 56 (3): 180.

Brooking, Mrs. A. M. 1934. Report in 1934 migration season. *Nebr. Bird Review*, 2 (2): 48.

_____. 1946. Whooping Cranes in Hall and Buffalo counties. *Nebr. Bird Review*, 14 (2): 46.

Brooks, Winthrop S. and S. Cobb. 1911. Notes from eastern Alberta. *Auk*, 28 (4): 466.

Browne, Eddie. 1942. The Whooping Crane at Lexington, Dawson County. *Nebr. Bird Review*, 10 (1): 30.

Bryant, Henry. 1853. Paper on the Sandhill Crane. *Proc. Boston Soc. Nat. Hist.*, Vol. 4, pp. 303-305.

Buck, Peter H. 1938. Vikings of the Sunrise. Phila., Lippincott.

Burleigh, Thomas D. 1944. The bird life of the Gulf Coast region of Mississippi. La Univ., *Occ. Papers Mus. Zool.*, 20: 363.

_____. 1958. Georgia birds. Univ. Okla. Press, Norman.

Burns, Frank L. 1932. Charles W. and Titian R. Peale and the Ornithological Section of the Philadelphia Museum. *Wilson Bulletin*, 44 (1): 23-35.

Burmood, Mrs. Will. 1934. Whooping Cranes near Wood River, Hall County. *Nebr. Bird Review*, 2 (4): 117.

Burrage, H. S. 1906. Early English and French Voyages, 1534-1608. New York, Scribner.

Butler, Amos W. 1898. The birds of Indiana. *22nd Ann. Rept., Ind. Dept. Geol. and Nat. Res.* (1897), pp. 515-1187.

Canfield, R. H. 1944. Measurement of grazing use by line intersection method. *J. Forestry*, 42 (3): 192.

Carmichael, Lloyd T. 1951. Whooping Cranes. *Blue Jay*, 9:7.

Carroll, James J. 1900. Notes on the birds of Refugio County, Texas. *Auk*, 17 (4): 340.

Cartwright, Bertram W. 1931. Notes and observations on some Manitoban birds. *Canadian Field-Naturalist*, 45 (8): 181-187.

Cary, Merritt. 1900. Some bird notes from the Upper Elkhorn. *Proc.*

Nebr. Orn. Union, 1899, p. 22.

Catesby, Mark. 1771. The natural history of Carolina, Florida, and the Bahama Islands. London, printed for B. White.

Chamberlain, Montague. 1887. A catalogue of Canadian Birds. St. John, N. B., J. and A. McMillan.

Champlain, Samuel De. 1604-10. Voyages of Samuel de Champlain. Otis trans. Boston, The Prince Society (1878-82).

Chapman, Frank M. 1891. On the birds observed near Corpus Christi, Texas, during parts of March and April, 1891. *Bull. Amer. Mus. Nat. Hist.*, 3 (2): 328.

———. 1912. Handbook of birds of eastern North America. New York, D. Appleton and Co.; 1932, 2nd ed.

Christy, Miller. 1885. Notes on the birds of Manitoba. *Zoologist*, 3rd ser., 9 (10):121-133.

Clarke, C. H. D. 1940. A biological investigation of the Thelon Game Sanctuary. *Bull. 96, Biol. ser. 25, Nat. Mus. Canada*, p.49.

Clarke, Franics E. 1930. Great wings and small. New York, Mac-millan.

Clement, Roland C. 1964. Whooping Crane. Today and tomorrow. *Audubon Magazine*, 66: 74-77.

Cobeaux, Eugene. 1960. Contributions to the natural history of the North West Territories. 1. The birds of Saskatchewan. *Ottawa Naturalist*, 14 (12): 26.

Conover, H. B. 1922. *Anas diazi novimexicana* and *Grus americana* in Nebraska. *Auk*, 39 (3): 412.

Conway, W. G. 1957. Three days with a family of Whooping Cranes. *Animal Kingdom*, 40 (4): 98-106.

Cooke, W. W. 1888. Report on bird migration in the Mississippi Valley . . . 1884 and 1885. U. S. Bur. of Biol. Surv., Bull. No. 2: 84-85.

———. 1897. Birds of Colorado. Colo. State Agr. Coll., Ft. Collins, Bull. No. 37 (Tech. Ser. No. 2).

———. 1914. Distribution and migration of North American Rails and their allies. U. S. Dept. Agr. Bull. 128: 1, 4-7.

Cory, C. B. 1909. The birds of Illinois and Wisconsin. *Field Mus. of Nat. Hist.*, 131. Zool. Ser., 9: 375-376.

Cosgrave, R. 1911. Notes on the Cranes at Lilford Hall. *Avicultural Magazine*, New Ser., 2 (5): 147-150.

———. 1912. The Whooping Crane. *Avicultural Magazine*, New Ser., 3 (10): 312.

Coues, Elliott. 1868. A list of the birds of New England. *Proc. Essex Inst.*, 5: 289.

———. 1868b. Synopsis of the birds of South Carolina. *Proc. Boston Soc. Nat. Hist.*, 12: 123.

———. 1874. Birds of the Northwest. U. S. Geol. Surv. Terr., Misc. Publ. No. 3.

———. 1874b. The Cranes of America. *Forest and Stream*, 3 (2): 20-21.

———. 1878. Field notes on birds observed in Dakota and Montana . . . 1873 and 1874. U. S. Geol. Surv. Terr., Bull. 4: 545-661.

———. 1882. Check List of North American birds. Boston, Estes and Lauriat.

———. History of the Expedition under the command of Lewis and Clark. Vols. 2 and 3., New York, Francis P. Harper.

Covert, A. B. 1876. Birds of Lower Michigan. *Forest and Stream*, 7 (1): 147.

Cracraft, Joel. 1968. The Whooping Crane from the Lower Pleistocene of Arizona. *Wilson Bulletin*, 80 (4): 490.

Craven, Earl. 1946. The status of the Whooping Crane on the Aransas Refuge, Texas. *Condor*, 48 (1): 37-39.

Cutting, Hiram A. 1884. Lectures on Milk, Forestry, our bird catalogue . . . , etc. Montpelier, Vt., Watchman and Journal Press.

Dambach, Charles A. 1944. Status of the Whooping Crane. *Wilson Bulletin*, 56 (4): 180.

"D. O. of B." 1876. A hunt in western Iowa. *Chicago Field*, 6 (14): 226.

Davie, Oliver. 1889. Nests and eggs of North American birds, 4th ed. Columbus, Hahn and Adair.

Davies, Freda. 1953. Can the Whooping Crane be saved? *Oryx*, 2

(3): 212-218.

Davis, Edwin C. n. d. Reduced price list of North American birds' eggs. Gainesville, Texas.

Davis, John H., Jr. 1943. The natural features of southern Florida, Tallahassee. *Fla. Geol. Surv. Bull. 25.*

Dawson, William Leon. 1903. The birds of Ohio. Columbus, Wheaton Publ. Co.

———. 1908. New and unpublished records from Washington. *Auk*, 25 (4): 484.

Dawson, William Leon, and J. H. Bowles. 1909. The birds of Washington. Vol. II, Seattle, Occidental Publ. Co.

Deane, Ruthvean. 1923. Extracts from the field notes of George B. Sennett. *Auk*, 40 (4): 627, 629-631.

Dekay, James E. 1844. Zoology of New York or the New York Fauna. Part II, Birds. Albany, Carroll and Cook.

De Laubenfels, Max W. 1954. A second flock of Whooping Cranes. *Wilson Bulletin*, 66 (2): 149.

DeMay, I. S. 1941. Quaternary bird life of the McKittrick Asphalt, California. Carnegie Inst. Washington, Publ. 530: 35-60.

Denver Wildlife Research Report. 1963. Annual progress report, 1962-63.

Dept. of the Interior Information Service. 1959. Fish and Wildlife Service Release, 19 June 1959.

———. 1963. Fish and Wildlife Service News Release, 7 April 1963.

Derby, Stafford. 1955. 'A White, Shining superb creature.' *Christian Science Monitor*, Sept. 26, 1955.

Douthitt, Bessie Price. 1918. Migration records for Kansas birds. *Wilson Bulletin*, 30 (4): 108.

Dresser, H. E. 1866. Notes on the birds of southern Texas. *Ibis*, 2nd ser., 2: 30.

Drury, Charles. 1900. Random notes on Natural history. *J. Cincinnati Soc. Nat. Hist.*, 19 (5): 174.

Dudley, William. 1854. Description of a species of Crane (*Grus hoyanus*) found in Wisconsin. Presumed to be new. *Proc. Acad. Nat. Sci., Phila.* 7: 64.

Dumont, Philip A. 1933. A revised list of the birds of Iowa. *Univ. Iowa studies in Nat. Hist.*, 15 (5): 59-60.

Dundas, Les. 1968. Whooping Crane record. *Flicker*, 40 (1): 21.

Eaton, Elon Howard. 1901. Birds of western New York. *Proc. Rochester Acad. Sci.*, 4: 25.

———. 1910. The birds of New York. *Memoir 12, N. Y. State Mus. Part 1.* Albany, Univ. of the state of N.Y.

Edwards, George. 1750. A natural history of birds the most of which have not hitherto been figured or described. Part III, Vols. 3 and 4 (original ed. 1743-51), London. W. Gardener (1802).

"Elanoides." 1890. A list of birds of McLennan County, Texas. *Ornith. and Oologist*, 15 (4): 57.

Emmons, Ebenezer. 1833. Birds. In Edward Hitchcock's *Catalogue of the Animals and Plants of Massachusetts.* Amherst, J. S. and C. Adams.

Erickson, Ray C. 1961. Production and survival of the Whooping Crane. Manuscript Report from the U. S. Bureau of Sport Fisheries and Wildlife, pp. 1-29.

Evenden, Fred G., Jr. 1952. Notes on Mexican bird distribution. *Wilson Bulletin*, 64 (2): 112-113.

Everts, Hal G. 1923. The last straggler. *Saturday Evening Post*, 196 (2): 48.

———. 1923b. The passing of the old west. Boston, Little, Brown.

Farb, P. . Porter Allen and the Whooping Crane. *Frontiers*, 26 (1): 3-6.

Farley, Frank L. 1932. Birds of the Battle River region, 1st ed. Inst. Appl. Art, Edmonton, Alberta.

———. 1944. Saskatchewan records of the Whooping Crane. *Canadian Field-Naturalist*, 58 (4): 142.

Faxon, Walter. 1915. Relics in Peale's Museum. *Bull. Mus. Comp. Zool.*, 59 (3): 131.

Federal Migratory Bird Law. 1916. Open season effective August 21, 1916. *Bull. Am. Game Prot. Assoc.*, 5 (3): 3, 6.

Feducia, J. Alan. 1967. *Ciconia maltha* and *Grus americana* from upper Pliocene of Idaho. *Wilson Bulletin*, 79 (3): 316-318.

Fenton, Carroll Lane. 1916. Preliminary list of the birds of Floyd County (Iowa). *Wilson Bulletin*, 28 (3): 133-134.

Fisher, Albert Kendrick. 1893. The Death Valley Expedition. U. S. Biol. Surv., *N. Amer. Fauna No. 7.*

Fisher, Harvey I., and Donald C. Goodman. 1955. The Myology of the Whooping Crane, *Grus americana.* Urbana, Univ. of Ill. Press.

Fisher, James. 1939. Birds as animals. London and Toronto. W. Heinemann.

Fleming, James H. 1901. A list of the birds of the districts of Parry Sound and Muskoka, Ontario. *Auk,* 18 (1): 36.

Forbush, Edward Howe. 1912. A history of the Game Birds, Wild-Fowl, and Shore-Birds of Massachusetts and adjacent states. Boston, Mass., State Board of Agriculture.

_____. 1925. Birds of Massachusetts and other New England States. Mass. Dept. of Agric. Vol. 1.

Ford, Edward R. 1936. Birds of the Chicago region. *Chi. Acad. Sci. Spec. Publ. No. 12.*

Ford, E. R., C. C. Sanborn, and C. B. Coursen. 1934. Birds of the Chicago region. *Pro. Act. Chi. Acad. Sci.,* 5 (2-3): 18-80.

Forest and Stream. 1881. An intelligent Crane. 16 (4): 67.

Fuertes, Louis Agassiz. 1923. Whooping Crane in Nebraska. *Auk,* 40 (1): 121.

G. M. 1876. The Game birds of Manitoba. *Forest and Stream,* 6 (14): 212-213.

Gabrielson, Ira N. 1917. A list of birds observed in Clay and O'Brien counties, Iowa. *Proc. Iowa Acad. Sci.,* 24: 264.

_____. 1943. Wildlife Refuges. New York, Macmillan Co.

Gabrielson, Ira N., and Stanley G. Jewett. 1940. Birds of Oregon. Oregon State Coll., Corvallis.

Gabrielson, Ira N., *et al.* 1950. Report of the A. O. U. Committee on Bird Protection, 1949. *Auk,* 67 (3): 321-322; 1954, 71: 186-190; 1956 (1955 Report), 73: 119-123; 1957 (1956 Report), 74: 90-93.

Gammell, Ann M. 1957. Regional reports, Northern Great Plains. *Audubon Field Notes,* 11: 34-35; 1960, 14: 397-398.

Gammell, Ann M., and Robert T. Gammell. 1953. Regional reports, Northern Great Plains. *Audubon Field Notes,* 7: 23-24.

Gammell, Ann M., Robert T. Gammell, and Howard S. Huenecke. 1954. Regional reports. Northern Great Plains. *Audubon Field Notes,* 8: 319-320.

Gammell, Ann M., and Howard S. Huenecke. 1955. Regional reports. Northern Great Plains. *Audubon Field Notes,* 8:34-36; 1956, 10: 32-37.

Gillese, John P. 1948. I shot a Whooping Crane. *Forest and Outdoors,* 44 (9): 29.

Giraud, Jacob P., Jr. 1844. The birds of Long Island. New York, Wiley and Putnam.

Glandon, Mr. and Mrs. Earl W. 1934. Notes on some Logan County birds. *Nebr. Bird Review,* 2 (2): 31-36.

Glisan, Rodney. 1874. Journal of Army life. San Francisco. A. L. Bancroft and Co.

Godfrey, Earl W. 1964. Review of Paul Hahn's book "Where is that vanished bird." *Canadian Field-Naturalist,* 78: 193-194.

_____. 1966. The birds of Canada. *Natl. Mus. Canada Bull. No. 203. Biol. Ser. No. 73,* Queen's Printer, Ottawa.

Goldman, Luther C. 1954. Regional reports, Southern Texas. *Audubon Field Notes,* 8 (1): 28-32.

Goldman, Luther C., and Frank G. Watson. 1953. Regional reports, Southern Texas. *Audubon Field Notes,* 7 (1): 39-40, (3): 223-224, (4): 282-285.

Golsan, L. S., and E. G. Holt. 1914. Birds of Autauga and Montgomery counties, Alabama. *Auk,* 31 (2): 218.

Goodrich, Arthur L., Jr. 1946. Birds of Kansas. *Kansas State Board Agric.,* Topeka. 64: 267: 190.

Gottschalk, John. 1968. U. S. Fish and Wildlife Service, Bureau of Sport Fisheries and Wildlife, release, 8 February 1968.

Gowanlock, James Nelson. 1939. Vanished Americans. *Louisiana Conservation Review,* 8 (1): 49.

Graham, Edward H. 1947. The Land and Wildlife. New York, Oxford Univ. Press.

Grave, B. H., and Ernest P. Walker. 1913. The birds of Wyoming. Laramie, Univ. of Wyoming.

Green, Dave. 1961. Whooping Crane monument. *Blue Jay,* 19 (2): 75.

Greene Smith Museum (Peterboro, N. Y.). 1881. Catalogue of birds, eggs, and nests. Morrisville, N. Y. Madison Observer offce.

Griffin, William W., and Annette McLean. 1957. A Whooping Crane from Macon (Ga.). *Oriole,* 22: 30.

Grinnell, George Bird. 1917. Dr. Grinnell writes of Native Cranes. *Bull. Am. Game Prot. and Prop. Assoc.,* 6 (1): 9-10.

Grinnell, Joseph. 1900. Birds of Kotzebue Sound region, Alaska. Cooper Ornith. Club of Calif., *Pacific Coast Avifauna,* No. 1.

Grinnell, Joseph, and Alden H. Miller. 1944. The distribution of the birds of California. *Cooper Ornith. Club. Pacific Coast Avifauna,* No. 27.

Griscom, Ludlow, and M. S. Crosby. 1925. Birds of the Brownsville region, southern Texas. *Auk,* 42 (4): 437, (4): 519-537.

Griswold, J. A. 1962. Proven methods of keeping and rearing Cranes in captivity. *Spec. Rept. International Wild Waterfowl Association, Inc.* 18 pp., illus. July 1962.

----. 1964. Raising Cranes in captivity. *America's first Zoo,* 14: 28.

Gunter, Gordon. 1938. The common blue crab in fresh waters. *Science,* 87: 2248: 87-88.

----. 1943. Remarks on the American bison in Louisiana. *J. Mammalogy,* 24 (3): 398-399.

----. 1943. Remarks on the American bison in Louisiana. *J. Mammlogy,* 24 (3): 398-399.

_____. 1945. Studies on marine fishes of Texas. *Pub. Inst. Marine Sci.,* 1: 1.

_____. 1947. Paleoecological import of certain relationships of marine animals to salinity. *J. Paleontology,* 21 (1): 77-79.

. 1950. Distribution and abundance of fishes on the Aransas National Wildlife Refuge . . . . *Publ. Inst. Marine Sci.,* 1 (2): 89-101.

_____. 1950b. Seasonal population changes and distributions . . . of the Texas Coast . . . . *Publ. Inst. Marine Sci.,* 1 (2): 7-51.

Gurney, J. H. 1921. Early annals of Ornithology. London, Witherby.

Gutherie, J. E. 1932. Snakes versus birds, Birds versus snakes. *Wilson Bulletin,* 44 (2): 88-113.

Hall, F. S. 1933. Studies in the history of Ornithology in the state of Washington (1792-1932) . . . . *Murrelet,* 14 (3): 70.

Harris, Harry. 1919. Birds of the Kansas City Region. *Trans. Acad. Sci. of St. Louis,* 23 (8): 244, 339.

Hatch, David R. M. 1966. Regional reports, Northern Great Plains. *Audubon Field Notes,* 20 (1): 61-64, (4): 519-522; 1968, 22 (1): 54-57, (4): 544-547; 1969, 23 (1): 70-74.

Hatch, P. L. 1892. Notes on the birds of Minnesota. Minn. Geol. and Nat. Hist. Surv. Zool. Ser. 1, Minneapolis.

Hearne, Samuel. 1795. Journey from Prince of Wales' Fort . . . 1769, 1770, 1771 & 1772. London, printed for A. Strahan and T. Caddell and sold by T. Caddell, Jun. and W. Davis.

Hedgpeth, Joel W. 1950. Notes on the marine invertebrate fauna of Salt Flat areas in Aransas National Wildlife Refuge, Texas. *Publ. Inst. Marine Sci.,* 1: 2.

Henniger, W. P. 1902. A preliminary list of the birds of Middle southern Ohio. *Wilson Bulletin,* 9 (3): 81.

Henry, Thomas Charlton. 1859. Catalogue of the birds of New Mexico . . . *Proc. Acad. Nat. Sci., Phila.,* 11: 108.

Henshaw, Henry W. 1915. American Game Birds. *National Geographic Magazine,* 28 (2): 122-123.

Hersey, L. J., and R. B. Rockwell. 1909. An annotated list of the birds of the Barr Lake District, Adams Co., Colorado. *Condor,* 11 (4): 114.

Hewitt, C. Gordon. 1921. The conservation of wildlife of Canada. New York, Scribner.

Hibbard, Edmund A. 1956. An old nesting record for the Whooping Crane in North Dakota. *Wilson Bulletin*, 68 (1): 73-74.

Hind, Henry Youle. 1860. Narrative of the Canadian Red River Exploring Expedition of 1847 and of the Assinboine and Saskatchewan Exploration of 1858. London, Longman, Green, Longman and Roberts.

Hoffman, W. J. 1882. List of birds observed at Fort Berthold, Dakota Territory during the month of September 1881. *Proc. Boston Soc. Nat. Hist.*, 2: 404.

Holmes, Charles F. 1945. A 1936 record of the Whooping Crane. *Canadian Field-Naturalist*, 59 (2): 69.

Hooey, George. 1950. Whooping Crane. *Blue Jay*, 8 (1): 8.

Hopkins, Sewell H. 1942. The crab fishery . . . . *Texas Game and Fish*, reprinted from the Feb. issue.

Hornaday, William T. 1913. Our vanishing wild life. N. Y. Zool. Society.

Hough, E. 1895. Round Rockport way in Texas. *Forest and Stream*, 44 (19): 366-367.

Houston, C. Stuart. 1947. *Blue Jay*, 6 (1): 4-5.

———. 1949. The birds of the Yorkton District, Saskatchewan. *Canadian Field-Naturalist*, 63 (6): 215-241.

Houston, C. Stuart, and Maurice F. Street. 1959. The Birds of the Saskatchewan River. Spec. Publ. No. 2, Sask. Nat. Hist. Soc.

Howard, Hildegarde. 1930. A census of the Pleistocene birds of Rancho la Brea from the Collections of the Los Angeles Museum. *Condor*, 32 (2): 81-88.

Howell, Arthur H. 1911. Birds of Arkansas. *U. S. Biol. Surv. Bull.* 38.

———. 1928. Birds of Alabama. Dept. of Game and Fisheries, Montgomery.

———. 1932. Florida Bird Life. Florida Dept. of Game and Fresh Water Fish, Tallahasee.

Hoy, Philo Romayne. 1844. (An account of the former and present status of 26 species). *Racine Advocate*, June 4, 1844.

———. 1864. Journal of an Exploration of western Missouri in 1854. *Ann. Rept. Smithsonian Inst. for 1864*, pp. 437-438.

———. 1874. Some of the peculiarities of the Fauna near Racine. *Trans. Wis. Acad. Sci.*, 2: 120-122.

———. 1885. Man's influence on the avifauna of southeastern Wisconsin. *Proc. Wis. Nat. Hist. Soc.*, March (1885): 4-9.

———. 1886. (Record of Whooping Crane shot in Nebraska and mounted by Hoy). *Racine Journal*, April 21, 1886.

Hubbard, William. 1630. General history of New England from the discovery to MDCXXX. *Coll. Mass. Hist. Soc.*, ser. 6: 672.

Hunter, J. S. 1900. The bird fauna of the Salt Basin near Lincoln. *Proc. Nebr. Ornith. Union*, for 1st meeting, 1899, p. 20.

Huntington, Dwight W. 1911. Our feathered game. New York, Scribner.

Imhof, Thomas A. 1962. Alabama birds. Ala. Dept. of Cons., Game and Fish. Div., Univ. Ala. Press.

Imler, Ralph H. 1936. An annotated list of the birds of Rooks County, Kansas, and vicinity. *Trans. Kans. Acad. Sci.*, No. 39, p. 301.

Ingersoll, A. M. 1887. Eggs! Eggs!! Eggs!!! (Classified Advertisement). *Oologist* (4): nos. 3-4.

Isley, Dwight. 1912. A list of the birds of Sedgwick County, Kansas. *Auk*, 29 (1): 40.

J. F. L. 1887. Whooping Cranes. *Forest and Stream*, 28 (2): 27.

Jackson, H. H. T. 1946. Conserving endangered wildlife species. *Ann. Rept. Smithsonian Inst. for 1945*, p. 261.

James, Edwin. 1823. Account of an expedition . . . in the years 1819, 1820 . . . . London, printed for Longman, Hurst, Rees, Orme, and Brown.

Job, Herbert K. 1923. Propagation of wild birds. New York, Garden City, Doubleday.

Johonnot, James. 1885. Neighbors with wings and fins and some others. New York, D. Appleton.

Jones, Joe. 1946. Letters. *Audubon Magazine*, 50 (5): 321.

Jouy, P. L. 1894. Notes on birds of central Mexico . . . . *Proc. U. S. Natl. Mus.*, 16: 771-795.

Judd, Elmer T. 1891. Dakota Game Birds. *Forest and Stream*, 36 (9): 169.

———. 1917. List of North Dakota birds . . . 1890 to 1896 . . . . Cando, N. D. Author.

Kalmbach, E. R. 1942. Whooping Cranes in eastern Colorado. *Auk*, 59 (2): 307.

Kalmbach, E. R., *et al.* 1960. Report to the American Ornithologists' Union by the Committee on Bird Protection, 1959. *Auk*, 77 (1): 73-77.

Kellogg, Vernon L. 1900. A list of the biting lice (*Mellophaga*) taken from birds and mammals of North America. *Proc. U. S. Natl. Mus.*, 22: 1183: 72,86.

Kelsey, Carl. 1891. Birds of Poweshiek County, Iowa. *Ornith. and Oologist*, 16 (9): 131.

Kelsall, John P. 1966. Additional bird observations at Bathurst Inlet, N. W. T. *Canadian Field-Naturalist*, 80 (3): 179.

Kemsies, Emerson. 1930. Birds of Yellowstone National Park, with some recent additions. *Wilson Bulletin*, 42 (3): 198-210.

———. 1935. Changes in the list of birds of Yellowstone National Park. *Wilson Bulletin*, 47 (1): 68-70.

Kennedy, John P. 1934. The Whooping Crane in Nebraska in forty years of observations. *Nebr. Bird Review*, 2 (4): 117.

Kennicott, Robert. 1853-54. *Transactions of the Illinois State Agricultural Society*, 1: 587.

Keyes, C. R., and H. S. Williams. 1888. Preliminary annotated catalogue of the birds of Iowa. *Proc. Davenport Acad. Nat. Sci. Pub. Mus.*, Vol. 5.

Kimball, H. H. 1923. Bird notes from Arizona and California. *Condor*. 25 (3): 109.

King, Richard. 1836. Narrative of a journey to the shores of the Arctic Ocean in 1833, 1834 and 1835. Vol. 2, London, Richard and Bentley.

Kingsley, F. R. 1935. Whooping Cranes in Kearney County, Nebraska. *Nebr. Bird Review*, 3 (2): 57.

———. 1935b. More Whooping Cranes seen in Kearney County, Nebraska. *Nebr. Bird Review*, 3 (3): 84.

———. 1937. The Whooping Crane in northeastern Gosper County. *Nebr. Bird Rev.*, 5 (3): 57-58.

Kiracofe, Jack. 1969. Whooping Crane eggs hatch. *Modern Game Breeding*, 5 (9): 21.

Knight, Wilbur C. 1902. The birds of Wyoming. *Wyo. Agr. Exp. Sta.*, Laramie, Bull. 55.

Knoder, C. Eugene. 1965. Reported use of anesthetic for Cranes— Equisthesin 14 cc intravenous. Whooping Crane conference, Washington, D. C., 9 March 1965.

Knowlton, Frank H. 1909. Birds of the World. New York, Holt.

Krider, John. 1873. Game in season for November. *Forest and Stream*, 1 (15): 235.

———. 1879. Forty years' notes of a field ornithologist. Philadelphia, Jos. H. Weston.

Krause, Herbert. 1958. Regional Reports, Northern Great Plains. *Audubon Field Notes*, 12 (3): 362-364; 1959, 13 (1): 41-43; 1961, 15 (1): 51-54.

Kumlien, L. 1879. Contributions to the natural history of Arctic America. *U. S. Natl. Mus. Bull.* 15.

Kumlien, L., and N. Hollister. 1903. The birds of Wisconsin. *Bull. Wis. Nat. Soc.*, Vol. 3 (new ser.), 1, 2, 3.

———. 1948. The birds of Wisconsin. *Passenger Pigeon*, 10 (3): 107-113 (in part) (with revisions by A. W. Schorger).

Lahrman, F. W. 1957. Aggressive behavior of Whooping Crane. *Blue Jay*, 15 (1): 14-15.

———. 1959. Whooping Cranes dance during migration. *Blue Jay*, 17 (3): 91-93.

Lahrman, Fred W., and Lorne Scott. 1969. Whooping Crane at Glaslyn, Saskatchewan, 1969. *Blue Jay*, 27: 213.

Langdon, Frank W. 1877. A catalogue of the birds of the vicinity of Cincinnati, with notes. Salem, Mass., The Naturalists' Agency.

Langille, J. Hibbert. 1884. Our birds and their haunts. Boston, S. E. Casino and Co.

Lantz, David E. 1896-97. Review of Kansas Ornithology. *Proc. Kan. Acad. Sci.*, 16 : 224-376.

_____. 1907. An economic study of the field mice (Genus *Microtus*). *U. S. Biol. Surv. Bull. 31*, p. 53.

Larson, Adrian. 1907. A preliminary list of the birds of western Lyman County, South Dakota. *Wilson Bulletin*, 19 (3): 114.

_____. 1925. The birds of Sioux Falls, S. D., and vicinity. *Wilson Bulletin*, 37 (1): 24.

Latham, J. 1824. General History of birds. Vol. 9, Winchester, author.

Latrobe, Charles J. 1836. The rambler in North America. 2nd ed. London, Seeley and Burnside.

Lawson, John. 1709. The history of Carolina, containing the exact description and natural history of that country. Raleigh, N. C., printed by Strother and Marcom (1860).

Lewis, Harrison F. 1946. Management of Canada's wildlife resources. *Trans. 11th N. Amer. Wildlife Conference.*

Lewis, Meriwether. 1804-05-06. History of the expedition . . . performed during the years 1804-05-06. New ed. with copious notes by E. Coues. New York, Harper (1893).

Lewis, Walter E. 1930. Water birds on dry land. *Wilson Bulletin*, 42 (1): 36-44.

Licking, Clyde L. 1940. The 1939 spring flight of migratory birds in Nebraska. *Nebr. Bird Review*, 8 (1): 10, 11.

Lister, Robert. 1964. Regional reports, Northern Great Plains. *Audubon Field Notes*, 18 (4): 460-464; 19 (1): 53.

Lloyd, Hoyes. 1922. . . . observations on the birds of Baffin Island and vicinity. *Canadian Field-Naturalist*, 36 (3): 49-50.

Lloyd, William. 1887. Birds of Tom Green and Concho Counties, Texas. *Auk*, 4 (3): 185.

Long, W. S. 1940. Check-list of Kansas birds. *Trans. Kan. Acad. Sci.* 43: 441.

Louisiana Dept. of Conservation. 1914-1916. Report of the Conservation Commission of Louisiana, p. 19.

_____. 1921. Wildlife resources of Louisiana; their nature, value, and protection. New Orleans. Bull. 10, 151-152.

Ludlow, Charles S. 1935. A Quarter century of spring bird migration records at Red Cloud, Nebraska. *Nebr. Bird Rev.* 3 (1): 3-25.

McAtee, Waldo Lee. 1923. Local names of migratory game birds. *U. S. Dept. Agr. Miscel. Circ. No. 13.*

_____. 1955. Folk names of Florida birds. Part 2. *Florida Naturalist*, 28 (3): 83-91.

McCall, George A. 1851. Some remarks on the habits, etc. of birds met with in western Texas . . . . *Proc. Acad. Nat. Sci., Phila.*, 5: 223.

McCaskie, Guy. 1969. Regional Reports, Southern Pacific Coast. *Audubon Field Notes*, 23 (1): 106-112.

McChesney, Charles E. 1877. Birds of the Coteau des Prairies of eastern Dakota. *Forest and Stream*, 8 (16): 241.

_____. 1879. Notes on the birds of Fort Sisseton, Dakota Territory. Extracted from *Bull. U. S. Geol. and Geog. Survey*, 5 (1): 94.

McCollum, C. 1884. Wisconsin birds. *Young Oologist*, 1 (6): 93.

McCoy, J. J. 1966. The hunt for the Whooping Cranes. New York, Lothrop, Lee & Shephard Co.

McCreary, Otto. 1937. Wyoming birds life. Minneapolis, Burgess Publ. Co.

MacFarlane, R. R. 1891. Notes on and list of birds and eggs collected in Arctic America, 1861-1866. *Proc. U. S. Natl. Mus.*, 14: 413-466.

McIlhenny, Edward Avery. 1938. Whooping Crane in Louisiana. *Auk*, 55 (4): 670.

_____. 1943. Major changes in the bird life of southern Louisiana during sixty years. *Auk*, 60 (4): 541-549.

McIlwraith, Thomas. 1894. The birds of Ontario. Toronto, Wm. Briggs.

MacKay, R. H. 1963. Release, Canadian Wildlife Service, Results of Whooping Crane aerial survey, 5 Sept. 1963.

McNulty, Faith. 1966. Reporter at large: wild and captive Whooping Cranes. *New Yorker*, 42: 31-36.

_____. 1966b. The Whooping Crane. New York, E. P. Dutton.

_____. 1966c. (Review) Whooping Crane. *Time*, 88: 126-.

Macoun, John. 1882. Manitoba and the Great North-west. Guelph, Ontario, World Publ. Co.

_____. 1900. Catalogue of Canadian birds. Part 1. Ottawa. (Can. Geol. Surv.).

Mair, Charles, and R. R. MacFarlane. 1908. Through the Mackenzie Basin. Toronto, Wm. Briggs.

Mann, William M. 1938. Wild animals in and out of the Zoo. New York. Smithsonian Inst. Ser. 6.

Maynard, C. J. 1896. The birds of eastern North America, ... Rev. ed. Newtonville, Mass., C. J. Maynard.

Mayr, Ernst. 1942. Systematics and the origin of species. New York, Columbia Univ. Press.

Merriam, Clinton Hart. 1891. Results of the Biological Reconnoissance of south-central Idaho. *U. S. Bureau of Biol. Surv. N. A. Fauna No. 5.*

Mershon, William B. 1923. Recollections of my fifty years hunting and fishing. Boston, Stratford.

_____. 1928. Whooping Crane in Saskatchewan. *Auk* 45 (2): 202-203.

_____. 1934. A recent and former occurrence of the Whooping Crane in Saskatchewan and North Dakota. *Nebr. Bird Rev.*, 2 (2): 39

Miller, A. H., and C. G. Sibley. 1942. A new species of Crane from the Pliocene of California. *Condor*, 44 (3): 126-127.

Miller, Leah R. 1951. Stockbridge Chapter, North East District. *Indiana Audubon Quarterly*, 29 (3): 49.

Miller, Loye. 1925. The birds of Rancho la Brea. Carnegie Inst. Washington Publ. 349: 63-106.

_____. 1944. Some Pliocene birds from Oregon and Idaho. *Condor*, 46 (1): 26, 30.

Miller, Loye, and I. DeMay. 1942. The Fossil birds of California . . . . *Univ. Calif. Publ.* 47 (4): 109.

Mills, Harlow B., and Frank C. Bellrose. 1959. Whooping Crane in Mid-west. *Auk*, 76: 234-235.

Mitchell, H. Hedley. 1924. Birds of Saskatchewan. *Canadian Field-Naturalist*, 38 (6): 101-118.

Moody, A. F. 1931. Death of an American Whooping Crane. *Avicultural Magazine*, 4th ser., 9 (1): 8-11.

Moos, Louis L. 1937. Interesting records of birds of western South Dakota. *Journ. Minn. Ornith.*, 1 (2): 11-12.

Morrison, Charles F. 1888. A list of the birds of Colorado. *Ornith. and Oologist*, 13 (11): 166.

Mowat, Farley M., and Andrew H. Lawrie. 1955. Bird observations from southern Keewatin and the interior of Northern Manitoba. *Canadian Field-Naturalist*, 69 (3): 93-116.

Mumford, Russell E. 1959. Regional Reports, Middlewestern Prairie. *Audubon Field Notes*, 13 (1): 33-37.

Nauman, E. D. 1931. Birds of early Iowa. *Iowa Bird Life*, 1: 3-4.

Nehrling, H. 1882. List of birds observed at Houston, Harris County, Texas . . . . *Bull. Nuttall Ornith. Club*, 7 (3): 223.

Nelson, E. W. 1876. Birds of Northeastern Illinois. *Bull. Essex Inst.*, 8: 90-155; 1877, 8:9-12, 133.

_____. 1929. The Whooping Crane continues to visit Louisiana. *Condor*, 3 (4): 146-147.

Nero, Robert W. 1961. Regional Reports, Northern Great Plains. *Audubon Field Notes*, 15 (4): 419-422; 1962, 16 (1): 47-50, (4): 423-426; 1963, 17 (1): 40-44.

Newcombe, Curtis L. 1945. The biology and conservation of the blue crab, *Callinectes sapidus* Rathbun. *Educ. Ser. No. 4.* William and Mary College, Fisheries Lab. and Va. Comm. of Fisheries, Richmond.

New Jersey State Museum, Trenton. 1903. Annual report (list of the birds of N. J.), p. 66 (1904).

Nice, Margaret Morse. 1931. Birds of Oklahoma, rev. ed. *Univ. Okla. Biol. Surv.*, Vol. III, No. 1, pp. 1-224.

Novakowski, N. S. 1965. The day we rescued a Whooping Crane. *Audubon Magazine*, 67 (4): 230-233.

_____. 1966. Whooping Crane population dynamics on the nesting grounds . . . . *Canadian Wildlife Service Report Series, No. 1*, 20 pp., illus.

Nuttall, Thomas. 1834. A manual of the ornithology of the United States and of Canada. Water Birds. Boston, Hilliard and Brown.

Nutting, C. C. 1893. Report on zoological explorations on the Lower Saskatchewan River. *Bull. Lab. Nat. Hist.*, Iowa State Univ., 2: 235-293.

Oberholser, Harry C. 1938. The bird life of Louisiana. *La. Dept. of Cons. Bull. 28.*

Oberholser, Harry C., and W. L. McAtee. 1920. Waterfowl and their food plants in the Sandhill Region of Nebraska. *U. S. Dept. Agr. Bull.* 794: 28.

Oliver, S. W. 1948. A Whooping Crane named Bill. *Audubon Magazine*, 50 (4): 226-231; 1949, 51 (6): 403.

Ornithologist and Oologist. 1890. A list of the birds of Minnesota. 15 (9): 130.

Palmer, Theodore Sherman. 1902. Legislation for the protection of birds other than Game Birds. *U. S. Bur. of Biol. Surv. Bull. 12.* rev. ed., p. 22.

Parker, H. W. 1871. Iowa birds. *American Naturalist*, 5 (3): 169.

Pearson, Thomas Gilbert. 1922. Whooping Cranes (*Grus americana*) in Texas. *Auk*, 39 (3): 412-413.

_____. 1932. Notes on some extinct, rare and vanishing birds. *Maryland Conservationist*, 9 (4): 9.

Peters, James Lee. 1934. Check-list of the birds of the World. Vol. 2. Cambridge, Harvard Univ. Press.

Peterson, Roger Tory. 1948. Birds over America. New York, Dodd Mead.

Pettingill, Olin Sewall, Jr. 1947. Progress report on the Whooping Crane. Abstract. Paper given at 28th Annual Meeting. Wilson Orn. Soc. *Wilson Bulletin*, 59: 62.

Phillips, John Charles. 1912. Wintering Cranes in New England. *Avicultural Magazine*, 3rd ser., 3 (8): 222-224.

_____. The Whooping Crane. *Avicultural Magazine*, 3rd ser., 3 (1): 288.

_____. An attempt to list the extinct and vanishing birds of the Western Hemisphere . . . . Reprinted from *Proc. VI Internat. Ornith. Cong.*, p. 510, Copenhagen.

Picket, . 1883. The Whooping Crane. *Forest and Stream*, 21 (21): 407.

Pindar, J. Otley. 1887. A list of the birds of Fulton County, Ky. *Ornith. and Oologist*, 12 (4): 55.

_____. 1924. Winter birds of eastern Arkansas. *Wilson Bulletin*, 36 (4): 204.

_____. 1925. Birds of Fulton County, Ky. *Wilson Bulletin*, 37 (2): 77-88.

Pittman, H. H. 1957. Saving the Cranes. *Blue Jay*, 15 (2): 58-59.

Porsild, A. E. 1943. Birds of the Mackenzie Delta. *Canadian Field-Naturalist*, 57 (2 & 3): 19-35.

Pough, Richard H. 1952. Bird protection in the United States. *Passenger Pigeon*, 14 (4): 141-148.

Pratt, Jerome J. 1961. Transactions of the Whooping Crane Cons. Conf. *Modern Game Breeding*, April.

_____. 1962. News items. Whooping Crane. Whooping Crane Cons. Assoc. Items, Dec.; 1963, Dec.

_____. 1964. Whooping Crane Cons. assoc. News Items, March, May, June, Dec.

_____. 1964b. *Newsletter No. 8, Sask. Nat. Hist. Soc.* 1.

_____. 1965. Whooping Crane Cons. Assoc., Spec. Bull., Jan.

_____. 1967. Fred Stark. *Grus Americana*, 6 (4): 1.

_____. 1968. Whooper shot. *Grus Americana*, 7 (1): 1.

_____. 1969. Migration (Whooping Crane). *Grus Americana*, 8 (2): 2.

Preble, Edward A. 1902. A biological investigation of the Hudson Bay region. *U. S. Bur. of Biol. Surv., N. Amer. Fauna No. 22.*

_____. 1908. A biological investigation of the Athabaska-Mackenzie region. *U. S. Bur. of Biol. Surv., N. Amer. Fauna No. 27.*

Preston, J. W. 1886. My first White Crane's nest. *Oologist*, 3 (4): 43-44.

_____. 1893. Some prairie birds. *Ornith. and Oologist*, 18 (6): 81.

Raine, Walter. 1892. Bird-nesting in North West Canada. Toronto, printed by Hunter, Rose and Co.

Rapp, William F., Jr. 1954. Status of cranes in Nebraska. *Wilson Bulletin*, 66: 218-219.

Reagan, Albert B. 1908. The birds of the Rosebud Indian Reservation, S. D. *Auk*, 25 (4): 463.

Red Triangle. 1949. Conoco turns an ear to the plight of the rare Whooping Crane. March.

Reed, Chester Albert. 1904. North American birds' eggs. New York, Doubleday, Page.

Reid, Russell. 1946. The Whooping Crane. *N. Dak. Outdoors*, 8 (10): 12-13.

Reynolds, D. L. 1959. A Whooping Crane in northwest Missouri. *Audubon Magazine*, 61: 32-33.

Rice, Dale W. 1949. In quest of the Whooping Crane. *Yearbook of the Indiana Audubon Society*, 27: 14-17.

Richardson, Sir John, and W. Swainson. 1831. Fauna Boreali-Americana, or the zoology of the northern parts of British America. 2: 372. London, Murray.

Ridgway, Robert. 1873. Birds of Colorado. *Bull. Essex Inst.*, 5 (11): 177.

_____. 1877. Ornithology. In Clarence King's report of the Geological exploration of the 40th Parallel. *U. S. Army Eng. Dept. Prof. Papers No. 18*, Vol. 4, Pt. 3: 303-643, 652-669.

_____. 1895. The ornithology of Illinois. *Ill. Lab. Nat. Hist.*, Vol. 2. Springfield, H. W. Rokker, Printer.

_____. 1915. Bird-life in southern Illinois. Pt. IV. Changes which have taken place in half a century. *Bird-Lore*, 15 (3): 192, 195.

Ridgway, Robert, and Herbert Friedmann. 1941. The birds of North and Middle America. *U. S. Natl. Mus. Bull. 50*, Pt. 9.

Roberts, Thomas Sadler. 1880. The convolutions of the trachea in the Sandhill and Whooping Cranes. *American Naturalist*, 14: 108-114.

_____. 1919. Water birds of Minnesota, past and present. *Minn. Game and Fish Comm., Bienn. Report, Period ending July 31, 1918.* pp. 70-71.

_____. 1919b. A Review of the ornithology of Minnesota. *Research Public. Univ. Minn.*, 7:31.

_____. 1932. The birds of Minnesota. Vol. 1, Univ. of Minn. Press, Minneapolis; 1936, 2nd rev. ed., Vol. 1.

Roberts, Thomas Sadler, and F. Benner. 1880. A contribution to the ornithology of Minnesota. *Bull. Nuttall Ornith. Club*, 5 (1): 19.

Robinson, Thane S. 1953. Whooping Cranes in Kansas in 1952. *Wilson Bulletin*, 65: 211.

Rolfe, Eugene S. 1896. The passing of species. *Oologist*, 13 (5): 42-44.

Ronning, Rudolph. 1966. Whooping Cranes in 1938. *Blue Jay*, 24 (2): 100.

Rooke, R. P. 1947. Bird life in the Yorkton district in the 1890's. *Blue Jay*, 5 (3 and 4): 26-27.

Ross, Alexander Milton. 1872. The birds of Canada. Toronto, Rosswell and Hutchinson.

Ross, Bernard Rogan. 1862. On the mammals, birds. etc. of the Mackenzie River District. *Nat. Hist. Rev.*, 2nd ser. 2: 284.

_____. 1942. Letter to Spencer Fullerton Baird, 26 Nov. 1859. *Canadian Field-Naturalist*, 56: 120-121.

Salt, W. Ray, and A. L. Wilk. 1966. The birds of Alberta. rev. ed. The Queen's Printer, Edmonton.

Salvin, Osbert, and F. D. Godman. 1903. Biologia Centrali-Americana. *Aves*, 3. London, Taylor and Francis.

Saunders, Aretas A. 1921. A distributional list of the birds of Montana. Cooper Ornith. Club of California. *Pacific Coast Avifauna*, No. 14.

Saunders, W. E. 1910. Birds of central Alberta. *Auk*, 27 (1): 89.

_____. 1910b. Birds of Alberta. *Ottawa Nat.*, 24: 21-22.

Schaars, H. W. 1959. The origin of the common names of Wisconsin birds. *Passenger Pigeon*, 11 (4): 143-154.

362

Schorger, A. W. 1944. Philo Romayne Hoy; Wisconsin's greatest pioneer zoologist. *Passenger Pigeon*, 6 (3): 55-59.

_____. 1944b. Benjamin Franklin Goss. *Passenger Pigeon*, 6 (4): 85.

Sennett, George B. 1878. Notes on the Ornithology of the Lower Rio Grande, Texas . . . 1877. *Bull. U. S. Geol. and Geog. Surv. of the Terr.*, 4 (1): 61.

_____. 1879. Further notes on the ornithology of the Lower Rio Grande of Texas . . . 1878. *Bull. U. S. Geol. and Geog. Surv. of the Terr.*, 5: 371-440.

Seton, Ernest Thompson. 1886. The birds of western Manitoba. *Auk*, 3 (2): 150.

_____. 1891. The birds of Manitoba. *Proc. U. S. Natl. Mus.*, 13: 841: 457-643.

_____. 1911. The Arctic prairies. New York, Scribner.

_____. 1940. Trail of an Artist-Naturalist. The Autobiography of Ernest Thompson Seton. New York, Scribner.

Shields, Robert H., and Earl L. Benham. 1968. Migratory behavior of Whooping Cranes. *Auk*, 85: 318.

Shufeldt, R. W. 1894. On the Osteology of certain Cranes . . . . *J. Anat. and Phys.*, 29 (21): 29, 31.

Simmons, Albert Dixon. 1937. Letter. *Bird-Lore*, 39 (3): 220.

_____. 1937b. A Trumpeter of the marshlands. *Nature Magazine*, 30 (3): 142-143.

Simmons, George Finlay. 1925. Birds of the Austin region. Austin, University of Texas.

Smith, H. R., and P. W. Parmalee. 1955. A distributional check list of the birds of Illinois. *Ill. State Mus. Pop. Sci. Ser.*, 1-62.

Smith, Robert H., and Robert P. Allen. 1948. An aerial waterfowl reconnaissance in the Far North. *U. S. Fish and Wildlife Service, Spec. Scientific Report No. 60*, pp. 5-12.

Smith, Robert H., and Everett L. Sutton. 1952. Breeding grounds located. *Blue Jay*, 10 (3): 24.

Snow, Francis Huntington. 1875. A catalogue of the birds of Kansas, 3rd ed. Kansas City, author.

_____. 1903. Notes on the birds of Kansas and a revised catalogue, 5th ed. *Trans. Kansas Acad. Sci.*, 18: 154-176.

Soper, J. Dewey. 1921. Gleanings from the Canadian west. Pt. 1. Avian fauna of Islay, Alberta. *Canadian Field-Naturalist*, 25: 50-54.

_____. 1928. A faunal investigation of southern Baffin Island. *Bull. Natl. Mus. Canada*, p. 95.

Sprunt, Alexander, Jr. 1929. The White legions. *Nature Magazine*, 14 (3): 168-170.

_____. 1941. Wings along the coast of Texas. *Audubon Magazine*, 45 (3): 243-244.

_____. 1945. The Vanished legions. *Audubon Magazine*, 47 (3): 130-133.

_____. 1954. Florida bird life. Coward-McCann, New York.

Spurrell, J. A. 1917. Annotated list of water birds, game birds and birds of prey of Sac County, Iowa. *Wilson Bulletin*, 29 (3): 152-153.

Stansell, Sidney S. S. 1909. Birds of central Alberta. *Auk*, 26 (4): 392.

Stearns, R. E. C. 1869. Rambles in Florida. *American Naturalist*, 3 (8): 401.

Stephens, T. C. 1943. Early bird life in Clay County, Iowa. *Iowa Bird Life*, 13 (4): 65.

_____. 1944. The makers of ornithology in north-western Iowa. *Iowa Bird Life*, 14 (2): 25.

Stevenson, James Osborne. 1942. Whooping Cranes in Texas in summer. *Condor*, 44 (1): 40-41.

_____. 1943. Will bugles blow no more? *Audubon Magazine*, 45 (3): 134-139.

_____. 1943b. Will bugles blow no more? *Texas Game and Fish*, 1 (11): 5, 17-19.

_____. 1946. An old account of the Whooping Crane in Nebraska. *Nebr. Bird Rev.*, 14 (1): 21-22.

Stevenson, James Osborne, and R. E. Griffith. 1946. Winter life of the Whooping Crane. *Condor*, 48 (4): 160-178.

Stillwell, Jerry Edward. 1939. Check list of the birds of Dallas County, Texas, 3rd ed. Dallas, printed by Boyd Printing Co.

Stone, Witmer. 1894. The birds of eastern Pennsylvania and New Jersey. Philadelphia, Del. Ornith. Club.

_____. 1908. The birds of New Jersey. *N. J. State Mus. Ann. Rept.* Pt. 1, pp. 108-109.

_____. 1937. Bird studies at old Cape May. *Del. Valley Ornith. Club*, Phila.

Strecker, John K., Jr. 1912. The birds of Texas. *Baylor Univ. Bull.*, 15 (1): 18.

_____. 1927. Notes on the ornithology of McLennan County, Texas. *Baylor Univ. Spec. Bull.*, 1: 27.

Street, Maurice. 1943. A list of the birds of Nipawin, Sask. Contribution No. 2 of Yorkton Nat. Hist. Soc.

_____. 1946. Whooping Crane records. *Blue Jay, Bull. Sask. Nat. Hist. Soc.*,

_____. 1946b. Additions to a list of the birds of Nipawin, Sask. *Blue Jay*, 4: 45.

Sutton, George Miksch. 1931. Notes on the birds observed along the west coast of Hudson's Bay. *Condor*, 33 (4): 57.

_____. 1932. The exploration of Southampton Island, Hudson Bay. Part II. Zool., sec. 2. The birds of Southampton Island. *Memoirs Carnegie Mus.*, Vol. XII, Part II, Sect. 2.

_____. 1967. Oklahoma birds. Norman, Univ. Okla. Press.

Stewart, Robert E. 1966. Notes on birds and other animals in the Slave River-Little Buffalo River area, N. W. T. *Blue Jay*, 24 (1): 22-32.

Swenk, Myron H. 1913. The Whooping Crane (*Grus americana*) in Nebraska. *Auk*, 30 (3): 430.

_____. 1921. The present status of the Whooping Crane. *Wilson Bulletin*, 33 (1): 57-58.

_____. 1933. The present status of the Whooping Crane. *Nebr. Bird Review*, 1 (4): 111-129.

Taverner, Percy Algernon. 1919. The birds of the Red River, Alberta. *Auk*, 36 (2): 264.

_____. 1919b. The birds of Shoal Lake, Manitoba. *Ottawa Naturalist*, 32 (9): 157.

_____. 1934. Birds of Canada. Natl. Mus. Canada, Ottawa.

_____. 1939. Canadian water birds. Phila., McKay.

_____. 1949. Birds of Canada, rev. ed. Toronto, Musson Book Co.

Taverner, Percy Algernon, and George M. Sutton. 1934. The birds of Churchill, Manitoba. *Ann. Carnegie Mus.*, 23: 31-32.

Taylor, W. Edgar, and A. H. VanVleet. 1888. Notes on Nebraska birds. *Ornith. and Oologist*, 13 (11): 170.

Tout, Wilson. 1947. Lincoln County, Birds: Lincoln Co., Nebraska. North Platte, author.

Townsend, John Kirk. 1839. Narrative of a journey across the Rocky Mountains to the Columbia River . . . . Phila., Henry Perkins.

Trine, Mrs. George W. 1935. Whooping Cranes present and lingering near Red Cloud. *Nebr. Bird Review*, 3 (3): 84.

Trippe, T. Martin. 1871. Notes on the birds of Minnesota. *Proc. Essex Inst.*, 6 (6): 118.

_____. 1872. Notes on the birds of southern Iowa. *Proc. Boston Soc. Nat. Hist.*, 15: 240.

Tufty, B. 1963. Twenty-eight Whooping Cranes left. *Science N L*, 83: 245 Ap. 20.

_____. 1964. Whooping Crane lives. *Science N L*, 85: 310 May 16.

_____. 1946b. Whooping Crane safe. *Science N L* 86: 262.0.24.

Turnbull, William Patterson. 1869. The birds of east Pennsylvania and New Jersey. Glasgow, printed for private circulation.

Uhler, F. M., and L. N. Locke. 1970. A note on the stomach contents of two Whooping Cranes. *Condor*, 72: 246.

U. S. National Park Service. 1942. Fading Trails. The story of endangered American Wildlife. New York, Macmillan.

Visher, Stephen Sargent. 1911. Annotated list of the birds of Harding County, NW South Dakota. *Auk*, 28 (1): 5-16.

_____. 1913. An annotated list of the birds of Sanborn County, SE-C South Dakota. *Auk*, 30 (4): 565.

———. 1915. A list of the birds of Clay County, SE South Dakota. *Wilson Bulletin,*, 37 (2): 325.

W. L. B. 1887. Whooping Cranes. *Forest and Stream*, 28 (2): 27.

Walkinshaw, Lawrence H. 1949. Apparent observations of the Whooping Crane in central Saskatchewan. *Canadian Field-Naturalist*, 63 (2): 78-80.

———. 1965. Whooper nest sits for a rare portrait. *Audubon*, 67 (5): 299-301.

———. 1965b. Attentiveness of Cranes at their nests. *Auk*, 82: 465-476.

Ward, F. C. 1943. Whooping Cranes at Shoal Lake, Manitoba. *Wilson Bulletin*, 55 (4): 245.

Watson, Frank G. 1955. Regional reports, South Texas. *Audubon Field Notes*, 6 (4): 254-257.

Wayne, Arthur Trezevant. 1910. Birds of South Carolina. *Cont. Charleston Mus.*, Charleston, S. C.

Weakly, Harry E. 1937. The Whooping Crane in North Platte, Lincoln County. *Nebr. Bird Rev.*, 5 (3): 58.

———. 1939. The Whooping Crane and other birds seen in Lincoln County in the spring of 1939. *Nebr. Bird Rev.*, 7 (1): 30.

———. 1940. Some recent Nebraska records of the Whooping Crane. *Nebr. Bird Rev.*, 8 (1): 32.

———. 1945. Whooping Cranes again seen in Lincoln County. *Nebr. Bird Rev.*, 15 (1): 43.

Webster, Fred S., Jr. 1956. Regional Reports, Southern Texas. *Audubon Field Notes*, 10 (1): 37-40; 1958, 12 (1): 41-44, (3): 365-370; 1959, 13 (1): 45-49, (3): 383-388; 1960, 14 (1): 52-56, (3): 401-407, (4): 460-465; 1961, 15 (1): 56-59, (4): 424-427; 1962, 16 (1): 52-58, (3): 347-350, (4): 428-433; 1963, 17 (1): 46-50, (4): 415-419; 1965, 19 (1): 56-60, (4): 490-497; 1966, 20 (1): 66-72, (4): 525-532; 1967, 21 (1): 54-59, (4): 520-524; 1968, 22 (1): 61-69, (4): 550-557; 1969, 23 (1): 77-81.

Wetmore, Alexander. 1931. The avifauna of the Pleistocene of Florida. *Smithsonian Miscel. Coll.*, 85 (2): 35-36.

Wheaton, John M. 1882. Report on the birds of Ohio. (Ohio Geol. Surv.). Columbus, Nevins and Myers.

Whitney, H. H. 1948. Letters. *Audubon Magazine*, 50 (5): 322-323.

Widmann, Otto. 1907. A preliminary catalogue of the birds of Missouri. *Trans. Acad. Sci., St. Louis*, 17: 56-57.

Williams, Mrs. C. S. 1967. Save the Whooping Crane. *Blue Jay*, 25 (3): 118-119.

Williams, Frances. 1966. Regional Reports, Southern Great Plains. *Audubon Field Notes*, 20 (1): 64-66; 1967, 21 (1): 51-54; 1968, 22 (4): 547.

Williams, George C. 1941. The season. Texas coastal region. *Audubon Magazine*, (No. 5, sect. 2): 477-478, (No. 6, sect. 2): 575-576.

———. 1945. Winter season, Texas coastal region. *Audubon Magazine*, (No. 3, sect. 2) 47: 25-26.

———. 1949. Winter season, Dec. 1, 1948 to Mar. 31, 1949., So. Texas region, *Audubon Field Notes*, 3: 176-177.

———. 1950. Regional Reports, Southern Texas. *Audubon Field Notes*, 4 (1): 14-15; 1951, 5 (1): 27-29.

Williams, H. V. 1926. Birds of the Red River Valley of northeastern North Dakota. *Wilson Bulletin*, 38: 17-33.

Wilson, Alexander. 1814. American Ornithology. Vol. 3. New York, Collins and Co., Phila., Harrison Hall.

Wilson, Ellis E. 1933. A wounded Whooping Crane. *Iowa Bird Life*, 3 (2): 25-26.

Wilson, J. H. 1944. Bird notes. *Blue Jay*, 2 (2): 11.

Wilson Bulletin, 1945. Ornithological News. 57 (2): 134-135.

Wolcott, Robert H. 1909. An analysis of Nebraska's bird fauna. *Proc. Nebr. Ornith. Union*, 4 (2): 35.

Wood, Norman A. 1923. A preliminary survey of the bird life of North Dakota. *Univ. Mich. Mus. Zool., Misc. Publ.*, 10: 10, 24-25.

———. 1923b. Whooping Cranes in North Dakota. *Auk*, 40: 692.

———. 1925. New and rare birds in North Dakota. *Auk*, 42: 452.

Woodruff, Frank Morley. 1907. The birds of the Chicago area. *Chicago Acad. Sci., Nat. Hist. Surv., Bull.* 6: 56-57.

Youngworth, William. 1931. Notes from Sioux City. *Iowa Bird Life*, 1 (1): 11.

———. 1935. The birds of Fort Sisseton, South Dakota; a sixty-year comparison. *Wilson Bulletin*, 47 (3): 217.

Grus vipio

Austin, Oliver L., Jr. and N. Kuroda. 1953. The birds of Japan, their status and distribution. *Bull. Mus. Comp. Zool.*, Harvard College, Vol. 109 (No. 4), pp. 279-637.

Blakiston, T., and H. Pryer. 1878. A catalogue of the birds of Japan. *Ibis*, 1878:209-250.

Blaauw, F. E. 1897. A monograph of the cranes. E. J. Brill, Leiden. viii + 64 pp.

Crandall, L. S. 1944. A rare baby crane. *Animal Kingdom*, 47:125-127.

Griswold, John A. 1962. Proven methods of keeping and rearing cranes in captivity. Spec. Rept. International Wild Waterfowl Assoc., Inc. 19 pp.

Hand-List of Japanese Birds. 1958. Ornithological Society of Japan, Yamashina Institute of Ornithology and Zoology, Tokyo, viii + 264 pp.

Ivanov, A. I., E. B. Koslova, L. A. Portenko, and A. Ya. Tugarinov. 1951. Birds of the USSR. Vol. 2. Academy of Sciences, Moscow.

Kreag, K. 1946. Rare baby crane. *Your Zoo* (Detroit Zool. Soc.) (3):4.

LaTouche, J. D. D. 1933. A Handbook of the birds of eastern China. Vol. 2. xxiii + 566 pp.

Przhevalsky, N. 1870. Journey in the Ussuri region in 1867-1869.

———. 1877. The birds of Mongolia, the Tangut Country, and the solitudes of northern Tibet. *In*, G. D. Rowley's 'Ornith. Misc.' 2(3):417-438.

Uchinda, S. 1930. Photographs of bird-life in Japan. Vol. 1, 112 pp. Sanseide Co., Ltd., Tokyo, Osaka.

Walkinshaw, L. H. 1951. Nesting of the White-naped Crane in Detroit Zoological Park. *Auk*, 68 (2):194-202.

Grus antigone

Acharya, Hari Narayan G. 1936. Sarus flocks. *Journ. Bombay Nat. Hist. Soc.*, 38:831.

Ali, Salim. 1927. The Moghul Emperors of India as Naturalists and Sportsmen. Pt. 2. *J. Bombay Nat. Hist. Soc.*, 32:34-63.

———. 1940. The birds of Central India (Pt. 2). *J. Bombay Nat. Hist. Soc.*, 41:470-488.

———. 1945. *The birds of Kutch*. Oxford Univ. Press, Brit. Indian Press, Bombay. xviii + 175 pp.

———. 1953. The Keoladeo Ghana (Bird Sanctuary) of Bharatpur (Rajasthan). *J. Bombay Nat. Hist. Soc.*, 51:531-536.

Ali, Salim, and Humayun Abdulali. 1939. The birds of Bombay and Salsette. Pt. 6. *J. Bombay Nat. Hist. Soc.*, 40:628-652.

Baker, E. C. Stuart. 1899. The birds of North Cachar. Pt. 10. *J. Bombay Nat. Hist. Soc.*, 12:486-510.

———. 1922. Hand-list of the birds of India. Pt. 7. *J. Bombay Nat. Hist. Soc.*, 28:830-873.

———. 1928. The fauna of British India, including Ceylon and Burma. 2. ed. London. Vol. 6, xxxv + 449 pp.

———. 1929. The game birds of the Indian Empire. Vol. 5., Pt. 5. *J. Bombay Nat. Hist. Soc.*, 33:1-6.

Barnes, Lieut. H. Edwin. 1885. *Handbook of the birds of the Bombay Presidency*. Calcutta, Central Press Co., Ltd. xxiv + 1-499 + xi pp.

———. 1886. Birds nesting in Rajpootana. *J. Bombay Nat. Hist. Soc.*, 1 (1):38-62.

Basil-Edwardes, S. 1926. A Contribution to the ornithology of Delhi. *J. Bombay Nat. Hist. Soc.*, 31:567-578.

Bates, R. S. P. 1925. Birds nesting with a camera in India. Pt. 3. *J. Bombay Nat. Hist. Soc.*, 30:306-313.

Blaauw, F. E. 1897. *A monograph of the Cranes*. E. J. Brill, Leiden and London. viii + 64 pp.

Blackman, J. G. 1971. Distribution of the Sarus Crane in northern Queensland. *Emu*, 71 (3):137-138.

Blanford, . 1896. *Bull. Brit. Orn. Club*, 5:7.

Bravery, J. A. 1969. The Sarus Crane in north-eastern Queensland. *Emu*, 69 (1):52-53.

Cook, Bruce. 1969. Photograph adult Burmese Sarus Crane, Normanton, Queensland, *Emu*, 69 (1): Plate 1.

Cook, J. P. 1913. A list of the Kalaw birds, with bird-nesting notes. *J. Bombay Nat. Hist. Soc.*, 22:260-270.

D'Abreu, E. A. 1912. Notes on the bird collecting trip in the Balaghat District of the Central Provinces (India). *J. Bombay Nat. Hist. Soc.*, 21:1158-1169.

————. 1935. A list of birds of the Central Provinces. *J. Bombay Nat. Hist. Soc.*, 38:95-116.

Deignan, H. G. 1945. The birds of northern Thailand. U.S. Natl. Mus., Bull. 186, v + 616 pp.

Delacour, Jean. 1947. Birds of Malaysia. The Macmillan Co., N.Y. xvi + 382 pp.

Delacour, J., and P. Jabouille. 1931. Les Oiseaux de l'Indochine Francaise. l, lvi + 280 + xlvi pp.

Delacour, J., P. Jabouille, and W. P. Lowe. 1928. On the birds collected during the Third Expedition to French Indo-China. Pt. 1. *Ibis*, 12th ser., 4:23-51, 4 pls.

Delacour, J., and Ernst Mayr. 1946. *Birds of the Philippines.*, Macmillan Co., N.Y. xv + 309 pp.

Dementiev, G. P., and N. A. Gladkov, *et al.* 1951. *The birds of the Soviet Union*. Vol. 2. Moscow.

De Schauensee, Rodolphe Meyer. 1929. *Proc. Acad. Nat. Sci.*, Philadelphia.

Dharmakumarsinhji, R. S. 1955. *Birds of Saurashtra, India*. Times of India Press, Bombay, liii + 561 pp.

Frome, N. F. 1947. The birds of Delhi and district. *J. Bombay Nat. Hist. Soc.*, 47:277-300, map.

Gee, E. P. 1964. *The wildlife of India*. Collins, St. James Place, London. 192 pp.

Gill, Mrs. H. B. 1969. First record of the Sarus Crane in Australia. *Emu*, 69 (1):49-52.

Hill, A. J. R. 1930. Nesting of the Sarus (*Antigone antigone*). *J. Bombay Nat. Hist. Soc.*, 34:582.

Hingston, R. W. G. 1921. A list of the birds of Dharmsala. *J. Bombay Nat. Hist. Soc.*, 27:555-572.

————. 1927. Bird notes from the Mount Everest Expedition of 1924. *J. Bombay Nat. Hist. Soc.*, 32:320-329.

Hopwood, Cyril. 1912. A list of birds from Arakan. *J. Bombay Nat. Hist. Soc.*, 21:1196-1221.

————. 1912b. Notes on some birds from the Chindwin Valley. *J. Bombay Nat. Hist. Soc.*, 21:1089-1090.

Inglis, C. M. 1903. The birds of the Madhubani sub-division of the Darbhanga District, Tirhut, with notes on species noticed elsewhere in the district. *J. Bombay Nat. Hist. Soc.*, 14:764-771.

King, R. C. H. Moss. 1911. The resident birds of the Sauger and Damon districts, Central Provinces. *J. Bombay Nat. Hist. Soc.*, 21:87-103.

Kiracofe, Jack. 1964. The Sarus Crane *Grus collaris*. Successful breeding and other observations. *Modern Game Breeding*, 1 (2):12-18.

Law, Satya Churn. 1930. Fish-eating habit of the Sarus Crane (*Antigone antigone*). *J. Bombay Nat. Hist. Soc.*, 34:582-583.

Livesey, T. R. 1937. Sarus flocks. *J. Bombay Nat. Hist. Soc.*, 39:420.

Lowther, E. H. N. 1941. Notes on some Indian birds. VI. An Indian River bed. *J. Bombay Nat. Hist. Soc.*, 42:782-795.

MacDonald, K. C. 1906. A list of birds found in Myingyan district of Burma. Pt. 2. *J. Bombay Nat. Hist. Soc.*, 17:492-504.

McGregor, Richard C. 1905. Notes on three rare Luzon birds. Dept. of Interior, Bur. Govt. Lab., Pt. 2, 29.

McGregor, R. C., and D. C. Worcester. 1906. A Hand-list of the birds of the Philippine Islands. Bur. Govt. Lab., Dept. of Interior, No. 36, Manila. pp. 1-123.

Mosse, A. H. 1910. Nidification of the Sarus Crane. *J. Bombay Nat. Hist. Soc.*, 20:218.

O'Brien, E. 1909. Nidification of the Sarus Crane (*Grus antigone*). *J. Bombay Nat. Hist. Soc.*, 19:524.

Osmaston, A. E. 1913. The birds of Gorakhpur. *J. Bombay Nat. Hist. Soc.*, 22:532-549.

Pershouse, Stanley. 1911. Nidification of the Sarus Crane (*Grus antigone*). *J. Bombay Nat. Hist. Soc.*, 20:854.

Rand, Austin L., and Robert L. Fleming. 1957. Birds of Nepal. *Fieldiana: Chi. Nat. Hist. Mus.*, 41, 218 pp.

Roseveare, W. L. 1949. Notes on birds of the irrigated area of Shwebo District, Burma. Pt. 2. *J. Bombay Nat. Hist. Soc.*, 48:729-749.

Ward, A. E. 1907. Birds of the Province of Kashmir and Jammu and adjacent districts. *J. Bombay Nat. Hist. Soc.*, 17:943-949.

Whistler, H. 1918. Notes on the birds of Ambala District, Punjab. Pt. 2. *J. Bombay Nat. Hist. Soc.*, 26:172-191.

————. 1938. The Ornithological Survey of Jodhpur State. *J. Bombay Nat. Hist. Soc.*, 40:213-235.

Wickham, P. F. 1930. Notes on the birds of the upper Burma Hills. *J. Bombay Nat. Hist. Soc.*, 34:337-349.

Whitehead, C. H. T. 1911. Notes on the birds of Sehore, Central India, with special reference to migration. *J. Bombay Nat. Hist. Soc.*, 21:153-170.

————. 1911. On the birds of Kohat and Kurram Valley, No. India. *J. Bombay Nat. Hist. Soc.*, 20:954-980.

Grus rubicundus

Agnew, Noel V. I. 1921. Further notes from Peel Island, Moreton Bay, Queensland. *Emu*, 21:131-137.

Alexander, W. B. 1923. A week in the Upper Barcoo, Central Queensland, *Emu*, 23:86.

Ashby, E. 1906. Northern notes. *Emu*, 6:72-74.

Astley, H. D. 1900. Review of November issue of Aviculture Magazine. *Emu*, 1:151.

Austin, Thos. B. 1907. Field notes on birds from Talbragar River, New South Wales. Pt. 2. *Emu*, 7:74-79.

Barnard, H. G. 1911. Notes from Cape York. *Emu*, 11:17-32.

————. 1914a. Birds of Brunette Downs (N.T.). *Emu*, 13:205-210.

————. 1914b. Northern Territory Birds. *Emu*, 14:39-57.

————. 1926. Birds of the Cardwell District, Queensland. *Emu*, 26:1-13.

Barnard, H. G., and Chas. A. Barnard. 1925. A review of Bird life on Coomooboolaroo Station, Dauringa Dist., Queensland during the past 50 years. *Emu*, 24:252-265.

Barrett, Charles. 1916. Bird life on Yanko Creek (N.S.W.). *Emu*, 16:15-23.

————. 1924. The Brolga. *Emu*, 23:236.

————. 1925. Rockhampton Outings. *Emu*, 24:217-221.

Batey, Isaac. 1907. On fifteen thousand acres: Its Bird-life sixty years ago. *Emu*, 7:1-17.

Bedggood, G. W. 1959. Brolgas at Corop., *Emu*, 59:288.

Berney, F. L. 1907. Field notes. Birds of Richmond District, North Queensland. (Pt. 4). *Emu*, 6 (3):106-115.

Binns, Gordon. 1953. Birds of Terang, South-western Victoria. *Emu*, 53 (3):211-221.

————. 1954. The Camp-out at Lake Barrine, Atherton Tableland, North Queensland. *Emu*, 54:29-46.

Blaauw, F. E. 1897. A Monograph of the Cranes. Leiden and London, viii + 64 pp.

Blackman, J. G. Unpublished Thesis for Master Degree on the Brolga.

Bourke, P. A., and A. F. Austin. 1947. The Atherton Tablelands and its Avifauna. *Emu*, 47:87-116.

Broadbent, K. 1910. Birds of Cardwell and Herbert River Districts (N.Q.). *Emu*, 10:233-245.

Brown, A. Graham. 1950. (Notes from the Diary of the late Urquhart Ramsay). The Birds of 'Turkeith', Victoria. *Emu*, 50:105-113.

Bryant, C. E. 1931. Excursions to Biggenden and Fraser Island. *Emu*, 30:180-187.

————. 1934. The Camp-Out at Moree, N.S.W. and the birds observed. *Emu*, 33:159-173.

Buturlin, Sergius A. 1911. Australian birds in Siberia. *Emu*, 11:95-98.

Caley, Neville W. 1967. What Bird is that. (4th ed. reprinted). xv + 344 pp. Halstead Press, Sydney.

Campbell, A. J. 1901. Nest and eggs of Australian Birds. Dawson and Brailsford, Sheffield. xl + 1102 pp. (pp. 760-762).

————. 1902. Birds of N.E. Victoria. *Emu*, 2:9-18.

————. 1903. The protection of native birds. *Emu*, 2 (4):187-194.

————. 1913. Commonwealth Collection. *Emu*, 13:65-74.

Campbell, A. J. and H. G. Barnard. 1917. Birds of the Rockingham Bay District, North Queensland. *Emu*, 17 (2):2-38.

Chalmers, C. O. 1934. Bird notes from Macdonald Downs, 150 miles North-East of Alice Springs, C.A. *So. Australian Ornithologist*, 6:211-213.

Check-List. 1913. Check-list of the Birds of Australia. *Emu*, 12 (Sup.). 38.

Chisholm, A. H. 1944. Birds of the Gilbert Diary. *Emu*, 44 (2):131-150 (pt. 1).

Chisholm, E. C. 1929. Birds of the East Bogan District, County of Flinders, New South Wales. *Emu*, (2):143-151.

Church, A. E. 1925. Birds observed at Burketown, North Queensland. *Emu*, 24 (4):290-295.

Cohn, Marc. 1926. Records of Birds movements. Report of migration committee for quarter ending 3/9/25. *Emu*, 25 (4):282-286.

Cole, C. F. 1920. Native Companions. *Emu*, 20 (1):37-38.

Condon, H. T. 1938. Some Birds of the South and Central Australian border. *So. Australian Ornithologist*, 10:146-151.

Cornwall, E. M. 1910. Notes on the Great-billed Heron (*Ardea sumatrana*). *Emu*, (3):138-141.

Crossman, Alan F. 1910. Birds seen in and around Broome, North-Western Australia. *Emu*, 9 (3):138-150.

Dennis, R. F. 1933. Nest of Brolga. *Emu*, 33 (3):223.

Dickison, D. J. 1932. History and early records of Ornithology in Victoria. *Emu*, 31 (3):175-196.

D'Ombrain, . 1921. Trip to the "Watercourse," North West, N.S.W. *Emu*, 21:59-67.

Elliott, A. J. 1938. Birds of the Moonie River District adjacent to the border of New South Wales and Queensland. *Emu*, 38 (1):30-49.

Francis, L. S. 1949. A trip to Darwin via Alice Springs. *So. Australian Ornithologist*, 21 (Summer):35-38.

Frith, H. J., and S. J. J. F. Davies. 1961. Breeding seasons of Birds in subcoastal Northern Territory. *Emu*, 61:97-111.

Glover, Brian. 1956. Movements of Birds—Part III in other states. *So. Australian Ornithologist*, 28 (Aug.):25-28.

Hill, G. F. 1907. Birds of Ararat District. Pt. 2. *Emu*, 7 (1):18-23.

————. 1911. Field notes on the Birds of Kimberley, North-West Australia. *Emu*, 10 (4):258-290.

————. 1913. Ornithological notes, Barclay Expedition. *Emu*, 12 (4):238-262.

Hindwood, K. A. 1940. Birds of Murrumbidgee Irrigation Area, N.S.W. *Emu*, 39 (3):219-232.

Hindwood, K. A., and A. R. McGill. 1951. The 'Derra Derra' 1950 Camp-out of the R.A.O.U. *Emu*, 50 (4):217-238.

Hogan, J. 1925. Bird notes from Willis Island. *Emu*, 24 (4):266-275.

Howe, Frank E. 1928. Notes on some Victorian Birds. *Emu*, 27 (4): 252-265.

Humphries, Cyril P. 1947. Among the Birds of Melville Bay. *Emu*, 47 (2):130-136.

Jackson, Sidney Wm. 1912. Haunts of the Spotted Bower-bird (*Chlamydodera maculata*, Gld.). *Emu*, 12 (2):65-104.

Jarman, Howard E. 1945. The Birds of Elliott and Newcastle Waters, Northern Territory. *South Australian Ornithologist*, 17 (7):74-78.

Jenkins, C. F. H. 1933. Branch Report. Western Australia. *Emu*, 32 (3):180-181.

————. 1947. Overland to the Ord River. *Emu*, 47 (1):35-41.

Jones, Jack. 1952. The Hattah Lakes Camp-out, October 1951 with general notes on the Birds of the Kulkyne State Forest. *Emu*, 52 (4):225-254.

Kilgour, James F. 1904. A trip to the Ord River (N.W.A.). *Emu*, 4 (2):37-43.

Lansell, G. L. 1933. Birds of Moulamein District (Riverina), N.S.W., *Emu*, 33 (2):122-127.

Lavery, H. J. 1965. The Brolga, *Grus rubicundus* (PERRY), on some Coastal Areas in north Queensland: Fluctuations in Populations, and Economic Aspects. *Queensland Journal of Agricultural Science*, 21:261-264.

————. 1968. List of Birds in Queensland. (Mimeographed). 19 pp.

————. 1968b. Mammals and Birds of the Townsville District, North Queensland. 2. Birds. *Queensland Journ. Agricultural and Animal Sciences*, 25:243-254.

Lavery, H. J., and J. G. Blackman. 1969. The Cranes of Australia. *Queensland Agricultural Journal*, 95 (3):156-162.

Lavery, H. J., and Nancy Hopkins. 1963. Birds of the Townsville District of North Queensland. *Emu*, 63:242-252.

Le Soüef, W. H. D. 1901. Descriptions of Birds' Eggs from the Port Darwin District, Northern Australia. *Emu*, 1:128-132.

————. 1903a. Descriptions of Birds' eggs from the Port Darwin District, Northern Australia. Pt. 2. *Emu*, 2 (3):139-159.

————. 1903b. Notable migration of Native Companions. *Emu*, 2 (3):174.

————. 1918. Queensland notes. *Emu*, 18 (1):43-49.

Lord, E. A. R. 1956. Birds of Murphy's Creek Dist., So. Queensland. *Emu*, 56:100-128.

Lyons, O. M. 1901-2. Some notes on the Birds of Lake Eyre District. *Emu*, 1:133-138.

MacGillivray, Wm. 1910. Along the Great Barrier Reef. *Emu*, 10 (3):216-233.

————. 1914. Notes on some North Queensland Birds. *Emu*, 13 (3):132-186.

————. 1918. Ornithologists in North Queensland. Pt. 2. *Emu*, 17 (3):145-148.

————. 1924. A spring excursion into south-western Queensland. Pt. 2. *Emu*, 24 (2):90-101.

————. 1929. Through a drought-stricken land. Pt. 2. *Emu*, 29 (2):113-128.

McGilp, J. Neil. 1924. Birds of Lake Frome Dist., South Australia. *Emu*, 23 (3):237-243.

McLennan, C. H. 1908. Ways of the Emu. *Emu*, 8 (1):42-45. (43).

McLennan, W. R. 1917. North Australian Birds. *Emu*, 16:117-158; 205-231 (communicated by H. L. White.).

Makatsch, Wolfgang. 1959. Der Kranich. A Zeimsen Verlag. Wittenberg-Lutherstadt. 99-100.

Mathews, Gregory. 1908. Handlist of the Birds of Australasia. *Emu*, 7 (Sup.):30.

————. 1909. Birds of North-west Australia. Pt. 2. Birds from Wyndham (With field Notes by the collector, J. P. Rogers.) Pt. 2. *Emu*, 9 (2):53-66.

————. 1910a. List of Birds observed on Parry's Creek, North-West Australia. *Emu*, 9 (4):238-241.

————. 1910b. On the Birds of Northwest Australia. Pt. 3. *Emu*, 10 (2):103-109.

————. 1911. Alterations in the Nomenclature of "Handlist of the Birds of Australia." *Emu*, 10 (5):317-326.

————. 1912. Nov. Zool. 18:227.

————. 1913-14. Birds of Australia. Vol. 3. pp. 512.

————. 1914. Austral. Av. Record. 2 (5).

Mathews, Gregory M., and Tom Iredale. 1921. The Manual of the Birds of Australia. Vol. 1. H. F. Witherby, London. xxiv + 279 pp.

Mayo, Lila M. 1931. A Queensland 'Sancturary.' *Emu*, 31:71-76.

Mayr, Ernst. 1941. List of New Guinea Birds. Am. Mus. Nat. Hist. publ. xi + 260 pp.

Morse, F. C. 1922. Birds of the Moree District. *Emu*, 22 (1):24-38.

Nicholls, Brooke. 1924. A trip to Munderanie, Central Australia. *Emu*, 24 (1):45-59.

North, Alfred J. 1896. Aves; Report . . . Horn Scientific Expedition to Central Australia. Ed. by Baldwin Spencer, London, Dulau, 4 parts. Part 2, pp. 53-111.

————. 1913. Nest and eggs of Birds found breeding in Australia and Tasmania. F. W. White, Sydney. Vol. 4, Pt. 3, pp. 201-300.

Oates, Eugene W. 1902. Catalogue of the collection of Birds eggs in the British Museum (Natural History) vol. ii. London, 8vo. pp. xx + 400.

Oliver, W. R. B. 1945. Avian Evolution in New Zealand and Australia. *Emu*, 45 (2):128-152.

Pawsey, C. F. 1906. Bird census of the Stawell District. *Emu*, 6 (2):70.

Rand, A. L., and E. Thomas Gilliard. 1967. Handbook of New Guinea Birds, Weidenfeld and Nicolson, London. x + 612 pp.

Rhodes, Lyle J. 1944. Birds of the Adelaide River District, Northern Territory. *Emu*, 44 (2):87-93.

Russell, James. 1921. Birds of the Barunah Plains and district. *Emu*, 21 (2):137-142.

Sedgwick, Eric H. 1947. Northern Territory Bird notes. *Emu*, 46 (4):294-308.

Sefton, A. R. 1958. Bird notes from the Illawarra District, New South Wales. *Emu*, 58:393-394.

Serventy, D. L., and H. M. Whittell. 1962. Birds of Western Australia. Third ed. Peterson Brokensha, Pty., Ltd., Perth, 327 pp.

Serventy, Vincent. 1959. Birds of Willis Island (Queensland). *Emu*, 59:167-176.

Shilling, David. 1948. The Birds of Upper Liveringa Station, Western Australia. *Emu*, 48 (1):64-72.

Simpson, A. J. 1903. Native Companions. *Emu*, 2 (4):217.

Stone, A. Charles. 1912. Birds of Lake Boga, Victoria. *Emu*, 12 (2):112-122.

————. 1913. Some Swamp Birds. *Emu*, 13 (1):82-86.

Storr, G. M. 1953. Birds of the Cooktown and Laura Districts, No. Queensland. *Emu*, 53:225-248.

————. 1967. List of Northern Territory Birds. Western Australia Museum Spec. Publication No. 4, Govt. Printer, Perth, W.A. 90 pp.

Sullivan, C. 1931. Notes from North-Western New South Wales. *Emu*, 31 (2):124-135.

Sutton, J. 1927. Birds of South Australia (Reprinted from the South Australian Ornithologist.).

Wheeler, W. Roy. 1959. The R.A.O.U. Camp-Out at Noosa Heads, Queensland, 1958. *Emu*, 59:229-249.

————. 1967. A Handlist of the Birds of Victoria. Victorian Ornithological Research Group. Melbourne University Press, Carlton, Victoria. 88 pp.

White, H. L. 1917. North Australian Birds. *Emu*, 16 (3):117-158; (4):205-231.

————. 1922. A Collecting trip to Cape York Peninsula. *Emu*, 22 (2):99-116.

————. 1923. North Queensland Notes. *Emu*, 23:143-144.

White, S. A. 1923. The most extensive Ornithological tour ever accomplished in Australia. *Emu*, 22 (3):218-236.

White, S. R. 1946. Notes on the Bird life of Australia's Heaviest Rainfall Region. *Emu*, 46 (2):81-122.

Whitlock, F. Lawson. 1925. Ten months on the Fitzroy River, Northwestern Australia (with an introduction by A. J. Campbell).

Emu, 25 (2):69-89.

Wilson, A. H. R. 1928. Bird notes from Yarraberb. *Emu*, 28 (2):121-127.

Wolstenholme, H. 1925. Notes on the birds observed during the Queensland Congress and Camp-Out, 1924. *Emu*, 24:230-236.

Wood, P. J. 1955. Brolga Breeding in the Geelong District. *Emu*, 55:158.

————. 1959. 'Rare' Birds of the Geelong District. *Emu*, 59:211.

Grus leucogeranus

Amadon, Dean. 1949. Further record of *Grus leucogeranus* from Japan. *Tori*, 12:No. 29:271-272.

Baker, E. C. Stuart. 1929. *The fauna of British India, including Ceylon and Burma*. Sec. ed. London. Vol. 6, xxxv + 499 pp.

Barnes, H. Edwin. 1885. *Handbook to the birds of the Bombay Presidency*. Calcutta Central Press Co., Ltd., Calcutta. xxiv + 149 + xi pp.

Blaauw, F. E. 1897. A monograph of the Cranes. E. J. Brill, Leiden and London, viii + 64 pp.

Blyth, E., and W. B. Tegetmeier. 1881. The natural history of the Cranes. Horace Cox, London. viii + 92 pp. 20 illus.

Chekmenev, D. I. 1960. The Biology of the Demoiselle Crane in Central Kazakhstan. Trudy Inst. Zool. Akad. Nauk. Nazakh, SSR. Alma Ata 13:142-147.

D'Abreu, E. A. 1935. A list of the birds of the Central Provinces. *J. Bombay Nat. Hist. Soc.*, 38:95-116.

Dementiev, G. P., and N. A. Gladkov, *et al.* 1951. Birds of the Soviet Union. Vol. 2, pp. 123-128.

Donald, C. H. 1952. Bird migration across the Himalayas. *J. Bombay Nat. Hist. Soc.*, 51:269-271.

Dresser, H. E. 1908. On the Russian Arctic Expedition of 1900-1903. Pt. 2. *Ibis*, 9th ser., 2:593-599.

Frome, N. F. 1947. The birds of Delhi and district. *J. Bombay Nat. Hist. Soc.*, 47:277-300.

Handlist of Japanese Birds. 1958. The Ornithological Society of Japan, Yamashina Institute for Ornithology and Zoology. ix + 264 pp.

Hume, A. 1868. II. Stray notes on Ornithology in India. *Ibis*, 28-40.

Inglis, C. M. 1903. The birds of the Madhubani sub-division of the Darbhanga district with notes on species noted elsewhere in the district. *J. Bombay Nat. Hist. Soc.*, 14:764-771.

La Touche, J. D. D. 1933. A Handbook of the birds of Eastern China, Vol. 2, Pt. 4, pp. 229-400.

Maries, C. List of Birds in the Gwalior State Museum, collected in the Gwalior State. *J. Bombay Nat. Hist. Soc.*, 11:136-140.

Seebohm, Henry. 1890. The Birds of the Japanese Empire. 8vo. London.

Temminck, C. T., and H. Schlegel. 1849. Aves. *In* Siebold's Fauna Japonica.

Ticehurst, Claud B. 1926. On the downy plumages of some Indian Birds. *J. Bombay Nat. Hist. Soc.*, 31:368-378.

Bugeranus carunculatus

Belcher, C. F. 1927. Some African rarities. *Oologists' Record*, 7:73-76.

————. 1950. Notes on some eggs collected in northern Nyasaland. *Oologists' Record*, 24:2-10.

Benson, C. W. 1940. Notes on Nyasaland birds. Pt. 2. *Ibis*, 14th ser., 4:387-433.

————. 1942. Additional notes on Nyasaland birds. Pt. 1. *Ibis*, 14th ser., 6:197-224.

————. 1953. A Check List of the birds of Nyasaland. Heatherwick Press, Church of Scotland Mission, Blantyre, Nyasaland.

––––. 1960. Breeding seasons of some game and protected birds of Northern Rhodesia. *Black Lechwe*, 2:149-158.

Benson, C. W., and C. R. S. Pitman. 1959. Further breeding records from Northern Rhodesia. Pt. 3. *Bull. Brit. Orn. Club*, 79:18-22.

Benson, C. W., and C. M. N. White. 1957. Check List of the birds of Northern Rhodesia. Govt. Printer, Lusaka. xxii + 166 pp.

Blaauw, F. E. 1897. A Monograph of the Cranes. E. J. Brill, Leiden. viii + 64 pp.

Brelsford, V. 1947. Notes on the birds of the Lake Bangweulu area in Northern Rhodesia. *Ibis*, 89:57-77.

Brooke, R. K., and W. Tarboton. 1964. Birds of the West Sinoia District of Southern Rhodesia. *So. African Avifauna Ser.*, No. 23. 28 pp.

Chapin, J. P. 1939. The birds of the Belgian Congo. Pt. 2. *Bull. Amer. Mus. Nat. Hist.*, 75 + vii + 632 pp.

Cheeseman, R. E., and W. L. Sclater. 1935. On a collection of birds from North-western Abyssinia. Pt. 2. *Ibis*, 77:297-329.

Clay, G. 1953. Some notes on the birds of the Isoka District of the northern Province of Northern Rhodesia. *Ostrich*, 24:76-97.

Crandall, L. S. 1945. We have two of the rarest chicks in the World. *Animal Kingdom*, 48:119.

Gloger, . 1842. Handb. Naturg.

Gmelin, J. G. 1789. Syst. Nat. I, Part 2:643.

Guichard, K. 1950. A summary of the birds of the Addis Ababa Region, Ethiopia. *Jour. East. Africa Nat. Hist. Soc.*, 19:154-178.

Gurney, J. H. 1864. A sixth additional list of birds from Natal. *Ibis*, 6:346-361.

––––. 1868. A ninth additional list of birds from Natal. *Ibis*, new ser. 4:460-471.

Haagner, A. K. 1948. A list of the birds observed in Beira and neighbourhood, with some notes on habits, etc. Pt. 2. *Ostrich*, 19:211-217.

Hewitt, J. 1931. A guide to the vertebrate fauna of the eastern Cape Province. Pt. 1. Mammals and birds. The Modern Printing Works, Grahamtown.

Hulett, J. 1953. The Wattled Crane. *Natal Soc. for the Preservation of Wildlife and Natural Resorts*, 2 (No. 2):6-7.

Jackson, F. J. 1938. The birds of Kenya Colony and the Uganda Protectorate. Gurney and Jackson, London.

Jourdain, F. C. R. 1935. The eggs of the Wattled Crane. *Oologists' Record*, 15:53-54.

Latham, J. 1785. Gen. Syst. III, Pt. 1, p. 82.

Layard, E. L. 1875. The birds of South Africa. Bernard Quaritch, London. xxvii + 890 pp.

Mackworth-Praed, C. W., and C. H. B. Grant. 1952. Birds of eastern and north eastern Africa. African Handbook of birds. Ser. 1, Vol. 1. Longmans, Green and Co., London. xxv + 836 pp.

Neave, S. A. 1910. On the birds of Northern Rhodesia and the Katanga District of Congoland. Pt. 1. *Ibis*, ninth ser., 4:78-155.

Pitman, C. R. S. 1935. The eggs of *Bugeranus carunculatus* (Gmelin)—Wattled Crane. *Oologists' Record*, 15:49-53.

Priest, C. D. 1934. The birds of Southern Rhodesia. Vol. 2:39-43.

Roberts, A. 1951. The birds of South Africa. H. F. & G. Witherby, Ltd., London and Central News Agency, Ltd., Johannesburg. xxxvi + 463 pp.

Shelley, G. E. 1899. On a collection of birds from Tanganyika Plateau, in British East Africa. *Ibis*, 7th ser., 5:364-380.

Smithers, R. H. N. 1964. A Check List of the birds of the Bechuanaland Protectorate and the Caprivi Strip. Trustees of the Natl. Mus. of Southern Rhodesia, Univ. Printing House, Cambridge, England. ix + 161 pp., 1 map.

Sparrow, R. 1935. The eggs of the Wattled Crane, *Bugeranus carunculatus* (Gm.), and other cranes. *Oologists' Record*, 15:77-78.

Stark, A., and W. L. Sclater. 1906. The birds of South Africa. Vol. 4, xvii + 545 pp.

Traylor, M. L. 1963. Check-list of Angolan birds. Estudo de Biologia na Lunda Museo de Dundo. Cultural Publications, No. 61. 250 pp.

––––. 1965. A collection of birds from Barotseland and Bechuanaland. Pt. 1, *Ibis*, 107:137-172.

Urban, E. K. and L. H. Walkinshaw. 1967. The Wattled Crane in Ethiopia. *Auk*, 84 (2):263-264.

Vincent, A. W. 1945. On the breeding habits of some African birds. Pt. 3. *Ibis*, 87:345-365.

Walkinshaw, L. H. 1965. The Wattled Crane *Bugeranus carunculatus* (Gmelin). *Ostrich*, 36:73-81.

––––. 1965b. Territories of Cranes. *Papers of the Michigan Academy of Science, Arts, and Letters*, Vol. L (1964 meeting): 75-88.

––––. 1965c. Attentiveness of cranes at their nests. *Auk*, 82 (3):465-476.

West, O. 1956. Nesting plumage, Wattled Crane. *Ostrich*, 27:41.

––––. 1963. Notes on the Wattled Crane *Bugeranus carunculatus* (Gmelin). *Ostrich*, 34:63-77.

White, C. M. N. 1945. The Ornithology of Kaonde Lunda Province, Northern Rhodesia. *Ibis*, 87:309-345.

Winterbottom, J. M. 1965. A preliminary list of the birds of South West Africa. *So. African Avi. Ser.*, No. 25, 38 pp.

Anthropoides virgo

Baker, E. C. S. 1928. The game birds of the Indian Empire. The waders and other semi-sporting birds. Pt. 5. *Journ. Bombay Nat. Hist. Soc.*, 32:397-407.

Berg, Bengt. 1930. To Africa with the migratory birds. G. P. Putnam's Sons, N.Y. 274 pp.

Chekmenev, D. I. 1960. The Biology of the Demoiselle Crane in Central Kazakhstan. *Trudy Inst. Zool. Akad. Nauk. Nazakh, SSR*, Alma Ata 13, 142-147.

Cullen, C. A. 1869. Account of the breeding habits in Dobrudscha (Turkey) *Grus virgo. The Field*, 11, September 1869.

Dementiev, G. P., and N. A. Gladkov, *et al.* 1951. Birds of the Soviet Union. Moscow. Vol. 2, pp. 133-138.

Elgood, J. H. 1964. Provisional Check-list of the birds of Nigeria. *Nigerian Ornith. Soc. Bull.*, No. 1:13-25.

Elgood, J. H., R. E. Sharland, and P. Ward. 1966. Palearctic migrants in Nigeria. *Ibis*, 108:84-116.

La Touche, J. D. D. 1933. A handbook of the birds of eastern China. Vol. 2. xxiii + 506 pp.

Mathiasson, S. 1963. Visible diurnal migration in the Sudan. *Proc. XIIIth Int. Orn. Congress, Ithaca, N.Y., June 1962*. Baton Rouge. pp. 430-435.

Anthropoides paradisea

Blaauw, F. E. 1897. A monograph of the Cranes. E. J. Brill, Leiden. viii + 64 pp.

Boddam-Whetham, A. D. 1965. The Birds of Kirklington, O.F.S., *So. African Avi. Ser.*, No. 32. 35 pp.

Courtenay-Latimer, Miss M. 1964. Check List of the Birds of the East London Area. *So African Avi. Ser.*, No. 20. 76 pp.

Hewitt, J. 1931. A guide to the Vertebrate Fauna of the Eastern Cape Province. Pt. 1. Mammals and Birds. Modern Printing Works, Grahamtown.

Jones, E. Morse. 1965. The Birds of Salt Vlei, Bathurst Division, C.P., *So. African Avi. Ser.*, No. 28, 34 pp.

Jourdain, F. C. R. 1935. The eggs of the Wattled Crane. *Oologists' Record*, 15:53-54.

Lichtenstein, A. A. H. 1793. Catalogus rerum naturalium rarissimarum. 60 pp.

Little, Jeanne de V. 1963. List of the Birds of the Caroline District. *So. African Avi. Ser.*, No. 11. 27 pp.

Markus, Miles B. 1964. An Annotated list of the Birds of Pretoria City., *So African Avi. Ser.*, No. 18. 50 pp.

Milstein, P. le S. 1962. Birds of the Mineral Range, Groblersdal District. *So African Avi. Ser.*, No. 4. 36 pp.

Niven, C. K., and P. N. F. Niven. 1966. The Birds of Amanzi, Uitenhage District, C.P., *So. African Avi. Ser.*, No. 34. 55 pp.

Roberts, A. 1951. *The Birds of South Africa.*, H. F. & G. Witherby, Ltd., London and Central News Agency, Ltd., Johannesburg. xxxvi + 463 pp.

Shephard, J. B. 1962. Check List of Birds of Swartberg Dist. *So. African Avi. Ser.*, No. 6. 17 pp.

Skead, C. J. 1964. The Birds of King William's Town Dist. *So African Avi. Ser.*, No. 15. 70 pp.

————. 1965a. A Revised list of the Birds of the Bloemhof District. *So. African Avi. Ser.*, No. 26. 31 pp.

————. 1965b. Birds of the Albany (Grahamstown) Dist. *So. African Avi. Ser.*, No. 30, 46 pp.

Smithers, R. H. N. 1964. A Check List of the Birds of Bechuanaland Protectorate and the Caprivi Strip. Trustees of the Natl. Mus. of Southern Rhodesia. Univ. Printing House, Cambridge, England. ix + 161 pp., 1 map.

Sparrow, R. 1935. The eggs of the Wattled Crane, *Bugeranus carunculatus* (Gm.), and other Cranes. *Oologists' Record*, 15:77-78.

Stark, A., and W. L. Sclater. 1906. The Birds of South Africa. Vol. 4. xvii + 545 pp.

Taylor, J. S. 1964. The Birds of Fort Beaufort and Adelaide, C.P. *So. African Avi. Ser.*, No. 22. 40 pp.

Thorrington-Smith, E. 1960. Towards a plan for the Tugela Basin. Natal Town and Reg. Planning Comm., Pietermaritzburg. 266 pp., 72 maps.

Van Ee, C. A. 1966. Notes on the Breeding Behaviour of the Blue Crane *Tetrapteryx paradisea*. *Ostrich*, 37:23-29.

Walkinshaw, L. H. 1963. Some Life History Studies of the Stanley Crane. *Proc. XIIIth International Ornithological Congress, Ithaca, N.Y., June 1962.* Baton Rouge, pp. 344-353.

West, O., P. B. Wright, and G. Symons. 1964. The Birds of Weenan County, Natal. *So. African Avi. Ser.*, No. 14. 50 pp.

Winterbottom, J. M. 1962a. List of the Birds of Swellendam Dist. *So. African Avi. Ser.*, No. 5. 20 pp.

————. 1962b. List of Birds of Worcester District. *So. African Avi. Ser.*, No. 7. 19 pp.

————. 1964. Some MS. notes on Basutoland Birds by J. P. Murray. *So. African Avi. Ser.*, No. 21. 10 pp.

————. 1965. A Preliminary list of the Birds of South West Africa. *So. African Avi. Ser.*, No. 25. 38 pp.

————. 1966. The Comparative Ecology of the Birds of some Karoo Habitats in the Cape Province. *Ostrich*, 37:109-127.

Balearica

Bannerman, D. A. 1931. The birds of tropical West Africa. The Crown Agents for the Colonies, London. Vol. 2, xxix + 428 pp.

————. 1951. The birds of tropical West Africa. Vol. 8. Oliver and Boyd, London. xxiv + 552 pp.

Bennett, E. T. 1833. (1834). On several animals recently added to the Society's menageria. *Proc. Zool. Soc. London*, pp. 118-119.

Benson, C. W. 1940. Notes on Nyasaland birds (with particular reference to those of the Northern Province). Part 2. *Ibis*, 14th ser., 4:387-433.

————. 1953. A Check list of the birds of Nyasaland. Publ. by the Nyasaland Society and Publ. Bur. Blantyre and Lusaka. The Heatherwick Press, Church of Scotland Mission, Blantyre, Nyasaland, 118 pp.

————. 1960. Breeding seasons of some game and protected birds in Northern Rhodesia. *Black Lechwe*, 2:149-158.

Benson, C. W., and C. M. N. White. 1957. Check list of the birds of Northern Rhodesia. Govt. Printer, Lusaka. xxii + 166 pp. 20 photos.

Blaauw, F. E. 1897. A monograph of the Cranes. E. J. Brill, Leiden. viii + 64 pp.

Blyth, E., and W. B. Tegetmeier. 1881. The natural history of the Cranes. Horace Cox, London. viii + 92 pp., 20 illus.

Brasil, L. 1913. P. Wytsman's 19 Part Genera Avium. Grues. Louis Desmet-Vertenfeuil, Publishers and Printers, Brussels.

Brooke, R. K., and K. E. Cackett. 1965. Preliminary list of birds of the central Sabi valley, southern Rhodesia. *S. African Avi. Ser.*, No. 31. 34 pp.

Cave, F. O., and J. D. MacDonald. 1955. Birds of the Sudan. Oliver & Boyd, Edinburgh. xxvii + 444 pp.

Cawkell, E. M., and R. E. Moreau. 1963. Notes on birds in the Gambia. *Ibis*, 105:156-178.

Chapin, J. B. 1939. Birds of the Belgian Congo. *Bull. Amer. Mus. Nat. Hist.*, New York, Vol. LXXV, Pt. 2, 632 pp.

Cheeseman, R. E., and W. L. Sclater. 1935. On a collection of birds from north-western Abyssinia (Part 2). *Ibis*, 77:297-329.

Courtenay-Latimer, Miss M. 1964. Check List of the birds of the East London area. *So. African Avi. Ser.*, No. 20. 76 pp.

Cusack, Miss E. B. 1943. The Crowned Crane (*Balearica regulorum*). *Ostrich*, 13:212-218.

Davison, E. 1963. Check list of the birds of Wankie National Park, *So. African Avi. Ser.*, No. 13. 50 pp.

Fry, V. H. 1962. Birds of the Zaria area. *Nigerian Ornith. Union Circular*, No. 1. 11 pp.

Guichard, K. 1950. A summary of the birds of the Addis Ababa region, Ethiopia. *J. East Africa Nat. Hist. Soc.*, 19:154-178.

Haagner, A. K. 1948. A list of the birds observed in Beira and neighbourhood, with some notes on habits, etc. Part 2, *Ostrich*, 19:211-217.

Jackson, F. J. 1938. The birds of Kenya Colony and Uganda Protectorate. Gurney and Jackson, London. Vol. 1. lii + 542 pp.

Jensen, R. A. C. 1966. The birds of the Victoria Falls National Park, Rhodesia. *So. African Avi. Ser.*, No. 33, 35 pp.

Keith, Stuart. 1968. Notes on birds of East Africa, including additions to the Avifauna. *American Mus. Nov.*, No. 2321, June 19, 1958. 15 pp.

Layard, E. L. 1875. *The birds of South Africa.* Bernard Quaritch, London. xxvi + 890 pp.

Little, Jeanne de V. 1963. List of birds of the Caroline District. *So. African Avi. Ser.*, No. 11. 27 pp.

Mackworth-Praed, C. W., and C. H. B. Grant. 1952. Birds of eastern and northeastern Africa. African Handbook of birds. Ser. 1, Vol. 1. Longmans, Green and Co., London. xxv + 836 pp.

Mitchell, P. C. 1904a. Abstracts of *Proc. Zool. Soc. London*, 15 Nov. 1904, No. 10, p. 13.

————. 1904b. on the species of Crowned Cranes. *Proc. Zool. Soc. London*, 2:200-205.

Owre, Oscar T. 1966. The Crowned Crane at Lake Rudolf. *Bull. Brit. Ornith. Club*, 86:54-56.

Page, Ernie V. 1948. Some notes on the birds of Kei Mouth, Cape Province. *Ostrich*, 19:89-93.

Pike, E. O. 1954. The birds of Blythswood and some notes on birds of the district. *Ostrich*, 25:115-129.

————. 1965. The birds of Kobonqaba, Transkei. *So. African Avi. Ser.*, No. 24. 22 pp.

Roberts, A., G. R. McLachlan, and R. Liversidge. 1958. Birds of South Africa. Cape Times Ltd., Cape Town. 504 pp.

Shephard, J. B. 1962. A Check List of the birds of Swartberg District. *So. African Avi. Ser.*, No. 6. 17 pp.

Skead, C. J. 1964a. The birds of King William's Town District. *So. African Avi. Ser.*, No. 15. 70 pp.

Skead, D. M. 1964. A Revised list of the birds of the Bloemhoef District. *So. African Avi. Ser.*, No. 26. 32 pp.

Skilleter, M. 1963. Some notes of Kaduna birds. *The Nigerian Field*, 28:34-42.

Smith, V. W. 1962. Some birds which breed near Vom, Northern Nigeria. *The Nigerian Field*, 27:4-34.

————. 1964. Further notes on birds breeding near Vom, Northern

Nigeria. *The Nigerian Field*, 29:100-117.

Smithers, R. H. N. 1964. A Check List of the birds of the Bechuanaland Protectorate and the Caprivi Strip. Trustees of the Natl. Mus. of So. Rhodesia. University Printing House, Cambridge, England. ix + 161 pp.

Smithers, R. H. N., M. P. Stuart Irwin, and M. L. Patterson. 1957. A Checklist of the birds of Southern Rhodesia. Rhodesia Ornith. Soc. ix + 175 pp.

Sparrow, R. 1935. The eggs of the Wattled Crane *Bugeranus carunculatus* (Gm.), and and other cranes. *Ooologists' Record*, 15 (No. 4):77-78.

Stark, A., and W. L. Sclater. 1906. The birds of South Africa. Vol. 4, xvii + 545 pp.

Taylor, J. S. 1964. The birds of Fort Beaufort and Adelaide, C.P. *So. African Avi. Ser.*, No. 22. 40 pp.

Traylor, M. L. 1963. Check-list of Angolan birds. Estudo da Biologia na Lunda Museo de Dundo. Cultural Publications No. 61, 250 pp.

————. 1965. A collection of birds from Barotseland and Bechuanaland. Pt. 1, *Ibis*, 107:137-172.

Urban, E. K., and L. H. Walkinshaw. 1967. The Sudan Crowned Crane in Ethiopia. *Ibis*, 109:431-433.

Vincent, J. 1934. The birds of northern Portuguese East Africa. Comprising a list of, and observations on, the collections made during the British Museum Expedition of 1931-32. Part 4. *Ibis*, 76:495-527.

Walkinshaw, L. H. 1964. The African Crowned Cranes. *Wilson Bull.*, 76:355-377.

————. 1965a. Territories of Cranes. *Papers of the Michigan Academy of Science, Arts, and Letters*, Vol. L (1964 meeting): 75-88.

————. 1965b. Attentiveness of Cranes at their nests. *Auk*, 82:465-476.

————. 1966. The Crowned Crane on the Jos Plateau, Northern Nigeria. *Nigerian Ornith. Soc. Bull.*, No. 9, vol. 3:6-10.

West, O., P. B. Wright, and G. Symons. 1964. The birds of Weenan County, Natal. *So. African Avi. Ser.*, No. 14, 50 pp.

Wilkes, A. H. Paget. 1928. The birds of the region south of Lake Nyasa. Pt. 1. Non-Passerine Birds. *Ibis*, 12th ser., Vol. 4:690-748.

Winterbottom, J. M. 1964. Some MS. notes on Basutoland birds by J. P. Murray. *So. Afr. Avi. Ser.*, No. 21. 10 pp.

Wyndham, Chas. 1940. The Crowned Crane (*Balearica regulorum*). *Ostrich*, 9 (1): 45-48.